SPOKESMEN
FOR THE
DESPISED

EDITED BY
R. SCOTT APPLEBY

SPOKESMEN

FOR THE

DESPISED

Fundamentalist Leaders
of the Middle East

THE UNIVERSITY OF CHICAGO PRESS
CHICAGO & LONDON

R. SCOTT APPLEBY is associate professor of history and director of the Cushwa Center for the Study of American Catholicism at the University of Notre Dame. With Martin E. Marty he co-edited the five volumes of the Fundamentalism Project, published by the University of Chicago Press.

The University of Chicago Press, Chicago 60637
The University of Chicago Press, Ltd., London
© 1997 by The University of Chicago
All rights reserved. Published 1997
Printed in the United States of America
05 04 03 02 01 00 99 98 97   1 2 3 4 5

ISBN: 0-226-02124-6 (cloth)
0-226-02125-4 (paper)

Library of Congress Cataloging-in-Publication Data

Spokesmen for the despised : fundamentalist leaders of the Middle East
/ edited by R. Scott Appleby.
    p.   cm.
    Includes index.
    ISBN 0-226-02124-6 (cloth : alk. paper). — ISBN 0-226-02125-4
(pbk. : alk. paper)
    1. Muslims—Biography. 2. Islamic fundamentalism. I. Appleby,
R. Scott, 1956–   .
BP70.S67   1997
291.6'1'0956—dc20   96-20600
                                                              CIP

CONTENTS

ACKNOWLEDGMENTS

Planning for this book began during the final phase of the Fundamentalism Project, an international public policy study conducted under the auspices of the American Academy of Arts and Sciences and supported by a grant from the John D. and Catherine T. MacArthur Foundation. The opinions expressed, of course, are those of the individual authors only, and do not necessarily reflect the views of the American Academy or the supporting foundation.

Martin E. Marty, the director of the Fundamentalism Project, is mentor, friend, and the empowering spirit behind this and other worthy initiatives. Martin Kramer provided the volume's title, one of its richest portraits, and sensible editorial and procedural advice at crucial points along the way. Alan Thomas and Randolph Petilos of the University of Chicago Press supervised the publication process with the same alacrity and skill they devoted to the five volumes of the Fundamentalism Project. Joel Score displayed impressive expertise, sound judgment, and considerable insight in copyediting the manuscript. The important tasks of proofreading the copyedited manuscript and preparing the index were an Appleby family effort, with major contributions coming from Peg, Ben, and my sister Angie Appleby-Purcell.

At the University of Notre Dame, where the editorial work was completed, historian John Haas became the resident expert on charismatic leadership and contributed material to that section of the introduction. Barbara Lockwood of Notre Dame's Cushwa Center for the Study of American Catholicism contributed her peerless secretarial and management abilities; as usual, she was the person indispensable to the successful completion of the project.

I am still learning how to think about comparative politics and religion in general, and fundamentalism and the Middle East in particular.

I have learned most about the latter from Emmanuel Sivan of Hebrew University, Jerusalem, and a great deal about the former from Gabriel A. Almond, emeritus professor of political science at Stanford University. This book is dedicated to Professor Almond, with thanks for his generous spirit and enduring brilliance as a scholar and teacher.

INTRODUCTION

R. Scott Appleby

How shall we characterize our times? In George Steiner's apt epigram: "We come after." After, certainly, a century of genocide and holocaust, after the rise and fall of Marxist ideology, after "the end of History."

In the waning years of the twentieth century the people of the Middle East, caught in religiously inspired wars and acts of war, come a full generation after Sayyid Qutb radicalized segments of Sunni Islam with the notion that society, even so-called Islamic society, is decadent and ripe for revolution. They come after the Iranian revolution, led by a Shi'ite scholar, transformed the political dynamics of the region and sent shock waves throughout much of Africa, as well as central and south Asia. They live in the bloody wake of the massacre of Muslim worshipers by a Jewish extremist at the Tomb of the Patriarchs in Hebron, and in the shadow of a terrible string of suicide bombings against Jews in Israel by the young militants of Hamas (the Islamic Resistance Movement of Palestine) intent on destroying the peace process. They live in the days of the Sudanese civil war and armed struggles for the Islamization of Algeria and Egypt. And they come two decades after the New Christian Right emerged in the United States and fervently embraced the state of Israel as the site of the longed-for second coming of Christ.

Future historians venturing to reconstruct the last quarter of the twentieth century will surely grapple with the meaning of these disparate phenomena, and with the potentially confusing fact that mass communicators and some educators applied the same word—*fundamentalism*—to characterize each of them. Were such historians to rely in the first instance on the records available in the print and electronic media, they would discover that the label became ubiquitous in news reports filed

I

around the time of the 1979 Iranian revolution and continued to appear regularly thereafter, serving as journalistic shorthand for uncompromising, militant religious activists and ideologues around the world.

The discerning researcher may be intrigued to note that the word *fundamentalist,* coined by a North American Baptist in 1920 to refer to Bible-believing Christians in the United States, was frequently applied in the 1990s to Muslims and Jews—and primarily to Muslims and Jews of the Middle East.[1] Our intrepid historian would discover, for example, that "Islamic fundamentalists" (a.k.a. "Islamic terrorists") were initially thought to be responsible for the deadly explosion at the Alfred P. Murrah Federal Building in Oklahoma City, Oklahoma, on 19 April 1995. Television commentators publicized remarks to that effect made by former U.S. congressman Dave McCurdy, and subsequently reported that three men of dark complexion, "presumed to be from the Middle East," had been observed fleeing the scene of the crime. A brief but ugly backlash against Arab-Americans ensued.[2] Timothy McVeigh, an American of Irish descent, with no known ties to Islam or to the Middle East, was subsequently arrested in connection with the bombing.

The rush to judgment was not surprising given the recent, sensational history of religiously motivated acts of terrorism emanating from the Middle East. Americans bear vivid memories of the October 1983 suicide bombing that claimed the lives of 241 American marines stationed in Lebanon, and of the 1994 explosion at the World Trade Center in New York City, engineered by followers of the Egyptian preacher Shaykh 'Umar 'Abd al-Rahman. As the region of the world that gave birth to the "Peoples of the Book"—Jews, Christians, and Muslims, all of whom claim a spiritual ancestor in the patriarch Abraham—the Middle East is the place to which prayerful women and men turn, figuratively and literally, in their hope for the dawning of world peace. It is also a place, sadly, where Jews, Christians, and Muslims are often bitterly divided and locked in long-standing disputes over territorial rights, sacred land, and the holy city of Jerusalem.

Among the peoples of Judaism, Christianity, and Islam, at different times in the long histories of those traditions, there have emerged charismatic figures dedicated to the task of renewing the religious fervor and communal identity of their followers. This book is about the contemporary charismatic leader in the Middle East, the radical "man of religion" who articulates the plight of the "oppressed and righteous" ones, whose cause he embodies or claims to represent. He magnifies, through vivid words and dramatic actions, the virtues and beliefs that set his religious community apart from the infidel—and apart from lukewarm or compromising adherents of his own faith.[3] The individuals described in this book have added a new wrinkle to this role by adopting a unique style of political activism, which the Western media has come to describe as "fundamentalism."

FUNDAMENTALISM: POLITICIZED TRADITIONAL RELIGION

To suggest that certain Muslim religious scholars,[4] Jewish rabbis, and Christian preachers have something substantial in common beyond a zealous dedication to their own particular religious traditions and communities, is not to imply that they share the same worldview, much less that they are allied against the irreligious forces they confront in the modern world. Nor do the contributors to this volume take at face value the fundamentalist leader's claim that he presents the genuine face of the religious tradition. Fundamentalists are in the minority in Judaism, Christianity, and Islam; they do not speak for millions of their nonfundamentalist coreligionists and cannot always count on the allegiance even of fellow radicals within the religious community. If and when the authors refer to fundamentalists as "true believers," therefore, they are merely echoing their subjects' self-descriptions, not making normative judgments.

Why, then, apply a North American Protestant term to Muslim and Jewish activists of the Middle East? Might not this decision induce careful scholars to engage in a form of cultural imperialism, interpreting indigenous movements and individuals through the distorting lens of Euro-American sensibilities? Certainly it would be a mistake were we to insist that all "fundamentalists" exhibit the characteristics of North American Protestants. If we claimed, for example, that a belief in scriptural inerrancy is the defining mark of the fundamentalist, the category would become virtually meaningless. How could we hope, in the case of Islam, to distinguish fundamentalist Muslims from the far greater number of nonfundamentalist Muslims, who also believe the Qur'an to be the infallible word of Allah? The shared characteristics or "family resemblances" of Jewish, Christian, and Muslim fundamentalists must be found elsewhere.

The actual resemblances are found not in specific doctrines or religious practices, but in a shared attitude toward religion itself, and in a specifiable process of using religion to construct ideologies and organize movements. As a distinctive attitude or habit of mind, fundamentalism divides the world into realms of absolute good and absolute evil, claims exclusive possession of divine truth, and thrives on the identification and unmasking of the enemy. In particular, religious fundamentalists deeply mistrust secular or "godless" ways of knowing. And they oppose the ideas and practices that gain favor as a result of secularism, including *pluralism* (the acceptance of the existence of many different types of belief and practice, religious as well as nonreligious), *relativism* (the conviction that no belief is inherently superior to any other), and *radical individualism* (the idea that the individual rather than the community is the final arbiter of belief and practice). Finally, fundamentalists see revived, militant religion, characterized by absolutism and moral dualism, as the best defense against the threatening encroachments of secularism.[5]

As an ideological and organizational process fundamentalism entails the selective retrieval of religious doctrines and practices for the purpose of building a viable political movement. Politics is the organized pursuit of power, and fundamentalists seek power over, variously, the family's reproductive practices and child rearing, the school board, the seminary, the religious endowment, the denomination, the political party, the military, the government, and "outsiders," however the latter are defined. In this process fundamentalists reveal themselves to be quite at home in the modern world; indeed, they are instrumental if not philosophical modernists, appropriating (or even inventing) the latest technologies and employing the most sophisticated political stratagems.

To state this point another way, religious sensibilities animate the fundamentalist use of modern instruments and processes. If Shiʻite fundamentalists are to form a modern political party in Lebanon, it will be the "party of God" (see chapter 2). If Jewish fundamentalists are to justify the assassination of the prime minister of Israel, it will be through condemnations of the traitor or "pursuer" *(rodef),* a concept taken from Jewish religious law (see chapter 7). If Protestant fundamentalists are to establish a diplomatic outpost in Jerusalem, it will be the *Christian* Embassy, the political contrivances of which are shaped by the biblically derived, apocalyptic system of thought known as dispensational premillennialism (see chapter 8).

The word *fundamentalism,* therefore, aptly describes the basic method of the modern religious leader who reaches into the sacred past, selects and develops politically useful (if sometimes obscure) teachings or traditions, and builds around these so-called fundamentals an ideology and a program of action. What we mean by fundamentalism, in other words, is the blending of traditional religion and its politicized, ideological defense.[6]

It should be clear that fundamentalism is traditional religion only in a qualified sense. But we should be equally clear as to where the qualification lies. The process of treating the contents of sacred scripture or religious doctrine as the raw material for a new synthesis with elements of contemporary society is not unique to the twentieth century or to fundamentalists. Students of religion have long recognized that tradition is a dynamic and fluid process, not a static "essence," in every historical period. "Traditional," in short, is not synonymous with "unchanging" or "timeless."[7] If fundamentalists adapt inherited teachings and practices to the needs of the day, this hardly disqualifies them from being traditionalists. Yet fundamentalist leaders want their followers—who include university-educated doctors, lawyers, and engineers—to believe that the political message they preach is also grounded in unchanging and absolute authority and that the leader holds this authority from God. The particulars of his message may change according to the concrete circumstances; but if the source of religious authority is secure, the act of adaptation will not undermine the leader's status.

THE CONTRADICTIONS OF FUNDAMENTALIST LEADERSHIP

Thus the presentation of religion as immutable truth, as a solid rock in a sea of uncertainty, is the key to the fundamentalist leader's worldview and political ambitions. In times of political, economic, or religious crisis, the leader answers the call for certainty. He provides a stable foundation, immune from the terrifyingly rapid changes and dislocations meted out by seemingly random historical processes; he offers hope for the reintegration of personal and social identities.

In some settings fundamentalism is closely related to nationalism, as in the case of Hamas's rivalry with the secular nationalist forces of the Palestine Liberation Organization (chapter 4). But the fundamentalist leader—in the case of Hamas, Shaykh Ahmad Yasin—brings more than the usual political considerations to the situation, emphasizing also a distinctive religious content. (This too is a political consideration, of course, in that Yasin's "constituency" is made up of true believers who evaluate political realities according to spiritual imperatives.) Indeed, it is precisely their allegiance to a transcendent source of knowledge that causes fundamentalist leaders to be, or at least appear to be, uncompromising absolutists.

Yet fundamentalists practice a politicized form of religion and play religiously informed politics. And because politics is the art of compromise, the leader's dramatically proclaimed allegiance to God must be a coded allegiance. The divine will may be unbending, but the fundamentalist leader—or his operatives in the field—must be flexible in their pursuit and wielding of power. This tension between the absolutism of religious devotion and the calculation and compromise of politics, means that the fundamentalist leader will move uneasily back and forth between his dual identities, attempting to negotiate their competing universes of discourse and moral responsibilities. How is one to balance fidelity to a source of truth immune to historical change, on the one hand, and the constantly shifting demands of temporal political leadership, on the other?

Judith Miller reports the seemingly schizoid quality of the pronouncements of Sudan's Hassan al-Turabi (chapter 3), the Muslim leader of the National Islamic Front, who denies involvement in a regime whose policies he clearly shapes and who cavalierly dismisses overwhelming empirical evidence of official human rights violations, suggesting that it is all a gigantic misunderstanding. Miller wonders aloud whether the man has lost touch with reality or is distancing himself shrewdly, if transparently, from the regime's failed policies. In a similar vein Samuel Heilman, in his discussion of possible religious motivations behind the assassination of Israeli prime minister Yitzhak Rabin by a Jewish fundamentalist (chapter 7), notes the ambiguous relationship between the recondite debates and rulings of the religious Zionist rabbis and the actual conduct of the assassin, Yigal Amir. No matter how much the rabbis hide behind the ambiguity, however, Heilman holds them ultimately responsible for the climate of hatred and disdain for the Israeli government that made such an act plausible.

Other authors of this volume also use phrases like "studied ambiguity" to describe the utterances and actions of their subjects, as least as often as they use words conveying decisive action of unmistakable intent. Would the dying Khomeini throw his weight behind the pragmatists vying for his legacy, or would he support the uncompromising clerical radicals? The answer was not clear, Daniel Brumberg tells us, until the pragmatists in the Iranian government succeeded in promoting their self-serving interpretation of the Imam's ambiguous legacy. And if the Ayatollah Khomeini, whose image in the West is that of a steely-eyed fanatic, sometimes veered erratically in his political judgments and even reversed himself periodically, should we expect that Sayyid Muhammad Fadlallah, the spiritual mentor of the Lebanese Shi'ite movement known as Hizbullah, would better satisfy our stereotypical view of the unwavering fundamentalist leader? To the contrary, as Martin Kramer points out in chapter 2, Fadlallah was the master of ambiguity and double-talk, especially when reporters inquired about his opinions regarding the latest act of terror perpetrated by Hizbullah. Fadlallah, like Turabi, sometimes found it impolitic to stand too close in the spotlight to the radical forces he had helped to unleash. Politics is indeed a dirty business, especially for holy men whose spiritual discipline and personal detachment feeds the expectation that they might somehow be above it all.

THE CHARISMATIC LEADER

The fundamentalist leader of the Middle East is usually a charismatic figure. If *fundamentalist* is a useful but broad label constantly in need of nuancing, the term *charismatic* comes equally laden with misleading stereotypes. As Martin Klein notes:

> The popular press has deprived the word *charisma* of much of its meaning by using it to refer to any politician who is either handsome or articulate or any chief of state with an efficient propaganda machine. Used precisely, however, it remains an important analytic concept. Charismatic authority is religious or revolutionary. It emerges in response to social crisis or a perception of social crisis. When legitimacy is called into question, the charismatic leader is a new source of legitimacy. There are no rules, but to persist the charismatic authority must transform itself or must create a structure of rules.[8]

Like *fundamentalism* the term *charisma* is a Western construct with a revealing history. The ancient Greek word *kharisma*—meaning "grace," "favor," or, in certain contexts, "a free gift"—was adapted by the sociologist Max Weber and given a new application. In his 1930 translation of Weber's *The Protestant Ethic and the Spirit of Capitalism*, Talcott Parsons explained that "*charisma* is a sociological term coined by Weber himself. . . . It refers to the quality of leadership which appeals to non-rational motives."[9] The Weberian charismatic leader, sociologist Luciano Cavalli explains, "brings about a new order, a new social and personal integration. In principle, he lifts people from a state of regression towards the dimension of the extraordinary and the divine, from where true values and norms guide both the individual and social life, endowing them with complete meaning."[10] For Weber, Cavalli says, a charismatic leader is "the source of law, in a sense that includes the moral principles as well." He liberates his followers from any sense of guilt towards the old laws and principles that he has discarded, and "gives them new laws and principles, arousing a sense of obligation and of moral duty toward them."[11]

Weber's concept of charisma, Parsons adds, "focuses on the individual person who takes responsibility for announcing a break in the established normative order and declaring this break to be morally legitimate, thereby setting himself in significant respects in explicit opposition to the established order."[12] In this respect charismatic authority differs from both rational-legal and traditional authority. The charismatic leader makes "a kind of claim to authority which is specifically in conflict with the bases of legitimacy of an established, fully institutionalized order. The charismatic leader is always in some sense a revolutionary, setting himself in conscious opposition to some established aspects of the society in which he works."[13]

In the contemporary Middle East, we have seen what happens when a charismatic leader announces "a break in the established normative order." Under particular kinds of conditions he thereby unleashes forces beyond his control. This is certainly one of the lessons of Kramer's rich profile of Fadlallah. As a scholar of Islamic law, the spiritual mentor of Hizbullah followed a very precise legal formula in justifying suicide bombings (normally, suicide is a clear violation of Islamic law), and he studiously imposed religiously derived restrictions on the use of violence in general (insisting, for example, that Hizbullah avoid the death of innocents whenever possible). But Fadlallah found that his young, undisciplined Shi'ite followers, inflamed by the religious zeal he and others had helped to kindle in their hearts, had little use for the fine distinctions of the religious lawyer.

In other words, the dynamic of religious violence, once set into motion, follows a logic of its own; and this fact places the fundamentalist leader in a quandary. Charismatic authority depends on what Weber called *Ausseralltäglichkeit,* the emancipation from routine. Yet the fundamentalist leader is not antinomian; rather, he introduces "a pattern of conformity with . . . *a definite duty* . . . and he claims moral authority and hence legitimacy for giving orders to his followers, or whoever falls within the scope of the pattern." The authority of the charismatic leader is recognized by his followers and not, as in a democracy, derived from their consent. The salient element is therefore not the will of the followers, but their duty or obligation. Accordingly, the charismatic leader's claim to authority involves the ability "to impose obligations in conflict with ordinary routine roles and status."[14] In short, the fundamentalist leader must use his charismatic powers not only to unleash revolutionary energies in his followers, but also to contain and channel those energies toward the rebuilding of the social order.

Weber's concept of *routinized charisma* is therefore particularly useful in explaining Khomeini's struggle to ensure that the Islamic republic would be sustained in a fundamentalist mode long after the revolutionary period (and his own life) had ended. Brumberg makes this struggle the centerpiece of his profile of the Shi'ite "Imam." Because it is "a revolutionary force, tending to upset the stability of institutionalized orders . . .

[charismatic authority] cannot itself become the basis of a stabilized order without undergoing profound structural changes," Parsons writes.[15] The original force of the revolutionary charismatic authority involves the assertion of "an individual against the established order," but if the movement grows and gains recognition, becomes an organization or institution in its own right, successive leaders cannot base their claims to authority on the same grounds. Charisma then becomes part of the normative order, as in hereditary succession or the succession of an office. While a "process of routinization" is therefore unavoidable, "the charismatic element does not necessarily disappear."[16] Khomeini's goal was precisely to routinize his authority without losing its charismatic force.

This is an elusive goal, however, for charismatic authority ultimately depends on the personal qualities of the leader, and these qualities vary from person to person. Mesmerizing oratory is frequently cited, and Patrick Gaffney analyzes the discursive system of radical Islam by presenting the case of Shaykh Ahmad Isma'il, a charismatic preacher who held sway in Upper Egypt in the 1970s and early 1980s (chapter 5). Gaffney's examination of the shaykh's rhetoric—a complex farrago of rolling cadences, staccato outbursts of emotion, extemporaneous ejaculations of piety, convoluted scriptural exegesis, and astute political commentary—demonstrates the virtuosity and power of the charismatic preacher. The reader would do well to consider the profiles of Khomeini, Fadlallah, and Turabi—each of whom developed a reputation for searing, inspirational oratory—in light of Gaffney's discussion of fundamentalist Muslim preaching.

Other leaders profiled in this volume exude charismatic authority by virtue of different kinds of personal qualities. Hamas's Shaykh Ahmad Yasin injured his spine in a boyhood accident and was left partially paralyzed but spiritually unbowed; his moral courage and faith-filled endurance of suffering is perhaps more striking than his rhetorical skills or the originality of his message, according to Ziad Abu-Amr. Rabbi Moshe Levinger, Professor Heilman tells us, captivated his followers by his intense zeal and fearless pursuit of his religious convictions: he led the first illegal settler's band to Hebron and has seemed indifferent, throughout his career, to the personal price exacted by his pioneering initiatives. Gideon Aran's essay on the ideological mentors of Gush Emunim, the Jewish "Bloc of the Faithful," who pioneered the West Bank settlements, suggests that there is a charismatic quality to ideas themselves. The rather eccentric ideas of Rabbi Abraham Kook—the kabbalistic notion, for example, that every Jew harbors a "sacred spark" in his soul, leading him to support God's plan of redemption—were personalized and "operationalized" by his son, Rabbi Zvi Yehuda Kook, Aran notes. In a similar vein, Ya'akov Ariel locates the charisma of the Christian fundamentalist Jan Willem van der Hoeven in the power of an idea: the conviction that Israel will be the site of Armageddon, the final battle prophesied in the Book of Revelation, and that Jews must regain every inch of the Holy Land in order for the events of the Last Days to unfold.

To say that a person has charisma, however defined, is also to say that he or she has an audience. Charisma does not exist in isolation from human relations; it is essentially interactive, called into being and sustained through constant contact with the expectations, hopes, and fears of other human beings. The cultural and social horizons of the audience constitute the framework within which a charismatic person becomes a social leader. In this general context the sociologist Edward Shils famously discussed the decidedly nontraditional ends to which charismatic power could be turned.[17]

Writing in the late 1950s of the so-called third world, Shils observed that the charismatic authority of local tribal chieftains was being transferred to the political leaders of the developing nations. These new national leaders spoke of "the sacredness of the nation" and used their quasi-religious authority to pursue solely secular, economic ends. The lack of economic ambition in these developing countries, and their socialist economic orientation, was a function, Shils argued, of "ancestral sensitivity to charismatic things" and the muted individuality fostered by traditional societies.[18] Thus, when the political leadership fostered support for state-directed economic goals among the peasantry, it appealed not to individual interest or ambition, but to the glory of the nation.

A cultural policy designed to undermine traditionalism, Shils advised, "might help to create more favorable conditions for economizing action." Such a policy might destabilize these societies, he admitted, but "the very situation which stimulates anomie also releases creative potentialities. . . . The loosening of the hold of the ties of the extended family which is the chief bearer and mediator of tradition is essential, if any of the potentialities are to become economically productive." In short, the deliberate disruption of tradition is "a necessary precondition for the dispersion of charisma."[19]

In this view, which Shils later elaborated, the force of charisma, if channeled properly, could liberate underdeveloped societies from a passive traditionalism and move them toward a creative engagement with nature and with the world outside the tribe.[20] Shils had in mind a creative engagement that would take the form of capitalism at the expense of traditional patterns of life centering on the family and kinship network. Contemporary fundamentalist leaders, however, "come after" the manifest failure of such Western-inspired schemes of development. They place charismatic authority at the service of reconfiguring traditional society both to liberate it for greater productivity and to protect it from the kind of globalizing, homogenizing forces Shils anticipated. Shils's stated goal—to discredit the authority of the elders in order to free the individual's "libido," thereby encouraging "individual differentiation and . . . individual attachments to objects"—is precisely the kind of vision of society denounced to such effect by fundamentalist religious leaders of the Middle East.[21]

The fundamentalist leaders claim to speak for the dispossessed and despised masses—the generation that modernizing economies and Westernizing cultural revolutions failed to liberate. In the case of Islam, the despised are "millions of the unhappily ruled, the educated-but-unemployable, futureless young, the poor, the dispossessed—those whom Muslims call 'the disinherited' and whom they recruit by the tens of thousands."[22] In the case of Israel's radical Jews, the despised are the religious Zionist rabbis and their brilliant young yeshiva students who refuse to accommodate the Israeli government's plans for peace with the Arabs and who seek a Jewish theocracy in the Holy Land.

Each of these groups of religious fundamentalists provokes outrage on the part of their coreligionists who prefer moderation in the pursuit of societal and political reform, or who do not share the exclusivist religious vision of the fundamentalists. The "yeshiva boys" who make up the corps of radical religious Zionists, for example, stir up the resentment of their fellow Israelis because they take advantage of their religious identity to avoid military service but never fail to criticize the government for inadequate use of military force to restrain or extradite threatening Arab elements in the occupied territories. Islamic radicals fare no better in the eyes of their peers: Hamas is increasingly unpopular among the very Palestinian population it seeks to liberate from Israeli rule. In 1996 the desperate campaign of suicide bombings conducted by the movement's militant wing, or by its splinter groups, led to massive and indiscriminate retaliation by the Israeli government, which sealed off the West Bank and Gaza and shut down social service institutions suspected of harboring Hamas operatives. Outraged Palestinians caught in the crossfire joined rallies in support of Yasir Arafat's administration. In the face of such widespread scorn, the fundamentalist leader's charismatic authority binds together the true believers in solidarity against the outside world.

NUANCING THE CATEGORIES

If accuracy is embedded in the details, then the comparativist must constantly test the theoretical constructs "fundamentalism" and "charismatic authority" against the theory-confounding particulars of human lives. The turn to biography or life story is the way we have chosen to accomplish this task. As Martin Kramer writes, however, it is an appropriate but particularly exacting method of studying the Middle East:

> The "new" biographer, like the "new" historian, cannot discount the dearth of intimate source materials. There are no comprehensive and accessible source materials. There are no comprehensive and accessible collections of private papers, no confidential diaries deposited for the scrutiny of all. . . . There were too few intimate documents to surround public text with context. . . . No one can say how many lives of Muslim intellectuals might be turned over by the discovery of a trunk of letters. But these lives were not lived in Bloomsbury. Cairo, Damascus, Istanbul, Tehran—these cities insisted on conformity, in politics, literature, and art. An intellectual might dare to stretch these conventions but could never openly defy them. And so it is almost impossible to strip away the heavy layers of self-imposed censorship; in many instances, the absence of letters and diaries means that the private voice is forever lost.
>
> The intimate sources for the lives of rulers and leaders remain even more inaccessible.[23]

Tracking the life stories of Middle Eastern fundamentalists is perhaps even more vexing an assignment, given the studied ambiguity of their public discourse and the pronounced level of secrecy surrounding their affairs. Six of the authors of the present volume—Miller, Abu-Amr, Ariel, Gaffney, Aran, and Heilman—tried with some success to penetrate these veils by conducting extensive personal interviews either with the fundamentalist leaders themselves or with their followers; all of the contributors relied on primary sources produced by the fundamentalist leader in question or by his movement.

The resulting biographical profiles, in their richness of detail, reveal both the inadequacy and the necessity of generalizing labels and categories. The specificity of each individual's story, including its incomparable elements, does not diminish our perception that the collected stories bear substantial "family resemblances"; rather, the focus on the particular sharpens that perception, even as it guides us in refining the contents of the broad comparative categories. Certain themes and patterns of fundamentalist leadership are striking precisely because they recur in the very different social, cultural, political, and religious environments—and in the lives of the very different men—described in the following portraits. The concluding chapter discusses these notable points of comparison.

Notes

1. Christian political activists have come to prefer the term *conservative*, in part to escape the pejorative connotations attached to the term *fundamentalist*. For a thorough discussion of the application of the term *fundamentalism* in the 1990s, see the winter and spring 1995 issues of *Contention: Debates in Society, Culture, and Science*. For an example of the media's use of the term, cf. Steven Emerson, "The Other Fundamentalists," *New Republic,* 12 June 1995; Emerson discusses radical Islamists operating from the Middle East and establishing a network in the United States. On the presentation of Islam, cf. Edward W. Said, *Covering Islam: How the Media and the Experts Determine How We See the Rest of the World* (New York: Pantheon, 1981).

2. Richard Lacayo, "Rushing to Bash Outsiders," *Time,* 1 May 1995, 70.

3. For an elaboration of the argument that fundamentalism has antecedents but no precedents, see Bruce B. Lawrence, *Defenders of God: The Fundamentalist Revolt against the Modern Age* (San Francisco: Harper & Row, 1989).

4. Strictly speaking, Islam has no official "clergy"; there is, therefore, no Arabic or Turkish equivalent to the Western term *layman*. Nor has Islam historically recognized the distinction between "church" and state, the spiritual and the temporal as such. Bernard Lewis writes: "One might perhaps discern, in the postclassical evolution of the professional men of religion, some approximation to a clergy, and such terms as 'ulema' and 'mullahs' almost acquire this sense. But there is no equivalent to the term 'laity,' a meaningless expression in the context of Islam. At the present time, the very notion of a secular jurisdiction and authority—of a so-to-speak unsanctified part of life that lies outside the scope of religious law and those who uphold it—is seen as an impiety, indeed as the ultimate betrayal of Islam. The righting of this wrong is the principal aim of Islamic revolutionaries and, in general, of those described as Islamic fundamentalists." Bernard Lewis, *The Political Language of Islam* (Chicago: University of Chicago Press, 1988), 3.

5. For an elaboration of these traits, see Gabriel A. Almond, Emmanuel Sivan, and R. Scott Appleby, "Fundamentalism: Genus and Species," in Martin E. Marty and R. Scott Appleby, eds., *Fundamentalisms Comprehended* (Chicago: University of Chicago Press, 1995), 399–424.

6. There is a growing literature on the defining traits of the religiopolitical style known as fundamentalism. The first comparative work to employ this term was Lionel Caplan, ed., *Studies in Religious Fundamentalism* (Albany, N.Y.: State University of New York Press, 1987). Of the recent collections of essays on the topic, see also Richard T. Antoun and Mary Elaine Hegland, eds., *Religious Resurgence: Contemporary Cases in Islam, Christianity, and Judaism* (Syracuse, N.Y.: Syracuse University Press, 1987); Lawrence Kaplan, ed., *Fundamentalism in Comparative Perspective* (Amherst, Mass.: University of Massachusetts Press, 1992); Emile Sahliyeh, ed., *Religious Resurgence and Politics in the Contemporary World* (Albany, N.Y.: State University of New York Press, 1990); and Broni-

slaw Misztal and Anson Shupe, eds., *Religion and Politics in Comparative Perspective: Revival of Religious Fundamentalism in East and West* (Westport, Conn.: Praeger, 1992).

The first single-author volume to provide a coherent and influential theory of "comparative fundamentalism" was the aforementioned *Defenders of God: The Fundamentalist Revolt against the Modern Age* by Bruce Lawrence. The University of Chicago Press has published a series of encyclopedic volumes of commissioned essays on the topic of global fundamentalism, replete with theories, definitions, antidefinitions, and case studies. Edited by Martin E. Marty and R. Scott Appleby, the Fundamentalism Project Series includes *Fundamentalisms Observed* (1991), *Fundamentalisms and Society: Reclaiming the Sciences, the Family, and Education* (1993), *Fundamentalisms and the State: Remaking Politics, Economics, and Militance* (1993), *Accounting for Fundamentalisms: The Dynamic Character of Movements* (1994), and *Fundamentalisms Comprehended* (1995).

Volumes devoted exclusively to fundamentalism or religious resurgence in the Middle East include John L. Esposito, ed., *Voices of Resurgent Islam* (New York: Oxford University Press, 1983); Shireen T. Hunter, ed., *The Politics of Islamic Revivalism* (Bloomington, Ind.: Indiana University Press, 1988); Emmanuel Sivan and Menachem Friedman, eds., *Religious Radicalism and Politics in the Middle East* (Albany, N.Y.: State University of New York Press, 1990); and Laurence J. Silberstein, ed., *Jewish Fundamentalism in Comparative Perspective: Religion, Ideology, and the Crisis of Modernity* (New York: New York University Press, 1993).

7. On this point, see Edward Shils, *Tradition* (Chicago: University of Chicago Press, 1981), esp. 44–46, 94–100.

8. Martin A. Klein, "Muslim Authority," *Journal of African History* 31, no. 1 (1990): 158–59. Klein's article is a review of Donald B. Cruise O'Brien and Christian Coulon, eds., *Charisma and Brotherhood in African Islam* (Oxford: Clarendon Press, 1988).

9. Max Weber, *The Protestant Ethic and the Spirit of Capitalism,* trans. Talcott Parsons (1930; New York: Charles Scribner's Sons, 1958), 281. See also Talcott Parsons, *The Structure of Social Action* (Glencoe, Ill.: Free Press, 1949), 658–72. Parsons was in error according to Luciano Cavalli, who notes that Weber used the word in its "traditional Christian sense" in *Protestant Ethic,* borrowing the term from the first volume of Rudolph Sohm's *Kirchenrecht* (1892). Cf. Luciano Cavalli, "Charisma and Twentieth-Century Politics," in Scott Lash and Sam Whimster, eds. *Max Weber, Rationality and Modernity* (London: Allen & Unwin, 1987), 317.

10. Cavalli, "Charisma and Twentieth-Century Politics," 325.

11. Ibid.

12. Talcott Parsons, Introduction to Max Weber, *The Sociology of Religion,* trans. Ephraim Fischoff (Boston: Beacon, 1963), xxxiii–xxxiv.

13. Talcott Parsons, *Essays in Sociological Theory Pure and Applied* (Glencoe, Ill.: Free Press, 1949), 118.

14. Ibid., 125.

15. Ibid., 126.

16. Ibid., 128.

17. Edward Shils, "The Concentration and Dispersion of Charisma: Their

Bearing on Economic Policy in Underdeveloped Countries," reprinted in *Selected Essays by Edward Shils* (Chicago: Center for Organizational Studies, Department of Sociology, University of Chicago, 1970), 53–71.

18. Ibid., 54–58.

19. Ibid., 67–68.

20. Edward Shils, "Charisma, Order, and Status," *American Sociological Review* 30 (April 1965): 199. For critical appraisals of this article, see Joseph Bensman and Michael Givant, "Charisma and Modernity: The Use and Abuse of a Concept" (1975), in Ronald M. Glassman and William H. Swatos Jr., eds., *Charisma, History, and Social Structure* (New York: Greenwood Press, 1986), esp. 35–41; and, Bryan R. Wilson, *The Noble Savages: The Primitive Origins of Charisma and Its Contemporary Survival* (Berkeley: University of California Press, 1975), 10–13. See also Edward Shils, "Charisma," in David L. Sills, ed., *International Encyclopedia of the Social Sciences* (New York: Macmillan and Free Press, 1968) 2: 386–90.

21. Shils, "Concentration and Dispersion of Charisma," 68. Also cf. Daniel Lerner, *The Passing of Traditional Society. Modernizing the Middle East* (Glencoe, Ill.: Free Press, 1958), passim.

22. Judith Miller, *God Has Ninety-nine Names: A Reporter's Journey through a Militant Middle East* (New York: Simon & Schuster, 1996), 13.

23. Introduction, in Martin Kramer, ed., *Middle Eastern Lives: The Practice of Biography and Self-Narrative* (Syracuse, N.Y.: Syracuse University Press, 1991), 6–8.

ONE

KHOMEINI'S LEGACY

Islamic Rule and Islamic Social Justice

Daniel Brumberg

> Imam Ruhullah Khomeini is no longer with us, but his spirit is
> very much alive, and his inspirations and commands continue to
> guide millions of Muslims around the world forever to come.
> The passing away of "the Man of the Century"
> has made planet Earth all the more poor.
>
> *Imam Khomeini's Last Will and Testament,* introduction

Few would deny that Ayatollah Khomeini's intellectual and spiritual legacy remains "very much alive." That most Westerners would prefer to
forget that legacy while many Iranians fervently cling to it years after
Khomeini's death is a tribute to its enduring significance.

Khomeini's lasting influence can be traced to one simple fact: he was
the first successful Islamic revolutionary in modern times. Coups d'état
have come and gone in the Islamic world, Islamic movements have assailed secular governments, and leaders as diverse as Hassan al-Turabi
of the Sudan, Sayyid Muhammad Husayn Fadlallah of Lebanon, Shaykh

Ahmad Yasin of Palestine, and King Fahd of Saudi Arabia have claimed to rule or lead in the name of Islam. But only Khomeini led a popular revolution that overturned a social order; only Khomeini brought about the creation of an Islamic state whose leaders spoke on behalf of the world's downtrodden. The creation of an Islamic state by a mass uprising had a deep psychological impact on Muslims everywhere, particularly when the global significance of the event was dramatized by Iran's defiance of the "Great Satan" during the 1979–1981 hostage crisis.

Yet Khomeini's appeal was not without its paradoxes and mysteries. He came to power in a country dominated by Twelver Shi'ism, whose proponents reviled the traditions of the Sunni Muslims, by far the more numerous branch of Islam worldwide. Moreover, he reinterpreted Shi'-ism to justify what he called the *velayat-i faqih* (Rule of the Jurist). This doctrine called for a state ruled by a quasi-infallible *rahbar* (Leader) who would rule absolutely in his capacity as *marja' i taqlid,* or supreme religious guide of all Shi'ites. Most Sunnis rejected this notion and scorned Khomeini's claim that his return to Iran heralded the return of the Shi'ites' own messiah figure—the Twelfth, or Hidden, Imam. Yet despite this profound disagreement, Sunni activists from Algiers to Jakarta found inspiration in Khomeini's revolution.[1]

The mystery of Khomeini's legacy deepens when we consider the remarkable events that occurred during the last year of his life and immediately following his death in June 1989. In the year prior to his death Khomeini issued several edicts, the ambiguous wording of which set the stage for a transformation of Iran's political system that seemingly contradicted his greatest innovation, the Rule of the Jurist. At the vanguard of the campaign to realign the political system was the speaker of the Majlis (parliament), 'Ali-Akbar Hashemi Rafsanjani. Invoking Khomeini's own speeches, Rafsanjani secured a series of constitutional amendments that undermined clerical authority in two ways. First, it held that the Leader need not be a *marja',* but merely a man of "scholarship" and "piety" who had the "right political and social perspicacity." Second, it diminished the power of the Council of Guardians, a body of high-ranking clergy that had previously been able to veto legislation passed by the Majlis. Thus, in one fell swoop, the 1989 constitution effectively distanced "church" from state while robbing the Islamic republic of its Shi'ite core—and all in Khomeini's name.

This development may have strengthened Iran's appeal among Sunni Islamists who looked to Iran as a beacon, but it was scorned by Iran's radical clerics, who dismissed the very idea that Khomeini's legacy was mysterious or paradoxical. Rafsanjani, they asserted, had simply violated Khomeini's ideas in order to rob the Leader of his unrivaled authority over Shi'ites.

Who, then, was the *real* Khomeini? The man who professed a revolutionary Shi'ite theory, or the man whose last speeches and utterances—by design or default—helped subvert that theory in the name of a universal Islamic vision? His fundamentalist disciples advanced one simple and appealing explanation: Khomeini developed a clear and consistent ideology as a young man, then waited for the right moment to apply it; his life was one long prophetic mission culminating in his return to Tehran in February 1979.[2] Any interpretation that deviated from this view, they claimed, defamed the "true" Khomeini. Ironically, many Americans also subscribed to this view. Shaken by the humiliating encounter between the United States and the new Islamic republic, they readily accepted the portrayal of Khomeini as the Islamic world's most obstinate "religious fanatic," a man who had hidden his deepest religious convictions until his prey came within easy striking distance.[3]

Most scholars of Iran reject such stereotyping. Yet their view of the link between Khomeini's intellectual commitments and Iran's politics often replaces one simplistic explanation with another. The root of the problem is partly theoretical. It has become almost a matter of revealed truth among secular students of Islam that Islamic ideals do not "determine" politics in any fundamental way. Instead religious ideals are cleverly appropriated by leaders whose overriding goal is power.[4] Since ideals come and go while the universal desire for power remains constant, Khomeini's self-serving transformation of Shi'ism, and the ensuing efforts by Rafsanjani to appropriate his legacy, have a tenuous relationship to "genuine" Shi'ism.[5] What really counts, according to this received wisdom, are the political or social resources that allow a leader to make his views of Islam "hegemonic" within a constituency.

This reduction of Islamic leaders to crafty politicians or demagogues misses a key point: a leader succeeds by inspiring the imaginations of his followers. This cannot be done by crassly manipulating Islamic symbols, as if they were objects with little connection to the soul of religion itself, commodities that can be sold to gullible consumers. Nor can this link be based on blind adherence to a religious doctrine that only few can grasp. The cultural and religious aspirations of a people are inherently dynamic and diverse; a leader thus must show, by dint of character and action, that he can integrate the disparate intellectual and moral currents of his world in a manner, however unorthodox, that also strengthens and unifies society. The embrace and ordering of the confused and often competing yearnings of a people during a moment of shared crisis—this is what makes a "charismatic" leader. Such leaders are rare, exceptional individuals who benefit both from their protracted intellectual development and life experiences and from sheer luck, a fortuitous fit or "elective affinity" between their own commitments and the larger socioeconomic, cultural, and political conditions that imbues their ideas with an intensive mass appeal.[6]

Khomeini was one such individual. His life constituted a continual encounter with diverse spiritual and intellectual ideas deeply rooted in Iranian Shi'ite and wider Muslim society. Rather than clinging to any single creed, he combined these ideas into an ideology that was at once eclectic, even contradictory, and on another level deeply alluring precisely because it was so heterogeneous. At the same time he was assisted by the caprice of history; he did not plan his rise to power, but neither did he flinch when the political and cultural chaos of the 1970s presented him the chance to link his aspirations with those of the Iranian people.

This essay traces the roots of this extraordinary phenomenon in an effort to demystify Khomeini's ideology and to illuminate the link between that ideology and the dramatic reform of Iran's political system following his death in June 1989. It explores three central ideas that shaped Khomeini's thinking from the early 1920s through the late 1960s. The first of these was *mystical asceticism,* a tradition firmly rooted in his native soil; by renouncing worldly pleasures and probing the hidden spiritual world of mystical Islam, Khomeini would develop the moral fiber required to resist the corrupting forces of domestic tyranny and Western colonialism. The second idea, which Khomeini embraced in the 1950s and 1960s, was *utilitarianism,* the notion that the divine injunctions of Islam could not be followed in the abstract, but must be applied by leaders situationally for the purpose of protecting the political and moral unity of the Islamic community. The third "idea" was *revolutionary Shi'ism,* the ideology Khomeini began to articulate in the late 1960s and for which he later became famous. This ideology combined novel interpretations of the Shi'ite concepts of the ruling jurist and the infallibility of the imam with Khomeini's utilitarian and mystical ideas in a rich and complex pattern designed to legitimate his personal rule as "supreme leader" of Iran. Khomeini attempted to forge a bond between this theory of revolutionary Shi'ism and the aspirations of the Iranian people. In this he profited, as have other charismatic leaders, from the unpredictable turns of history: by exploiting a period of cultural and economic crisis through well-chosen words and dramatic actions, Khomeini embodied the link between his own authority and that of the Twelfth Imam.

These three approaches to religion and politics were joined in a tense and even contradictory relationship in the leadership Khomeini exercised. The sharpest tension was between his utilitarianism and the charismatic authority that lay at the core of his ideology. The utilitarian impulse would subordinate the specific doctrinal requirements of Shi'ism to the wider political challenge of unifying the Muslims, while the ideology of revolution aspired to a specifically Shi'ite state ruled by a charismatic *marja'* and his clerical allies. It was precisely his ability to transcend these tensions that made Khomeini an alluring leader. He strengthened the threads that united these different traditions in order to advance one core idea: the moral and political unity of Muslims in face of what he deemed an unholy alliance between local despots and Western imperialism.

During the 1980s, however, the human and social costs of the Iran-Iraq war, persistent economic crisis, and sharp clerical disputes threatened the legitimacy of the Islamic Republic of Iran. Khomeini discovered that the forces which gave rise to his quasi-divine authority could not last forever; each time he relied on his authority as imam to resolve a clerical dispute, he diminished the effectiveness and legitimacy of Iran's political institutions, in particular the Majlis. But if sociopolitical factors compelled Khomeini to confront the tension between his utilitarian commitment to government and his doctrinal devotion to the Rule of the Jurist, his way out of the bind was novel. The transfer of personal or divine authority to law and governmental institutions—what sociologist Max Weber called the "routinization of charisma"—usually occurs *after* the passing of a charismatic leader. Yet there is evidence that Khomeini was the agent of his own routinization—that he deliberately illuminated the path from his personal rule to the rule of institutions, thus enabling Rafsanjani and his allies to argue that their revision of the Iranian constitution honored Khomeini's legacy.

Paradoxical? Not if we keep in mind the goal at the core of Khomeini's ideology, at the center of the three intellectual-spiritual commitments that defined who he was: the goal of ensuring Islamic rule and Islamic social justice in the face of domestic and Western challenges to Islamic unity. Confronted by the possibility that the Islamic Republic of Iran might not survive his passing, and worried that clerical disputes might discredit the very principle of an Islamic state, Khomeini paved the way for the survival of that state.

THE STORY OF AN "ORPHAN"

In the early winter of 1903 a religious scholar named Sayyid Mostafa was murdered by assassins dispatched by an absentee landlord. This is the version of events told by his family and passed on to his descendants.[7] Such events were not unusual in the northeastern Iran during that period. By then, the ruling Qajar dynasty had ceded authority to landowners and their henchmen. These men imposed their own laws brutally on hapless villagers and their religious leaders. When Mostafa defied a landowner's dictates, he was struck down, six months after his son Ruhollah was born.

Ruhollah Khomeini, named after the destitute village of Khomein in which he was born, never knew his father. Yet he certainly knew of the struggles of his father and of those who had preceded him. Sayyid Mostafa came from a long line of sayyids who claimed descent from Musa al-Kazim, the seventh Shi'ite imam. In the late eighteenth century, Mostafa's grandfather moved his family from northeastern Iran to India, where the family split into two parts, one part settling in Lucknow and the other in Kintur. His son left Kintur for the holy city of Najaf, in Iraq, in the early nineteenth century, and settled in Khomein, where Sayyid Mostafa was born, around 1849. Like his father and grandfather before him, Sayyid Mostafa became a religious scholar. He began advanced studies in Esfahan, where he was the pupil of Mir Muhammad Taqi Modarrisi, the father of Sayyid Hasan Modarrisi, a prominent opponent of Reza Shah Pahlavi in the 1930s. Mostafa then trained in Najaf, taking classes with Mirza Hazan Shirazi (d. 1894), the famous cleric whose fatwa, or religious edict, initiated the 1892 tobacco boycott, which challenged British control of the tobacco market. Although he never publicly spoke of Sayyid Mostafa, Ruhollah Khomeini honored his father's legacy by following in his footsteps and by naming his first-born child after him. In choosing the path of a religious scholar, Ruhollah was encouraged by his elder brother—the future Ayatollah Pasandideh—who along with other religious instructors in the village of Khomein imparted the principles and ethos of the Shi'ite faith to the young Khomeini.[8]

Khomeini undoubtedly noticed the parallels between the story of the Shi'ites and that of his own family's last four generations, for the Shi'ites had always seen themselves as the righteous few struggling against the unjust many. This view had its roots in a seventh-century dispute over who was to succeed the Prophet as caliph, or leader of the Muslims. The Sunnis held that Abu Bakr, by virtue of the consensus of the community's leaders, was caliph. The minority Shi'ites insisted that the Prophet had designated 'Ali, his first cousin and son-in-law, as the caliph because 'Ali had acquired the Prophet's unparalleled knowledge of the Qur'an. 'Ali was acclaimed caliph in 656 despite the continued controversy over the succession. When he agreed to having the dispute over the caliphate arbitrated, however, 'Ali was murdered by a group of his most fanatical supporters. His son, Husayn, also met a violent death, murdered by the Sunni Umayyad caliph Yazid in 680 in the battle of Karbala.

In the ensuing centuries "Twelver Shi'ites" asserted that 'Ali and the ten "imams" directly succeeding him were the only legitimate leaders of Muslims. The twelfth imam was said to be in hiding or occultation, and Shi'ites believed that the creation of a fully legitimate Islamic state had to await his return. In the interim the *mujtahids,* or legal scholars, became the defenders of a persecuted minority who suffered at the hands of unjust rulers.[9] Khomeini was thus following a venerated path sanctified by the blood of many religious martyrs, including—some believed—his own father. Yet while his father labored in a geographically isolated area, Khomeini forged his religious commitments in a country that was being torn apart by civil war and interference by the great powers.

British and Russian imperialism reached its zenith in Iran within three years of Khomeini's birth, as both countries tried to shape the course of the 1905–1911 "constitutional revolution." Two central events marked that period: the August 1907 Anglo-Russian Convention, which divided Iran into three zones (Russian in the north, British in the southeast, with a "neutral sphere" along the Persian coast), and the dissolving of the Second Majlis in December 1911. The Russians, with British acquiescence, backed the Bakhtiyari tribal leaders who toppled Iran's first constitutional government, and they occupied northern Iran. One year later, Russian troops bombed the shrine of the eighth Shi'ite imam, Reza, the most hallowed Shi'ite site in Iran.

At the age of fifteen Ruhollah decided to pursue advanced studies in the town of Arak; the foreign intervention seemed to preclude his traveling to Najaf. As he grew to manhood, Khomeini came to abhor the injustice he saw in the foreign domination of his homeland, a situation he interpreted in the context not only of his father's supposed martyrdom but also of the rich Shi'ite lore of martyrdom and oppression.

KHOMEINI AS ASCETIC MYSTIC

Injustice can be resisted by individual acts of piety that explicitly or implicitly impugn the existing moral order, or it can be opposed by individual or collective deeds of revolt in the name of a new vision of the common good. The Shi'ite tradition in which Khomeini was educated emphasized the first of these two approaches. The leading religious scholars of the time asserted that any attempt to overthrow the existing rulers and replace them with an Islamic state was tantamount to blasphemy since a legitimate Islamic state could not be established in the absence of the Twelfth Imam. Taken to extremes, this view could rationalize suffering, since "from a . . . traditional perspective, the profusion of tyranny is a sign of the imminence of the return of the twelfth imam, and thus a 'preparation' for his coming."[10] Khomeini channeled his loathing of injustice into two streams of Shi'ite religiosity that emphasized the redeeming qualities of quiet suffering: asceticism and mysticism.

Asceticism entails the rejection of worldly goods and pleasures in favor of the contemplation of the spiritual. In denying all but the most basic needs—sometimes to the point of physical suffering—the ascetic tries to transcend his existence in order to reach a higher level of divine knowledge. The emotional roots of Khomeini's asceticism lie in his childhood in a remote and impoverished village, in a mud-brick house that one biographer has described as a "temporary abode, a chance dormitory on the roadside rather than a real home."[11] In this structure, which housed up to thirty people at any one time, the boy was raised by his mother, Hajar, and his paternal aunt Sahiba. Tragically, his aunt and then his mother died in 1917, leaving Khomeini under the supervision of his older brother, the future Ayatollah Pasandideh. As the unhappy chapters of Khomeini's boyhood unfolded, he learned to endure personal loss, physical hardship, and social deprivation by immersing himself in Qur'anic studies, and he apparently mastered the Qur'an at a very early age. Little else occupied his time during the ensuing years, so that by the age of seventeen, Khomeini knew two fundamental things: Qur'an and self-denial.

Khomeini brought this deeply ingrained asceticism with him to Arak, where he studied Islamic jurisprudence under the tutelage of Shaykh Abdel Karim Hairi. In 1920 Hairi moved to Qom to establish a new theological seminary. Khomeini followed shortly thereafter and became one of Hairi's prize students and eventually a leading scholar in Qom.[12] Hairi was a prominent advocate of clerical quietism. He not only insisted that the clergy remain aloof from politics, but rejected the notion that Shi'ites should model their lives after one supreme *marja' i taqlid al-mutlaq* (supreme source of imitation). Until the early eighteenth century, Shi'ites had chosen among a doctrinally diverse group of religious leaders, since according to tradition, only the Twelfth Imam had the knowledge of the Qur'an required to demand the absolute allegiance of the community. Thus Shi'ite traditionalists opposed the selection of a single supreme religious figure—the very idea of which was of relatively recent vintage—whose status might lead the masses to equate the worldly authority of the *marja'* with the divine mandate of the Twelfth Imam. But although he was a traditionalist, Hairi was hardly blind to the needs of his followers. He held that jurists, while abjuring formal participation in politics, had a duty to defend the moral and legal precepts of Shi'ism. Thus soon after arriving in Qom, where the "entire population" seemed to consist of "the blind, the lame, the hunchbacked, the sick and the mentally infirm,"[13] Hairi began building a *madrasa* (seminary) whose first mission was to tend to the religious and spiritual needs of the city's impoverished and neglected citizens.

During his first few years in Qom, Khomeini subscribed closely to the premises of his master's approach to Shi'ism. That he did so might be attributed to sheer expediency, given that political activities might have attracted the disapprobation of the authorities. But having arrived in Qom convinced that religious study and an ascetic lifestyle provided the surest path to defying injustice, Khomeini was predisposed to following in Hairi's footsteps, an inclination that was reinforced by Khomeini's exposure to mysticism during the 1920s. Mystical religious practice in Islam, known as Sufism, strives toward knowledge of the divine attained through direct emotional experiences of the divine energy or "light" of the Creator. Its practices are by definition nonintellectual and nonrational; they entail the creation of intense psychological states that sometime reach the level of otherworldly trances. That Khomeini took to such practices so avidly was logical in a way: the austere ethos of mysticism found a natural ally in his ascetic sensibilities. Thus Khomeini plunged into this mysterious world, studying with such leading scholars of mysticism as Mirza Ali Akbar Yazdi (d. ca. 1921) and Ayatollah Muhammad Ali Shahabadi (d. 1950). At the same time, Khomeini expressed his mystical devotion by writing Persian *ghazal,* or sonnets, and by authoring several studies in which he showed a mastery of gnostic discourse and mystical interpretation of prayer.[14]

Hamid Algar has noted that such activity was the "object of outright hostility" among some of the clergy, while Khomeini himself recalled the scrutiny to which he was subjected by the clerics of Qom, writing of his regret that "some of the ulema should . . . deprive themselves of the benefits to be gained from studying *irfan* [mysticism]."[15] Still, if the supernatural fervor of mysticism offended some of the clergy, its quietist overtones must have found favor among traditionalists such as Hairi. He and Khomeini maintained a distance from the temporal world of politics throughout the 1920s. Hairi said nothing when the British expelled Shi'ite leaders from Iraq in 1923, did not back Esfahan clerics when they rose against the government a year later, and failed to protest when Ayatollah Muhammad Taqi Bafqi was exiled by the royal court in 1929.

Such quietism is all the more impressive when we consider the remarkable changes that took place in Iran's political and social landscape during the 1920s. In February 1921 Reza Khan staged a coup d'état against the Qajar dynasty and installed himself as minister of war; four years later he proclaimed himself Reza Shah Pahlavi, Shah of Iran and founder of the Pahlavi dynasty. Following the example of Turkey's Kemal Atatürk, he began a modernization program that sought to secularize the society. Hairi endured this campaign for several years, but lost patience when in December 1928 the government passed a "uniformity of dress law" that called for banning the veil and replacing Islamic with Western dress. Convinced that this action violated the basic laws of Twelver Shi'ism, Hairi sent a telegram to the Shah condemning the law.[16] In the ensuing decade, however, the Shah accelerated his attempts to centralize the institutions of the state. Particularly galling were his efforts to place educational institutions and the administration of religious endowments *(Awqaf)* under the state's authority, a policy that threatened the financial and institutional independence of the clerics.

THE LATENT POLITICAL IMPULSE IN KHOMEINI'S MYSTICISM

As his story unfolded, Khomeini's attitude towards the regime shifted from irritation to outright hostility. Like many of his compatriots, he was enraged by the contempt Reza Shah showed toward many religious scholars. That scorn manifested itself brutally in 1935, when the Shah's troops massacred *madrasa* students in Mashhad during protests over the arrest of two clerics. Although he did not witness the violence, Khomeini was profoundly shaken by the sight of one of the shackled clerics "sitting under guard at the side of the road, with his turban removed."[17]

The Shah's mistreatment of the ulema inflamed Khomeini, as did the widely held belief that the Shah's modernization program was the result of foreign intervention. While Reza Shah dismissed such assertions, the British had been implicated in his 1921 coup and continued to exercise influence through the Anglo-Iranian Oil Company.[18] Moreover, the Shah invited French and Germans to help modernize the army and brought in Americans—through the 1922 Millspaugh Mission—to reorganize Iran's finances. The specter of foreign intervention became even more dramatic during World War II: in the summer of 1941 the Soviet Union and Britain invaded Iran, the former from the north and the latter from the south. In addition to the institutional manifestations of the invasion (troops, armor, trans-Iranian road and rail lines maintained by the United States) the occupying forces brought alien customs such as the free mixing of the sexes and the open consumption of alcohol. In this way a link between forced modernization, injustice, and imperialism was forged in the public mind.[19]

Khomeini sought the counsel of prominent religious scholars who publicly opposed the Shah. During the early 1930s he regularly visited the Shah's most virulent critic, Sayyid Hasan Mudarris, until the latter's assassination in 1934. In his most famous work of the time, *Kashf al-Asrar (The Discovery of Secrets),* a book published some months after the abdication of Reza Shah in 1941, Khomeini attacked the Shah for creating a government "at bayonet point."[20] Khomeini insisted that since the government had utterly failed to respect Islam and the ulema, "all orders issued by the dictatorial regime . . . have no value at all."[21] But although his writings reflected an abiding commitment to defending Islam, Khomeini never advocated clerical rule (that is, rule by Islamic religious scholars) during this period. On the contrary, he admitted that "the rule of the Jurist" had been an issue of great contention "from the first day." The clergy, he stated, "do not say that the government must be in the hands of the *faqih* [jurist]," but rather demand a "just monarch who will not violate God's laws."[22] Thus Khomeini implied that the mujtahids should appoint the monarch but declare him unfit to rule if he violated Islamic law.[23] Like Hairi, he remained dedicated to the notion that the religious scholars should serve, not as political figures, but only as a moral guides in order to preserve the purity required to defend their flock.

Khomeini's devotion to mysticism provided a powerful rationale for this mission. For at the heart of mysticism was the idea of the *insan-e kamel* (perfect man). This concept teaches that man must confront his innate moral deficiencies by striving for an awareness of all the divine attributes of God. An awareness of God and his laws, Khomeini held, provided the only means to ensure that "mankind is dissuaded from treachery and crime."[24] Because only a few gifted souls had the moral stamina and intelligence to seek the hidden meanings of God's word, Khomeini concluded that the clergy's primary duty was to help the common man strive for "totalness."[25] In this limited but important sense, Khomeini's ascetic mysticism had taken on a political trajectory. As his Tehran biographers observed, "*Irfan* . . . never implied social withdrawal or political quietism, but rather the building up of a fund of energy that finds its natural expression on the sociopolitical plane."[26]

The intellectually intense world of the Feziyeh seminary where Khomeini became a teacher offered him an ideal forum for realizing this goal. While his name had hardly been heard outside Qom, by the 1940s he had attracted a flock of loyal disciples to the seminary. The devotion of Khomeini's students was partly inspired by the moral probity he personified: he lived on a meager income, acquired no luxuries, and unlike other clerics took only one wife. Yet the roots of his charismatic appeal went beyond his ascetic example. What inspired awe in his peers and particularly his students was the skillful and alluring manner in which he combined ascetic mysticism with the study of law, philosophy, and ethics. Other teachers in Qom regarded his famous aloofness—Khomeini spoke in class without looking at his audience—with admiration, fear, or dislike. But most students and colleagues were impressed by the overtones of *irfan* that Khomeini introduced into his discussions of moral law and the Qur'an. The *talabehs* (religious students) heard these lectures as a powerful encouragement to the self-control that most of them struggled to exercise. Through this singular and even heterodox approach Khomeini formed a charismatic bond with a group of disciples, many of whom emerged decades later as his most loyal allies in the revolution.

During the 1930s and 1940s the political and social potential of Khomeini's ascetical mysticism found expression in the way he defined the mission of the religious scholars at Qom. They were to defend the morally fallible masses against the efforts of an unjust regime and its foreign backers to sabotage the social and political institutions of Shi'ism. The link between fighting injustice and opposing foreign interference would become the defining principle of Khomeini's life. By the late 1940s, Khomeini was reconsidering how to fight that battle, as events at home and abroad pushed him to conceive of the conflict in a new light.

KHOMEINI'S UTILITARIANISM

The abdication of Reza Shah in 1941 did not dampen Khomeini's anger. On the contrary, Mohammed Shah's efforts to pursue his father's modernization policies following World War II, together with repeated interventions in Iranian politics by the victorious allies, only deepened Khomeini's contempt for the regime. Nonetheless Khomeini backed the candidacy of Ayatollah Burujerdi for the position of grand ayatollah, even though the latter supported the regime.

The 1944 election of a fiery politician named Muhammad Mossadegh to Iran's parliament, and his 1951 nationalization of the Anglo-

Iranian Oil Company, transformed Iran's politics in ways that had a profound impact on Khomeini. Mossadegh's actions brought the country to the brink of bankruptcy but generated a wave of nationalist fervor. Dismayed by the prospect of civil insurrection, the Shah dismissed Mossadegh. When Mossadegh refused to go, the Shah lost his nerve and prepared to flee Iran.[27] The United States—with British support—responded by sponsoring a coup against Mossadegh in 1953, an act that allowed the Shah to return to Iran and solidify his rule in the following decade.[28] Henceforth Muhammad Shah—even more than his father—was seen by many Iranians as an instrument of Western imperialism. By turning Mossadegh into a hero, the coup engendered greater support for a nationalist ideology at the expense of Islam. Activist clerics such as Ayatollah Kashani, who had been a member of Mossadegh's National Front until Kashani broke with it in 1952, responded by trying to absorb nationalist and populist themes into Islamic ideology.[29] This trend caught Khomeini's attention. Although publicly he had kept his distance from such Shi'ite activists during the 1950s, privately he sought them out, meeting with Kashani and others to solicit their views.[30]

This development took place at a crucial moment for the entire Middle East. From Tehran to Algiers, clashes between nationalist leaders and discredited regimes were accompanied by successful efforts of Islamic groups to appropriate nationalist themes. Among these groups, the most important was the Muslim Brotherhood of Egypt. The Brotherhood's view of politics was partly influenced by the writings of the eleventh- and twelfth-century theorists of the caliphate, as recast in the works of modern Islamic thinkers such as Jamal al-Din "al-Afghani," Rashid Rida, and Hassan al-Banna, the founder of the Brotherhood. According to these advocates of "Sunni realism," the function of Islamic government is first and foremost the defense of the state and the wider Islamic community, or *umma*.[31] By making politics and power the first priority of Islam, al-Afghani, Rida, and others breathed a utilitarian spirit into Islamic thinking.

Of course, this spirit had always been present in Islam in so far as it calls for applying Islamic principles to all aspects of public life. But al-Afghani and his disciples pushed the pragmatic ethos one step further, teaching that Islam was not so much an end in itself as a useful tool for unifying all Muslims, whether Sunni or Shi'ite, against the threat of the West.[32] This utilitarian reasoning placed Islam in the service of the Muslim community's temporal needs rather than defining those needs solely according to the supreme spiritual dictates of Islam. Following this pragmatic logic, the Muslim Brotherhood insisted that they could work with a variety of regimes so long as they applied Islamic laws and secured Islamic unity against foreign encroachments.[33]

Khomeini read the writings of al-Banna and apparently met with leaders of the Muslim Brotherhood during a brief stay in Najaf in the 1930s.[34] The Brotherhood's utilitarianism found an echo in Khomeini's own religious training. Shi'ism emphasizes the pragmatic role of the mujtahids, who must use reason to engage in *ijtihad,* or legal interpretation. That Khomeini attached a mystical element to ijtihad does not diminish the importance of his work in the rational science of legal interpretation. This training, combined with his exposure to the nationalist and pan-Islamic ideas sweeping the region during the 1950s, instilled in Khomeini an affinity for utilitarian thinking—a penchant which grew as a result of a series of events in the 1960s. The death of Ayatollah Burujerdi in 1962 left Iran without a grand ayatollah or *marja' i taqlid.* By then Khomeini had developed a following in Qom sufficient to place him among the dozen or so leading ayatollahs.[35] Compared to his colleagues, however, Khomeini was an inferior scholar and mujtahid. As his Shi'ite biographers admit, it was not his knowledge of "technical procedures as such," but rather "his willingness to confront the Shah's regime at a time when few dared to do so" that eventually catapulted him to fame.[36]

The series of clashes that pushed Khomeini into the limelight were provoked by Mohammed Shah's modernization program, which Khomeini saw as more threatening to the social, economic, and intellectual interests of the clergy than anything that had been contrived by Reza Shah. Khomeini first clashed with the new regime in the fall of 1962, when he opposed a law providing for elected provincial and city councils because it failed to stipulate that only Muslims could hold public office. While this action was not noticed outside Qom, the Shah's proclamation of the "White Revolution"—and particularly the decision to give women the vote—infuriated the traditional ulema. Moreover, the Shah's decision to grant extraterritorial privileges to Americans linked "modernization" to imperialism in the eyes of many Iranians. In this context Khomeini emerged as a national figure in the spring of 1963.

Apparently aware that his fellow ayatollahs were afraid to denounce the White Revolution despite their opposition to its secularizing policies, Khomeini issued a fatwa in which he commanded Iranians not to mark the pre-Islamic Persian new year of Nowruz.[37] The regime responded by encouraging a mob to attack several students outside Khomeini's Feziyeh seminary, an action which resulted in the death of two religious students. Khomeini denounced the regime, which, he claimed, had "sealed it own doom; it is going to die and we shall be victorious."[38] The Shah retaliated

by mounting a public campaign vilifying the clergy. The campaign provoked violent protests, which, unfortunately for the Shah, fell on 2 June
1963, the holy day of 'Ashura, which marks the anniversary of Imam
Husayn's martyrdom at the hands of the Sunni caliph Yazid. Seizing on
the momentum generated by the Tehran protesters—who shouted "hail
to Khomeini" as they attacked official buildings—Khomeini publicly denounced the regime in an sermon, unprecedented in its ferocity, in which
he drew an explicit parallel between the Shah and Yazid.[39] Enraged by
this hitherto unheard-of equation with the Shi'ites' historical archenemy,
the Shah had Khomeini arrested. This led to riots in which the Shah's
security forces killed one hundred people in three days.

In the mythology of the Islamic revolution, this "second 'Ashura"
marked the beginning of a sixteen-year battle to destroy "the new Yazid."
The Shah played into this mythology by dragging out the confrontation
with Khomeini and his followers. He released Khomeini some weeks after
having him arrested, which only encouraged Khomeini to escalate his
attacks. In November 1964 the Shah expelled Khomeini to Turkey, and
in January 1965 exiled him to Najaf, Iraq. Khomeini's exile in Najaf was
the most vital link in a series of events that pushed him towards a utilitarian perspective. This development did not, however, signal a change in
Khomeini's earlier devotion to the notion of the clerics as moral guides.
As Hamid Dabashi observes, "It would be a mistake to assume that Ayatollah Khomeini went into exile determined to topple the Iranian monarchy."[40] From his seat in Najaf, however, Khomeini now had an unparalleled opportunity to sample the pan-Islamic thinking of a new generation
of radical clerics. Although further from his native land, he was in many
ways closer to the ideological transformations sweeping through the region.

In Najaf, the Shi'ite world's holiest city, a new generation of
religious scholars, fearing the growing popularity of socialist ideas and
movements, were promoting a pan-Islamic, quasi-socialist ideology in
an effort to head off leftist forces. Khomeini kept a distance from
these clerics for fear the Iraqi authorities would expel him, but he
did interact with Musa al-Sadr, a prominent leftist-Islamic cleric whose
niece was married to Khomeini's son Ahmad. More importantly,
Khomeini was exposed to the ideas of Najaf's leading radical cleric,
Ayatollah Muhammad Baqir al-Sadr. A prolific writer, Baqir al-Sadr
tried to show that Islam could incorporate Marxism's emphasis on
social justice and communitarian responsibility without compromising
its fundamental principles.[41] Moreover, he held that these principles
were broad enough to encompass both the Sunni and Shi'ite world,

an assertion that gave his ideas an ecumenical currency. Baqir al-Sadr brought his pan-Islamic concerns directly to Khomeini in 1967, just as the confrontation between Israel and the Arabs was heating up.[42] The defeat of the Arabs in the June 1967 war galvanized Khomeini. Having long argued that Islam's number-one enemy was the Jews and Israel, he now warned that Israel and its Western allies were ripping the Islamic world apart.[43] The only solution, he argued, was to strengthen the one force that could unite the Islamic world—Islam.

During the 1970s Khomeini promoted this ecumenical utilitarianism through his interactions with a myriad of Islamic student groups based in North America and western Europe.[44] In his communications with these groups, he encouraged students to find a common language that would unify the Islamic community against the West.[45] Khomeini looked to the new generation of Islamic thinkers to provide the populist themes that would inspire the youth of Iran and the wider Islamic world. Borrowing from lay Islamic intellectuals such as Ali Shari'ati (d. 1977), a leftist-Islamic sociologist who had close ties to the modernist Iran Liberation Movement, as well as from clerics such as Musa al-Sadr, who forged the populist notion of the Islamic state as defender of the *mustadh'af,* or underdog, Khomeini created an "Islamic ideology."[46] Central to this ideology was the instrumental notion that the exigencies of collective survival and social justice should dictate the principles of Islamic governance, rather than the other way around.

It bears repeating that this utilitarian approach did not imply a call for clerical rule as such. Quite the contrary: because his utilitarianism was principally concerned with issues of power and unity, Khomeini argued that any number of political institutions were equally suited to bringing about these ends. As he put it during the 1960s, the primary responsibility for reunifying the Islamic world rested with "Islamic governments, Islamic presidents, and Islamic kings."[47] Neither did this view conflict with Khomeini's insistence that religious scholars remain above politics. Indeed, if the quest for Islamic unity and justice required no particular form of government, it could be argued that a morally superior clergy that was distanced from political institutions and government would be best suited to guide the struggle.[48]

The struggle to restore unity and social justice to the Islamic community had always defined Khomeini's core principles and commitments. In the 1960s, he discovered a new means to advance these principles, setting aside issues of Shi'ite or Sunni doctrine in order to emphasize the Islamic world's common struggle for political power and unity in the face of domestic and foreign enemies. It remained to be seen if Khomeini's utilitarian commitments could be usefully merged with what came to be his revolutionary view of a specifically Shi'ite form of Islamic government.

Revolutionary Shi'ism

With its throngs of students and Islamic leaders from around the world, and the towering voice of its leading advocate of activist Islamic ecumenism, Baqir al-Sadr, Najaf was the center of what Chibli Mallat has called "the Shi'i international."[49] There Khomeini learned from emissaries that the Shah had launched a campaign to subordinate Shi'ism to a patriotic credo based on pre-Islamic Persian identity. This policy reached new heights with the October 1971 festivities held in Persepolis, Shiraz, and Pasargadae to commemorate the twenty-five hundredth anniversary of the founding of the Persian Empire. Faced with the Shah's attempts to strengthen state institutions and symbols at the expense of the moral and cultural authority of Shi'ite religious scholars, Khomeini concluded that he could no longer assume that the clerics' role as spiritual "guides" would be sufficient to safeguard Islam. And utilitarianism by itself provided no specific remedy for the political isolation of the ulema and the growing power of a secularizing state. In short, by the early 1970s Khomeini had to find a new means of defending his ideals. That solution, in its institutional form, entailed a radical revision of the doctrine of the Rule of the Jurist.

Islamic Government: Utilitarianism and Shi'ism United

The Rule of the Jurist had always been a controversial concept in the Shi'ite world. The theory of the "imamate" in Twelver Shi'ism holds that a fully legitimate Islamic state must await the return of the Twelfth Imam, since only the imams inherited from 'Ali the divine infallibility, or *esmat,* without which the word of God could not be completely revealed.[50] The corollary of this theory is that jurists cannot rule an Islamic state. At most, the traditional theologians argued, the Rule of the Jurist might be interpreted to allow for the mujtahids' jurisdiction over legal and ethical matters; but it did not allow for executive and legislative power, both of which had to be left to secular powers until the return of the "Redeemer."[51]

In adhering to the notion of Muslim religious scholars as guides Khomeini had in effect upheld the traditionalist view. But the news from Iran convinced him that this approach no longer guaranteed clerics the degree of spiritual authority they required to enforce the precepts of Islam. What, then, was to be done? Khomeini could not propose that clerics, and in particular one leading mujtahid, should actually rule an Islamic state without implying either that the Twelfth Imam had returned, or that someone with spiritual qualities similar to those of the Twelfth Imam had emerged. From a traditional vantage point both ideas were revolutionary and potentially blasphemous. Khomeini's solution to this problem consisted of two related parts. The first, forged in the early 1970s, entailed a theoretical exercise by which he drew upon his commitments to mysticism and utilitarianism to show that the Rule of the Jurist demanded a government based on both institutions and charismatic clerical rule. The second, devised immediately prior to the Islamic revolution of 1978–1979, was to show through words and actions how this novel meshing of personal-charismatic and rational-institutional authority could remedy the cultural-spiritual crisis facing Iran.

In lectures delivered in 1969 and 1970 (later collected under the title *Islamic Government*), Khomeini developed an argument for expanding the role of the Jurist from the narrow realm of law to the arena of executive and legislative rule.[52] The lectures mirrored Khomeini's enduring belief that a mystically inspired clerical elite should guide the fallible masses, and he relied on utilitarian premises to make the case for the Rule of the Jurist. He began with the familiar premise that the "Glorious Qur'an and the Sunna contain all the laws and ordinances that man needs in order to attain happiness and the perfection of his state." "Law," he asserted in a memorable phrase, "is actually the ruler." Its purpose, Khomeini argued, was to prevent men from transgressing "against the rights of others for the sake of their personal pleasure."[53]

However, because law cannot be enforced without a structure of rule, it followed that Muslims need an "Islamic government," the meaning of which Khomeini did not clarify at this point. Instead, he advanced a utilitarian argument that emphasized the *purpose* rather than the *content* of government. Its object, he asserted, was to "prevent . . . anarchy and disorder": "Islam came . . . to establish order in society; leadership and government are for the sake of ordering the affairs of society." Indeed, he continued, "it is our duty to preserve Islam. This duty is one of the most important obligations incumbent upon us; it is more necessary even than prayer and fasting."[54] Having proffered this instrumental argument, Khomeini then offered a specifically Shi'ite justification for making the clergy and its leading jurist the chief vehicle of Islamic government. He began by applying deductive logic, using the Socratic skills that were a central part of his training as mujtahid. It would be ridiculous, he suggested, to believe that God wanted man to enforce his divine law "only in the time of the Commander of the Faithful ['Ali], . . . and that afterwards, men became angels." Since man was still evil, God surely wanted man to observe his laws forever. "The wisdom of the Creator," Khomeini asserted, "is eternal and immutable."[55]

This argument, however, did not address the traditional objections against clerical rule, namely that God's laws could only be fully illuminated by the Twelfth Imam. To address this concern and create a specifically Shi'ite ideology of clerical rule, Khomeini recast the concepts of the imamate and infallibility. In *Islamic Government* he advanced another utilitarian argument to support this move. Citing the Qur'an's "authorization" suras[56] and *hadiths,* or stories, attributed to the Prophet and the imams, Khomeini argued that both the Prophet and 'Ali intended religious scholars to enforce the law pending the return of the Twelfth Imam. This did not mean, he added, that "the status of the faqih is identical to that of the Imams and the Prophet": "No one," he insisted, "can attain the spiritual status of the Imams."[57] Yet this status was "unconnected with the function as ruler," which derived from "government powers" whose source is a "rational and extrinsic matter." In other words, the critical thing about ruling was its function—the exercise of power in a "rational" manner. This duty to rule was no less incumbent on the clerics now than it was on their "functional" predecessors during the early years of Islam.[58]

This ingenious utilitarian distinction between spiritual "status" and political "function" notwithstanding, Khomeini admitted that there was one critical difference between the era of the imams and that which followed: in the latter "no single individual has been designated for the task" of rule.[59] How, then, was the religious leader to be selected? In answering this question, Khomeini cited the Qur'an and several hadiths about the imams as evidence that the ruling jurist must have three qualities: he must know the law, he must be morally just, and he must be an imam. By "imam," Khomeini hastened to emphasize, he meant a religious leader or guide—the common Arabic meaning of the term—and not one of the Shi'ite imams.[60] When a man with these three attributes emerges, Khomeini wrote, "he will possess the same authority as the Most Noble Messenger [the Prophet Muhammad] . . . and it will be the duty of the people to obey him."[61]

On what basis could one ascertain whether a leader was just and moral? The subjective nature of these qualities hardly lent themselves to rational measurement. And : How could a man who possesses "the same authority as the Most Noble Messenger" be chosen *without* reference to the intangibles of personality? Khomeini's circular argument in *Islamic Government,* that the ruling jurist should be chosen according to his leadership attributes, only begged the question. The position of ruling jurist, he insisted, in a phrase that reflected the elitist premises of Shi'ism, would "fall" to a scholar who had achieved a level of ijtihad sufficient to "discern the true practices of the Messenger of God."[62] If such a person could not be found, the task would "fall" to a group of scholars. But Khomeini did not say how these abilities were to be demonstrated or measured.

In 1972 Khomeini proposed an ingenious solution to this problem in a publication called "The Greater Jihad" (also known as "The Struggle against the Appetitive Soul"). His argument was based on a mystical reinterpretation of the concept of infallibility which implied that infallibility could be attained through earthly actions—through the acquisition, in other words, of charismatic authority. Thus Khomeini argued that infallibility was not exclusively a quality of divinity passed on from Imam 'Ali to his eleven heirs. Infallibility could also derive "from the perfection of faith. . . . If a man believes in God Almighty and with the eye of his heart sees Him as clearly as he sees the sun, it is impossible for him to commit any act of sin." Man acquires this "extrinsic" infallibility, Khomeini asserted, when he renounces "the desire of his carnal self." Shorn of the "veils of darkness" and "attachment to the world,"[63] he is spiritually reborn before "an armed powerful (master)."[64] Indeed, the imams themselves, Khomeini insisted, attained this kind of earthy esmat through "asceticism, acquisition of illumination, and virtuous dispositions."[65] The logical corollary of this argument was that those rare mortals who were capable of achieving—as opposed to intrinsically possessing—"perfect faith" could follow in the footsteps of the imams, since they would possess the extrinsic infallibility required to perform the political functions of the latter.

Thus Khomeini linked the practical and charismatic to conclude that the Rule of the Jurist could entail the rule of a quasi-infallible but mortal leader. Whether he anticipated in 1972 that he would be that leader is, however, difficult to say. It may not have been entirely coincidental that his own charisma echoed the "extrinsic infallibility" he depicted in his mystical tract. Indeed, his students and closest allies had been calling him "Imam" since 1970. Nevertheless, as Khomeini's own argument implied, charisma could not be attained by theory alone, nor from the adulation of his immediate disciples. The extrinsic infallibility of which he had written—the worldly evocation of a spiritual light that shows God's favor—had to flow from actions and words whose miraculous aura "spoke" in some profound and magical manner to the yearnings and aspirations of a leader's following. If the notion of the Rule of the Jurist was to spark the imaginations of the Iranian people, if Khomeini himself was to assume the mantle of the jurist, he would have to show by his words and deeds that he could remedy the ills from which the Iranian people were suffering.

THE RISE OF THE IMAM

The crisis that gripped Iran during the late 1970s provided the context in which Khomeini demonstrated to the Iranian people that his theory of Islamic rule was the antidote for their suffering. This crisis was first and foremost one of identity. We have already noted that the Shah's modernization program deliberately belittled indigenous Shi'ite traditions in favor of a pre-Islamic nationalist credo represented in the symbols of the "Pahlavi monarchy." This campaign to redefine Iran's national identity began with the crowning of the Shah in 1967 and seemed to reach its zenith in 1971 with the lavish celebrations marking the twenty-five hundredth anniversary of the founding of the Persian Empire. But the festivities in Persepolis and elsewhere—at which foreign dignitaries feasted on fowl, champagne, and caviar—were just the beginning. In 1975, with the onset of the oil boom and huge profits accruing to the state's coffers, the Shah's "imperial grandeur" reached unheard-of heights. From his perch upon the gold-encrusted "peacock throne," the Shah tried to reshape the consciousness of the Iranian people according to his own pre-Islamic, Persian image. He began by sponsoring international meetings at Persepolis and other cities to discuss the contributions of pre-Islamic religions and cults to Iranian history. One year later, in 1976, he replaced the Iranian-Islamic calendar with the "Sal-e Shahanshahi, the . . . 'Year of the King of Kings' based on the putative founding of the first Iranian kingdom."[66] Overnight, the Iranians were told that it was no longer 1355, but 2535!

Few people enjoy being told that the cultural symbols that give them a sense of common identity are trivial or even meaningless.[67] But the Shah's offense was compounded by the socioeconomic effects of rapid, oil-financed industrialization and the widespread perception among Iranians that American political and cultural connivance was responsible for the Shah's campaign to modernize the country. This campaign brought thousands of Iranian youth from the villages and towns to the cities. There they suffered from the unemployment, crowding, and poverty that is so often the fodder for urban rebellion in third-world metropolises. Those who bore the brunt of this process were enraged by the conspicuous consumption of Western luxuries displayed by Shah's family members and political cronies. Confronted by such extreme disparities in income and lifestyle, these young people sensed that their country was being torn apart by the seductions of Western material goods. The corrupt elite that ruled Iran did little to mitigate the popular perception of social and cultural fragmentation and dependence on the United States. By the mid-1970s, Washington was heavily implicated in providing the Shah with military hardware and political support, and American products and businesses had inundated the Iranian media and economy. In 1976 and 1977 the United States did push for a degree of political liberalization in Iran, but this pressure, rather than bolstering the Shah's position, helped to prepare the way for his downfall.

Iran's traditional merchants and craftsmen paid a particularly high price under the Shah's modernization campaign. With oil-fed industrialization breeding a rush for Western products, the "bazaaris," as this class was called, lost not only money but also the pride that came from producing the arts and crafts of a national culture. The close relationship between this class and the clergy made this combination of economic and cultural loss especially explosive.[68] This process of economic dislocation and cultural fragmentation culminated in the late 1970s. With some six hundred thousand tourists visiting the country each year, and no fewer than fifty thousand Americans residing in Iran on the eve of the 1978 revolution, many Iranians felt their country was again under siege. What made the American "invasion" particularly infuriating was the popular conviction that it advanced the Shah's assault on Shi'ite identity.[69]

MARTYRDOM AND THE MESSIANIC MOMENT

If the onslaught against Shi'ism was perceived as the outcome of a conspiracy between the Shah and his American supporters, then the logical conclusion was that the domestic and foreign foundations of the Shah's regime had to be destroyed. This growing conviction, especially among Iran's urban lower-middle classes, helped Khomeini build an ideological bridge between his new theory of Islamic rule and the yearnings of the Iranian masses. He began in 1977 by instructing his disciples to distribute audiocassettes of his preaching throughout Iran. In Qom Khomeini had taught upwards of twelve thousand students and he mobilized several thousand of these young men to spread his condemnations of the Shah's regime throughout the cities and towns of Iran.

Khomeini's ability to reach the Iranian masses was also facilitated by his expulsion from Iraq in September 1978. In his new headquarters outside Paris, few restraints were placed on his political activities, while the international press gained unprecedented access to him. In the cassettes distributed from Iraq and Paris, Khomeini was careful *not* to advocate clerical rule for fear of alienating potential allies among liberals and leftists. What he did do was inspire the youth to take to the streets. In retrospect, it is clear that Khomeini hoped the anticipated killings of protestors by the Shah's troops would persuade Iranians that they themselves were enduring the martyrdom of Imam Husayn and his supporters at the hands of Yazid. In such an atmosphere of mass suffering, a leader perceived as absolutely good and imbued with a clear determination to resist evil—a this-worldly imam—would then reappear to lead the people from darkness into light.

This apocalyptic drama began to unfold in October 1977 with the sudden death of Khomeini's son Mostafa. Khomeini was apparently crushed by the loss. Khomeini believed that his favorite son—the "light of my eyes" and the namesake of Khomeini's supposedly martyred father—had been murdered by the Shah's secret service, the SAVAK. But as miserable as he was, Khomeini did not publicly mourn his son's death. Instead, as his official biographers remind us, he "bore this blow stoically."[70] This demonstration of quiet suffering and unbending defiance had its intended effect. Within days of Mostafa's death, Khomeini's father-in-law, Ayatollah Saqafi-Tehrani, published an obituary that referred to Mostafa as "the offspring of the Exalted Leader of All Shi'ites of the World." Emboldened, Khomeini's supporters flooded him with condolences, an act which obliged the grand ayatollahs of Qom to hold their own memorial service, "thus indirectly acknowledging Khomeini's position as supreme leader."[71]

The Shah's court retaliated by having the daily newspaper *Ettela'at* publish an article describing Khomeini as a British agent and a "mad Indian poet with homosexual tendencies."[72] Outraged, Khomeini's supporters took to the streets of Qom on 8 January 1978. As more young "martyrs" perished, Khomeini hailed "the people of Iran [who] have proven how fully alive they are."[73] Such "proof" reached new peaks on 8 September 1978, when hundreds of Iranians were shot down in Tehran's Jaleh Square in what came to be known as "Black Friday." With the approach of Muharram—the month in which the martyrdom of Imam Husayn is commemorated—Khomeini found his moment. Evoking Husayn, he issued a rousing call "to begin the month of epic heroism . . . the month in which the leader of the Muslims taught us how to struggle against all tyrants."[74]

In the following weeks fifteen hundred Iranians were killed in clashes with the Shah's troops. Then, on December 10 and 11, the days of Tasu'a and 'Ashura—the holiest days of the Shi'ite calendar, marking the eve and the day of Husayn's martyrdom—a miracle of sorts occurred. As more than a million Iranians filled the streets, a group of officers and enlisted men attacked the officers' mess of the Shah's Imperial Guard.[75] The ensuing desertions from the military left the regime defenseless. On 17 January the Shah and his family quit Iran. Two weeks later, on 1 February 1979, "Imam Khomeini" returned "to his homeland." This event "signaled the ushering in a new era for Iran and the world. . . . By the time he returned to Iran, the Imam, with no material resources . . . had established himself as the undisputed leader . . . (and) above all, a perfect exemplification of Islam in practice."[76] That Khomeini's return was made aboard an Air France 747 should not obscure just how miraculous this event appeared to be to his people. His stoic example had inspired the nation to topple a despised monarch. Now as processions of cars made their way into Tehran, million of Iranians hailed Khomeini as the "Imam." Thus Khomeini achieved the extrinsic infallibility he had written about less than a decade earlier.

Khomeini never called himself "Imam," but he did nothing to discourage his followers from doing so. Traditional clerics such as Ayatollah Shariatmadari warned Khomeini that this unprecedented use of the term posed unknown dangers. But this was beside the point.[77] Khomeini knew that his courageous example, combined with the adulation of the masses, had turned him into Imam Khomeini. The mere use of this term, as Dabashi writes, "in defiance of all historical or doctrinal prohibitions . . . demands, indeed exacts, obedience with the combined force of facts and fantasies."[78]

The Remedy: Reviving the Clergy and "Slapping" the West

Khomeini completed his metamorphosis into Imam by explaining to Iranians how clerical rule would restore the sense of dignity and social justice denied them by the Shah. Khomeini delivered this message in a series of Friday sermons with the same stern but penetrating detachment that had made him a popular and feared teacher years before. Standing erect in a flowing black robe, his austere black turban setting off his striking white beard, Khomeini would never make eye contact with his listeners, as if to tell his followers that the world was his audience. He invoked the themes that had shaped his own life, knowing that each of them found an echo in the yearnings of his followers. Making use of the simple populist terms he had imbibed in the 1960s, he would weave references to martyrdom, ascetic mysticism, and the quest for political power into a powerful ideological tapestry of regained unity and community.

The speeches Khomeini made during the first year of his rule capture the central themes that made his theory of revolutionary Shi'ism appealing. He began one of his most famous speeches, delivered in December 1979 to an audience of craftsmen, by asserting that the isolation of Islam under "this corrupt father and son . . . was mainly due to foreign propaganda."[79] Westerners and their Iranian supporters, he asserted, were responsible for "imprisoning" Islam in two false realms. The first consisted of the "schools and mosques" over which the clergy presided. These clerics behaved as if Islam "allowed only spiritual aspects," failing to notice that in the Qur'an "there are also chapters on government . . . laws and all that is related to . . . government." The second realm was filled with those who "sacrificed spiritual values for material considerations." These "materialists"—by which Khomeini meant liberals and Marxists, and particularly Islamic Marxists—turned "every chapter of the Qur'an" into "a worldly issue," as if "nothing existed in the invisible world." Worse, the materialists claimed the revolution was about "democracy, when most of (the Iranian people) never heard of the word 'democracy.' " Nor was it about "an improvement in their material life." Such a claim, Khomeini implied, was ludicrous: "Does it seem reasonable for a person to shout for his stomach and then give up his life, is this reasonable?" "Could anyone," he asked, "wish his child to be martyred in order to obtain a good house? This is not the issue. The issue is another world. Martyrdom is meant for another world. This is a martyrdom sought by all of God's saints and prophets. . . . The people want this meaning."

Islam was limited neither to mundane nor to spiritual concerns, Khomeini asserted: "Islam is everything." It "transform[s] man" by uniting his spiritual and physical existence, for "man is a miniature universe. . . . Man embodies all the things that exist in all things . . . good and evil." But man by himself cannot bring body and spirit together, Khomeini explained. Thus it was the task of the prophets "to take man by the hand . . . and guide him to the light . . . through teaching." This evocation of Khomeini's lifelong devotion to mystical philosophy struck a chord among his audience because it addressed the spiritual and social alienation of so many Iranians in the late 1970s. Khomeini understood that in their readiness to die, Iranian youth were paradoxically expressing a desperate desire to regain their humanity. As he put it on another occasion, "Dying does not mean nothingness: it is life."[80]

Khomeini never let his audience forget who was responsible for taking their humanity away. "The superpowers," he warned, "are stripping us naked. . . . One of their big plans is to rob us of our brains and replace them with European ones: To make us so European that we will think everything we have comes from Europe, to rob us of our intellectual independence." This appeal to the populist theme of dependency found a receptive audience among those classes that had paid the highest economic and spiritual price for the Shah's modernizing regime. Addressing the assembled craftsmen Khomeini warned that "our brains have become empty, we have forgotten our industries: tile work, inlaid work, carpet-weaving. . . . We forgot these things because they made us fall in love with the West." Indeed, he asserted, things had gotten so bad that when one of the Shah's relatives developed tonsillitis, "a doctor was fetched from abroad. . . . This was such a slap to our doctors . . . it was such a slap in the face to these people. . . . What shame and degradation it is for a country that it has to stretch its hands toward America." Tapping into the vein of humiliation and self-reproach many Iranians felt at being made to "fall in love with the West," Khomeini declared that the time had arrived to replace our colonialist brain with "an independent brain." But he also insisted that Iranians could not attain this goal if they remained fatalistic, if they were "satisfied with saying 'God Willing' . . . or just praying." Instead, he asserted, "you should act."

Invariably, Khomeini prescribed three closely related courses of action. First, he insisted that Iranians sever all "economic and cultural links with foreign countries." But this divorce could not be effected, he argued, without humiliating the party most responsible for their sufferings—the American government. Khomeini insisted that the American government be "slapped in the face" and "punched in the mouth."[81] On 4 November 1979, Islamic students engineered perhaps the most dramatic manifestation of Khomeini's words when they overran the American embassy and took hostages. Second, Khomeini asserted that the moment had arrived to replace "this Western pattern . . . with an eastern pattern . . . an Islamic pattern." By "eastern pattern" he meant an ethical approach to life in which man's physical and spiritual sides were unified in a way that checked his natural propensity for evil and self-indulgence. This, Khomeini insisted, was this approach of the prophets, who "would never fight among themselves because fighting comes from selfishness and flaws in the human being."[82] In the absence of the prophets, the clergy were most qualified to pursue the war against corruption and the evils of egoism. "The power of the clergy . . . unified the people and made them rise against the regime," he observed.[83] Thus it followed that the clerics should now rule Iran, in order to maintain social peace and harmony. Third, Khomeini held that clerical rule required an arbiter, an ultimate source of moral authority who would, as it were, shepherd over the other shepherds. The supreme authority was the ruling jurist. "I assure the nation," Khomeini announced,

> that if Islamic government works under the supervision of the vice-regency of the chief theologian . . . no harm will befall the country. . . . The chief theologian will control and prevent any measures taken by the government, the president or anyone else if they are contrary to the path taken by the nation or the interests of the country.[84]

In establishing himself as the final arbiter of the nation's interests, Khomeini offered a powerful combination of Shi'ite utilitarianism and mystical philosophy. He realized that a synthesis might be seen as a prescription for tyranny, and he reassured his audience that *"velayat-i faqih* [the Rule of the Jurist] will not create a dictatorship."[85] Khomeini also understood, however, that Iranians felt a pervasive longing for someone to put the country back together again. The eclectic ideology that underlined the Rule of the Jurist promised to do just that. By proposing methods of regaining a sense of spiritual "wholeness" that were both practical and cathartic, Khomeini captured the imaginations of millions of people. At the heart of this multifaceted project was Imam Khomeini himself. His actions and words offered Iranians a unsurpassed example of what could be achieved by selfless and resolute devotion to a basic set of principles. When Khomeini accepted the mantle of leadership in 1979, he assumed that he had finally discovered the most effective means of realizing these ideals. But as he would soon learn, the Rule of the Jurist ignited as many fires as it was designed to extinguish.

KHOMEINI AND THE REVOLUTION

In December 1983 Khomeini made this extraordinary statement:

> Before the revolution, I believed that once the revolution succeeded then there would be honest people to carry out the task. . . . Therefore I . . . stated that the clergy would leave and attend to their own profession. However, I later realized that . . . most of . . . (the honest people) were dishonest. . . . I later stated . . . that I had made a mistake. This is because we intend to implement Islam. Accordingly . . . I may have said something yesterday, changed it today, and will again change it tomorrow. This does not mean that simply because I made a statement yesterday, I should adhere to it. Today I am saying that . . . the ulema should continue with their jobs.[86]

Having defeated his enemies and secured his power in the name of the Rule of the Jurist, he admitted that initially he had wanted to restrict the ulema's activities to what he called their "own profession." More remarkably, he acknowledged that he would not cling to past statements if he concluded he had been mistaken. To those who believe Khomeini brought to his stewardship of the Islamic republic a coherent and internally consistent ideology, this remark sounds strange. But as we have seen, the ideology of revolutionary Shi'ism—of which the Rule of the Jurist was a part—incorporated an eclectic mix of philosophical and political ideas. These ideas were bound together by a core theme to which Khomeini alluded in the above remarks: "We intend to implement Islam." In pursuit of this pragmatic goal Khomeini claimed he had a right to change his mind from one day to the next. In the final analysis, what counted was devising the most effective means of achieving Islamic unity and social justice.

This practical approach to ideology had served Khomeini well all his life. But it had done so as a doctrine of protest or opposition rather than an ideology of actual power. Once Khomeini became rahbar, it was possible that the eclectic nature of this ideology would become a liability. Khomeini's utilitarian or pragmatic tendency led him to call for mechanisms that would sustain Islamic unity and power, while his traditional elitism led him to call for a divinely inspired ruler whose authority emanated from his personality. While both approaches had played vital parts in bringing him to power, Khomeini was bound to discover that utilitarianism and charisma were not easily reconciled when it came to building and sustaining an Islamic state. Such a state required an institutional foundation that would outlive its charismatic, yet mortal, supreme leader.

The problem of succession was hardly unique to Khomeini. All revolutions born under charismatic leadership must one day confront the task of moving from what Weber called "charismatic" to "rational" or institutionalized authority.[87] Charismatic authority derives from the alluring power that a leader's personality exercises over his followers. But while emotional appeal may attract adherents, it cannot be the basis of a lasting political order. Eventually, solid institutions and laws that transcend the personal authority of the leader must be created. Without institutionalizing authority, the new political order will not easily survive the passing of its founding figure.

This raises an interesting question: Are revolutionary leaders aware of the need, in Weber's phrase, to "routinize charisma"? Or must this process await the emergence of new leaders with the ability to see, as it were, into the institutional hereafter?[88] Khomeini was aware of the tensions in his ideology and consciously wrestled with them from the moment he became leader of the Islamic republic in 1979 until his death in 1989. Cognizant of the need to forge institutions that would survive, Khomeini took several decisions during the last two years of his life that effectively transferred his authority to the institutions and laws of the Islamic republic. In this way, he was the agent of his own routinization. In telling this story, we will not give a detailed history of the first decade of the Islamic Republic of Iran. Rather, we will focus on how Khomeini wrestled with the dilemmas of charismatic rule that his elevation to Imam had created, examining his public speeches and pronouncements in the context of Iran's changing social, economic, and political conditions.

Khomeini's struggle to reconcile charismatic and rational authority revealed itself in sometimes contradictory pronouncements; we will consider examples in four domains. First, he showed ambivalence regarding the costs of "revolutionary action," promoting such activity during his first turbulent year as leader in a bid to keep the mobilizing fires of the revolution burning, yet bemoaning the political and social chaos it engendered and often condemning actions as "un-Islamic." In so doing he sent mixed signals to his followers, one day calling for purges, the next insisting that law and order prevail. Second, Khomeini evinced apprehension regarding clerical involvement in politics. Although his devotion to mystical Islam and Shi'ite political theory convinced him that clerics had to have some political power or influence, he feared that their moral stature would be compromised by the unseemly public struggle to determine policy. Thus he would promote religious scholars' involvement in politics, only to assail them for not adhering to their "profession" when their actions produced political strife. Third, Khomeini attempted to arbitrate the dramatic disputes between the Majlis and the Council of Guardians, the body of high-ranking ulema empowered to approve or reject all legislation, without preference for either, rather than breaking the standoff that resulted from their overlapping authority under the 1979 constitution. This legislative paralysis proved disastrous for Iran's economic and political stability as early as 1982.

Finally, Khomeini evinced ambivalence about his own role as "supreme leader." The constitution rendered the Majlis relatively impotent vis-à-vis the Council of Guardians, a situation that frequently obliged him to intervene in politics, particularly during the first year and a half of his rule. Nonetheless, he demonstrated a preference for transferring authority to the Majlis, which he often called—in contradiction of the constitution—the "paramount source of authority," rather than exercising his authority as rahbar. Such interventions only emphasized how dependent the entire political system was on his own charismatic authority, but barring a change in the constitution, Khomeini could not remedy this imbalance.

By the mid-1980s the costs of continuing this cycle had become prohibitive. The Council of Guardian's repeated vetoes of social reform laws, compounded by the human and economic costs of the Iran-Iraq war, had left the economy in shambles. Constant infighting among the clergy was producing precisely the consequences Khomeini most feared: in their struggle for power, the upholders of moral order were impugning the sanctity of the Islamic republic. Consequently, the ideals Khomeini cherished above all others—unity and independence—were threatened. Faced with this crisis, Khomeini turned to ascetic mysticism. The clerics, he insisted, would regain their unity and moral authority by abandoning their egotistical quest for power in favor of contemplation of the divine. During the war with Iraq Khomeini took this notion of self-denial to the limit by equating mystical asceticism with mass martyrdom. When this approach failed, Khomeini invoked utilitarian principles of "ultimate necessity" and "secondary ordinances" in a bid to bypass the authority of the Council of Guardians.

As these attempts proved futile and his health grew worse, Khomeini advanced a novel solution to the crisis of governmental authority: in a series of statements in late 1987 and early 1988, he proposed that the government, insofar as it was part of the "vice-regency" of the Prophet, had a right to define Islamic "interests" as it saw fit. This utilitarian declaration opened the door to pragmatists within the regime. Led by Hashemi Rafsanjani, they invoked the Imam's words, often with his blessing, to justify a revision of the constitution that weakened the authority of the ruling jurist and the Council of Guardians and in theory increased that of the Majlis.

The First Stage: February 1979 to December 1980

Historians have argued that during the first year of the revolution, Khomeini tricked his opponents. By inviting modernist Islamic leaders such as Mehdi Bazargan and Abul Hassan Bani-Sadr to share power, then crushing them when their support was no longer needed, Khomeini supposedly executed a carefully designed plan to impose the Rule of the Jurist.[89] In a general sense this interpretation is correct. Khomeini wanted to derive legitimacy from these modernist intellectuals' quasi-socialist agenda without subordinating his revolutionary agenda to the them. But this explanation simplifies reality by confounding the results of a complex historical process with Khomeini's intentions. Looking closely at the chaotic process by which he consolidated power, there is evidence that Khomeini initially took a flexible approach to instituting the Rule of the Jurist. Such flexibility was not merely the result of political expediency; it reflected a desire to integrate his diverse political ideas into a workable plan of Islamic rule.

Khomeini found, however, that his vision of an Islamic system and that of the modernists were not easily reconciled. Indeed, he correctly assumed that the liberal approach to Islam advocated by Bazargan would lead to the effective separation of religion and politics. After his triumphal return to Iran in February 1979, Khomeini linked the traditional notion of clerics as ethical guides to a pragmatic concern with maintaining order. To prevent "anarchy and chaos," he insisted, "the ulema and the preachers (must) . . . go to mosques and call on the people to observe peace and friendship."[90] In the ensuing weeks the multiplication of "revolutionary committees" brought the very chaos he feared. Khomeini responded by outlining a functional view of government, according to which revolutionary zealotry would be tamed by the compartmentalization of governmental tasks. "Islamic revolutionary committees," he warned in a fourteen-point decree, "are duty-bound . . . to refrain from interfering in government." To ensure that they acquitted themselves in a "humanitarian fashion," the ulema, as "guardians of the Qur'an and Islam," were "not to allow anyone to deprive anyone else of his freedom."[91]

As the 30 March referendum on the creation of an Islamic republic approached, Khomeini expressed a hesitancy about the unrestrained use of his own authority—a hesitancy that would surface time and again in the ensuing months and years. "I demand of you, my sisters and brothers, to go and drop that ballot card . . . which says 'yes.' "[92] The next day, however, he insisted that "you are free to vote for whatever you like. . . . But I recommend that . . . to obey the orders of God . . . you should try and vote for the Islamic Republic."[93] After the overwhelming vote in favor of a Islamic republic, Khomeini continued to prefer political cooperation over revolutionary action. Thus he attempted to cooperate with Prime Minster Mehdi Bazargan, who had been appointed a month before the March referendum. An engineer by training and a leader of the modernist Iran Liberation Movement, Bazargan favored a liberal approach to Shi'ism. Thus he had advocated a draft constitution that provided for a Council of Guardians consisting of five clerics and six lay legal experts. The idea, inspired by the 1906 constitution, was to limit the clerics to their traditional domain as legal guardians, while placing real executive and legislative power in the parliament.[94]

Despite opposition to Bazargan's modernist views within radical Islamic circles, Khomeini supported his prime minister until the first days of spring 1979. But in the following months he began to see in Bazargan's plan the makings of a counterrevolution whose aim was to subvert the principle of Islamic rule. Khomeini's suspicions were heightened by several attacks on leading clerics, including the 1 May assassination of his longtime disciple (and chairman of the Revolutionary Council), Ayatollah Morteza Motahhari. When Bazargan submitted the draft constitution a month later, Khomeini vetoed his proposal to create a "constituent assembly" to consider the constitution. Instead, he created a seventy-three-seat "assembly of experts," whose task was to draft a constitution without the interference of lay political leaders. This was followed by the election of the Assembly in August, the takeover of the American Embassy by Islamic radicals on 4 November, and Bazargan's resignation two days later.

As these events unfolded, Imam Khomeini became more hostile toward anyone he suspected of rejecting the principle of clerical rule. He was especially suspicious of traditional clerics and lay Islamic intellectuals, "those who want to speak behind a veil . . . (of a) democratic Islamic Republic." They "want freedom but without Islam," he insisted. "We hate freedom without the Qur'an. . . . We hate their saying: Islam without the clergy." This talk was unacceptable. "The slightest deviation from the Islamic Republic," Khomeini warned, "is against the course of Islam."[95] A month later Khomeini lashed out at the modernist forces, who wanted a constituent assembly to draft the constitution. "This presents a danger for Islam and for the Prophet of God," the Imam said. "The ratification of the constitution by the constituent assembly . . . poses a danger for the Hidden Imam." Thus, he warned, the misguided intellectuals who supported this idea should "know that I . . . do not want them to be suspected of ill intentions."[96]

Having exhibited such clear hostility to the opponents of clerical rule, Khomeini wavered. In theory rule by the religious scholars was legitimate. But in practice, he found it could backfire when the ulema competed for power in a manner that blemished their reputation as upholders of the collective moral order. In this sense, Khomeini warned, "we are facing a . . . danger greater than that posed by the former regime. This is the danger of unbridledness *(afsar gosikhteh),* which means that (when) . . . the walls of dictatorship are crumbling . . . (man) commits any deed his heart desires." This debilitating condition had infected the ulema in its bid for power. Zealous religious scholars "had given people the impression that "we are ensnared by the tyranny of the clergy, (that) the clergy is a dictator." If this situation persisted, the very survival of the republic would be in jeopardy. "Even Imam Ali was defeated by Muawiyah," Khomeini reminded his audience.[97]

In these warnings Khomeini addressed the revolutionary committees, whose revolutionary justice was fomenting chaos. "If the committees . . . God forbid, should act against the rules of Islam," Khomeini warned, "they have failed our school." The task of spreading the revolution, he went on, "is a great undertaking for the clergy." But in overstepping proper bounds, "you are losing the key to the nation's victory." That key was the principle to which Khomeini was most devoted: "unity of expression."[98]

Khomeini's attempt to mitigate the negative effects of clerical activism had a schizophrenic quality to it. On the one hand it was marked by calls for harmony and fairness. "Set aside other objectives in the interest of Islam and . . . join hands," he told the clerics. On the other hand it was characterized by a demand for revolutionary action against all forces which threatened this quest for harmony. "I pray to Almighty for Strength for Islam," Khomeini asserted, and "I issue the same emphatic warning to the press. . . . If I should sense a serious danger, I will bring up the problem with my dear nation."[99] Two months later he went even farther. Reacting to a rebellion in Kurdistan he warned, "We will give these corrupt strata a little longer. . . . If they do not put their affairs in order . . . God knows that I will act as a revolutionary."[100] In this candid admission that events were pressing him to "act as a revolutionary," the Imam also challenged the clergy to join in him in his crusade to destroy all the forces opposed to clerical rule. Harmony and unity would thus have to be brought about by revolutionary action, with all the paradoxes that implied:

> Theocracy is something that God, the exalted, has ordained. . . . Wake up, you gentlemen . . . because the deviationists are trying to smash our movement. . . . (They) speak out (against) the concept of theocracy. . . . I shall strike you in the mouth. Stop this talk, . . . Enough is enough: what ought to be done must be done.[101]

By November 1979 Khomeini had in fact achieved "what ought to be done." On the fifteenth of that month, the Assembly of Experts approved the new constitution. While this document marked a watershed for Iran in that it enshrined Khomeini's view of the Rule of the Jurist, it also reflected the tensions embedded in Khomeini's ideology of revolutionary Shi'ism—particularly the tension between his utilitarian aspiration for political power and his charismatic quest for clerical rule. The charismatic authority of Imam Khomeini was enshrined in articles 5 and 107. The former reads as follows:

> During the Occultation of the Glorious Lord of the Age . . . The Mandate to Rule *(velayat amr)* and The Imamate of the People *(Umamate Umat)* devolve upon a just and pious *faqih*, well-informed with his times, coura- geous, resourceful, . . . recognized and accepted by the majority of the peo- ple as a leader *(rahbari)*. Should there be no jurist endowed with such quali- fications . . . his role will be undertaken by a Leadership Council consisting of religious jurists meeting the above mentioned requirements in accor- dance with Article 107.

Article 107 reiterated the main points of the above article, but related them directly to Khomeini as rahbar:

> When one of the *fuquha* [scholars of Islamic law] who fulfills the conditions mentioned in Principle 5 . . . is recognized . . . by a decisive majority of the people for the position of *marja'* and leader *(rahbari)*—as is the case with the Exalted and Source of Imitation *(marja' i taqlid)* and leader *(rahbar)* of the Revolution Ayatollah Al-Uzma Imam Khomeini—then this leader will have charge of governing and all the responsibilities arising from it.[102]

These articles resolved Khomeini's earlier failure to define how a leader would be selected. In holding that leadership was determined by popular "recognition"—in other words, by a charismatic bond between the "leader" and the "people" created through a form of popular acclama- tion—the constitution determined that the role of a moral and religious guide and political leader were to be fused into one office: that of rahbar, or Leader.[103]

The constitution did not, however, equate Islamic government with the power of the Leader. Instead, reflecting the diverse content of Kho- meini's political thought, it attempted to accommodate the charismatic logic of the Rule of the Jurist to the rationalist demands of "Islamic gov- ernment." The result was twelve chapters and 175 articles of constitu- tional confusion. For example, articles 2 and 56 echoed the charismatic- elitist principles proclaimed in articles 5 and 107, stating that sovereignty belonged to God while the duty of "continuous leadership" fell on the *fuquha*. But articles 71 and 113 contravened these provisions, the former by providing for a elected "consultative assembly" (the Majlis), which was empowered to "establish laws on all matters, within the limit of its competence as laid down in the Constitution," the latter by providing for a popularly elected president, who "after the leadership . . . is the highest official position in the country." Similarly, Article 57 held that the legislative, executive, and judicial branches were "independent of each other," but then undermined this provision by placing these branches under the supervision of the rahbar. Finally, the constitution undermined the Majlis's authority by providing in Article 96 for a clerically dominated Council of Guardians empowered to veto any laws that it deemed un-Islamic. The constitution made no provision, however, for settling disputes between the Majlis and the Council, or between the president and the prime minister. Instead, Article 107 and several other articles gave ultimate authority to settle such conflicts to Khomeini.

In time these provisions were to wreak havoc. As we shall see, they set up a damaging conflict between the authority of the Majlis and that of the Council of Guardians. Since only Khomeini had the power to settle this conflict, the constitution ensured that his charisma would be the ultimate fount of authority.

Bani-Sadr, Khomeini, and the Clerics: Harmony versus Zealotry

After winning this crucial victory, Khomeini tried to back away from his earlier revolutionary statements in favor of a pragmatic approach that emphasized the authority of the Majlis over that of the Council of Guardians. Circumstances, however, pushed him to a more radical position. With presidential elections about to be held, he vetoed Ayatollah Beheshti's quest for the presidency in January 1980. A longtime clerical ally, Beheshti zealously advocated Khomeini's version of *velayat-i faqih*. Nevertheless, Khomeini held that the ulema should not occupy high government positions.[104] Not only was Khomeini opposed to clerics running for high office, he also refused to exercise his constitutional authority as rahbar to affirm the eligibility of the candidates. "I do not intend to recommend anyone," he explained. "I ask the parties, groups and individuals not to attribute their candidacies to me."[105] The only specific stipulation he made at the time was that those who had voted against the constitution be barred from running. This condition left the field open to a wide spectrum of Islamic candidates, including Bani-Sadr, a French-trained Islamic modernist who proceeded to win the election.

While Khomeini's acceptance of Bani-Sadr's election and his subsequent appointment of him as head of the Revolutionary Council can be seen as an effort to co-opt the modernists, it also reflected Khomeini's pan-Islamic approach to politics. Bani-Sadr, who was considered by many to be Khomeini's "spiritual son," represented the modernist movement from which Khomeini had borrowed many of his utilitarian notions of social justice.[106] For Khomeini to have rejected Bani-Sadr would have amounted to rejecting one of the principle bases of his own political thought.

Three months after Bani-Sadr became president, elections were held for the Majlis. Marking this event, Khomeini insisted that all candidates put aside their differences to create a "central power on which all other powers will depend." Remarkably, he then said that the "Majlis is higher than all the positions which exist in the country."[107] While this claim blatantly contradicted Khomeini's constitutional powers as rahbar, it attested to his enduring desire to create a rational basis for the assembly's authority. Yet it was not easy to adjust this desire to institutionalize the revolution to the demands of sustaining revolutionary fervor. In the ensuing weeks and months, Khomeini again tried to have it both ways. In March 1980, for example, he issued a series of guidelines to revolutionary organizations. While supporting the existence of the Revolutionary Guard Corps, he warned that the "slightest violation (of someone's rights) would lead to prosecution." The corps, he insisted, must "deal with all people with kindness and with Islamic manners." Khomeini then turned to the revolutionary courts, which he held "have no right to have armed forces of their own. They should act according to the Constitution and, gradually, the Islamic judicial system should take over." Yet after repeating this judicious message, Khomeini called for a "revolution . . . in all the universities" and a "purging" of all "deviant groups . . . engaged in mixing Islamic ideas with Marxist ideas."[108] One month later, he proclaimed an "Islamic cultural revolution," whose purpose was to purge the universities, the judiciary, and other public institutions of all "un-Islamic" elements. Speaking to a large crowd in Qom, Khomeini insisted that "you should make sure that these people who indulge in corruption . . . are crushed with full force. Such people, wherever they are, should be sentenced to death."[109]

Khomeini's increasingly strident language can be attributed in part to the hostage crisis, which gave the radical students an ideal means to humiliate the United States and isolate Iranians who favored reconciliation with Washington. The failure of the Carter administration to free the hostages in April 1980 only strengthened these students at the expense of Bani-Sadr and others who sought such reconciliation. But despite having issued this violent summons, Khomeini marked the opening of the Majlis six days later by warning the deputies to "act with calm and mutual respect and . . . shun . . . the unprincipled taking of sides in order to crush the opposition."

Moreover, in an implicit reference to conflicts between the Majlis and President Bani-Sadr, Khomeini insisted that the "Majlis and the gov-

ernment act harmoniously . . . to overcome the difficulties of the country."[110] This was not the first time Khomeini had tried to promote cooperation between Bani-Sadr and the clerics. Indeed, prior to the March 1980
Majlis elections, Bani-Sadr had attempted to form a cabinet dominated
by technocrats, only to find his nominees for the post of prime minister
repeatedly vetoed by the clerically dominated Revolutionary Council.
After the elections, this conflict was played out in the Majlis itself. Dominated by clerics and lay activists from the Islamic Republican Party,
the Majlis rejected Bani-Sadr's nominees in favor of their own candidate,
Mohammad Ali Rajai. Initially, Khomeini tried to stay out of the conflict.
But by the summer of 1980, he appeared set on a course which would
compel him to move against Bani-Sadr and assert his authority as
Imam.

The Emergence of Khomeini as "Imam"

While the ongoing hostage crisis played a role in Khomeini's decision to
move against Bani-Sadr, several other factors also pushed him in a more
defiant direction. Among them was the discovery of no fewer than four
coup plots by army officers between late May and mid-July 1980. More
important, as far as Khomeini was concerned, was the persistent opposition of traditionalist clerics such as Ayatollah Shariatmadari who, together with many lay Islamic activists from the left, rejected the notion
of clerical rule. The leftists' support for Bani-Sadr made it increasingly
difficult for Khomeini to refrain from intervening in the conflict between
the president and the Majlis. Frustrated, Khomeini first lashed out at his
opponents among the Islamic leftists and the clergy. These clerics, he
claimed, had mistakenly believed they could "deceive me [with] words
. . . from the Qur'an and the *Nahej al-Balagha* [a book attributed to
Imam 'Ali]." Furiously rejecting those who dared speak another Islamic
language, Khomeini dismissed the "turbaned" impostors he asserted were
"infiltrating the clergy and engaging in sabotage." What is more, he
added indignantly, they had formed imam committees. "Who is this
imam? . . . Anybody who wishes to do something puts it under the name
of the imam." This was totally unacceptable. "I warn the clergy," Khomeini said. "I tell them all and discharge myself of my final responsibility,
to repulse all these mullahs."[111]

Several days later, Khomeini turned his attention to Bani-Sadr himself. Unless the president moved quickly to rid his government of any
vestiges of the Pahlavi regime, Khomeini warned, "I will urge the nation
to do the same thing with you as they did with the shah. . . . Resign if
you are unable."[112] One month later, in a veiled attack on Bani-Sadr and

his allies, Khomeini hinted that he had arrived at a decision. In the beginning of the revolution, he explained, "we were two groups; one . . . from the seminary and the other . . . from abroad [i.e., modernists such as Bani-Sadr]. They [the modernists] had revolutionary experience, but these people from the seminary made the revolution." Counting on those "from abroad" was wrong, Khomeini implied. "Right from the beginning we made mistakes . . . we were not experienced . . . and a person [i.e., Bani-Sadr] was elected." But such errors would not be repeated. Henceforth, Khomeini insisted, the "Majlis must be 100 percent religious . . . 100 percent revolutionary and ideologically motivated."[113] Bani-Sadr had permitted people "whose thoughts are not revolutionary" to head ministries. "Mr. Bani-Sadr should not introduce such people into the Majlis, or if he does the Majlis should reject them." From now on, Khomeini insisted, all those opposed to Islam "should be purged. I cannot tolerate seeing anyone changing his mind about what he wants to be."[114]

Khomeini kept the pressure on Bani-Sadr throughout the summer. In August, Bani-Sadr finally acquiesced to the selection of Rajai as prime minister, and he quickly found himself in a public row with his Rajai regarding the prospective members of the new cabinet. Iraq's invasion of Iran in September 1980 temporarily saved the president from Khomeini's wrath. With Iraqi forces on the offensive, Khomeini asked Bani-Sadr to take charge of the military. Thus for a time Bani-Sadr could protect himself from his domestic enemies. By the winter of 1981, however, tensions between Bani-Sadr and Rajai were reaching a boiling point. First a group of prominent intellectuals led by Bazargan sent a letter to the government attacking it for violating human rights. This was followed, in March and June, by violent clashes between supporters of Bani-Sadr and backers of Khomeini.

As these events unfolded, Khomeini came under pressure to take action against his "spiritual son." But he still hesitated to use his power as rahbar to remove Bani-Sadr. Such an action would not only signal the regime's final rupture with the modernist forces Bani-Sadr represented, but would emphasize the political system's dependence on Khomeini's charisma. Khomeini preferred avoiding this day of reckoning and signaled Bani-Sadr to that effect. Four months later, however, a march by the National Front against Islamic legislation proposed by the Majlis enraged Khomeini, who condemned it as nothing less than an "invitation to rebellion . . . against the explicit direction of the Qur'an." He then issued a remarkable statement which effectively equated his authority with that of Imam 'Ali: "What makes me feel sorry is . . . to face those who did not let Imam Ali finish his duties." Such behavior, he said, left him little choice but to invoke his powers. "What can I do. You did not listen to my advice. . . . The National Front is condemned as of today."[115] Several days later one of Khomeini's disciples, minister of justice Ayatollah Beheshti, suggested that Bani-Sadr be tried for treason. The besieged president went into hiding, and on 16 June the Majlis began impeachment proceedings. These events were followed by the 28 June bombing of the headquarters of the Islamic Republic Party, in which seventy of Khomeini's supporters, including Beheshti, were killed. Two months later, two more allies of Khomeini died in another bomb blast.

Enraged by the deaths of his allies, Khomeini decided to stop excluding the clergy from top governmental posts. In August 1981 he appointed a Presidential Council consisting of Ayatollah Musavi-Ardabilli, Rafsanjani, and Ayatollah Mahdavi Kani. Two months later, Ayatollah Ali Khamenei's election as president signaled the demise of the modernists. Khomeini then launched a campaign against his clerical foes. This crusade would eventually culminate in the April 1982 "defrocking" of Ayatollah Shariatmadari and the purging of Khomeini's clerical opponents in the seminaries of Qom.

1981–1982: The Trials and Tribulations of Clerical Rule

Khomeini's victory was bittersweet. The direct involvement of leading clerics in politics ensured that their differences would become a matter of public record. Khomeini, as we have seen, understood the dangers; he had already warned that the clergy "should in no way interfere in matters for which they are not qualified." Such interference, he warned, "would be an unforgivable sin, because it will lead to the nation's mistrust of the clergy."[116] Despite Khomeini's warnings, the ulema's assignment expanded in direct proportion to its incompetence. As a result, Khomeini's worst nightmares were realized. Not only did the clergy's public disputes tarnish its image; by late 1981 they produced a legislative deadlock due to the Council of Guardians' repeated vetoes of land-reform legislation passed by the Majlis.[117] At the heart of this dispute was a fundamental ideological difference regarding the role of the state in managing the economy. The Council's senior members, some of whom were landowners, advocated a procapitalist position, while the Majlis, representing a more populist social base, advocated state intervention. Khomeini was sympathetic to the populist orientation of the Majlis.

The failure of the Majlis to advance its social policies came at a particularly difficult moment for Iran. To finance the war with Iraq on the country's southern border, which was disrupting oil exports, the regime had to reduce

funding of social welfare programs. As a result, one of Khomeini's fundamental goals, social justice, was severely undermined. The only immediate
solution was to intervene in the standoff between the Majlis and the Council. But to have done so would have again represented a victory for Khomeini's charismatic authority at the expense of the Majlis. Thus the Imam
was caught in a web he himself had helped spin.

Martyrdom and Ascetic Mysticism versus Utilitarian Politics

As Khomeini became more frustrated with this situation, he groped in
various directions for a solution. The search took him toward both extremes of the rational-charismatic spectrum—sometimes to mystical philosophy and asceticism, other times to utilitarian politics. Such bouncing
back and forth only emphasized how difficult it was to reconcile the two
forms of authority. To appreciate why Khomeini sought a solution in
ascetic-mystical philosophy we must recall that he believed that the only
way to overcome man's egotistical, self-serving nature was through contemplation of God's spiritual light. Where man failed to strive for this
light, he fell into disputes with others. Thus, Khomeini reasoned, the only
way to dissuade clerics from engaging in petty political battles was to
push them back towards the practice of ascetic self-denial and spiritual
reflection. The challenge was to make this case in a way that would put
maximum pressure on the clergy.

The Iran-Iraq war provided an ideal arena in which to make this
case. From the start of the war in November 1980, Khomeini invoked
the youth's acts of martyrdom on the field of battle to show the clergy
and entire nation what could be achieved when men forfeited their supreme self-interest to defend the common good. It is true that in making
this case, Khomeini also looked for a means to mobilize the youth in a
war for which Iran was technologically unequipped by comparison to its
foe. Indeed, he unabashedly defended the instrumental use of martyrdom.
For example, two months after the invasion and on the eve of Muharram,
Khomeini told a group of clerics:

> Do not imagine that in the mourning ceremonies you are weeping for the
> sake of the Lord of Martyrs. No, the Lord of Martyrs has no need for
> this weeping. (Do not imagine) that these ceremonies achieve anything by
> themselves. However . . . (they) unify the people. . . . The prophets with
> their divine mission wished to mobilize . . . the nations through various
> *means.* Islamic issues are political issues and the political aspects predomi-
> nate over its other aspects.[118]

Something more profound than mere opportunism was going on here. Over time, it appears that Khomeini became convinced that martyrdom was the supreme form of asceticism; by giving of one's life, he argued, a Muslim would transcend his "self" and thus achieve a mystical bond with God. He had hinted at this link between asceticism and martyrdom in October 1980. In speech that echoed his mystical belief in man's incompleteness, he argued that "the natural world is the lowest part of creation, the dregs of creation. The true arena is the divine world which is inexhaustible." That world "was the standard of defeat and victory, not the world of nature." However, he continued, "even in animal ambitions man is different from the rest of the animals." Man can reach his "divinity" by ceasing to be a "slave of nature" and turning instead to the "path of God." That change, in fact, was demonstrated by "our youngsters" who "welcome martyrdom." By not being "a material being," Khomeini claimed, these young people were helping Iran achieve "a situation which we cannot describe in any other way except to say that it is a divine country."[119]

Khomeini expanded on this theme before a group of clerics in March 1981. "One should not expect, without having been reformed himself, to attempt to reform another," he warned. Self-reform began with the realization that "mankind is endowed with . . . the desire for absolute . . . power." Since this desire was ripping the clergy apart, the only solution was to "reach the stage where you . . . overlook yourself." "When there is no self to contend with," Khomeini claimed, "there is no dispute, no quarrel."[120]

While such appeals inspired thousands of Iranian youths to forfeit their lives, they did not quell the disputes within the clergy. Clearly upset, Khomeini again shifted towards a utilitarian approach to resolve the Council-Majlis deadlock. Khomeini's efforts in this regard were encouraged by Majlis speaker Hashemi Rafsanjani. A loyal ally of Khomeini for many years, Rafsanjani sought his leader's backing in the dispute with the Council of Guardians. In October 1981, in the wake of the Council's veto of a bill providing for land ownership in the cities, he asked the Imam to proclaim his support for the Majlis's bill. Such intervention, Rafsanjani implied, was justified by the principle of public necessity, a principle which holds that when the interests of the Islamic community are at stake, clerics can legislate "secondary ordinances" regarding issues not directly legislated on in the Qur'an or the Sunna.[121] Khomeini endorsed this request, thus legitimizing the utilitarian logic that underlined Rafsanjani's appeal. But instead of exercising his constitutional authority to legislate "secondary ordinances," Khomeini turned around and delegated this authority to the Majlis. "Whatever concerns the safeguarding of the Islamic Republic order," he wrote, "and whichever is necessary . . . once the majority of deputies . . . recognize the topic in question, they are authorized to . . . implement it, while stressing its temporary nature."[122] This effort to routinize his charisma by delegating authority to the Majlis was doomed to fail, however, because it did not provide a solution to the conflict between the Majlis and the Council. As long as the Council had the right to veto the Majlis's laws, the stalemate would continue.

It was somewhat bizarre, therefore, that only two months after making this halfhearted effort to shift his authority to the Majlis, Khomeini issued a decree that virtually heralded the institutionalization of his revolution. In a kind of Islamic Bill of Rights, he held that "it is not acceptable . . . that in the name of revolution . . . somebody should be oppressed. From now on, (this) is the time for stability and construction."[123] A week later he added a utilitarian twist to the above decree, declaring that "serving the government is the same as serving Islam. . . . We should no longer say we are in a revolutionary situation."[124]

1983: EXERCISING POWER — A NO-WIN PROPOSITION?

The institutionalization of Khomeini's revolution could not be achieved merely by the Imam's pronouncements. Even his charisma had its limits. Thus barely a week after proclaiming that Iran was no longer in a revolutionary situation, Khomeini found the Majlis again locked in a fierce battle with the Council of Guardians over the direction of social reform. Again Khomeini invoked the concept of secondary ordinances in an effort to break the deadlock, but this time, he gave it a novel interpretation. Conventional wisdom held that clerics could issue such ordinances when ruling on questions not explicitly addressed in the Qur'an or Sunna. But now Khomeini told the Majlis that "we cannot imagine that God would not have looked at every aspect of any problem." This dictum, he claimed, even applied to "secondary provisions (which) . . . have been ordained for the very reason that problems may arise in a particular society. . . . These are also ordinances from God."[125] By implying that secondary rulings were also mandated by God, Khomeini virtually equated the clerical power to issue such rulings with the authority of Allah. This turned out to be a dress rehearsal for a transformation that took another eight months to unfold. For within days of making his appearance, the Imam withdrew from the stage, and instead of exercising his powers to break the impasse again assigned the task of determining secondary principles to the Majlis, thus failing to address the basic source of the political crisis.

As Khomeini recognized his failure to find a workable solution to this crisis, he again sought solace in mysticism. In a speech that celebrated the successes of the revolution, Khomeini exclaimed, "Your youths have crossed the border in one night. . . . They have suddenly achieved what the mystics and mystical poets have been dreaming of for many years."[126] Three months later, he declared that the "trenches . . . are centers for worship of God"; there, Khomeini asserted, the martyrs had attained "mystical and divine stages."[127] Khomeini then extended his argument another step, recasting the concept of martyrdom in a speech to high-ranking clerics. Instead of defining it as an unforeseen act by which Muslims inadvertently sacrifice themselves in the defense of Islam, Khomeini now held that the survival of the Islamic republic required the deliberate pursuit of martyrdom. As he put it:

> If the great martyr . . . confined himself to praying . . . the great tragedy
> of Kerbela would *not* have come about. . . . Among the contemporary
> ulema, if the great Ayatollah . . . Shirazi . . . thought like these people [who
> do not fight for Islam] a war would *not* have taken place in Iraq . . . all
> those Muslims would *not* have been martyred.[128]

While these statements pushed the concept of martyrdom in unprecedented directions, they proved no more effective in 1983 than they had in 1982. By the end of 1983, the Imam admitted his failure to institutionalize the revolution. As he put it, "My only fear is that we may fail to hand over things to the next generation in a consolidated manner."[129]

This failure was the product of a basic dilemma that had haunted him since he became rahbar. Khomeini wanted to advance a utilitarian view of politics that transcended his person, and tried to do so by delegating his authority on secondary provisions to the Majlis. But because the Majlis lacked a clear constitutional authority to legislate, or an authority which could match that of the Imam, Khomeini's actions had only accentuated the dependence of the political system on his charismatic power.

Khomeini could have tried to resolve this dilemma by invoking his right as Imam to impose the law. But in doing so, he would have further solidified the very authority he wished to shift to the Majlis. In short, whether by action or inaction, Khomeini impeded the institutionalization of revolution, whether by accentuating the Majlis's lack of authority, or by equating the revolution with the power of a charismatic yet mortal man.

1984–1988: VELAYAT-I FAQIH AS GOVERNMENT

The country could tolerate the dilemmas of clerical rule so long as Khomeini remained to impose his will when all else failed. By the summer of 1987, however, illness had begun to take a toll on the revolution's charismatic innovator. Sensing that time was running out, Rafsanjani again asked Khomeini to intervene, this time to support a labor law that the Council of Guardians had vetoed. To Rafsanjani's apparent dismay, however, Khomeini not only refused to invoke his authority as Imam, he even declined to delegate this authority to the Majlis. Weakened by sickness, all he would do was allude to the mystical encounters that awaited him in the next life. Thus Khomeini would speak of "Islam's mysticism, Islam's gnosticism, at the head of which are the spiritualities of Islam."[130] "This is a transitional world," he told Majlis deputies some time later. "Everyone's time will come. I will part first, and you will follow later."[131]

Although this recourse to mysticism proved no more effective than it had in the past, the possibility of death began to concentrate Khomeini's mind. He abandoned talking about the hereafter and turned his attention to devising a durable solution to the crisis that had immobilized the country's political leadership. This solution was presaged by a series of events that began to unfold in December 1987. Angered by the persistent refusal of the Council of Guardians to accept the labor law, and frustrated by his own failure to end the stalemate, the Imam took the one step that he had so long avoided: in a blunt speech, he commanded the Council of Guardians to accept the labor law in words that unambiguously upheld the utilitarian prerogatives of government. "The state can," Khomeini insisted,

> by using this power, replace those fundamental . . . Islamic systems, by any kind of social, economy, labor . . . commercial, urban affairs, agricultural, or other system, and can make the services . . . that are the monopoly of the state . . . into an instrument for the implementation of general and comprehensive policies.[132]

Two weeks later, Khomeini extended the notion that the state could replace fundamental Islamic systems. He did so in response to a speech given by President Khamenei, who had cited Khomeini's own remarks to argue that the ruling jurist had a right to interpret the law. This formulation did not satisfy Khomeini, who rebuked the president for failing to clarify that the ruling jurist was not merely the interpreter of the law, but in some sense the vehicle of law itself. As Khomeini put it:

Government is among the most important divine injunctions and has priority over all peripheral divine orders. Your interpretation of what I said,
that is, the government has jurisdiction within the framework of divine
injunctions, is . . . contradictory to what I said. . . . The government, which
is part of the total vice-regency of the Prophet . . . is one of the foremost
injunctions of Islam and has priority over all other secondary injunctions,
even prayers, fasting and the hajj. . . . The government is empowered to
unilaterally revoke any lawful agreement . . . if the agreement contravenes
the *interests* of Islam and the country. It can prevent any matter, whether
religious or secular, if it is against the *interests* of Islam.[133]

By equating the "divine injunction" of government with the "total vice-
regency of the Prophet," and by asserting that the vice-regent could take
any action to defend the "interests of Islam and the country"—interests
defined by the vice-regent —Khomeini implied that vice-regent had the
authority to determine both "divine" and secondary injunctions. This
utilitarian formulation did not come out of the blue. But now Khomeini
apparently embraced an absolute utilitarianism that seemed to defy the
most sacred principles of Islam by implying that sovereignty no longer
belonged to God, but to the vice-regent himself. Yet it was far from
clear that Khomeini's concept of the "total vice-regency" could provide
an enduring solution to the constitutional crisis that still engulfed his
country. On the contrary, this formulation appeared on the surface to
enshrine the principle of charismatic leadership. How then, could such
a statement provide a rationale for shifting authority into the hands of
the Majlis?

The answer is that Khomeini's formulation was far from as definitive
and clear as it seemed on the surface. Whether by design or by default,
his statement was riddled with ambiguities. For example, although Khomeini had spoken of the "total vice-regency of the Prophet," he had
linked this vice-regency *not* exclusively to himself, but to a nebulous entity he called the "government." Yet Khomeini was unclear about what
constituted government, how it was part of the vice-regency, and what
or who was to define state interests.[134] This ambiguity opened the door
to the possibility that Khomeini was not speaking about the personal
power of the vice-regent, but rather the institutional power of government itself. This possibility set the stage for a complex political battle, in
which those forces that wanted to create an institutional basis for political
power that transcended the Imam's charisma found ample ammunition
in the words of the Imam himself.

STRUGGLING TO DEFINE "WHAT THE IMAM TRULY BELIEVED"

The struggle over a charismatic leader's legacy usually awaits his passing; few risk incurring the wrath of a popular leader by seeming to misrepresent or abuse his wishes. Khomeini, however, was still alive—albeit not well—when the battle to define what "the Imam truly believed" began in earnest. The heterogeneous nature of Khomeini's ideology invited this contest. On one side were the *institutional-pragmatists*. This group, led by then speaker of the Majlis Rafsanjani, was pragmatic in that it emphasized economic reconstruction and political reconciliation at home and abroad, and institutional because it sought to reduce the role of the clergy—and its charismatic leader, the rahbar—in favor of the legal and institutional authority of the Majlis.[135] On the other side were the *charismatic radicals*. Led by interior minister Ali Akbar Motashemi, this group was charismatic in that it treated Khomeini's political and social dictums as divine revelations, and radical in the sense that it opposed all reconciliation with potential ideological foes, whether in Iran or abroad.

Each faction attempted to exploit Khomeini's sayings to legitimate its own political agenda. The institutional pragmatists, however, initially had several advantages. First, by 1988 the Iran-Iraq war had turned against Iran; with tens of thousands dead, the utility of glorifying, even promoting, martyrdom was exhausted. Second, as economic conditions worsened—industrial and agricultural output, as well as per capita GNP, had been reduced to pre-1960 levels—it became easier to argue that it was time to stabilize the revolution and begin domestic reconstruction. Finally, and perhaps most importantly, the Imam supported the pragmatists' call to revise the constitution. While Khomeini did not live to see this project through, his pronouncements on the role of government and the need to defend Islamic interests provided the ideological foundation from which Rafsanjani and his allies launched their reform campaign.

The ink was barely dry on Khomeini's 7 January 1988 edict concerning *velayat-i faqih* when Rafsanjani and his allies realized that the edict offered a potential solution to the political crisis that had paralyzed the country for years. As we have noted, Khomeini left open the possibility that the Rule of the Jurist had more to do with governing institutions than with the authority of the ruler; if a case could be made for this interpretation, then Rafsanjani could argue that a reform of the constitution that strengthened governmental institutions (even at the expense of the clerics) was in line with the Imam's wishes. The pragmatists wasted no time in exploiting this possibility. As Rafsanjani put it five days after Khomeini had made his famous pronouncement: "The views expressed by his holiness the imam . . . illustrate the depth of his . . . leadership. . . . The meaning of proper leadership," Rafsanjani claimed, in a elliptical reference to Khomeini's utilitarianism, "is that leadership should respond to the call of the people." In answering the people's call, Rafsanjani continued, "the imam's line has become clear." Islam, he insisted, must "demonstrate its power on essential issues of the state."

By suggesting that Khomeini had delegated his absolute authority to the Majlis, Rafsanjani sought to diminish the ruling jurist's power while appearing to defend Khomeini and the nation. "Today the views of the leader are our final authority," Rafsanjani asserted. "If everyone accepts the imam's line, there should no longer be any division among us."[136] Prime Minister Musavi then took a cue from Rafsanjani. In an interview with Tehran radio, he expressed his delight with "the recent message of his eminence the imam." The cabinet, he emphasized, "treated this message seriously" because it "clarifies a great number of ambiguities" and enables "the holy system of the Islamic Republic to deal with the . . . problems it is facing." Given this progress, it was time to "implement" Khomeini's message through "the formation of the required Majlis committees" and the appointment of "revolutionary specialists who follow the imam's line." Such a policy, he added for good measure, was the foundation of the "Imam's *Islamic Government*." That book, the prime minister claimed, outlined a "concept of an Islamic government" that was capable of solving "various problems."[137]

Rafsanjani's opponents quickly caught on to the transformation that was occurring. "O Imam," they warned two days after Musavi's interview,

> The enemies of Islam and the opportunists made diverse interpretations regarding the response of the Master [Khomeini] and the query of the student [Khamenei] which cast doubt in the minds of the divine nation. . . . In the name of defending . . . jurisconsult and imamate, they had engaged in insinuation. . . . Their main aim was to . . . destroy the man who raised the call of the Islamic Revolution . . . rather than to explain the absolute divine jurisconsult.[138]

Rafsanjani's allies, however, were unrelenting. Students at Tehran University proclaimed their absolute support for Khomeini: "[Because] his holiness the imam . . . described government as one of the primary principles of Islam, there is no longer any ambiguity in the Islamic government's plans for solving the country's economic and social problems."[139] Appar-

ently emboldened by this popular celebration of Khomeini's utilitarianism, Rafsanjani gave an extraordinary sermon in which he interpreted
the Imam's 7 January declaration in a way Khomeini himself might have
found dubious. Rafsanjani implied that the dispute over Khomeini's
words amounted to a simple misunderstanding rather than a political
contest. There was, Rafsanjani insisted, no power struggle in Tehran as
the foreign press had reported; the Imam was simply defining "the reality
of *Velayat-e Faqih* and Islamic government . . . for it is something which
is not yet clear to the people." The speaker went on to emphasize that
the Imam's recent edict concerned the institutions and prerogatives of
government. It was government, Rafsanjani explained, that "is responsible for implementing affairs and regulation." In this regard, "the Majlis,
as his holiness has repeatedly said, is above all affairs, it is the axis of
things." Indeed, the Majlis was responsible for passing "laws within the
framework of Islam." "Not all the laws which were implemented during
the time of the Prophet were divine rules communicated in the Qur'an,"
Rafsanjani explained; instead "there were certain matters in governmental affairs which were left to the Prophet . . . as a ruler and vice regent
. . . that was his government authority."[140] The Imam's delegation of this
authority, Rafsanjani insisted, allowed the Majlis to pass social legislation:

> Our legitimate right to interfere comes from the imam, since you know
> that this is the issue of *Velayat-e-Faqih*. . . . I am Hashemi Rafsanjani. . . .
> I have no right to enact laws for people. I am their representative, yet I . . .
> do not have this right. The imam can give me this right. *Velayat-e-Faqih*
> gives me this right. . . . The entire system's legitimacy stems from the posi-
> tion of the imam.

Did the delegation of the absolute authority of the Imam mean the
creation of a new despotism? No, Rafsanjani insisted, "all those analysts
who . . . reason dictatorship out of this are very wrong." The Rule of
the Jurist had in fact created a "democratic system. . . . There are councils,
the Majlis, and the right to vote. Decisions start with the people. They
all have the soul of Velayat. . . . So, as you see, democracy is present
in a form better than in the West." Rafsanjani concluded in words that
momentarily placed him closer to Gettysburg than to Tehran, saying that
"the system is not moving towards . . . absolutism. . . . This healthy style
of government of the people by the people, with the permission of Velayat-e Faqih, will continue."[141] Rafsanjani's allies subsequently echoed
this theme. President Khamenei, for example, declared that "the legitimacy of all bodies—legislative, executive or judicial—is a product of

their affiliation with the rule of jurisconsultant. . . . It is the supreme jurisconsult who creates . . . the system." Yet, the president added almost as an aside, "if the supreme jurisconsult gives some of these powers to a person or body, that person or body will possess (these) powers."[142]

Khomeini Supports the Pragmatists

By seizing the initiative, the pragmatists created a political climate receptive to the notion that Khomeini's words required a reinvigoration of the Majlis and a diminution of the power of the high-ranking clergy. Khomeini's subsequent actions strongly suggest that he supported Rafsanjani and recognized the necessity of routinizing his own charisma. In February 1988, several Majlis deputies again demanded that Khomeini intervene against the Council of Guardians. Khomeini hesitated at first, reluctant openly to oppose a body whose existence reflected his enduring belief in the moral leadership of the clergy. But a choice had to be made, lest a more important ideal—the unity and efficacy of the Islamic republic—be sacrificed. Thus he agreed to form a "consultative council to ascertain the interest of the state."[143]

More than any other political institution, this council reflected and enshrined Khomeini's utilitarianism. Known also as the Expediency Discernment Council, it was empowered to overturn the veto of the Council of Guardians. It consisted of six members of the Council of Guardians; six deputies, including Rafsanjani and two of his allies, President Khamenei and Musavi Kho'iniha; and the minister concerned with the relevant legislation. By adding this thirteenth member, Khomeini insured that the balance of power favored the council's "politicians" (that is, the pragmatists) over its "theologians." The pragmatists on the council used their majority to compel the clerics to accept some of the social reform laws that had previously been rejected by the Council of Guardians. In fact, the new council was so effective in "ascertaining the interests of state" that Khomeini acted to diminish its powers by the end of 1988.

Khomeini also backed the pragmatists by favoring the technical "specialists" during the April and May 1988 elections for the Third Majlis. Several weeks prior to the voting, Khomeini insisted that "the people act freely in these elections, they do not need guardians." The absence in this speech of *any* reference to the role of clerics in the elections indicates a subtle reproach to the clergy. The only advice from this "old father" (as Khomeini called himself), was that the people should vote "for those representatives who are committed to Islam, who are faithful to the people." The Majlis, he asserted, "is the house of all the people and the source of hope for the deprived."[144] The returns seemed to follow Khomeini's wishes. The "professional clerics" (or *mo'ammamim*, "those who wore the turban") lost nearly half of their seats in the 270-member assembly; from 122 seats in the Second Majlis the clerics fell to a paltry 71. Meanwhile, the politicians won an overwhelming majority of 189 seats, 42 more than in the previous Majlis. What is more, only 68 members of the new assembly had a traditional or religious education, as compared to 153 in the Second Majlis.[145]

Khomeini appeared pleased with the results of the elections. In a message to the Majlis read by his son Ahmad he expressed his thanks to God that "the elections . . . were carried out in a sound manner." It was the "people's only desire," Khomeini insisted, "for the Majlis to resolve problems . . . and alter the country's extremely complicated administrative system." Towards this end, Khomeini instructed the Majlis to "propound laws and bills in the committees on the basis of dear Islam" and to give "priority to implementing the country's infrastructural policies."[146] Clearly, the Imam had taken the side of Rafsanjani and those who wanted to institutionalize political power. In the ensuing six months the pragmatists moved quickly to translate the Imam's call into reality. The central feature of this process was a wholesale amending of the constitution itself. Several factors encouraged Khomeini and the pragmatists to push for changes in the constitution. By mid-1988, the Iraqis had scored several victories in their eight-year battle with Iran. The downing of an Iranian airbus on 3 July 1988 — which Khomeini believed was perpetrated deliberately by the United States in order to aid the Iraqis—apparently convinced the Imam that Iran had to choose between pursuing the war abroad or initiating reconstruction at home. Within three weeks Khomeini decided in favor of the latter. In a bitter speech, he accepted United Nations Resolution 598, which set out the terms for a cease-fire and negotiations with Iraq.[147]

This choice was made easier and even necessary by the disastrous condition of the economy. Industrial and agricultural production had plummeted, and the regime, deprived of oil income by what was in effect a Western embargo on Iran, could not raise the hard currency for vital imports. This spelled disaster for a regime whose legitimacy was based on the promise of striving for the downtrodden. And while Rafsanjani had successfully invoked Khomeini's 7 January edict in his bid to legitimate the role of government, he had not resolved the fundamental problem: the failure of the constitution to provide the Majlis with a clear basis of institutional authority. Moreover, there was the question of succession. It was apparent that no one leader could replicate Khomeini's charisma and thus endow the position of Leader with the sacredness it required.

Ayatollah Montazeri had been nominated as Khomeini's heir in 1985 but was not truly qualified to be rahbar, because the constitution specified that the Leader had to be a *marja'*, or "source of imitation." Khomeini finally asked Montazeri to withdraw his candidacy in March 1989.[148]

In the absence of someone who could match Khomeini's charisma, the only alternative allowed by the constitution was to create a "leadership council" of three or five grand ayatollahs. Together these men were to exercise the authority of one ruling jurist. With the exception of Montazeri, however, none of the grand ayatollahs had accepted Khomeini's concept of the ruling jurist. Moreover, it was unlikely that a three- or five-member council could replicate the authority of a single charismatic leader. As Ayatollah Ahmad Azari-Qomi put it, it was ridiculous to expect the masses to replace their acclamation for the Imam with "slogans like: 'We are your soldiers, Oh Council of Leadership.' "[149]

Given the fact that neither a qualified *marja'* nor an effective leadership council could assume the mantle of the ruling jurist, the only solution was to amend the constitution in a manner that diminished the political authority of the ruling jurist. In the winter of 1988 the pragmatists began a campaign to gain the Imam's blessing for such a revision, a goal they linked to economic reconstruction. Khomeini gave the pragmatists the opening they wanted. He repeated his policy of "neither East nor West" but added that the "strategy of reconstruction" was to be led by "experts, in particular cabinet ministers, the appropriate Majlis committees . . . scientific and research centers . . . inventors, discoverers, and committed specialists."[150] These words were a clear signal of support to the pragmatists. Encouraged, they turned directly to the issue of constitutional reform.

President Khamenei raised the issue in a Friday sermon. The constitution, he argued, "is the embodiment and manifestation of the revolution." In cases, however, of difficulties not anticipated in the constitution—such as the deadlock between the Majlis and the Council of Guardians—the "chief jurisconsult creates an assembly . . . and [resolves] the difficulty through this body." Such extraconstitutional bodies did not resolve the central problem, however: the failure of the constitution itself to clearly provide for authoritative institutions.[151] Khamenei's bold critique was echoed by other Majlis deputies. In a gathering at Tehran University on 5 December, one hundred deputies addressed a letter to Khomeini in which they called for the creation of a committee for amending the constitution. Within three months, the Imam gave his full backing to this proposal by forming a "council for the reappraisal of the constitution" chaired by Ayatollah Meshkini.

Khomeini's Death and the Amending of the Constitution

Khomeini's death on 3 June 1989 was, of course, an extraordinary event for the entire country. Millions of people jammed the streets of Tehran to touch his coffin and feel the Imam's immense charisma. In the resulting frenzy of tears and cries, Khomeini's body fell out of the coffin, as if responding to the Iranian people's unwillingness to release their cherished leader. The pragmatists mourned his passing as much as anyone, but solidified their gains by electing Khamenei "Leader" only a day later. Several draft amendments had circulated in the press already in the spring of 1989. Now, with the radicals robbed of their court of final appeals, the pragmatists quickly enacted an array of amendments and incorporated them into a new constitution, which was approved in a national referendum on 9 July 1989.

The most important amendments were those that strengthened the authority of the Majlis and government while diminishing the constitutional powers of the rahbar and the Council of Guardians. The first goal was achieved by abolishing the post of prime minister and transferring its authority to the presidency. In theory this change did not make the president more powerful than the Leader. However, the rahbar's position was weakened, at least in relative terms, by amendments to articles 5, 107, and 109 that stripped him of his charismatic base.[152] The new version of Article 5 dropped all reference to popular acclamation of the Leader. Article 109 redefined the qualities of the Leader in strictly political or rational terms, replacing the requirement that he be a *marja'* with the weaker stipulation that he demonstrate "scholarship, as required for performing the function of *mufti* in . . . fields of *fiqh*," or Islamic law. To reinforce this point, Article 109 article held that "in case of a multiplicity of persons fulfilling the above qualifications, the person possessing the better jurisprudential and *political perspicacity* will be given preference."[153] This critical change was reaffirmed in Article 107, which specified that, henceforth, the Leader would be chosen by "experts elected by the people" from among the scholars of religious law with the requisite legal and political skills. Article 107 concluded with the stipulation that "the Leader is equal with the rest of the people . . . in the eyes of the law."

The other crucial change in the Constitution concerned the Council of Guardians. While the council retained its veto power, Article 112 turned the Expediency Discernment Council into a permanent body. Empowered to "discern the interest in matters arising between Parliament and the Council of Guardians," its membership was stacked to ensure that the six Council of Guardians *fuqaha* who sat on it were in the minority.[154] Thus the council's political power was substantially reduced. In the ensuing year the Majlis took advantage of this critical change, enacting a series of pieces of reform legislation that had previously been blocked by the council.

Khamenei surely understood that the adoption of the new constitution only three weeks following his selection as Leader was no coincidence. As amended, it specified qualifications for his office that he possessed; he was neither a grand ayatollah nor a *marja'* but merely an "equal with the rest of the people." What is more, his ability to build a popular base was severely hampered, not only by his lack of charisma but by the new constitution, which stipulated that the rahbar be chosen by a small group of clerics rather than acclaimed by the people. By contrast, the position of the president, technically below that of the rahbar, had the advantage of being chosen by popular election. Thus when Rafsanjani was elected president on 28 July, his position relative to that of the rahbar was in many respects enviable.

A month after his election, Rafsanjani appointed a cabinet whose members reflected the movement towards rationality in the regime. The new cabinet excluded radicals and replaced them with technocrats, a third of whom had studied in the West.[155] These technocrats—to the dismay of the radicals—advocated a diminished role for government in economic affairs and an enlarged role for Western investment—excluding, of course, funds from the United States.

Rafsanjani and his allies tried to portray these policies as totally compatible with the Imam's wishes. Indeed, even while he was still alive they had invoked Khomeini's own utilitarian arguments to show why the constitutional demotion of the Leader would protect the sanctity of Islam. Asked by a reporter whether the regime was "in effect, separating religion from politics" by separating the position of Leader from that of *marja'*, Prosecutor General Musavi Kho'iniha had replied that "it is not logical to say that the condition for leadership is to be a source of emulation." In fact Kho'iniha had retrieved an argument that had always been at the core of Shi'ite traditional thinking: "The issue of emulation," he insisted, "is a personal matter, quite separate from the affairs of . . . running the country." Indeed, the true measure of Islam's influence was *not* the presence or absence of clerical rule; rather it was "how much the regime pays attention to religion. If the Islamic Republic . . . stresses religious and Islamic principles, the Muslim people will support it."

How could Rafsanjani and his colleagues exploit Khomeini's legacy without appearing to denigrate the memory and reputation of the Imam? The pragmatists devised a clever and wholly plausible solution to this dilemma: instead of alluding to Khomeini's ambivalence, they redefined his identity. The Imam was a man of many dimensions. As Khamenei put it in an extraordinary speech:

> It would be wrong to say that one can only detect what the Imam really had at heart, by looking at his political vision. What the Imam truly believed can be grasped by looking at all aspects and dimensions of his being and thought . . . such as his political cries; mystical poetry; his smile; or even when he shed a tear.[156]

Khamenei seemed to imply that once Khomeini's many dimensions were grasped in the totality of his being, one could correctly understand the real meaning of any particular political vision he had expressed.

The radicals would not tolerate such blasphemy. Not only did they insist that there was one and only one Khomeini; they suggested the potentially explosive idea that the Imam was a prophet whose utterances consisted of divine and unalterable truths. "Our people are the imam's followers, and no distortion or fallacy can conceal these facts," said Majlis speaker Mehdi Karrubi. "Obeying the imam means that the modus operandi and the directions and exhortations are those that the imam specified."[157]

The difficulty with this argument was not merely that it appeared to deify Khomeini. Given the many statements that the Imam had issued, it was difficult if not impossible to say which ones constituted the revealed truth out of which a new Shi'ite "fundamentalism" was to be constructed. But the radicals were not deterred. Instead, they found their revealed truth in *Imam Khomeini's Last Will and Testament,* a document that the government had released several months after Khomeini's death. The radicals' claim that the will enshrined Khomeini's principles was not altogether fanciful. Khomeini had described his will in grandiose terms, insisting that he intended it not only for Iranians, but also as a "recommendation to all Muslim nations."[158] The will's specific recommendations failed, however, to convey the tensions and complexities of Khomeini's thought. Instead, they amounted to a simplistic rendition of the Imam's populist principles—such as clerical rule and the role of the Leader, Muslim independence, social justice, and defiance of the "Great Satan." The one-dimensional nature of Khomeini's will was in one sense an asset; its lack of nuance meant that it could be readily understood by the masses. Thus Karrubi argued, "The political, economic and cultural bases that the imam propounded . . . in his will are important. . . . The provisions of the will are for the post-imam period. . . . [T]he imam's principles . . . are to guide the people after him."[159]

In their subsequent attempts to transform the will into a prophetic document, the radical fundamentalists paid less heed to Khomeini's concept of *velayat-e faqih* than to his principles of Muslim resistance to the West and support of the downtrodden classes. This lapse may sound paradoxical, given the centrality of this concept to Khomeini's thought. But the radicals understood that in a doctrinal sense, they were in a weak position. They could not argue that the ruling jurist was the ultimate authority without accepting the authority of the new Leader, Khamenei, to define the political agenda. Faced by a choice between obeying a rahbar whose charismatic authority had been undermined and treating the "advice" of the departed Khomeini as revealed truth, they chose the latter path.

In 1990 the pragmatists skillfully exploited the theological contradictions that marred the radicals' "canonization" of Khomeini. In an editorial in *Resalat,* a newspaper closely affiliated with Rafsanjani, Council of Guardians member Ayatollah Azari-Qomi and editor of *Resalat* assailed Karrubi's recent remarks as indicating "his inadequate information about our dear departed imam's culture regarding the absoluteness of the vice regency." Since "Ayatollah Khamenei and his auspicious leadership have the dear imam's endorsement," they continued, "they have absolute *velayat* [and thus the] power of the Majlis, the Cabinet, the judiciary, the Armed Forces, and everyone else." Given this authority, Azari-Qom asked, can it be claimed that the "absolute velayat pertains basically to two people? Is it possible that during the imam's life, he was the absolute Ruler, along with Ayatollah Khamenei?" Such a notion, Azari-Qomi implied, was ludicrous. Had this same logic prevailed after the Prophet's death, it would have implied that 'Ali's leadership constituted a "sacrilege regarding the holy Prophet." In other words, it would have obviated the need for leadership, a need which was at the very heart of Shi'ism! "By the same logic," Azari-Qomi wrote, "where is the need for the imam! This is Americanized Islam, according to which some people ignore the Leader's . . . rulings on the pretext of using 'the imam's traditions.' By using his eminence the imam . . . and showing respect and reverence to him, they are ignoring his most important precept—the rule of Islam."

In branding the Islam of his foes "Americanized Islam," Azari-Qomi was implying that the radicals' veneration of Khomeini had stripped Islam of its most vital element—its ability to rule via the authority of the Leader. This authority, Azari-Qomi implied, had to be a living reality, it could not be relegated to the heavens. By placing the Leader beyond man's reach, the radicals had Christianized Islam, an act Azari-Qomi suggested was not a celebration of Khomeini's legacy but a defiance and corruption of it. Those who truly wanted to "love the imam," he went on, "should implement his most important bequest . . . (his) most important precept—the rule of the supreme jurisconsult, which today is on his Eminence Ayatollah Khamenei's shoulders with all its absoluteness."[160]

The pragmatists had simply carried Khomeini's declaration to its logical conclusion. By early 1991, they had forged an "Islamic government" in which the authority of the Council of Guardians, and most importantly that of rahbar himself, had been diminished—in Khomeini's name.

KHOMEINI'S ENDURING LEGACY

Neither religions nor men are open books. They have been historical rather than logical or even psychological constructions without contradiction. Often they have borne within themselves a series of motives, each of which, if separately and consistently followed through, would have stood in the way of the others or run against them head-on.

Max Weber[161]

Great leaders can live with the anomalies that animate their ideas so long as they are not challenged by the facts of history and the complexities of political experience. Once the task of rule is thrust upon them, they must often sort out the historical motives that have shaped their lives. This process often requires a painful choice between different values, all of which seem as integral to their identities as life itself. In coming to terms with the personal and intellectual forces that shaped the "Imam," Ayatollah Khomeini was obliged to make such a choice. Having battled for nearly a decade to accommodate his desire for divinely inspired clerical rule to his aspiration for effective and enduring Islamic government, Khomeini chose in favor of his utilitarian commitments.

The process by which the incongruities of identity adjust to the exigencies of historical reality is complex and multidetermined. Khomeini failed to establish a political order based on the absolute and divinely inspired authority of the ruling jurist in part because the religion itself required a squaring of the circle: velayat-i faqih demanded the constant intercession of a charismatic leader, but sustaining the Islamic republic demanded institutions and laws that transcended the authority of the rahbar. At the same time, political and socioeconomic forces came into play. After the Islamic republic was established, the demands of governance pushed Khomeini and the pragmatists to infuse the Majlis with the authority to resolve problems. The debilitating centralization of Iran's economy and the war with Iraq accelerated this trend. As the economy floundered, the regime adopted a reconstruction policy which required the rationalization of political authority. Thus ideal, political, and economic forces fused in a manner that spoke persuasively to the most enduring and powerful element of Khomeini's political thinking, his devotion to the cause of Islamic unity and social justice. In the final analysis, Khomeini's devotion to utilitarianism prevailed because it provided the most effective means of realizing his most cherished goals.

This does not meant that the Imam completely anticipated or wholly embraced every change that Rafsanjani and his allies brought about. But neither was he "defeated"—as one scholar has put it—"by the cunning of history."[162] In some respects, Khomeini was the agent of his own charisma's "rationalization." That he was aware of the dilemmas of charismatic rule and attempted to address them was wholly in keeping with his practical approach to politics and his enduring commitment to the utilitarian principle of power and unity. For this reason, Rafsanjani could *credibly* argue that shifting the Leader's authority to the Majlis entailed a victory for Khomeini and the revolution. By welding this argument to a powerful political alliance, the pragmatists created the foundations for an Islamic republic in which the interests of state increasingly defined the boundaries of Islamic practice. In doing so, they remained loyal to Khomeini's core principles.

While the passing of Khomeini in 1989 and the subsequent revision of the constitution was a watershed for the Islamic republic, the long-term implications of these developments are as yet unclear. Indeed, within three years of Rafsanjani's victory, Khamenei had moved closer to the radicals, and his supporters were proposing that he be declared *marja'*, or "source of imitation" of all Shi'ites! This effort was resisted, even by Shi'ite clerics in Lebanon and in the Iraqi Shi'ite organization 'Al-Dawa. In keeping with the logic of the revised Iranian constitution, they insisted Shi'ites were free to follow the example of whichever *marja'* they most favored. Shaykh Fadlallah of Lebanon, as the following chapter by Martin Kramer demonstrates, certainly adopted this approach to Khomeini's legacy. Such defiance of Iran's rahbar offered another reminder that Khomeini's rise to power was a singular event, the product of the fortuitous meshing of his extraordinary charisma and his extraordinary times.

It is doubtful that Khamenei—or any Shi'ite leader—will ever be so gifted or so lucky.

Still, some scholars in the West expect that Rafsanjani's victory may prove to be a Pyrrhic one. Inspired by the teleological ethic of Western social science, they suggest that the division of political and religious authority enshrined in Iran's new constitution might lead to a secularization of the political system.[163] Such an expectation is not unreasonable. Indeed, there is historical precedent for it, as Albert Hourani has shown in his study of the reformist ideas of Muhammad Abduh and other Arab thinkers. Hourani observed that by advancing an instrumentalist view that equated Islam with whatever form of politics are supposed to serve the public interest, Abduh and his followers ironically opened "another door to secular nationalism."[164] Rafsanjani's fundamentalist opponents might endorse Hourani's conclusions. They spurned utilitarianism precisely because it denies that ideals can be anchored in the revealed truth of God or any one of his messengers.

Yet it would be misleading to assume that history must repeat itself in Iran—or, for that matter, in any other arena of the Islamic world. A utilitarian Shi'ism may not necessarily create an opening to secularism as we know it in the West. On the contrary, it might secure the foundations for an Islamic republic whose institutions will prove as enduring as those of any other modern state. Rather than strip the Islamic republic of its religious base, strengthening the state's political arm may allow politicians to restrict the influence of the religious authorities to specific domains such as education and cultural affairs, while permitting the political class to retain ultimate political power. As in Pakistan and Israel, religion and politics in Iran might eventually be joined through their functional partition.

While this development may seem strange to those who view it through the prism of Western experience, the real paradox lies elsewhere. For although a reinterpreted vision of Shi'ism inspired the creation of the Islamic Republic of Iran, the institutionalization of the revolution has been legitimated by utilitarian principles that echo the Sunni theory of the caliphate. This twelfth-century theory held that the "supreme value in politics (is) . . . not justice but security—a state of mind which set a high premium on the ability to rule and maintain 'law and order,' rather than on piety."[165] Some eight centuries later, it is worth repeating, Khomeini evoked this theme when he wrote in *Islamic Government* that "Islam came in order to establish order. . . . It is our duty to preserve Islam. This duty is . . . more necessary even than prayer."[166]

Rafsanjani's adoption of this principle did not mean that he was trying to establish a new caliphate. Nevertheless, by divesting the Islamic revolution of its most outwardly Shi'ite symbol—the rule of a divinely inspired Leader—the pragmatists strengthened Iran's appeal among Sunni Muslims. Although it seems paradoxical to claim that Iran advanced a more ecumenical message *because* Khomeini has passed on, we must remember that the Imam had extolled utilitarianism in the name of Islamic unity. Through their support of Islamic activists in Lebanon, Sudan, Palestine, and Algeria, Iran's leaders are today honoring Khomeini's most enduring legacy.

Acknowledgments

I would like to thank Professor Scott Appleby for his editorial comments and his boundless patience over the course of this work's preparation. I would also like to thank David Menashri, James Piscatori, Sole Ozel, and Marvin Zonis for their comments. This essay began as a presentation in the spring of 1991 at the Institute for the Advanced Study of Religion of the University of Chicago. Colleagues' comments there and, later, in the Department of Religion of Emory University were very helpful. I would also like to thank my student Lisa Tadayun for helping me to translate Persian material, and my graduate research assistant Jessica Cashdan for doing a superb editing job. The essay is dedicated to my wife, Laurie.

Notes

1. See Marvin Zonis and Daniel Brumberg, "Khomeini, the Islamic Republic of Iran and the Arab World," *Harvard Middle East Papers,* modern series no. 5, Center for Middle Eastern Studies, Harvard University, 1987.

2. This view is reflected in the official biographies of Khomeini published by the Islamic Republic of Iran. See "Biography of Imam Ayatullah Ruhullah Khomeini," in *Imam Khomeini's Last Will and Testament* (Washington, D.C.: Interest Section of the Islamic Republic of Iran, Sola Publishing, n.d.); *Biography of Ayatollah Khomeini* (Tehran: Ministry of Islamic Guidance, Council for the Celebration of the Third Anniversary of the Victory of the Islamic Revolution, 1982). It is also echoed in Hamid Algar, "Imam Khomeini, 1902–1962: The Pre-Revolutionary Years," in Edmund Burke III and Ira M. Lapidus, *Islam, Politics and Social Movements* (Berkeley: University of California Press, 1988), 263–88.

3. See for example Clive Irving's introduction to *The Little Green Book: The Sayings of the Ayatollah Khomeini* (New York: Bantam Books, 1980).

4. See Nikki R. Keddie, *An Islamic Response to Imperialism: Political and Religious Writings of Sayyid Jamal ad-Din "al-Afghani"* (Berkeley: University of California Press, 1983), and Nikki R. Keddie and Farah Monian, "Militancy and Religion in Contemporary Iran," in Martin E. Marty and R. Scott Appleby, eds., *Fundamentalisms and the State: Remaking Polities, Economies, and Militance* (Chicago: University of Chicago Press, 1993), 511–38. For a good example of the "rational choice" method, see Abner Cohen, *Two-Dimensional Man: An Es-*

say on the Anthropology of Power and Symbolism in Complex Society (Berkeley: University of California Press, 1974).

5. Keddie and Monian, "Militancy and Religion," 523–33. Keddie and Monian argue that Khomeini's ideology had less to with Islam than with the universal forces promoting the struggle of third-world countries to "free their nations from Western control."

6. On Weber's concept of "elective affinity," see "The Social Psychology of World Religions," in H. H. Gerth and C. Wright Mills, eds., *From Max Weber: Essays in Sociology* (New York: Oxford University Press, 1946), 267–301.

7. Works on Khomeini can be divided into at least five genres. There are popular biographies written mostly by his detractors, the most comprehensive of which is Amir Taheri, *The Spirit of Allah Khomeini and the Islamic Revolution* (Bethesda, Md.: Adler and Adler, 1985). Taheri portrays Khomeini largely as an opportunist. The work is filled with personal detail but is often inadequately documented and suffers from inaccuracies and contradictions in the narrative. There are also sympathetic biographies that attribute a kind of prophetic consistency to Khomeini's life. These include official biographies published by the Islamic Republic of Iran, such as the previously cited *Biography of Ayatollah Khomeini* and "Biography of Imam Ayatullah Ruhullah Khomeini." Hamid Algar's short biographical essay, while scholarly and well documented, echoes the official line; see Algar, "Imam Khomeini." One of the most balanced studies of Khomeini's life, which identifies the common threads as well as the historical breaks, can be found in Hamid Dabashi, *Theology of Discontent: The Ideological Foundation of the Islamic Revolution in Iran* (New York: New York University, 1993), 409–84. A "psychobiographical" approach is adopted by Bruce Mazlish in "The Hidden Khomeini," *New York Magazine,* 24 December 1979, 50–55. Also highly recommended is Roy Mottahedeh, *The Mantle of the Prophet* (New York: Pantheon, 1985); while not a biography of Khomeini as such, it contains much useful information about his life and times. Finally, there are interpretive works which borrow from history, sociology, and anthropology to illuminate the subjective and objective factors shaping Khomeini's political action and ideology. These include Michael Fischer's short but intriguing "Imam Khomeini: Four Levels of Understanding," in John Esposito, ed., *Voices of Resurgent Islam* (New York: Oxford University Press, 1983), 150–74, as well as the present study.

8. Dabashi, *Theology of Discontent,* 410.

9. Hamid Enayat, *Modern Islamic Political Thought* (Austin: University of Texas Press, 1982), 18–51; Shahrough Akhavi, *Religion and Politics in Contemporary Iran: Clergy-State Relations in the Pahlavi Period* (Albany: State University Press of New York, 1980), pp. 1–22. It should be noted that while many clerics adopted this oppositional role, a minority maintained relations with the ruling authorities.

10. Hamid Algar, "The Role of the Ulema in Twentieth Century Iran," in Nikki R. Keddie, ed., *Scholars, Saints and Sufis* (Berkeley: University of California Press, 1972), 232 n. 3.

11. Taheri, *Spirit of Allah,* 30.

12. During his first five years in Qom, Khomeini studied with a number of scholars, but began direct study under Hairi in 1926.

13. Taheri, *Spirit of Allah,* 49.

14. Among these works were *Mesbah al-Hedayeh* (1928) and *Sharh Do'a al-Sahar* (1930). See the chapter "Ayatollah Khomeini," in Dabashi, *Theology of Discontent,* 411; Algar, "Imam Khomeini," 269.

15. See Algar, "Imam Khomeini," 268–69.

16. Akhavi, *Religion and Politics,* 44.

17. Algar, "Imam Khomeini," 274; see also Taheri, *Spirit of Allah,* 93–94. In 1979, Taheri notes, Khomeini had the commander of the troops responsible for the massacre, Captain Iraj Matbu'i, executed at the age of ninety-six.

18. See Marvin Zonis, *Majestic Failure: The Fall of the Shah* (Chicago: University of Chicago Press, 1991), esp. "Xenophobia and Emulation," 166–206.

19. See Said A. Arjomand's astute analysis of this period in his *Turban for the Crown: The Islamic Revolution in Iran* (New York: Oxford University Press, 1988), 59–87.

20. Algar, "Imam Khomeini," 276.

21. "Biography of Imam Ayatullah Ruhullah Khomeini," 3.

22. Ayatollah Khomeini, "A Warning to the Nation," in Hamid Algar, trans., *Islam and Revolution: Writings and Declarations of Imam Khomeini* (Berkeley: Mizan Press, 1981), 170.

23. Algar, "Imam Khomeini," 276–77. Khomeini, in fact, stated that the 1907 constitution, which provided for clerical supervision of laws drafted by the parliament, offered an acceptable procedure for clerical guidance; see Khomeini, "Warning to the Nation," 170.

24. Khomeini, quoted in *Biography of Ayatollah Khomeini,* 5–6.

25. Dabashi, "Ayatollah Khomeini," 442.

26. "Biography of Imam Ayatullah Ruhullah Khomeini," 2.

27. Zonis, *Majestic Failure,* 99–107.

28. Kermit Roosevelt, *Countercoup: The Struggle for the Control of Iran* (New York: McGraw Hill, 1979).

29. Mottahedeh, *Mantle of the Prophet,* 131.

30. Taheri reports that in his effort to back Burujerdi for position of grand ayatollah, and in connection with the case of Hussein Emami, a member of the Fedayeen of Islam, Khomeini actually visited with the Shah in 1945. Another ayatollah present at the meeting reports that "this hate was at first sight." See Taheri, *Spirit of Allah,* 108.

31. Enayat, *Modern Islamic Political Thought,* 12. The term *Sunni realism* is Enayat's own.

32. Nikki R. Keddie, *An Islamic Response to Imperialism: Political and Religious Writings of Sayyid Jamal ad-Din "al-Afghani"* (Berkeley: University of California Press, 1968).

33. See Enayat, *Modern Islamic Political Thought,* 71, 89; Richard Mitchell, *The Society of Muslim Brothers* (London, 1969), 232. On Rida see Nadav Safran, *Egypt in Search of Political Community* (Cambridge: Harvard University Press, 1961), 76.

34. Taheri, *Spirit of Allah,* 97.

35. "Ayatollah" is an unofficial title meaning "miraculous sign of god." As Mottahedeh observes, the title was "originally conferred on a few of the very greatest jurisconsults at the end of the century" but is "now given to hundreds" (Mottahedeh, *Mantle of the Prophet,* 233). However, the term "grand ayatollah"

came to be accorded only to a select few, with the term "the grand ayatollah" reserved for the ayatollah generally accepted as the most advanced and renowned.

36. See "Biography of Imam Ayatollah Ruhullah Khomeini," 3.

37. Taheri, *Spirit of Allah*, 126.

38. Ibid., 128.

39. Ibid., 136.

40. Dabashi, "Ayatollah Khomeini," 425.

41. See Chibli Mallat, *The Renewal of Islamic Law: Muhammad Baqer as-Sadr, Najaf and the Shi'i International* (Cambridge: Cambridge University Press, 1993), 28–58.

42. Ibid., 51.

43. Mottahedeh notes that in his famous 1973 speech denouncing the Shah's shooting of students at the Feziyeh seminary, Khomeini claimed that "Israel assaulted the Faizeyeh *madrasa* by means of its sinister agents" (i.e., the Shah); see Mottahedeh, *Mantle of the Prophet*, 190.

44. See Dabashi, 472–74.

45. See "Message to the Muslim Students in North America," 10 July 1972, in Khomeini, *Islam and Revolution*, 209–11.

46. Taheri, *Spirit of Allah*, 163–64; H. E. Chehabi, *Iranian Politics and Religious Modernism: The Liberation Movement of Iran under the Shah and Khomeini* (Ithaca: Cornell University Press, 1990); Dabashi, *Theology of Discontent*, 424–25.

47. See Dabashi, *Theology of Discontent*, 427.

48. We shall see below that this was precisely the argument Khomeini made during the late 1980s, when clerical disputes threatened the unity of the Islamic Republic of Iran.

49. Mallat, *Renewal of Islamic Law*.

50. The Safavid Empire (1501–1722) offers a partial exception to this historical rule; see Arjomand, *Turban for the Crown*, 152.

51. Indeed, during the nineteenth century, when Iran was ruled by the Qajars (1785–1925) certain Shi'ite legal scholars emerged as popular defenders of Shi'ite society in opposition to the state; see Algar, "Role of the Ulema," 232.

52. Ruhollah Khomeini, *Islamic Government;* I have relied on Algar's translation in *Islam and Revolution*, 27–159. I have also consulted Hamid Enayat's "Iran: Khumayni's Concept of the 'Guardian of the Jurisconsult,'" in James Piscatori, ed., *Islam in the Political Process* (Cambridge: Cambridge University Press, 1983), 160–80.

53. Khomeini, *Islamic Government*, 44, 79, 53.

54. Ibid., 42, 75.

55. Ibid., 53.

56. "O you who believe, obey God and obey the Messenger and the holder of authority from among you. When you dispute with each other concerning a thing, refer it to God and his Messenger" (Qur'an 4:58–59).

57. Khomeini, *Islamic Government*, 62, 64.

58. Ibid., 64.

59. Ibid., 54–55.

60. Ibid., 82–83.

61. Ibid., 62.

62. Ibid., 70.

63. Ruhollah Khomeini, "The Greater Jihad," in Algar, *Islam and Revolution,* 353, 352.

64. See Dabashi, "Ayatollah Khomeini," 463. Dabashi provides a remarkable discussion of Khomeini's concept of infallibility.

65. Ibid., 463.

66. Zonis, *Majestic Failure,* 81.

67. Clifford Geertz, "Ideology as a Cultural System," in Clifford Geertz, *The Interpretation of Cultures* (New York: Basic Books, 1973), 193–233.

68. Mottahedeh, *Mantle of the Prophet,* 347–50.

69. Ibid., 222–23.

70. "Biography of Imam Ayatullah Ruhullah Khomeini," 6.

71. Taheri, *Spirit of Allah,* 185.

72. Ibid., 203.

73. Ruhollah Khomeini, "In Commemoration of the First Martyrs of the Revolution," 19 February 1978, in Algar, *Islam and Revolution,* 216.

74. Ruhollah Khomeini, "Muharram: The Triumph of Blood over the Sword," 23 November 1978, in Algar, *Islam and Revolution,* 242.

75. Arjomand, *Turban for the Crown,* 121.

76. "Biography of Imam Ayatullah Ruhullah Khomeini," 8–9.

77. See Algar, Foreword, in *Islam and Revolution,* 10. Algar reproduces Khomeini's theoretical distinction between "Imam," meaning the Twelfth Imam, and "imam," meaning a leader. In doing so he implicitly backs a conceptual distinction that served to obscure the real sources of Khomeini's authority as "Imam."

78. Dabashi, "Ayatollah Khomeini," 483.

79. Unless otherwise noted, the following quotes are from the speech "Khomeyni to the Craftsmen," Foreign Broadcasting Information Service, South Asia Section, Washington, D.C. (henceforth FBIS–SAS), 14 December 1979, broadcast on Tehran Domestic Service 13 December 1979; broadcast dates for subsequent speeches also refer to Tehran Domestic Service.

80. "Khomeini Delivers Oration," FBIS–SAS, 7 May 1979, broadcast 4 May 1979.

81. Marvin Zonis and Daniel Brumberg, "Shi'ism as Interpreted by Khomeini," in Martin Kramer, ed., *Shi'ism and Revolution* (Boulder: Westview Press, 1987), 52–53.

82. "Khomeini Tells Student of Importance of National Unity," FBIS–SAS, 24 December 1979, broadcast 23 December 1979.

83. "Khomeini Denies Islam Opiate of the Masses," FBIS–SAS, 28 June 1979, broadcast 27 June 1979.

84. "Khomeyni Urges Acceptance of Vice-Regency Plan," FBIS–SAS, 24 September 1979, broadcast 21 September 1979.

85. Ibid.

86. "Khomeyni Discusses Guardians Council Tasks," FBIS–SAS 83-060, 12 December 1983, broadcast 11 December 1983.

87. Max Weber, "The Types of Legitimate Domination," in Max Weber, *Economy and Society,* vol. 1, Buenther Roth and Clause Wittich, eds. (Berkeley: University of California Press, 1978), 212–45.

88. Max Weber, "The Routinization of Charisma," in *Economy*, 246–50. Weber held that a leader can delegate his authority to others, but that the "routinization of authority"—its institutionalization in a body of written laws and bureaucratic organizations—is a protracted process that occurs after the passing of the leader.

89. See, for example, Arjomand, *Turban for the Crown*.

90. "Six Point Message from Khomeini," Foreign Broadcasting Information Service, Middle East Area (henceforth FBIS–MEA), 79-031-A, 13 February 1979, broadcast 12 February 1979.

91. "Khomeyni Address to Nation," FBIS–MEA 79-042, 1 March 1979, broadcast 28 February 1979.

92. "Khomeyni Call," FBIS–MEA 79-062, 30 March 1979, broadcast 29 March 1979.

93. "Khomeyni Statement after Voting," FBIS–MEA 79-064, 2 April 1979, broadcast 30 March 1979.

94. Said Amir Arjomand, "Shi'ite Jurisprudence and Constitution Making in the Islamic Republic of Iran," in Martin E. Marty and R. Scott Appleby, eds., *Fundamentalisms and the State: Remaking Polities, Economies and Militance* (Chicago: University of Chicago Press, 1993), 90.

95. "Khomeini Delivers Speech on Freedom, Plots," FBIS–MEA 79-103, 29 May 1979, broadcast 25 May 1979.

96. "Khomeini Discusses Constitution," FBIS–MEA 79-118, 18 June 1979, broadcast 16 June 1979.

97. "Khomeini Says Iran Facing 'Danger of Unbridledness,' " FBIS–MEA 79-123, 25 June 1979, broadcast 24 June 1979. Muawiyah, who established the Umayyad dynasty in 661, opposed 'Ali's claim to the caliphate by calling for the arbitration of his claim. Khomeini's point seems to be twofold: first, even Islamic leaders can act in an evil fashion, and, second, differences within the Islamic camp can open the door to evil leaders such as Muawiyah.

98. "Khomeyni Warns Nation Losing Key to Victory," FBIS–MEA 79-132-A, 9 July 1979, broadcast 7 July 1979.

99. "Khomeini Urges Unity in Selection Draft Constitution," FBIS–MEA 79-145, 26 July 1979, broadcast 25 July 1979.

100. "Khomeyni: Army Must Act with Severity in Kordistan," FBIS–MEA 79-162-A, broadcast 17 August 1979.

101. "Khomeyni Defends Concept of Theocracy in 22 October Speech," FBIS–MEA 79-206, vol. 5, no. 206, 22 October 1979.

102. Qanoun Asasi Jumhouriyya Islami Iran 1980 (Constitution of the Islamic Republic of Iran 1980). For an English version, see *Constitution of the Islamic Republic of Iran*, trans. Hamid Algar (Berkeley: Mizan Press, 1980). My thanks to William Zeiske, assistant Middle East bibliographer at the University of Chicago Library, for providing the original Persian version of the 1980 constitution. See also Marvin Zonis and Daniel Brumberg, "Interpreting Islam: Human Rights in the Islamic Republic of Iran," in Heshmat Moayyad, ed., *The Baha'i Faith and Islam: Proceedings of a Symposium on the Baha'i Faith and Islam* (Ottawa: Association of Baha'i Studies, 1990).

103. Although in *Islamic Government* Khomeini had used the word *imam* to mean "leader," in the constitution he used the Persian word *rahbar* for "leader"

and the term *Imam* in its official Shi'ite sense, with a capital *I*, leaving little doubt as to the meaning of "Imam Khomeini."

104. Another interpretation of Khomeini's behavior might be that he wanted no competitors in the political hierarchy. While this may be true, his repeated statements suggest a genuine fear of the paradoxical consequences of clerical rule.

105. "Khomeyni Asks Public to Select Presidential Candidates," FBIS–MEA 80-00J, vol. 5, supp. 007, 8 January 1980, broadcast 4 January 1980.

106. A close ally of Bazargan, Bani-Sadr was also one of a group of three men who managed Khomeini's affairs in Paris. See H. E. Chehabi, *Iranian Politics and Religious Modernism* (Ithaca: Cornell University Press, 1990), 242.

107. "Address by Ayatollah Khomeini on the Occasion of the Iranian New Year," FBIS–MEA 80-056, 21 March 1980, broadcast 20 March 1980.

108. "Ayatollah Khomeyni Addresses Nation," FBIS–MEA 80-038, 24 March 1980, broadcast 21 March 1980.

109. "Khomeyni Addresses Youth on Corruption in Society," FBIS–SAS 80-100, 21 May 1980, broadcast 20 May 1980.

110. "Khomeyni Majlis Message," FBIS–SAS 80-104, 28 May 1980, broadcast 28 May 1980.

111. "Text of Khomeyni Speech to a Group of Workers," FBIS–SAS 80-125, 26 June 1980, broadcast 25 June 1981.

112. Robin B. Wright, *In the Name of God: The Khomeini Decade* (New York: Simon and Schuster, 1989), 92.

113. "Speech to Council," FBIS–SAS 80-141, 21 July 1980, broadcast 21 July 1980.

114. "20 July Speech," FBIS–SAS 80-143, 23 July 1980, broadcast 29 July 1980.

115. "Khomeyni Condemns National Front," FBIS–SAS 81-115, 16 June 1981, broadcast 15 June 1981.

116. "Khomeyni Message to the Nation," FBIS–SAS 81-029, 12 February 1981, broadcast 11 February 1981. It should be noted that Khomeini had only recently attacked those who opposed the clergy because they lacked the "technical" skills required for the management of public affairs.

117. Shaul Bakhash, *The Reign of the Ayatollahs: Iran and the Islamic Revolution* (New York: Basic Books, 1984), 166–216.

118. "Khomeyni Addresses Muslim Clergy on Eve of Muharram," FBIS–SAS 80-217, 6 November 1980, broadcast 5 November 1980; my emphasis.

119. "Khomeyni Id Ghadir Address on Islam, War," FBIS–SAS 80-211, 29 October 1980, broadcast 29 October 1980.

120. "Khomeyni Addresses Majlis Deputies March 19," FBIS–SAS 81-282, 21 March 1981, broadcast 19 March 1981.

121. See Arjomand, "Shi'ite Jurisprudence," 96.

122. "Majlis Speaker Requests Khomeyni Guidance on Laws," FBIS–SAS 81-198, 14 October 1981, broadcast 11 October 1981.

123. "Khomeyni Issues Message on Islamization," FBIS–SAS 82-242, 16 December 1982, broadcast 15 December 1982.

124. "Khomeyni Speaks of Civil, Property Rights," FBIS–SAS 82-24, 23 December 1982, broadcast 22 December 1982.

125. "Khomeyni Addresses Majlis Deputies January 24," FBIS–SAS 82-018, 26 January 1983, broadcast 24 January 1983.

126. "Khomeyni 10 February Message to Revolution Ceremony," FBIS–SAS 83-030, 11 February 1983, broadcast 10 February 1983.

127. "Khomeyni Issues Statement on Tudeh Leaders Arrest," FBIS–SAS 83-088, 5 May 1983, broadcast 4 May 1983.

128. "Ayatollah Khomeyni Message to Council of Experts," FBIS–SAS 83-137, 15 July 1983, broadcast 14 July 1983; my emphasis and additional explanations.

129. "Khomeyni Discusses Guardian Council Tasks," FBIS, SAS 83-239, 12 December 1983, broadcast 11 December 1983.

130. "Khomeyni Addresses Member of Council of Experts," Foreign Broadcasting Information Service, Near East Section (henceforth FBIS–NES), 87-128, 6 July 1987, broadcast 2 July 1987.

131. "Khomeyni Addresses Friday Imams 29 September," FBIS–NES 87-188, 29 September 1987, broadcast 29 September 1987.

132. "Khomeyni Ruling on State Powers Report," FBIS–NES 87-247, 24 December 1987, broadcast 23 December 1987.

133. "Khomeyni Answers Khamanei Letter on Authority," FBIS–NES 88-004, 7 January 1988, broadcast 7 January 1988; my emphasis.

134. See Millat, *Renewal of Islamic Law*, 91–93 for a somewhat different interpretation of this event.

135. The term *pragmatist* is used here in a nonevaluative sense to indicate a utilitarian approach to political action. It should not be equated, as it often is in the West, with "moderation." The history books are filled with the victims of "pragmatists."

136. "Majlis Speaker on Khomeyni Reply," FBIS–NES 88-004, 7 January 1988, broadcast 7 January 1988.

137. "Musavi on Khomeyni's Views, Decrees," FBIS–NES 88-006, 11 January 1988, broadcast 10 January 1988.

138. "Deputies Thank Khomeyni," FBIS–NES 88-008, 13 January 1988, broadcast 12 January 1988.

139. Ibid.

140. Indeed, Rafsanjani could have made an even bolder argument, one that was suggested by Khomeini's dictum, i.e., that "government," being a "divine injunction," was empowered to conceive all legislation, whether primary or secondary. Rafsanjani did not go this far.

141. "First Sermon on Islamic Government," FBIS–NES 88-011, 19 January 1988, broadcast 15 January 1988.

142. "Khamene'i Delivers Tehran Friday Prayer Sermons," FBIS–NES 88-015, 25 January 1988, broadcast 22 January 1988.

143. See Mallat, *Renewal of Islamic Law*, 105.

144. "Khomeyni Address on Majlis Elections," FBIS–NES 88-062, 31 March 1988, broadcast 31 March 1988.

145. David Menashri, "Iran," in Ami Ayalon and Haim Shaked, eds., *Middle East Contemporary Survey*, vol. 12 (1988), Moshe Dayan Center for Middle Eastern and African Studies, Shiloah Institute, Tel Aviv University (Boulder: Westview, 1990), 490.

146. "Khomeyni Message to Majlis," FBIS–NES 88-104, 31 May 1988, broadcast 28 May 1988.

147. Although Khomeini admitted that this act was "more lethal for me than poison," he added that was drinking the poison "for the sake of God's satisfaction," for the sake of protecting the revolution. "Khomeyni Message on Hajj, Resolution 598," FBIS–NES 88-140, 21 July 1988, broadcast 20 July 1988.

148. The task of leadership, Khomeini told his devoted disciple, was a "heavy and august responsibility" that "requires more strength" than you have. David Menashri, "Iran," in Ami Ayalon, ed., *Middle East Contemporary Survey,* vol. 13 (1989) (Boulder: Westview, 1991), 342.

149. David Menashri, "Iran," in Itamar Rabinovoch and Haim Shaked, eds., *Middle East Contemporary Survey,* vol. 11 (1987) (Boulder: Westview, 1989), 395.

150. "Khomeyni Letter on Guidelines for Reconstruction," FBIS–NES 88-192, 4 October 1988, broadcast 3 October 1988.

151. "Khamene'i Delivers Friday Prayers Sermon," FBIS–NES 88-233, 5 December 1988, broadcast 2 December 1988; my emphasis.

152. See "Islamic Republic of Iran," in Albert Blaustein and Gisbert Flanz, eds., *Constitutions of the Countries of the World* (Dobbs Ferry: Oceana Publications, 1992), in English and Persian.

153. My emphasis.

154. Mallat, *Renewal of Islamic Law,* 106–7.

155. Ibid., 356–57.

156. FBIS–NES 90-101, 24 May 1990, broadcast 22 May 1990.

157. FBIS–NES 90-045, 7 March 1990; published in *Keyhan,* 25 February 1990.

158. *Imam Khomeini's Last Will and Testament,* 16.

159. "Karrubi Speaks to Majlis," FBIS–NES 90-045, 7 March 1990, broadcast 25 February 1990.

160. "Azari-Qomi Responds to Karrubi," FBIS–NES 90-045, 7 March 1990, broadcast 26 February 1990.

161. Gerth and Mills, *From Max Weber,"* 291.

162. See Arjomand, "Shi'ite Jurisprudence," 105.

163. This argument is implied in Arjomand's essay cited above. See also H. E. Chehabi, "Religion and Politics in Iran: How Theocratic is the Islamic Republic?," *Daedalus* 120, no. 3 (summer 1991): 69–93.

164. Albert Hourani, *Arabic Thought in the Liberal Age 1798–1939* (London: Oxford University Press, 1970), 344.

165. Enayat, *Modern Islamic Political Thought,* 12.

166. Khomeini, *Islamic Government,* 75.

TWO

THE ORACLE OF HIZBULLAH

Sayyid Muhammad Husayn Fadlallah

Martin Kramer

The prerecorded audiocassette market of Beirut is one of the more sensitive measures of the city's fever. In the 1970s it was dominated by immensely popular tapes of Palestinian nationalist hymns. But in the mid-1980s, according to a Lebanese weekly, these lost their market share to the record-breaking sales of cassettes bearing the voice of a Shi'ite cleric. In the marketplace of inspiration-on-demand, nothing could match the tapes of Friday sermons delivered by Ayatollah Sayyid Muhammad Husayn Fadlallah. One vendor, operating from a cassette store in the neighborhood of Fadlallah's mosque in a poor Shi'ite quarter of Beirut, taped the sermon each week from the pulpit. The entrepreneur claimed to have sold more than a hundred thousand copies throughout Lebanon. Orders also arrived from West Africa and the United States, centers of the Lebanese Shi'ite diaspora. Heavy demand doubled the price of many tapes.[1]

Fadlallah spoke for Hizbullah, the "party of God," a movement of Lebanese Shi'ites that captured the world's attention beginning in 1982. Obscure men carried out the acts of violence that made Hizbullah renowned—suicide bombings, airliner hijackings, hostage takings. But it was the ubiquitous Fadlallah who processed the rage of Hizbullah into speech, in sermons and lectures, on tape and in print. Borne aloft on a wind of words, he made himself the voice of Hizbullah's conscience and its spokesman to the world. His very ubiquity suggested that he led the movement, a supposition that drew diplomats, mediators, and assassins to his door. Turban, beard, and spectacles combined in a countenance that, alone among the faces of God's partisans in Lebanon, became internationally famous and infamous. Fadlallah's place in the movement eluded definition; the precise boundaries of his role ran through Hizbullah's secret space. But in no other single instance did individual and collective needs so obviously combine for mutual gratification. Hizbullah's deeds amplified Fadlallah's words, carrying his voice far beyond his own pulpit to the wider world. Fadlallah's words interpreted and justified Hizbullah's deeds, transforming resentment into resistance.

Fadlallah personified the role of leaders in the emergence and transformation of contemporary Islamic movements. Islamic fundamentalism is deeply rooted in the social and economic crisis that has overwhelmed so many peoples of the Middle East and North Africa, and its power cannot be understood as the achievement of a few individual leaders. Yet the appearance of dynamic leaders has constituted a necessary condition for the forging of discontent into discipline, and the creation of organized movements. When Bernard Lewis wrote his prescient essay on "The Return of Islam" in 1975, he attributed the failure of earlier Islamic movements to an absence of such leadership:

> One reason for their lack of success is that those who have made the attempt have been so unconvincing. This still leaves the possibility of a more convincing leadership, and there is ample evidence in virtually all Muslim countries of the deep yearning for such a leadership and a readiness to respond to it. The lack of an educated and modern leadership has so far restricted the scope of Islam and inhibited religious movements from being serious contenders for power. But it is already effective as a limiting factor and may yet become a powerful domestic political force if the right kind of leadership emerges.[2]

Such leadership appeared a few years later in the person of Ayatollah Ruhollah Khomeini, who launched a movement that swept aside Iran's monarchy and established a regime of divine justice. As the 1980s unfolded, more leaders emerged as additional Islamic movements gained momentum—leaders who had mastered the power to persuade, and who knew enough of the discourse of modernity to puncture it. They convinced masses of people that a return to Islam meant not a step backward, but a leap forward into a postmodern world where the preeminent values of the West would be challenged by their own adherents. The certainties of Islam would prevail, and believers who held tightly to them would be empowered. The logic of these new leaders was a combination of the Cartesian and the Qur'anic, and they appealed directly to those scarred deeply by religious doubt, especially the ever more numerous young. In the span of a few years, these leaders came to stand at the head of mass movements, well positioned to bid for ultimate political power.

Hizbullah arose in Lebanon from a fusion of many discontents. It drew upon Shi'ite frustration with endemic poverty and the collapse of civil society into civil war. It received inspiration and direct support from Islamic Iran and won a following among those who suffered as a result of Israel's 1982 invasion of Lebanon.[3] It benefited from the indulgence of Syria and the fragmentation of Lebanon's Shi'ites themselves. Yet it is difficult to imagine how Hizbullah would have evolved without the omnipresence of Fadlallah. Others may have made Hizbullah's choices, but the movement bore his mark. For he was Hizbullah's oracle—a fount of infallible (if ambiguous) guidance, fed by an unfathomably deep well of wisdom. He rallied the masses to the movement, then kept them from following paths to self-destruction. The movement and the man guaranteed one another's survival—and together they wrote history.[4]

PRECOCIOUS POET

Fadlallah was born in the Iraqi Shi'ite shrine city of Najaf on 16 November 1935. His father, Sayyid 'Abd al-Ra'uf Fadlallah, had migrated there from the village of 'Aynata in South Lebanon in 1928 to pursue religious learning.[5] Najaf sits astride the sluggish Euphrates, on a baked plain 150 kilometers south of Baghdad. At the heart of this city of domes is the revered tomb of the Imam 'Ali, the Prophet Muhammad's cousin and son-in-law. In past times of prosperity and peace, this gateway to the predominantly Shi'ite south of Iraq teemed with pilgrims from throughout the Shi'ite world, who sought communion with God and fed the city's hoards of beggars. But Najaf also encouraged another kind of purposeful travel, for alongside the shrines were some of the most renowned Shi'ite seminaries. Great ayatollahs, scholars, and students assembled from throughout the Shi'ite world—the majority from Iran, others from Iraq, Lebanon, the Arab Gulf, Afghanistan, and the Indian subcontinent. In Najaf they studied sacred law, theology, and philosophy, according to the medieval pedagogical methods of the Islamic seminary. The schools were free of government control and submitted to no external academic authority. No presidents, deans, or masters presided. The ayatollahs maintained their seminaries through donations and alms, which arrived from throughout the Shi'ite world. Students paid no tuition, teachers received no salaries; all drew small stipends which allowed them to pursue pious learning in conditions of the utmost austerity. Some eventually returned to their own lands to preach; others spent lifetimes in the seminaries. Stories of deprivation and hunger suffered by students and teachers filled many memoirs of life in Najaf, but all attested to the city's tenacious hold upon those who dwelled within it.[6]

Upon entering the city, pilgrims and scholars stepped out of time. Shi'ism had survived as a negation of temporal Islamic history. In the Shi'ite view, the ship of Islam had been run aground immediately after the death of the Prophet by those who ignored his specific instruction that his son-in-law 'Ali be placed at its helm. Later the usurpers would compound the crime of disobedience with that of murder, when they slew 'Ali's son Husayn rather than recognize his divine right to rule. There followed a succession of violations against the just claims of 'Ali's descendants and their supporters. They and their truths were forced underground by a false Islam. So thoroughly did the usurpers suppress truth that the Shi'ite tradition did not expect wrongs to be righted before the end of eschatological time. The partisans of 'Ali nursed their grievances, mourned their martyrs, and scoffed at the wars waged by false Muslims for the expansion and defense of Islam. For them, history itself had gone into hiding. Nowhere did temporal time seem so completely suspended as in Najaf and Karbala, the burial places of 'Ali and Husayn. There Shi'ites came as pilgrims to lament the injustices of this world, and there they were brought for burial to speed them to the next. Najaf did not always know tranquility, but a succession of Sunni Islamic empires recognized its sacred character and granted immunities that formed a wall around the city.

The sacred space on the Euphrates traditionally gripped the imagination of young Shi'ites in Jabal 'Amil, the mountainous south of Lebanon. Through some study in Najaf, one might become a shaykh and gain some of the prestige traditionally accorded to the learned. But Najaf exercised a particular pull upon those who already claimed authority by descent and for whom acquired learning compounded distinguished lineage. They were *sayyids*, descendants of the Prophet Muhammad through the Imam Husayn, who were believed to possess *baraka*, an inherited grace that infused their blessings with potency. They were much in demand in all forms of religious ritual; in return, they laid a recognized claim to the alms due to the Imam. While shaykhs of undistinguished lineage wore white turbans, sayyids were entitled to wear black or green.

Beyond the hereditary title of sayyid, affirmed for the world by the color of one's turban, there were other, more prestigious titles associated with learning. Through a short period of study in Najaf, one might aspire to the title of *imam* and *khatib,* prayer leader and sermonizer in a mosque. More protracted study in Islamic law might earn one the formal title of *mujtahid,* one empowered to interpret the law in binding ways for believers. When respect for one's learning became great enough that one could accredit others as mujtahids, the title of ayatollah might be accorded by informal acclamation. Such titles could only be acquired through study in Najaf. Thus learning was pursued both for its own sake and as a credential of spiritual authority and social preeminence.

When Sayyid 'Abd al-Ra'uf departed for Najaf, he did what was expected of him. His family were the most notable sayyids of the village of 'Aynata, which sat astride the then-open frontier between Lebanon and Palestine; his father, one of the foremost clerics in the district, supervised a local seminary. Najaf captured Sayyid 'Abd al-Ra'uf as a young man, and held him close for thirty years. He finished his own studies under the leading teachers of the city, and taught a generation of aspiring young scholars from Iran, Iraq, and Lebanon. He returned to south Lebanon in the summer of 1956, but the scholarly ways of the shrine city did not leave him. When he died in 1984, his body was flown back to Iraq for burial in Najaf, far from his place of birth but at the sacred center of rebirth, so that he might be among the first to be resurrected on the appointed day.[7]

His son, Sayyid Muhammad Husayn Fadlallah, passed his formative years in Najaf's rarefied climate of scholastic piety. Like his fellow students, the young Fadlallah had to master a curriculum unaltered by the passage of time, which stressed grammar, logic, and rhetoric in the early years of study. This emphasis reflected a deep-rooted appreciation for the relationship between formalized language and power. A mastery of formal conventions of speech set a Najaf-educated man apart from all others; the mark of learning was an instrument of social power. The elements of this formalized language were control of classical Arabic combined with appropriate and precise quotation of the Qur'an and the sayings of the Prophet Muhammad and the Imams. These conventions, rigorously cultivated in seminary and mosque, affirmed the power of the speaker over his listeners.

Fadlallah was gifted and precocious. At the age of ten, he and some friends even put out a handwritten literary journal.[8] His mastery of the word distinguished him from his contemporaries, and he progressively advanced to the highest stages of learning in theology and law under Najaf's most esteemed teachers. The most venerated of these were ayatollahs Muhsin al-Hakim and Abu al-Qasim Kho'i—the former an Arab (and related to Fadlallah through his mother), the latter an Azeri. Yet from the outset, Fadlallah demonstrated a will and a talent for stretching convention, for putting his mastery of language to original use. He first did so in poetry, which constituted the most intimate and original form of expression among the ostensibly staid scholars of Najaf. After prayer or a visit to the public baths, students and teachers alike would meet in séances where they exchanged gossip and recited verse.[9]

> I cannot remember myself when I was not writing poetry because I began writing poetry when I was ten years old. . . . My presence in holy Najaf where I was born caused me to be deeply influenced by the poetic atmosphere which existed in this stage and by the experiment which was active at that time. . . . I was perhaps, with some fellow poets in Najaf, one of the first persons to write free verse in Najaf, which we published in the Iraqi papers at that time.[10]

In 1953, at the age of sixteen, Fadlallah visited Lebanon to attend a commemorative ceremony for a leading Shi'ite cleric. The teenager appeared wearing the turban of a learned man and recited a poem "which astonished people at the time." As a result, the young prodigy from Najaf stirred some comment in the Lebanese press.[11] In later life he continued to write poetry, in his spare time and on plane flights, and published several books of collected verse, almost all on Islamic themes.[12]

Fadlallah's composition of free verse hinted at a daring willingness to defy convention, even while mastering its complex forms. But he was not alone in testing the limits of convention. While he acquired the practical tools of a scholar and jurist, winds of change blew through Najaf, scattering timeworn assumptions about the role of Shi'ism in the temporal world. The collapse of the Ottoman Empire had breached the walls that separated Najaf from the tumult of this world. When Fadlallah's father arrived there in 1928, the city was already under the rule of British unbelievers. Many of the leading Shi'ite clerics had fled to the city of Qom in Iran, after supporting a failed rebellion against the English occupation in 1920. Qom had thus come to rival Najaf as a center of Shi'ite learning, and would later surpass it. When Iraq became nominally independent in 1932, and again after the revolution of 1958, the centralizing nationalist state sought to establish control over the autonomous Shi'ite shrine cities. While the state tightened its grip, contenders for power bombarded the new generation of young Shi'ites with the ideological messages of Arab nationalism, Arab socialism, and communism. Redemption from oppression, alienation, and poverty need not wait, proclaimed the new ideologies. Leave the clerics to their redemptive suffering and dogmatic messianism, and join the struggle for liberation.

Younger Shi'ite clerics understood the threat to their standing, their autonomy, and their survival. Fadlallah recollected that after the fall of the Iraqi monarchy in 1958, confronting communism became the great preoccupation of Najaf's clerics.[13] Islam would remain relevant to the needs of a doubting generation only if it became a theology of liberation. The young would go elsewhere unless given a Shi'ite Islamic response to their yearnings for political, social, and economic justice. Clerics could not continue to preach patience and damn politics as hubris. So began the revolution that would turn Shi'ism inside out, from a creed of pious resignation to a slogan of liberation. The best young talents of Najaf began to think, lecture, and write on such subjects as Islamic government, Islamic economics, and the ideal Islamic state. Justice could no longer be deferred, they proclaimed; Muslims had a duty to pursue it here and now. They should not wait passively for divine redemption, but must plan for it now, as though the fate of God's creation depended solely upon their own acts.

"My studies, which were supposed to be traditional, rebelled against tradition and all familiar things," Fadlallah later said.[14] He felt an irresistible attraction to this new reading of Islam, and particularly its presentation by his Najaf contemporary, Sayyid Muhammad Baqir al-Sadr, a brilliant scion of one of contemporary Shi'ism's leading families. Together the two young scholars collaborated on a journal. Fadlallah's own editorials dealt with the need to make the teachings of Islam relevant to changing circumstances and called for a more open approach to Islamic studies among the scholars themselves. These essays conveyed the vitality and originality of his intellect, and above all his ability to stretch convention without breaking it.[15] But Baqir al-Sadr wished to take his message beyond the seminaries, to the displaced Shi'ite masses who had left the countryside for Iraq's cities. These could not be reached through learned articles in journals. And so the clerical theorists of an Islamic state wove a clandestine network that became known as Hizb al-Da'wa—the "Party of the Calling." The Iraqi regime regarded this passage from arid intellectualism to committed activism as an impertinent challenge to its own legitimacy and began to intimidate the clerics and laymen who had joined together in the network of Al-Da'wa.[16]

The electrifying atmosphere of Najaf, the controversies that raged there, the inspiration of great teachers, the growing repression by the Iraqi regime—all of these left their mark on Fadlallah's character, his beliefs, his understanding of the world. He came to personify the great tradition of the seminaries of Najaf. In any other generation, he might have moved inexorably toward recognition as a first-rank academic scholar. Such standing had its rewards, and Fadlallah could have laid claim to a place on the higher faculty of an esteemed seminary. But he had matured on the brink of a war—an undeclared war against Islam, waged by the forces of alienation and secularization. In Najaf Fadlallah made a commitment that would bind him—a commitment to the survival of an Islam besieged by daunting enemies. Even for those who would have preferred to avoid the brewing battle, the seminaries could not offer sanctuary. With the emergence of Al-Da'wa, the Iraqi regime began to show a heavier hand in its intimidation of leading Shi'ite clerics and their disciples. The regime well understood the dangers implicit in the network's new preaching and threatened its members with imprisonment or exile. The ever-encroaching state seemed poised to throw out that most fundamental of all immunities, the physical inviolability of the clerics themselves.

At the same time, Lebanon beckoned. Fadlallah had maintained his ties to the country and had visited it occasionally over the years. He knew that there no government cajoled or threatened Shi'ite clerics. Lebanon had become a sanctuary for ideas and people unwelcome anywhere else in the Middle East. Why not for Shi'ism's theologians of liberation? In Lebanon, an enterprising young cleric could also make a mark; before Fadlallah lay the example of Sayyid Musa al-Sadr, a Shi'ite cleric about seven years his senior, whose family had deep roots in Najaf but who had been born in Qom in Iran. Sayyid Musa had spent four years studying in Najaf, and had been persuaded to go to Lebanon by Ayatollah Muhsin al-Hakim, one of Fadlallah's own mentors. Sayyid Musa did so in 1959, and by the mid-1960s he had won a considerable following. Soon he would be acclaimed the Imam Sadr by his supporters.

Fadlallah's decision might have been influenced by Sayyid Musa's success. In 1962 Fadlallah visited Tyre, in Lebanon, and helped Sayyid Musa draft a protest against the policies of the Shah of Iran.[17] He saw how Sayyid Musa had become a maker of Lebanese politics, despite his foreign birth. But Fadlallah's move to Lebanon may also have been encouraged by those who wished to bring down Sayyid Musa's rising star. Sayyid Musa had antagonized many of the landed families in south Lebanon, whom he accused of exploiting and misrepresenting the Shi'ite community. As it happened, Fadlallah's maternal grandfather had been the baron of the powerful and landed Bazzi clan of Bint Jubayl. They had bought and elbowed their way to respectability, eventually installing Fadlallah's maternal uncle as a parliamentary deputy from Bint Jubayl and then as a government minister. They would have been eager to groom one of their own as a counter to Sayyid Musa, whose call for internal social reform threatened to erode what remained of their privilege.[18]

FIRST PULPIT

It would be difficult to find two more apparently irreconcilable cities than Najaf and Beirut in the 1960s. Najaf's domes professed the sublime nature of God and submission to his will; Beirut's concrete citadels declared the supremacy of secular man, in commerce, journalism, literature, art, and revolution. Yet both were cities under siege. In the heart of Beirut, the Arab world came the closest to creating an island of secular tolerance and intellectual freedom; the American University of Beirut, in particular, had become a byword for provocative thought and free expression. "There was room for everyone," remembered one observer of Beirut's freewheeling ambience: "the devout and heathen, pious puritans and graceless hedonists, left-wing radicals and ardent conservatives, footloose and self-centered Bohemians and steadfast chauvinists and conventional patriots." The city was governed by "respect for differences."[19] Yet like Najaf, Beirut had come under relentless pressure, not from a centralizing state, but from masses of refugees from the despair and deprivation that surrounded the island. Like Najaf, Beirut saw its defenses crumbling.

And like Najaf, Beirut rewarded the talented manipulation of words. When Fadlallah decided to come to his ancestral Lebanon, the eloquent and slightly unconventional cleric knew where his art would be most appreciated. He arrived in Beirut in 1966 and selected as his arena the mixed Shi'ite-Palestinian shantytown of Nabaa in East Beirut. Nabaa was the poor relation of the neighboring Burj Hammud, one of the oldest of the city's Shi'ite communities, dating back to the 1940s, when Shi'ites first began to leave the countryside in pursuit of economic opportunity. The Shi'ites, made to feel unwelcome in Sunni West Beirut, had preferred Burj Hammud, settled between the world wars by Armenian refugees. Poorer and more recent Shi'ite arrivals squatted in neighboring Nabaa and were joined by Palestinian refugees of war. In Burj Hammud and Nabaa, Shi'ite entrepreneurs had opened workshops and small factories. Those Shi'ites who came from the southern town of Bint Jubayl and its vicinity brought with them their traditional craft of shoemaking and established a number of shoe factories which supplied the Lebanese market. There were as many people from Bint Jubayl in Nabaa, as in Bint Jubayl itself, and the transplanted community readily accepted this brilliant native son, who had all the right credentials of descent and learning. Community leaders welcomed Fadlallah for their children's sake as well. In the crush of the city, young people were moving away from their rural ways and even their faith. Their confusion could not be addressed by the corrupt and obscurantist shaykh who presided over the neighborhood before Fadlallah arrived.[20]

Fadlallah immediately identified the malaise of the confused young men and women who had distanced themselves from religious belief, and set out to redeem them through a socially aware reading of Islam. He opened a *husayniyya,* a place of communal gathering where Shi'ites mourn the martyrdom of the Imam Husayn. There he established a social and cultural association known as the Family of Fraternity (*Usrat al-Ta'akhi),* which supervised clinics, youth clubs, and a middle school for Islamic studies called the Islamic Law Institute (*Al-Ma'had al-Shar'i al-Islami).* The best of the students at the institute went on to Najaf for further studies. The Family of Fraternity also published a journal, *Al-Hikma,* which gave Fadlallah's writings a wide circulation.

Fadlallah now made excellent use of the sermonizing conventions he had acquired in Najaf. He would begin his sermons with formal invocations and quotations from the Qur'an, intoned sonorously as though to cast a spell. This would draw the audience into a state of attentiveness, and confirm his authority as a master of the sacred text. Then he would introduce his general theme, discussed on a high level of abstraction in the formal cadences of classical Arabic. In many of Fadlallah's written pieces, he went no further, leaving the reader with an impression of a rather formal brilliance. But in sermons, a clear break would occur, signified by his passage to a more colloquial Arabic. Here came the transition from the sacred to the temporal, as Fadlallah descended from his broad theme to the trying questions posed by the present. At this point, his speech became feverish; in an arresting mannerism, he would wipe his high forehead with a handkerchief, as if to cool a mind racing past safe limits. Fadlallah performed like an artist on the pulpit, deftly weaving words into a dense and intricate carpet of quotations and allusions of immense suggestive power.

Fadlallah simultaneously developed a freer style of lecturing for youth clubs and groups. A lecture differed in many subtle ways from a sermon, but the most obvious departure came at the end, in the question-and-answer period. Not every sermonizer could think quickly enough on his feet to answer impromptu questions and summon the necessary quotations from Islamic sources. Fadlallah had that talent, and it endeared him to the inquisitive young, who were eager for dialogue and wrestled with difficult dilemmas that other clerics preferred to avoid.

Fadlallah's words derived their power from their combination of traditional Islamic themes and the fashionable rhetoric of anti-imperialist nationalism. The young generation that Fadlallah sought to touch had been nurtured on the ideas of Arab revolution championed by Egypt's Gamal Abdel Nasser, the paladin of pan-Arabism. These ideas revolved around the belief that, despite the coming of formal political independence, a disguised imperialism thwarted the Arab advance toward true independence. Fadlallah, too, believed that imperialism remained the paramount obstacle to self-fulfillment, and he borrowed heavily from the vocabulary of Arab revolution. Fadlallah held that "imperialism cannot bear having Muslims proceed from a premise of intellectual self-reliance and it cannot bear having the Muslims act through economic and political self-sufficiency. It wants us to continue sitting at its table, feeding ourselves with the thought and consumer products it offers us."[21]

There was nothing original in this idea of economic and cultural imperialism sucking the lifeblood of its victims. But Fadlallah's formulations diverged from the prevailing discourse of pan-Arabism in this important respect: for the Arabs, Fadlallah substituted the Muslims, and for Arabism he substituted Islam. Imperialism had to be fought "in order to weaken it, limit its interests and break its spine, exactly as imperialism endeavors to weaken poor peoples economically, politically, militarily, by all available means."[22] But Arabism was a false god; only Islam could serve as the basis for a viable struggle against imperialism. Unlike some Islamic theorists, Fadlallah did not deny the values of Arab nationalism, particularly its emphasis upon unity in the struggle for liberation. But the ethos of Arabism had failed to unify the Arabs. Nationalism's incapacity to stir the deepest commitment was demonstrated by the failure to liberate Palestine. Most of the positive values of Arab nationalism had been derived from Islam in the first place, and the liberation of Palestine and the Arabs could be hastened only by returning to an Islamic conceptualization of struggle and sacrifice.[23]

The searing issue of the early 1970s for Lebanon's Shi'ites was the emergence of a Palestinian resistance on Shi'ite ground. Expelled from Jordan in 1970, Palestinian armed organizations relocated to Lebanon and began to attack Israel across Lebanon's border. Israel retaliated with uneven accuracy, often at the expense of Shi'ite bystanders. Should the Shi'ites turn their backs on the Palestinians or demonstrate solidarity by facilitating the attacks and sharing the consequences? This dilemma confronted Shi'ites not only in the south, in places like Bint Jubayl, but also in Beirut, where their Palestinian neighbors—including those in Fadlallah's own Nabaa quarter—had also armed themselves.

Sayyid Musa al-Sadr could never give Shi'ites a straightforward answer to their own Palestinian question. While he felt the pull of solidarity, he dreaded the inclusion of the Shi'ites in the ring of suffering that surrounded the Palestinians. After all, peace had prevailed for a generation along the frontier between Lebanon and Israel. The south had been transformed into a battleground only after the emergence of an armed Palestinian resistance, which used the region as a platform for attacks against Israel. Not a few Shi'ites shared the view, widespread in Lebanon, that the Palestinians were pursuing their war of liberation at Lebanon's expense and bore responsibility for the hellish Israeli reprisals upon the villages of the south. Sayyid Musa sympathized with Palestinian aspirations because the Palestinians had been dispossessed, but he did not believe that the Shi'ites, alone among all Arabs, should bear the burden of their struggle. As he said in private conversation in 1973, "Our sympathy no longer extends to actions which expose our people to additional misery and deprivation."[24]

Fadlallah understood the dilemma differently. Formed in the Arab world of the 1950s, he knew the language of Arab unity, Arab liberation, and Arab socialism. The whole enterprise of the younger generation of Najaf clerics had been the appropriation of that language and its translation into the categories of Islam. Najaf's poets also had vied with one another in spinning words on Palestine. Fadlallah shared the Arab nationalist conviction that Israel was the instrument of a wider Western plot to dominate the Arab and Muslim worlds. The conflict to the south was not a problem between Jews and Arabs in Palestine, but between two blocs contending for the world. The Shi'ites, Fadlallah warned, could not opt out of this conflict, for they too were slated for victimization. "The problem of the South is part of the Palestinian problem," he said in a lecture delivered in Bint Jubayl in 1972. "The claim of politicians and some others, that the departure of the Palestinian fedayeen from the region will solve the problem, is talk for the sake of talk, anachronistic words, a temporary anesthetic." Israel did not strike the south only in reaction to Palestinian attacks. Israel coveted the south and wished to possess it. Israel had taken territory in each of its previous three wars, declared Fadlallah, and would provoke yet another war to gain more.[25] Fadlallah understood the Shi'ite fear of taking a stand against Israel. "Israel frightened the entire Islamic world and appeared as the invincible element in 1967," he later said. "The Islamic world, and especially the Arab world, experienced such a psychological defeat that if any of us heard the word 'Israel' he trembled in fear, as many of us did with regard to the agents of Israel."[26] So to embolden his listeners, Fadlallah conjured up another fear—of eventual displacement, by an Israel which would grow like a cancer unless it was excised.

This argument set Fadlallah apart from Sayyid Musa al-Sadr. Its premises lay deep in the discourse of pan-Arabism, which Sayyid Musa never fully mastered. For Sayyid Musa, the salvation of the Shiʻites lay in Lebanon's recognition of their place in the mosaic. He appealed to those who clung to their Shiʻism and preserved their faith in Lebanon. But Fadlallah spoke to the young Shiʻites who were beyond the reach of Sayyid Musa, those who scoffed not only at Shiʻism but at Lebanon, and who believed that by espousing causes larger than both they might lose themselves in the revolutionary mass. Seeing no reason to cling to a sectarian Shiʻism, they instead offered their services to the leftist militias and the Palestinian organizations. To these young Shiʻites yearning to identify with anything but Shiʻism, Fadlallah offered the alternative of an ecumenical Islam. Embrace the cause of Palestine, he urged, but do so in the spirit and name of Islam.

This did not mean that Fadlallah endorsed the wild fury of the Palestinian attacks on Israel. The Shiʻites, the Palestinians, and the Arabs as a whole, had to face the limitations imposed by their situation. The people had to overcome the effects of the feudal order and the quarreling Arab regimes, in order to challenge an Israel supported by the greatest power in the West, the United States.

> The problem is what we are able to do, on the basis of the forces we can muster on the local level at a given moment in time. Emotion might push you towards thinking about revolting against your situation, but this alone will not bring you any result on the road to a solution. Perhaps an individual, in certain emotional states and in certain situations, may feel the urge to destroy himself and all that is around him. This might be a way to release rage and suppression through an explosion, but this has never solved a problem.[27]

This emotionalism was the bane of the Arab world. The Arabs primed themselves to expect a quick fix, and avoided long-term planning, while the aggressors unfolded their multistage plan "to gain control of our country and our resources, and then remove us from our homelands under the slogan 'a land without a people for a people without a land.'" The Arabs had to set aside their daydreams and begin by taking a profound look at the enemy's future plans, on the basis of present and past experience. "We should then plan our political, economic, and military life accordingly."[28] Fadlallah was too cautious to spell out a precise plan of action. He spoke instead of the necessity of individual transformation from within. "It is the individual who will grasp the gun, who will fly the plane. Tell me, by God, how will the individual advance this fateful cause, unless he possesses profound faith and moral fortitude, so that he will not yield to temptation?"[29] Fadlallah proclaimed Islam a theology of liberation at a moment when Arab revolutionaries and intellectuals denounced it as the paramount obstacle to an effective Arab challenge to Israel.

But Fadlallah's message did not resonate beyond a few Beirut neighborhoods. Sayyid Musa al-Sadr's voice carried much further, because he spoke directly to the strong sense of Shi'ite particularity which still gripped the community. Both men wore the same turban, but their differences were profound. The physically towering Sadr possessed an informal dignity that reflected the self-confidence of someone of the most noble descent. He relied heavily upon that pedigree, for when he spoke, his Persianized Arabic betrayed his foreign roots. Fadlallah was short and stocky, and could readily be mistaken for an acolyte. But his effortless and flowing Arabic proclaimed him the most Arab of Arabs.

The Shi'ites showed their preference. Sayyid Musa's deportment, lineage, winning manner, and message of hope captured the imagination and won the loyalty of many of Lebanon's Shi'ites. That Sadr spoke accented Arabic hardly mattered. Bereft of self-confidence, the Shi'ites of Lebanon were eager to defer to outside authority. Still strongly Shi'ite in identity, they were not embarrassed to look for leadership beyond the Arab world, to the seat of contemporary Shi'ite culture in Iran. Fadlallah had a much narrower appeal, which did not extend much past his own neighborhood. He won favor particularly with Shi'ites who shared his reading of the Palestinian problem as fateful for the Shi'ite community itself. Among these followers, young Shi'ites who had joined Palestinian organizations, and even risen to positions of some prominence, looked to Fadlallah as the cleric whose words most perfectly justified their choice.

But they were too few. Fadlallah remained in the shadows, while Sayyid Musa became Imam Sadr, hailed by many of Lebanon's Shi'ites as leader and savior. Fadlallah used his time to cultivate his support at the most local level, and to bolster his scholarly credentials. Later, when asked what he did during these years, Fadlallah said that he spent them laying "foundations" and sharing the suffering of the poor.[30] He also wrote his first full-length book, about methods of propagating Islam in the Qur'an, and he began work on a second, about the relationship of Islam to the use of force. The theme would soon prove timely as Lebanon began its descent into civil war.

A LOGIC OF POWER

The battle began in 1975, and the following year the Maronite-dominated Phalangist militia began a campaign to excise the Palestinians from their armed redoubts in the eastern part of Beirut. Nabaa, it turned out, rested squarely on Lebanon's fault line. An earthquake now began which would leave Beirut a divided city, the two halves separated by a vast chasm. The dilemma faced by the Shi'ites of the south suddenly confronted many in Beirut. The Phalangist militia laid siege to the Palestinians in Nabaa, blockading and shelling the shantytown. In 1976 the Shi'ites found themselves caught between two ruthless opponents and subject to Palestinian demands for solidarity. Some Shi'ites would have fought for their homes alongside the Palestinians, but Sayyid Musa al-Sadr feared for the fate of the community and struck a deal with the Phalangist militia that allowed the Shi'ites safe passage out of the neighborhood. Upon their departure, the Phalangist militia overran Nabaa, crushing the remnants of Palestinian resistance.

Among those Shi'ites who favored resistance, the evacuation agreement reached by Sayyid Musa smacked of defeatism and betrayal.[31] If Fadlallah shared this view, he did not voice it publicly. He left Nabaa with perhaps a hundred thousand others, abandoning the labor of a decade. However, he claimed to have done so outside the framework of the demeaning capitulation negotiated by Sayyid Musa.[32] Fadlallah would not return to Nabaa. Later he received a telephone message from Amin Gemayel, the Phalangist commander who had taken Nabaa and who would later be president of Lebanon. Fadlallah knew that the overture concerned the possibility of reopening a clinic which he had sponsored in the quarter. He did not return the call.[33]

As the shells fell during the long siege of Nabaa, Fadlallah wrote a book, mostly by candlelight. *Islam and the Logic of Power* was Fadlallah's most systematic polemic in favor of the empowerment of Islam.[34] When Fadlallah wrote it, the militarization of the Shi'ite community was already under way; Sayyid Musa al-Sadr and his followers had taken the first steps toward the arming and training of the Shi'ite militia known as Amal. Yet the founders of Amal narrowly conceived their purpose as the defense of Shi'ite interests and lives in a Lebanon gone mad with sectarian violence. Sayyid Musa argued that the Shi'ites must no longer allow themselves to be victimized, that they must arm themselves, as did all of Lebanon's other communities. Amal sought to guarantee Shi'ite survival among the wolves—and little more.

Fadlallah's book made the very different argument that the acquisition of power must serve not the ends of a sect, but those of all Islam in its confrontation with error, disbelief, and imperialism. Shi'ites must act, Fadlallah wrote, because Islam was endangered by the threat of an aggressive imperialism; Lebanon's strife was really a flash point in the global confrontation between Islam and imperialism. And so Fadlallah differed with Sayyid Musa over the uses to which emerging Shi'ite power should be put. Sayyid Musa saw the armed Shi'ite as a defender of his sect, which sought parity with other sects. Fadlallah saw the armed Shi'ite as an asset of Islam in a comprehensive confrontation with unbelief.

For many Shi'ites, Fadlallah's vision seemed to fly in the face of common sense. They thought Lebanon's Shi'ites would be fortunate to match the power of Lebanon's other sects. Was it not sheer fantasy to imagine the dispossessed and deprived Shi'ites of Lebanon mounting a defense of all Islam? In his book, Fadlallah said it was not. The power imperialism enjoyed over Islam was temporary and could be defeated, because it rested upon unbelief and exploitation. The Muslims did not have the same instruments of oppression and war that imperialism wielded, but power did not reside only in quantitative advantage or physical force. Strikes, demonstrations, civil disobedience, preaching—these too were forms of power. The precondition to such empowerment was a setting aside of fear; this in turn required that Muslims believe in the truth of their cause and have faith that martyrdom brings reward in the hereafter. Once they believed, they themselves would stir fear in the breasts of their most powerful adversaries.

At the same time, Fadlallah warned against such wanton and reckless violence as had backed the Palestinians into their pitiful corner. Legitimate and effective violence could only proceed from belief wedded to sober calculation. It had to be conceived as part of an overall plan of liberation. He repeated the warning first made in his Bint Jubayl lectures, against the surrender to emotion and impulse that underlined Palestinian violence. Fadlallah knew there were Shi'ites inspired by the Palestinians' theatrical acts of violence. But he regarded many of the actions of the Palestinian resistance as spasms of unguided emotion that produced nothing and signaled weakness.

In *Islam and the Logic of Power,* the dynamic tension in Fadlallah's thought found full expression. With one voice, he worked to convince the weak and doubting that they could acquire power through sacrifice.

With another voice, he sought to restrain the zealous and harness their willingness for sacrifice to a carefully considered plan of action. His ideal of virtue was the achievement of a perfect balance between these two voices—a seamless harmony, in politics as in poetry. This required an inner philosophical balance—between persuasion and violence, logic and emotion, sacrifice and ambition, belief and skepticism. By the time Nabaa fell, Fadlallah had struck that balance. The self-master could now master others.

STARTING ANEW

After the debacle of Nabaa, Fadlallah briefly retreated to Bint Jubayl in the south, where he fell back upon the patronage of his mother's powerful clan and the support of his father. The natives of Bint Jubayl who had fled Nabaa did the same. The town's population swelled from thirteen thousand to twenty-four thousand. Families took in destitute relations, and the houses filled to overflowing. Some two hundred families with no place to stay lived in the schools, which had emptied for summer vacation. Many families slept out in the open. The new arrivals depended completely upon their brethren for food, and prices skyrocketed. A six-month delay in the payment for the tobacco crop by the state monopoly created a terrible shortage of cash. Only the charity of Bint Jubayl's native sons in distant Michigan and West Africa saved the town from hunger.[35] These Shi'ites, including Fadlallah, were among the first refugees of Lebanon's civil war.

The loss of his congregation was a personal and professional setback to Fadlallah. He might have started again in Bint Jubayl, but he lacked the temperament of a provincial cleric and knew that his message of power did not resonate among the hills of the south. More important, Bint Jubayl began to empty as the war between Israelis and Palestinians overflowed into its streets. In October 1976, after a series of incidents, Israeli shells fell in the midst of a market-day crowd, killing seven people. A mass exodus began, carrying almost the entire population to Beirut's southern suburbs, the Dahiya. Fadlallah again joined the wandering flock, eventually settling in the crumbling Bir al-'Abd neighborhood, and began to raise a congregation. Good fortune shined when a wealthy Shi'ite émigré provided him with funds to expand an existing mosque. The Imam al-Rida mosque was a modern and spacious structure with a high ceiling and a balcony in the rear. A wall of glass admitted light. The place of worship was a much more confident structure than the self-effacing husayniyyas of the Dahiya, and its outspoken style perfectly suited its new denizen.

In making this new beginning, Fadlallah had the benefit of some additional support. Ayatollah Muhsin al-Hakim had died in Najaf in 1970, and most Lebanese Shi'ites chose to recognize the religious rulings of Ayatollah Abu al-Qasim Kho'i as binding. At that time, both Fadlallah and Sayyid Musa al-Sadr pledged their allegiance to Kho'i, whose seminary in Najaf was supported by donations from Lebanon and elsewhere in the Shi'ite world. But priorities shifted following the outbreak of the civil war in Lebanon, as increasing numbers of Shi'ites lost their homes and many children were orphaned. Now Kho'i asked that Lebanese Shi'ite clerics establish a committee to create charitable institutions in Lebanon, to be supported with funds collected in Kho'i's name, and he named Fadlallah his representative in Lebanon. Who better to understand the sufferings of orphans and others driven from their homes than a guardian who also had lost everything? The appointment made Fadlallah trustee for the sizable contributions made to Kho'i's Lebanese accounts. In Kho'i's name, Fadlallah established a large charitable institution (*mabarra*) in the neighborhood of al-Duha, which grew to include an orphanage, school, and mosque. In its first year, the school enrolled 275 students; a photograph from the summer of 1978 shows Fadlallah surrounded by youngsters, graduates of the school's first Qur'an recital class.[36] In subsequent years, the activities of the institution broadened to include courses for teachers of orphans.[37] Fadlallah's relationship with Kho'i gave him a base from which to rebuild his influence, this time among the inhabitants of the hard-pressed Dahiya.

At the same time, Fadlallah greatly benefited from the return to Lebanon of a group of able young theological students. Serious disorders broke out in Najaf in 1977, and the Iraqi regime tightened its grip on the seminaries by expelling many of the foreign students, including more than a hundred Lebanese Shi'ites. A few proceeded to Qom in Iran, but learning in the religious seminaries there had been disrupted by the escalating confrontation with the Shah's regime. Many aspiring clerics preferred to return to Lebanon, where a number of new seminaries absorbed them as teachers and students. Some appear as teachers in that same photograph of the Qur'an recital class in Fadlallah's school. Others found their place in the Islamic Law Institute Fadlallah had founded in Nabaa, which had since moved to Bir Hasan in the Dahiya. Fadlallah now had his own protégés, whom he could reward with positions in his expanding enterprises.

Yet another development worked to Fadlallah's advantage in making his message audible. In 1978, Sayyid Musa al-Sadr disappeared while on a trip to Libya. He was quite probably murdered there, but his precise fate has never been determined. Fadlallah had his differences with Sayyid Musa but would not air them openly. "Sayyid Musa al-Sadr was a friend and a schoolmate long before he arrived in Lebanon," Fadlallah later recalled. "I was with him for four years in Najaf, during our studies. When we did not agree on particular points or methods, this did not affect our friendship."[38] Public airing of disagreement would have breached the etiquette of collegiality that governed Najaf's seminaries. It also would have been impolitic, given Sayyid Musa's undeniable popularity. "We hope Sadr will return," Fadlallah declared during one of the feverish rounds of rumor about Sayyid Musa's imminent return, "although there might be differences of opinion between him and us."[39] Fadlallah never spoke further about those differences. Yet he must have understood that his own voice could not be heard above the noisy preoccupation with the doings and sayings of the spellbinding Imam Sadr. The disappearance of Sayyid Musa, tragedy though it was, opened a gate of opportunity for Fadlallah and his message.

REVOLUTION IN ISLAM, PARTY OF GOD

Then the "earthquake" struck. This was Fadlallah's own metaphor for the Islamic revolution that swept Iran, creating the sensation that the ground had shifted under the pillars of power and his own feet. The epicenter lay in Iran, but the shock jolted the most remote corners of Islam and affected Lebanon's Shi'ites immediately. Until Iran's revolution, the ideal of the Islamic state had been a remote abstraction, discussed only in the theoretical studies of clerics. Now men who had spent their lives in the seminaries of Qom and Najaf were swept to power on a wave of popular revolutionary fervor. In proclaiming an Islamic state, they summoned fellow Shi'ite clerics in the wider world to acclaim their revolution and apply its lessons to their own countries. Many came to Lebanon as emissaries of Imam Khomeini, to preach the new dispensation. To the poor, they began to dispense money.

The revolution and the arrival of Iranian emissaries compelled Lebanon's leading Shi'ite clerics to choose between the battered idea of confessional Lebanon and the stirring slogan of an Islamic state. Lebanon's foremost Shi'ite clerics sought the good will of Islamic Iran and made formal obeisance to Imam Khomeini, but balked at the prospect of jeopardizing the formal recognition of the Lebanese state for their institutions, first won for them by Sayyid Musa. Under his leadership, they had been peti-

tioners of the Lebanese government, demanding no less—and no more—
than their rightful share of office and privilege. A demand for an Islamic
state would sever their link to the confessional system and compel dis-
avowal of the institutional recognition accorded them by the state. Titles
still meant a great deal to leading Shi'ite clerics such as the Acting Chairman of the Supreme Islamic Shi'ite Council, Shaykh Muhammad Mahdi
Shams al-Din, and the Shi'ite Mufti of Lebanon, Shaykh 'Abd al-Amir
Qabalan. They presided over an elaborate hierarchy of ritual and legal
functionaries, whose status and income were derived from the established
Shi'ite institutions of Lebanon. They naturally hesitated to forfeit tangible
assets for the promise of a millennium.

But Fadlallah did not hold any title in the Shi'ite clerical establishment. Like any cleric of his standing, he was a member of the Supreme
Islamic Shi'ite Council. He even claimed to have been "one of those who
worked to find a consensus among the various Shi'ite scholars regarding
the issue of the Council" when it was first created, mediating between
Sayyid Musa and "others who differed from him." But Fadlallah played
no official role there: "I said I would not elect and would not nominate
myself to be elected," since his philosophy was "different from the formula of religious councils."[40] Fadlallah claimed instead that his alle-
giances crossed the frontiers of Lebanon, binding him to an ecumenical
and universal Islam.

And many Shi'ites now felt the same way. Fadlallah had seen the
spontaneous Shi'ite demonstrations that filled the streets of West Beirut in
April 1979, demanding an Islamic state in Lebanon. These demonstrators
answered to none of the established leaders and might be drawn to his
flame if he could provide Arabic captions to the mute icons of the Imam
Khomeini now plastering the walls of the Dahiya. So while the coyness
of Lebanon's Shi'ite establishment exasperated the many official and
semiofficial emissaries who began to arrive from Iran, Fadlallah rushed
headlong into their embrace, proclaiming the moral debt of all Muslims
to Iran's revolution and hailing its crucial role in the reawakening of Islamic consciousness among Lebanon's Shi'ites. He cheered the revolution
as "the great dream of all those whose life is labor for Islam" and praised
the early purging of revolutionaries compromised by the Western-
inspired notion of "Islamic democracy." The revolution bore within it a
universal message valid throughout all time: "It cannot be limited to a
specific place except on a temporary basis." The spread of the revolution
was the duty of every individual, the society, and the state.[41]

Fadlallah even sanctioned the controversial holding of American diplomats hostage in Tehran by students claiming to follow the "line of the

Imam Khomeini." He noted the criticism "by some in the [Islamic] movement" that the hostage taking was done without planning as to its aims, and that it constituted an "emotional student reaction to the American threat." Given Fadlallah's aversion to the blind expression of rage, he probably shared this criticism. Yet he also understood the role of rage in the consolidation of a movement or state. Raw emotion could be controlled and harnessed to higher purpose. And so behind the hostage taking in Iran, Fadlallah saw a purpose: "I am inclined to say that the leadership was not far removed from all the planning done by those students who claimed to follow the line of the Imam. In light of this, I think that the issue of the hostages was submitted to Islamic planning, in order to deepen the independent content of the revolution in the consciousness of the nation."[42] In other words, Khomeini himself had sanctioned the move, in order to promote the consolidation of the revolution. His authority justified the means.

Finally, Fadlallah delighted Iran's agents by leading the charge against Iraq's presence in Lebanon. The long years of repression the Shi'ite clerics had suffered at the hands of the Iraqi regime now reached their culmination. The regime moved against the Shi'ite seminaries in Najaf and elsewhere, making membership in Al-Da'wa punishable by death and arresting Sayyid Muhammad Baqir al-Sadr, who it secretly put to death. In September 1980, Iraq invaded Iran in a bid to undermine the foundations of the revolution made by the clerics. During late 1980 and early 1981, Beirut became an arena of small-scale clashes between pro-Iraqi and pro-Iranian elements, as the embassies of both countries replicated the war waged on their common frontier. Fadlallah played an admitted role in the campaign against the Iraqi regime in Lebanon and soon found himself targeted by persons "backed by the Iraqi Ba'th Party, as the result of my opposition to the system of government in Iraq."[43] In November 1980 armed assailants in a passing car sprayed Fadlallah's car with gunfire. A bullet even struck his turban, but he emerged unscathed.[44] There were several more attempts on his life over the next two years, and Fadlallah began to surround himself with bodyguards.[45]

In the end, the distant earthquake of Iran's revolution began to topple the buildings of Beirut. In December 1981 Iraq's opponents in Lebanon leveled the Iraqi embassy with a car bomb, killing the ambassador and many of the staff. Iraq, hopelessly exposed and outgunned in Lebanon, allowed its influence in that country to wane. The Lebanese Shi'ite struggle against the Iraqi regime was a sideshow, one of the countless little wars waged on Lebanon's soil. Yet its outcome gratified Iran, as did Fadlallah's continued preaching against the regime of Saddam Hussein. After the failed assassination attempt against him in 1980, he received a personal visit in his home from the speaker of Iran's parliament, 'Ali-Akbar Hashemi Rafsanjani—a demonstrative gesture of gratitude to the still-obscure cleric.[46]

Fadlallah's endorsements of the revolution and his condemnations of its enemies, all pronounced in a flawless Arabic, were music to the ears of Iran's emissaries to Lebanon. The triumph of the revolution had moved Lebanese Shi'ites, but it had occurred on the other side of a linguistic and cultural divide. Its message needed to be translated and interpreted for a Lebanese Shi'ite audience. The despised of the villages and slums might be won by the mute symbolism of posters of Khomeini, or swayed by the material favors handed out by Iran's representatives. Not so the newly literate and educated classes—avid consumers of words in Lebanon's emporium of ideas. They were potentially receptive to the message, for they had grown to maturity in a civil war, and knew Lebanon as little more than a broken abstraction. Many longed for a voice to lift them out of the rubble and reconcile the claims of Shi'ite identity with their revolutionary ideals. But emissaries from afar could not fathom the depths of their dilemma, let alone resolve it. Nor could they employ Arabic with the finesse needed to sway the educated young, who demanded a particularly Lebanese sophistication in the style and content of the message.

Fadlallah understood the problem perfectly. For over a decade he had worked with the disillusioned young, refining his message of Islam to respond to each new wave of millenarian fad and ideological fashion. He had a particular way with Shi'ite students in the city's several universities, who constituted an untapped resource for the cause of Islam. Fadlallah reached out to them partly through the Lebanese Union of Muslim Students *(Al-Ittihad al-Lubnani lil-talaba al-Muslimin),* an organization created with the support of clerics in the early 1970s to counter the temptations of secular ideologies among Shi'ite university students. The union began by organizing conferences, seminars, and a weekly lecture series in its own hall and reading room in the quarter of Al-Ghubayri, in the Dahiya. But it reached a far wider audience through publication of a monthly intellectual journal, *Al-Muntalaq,* which first appeared in 1978. Fadlallah's name figured in the journal only occasionally in its first two years of publication, but his sermons and articles appeared with greater frequency after 1980 and eventually as the lead pieces in nearly every issue.[47] *Al-Muntalaq* proved important to Fadlallah in reaching students who frequented libraries rather than mosques. But as Fadlallah became better known, he also began to speak on campus, in the very citadels of secular education—including the inner sanctum, the Assembly Hall at the American University of Beirut. Iran's emissaries, who well understood the value of educated cadres, grew ever more anxious to harness Fadlallah's persuasive talents to their revolutionary juggernaut.

Mutual need lay at the foundation of this partnership between Fadlallah and Iran's emissaries. The cleric brought with him his own following and a willingness to work to awaken the latent potential of Islam in Lebanon; the emissaries allowed Fadlallah free and unencumbered use of their symbols and provided him with material support. Fadlallah did not owe his daily bread to Iranian bursars, and in an oft-repeated challenge he defied "any intelligence agency in the world to prove that I have a financial or semi-financial relationship with any state in the world, including Iran."[48] Fadlallah did have his own resources, assuring him a degree of financial independence unique among the clerics rallied by Iran's agents. But the claim was misleading. Iran supported institutions under his control and offered him an array of important services, from personal security to airline travel. And above all, it offered him a kind of franchise for invoking the name of the revolution.

Fadlallah's franchise, however, was never exclusive. He had to share it with Iran's men on the scene, other Lebanese Shi'ite clerics, and zealous strongmen who volunteered their services as militiamen for Iran. Fadlallah lost an important battle very early in the day when he privately opposed Iran's creation of a distinct organization to bring these disparate souls together in a disciplined framework. Most Shi'ites were affiliated with Amal, and the creation of another Shi'ite organization would split the Shi'ite camp, since many Shi'ites would not or could not join a new party. Far better, Fadlallah argued, to preach the cause of Islam in an attempt to transform Amal from within than to create a competing organization.[49] Fadlallah raised his objection as a matter of principle, positing a choice between building a clandestine party to seize power—a select "party of God"—or appealing to a mass following through the open call of Islam. Islam, he proclaimed, "is a movement open to all, whereas a movement of a party carefully selects the people who are devoted to its idea, adhere to its teachings, and live fully as members. This requires that the party distinguish between those who meet the conditions of membership, who are then acknowledged, and those who do not, who are rejected. This contradicts the nature of religious adherence." Furthermore, in Iran, the masses, not a party, made the revolution. "The many Islamic parties in the Islamic world have never achieved a comparable result."[50]

But by this time, Iran's diplomats in Lebanon and Syria had despaired of gaining a firm hold over Amal. They could break off branches, but the trunk of the movement remained firmly rooted in the ground marked off by Sayyid Musa. Fadlallah understood the determination of Iran's emissaries and finally acquiesced in the fateful decision to establish a separate party, reluctantly permitting his own closest followers to join the newly created Hizbullah. But he did so with a sense of resignation: "It is not necessary that party organization be the only technique for advancing the revolution or acquiring power, for life does not hold within it only one method for bringing about progressive change. But no one can deny the value of the party in this regard, in the successful experiences of many of the states in the Eastern and Western worlds." Hizbullah had a role to play, provided it did not seek "to abolish the traditional way of presenting Islam as religion and neglect general action for promoting Islam at the community level, in mosques and public fora."[51] Fadlallah thus insisted that the new party respect his own role and that of others, who summoned men and women to a belief that no party could impose.

Yet Fadlallah preferred to remain formally outside the bounds of Hizbullah. Anticipating that Hizbullah's creation would fragment the Shi'ites of Lebanon, he sought to build a personal constituency on both sides of the incipient fissure and even across the long-standing divide between Shi'ites and Sunnis. Fadlallah thus repeatedly denied any formal connection to Hizbullah:

> The claim that I am the leader of Hizbullah is baseless and untrue. I am not the leader of any organization or party. It seems that when they could not find any prominent figure to pin this label on, and when they observed that I was active in the Islamic field, they decided to settle on me. It could be that many of those who are considered to be part of Hizbullah live with us in the mosque and they might have confidence in me. Who is the leader of Hizbullah? Obviously, he is the one who has influence. So, when they cannot see anybody on the scene, no spokesman, no prominent political figure speaking out for Hizbullah, they try to nail it on a specific person, whose name is then linked to every incident.[52]

It was a typically evasive statement. By the time Fadlallah made it, his mosque had become the great meeting ground of Hizbullah. His remarks were reported at length in Hizbullah's weekly newspaper, which eventually accorded him an interview in every issue. The movement's followers already hailed him as "the Sayyid," for they too sought to fix their gaze on a single visible leader who would voice their aspirations. But the denial of formal position was not a bluff. Since Fadlallah did not wish to be narrowly identified with Hizbullah, Iran's emissaries felt free to withhold information from him and exclude him from the movement's inner councils. If Fadlallah preferred to remain at arm's length from Hizbullah, then Hizbullah's patrons would double that length. Fadlallah and Iran's emissaries consulted, of course, and carefully coordinated their actions and statements when they found themselves in agreement. But when they disagreed, they went their separate ways, Fadlallah stating one thing and Hizbullah often doing quite another.

Fadlallah thus preserved his independence, but at the cost of a certain intimacy with the process of decision making in Hizbullah. For Fadlallah, this was just as well, for he had already argued the necessity of resorting to force in desperate circumstances. If he were ever linked to actual decisions to employ force, he might have to bear the consequences. The safest course was to stand slightly aside—to use all his powers of suggestion, yet allow others to take and bear responsibility for operative decisions. It was not all dissimulation when he declared: "I am not responsible for the behavior of any armed or unarmed group that operates in the arena. Whoever errs, I criticize his error even if he is one of ours, and whoever is correct, I appreciate his correctness even if he is a communist."[53] This desire to maintain a formal distance led Fadlallah to deny not only the title of leader, but even the less decisive designation of spiritual guide. Fadlallah once refused an interview to a leading news agency because it would not promise to omit the ubiquitous tag.[54] The ever-cautious Fadlallah preferred to elude all definition, since no definition did him justice, and most could do him considerable harm. In Hizbullah he was simply known as "the Sayyid."

Yet it was inevitable that Fadlallah would become identified in Lebanon and abroad as mentor of Hizbullah. And this was not so inaccurate as to be a libel. True, he did not serve as mentor to all in Hizbullah and he also had admirers beyond Hizbullah. Yet the despised and aggrieved who filled the ranks of the movement did look first to Fadlallah to interpret their own predicament. And at times he did serve Iran's emissaries and Hizbullah's clerics as adviser, jurist, strategist, tactician, spokesman, and mediator. Despite the irregular boundaries of his influence and the complexity of his role, the fact remained that his fortunes and fate were inseparable from those of Hizbullah. Partnership had evolved into mutual dependence; as the man and the movement embraced, they began a dizzying ascent to success.

OUT OF OBSCURITY

The "earthquake" of Iran's revolution was followed by what Fadlallah called the "holocaust" of the Israeli invasion in 1982. As Israeli forces rolled through the south and then into the Dahiya and West Beirut, Fadlallah experienced his most trying moments since the siege of Nabaa. His position had drawn him closer than any Shi'ite cleric to the Palestinian cause, at a time when many Shi'ites gave up even the pretense of solidarity with the Palestinians. The Palestinians by their arrogance had lost their claim to Shi'ite sympathy; the Shi'ites now refused the bill for the spiraling cycle of violence between Israelis and Palestinians. During the months prior to the Israeli invasion, Shi'ite resentment against Palestinian hegemony in the south had grown so intense that Amal took up arms against the Palestine Liberation Organization in the south and in Beirut. And Shi'ites remained bystanders when Israel took to the roads and the skies of Lebanon in the summer of 1982 to finish off the PLO.

Fadlallah's message of solidarity with the Palestinians fell upon deaf ears. Indeed, most Shi'ites dared to hope that Israel would save Lebanon in spite of itself, restoring peace and security to a liberated south. Israel's conduct in Lebanon ultimately betrayed that hope, but many of Lebanon's Shi'ites then fixed their gaze upon the United States, which appeared as peace broker and eased both the Palestine Liberation Organization and Israel out of Beirut. The United States and France now seemed ready to commit their moral and material force to the solution of Lebanon's strife. Their troops stood sentry just outside the Dahiya.

While hopes ran feverishly high in the Shi'ite community, Fadlallah remained silent. He waited for disillusionment to seep under the new order—and it was not long in coming. As the United States became a party to Lebanon's feud, throwing its support behind the claims of Christian privilege and Israeli security, more Shi'ites turned against it. In March 1983, Islamic Jihad, the clandestine arm of Hizbullah, took the initiative against the "American occupation army," with a grenade attack against a Marine patrol. In April 1983, the same group claimed credit for an immense explosion that gutted the U.S. Embassy in West Beirut, killing seventeen Americans. Now the time had come to expose the American role for what it was.

Only a few blocks from the Marines, Fadlallah began to explain the "secret of secrets" behind the American presence. The United States had not "saved" Lebanon from Israel; rather, it had prompted Israel to extend its invasion as far as Beirut, "beyond what the Israeli plan called for," in an attempt to "create new realities in the arena, to secure political gains for the purpose of complete control over the region." Now the plan reached its sinister culmination. Battered by "the mad Israeli shelling," the people of Beirut placed their trust in America.

They panted after any alleviation or pause in the siege, which had deprived the people of water, food, and medications. America then began to take up the role of a mediator, working to secure a supply of fuel or food or water, then guaranteeing the exit of the Palestinians, then bringing around the Israelis a bit, then assuring the withdrawal of foreign forces. So began the panting after America, which worked to multiply the panting, to create a psychological situation favorable to its policies. . . . The people began to recite "Praise be to America" for protecting them and providing them with a magical solution, delivered by a beautiful white stallion at the break of dawn.[55]

All illusion, said Fadlallah. Submission to America meant servility to the very power that guaranteed Israel's existence and used Israel to pursue its selfish ends. For Fadlallah, the Israeli invasion and its American aftermath confirmed his concept of the essential unity of imperialism. Now the eyes of others were opening to his truth. "We believe that the future holds surprises," he announced in an article published in the middle of 1983. "There is no alternative to a bitter and difficult jihad, borne from within by the power of effort, patience and sacrifice—and the spirit of martyrdom."[56]

It was that spirit which inspired the two "self-martyring operations" directed against American marines and French paratroopers on one morning in October 1983. In both instances, nameless youths drove explosive-laden trucks into the barracks housing the foreign forces, blasting apart themselves and their enemies in two combined acts of sacrifice and self-sacrifice. The two bombings claimed over three hundred lives, and would eventually persuade the United States and France that the cost of patrolling the Dahiya was far more than they could bear. But the destruction first provoked a feverish American and French quest for a culpable individual—a quest that irrevocably altered Fadlallah's life. For within days of the attacks, the intelligence service of the Phalangist party put out the information that Fadlallah had blessed the two "self-martyrs" on the eve of their operation. A story to this effect appeared in the *Washington Post* and Fadlallah achieved worldwide notoriety overnight.[57]

The accusation could not be proved or disproved, and no irrefutable evidence ever came to light establishing Fadlallah's direct involvement in the attacks.[58] But it hardly mattered. If the accusation gained sufficient credence in Washington and Paris, or if demands for vengeance overrode considerations of evidence, Fadlallah would become a hunted man. In the past, his influence had rested upon his mastery of words and his aura of credibility. Now his very life depended upon them. And so Fadlallah began a campaign to sow the seeds of reasonable doubt in the minds of foreigners charged with assessing responsibility for the attacks. The task would not be easy, for the master of the word spoke no language other than Arabic.

A meeting was arranged between Fadlallah and a journalist from the *Washington Post,* his first encounter with the international press. Perhaps he hoped the newspaper would retract the story, but he soon learned otherwise: "I told the reporter from the *Washington Post:* 'Perhaps I'll file suit against you.' He answered: 'We maintained our journalistic credibility, because we said that the information sources that published the accusations were the Phalangists.'"[59] Fadlallah's denials would have to carry their own weight. And he made them: he professed to be mystified by the charges; he did not believe in the method of suicide bombings; he was in his apartment on the morning of the attack. The denials were enhanced by their surroundings. His American interviewer found him living in a "dank tenement," a "shabby seventh-floor walk-up in the slums." The "ambitious but obscure holy man" possessed "scant resources to counter the charges" against him, and unnamed diplomatic sources were quoted as doubting whether Fadlallah or his followers had "the skill or the resources to handle such an operation alone."[60]

Once this seed of doubt was sown, Fadlallah nurtured it with further denials. "In my situation, could I have visited the Marines barracks, planned the operation, met the persons that prepared themselves for it, and blessed them like the Pope blesses the faithful?"[61] His involvement was not only a logistical improbability, but a moral one as well. He announced that he had "reservations about resorting to suicidal tactics in political action," based upon his reading of Islamic law.[62] From his pulpit, in his first Friday sermon after the attacks, Fadlallah told his audience that he had warned the young men against "exploding the situation," for "we do not believe that our war against America or France will end this way." He urged economic and cultural resistance to imperialism, but insisted that "we are against political assassination, and we do not agree with these explosions and assassinations, because you have no monopoly on such means; others possess them as well."[63] Respectable friends also stepped forward on his behalf. Delegations flocked to his home to denounce the very mention of his name in connection with the attacks. A group of engineers paid him a visit. So, too, did a delegation of Muslim students from the Lebanese University, the Arab University of Beirut, and the American University of Beirut.[64] In short order, Fadlallah succeeded in throwing off the worst suspicions of the Americans and French, who

increasingly looked beyond Beirut for the masterminds of the disaster—
to the Bekaa, Damascus, and ultimately Tehran.

Yet the dodge was more artful still, for Fadlallah proceeded to sanction the bombings after the fact. Just as he understood the need to put
a distance between himself and the attacks, he also understood the tremendous popular gratification derived from the fearsome blows dealt by
the powerless to the powerful. He repeatedly proclaimed to the world
that he did not play any personal role in the attacks; but he also proclaimed that the deeds deserved to be applauded. The justification was
simple. The whole plan of introducing foreign forces "was a deceptive
façade hiding the intention to convert Lebanon into a strategic base for
U.S. political influence in the region." The driving out of foreign forces
represented a legitimate act of resistance, even if the method was controversial—"acceptable to some, unacceptable to others, or conditionally
accepted or rejected by still some other groups."[65]

The deaths of the bombers, not the deaths of the intruders, posed
the only moral dilemma. The fact that they perished with the enemy
hinted deeply at suicide and sacrifice, and both belonged to the realm of
unholy violence, well beyond the perimeters of Islamic law. Such acts
could be validated only if they were admitted by learned opinion as sacred
acts of jihad. And here too Fadlallah provided justification. If the aim of
such a "self-martyr" was "to have a political impact on an enemy whom
it is impossible to fight by conventional means, then his sacrifice can be
part of a jihad. Such an undertaking differs little from that of a soldier
who fights and knows that in the end he will be killed. The two situations
lead to death; except that one fits in with the conventional procedures of
war, and the other does not."[66] Since the Muslims had no conventional
means to wage their war successfully, necessity demanded that they act
outside the conventions created by the powerful:

> The oppressed nations do not have the technology and destructive weapons
> America and Europe have. They must thus fight with special means of their
> own. . . . [We] recognize the right of nations to use every unconventional
> method to fight these aggressor nations, and do not regard what oppressed
> Muslims of the world do with primitive and unconventional means to con-
> front aggressor powers as terrorism. We view this as religiously lawful war-
> fare against the world's imperialist and domineering powers.[67]

Fadlallah denied he had told anyone to "blow yourself up"—he never
neglected to establish his own distance from the attacks—but affirmed
that "the Muslims believe that you struggle by transforming yourself into
a living bomb like you struggle with a gun in your hand. There is no

difference between dying with a gun in your hand or exploding your-self."[68]

Yet the artful evasion went still further. For if "self-martyrdom" was justified from a legal point of view, why did Fadlallah not issue a fatwa—an opinion based on Islamic law—sanctioning the acts? Here Fadlallah's judgment was molded by the conflicting considerations of personal im-munity and personal prestige. Acts committed on the basis of fatwas given in Lebanon would directly link clerics like himself to specific acts or tech-niques of violence. The wall of plausible deniability would collapse, open-ing them to vengeful reprisal. As he well knew, "assassination is a two-edged sword: If you can assassinate others, then others can assassinate you."[69] So Fadlallah refrained from formalizing his endorsement of the bombings in a legal ruling. "I can say that I have not issued any fatwa since the beginning of these operations and up to now," he declared, justifying prudence by principle. "On the contrary, I am one of those who stood against all this commotion for fatwas. Despite the positive points which come out of this action, I believe that there are many nega-tive points."[70] A fatwa would have forced him to weigh those points in a systematic way, which would have made his position dangerously clear. Anyway, an explicit ruling would have been redundant. According to Hizbullah's clerics, Khomeini himself had issued the necessary fatwa—from the safe distance of Iran.[71]

Nonetheless, Fadlallah did not wish the absence of his fatwa to be interpreted as either a legal repudiation of "self-martyrdom," or an ad-mission that he did not have sufficient authority to write one. He made it known that while he had not issued a fatwa, this did not mean that his reservations applied to all circumstances. "I have received young per-sons, men and women, who have asked me to provide fatwas authorizing them to launch military operations in which they cannot escape death. When I refuse because they do not meet all the conditions, they beg me to reverse my decision, as if they were asking a favor of me."[72] This im-plied that Fadlallah's refusal to rule arose not from a repudiation of "self-martyrdom" but only from the unsuitability of candidates. And while Fadlallah consistently denied that he had authorized "self-martyrdom," he consistently implied that he had the authority to do so if he wished. "Sometimes you may find some situations where you have to take risks," he said years later, "when reality requires a shock, delivered with vio-lence, so you can call upon all those things buried within, and expand all the horizons around you—as, for example, in the self-martyrdom op-erations, which some called suicide operations."[73] While Khomeini may have taken the decision, it was Fadlallah who wound up taking the risk, and he found his reward in a subtle claim to comparable authority.

Justifying the attacks as religiously valid while withholding formal religious validation amounted to an intellectual tightrope act. Yet Fadlallah performed brilliantly, scattering dust in the eyes of his enemies and stardust in the eyes of his admirers. All became entangled in his words. Fadlallah had no intention of sinking back into the relative obscurity he had known prior to the attacks. The collapse of the American and French barracks had drawn the attention of the world to the Dahiya. The helicopters of American vice-president George Bush and French president François Mitterrand had touched down within view, to survey the scenes of disaster. An opportunity presented itself. People who had known little or nothing of Fadlallah suddenly were interested in hearing about his vision of Islam, his understanding of Lebanon's predicament, his thoughts on terrorism and imperialism. Fadlallah could claim his place in the theater of Beirut, provided he was prepared to talk.

Fadlallah was not only ready but eager; once he started talking, he never stopped. He was perfectly cast for the role of oracle, interpreting the anger and despair of the Shi'ite community to itself and the world. When Fadlallah was named in connection with the bombings, reports claimed that Lebanese security knew so little about him that "it has been searching libraries of local newspapers for photographs of him."[74] It would not have had to look far, for the gist of Fadlallah's sermons appeared occasionally in the influential daily *Al-Nahar*, along with his photograph. He was never as obscure as his Lebanese enemies pretended. But nothing in Fadlallah's long years of toil had prepared Lebanon for his swift emergence as a political force and media star. Soon there would hardly be a person in Lebanon who had not seen his photograph and heard or read his words.

This was largely Fadlallah's own doing. His easy accessibility, so unlike the remoteness of Iran's reticent emissaries and Hizbullah's suspicious clerics and strongmen, brought a steady stream of journalists to his door. To enhance the effect of these encounters, Fadlallah instituted routines that established an aura of dignity and authority. He set up a front office, which scrutinized all requests to see him. Arriving interviewers might be searched and kept waiting in an anteroom, where they would be served tea. Here, women who did not come in full chador were usually required to don a scarf, provided by the house.[75] Fadlallah received his guests in a sparsely furnished sitting room, lit by neon. An appropriately Persian rug provided the decor. On a side table or the wall there reposed a large portrait of Khomeini, who brooded over the proceedings. Body-guards armed with machine pistols were never far away. Then, from deep within his armchair, Fadlallah would speak—always to a tape recorder, lest he be misquoted.

His interviews once were described as "lucid, substantive, and detailed expositions."[76] Often they were intricate and brilliant pieces of analysis, reflecting a keen estimate of the forces at play, not only in Lebanon but in the region and the world. But Fadlallah was lucid only when lucidity served a purpose. Often it did not, and his elusiveness could drive journalists to distraction. Fadlallah perfected two methods of evasion. When it suited him, he delivered long and winding monologues in response to the simplest question, wearing down the resistance of the most persistent journalists. At other times he spoke in Delphic telegraphy, as demonstrated in this characteristic exchange:

> *Interviewer:* Do you believe the Hizbullah in Lebanon could eventually be friendly toward the United States?
> *Fadlallah:* My belief is that the situation is becoming gray.
> *Interviewer:* But are you optimistic?
> *Fadlallah:* I am realistic. I look for optimistic signs in reality.
> *Interviewer:* What does that mean?
> *Fadlallah:* When the issue is gray, you do not see clearly.[77]

Such exchanges, which seemed as though they had been pulled through the looking glass, made perfect sense within the self-imposed rules that governed Fadlallah's public performances, and which permitted him to appear to know everything and nothing at the same time. A journalist once asked him whether he was the "spiritual guide" of Hizbullah and the Islamic student movement. "I am all of these and none of them at the same time," he replied.[78] "This astonishing man knows how to cultivate his myth," wrote one journalist. "Imperturbable, he would be above the fray, yet no detail escapes him . . . a veritable enigma."[79] "Although he does not speak openly and frankly," wrote another, "he alludes to what he wants to say, and points indirectly to those he wants to accuse of something. With Master Fadlallah one has to read between the lines to find the truth."[80] But the space between the lines left ample room for more than one truth, and no interviewer ever parted with a journalistic scoop on tape. Fadlallah could not be led by the tongue.

RESISTANCE LEADER

Although Fadlallah parleyed with the journalists, he devoted the better part of his time to encouraging Shi'ite resistance to the Israeli occupation of the south. While its forces had left Beirut, Israel still sought a formal security agreement with the government of Lebanon, as a condition for further withdrawal. As the prospect of an indefinite and onerous occupation loomed larger, the Shi'ite inhabitants of the south resorted first to civil disobedience and then to violent resistance.[81] Fadlallah turned his efforts toward blocking the implementation of a security agreement, encouraging the struggle against Israel and claiming the resistance for Islam.

Fadlallah's stand against any negotiated agreement with Israel drew partly upon his understanding of Islamic principle. Time and again, he drove home the point of Israel's absolute and unalterable illegitimacy from the point of view of Islam. Israel rested upon dispossession and usurpation; moreover, the dispossessed were Muslims, and the usurped land was sacred to Islam. Israel could not be viewed "as a state with the right to security and peace just like any other state in the region. We cannot see Israel as a legal presence, considering that it is a conglomeration of people who came from all parts of the world to live in Palestine on the ruins of another people."[82] No process could confer legitimacy on Israel. The United Nations could not do so, the PLO could not do so, and indeed, "even if the Jews should suddenly become Muslims, we would ask them to leave Palestine, which was usurped by them."[83] "We as Muslims, if we wish to be in keeping with our faith, cannot for a moment recognize Israel's legality, just as we cannot deem alcohol or adultery to be legal."[84] In Palestine, as in South Africa, a minority had come to dominate the majority by force. But the situation in Palestine was worse, since the Israelis, unlike the whites of South Africa, had driven out the greater part of the majority group and Israel treated those Palestinians who remained in Palestine as "fourth- or fifth-class citizens in comparison to the Jews."[85]

Theft of the land constituted the first count in Fadlallah's indictment of Israel. And to those in Lebanon prepared to forgive Israel this original sin—committed, after all, against Palestinians—in exchange for a negotiated settlement that would restore tranquility to the south, he submitted a second charge, that Israel was inherently expansionist. Few had believed Fadlallah when he had argued, in his Bint Jubayl lectures, before Israel's systematic incursions into Lebanon, that Israel coveted the south. But now the south was occupied, and Israel had no clear plans to leave. Claiming vindication, Fadlallah returned to his argument that the Shi'ites were next in line to be dispossessed by an expanding Israel, and that no agreement could prevent it. Peace with Israel was impossible, since "peace for Israel represents only a transitional stage preparatory to jumping to another stage" in the pursuit of its "ambitions to extend from the Euphra-

tes to the Nile."[86] Muslims had to understand that Israel did not simply
seek to displace the Palestinians; it was "not merely a group that established a state at the expense of a people. It is a group which wants to
establish Jewish culture at the expense of Islamic culture or what some
call Arab culture." The very purpose of Israel was to bring "all the Jews
in the world to this region, to make it the nucleus for spreading their
economic and cultural domination."[87] From Israel's expanded territorial
base, the Jews would then proceed to their ultimate objective: the complete subordination and eradication of Islam. "We find that the struggle
against the Jewish state, in which the Muslims are engaged, is a continuation of the old struggle of the Muslims against the Jews' conspiracy
against Islam." There existed a "world Jewish movement working to deprive Islam of its positions of actual power—spiritually, on the question
of Jerusalem; geographically, on the question of Palestine; politically, by
bringing pressures to block Islam's movement at more than one place;
and economically, in an effort to control Islam's economic potential and
resources, in production and consumption."[88] In this light, only the naïve
could believe that Israel would be satisfied with an agreement over the
south. Regardless of the terms of any security arrangement, Israel would
"find justifications for reviving this problem in the future" in order to
continue its expansion.[89]

The third count in Fadlallah's indictment cited Israel's role in the
service of American imperialism. The "connection" between Israel and
the United States was "aimed at turning the entire region here into a
U.S.-Israeli zone of influence, as required by the strategic, political, and
economic interests of the United States."[90] The relationship, according to
Fadlallah, functioned in this manner: "America acts diplomatically and
tells Israel to move militarily. . . . America suggests peace and leaves Israel
to suggest war, so that if anyone rebels against the American peace, he is
threatened with an Israeli war."[91] Although the United States had greater
interests in the Arab world, that world was unstable. Israel served to keep
it in line, assuring America's access to oil.[92] Thus it was a fantasy for
Arabs to believe they could drive a wedge between Israel and the United
States. "We believe there is no difference between the United States and
Israel; the latter is a mere extension of the former. The United States is
ready to fight the whole world to defend Israel's existence and security.
The two countries are working in complete harmony, and the United
States is certainly not inclined to exert pressure on Israel."[93] As long as
Israel existed, it would continue to act in the interests of imperialism, to
dominate and oppress the region as a whole.

Fadlallah offered only one answer: the strategy of jihad, which "insists that the presence of Israel in Palestine is illegal and that it is an imperialist base which represents a great danger to the Arab and Islamic worlds. It must, therefore, be removed from the map completely. This is what the slogan of liberating Jerusalem represents, since Jerusalem is the Islamic symbol for all of Palestine."[94] Following the eventual dismantling of Israel, Jews who were indigenous to Palestine could remain, but those who had come from elsewhere—the Soviet Union, the United States, Iraq, Yemen, wherever—would have to leave.[95]

In this panoramic perspective, negotiation with Israel over the south was worse than useless. The only solution was to "confront the problem by converting ourselves into a society of war. We must not view the question as merely incursions on the South, but must rather consider the whole Israeli presence as illegitimate."[96] But what could Lebanon's pathetic Shi'ites, who possessed no nuclear weapons, jets, or artillery, do about a conspiracy on so massive a scale? Fadlallah heard people say that there was no point in resisting Israel, which had defeated so many Arab armies, both collectively and individually. To resist would be akin to "stoning a mountain." Better to speak the language of diplomacy with Israel, and get the United States to somehow satisfy Israel and bring about a withdrawal. Fadlallah answered by claiming to have uncovered Israel's weak point. Israel was unprepared spiritually to make the sacrifices demanded by its own ambitions and its American-assigned role. Israel's resolve in Lebanon could be undermined by Israeli casualties that even primitive resistance could inflict. To force Israel out, Lebanon's Shi'ites did not need sophisticated weapons or strategic parity. They needed only to banish their fear.

This was the message Fadlallah carried in an endless round of speeches throughout the Shi'ite community. Fridays were reserved for preaching from his own pulpit in the Imam al-Rida mosque in Bir al-'Abd, sermons recorded by the audiotape vendors. But during the week Fadlallah often spoke several times a day, from mosque pulpits and lecterns, and in the open air through microphones and bullhorns. Consider the range of audiences he addressed during ten days in November 1984, at the height of his campaign:

■ As the week begins, Fadlallah presides over a rally in his own mosque to protest Lebanon's negotiation of a security agreement with Israel. The Shi'ite crowd is young and eager to demonstrate its anger and resolve. A banner with the Star of David is spread on the portal of the mosque, to be trampled by those entering and leaving. Fadlallah is seated with a group of clerics; he speaks last, condemning any measure that might be construed as recognition of Israel.[97]

■ A few days later, Fadlallah addresses an evening lecture at the invitation of the Islamic Committee for Prisoners of Ansar. The occasion is the anniversary of the death of four detainees held by Israel in the Ansar prison camp in the south. The setting is a well-lit lecture hall on the campus of the Arab University of Beirut. An audience of intent students is seated behind the clerics who fill the front row. A few photographs of Khomeini temporarily adorn the walls for the occasion, but this is no rally. Fadlallah again speaks against a security agreement with Israel, but dwells at length on America's behind-the-scenes role. Despite the occasion, the students are more preoccupied with America than with Israel and want to hear about the precise relationship of the Israeli occupation to American imperialism. Fadlallah obliges: Henry Kissinger fomented Lebanon's civil war, he tells them; Israel's entry into Beirut was "more an American than an Israeli affair."[98]

■ A week later he omits this theme in addressing a gathering in the mosque attached to the Islamic seminary in Baalbek. The event is organized by the Islamic Resistance, Hizbullah's arm in the struggle against Israel, and it is from here that the fighters go forth to operations in the south. The audience and Fadlallah are seated in an intimate circle on the floor. In the circle are turbaned clerics, rural notables in white headdresses, and bearded young militiamen in flak jackets. The walls are plastered with banners, posters, and photographs of young men killed in battle. Among the speakers is a renowned commander of the Islamic Resistance, who later will be killed in an Israeli raid. The Islamic Resistance has little time for theory, and Fadlallah does not distract them with the discourse on American imperialism that he has employed at the university. With this front-line audience he emphasizes that it is Israel that is pitted against Islam, and he urges them to rise up against the occupation of the land.[99]

Many of the occasions on which Fadlallah spoke were contrived for the purposes of mass mobilization. But he did not neglect the opportunities provided by the Shi'ite religious calendar. 'Ashura, the day of mourning for the martyrdom of the Imam Husayn at Karbala, outstripped all of these commemorations in releasing the pent-up ritual fervor. There were some whose zeal for ritual self-flagellation on 'Ashura landed them in the hospital, especially in Nabatiyya in the south, where the practice had the longest tradition in Lebanon.[100] Fadlallah now sought to harness this spirit of self-immolation to the cause of resistance to Israel. On the occasion of 'Ashura in 1985, he called upon self-flagellants to desist from the practice and join the Islamic Resistance:

Do you want to suffer with Husayn? Then the setting is ready: the Karbala of the South. You can be wounded and inflict wounds, kill and be killed, and feel the spiritual joy that Husayn lived when he accepted the blood of his son, and the spiritual joy of Husayn when he accepted his own blood and wounds. The believing resisters in the border zone are the true self-flagellants, not the self-flagellants of Nabatiyya. Those who flog themselves with swords, they are our fighting youth. Those who are detained in [the detention camp in] Al-Khiyam, arrested by Israel in the region of Bint Ju-bayl, they are the ones who feel the suffering of Husayn and Zaynab. Those who suffer beatings on their chests and heads in a way that liberates, these are the ones who mark 'Ashura, in their prison cells.[101]

Fadlallah not only knew how to speak the modern rhetoric of resistance, but possessed a complete mastery of the peculiarly Shi'ite symbols of mar-tyrdom, which he invoked whenever the calendar of religious observance made it advantageous to do so.

Fadlallah not only called for struggle, but also sought to fashion the strategies and even the tactics of the Islamic Resistance whenever these had implications for his reading of Islamic law. He therefore sanctioned the tactics of "self-martyrdom," which, having been used successfully against the United States and France in Beirut, were being employed in the south against Israel. "What is the difference between setting out for battle knowing you will die *after* killing ten [of the enemy], and setting out to the field to kill ten and knowing you will die *while* killing them?"[102] The artist of fine distinction saw no real distinction at all. After an initial spate of successes, however, it became clear that this ten-to-one ratio could not be guaranteed. As Israeli forces took prudent countermeasures, such operations became less effective, producing few, if any, Israeli casu-alties. Still, there were those in the Islamic Resistance who felt that even failed operations had value, in that they demonstrated a willingness to sacrifice young men on the altar of the struggle. Fadlallah strongly opposed this transformation of a failing military tactic into a sacrificial rite. Already in the spring of 1985, he openly expressed doubts. "The self-martyring operation is not permitted unless it can convulse the en-emy," Fadlallah declared. "The believer cannot blow himself up unless the results will equal or exceed the [loss] of the believer's soul. Self-martyring operations are not fatal accidents but legal obligations gov-erned by rules, and the believers cannot transgress the rules of God."[103] By late 1985, he did not hesitate to opine that the day of the self-martyrs had passed. Fadlallah deemed past operations against Israeli forces "successful in that they significantly harmed the Israelis. But the present circumstances do not favor such operations anymore, and attacks that only inflict limited casualties (on the enemy) and destroy one building should not be encouraged, if the price is the death of the person who carries them out."[104] It was a view which largely carried the day, and demonstrated Fadlallah's determination not only to fuel the Islamic Resistance, but to guide it.

Fadlallah's own daunting persistence and his seemingly limitless energy did a great deal to fire the Islamic Resistance. He remained in constant touch with the clerics and commanders who led the fight and inspired them with the words they used to gather recruits. Gradually the Islamic Resistance began to claim success, wearing down Israeli forces through ambushes, roadside bombs, and the threat of suicide bombs. Fadlallah described the process by which the weak demoralized the strong:

> The Israeli soldier who could not be defeated was now killed, with an explosive charge here, and a bullet there. People were suddenly filled with power, and that power could be employed in new ways. It could not be expressed in the classical means of warfare, because the implements were lacking. But it employed small force and a war of nerves, which the enemy could not confront with its tanks and airplanes. It appeared in every place, and in more than one way. Thus our people in the South discovered their power, and could defeat Israel and all the forces of tyranny.[105]

Fadlallah's contribution to the growing resistance to Israel could not be isolated and measured with any precision. Yet no one in Hizbullah could match his sheer ability to conceptualize conflict. For many of those in the Islamic Resistance, he had become an infallible moral and political compass.

The struggle of the Islamic Resistance in Lebanon was meant to "make confrontation with Israel possible in the future on the grounds that Israel is not an irresistible power even if it is supported by the United States." Yet Fadlallah never deceived himself or others about the meaning of the successes of the Islamic Resistance. Even as he argued that Israel coveted the South, he understood that Israel was vulnerable in south Lebanon in part because its consensus ended at the border, that from the moment Israel entered Lebanon, Israelis began to look for a way out—a timetable, a security plan, guarantees. There was thus "a difference between the liberation of Palestine and the liberation of South Lebanon as far as the method of operation is concerned." The obstacles on the road from the border to Jerusalem would be far greater; Israel would stiffen over the defense of its heartland. The liberation of Palestine, where a tenacious Israel had struck root, would require the emergence of an Islamic resistance in Palestine itself, as well as a broad "Arab-Islamic plan for confrontation." Without such a plan, operations against Israel from Lebanon would become "mere acts of self-martyrdom. That is why we think differently about the post-Israeli withdrawal phase, differently from the way of the resistance in South Lebanon."[106]

The ultimate liberation would take much more time. Just how much more became a point of disagreement between Fadlallah and Iran's emissaries, who feared that promising too remote a redemption might create despair. The Iranian agents believed what they preached—that Iran's revolution had switched Muslim history to fast-forward—but Fadlallah was more concerned with encouraging persistence, viewing hopes of quick victory as the perennial bane of the Arabs. At times, Fadlallah's ambiguity accommodated those short of patience: "When we say that Israel will cease to exist, this does not mean tomorrow or the day after."[107] But usually he spoke of years, decades, generations, even centuries. Israel's elimination could not be achieved in "one, two, or ten years" but might require "one hundred years if necessary."[108] Or perhaps fifty years, "just as the Jews sought to reach Jerusalem, even if it took fifty years."[109] Fadlallah did not wish to "take from the public its dream and aspiration of destroying Israel"—a dream he shared—but the liberation of Jerusalem would be done "only in future generations."[110] "In this connection," he admitted, "we think of great periods of time."[111] There was now "no strategy in the operational sense for the liberation of Jerusalem."[112]

Fadlallah did not expect to enter the promised land. Instead he sought to purify the young generation and steer them from the worship of false gods, so that they or their children might regain lost Jerusalem. And because Fadlallah did not become intoxicated by the early gains of the Islamic Resistance, he did not become discouraged when Israel dug in its heels in 1985, establishing a security zone in the south. He continued to preach against Israel with an even resolve. But as the Islamic struggle against Israel entered a stalemate, Fadlallah's audiences began to pay closer attention to his vision of Lebanon itself.

BALM OF LEBANON

How did Fadlallah envision the Lebanon left behind by Israel's retreat, and how precisely did he expect Islam to resolve the country's deadlock? It was difficult to say. No clouds obstructed his discourse against Israel, for the conflict in the south represented a battle of absolutes. But the rest of Lebanon—free of foreign intruders but contested, often militarily, by indigenous forces—was a different matter. Among the parties whose claims on the hopelessly small country had to be reconciled were Shi'ite Muslims, Sunni Muslims, Maronite Christians, Greek Orthodox Christians, Armenians, and Druze. In addressing the question of Lebanon, Fadlallah brought his talent for advocacy brilliantly into play. It was obvious, he declared, that neither the existing confessional system nor any other confessional formula could ever reconcile the claims of these different religious groups. But they could all be accommodated with equity through the implementation of a comprehensive Islamic political, social, and legal order. Islam, declared Fadlallah, constituted a framework in which all Lebanese could live in harmony, regardless of their religious affiliation.

Yet when pressed to explain how Islam would achieve this, Fadlallah let ambiguity reign. At times, he seemed to predicate Islamic redemption on the dissolution of Lebanon itself. Fadlallah believed Lebanon's borders were arbitrarily tailored "by great powers . . . as the result of a political deal" to create a bastion from which the West could continue to dominate the surrounding Muslim world.[113] Lebanon "came into being to perform a specific mission for the West . . . to be a stage on which all the plans propounded for the region would be tested."[114] Thus Lebanon, an entity that existed only to satisfy external political interests, need not be preserved. Fadlallah held out the ultimate promise of Lebanon's disappearance: "If the political situation in the region changes, not only is Lebanon unlikely to survive; neither will many other entities in the region."[115] In this respect, Lebanon as an idea did not differ significantly from Israel as an idea. Both were foisted on the Muslims from the outside; both were destined to disappear. This was certainly the analysis adopted by Iran's emissaries, who promised Lebanon's disappearance into a "great Islamic state."

But Fadlallah did not believe Lebanon's demise was imminent. Too many obstacles, within the country and beyond its frontiers, stood in the path of its absorption into a great Islamic polity. The likelihood that such a polity would ever emerge was slim; in Fadlallah's view, "modern developments with which the Muslims now live . . . have made the single world state irrelevant from the point of view of objective possibilities."[116] Iran's emissaries sought to create the illusion that parts of Lebanon had been incorporated into Iran, but illusion was one thing, reality another. The best that Lebanon might hope for was the separate implementation of an Islamic state.

Yet even this limited goal could not be achieved immediately, for confessionalism constituted the hard soil of Lebanon, and the idea of an Islamic state was a vulnerable transplant. While Iran's emissaries dwelt upon the similarities between Iran and Lebanon, Fadlallah saw profound differences, which arose primarily from Lebanon's confessional diversity. In Iran, there was "a population composed of Muslims only, which accepts the line of Islam, and a regime that had become an obstacle in the way of Islamic rule. The only solution was to fight this regime." But such homogeneity did not obtain in Lebanon, and, Fadlallah acknowledged, "sometimes there are obstacles that a revolution cannot eliminate."[117]

The first obstacle lay in the fact that the Muslims of Lebanon were not of one school but were divided between Sunnis and Shi'ites. And among the Sunnis, there were many with a vested interest in the existing confessional formula. Their fortunes, which had declined since the outbreak of the civil war, plummeted following the expulsion of their Palestinian allies in 1982. Now the rising demographic and political tide of Shi'ism threatened to sweep away their supremacy over the Shi'ites. They had profited from their mediation between the surrounding Sunni Arab world and the West, in commerce, education, and the professions. Shi'ites could see this themselves: most of the prospering industries and warehouses in the Dahiya were owned by Sunnis. The confessional system also guaranteed Sunnis a share of the state that their numbers could no longer justify. For example, twenty seats in parliament were reserved for Sunnis and only nineteen for Shi'ites, although Shi'ites had come to outnumber Sunnis two to one. Now assertive Shi'ites began to argue that the primacy of the Sunni community on the Muslim side of the confessional equation had no legitimacy. But the idea of an Islamic state could never win a majority if the Muslims split, and unity could only be achieved by alleviating Sunni anxieties. As Fadlallah noted, "the majority of the armed elements within West Beirut are Shi'ites, and there is no real Sunni armed presence. When people who are unarmed are faced with armed people, especially when infractions and violations of the law occur, they are bound to feel insecure."[118]

Fadlallah therefore set out to dispel the growing mistrust between Shi'ites and Sunnis. The first step was to admit that the problem existed, to avoid the denial that prevented dialogue. The inner sectarianism of Islam, he announced, had had "a profound effect on the emotional content of the view held by Muslims of one another." It had now reached the point of gross exaggeration, where Muslim openly accused Muslim of unbelief and polytheism. Instead of seeing sectarian differences as matters of marginal disagreement over law or the interpretation of theological details, Muslims had come to regard them as fundamental differences in belief. Fadlallah offered no precise solutions to these differences. But while others magnified them, he sought to minimize them. They were not theological but philosophical, he declared; they could be transformed into "an intellectual problem, to be examined by researchers in a scholarly way so as to reach a solution."[119]

While Fadlallah offered no magical formula, his ecumenical style did build a measure of Sunni trust. His own discourse was remarkably free of Shi'ite symbolism. He did employ a Shi'ite rhetoric on the anniversaries and commemorations set by the Shi'ite religious calendar, and when addressing exclusively Shi'ite audiences. But such rhetoric, he stated, was intended only to motivate people.[120] Given a choice between an allusion to the Qur'an or to the Imam Husayn, he usually chose the former; it was often difficult to tell from the texts of his regular sermons that they were spoken by a Shi'ite cleric. He also appeared before Sunni audiences, giving his assurances the weight of his personality. In a typical instance, Fadlallah lectured before alumni of a prestigious Sunni school; the audience comprised lawyers, doctors, engineers, a former prime minister, parliamentary deputies, and the head of Beirut's chamber of commerce. A photograph shows an audience of respectable older men of means, mustached, white-haired or bald, arms folded across their jackets and ties. These were the pillars of the Sunni professional and commercial establishment, those who felt most threatened by the encroachment of the masses of Shi'ite poor in West Beirut. Fadlallah read his prepared remarks from a seat on the dais. In measured tones and without passion, he worked to assuage their fears, speaking about the need for the unity of Shi'ites and Sunnis and the common ground on which they stood.[121]

Such performances were augmented by personal efforts to defuse sectarian powder kegs. Members of the Lebanese Sunni elite, who had built personal fortunes from their Saudi connections, shuddered when Lebanese Shi'ites sacked and burned the Saudi consulate in Beirut in 1984, in protest against a Saudi refusal to issue them pilgrimage visas. Fadlallah was quick to condemn the violence: "We regard this as an act of mischief, and believe it might have been the result of misplaced zeal."[122] That same year, he sought to prevent the extension of the Shi'ite 'Ashura processions from the Dahiya into West Beirut. While the commemoration of Imam Husayn's martyrdom played an essential role in the ritual universe of Hizbullah, its recalling of the opening of the chasm within Islam bore the potential for sectarian strife.

The understanding Fadlallah promoted was fragile, and the mistrust between Sunnis and Shi'ites simmered. But Fadlallah had the best chance of any Shi'ite cleric to emerge as the linchpin of any coalition the two communities might form, as guide to Shi'ites and Sunnis alike. "My views have had an impact in Lebanon, among Sunnis as well as Shi'ites," he declared in an unusually boastful moment. "I do not work on a Lebanese level alone but also at the level of the Islamic world. We have excellent relations with the Hizbullah group and with most of the Amal members, as well as with Islamic non-Shi'ite groups and the Sunnis in Tripoli and Beirut."[123]

But Fadlallah could never be certain that any Sunnis—even those impressed by his ecumenism—would follow him down the road to an Islamic state. They saw how Iran's revolutionary constitution had de-clared Twelver Shi'ism to be the religion of state, despite the presence of a large Sunni minority. Were not the Sunnis better off remaining one confession among many, rather than a minority in a predominantly Shi'ite Islamic state? Again, Fadlallah sought to banish one fear by evok-ing a greater one. Certainly Muslims had their differences, but their shared belief, law, culture, resources, and security were threatened by unbelief. That threat demanded that the Muslims "strive for the establish-ment of a state, *any state,* which will counter these threats from the posi-tion of Islamic thought." The great Shi'ite clerics and the leaders of Sunni movements had to find a formula that would guarantee the freedom of believers in such a state, by drawing upon the Qur'an as its constitution. The state would have to locate the common ground shared by the schools of Islam and tolerate the long-standing differences among them. For the alternative to an Islamic state was "subjugation to unbelieving tyranny, which will extend its injustice to Islam as a whole, and to all Muslims." Unbelief would establish its rule, its law, its complete control. "And that would not be agreeable to any Islamic logic, opinion, or school."[124] To accommodate Lebanon's Sunnis, the implementation of an Islamic state in Lebanon would have to differ fundamentally from its implementation in Iran. Concessions would have to be made to Lebanon's diversity.

But that diversity hardly ended with the Sunnis. Fadlallah knew that Lebanon's Christians would resist any attempt to substitute the rule of Islam for the tattered confessional order that guaranteed their privileges, which were even more extensive than those of the Sunnis. Fadlallah also understood that they had an identity and an ethos of their own, largely formed in opposition to Islam, and he had seen them at their most tena-cious and ruthless in Nabaa. Unlike many of Iran's emissaries, Fadlallah never underestimated the Christians of Lebanon. Like the invading Jews, they were unbelievers; but unlike the Jews, they were rooted in the soil of Lebanon and would not flee in the face of car bombs and ambushes. They would simply return the same with a vengeance. As he once put it,

"Lebanon is a country in which both Muslims and Christians live. Neither can remove the other; that is why we must stop losing ourselves in conjecture."[125]

Fadlallah's straightforward advice to his adherents was not to tangle with the Christians if such entanglement could be avoided. As Israel retreated, he urged that Shi'ite rage against the Christians be displaced onto the Israelis, arguing that Israel represented the "head" and Lebanon's Christians the "tail." Once he was asked whether liberation of all Beirut from the Christians should not take precedence over the liberation of the south. "Confront Israel and leave the 'tail' aside. For if you defeat Israel, if you chop off the 'head,' where will the 'tail' be?"[126] This was an astute shift of grievance, since the Islamic Resistance could not break the resolve of Lebanon's Christians. But it could break the overextended Israelis, who were already looking for any possible exit from the Lebanese labyrinth.

Yet Fadlallah believed that the Christians, and especially the Maronites, were growing weaker. The Maronites had been a European project, at a time when Europe pursued a policy of cultivating minorities. But America, the heir of Europe, had penetrated the entire Islamic world and had no need of a small minority at odds with its more numerous Muslim friends in the region.[127] Fadlallah believed that in the long term, this made Lebanon's Christians insecure—and susceptible to persuasion. The Christians could not yet be forced into submission, but perhaps they could be cajoled, coaxed, seduced. Fadlallah understood that they were afraid, and that fear stiffened their will. But if that fear could be alleviated, might not their will be eroded?

Thus began Fadlallah's remote dialogue with Lebanon's Christians— conducted at first through the Lebanese media. Fadlallah went out of his way to grant interviews to newspapers and magazines published and widely read by Christians. The journalists for these publications inevitably pressed Fadlallah on the status of Christians in any future Islamic state. Right through the Ottoman period, they had lived under Islam as protected inferiors, bound by the provisions of a pact, or *dhimma,* which they remembered as a discriminatory system of subjugation, a kind of religious apartheid. Fadlallah still upheld the dhimma as an ideal arrangement between the Muslim majority and the Christian minority, and argued that on close examination it was not "the oppressive or inhumane system that some people imagine it to be." But he suggested an alternative: a treaty, or *mu'ahada,* between majority and minority. The prophet Muhammad, on coming to Medina, had concluded precisely this kind of treaty with the Jews. Unlike the dhimma, which was a concession by the

Islamic state, the muʿahada was a bilateral contract. The Islamic state could conclude such a treaty with any minority—with Christians or Jews, obviously, but also, for example, with Kurds or Turks. Such a treaty would guarantee cultural rights and respect for customs and traditions, while leaving politics to the Islamic state. Pressed still further, Fadlallah could envision an additional pact, or *mithaq*, between the state and its religious minorities. Such an agreement, while negotiated within the broad lines of Islam, would open all state offices, with the exception of the highest decision-making authority, to members of the religious minority.[128] "Because of the Muslim majority in Lebanon," he announced, "the president should be a Muslim."[129] But at the same time, "if the president is a Muslim, but a supporter of infidel regimes and arrogant powers, in our view he is not acceptable."[130] The president would have to be both a Muslim and an Islamist. In late 1987 a handbill circulated in West Beirut naming Fadlallah as a candidate for the presidency of Lebanon. Fadlallah saw no reason why a man of religion could not hold such an office, but he denied any connection with the handbill and denounced the floating of his name as an attempt to harm him.[131] With the presidency still reserved for a Maronite, he could hardly do otherwise.

Fadlallah thus offered a comprehensive Islamic solution, but he assured Christians that he did not seek to impose it by force. He distanced himself from the demand of Iran's emissaries that the "regime" be toppled. The people of Lebanon, he averred, had the right to decide their own future. Any solution would have to be acceptable to a majority. It was Fadlallah who prevailed upon the drafters of Hizbullah's programmatic "open letter" of February 1985 to include a passage that called for "allowing all of our people to decide their fate and choose the form of government they want with complete freedom."[132] Muslims were duty-bound only to present the alternative of Islam, not to impose it. Fadlallah did not imagine he could persuade all of Lebanon's Christians, but he did seek to build a reservoir of Christian trust, which might be tapped later to build a multiconfessional majority in favor of an Islamic state.

His growing reputation certainly piqued Christian interest, and Fadlallah held discussions with a long list of Christian figures whom he met in Damascus. His interlocutors included the patriarchs of the Greek Orthodox, Greek Catholic, and Syrian Orthodox churches, as well as the papal nuncio in Damascus and the cardinal who presided over the Vatican's Secretariat for Non-Christians. "I never felt there was any problem during our talks," claimed Fadlallah. "It was as though I was conversing with Muslim scholars."[133] In Lebanon itself, however, no religious dialogue took place, and Fadlallah admitted that politics posed "serious obstacles to any attempt at a frank discussion."[134] Still, this did not prevent him from conducting a monologue. One Christmas he gave a lengthy interview devoted to Muslim-Christian relations, arguing that "fundamentalist Islam" was far closer to Christianity than Lebanon's "confessional Islam."[135] One Easter he gave a mosque sermon commemorating "the sufferings of Jesus," one of Islam's prophets, even though "we may not concur with Christians on certain details of theology."[136] As with Sunnis, so with Christians, Fadlallah sought to talk the differences away.

And if, despite Fadlallah's efforts, the majority of Lebanese still rejected the creation of an Islamic state? In those circumstances, Fadlallah did not rule out a compromise solution. Above all, he sought social and economic justice for the oppressed. Perhaps Lebanon's diversity made it impossible to create a state led by a Muslim and based on Islamic law. That was no reason to despair. "If we as Muslims fail to achieve an Islamic state for everyone, we should not stop in our tracks. Instead, we must call for a humane state for everyone."[137] Such a state could never be just in an Islamic sense, but it could be humane, provided it alleviated the distress of the despised and downtrodden. To those who insisted on a Muslim head of state, Fadlallah noted that there were other states headed by Muslim kings, princes, and presidents "who steal the funds of the Muslims, and the treasury of the nation and its future." To those who demanded the implementation of Islamic law, Fadlallah pointed out that this did not automatically guarantee justice. In a veiled allusion to Saudi Arabia, Fadlallah decried Arab regimes that practiced theft and then cut off the hand of the thief, practiced fornication and then stoned the adulterer.[138]

Fadlallah continued to talk about the necessity of an Islamic state, but he actively pursued more attainable objectives. And if he sometimes asked for more than was reasonable, it was usually in order to get something reasonable. Demand Jerusalem, but settle (for now) for the south; demand an Islamic state, then settle (for now) for a "humane" state. In his plea for the despised, Fadlallah remained both pragmatic and principled. Of course there were Christians and Sunnis who viewed his vision as a deceit, meant to lure them to a feast where they would constitute the main course. But Fadlallah concealed nothing. He expected them to sacrifice privilege—political, social, economic—in return for the protection afforded by his Islam. They could accept his offer now, or gamble losing everything in a future upheaval driven by a less forgiving Islam. Thanks largely to Fadlallah's subtle advocacy—and implicit threat—the idea of an Islamic state provoked a lively intellectual debate, among adherents of all confessions.

Critics and Assassins

To many of Iran's emissaries, Fadlallah's apparent bargaining away of high principles seemed unconscionable. They would have preferred that he simply repeat their slogans, not interpret them, and they lost no opportunity to bring pressure to bear on this maddeningly obstinate client. They leaned on him in Damascus when he paid obligatory visits to the Iranian ambassador. They demanded that he fall in line during his visits to Tehran, where he attended conferences and met with leading figures, and sometimes with Khomeini. According to Sayyid Sadiq al-Musawi, the most hard-line of Hizbullah's leaders, Khomeini refused to meet with Fadlallah for three years because of Fadlallah's refusal to demand an Islamic state.[139]

But Fadlallah remained absolutely unshaken in his conviction that he alone knew how to promote the Islamic alternative in Lebanon. During his sojourns in Tehran, he lobbied hard against the claim that Lebanon stood on the brink of Islamic revolution. His technique was to cast doubt on the competence of Iran's own emissaries. "There are some Iranian scholars and some officials who are perhaps not fully aware of the situation in Lebanon," he announced following one trip to Tehran.[140] The words implicitly indicted Iran's emissaries for concealing the truth from decision makers in Iran. The emissaries, in turn, questioned Fadlallah's devotion to the common cause, and his views became the subject of some suspicion. "There were a few of the leading clerics in Iran whom we venerate, who had concluded that we had abandoned the slogan of Islamic rule in Lebanon in a fundamental way." To them, Fadlallah patiently explained his own concept of change. "We believe in exporting the revolution, but there is a difference between exporting the revolution as 'one unit' and exporting it as 'parts.' We believe that the nature of the actual circumstances necessitates its export as 'parts,' since only this will bring us actual results."[141] The process, he maintained, was limited by the power of the exporting state and "the objective and actual circumstances" of the "importing" country, some of which could only be changed "with the passage of time." Dismissing the upbeat reports of the emissaries, Fadlallah told his interlocutors in Tehran that conditions for the rule of Islam "do not exist in the Lebanese reality at the present stage, and in the immediate stages to follow."[142]

Fadlallah made this argument persuasively. He quickly built a constituency in Tehran, where some in high places regarded him as a more reliable guide to the intricacies of the Lebanese sideshow than their own emissaries. Certainly the force of his argument won him a following, but he strengthened his hand by his own keen appreciation of the factionalism within the revolution's leadership. He saw the signs of division in the conduct of Iran's emissaries, and took careful measure of the rivalries that divided the revolution. He soon understood that a group of revolutionaries with impeccable credentials—realistic, patient, calculating, and averse to adventurism—had gathered around the speaker of the Majlis, 'Ali-Akbar Hashemi Rafsanjani. They became Fadlallah's quarry, and he eventually claimed to have won them to his own views: "During my recent meeting with the Iranian decision-making officials I sensed that they are not at present thinking about an Islamic republic in Lebanon, not in the Iranian model. At present they believe that the Lebanese problem should be solved through democracy or democracy of the majority because Lebanon cannot bear any more suffering."[143] In truth, Iran's decision makers were divided, but Fadlallah had won the confidence of Rafsanjani, his pillar of support in the shifting sands of Iranian factional politics. Rafsanjani's own mastery of Iranian power politics reassured Fadlallah that he had made a sagacious choice. As early as 1986, Fadlallah declared Rafsanjani "undoubtedly the thinking head of the state," for having vanquished Mehdi Hashemi, one of Iran's most adventurous emissaries and a dangerous domestic opponent. On the same occasion, Fadlallah gave his backing to Rafsanjani's trading of American hostages for American arms—a deal criticized by Iranian hard-liners. Under Rafsanjani, Iran's "struggle against imperialism" would continue, "but in a studied and rational manner"—precisely the manner championed by Fadlallah himself.[144]

Fadlallah held up his hard-won autonomy as a badge of integrity. He did not fail to acknowledge his debt to Iran's revolution; even while trumpeting his freedom to think and act, he allowed that "in all circumstances," Iran's revolution represented "the pillar of all the pure Islamic movements in the world. We believe we should support it with all our might so that it will gain strength sufficient to defeat all the forces of evil in the world."[145] But he invariably stiffened his neck while bowing, always insisting that "I am not an agent for anybody's policy. I am simply trying to implement my policy, which is based on Islam and which complements all the Islamic world's forces."[146] He also refused to apologize for the excesses of the Iranian revolution: Iran had achieved only "70 percent of justice," he estimated.[147] None of Iran's emissaries ever found a way to bring Fadlallah to heel; he possessed too much of that wiliness known in Persian as *zerangi,* a guile he raised to the level of a political art. Depending upon their temperament, the emissaries could only shrug or simmer at his declarations of independence. "We have the freedom to have our own views on special Lebanese affairs when speaking to Iranian brothers and others," Fadlallah boldly declared to anyone who asked. "We have our own views even in international issues, methods of political work, and the lines of political thought."[148] Fadlallah earned that freedom through his exacting command of language, combined with an acute feel for the requirements of survival in a sea of zeal, ambition, violence, and intrigue.

Still, as Fadlallah's visibility increased, he loomed larger in the imagination of Hizbullah's adversaries. Arrangements for his personal security grew ever more elaborate as he became the subject of death threats. Had he been concerned only for his safety, he might have allowed Iran's emissaries to coax him to the Bekaa Valley. But there he would have been cut off from his reservoirs of support and the media, and would have become utterly dependent upon Iran. He chose to remain in the Dahiya, where the risks he ran grew with his reputation. In March 1985, an attempt against his life almost succeeded; its effect, however, was to deepen the popular veneration of Fadlallah as a man in the service of a divine mission. A car bomb intended for Fadlallah claimed eighty lives, including the residents of apartment buildings demolished by gas lines which exploded. Over 250 persons were injured. It was a familiar Beirut nightmare come to life: buckled concrete, dismembered bodies, howling ambulances, dazed passersby. The Dahiya had never known a moment of such intense collective grief and emotion, expressed in an outpouring of sentiment during the funerals of the dead. Fadlallah, bullhorn in hand, presided over the service for those victims who were buried in a communal grave in the Rawdat al-Shahidayn cemetery.[149]

Fadlallah immediately appreciated the necessity of transforming the horror into a step towards the consolidation of the movement. Properly interpreted, the deaths could be given meaning that would partially redeem lost lives. He began immediately by laying responsibility for the bombing upon the United States. Fadlallah had no solid evidence, but none was required, and it was of paramount importance that the deed confirm the malevolence of imperialism. A banner stretched across one of the demolished buildings, which read "Made in USA," graphically represented Fadlallah's claim. Later the *Washington Post* claimed to have traced the bombing to an American "counterterrorism" initiative gone awry.[150] Fadlallah did not hold up the report as vindication, for the same newspaper might print a damaging charge against him tomorrow, as it had done in the past. But the supposed corroboration, repeated in Lebanon's press, worked to buttress his claim.

At the same time, Fadlallah was concerned that some in Hizbullah might strike out indiscriminately against Americans. While it served his purpose that the United States be blamed, violence against innocent Americans would lose for Hizbullah the higher moral ground gained through the sacrifice of its own innocents. So Fadlallah immediately urged that there be no revenge. "The people will not react in an emotional way," he declared, "but in a comprehensive plan to bring down imperialist policy. We must know that we are not against the American people; in America there are many who do not agree with the policy of their government. . . . We will not unjustly treat Americans who are distant from the apparatus of espionage and destruction."[151] Fadlallah demanded not vengeance, but a renewed resolve to defeat imperialism.

It was a difficult distinction to maintain amid the passions of the bereaved Dahiya. And ultimately the demand for vengeance had to be appeased. Yet it was done in Fadlallah's way, not through victimization of innocents, but through the application of Islamic law. Hizbullah soon announced that it had arrested eleven Lebanese for their alleged role in the bombing and, a year after the bombing, released their videotaped confessions and announced their execution.[152] The secret trials and executions were a brilliant maneuver. They appeased the demand for vengeance, which otherwise might have escaped control. They proclaimed that Hizbullah's intelligence service could solve a crime that baffled the Lebanese police. And they established the efficacy of Islamic law in creating an island of justice amid injustice. Fadlallah claimed not to have intervened himself, but he declared that "those who investigated and judged were faithful elements."[153] The process, while clandestine, undoubtedly inspired the confidence of the inhabitants of the Dahiya, whatever outsiders may have thought of it.

Fadlallah's narrow escape also enhanced his own aura, especially among those whom he could not reach by preaching alone. Fadlallah's constituency among students and intellectuals knew that his escape was a matter of coincidence, and he did not present himself as the beneficiary of a miracle. But the meaning of his survival was self-evident to the despised poor of the Dahiya and beyond, who could not always follow the thread of his intricate preaching and elliptical writings. If they had cause to doubt his special grace, it was confirmed for them now. Nowhere was this more evident than among those who had lost family members in the bombing. "Praise be to God that the Sayyid was preserved," said one man whose daughter was killed in the explosion. "He would have been lost to all the Muslims. Praise be to God that the carnage ended as it did, and not otherwise."[154]

The near loss of Fadlallah also served to underline his indispensability, even among those who disapproved of his independent spirit. Without him Hizbullah would have no voice, so the movement had to assume responsibility for his protection. The increasingly stringent security that surrounded Fadlallah enhanced his stature, and made his arrival at any location a memorable event. A motorcade of Mercedes limousines swept him through the rubble-strewn streets of the Dahiya and West Beirut, and along crumbling roads to the Bekaa and the south. The smoke-tinted windows made it impossible for potential assailants to know which of the armor-plated automobiles carried Fadlallah. When he arrived at a destination, his many bearded bodyguards, armed with automatic rifles and pistols, would take up positions around the door of his car. Then he would emerge: a stout man in an 'aba, a full-sleeved dark cloak; a graying beard; the black turban of a sayyid; and a walking stick.[155] On one occasion in 1987, he made a condolence call in West Beirut with an escort of ten cars and forty armed bodyguards.[156]

The closing off of his street no longer sufficed. He moved from his run-down apartment block to a spacious residence in the formerly Christian quarter of Harat Hurayk in the Dahiya, a little more than a mile from his mosque. The complex was surrounded by a ten-foot wall and two dozen guards.[157] The move could not guarantee his safety, for shells fell on the house during clashes between Hizbullah and Amal in 1988, and again during shelling from the eastern side of the city in 1989.[158] The approaches to his mosque also remained dangerous: late in 1989, Hizbullah announced it had discovered a parked car rigged with a hundred kilograms of dynamite along the route.[159] And betrayal also remained a possibility, as dark rumors surfaced about a foiled plot by persons in his own entourage, who had planted a bomb in his mosque.[160]

The growth of his new enterprises provided the most tangible evidence of Fadlallah's new prominence. The increased flow of donations to his coffers allowed him to expand his activities far beyond the care of orphans and the schooling of clerics. In 1983 he established a new bureau for social welfare to assist needy families. Within five years, it regularly provided financial and medical assistance to nearly twenty-five hundred Shi'ite families throughout Lebanon.[161] Such operations obviously could not be run without supervision. His household eventually grew to employ several hundred persons, including front-office personnel, financial managers, bodyguards, drivers, and servants. Important positions in Fadlallah's enterprises were reserved for members of his family, who could be trusted with the large sums of money collected and spent under his auspices. A brother-in-law ran his office. A nephew ran the institutes in Beirut established by Fadlallah in the name of the Imam Kho'i. A cousin acted on his behalf in the south.[162] With an eye toward the future, Fadlallah groomed one of his sons, 'Ali, for the role of cleric, allowing the young man to assume the pulpit during his absences.[163] Fadlallah had learned from Lebanon's old warlords, and from the distant Khomeini himself, that as one ages, one can only trust a son.

As Fadlallah's visibility increased, he faced a growing number of deliberate attempts to discredit him and denials became an integral part of his repertoire. As always, it was impossible to determine the veracity of the many charges leveled against him. In 1987 a noted American journalist, claiming to have had conversations with the director of the Central Intelligence Agency, reported in a book that Fadlallah had been approached by the Saudis after the failed assassination attempt and offered two million dollars if "he would act as their early warning system for terrorist attacks on Saudi and American facilities." Fadlallah was said to have agreed, although he preferred to receive the payment in food, medicine, and education expenses for some of his followers. "It was easier to bribe him than to kill him," the Saudi ambassador to Washington reportedly commented.[164] Fadlallah vigorously denied the charge of corruption: "I challenge anyone or any side who can prove that such aid was provided to us."[165] His office called the report a "cheap trick" to discredit him.[166] To buttress the claim that Fadlallah had sold out to the Americans, another report noted that one of his eleven children had been admitted to the United States for study, which was indeed the case.[167] Fadlallah did not bother to answer this accusation: the presence of a son in an American university only confirmed his stature as a master of all possibilities. He needed not only one son who could preach in his stead, but another who could interpret the real America as experienced through Wayne State University. This was all the more important now that Fadlallah could not visit the United States on lecture tours, as he had done before winning American notoriety. But the charge that Fadlallah had been compromised by American money would not stick. When the offending book appeared in Arabic translation, the charges against Fadlallah were omitted.

Fadlallah's placement of family members in positions of trust also gave rise to rumors of corruption. In 1990, Fadlallah's brother-in-law and sons were accused by Amal sources of speculating in foreign currency, and even of dominating that market in West Beirut and the Dahiya. Millions of dollars were supposedly smuggled abroad. Local money changers allegedly complained to the police that Fadlallah's operatives had pressured them to reverse a (temporary) decline in the value of the American dollar vis-à-vis the Lebanese pound. At the same time, members of Fadlallah's family were reportedly buying up extensive properties in the Dahiya.[168] But corruption charges had no more effect than the accusations of complicity in violence. Was Fadlallah dangerous and corrupt? Moderate and principled? People believed what they wished—and clearly many Shi'ites wished him well.

Fadlallah faced a more subtle but substantial challenge in the form of Shaykh Muhammad Mahdi Shams al-Din, the white-bearded man who headed the Supreme Islamic Shi'ite Council.[169] This position, at the summit of the Shi'ite clerical establishment, assured him of control over substantial funds and powers of appointment. Whenever Iran's emissaries sought new avenues of influence or felt frustrated by Fadlallah, they began to talk with Shams al-Din. He also visited Iran, where he presented himself as that Shi'ite cleric who enjoyed the widest respect throughout the Shi'ite community.

This was precisely the claim made by Fadlallah, and persistent reports spoke of personal conflict between the two men. Fadlallah invariably denied the rivalry; it was ignoble to argue publicly with a colleague-in-turban. But Fadlallah publicly discounted the importance of the Supreme Islamic Shi'ite Council, Shams al-Din's lever of influence in the community. The council, Fadlallah remarked, enjoyed "a certain degree" of representative authority, since it included clerics, Shi'ite members of parliament, and heads of various associations, but it did not control "all the political cards."[170] Fadlallah delivered the jab diplomatically: "With all due respect to the leadership of the Shi'ite Council, we believe that the composition of the Council is not such as to inspire Islamic Shi'ite trust."[171] Such talk so strained the relationship between the two leaders that mediators often had to work to reconcile them. Fadlallah would then meet with Shams al-Din, declare that the two were not rivals, and affirm that the scope of their differences was confined to "tactics."[172] That hardly did justice to the depth of their disagreements, so complicated by the emotional residue of their childhood bond. But neither did it fairly reflect the depth of their attachment, which sometimes surfaced in dramatic ways. When Fadlallah's father died in 1984, it was Shams al-Din who spoke the eulogy; when the body was returned to Najaf and Fadlallah accepted condolences at Beirut's airport, Shams al-Din stood at his side.[173] They were brothers in all but name—and so long as Shams al-Din claimed an equal share of the legacy, Fadlallah's ambition could not fly.

HIJACKERS AND HOSTAGES

The emergence of the formidable Fadlallah had been sudden and unexpected. But the speed of his ascent also brought him quickly to his limits. Because Fadlallah had preserved a distance between himself and Hizbullah, his words could not always bear the full weight of their supposed significance. In fact, there were decision makers in Hizbullah who did not regard him as the ultimate authority on the proper conduct of Islam's struggle, some of whom even acted in direct contradiction to his teachings.

A challenge to Fadlallah's moral authority came in June 1985, three months after the attempt on his life. In a move that riveted the attention of the world, Hizbullah strongmen organized the hijacking of a TWA airliner to Beirut and demanded the release of Lebanese Shi'ites held in an Israeli prison. Fadlallah had sensed the growing despair among the families of Shi'ites detained by Israel, and only weeks before the hijacking had publicly urged that an effort be made to take Israeli soldiers hostage in the south. On that occasion, he had declared it more important to capture Israeli soldiers than to kill them, in order to force the release of the Shi'ite detainees.[174] But in the prevailing circumstances, this was a very tall order, and Hizbullah's impatient strongmen moved instead against a soft civilian target. As the hijacking unfolded, Hizbullah openly expressed its solidarity with the hijackers: "We stand with them in defense of the weak and oppressed. We announce that the political dimension of the detention of hostages is much more important than the humanitarian aspect which America has raised against the hijackers."[175] Hizbullah even organized an airport demonstration in their support. The hooded hijackers, surrounded by a group of Hizbullah's clerics, led the demonstrators in chants. One wing of the demonstration first assembled in the open square in front of Fadlallah's mosque.[176]

Fadlallah's name inevitably surfaced. It was reported that one of the hijackers came from his entourage of bodyguards; this Fadlallah denied.[177] But then he was pressed for his verdict on the acceptability of hijacking. Did he subscribe to the declared position of Hizbullah in support of the hijacking? On one hand, Fadlallah understood the "tight spot" in which those who had hijacked the plane found themselves. Word had come out that the Shi'ites imprisoned by Israel were being badly treated, and this had "created unrest among the detainees' families"; anxious for the safe return of their relatives, they "felt helpless to do anything to Israel that would make possible the release." Theirs too was a humanitarian cause.[178] And in retrospect, the hijacking had "many positive results."

It unified the ranks of the believers, directed world attention to the problem of Shi'ite detainees in Israel, and opened the eyes of some Americans to Israel's perfidy.[179]

Nevertheless, hijacking's "negative angles are more numerous," Fadlallah told his Friday prayer congregation. "We must not be enthusiastic about this method. There is no basis for our trying to put means of transportation in the world at the mercy of political slogans. Today you are a hijacker and tomorrow you are the one who is hijacked."[180] Nor was his objection limited to the fear of retribution. He had moral objections as well. Were the passengers on these aircraft "to be called criminals because they are citizens of countries who have interfered with us in certain cases?"[181] Fadlallah declared that "hijackings do not solve anything and do not wipe out American policy. . . . We are against hijackings as a means of political action. I am among those who believe that means of transport—of air, sea, or land—should be safeguarded and not tampered with."[182]

Fadlallah's careful calculation was not in harmony either with the hijackers or with Hizbullah's clerics, who had endorsed the action. Ultimately, it was Rafsanjani who proved decisive in bringing the TWA hijacking to an end and securing the release of Shi'ite detainees.[183] Fadlallah's arguments, while they complemented Rafsanjani's efforts, did not suffice to break the deadlock. Nor did they prevent a recurrence of such episodes, for the TWA hijacking had worked. Hijacking would be used by Hizbullah strongmen for several years to come, and only the absolute refusal of air controllers in Beirut to allow hijacked planes to land there prevented the TWA episode from being repeated in Fadlallah's backyard. The resort to hijacking, in clear repudiation of Fadlallah's logic, defined the limits of his influence too clearly for his comfort.

Apart from the hijackings, Fadlallah's suasion faced a perpetual challenge posed by the systematic taking of foreign hostages. Most of them were taken between 1984 and 1987, by groups bearing the names Islamic Jihad Organization, Revolutionary Justice Organization, and Islamic Jihad for the Liberation of Palestine.[184] In the seizure of the American embassy in Tehran, Fadlallah had witnessed how vented passion, producing immoral acts, might advance a moral cause. His logic had led him to accept the holding of American hostages in Tehran. But in the different circumstances of Lebanon, his calculation yielded a different verdict. Certainly, Fadlallah understood the motives of Iran's emissaries and the Hizbullah strongmen, who together conspired in the taking of the hostages; when hostages were held to secure the release of Hizbullah prisoners elsewhere, he held, the kidnappings could not be described as terrorism.

Had the Americans then responded in "a practical way," by accepting an exchange "according to the Lebanese practice," Fadlallah believed the hostage holding "would have ended and its file would have been closed without further suffering."[185] Instead the United States lost its composure, exploiting the hostage holding to declare a "war on terrorism."[186] Of course not all hostages were held against the release of relatives, and some were assigned a political price. Fadlallah did not completely discount the value of political hostage holding, such as was sanctioned by Iran as a means to force the United States and France to alter their policies. These abductions, despite their negative aspects, also might have certain "positive results."[187]

Yet when all was said and done, Fadlallah's opinion ran against hostage taking. His opening argument was couched in ethical terms and the moral philosophy of Islam, and drew upon the same sources as his opposition to hijacking. In his understanding, the seizure of innocent persons constituted wrongful punishment and contradicted the teachings of Islam. In support of his argument, Fadlallah consistently cited a verse from the Qur'an which said that "no burdened soul should be made to bear the burden of another"—applying it to the situation of innocent foreigners made to bear the burden of their governments' guilt.[188] Many of the hostages not only were personally innocent, but were "participants in cultural, medical, and social institutions" that benefited Muslims.[189] Nor was Fadlallah moved by the argument that the hostage taking defended the movement from the plots of foreign intelligence services. "With the kidnapping of foreigners, we lost much medical, scientific, and technical expertise. Some will say, 'There were spies among them.' True. But among ourselves there are thousands of spies. What of those who serve Israeli intelligence in the South, are they not from among us?"[190] "We know that foreign embassies deal in intelligence, as do many of the journalists. But we do not believe that kidnapping will achieve the goal it seeks, but rather will produce negative results. We can fight espionage in other ways."[191] Fadlallah was particularly resentful of the abduction of journalists, since his own burgeoning reputation owed so much to the ready access he granted to the press. Even if some were spies, they were sorely needed by the movement; therefore, he concluded, "we believe we should help journalists in their task to inform, whatever the negative aspects may be."[192]

Fadlallah thus rejected the practice of political hostage taking as "inhumane and irreligious."[193] As he tersely put it on one occasion, "We have actually not understood the nature of the Islamic thought of the Islamic Jihad Organization."[194] At first many hoped against hope that his influence, and that his power of persuasion, would prevail. Families of hostages, mediators, and Western ambassadors beat a path to his door. For a time it was flattering, as petitioners besieged his office and beseeched him for favors. He even took up the cause of a few hostages whose cases lay a special claim upon his conscience. One was the French sociologist Michel Seurat, a highly regarded student of Islam and ardent supporter of the Palestinian cause who was kidnapped by the Islamic Jihad Organization in 1985. "Countless are the people who have already intervened on your husband's behalf," Fadlallah told Seurat's Syrian wife during her audience. "You know I have done everything possible to try to find him."[195] No hostage could count on greater support among leading Shi'ite figures, and Fadlallah even signed a petition of Muslim leaders protesting Seurat's "unjustified detention" and calling for his "prompt release."[196] Another hostage who had a claim upon him was Terry Anderson, an American and chief Middle East correspondent of the Associated Press who was seized by the Islamic Jihad Organization in March 1985 — "a day after he had interviewed me," acknowledged Fadlallah.[197] Anderson's sister wrote to Fadlallah; he replied, expressing his sympathy and regret and affirming that he was doing all in his power to secure Anderson's release.[198] In 1989 Fadlallah claimed to have appealed directly for the release of hostages over fifty times.[199]

Fadlallah hoped his writ would run, that his preaching would "create a psychological situation that would bring pressure to bear on the kidnappers via the masses."[200] And among adherents of Hizbullah who venerated Fadlallah, especially the university students, he did succeed in fostering a sense that the holding of hostages was wrong.[201] But this did not suffice, and those who actually held the hostages, in consultation with Iran's emissaries, were completely unmoved by his moral and practical calculations. Fadlallah had to admit as much. "I wish that I could influence the people involved," he said. "I can confirm that I have done a great deal of work in this direction, but I have come across many closed paths."[202] Elsewhere he explained, "I stumbled against a wall because there is a mysterious force behind this practice."[203] That force prevented the release of Seurat even when he fell so ill that his continued detention meant death, and it made the incarceration of Anderson the longest of any hostage.

It was not only the reputation of Islam that suffered. The continued hostage holding fueled doubts about Fadlallah's own credibility and the extent of his moral influence. Some believed he was simply lying; Seurat's wife bitterly concluded that he was "involved in the kidnapping, up to his neck."[204] In one sense, he did conspire with the hostage holders: although his sources would have kept him current on the doings of the hostage holders, he kept his information to himself. Fadlallah would not threaten betrayal simply because his powers of suasion had failed. In return, the hostage holders did what they could to shore up his reputation, sometimes crediting him for staying their hands when they backed down from threats to kill hostages. These were token gestures, since cool calculation, not deference to Fadlallah, dictated the cycle of ultimatums. But in a typical instance, a group holding French hostages announced it had backed away from a death threat out of "appreciation and respect" for Fadlallah.[205] Was this complicity on his part with those who held the hostages, or with those who sought their release? Mediation, by its nature, held up ambiguity as a virtue. But however others interpreted his role, Fadlallah did not regard himself as a party to the hostage takings. Sincerity shone through his statement that "I would not have any self-respect if I had anything to do with them."[206]

The exquisite anomalies of this role defeated the analytical abilities of many an observer. In a characteristic instance, a foreign journalist dismissed Fadlallah as "little more than a façade," an actor reciting lines in a play directed by the hostage holders.[207] Quite the opposite: Fadlallah wrote his own script, forcing the hostage holders to make their own case in videotapes, telephone calls, and letters to the press. Occasionally he followed the cue of his ally Rafsanjani, who preferred to name the price for the exercise of his own influence indirectly. Fadlallah often obliged, issuing pronouncements on what the West should do next, incidentally getting his name in headlines and his photograph in the *Washington Post,* the *New York Times,* and *Time* magazine. As always, the publicity was welcome. He also had a hand in the back-channel transmission of negotiating positions, for he constituted a link in one of several winding chains of mediation between foreign governments and the hostage holders. He could communicate confidentially with the hostage holders, Iran's leaders and emissaries, and diplomats from mediating governments, especially that of Algeria. It was sometimes suggested that he exacted tribute for such services, but no one seemed to know this for a fact.[208] In any event, Fadlallah did not actively seek this role, and sometimes he dodged it, as in 1990 when former American president Jimmy Carter reportedly expressed an interest in meeting him. "I rejected this proposal," said Fadlallah, "because the subjects raised by Jimmy Carter are unrelated to me, especially the question of the hostages."[209] The really crucial negotiations circumvented him, and when credit was given for the successful release of hostages, it always went to governments and full-time mediators. The last French hostages were freed in 1988; the last Americans and British, in 1991; and the last Germans, in 1992. The carefully choreographed releases, which excluded Fadlallah altogether, brought the boundaries of his influence into striking relief. Or did they? In the end, his view prevailed. The debate he prompted had put the hostage holders in the moral docket before the only constituency that mattered: Muslim believers in the primacy of Islamic law. It is possible that hostage taking would have been practiced even more extensively had this debate never taken place, although no one could say this for certain.

SYRIA IN LEBANON

One thing, however, was certain: Syria garnered most of the credit for the releases, confirming its return to the Lebanese chessboard. Syria's military intervention in Lebanon began in 1976, and since then Syrian President Hafiz al-Assad had worked painstakingly to bring Lebanon into the orbit of Damascus. In 1982, Israel's invasion and America's deployment had disrupted Syria's plans; Syria reacted by opening Lebanon's back door to Iran's emissaries, who were invited to inspire resistance against the foreigners. Iranian Revolutionary Guards, money, weapons—everything on which Hizbullah depended passed through Syria. Damascus became the indispensable link in the import-export trade in Islamic revolution, and the partnership produced dramatic success.[210]

But secular Syria had its own vision for Lebanon, and it did not include an Islamic state. Indeed, Syria had a bloody record in dealing with Islamic movements, having pounded its own Islamic opposition to dust earlier in 1982 and shelled the Islamic movement in Tripoli into submission in 1985. Wasn't the Arab nationalist, Ba'thist creed of Syria intrinsically opposed to Islam? Now Syria seemed bent on gaining a hold upon all of Lebanon, including the strongholds of Shi'ism. Syria would collect the spoils from Islam's victory over Israel and the West. Why not resist the return of Syria, before it had a chance to entrench itself? Many turned to Fadlallah for an answer.

Once again, his answer demonstrated a finely-honed realism. Fadlallah knew that the ultimate aims of Syria and Hizbullah diverged. But it would be disastrous if they quarreled over those aims when they both still faced the imminent danger of Israeli domination. Yes, Israel appeared to be in retreat, but appearances deceived. Israel would not abandon its attempt to dominate Lebanon; without Syria's steadfastness, the country would be at Israel's mercy—and Iran would be powerless to save it. "Syria plays a positive role which benefits us," Fadlallah concluded in 1985. "It protects Lebanese Muslims and spares them forced cooperation with Israel."[211] Fadlallah's description of Syria as protector of the Muslims must have grated on many ears in Hizbullah, but this was a truth far too dangerous to ignore. "If relations with Syria were negative," warned Fadlallah, "the Muslims would have been squeezed into the Israeli corner."[212] Fadlallah did not become a supplicant at Syria's door, preferring to leave mundane dealings with Damascus to the functionaries of Hizbullah. But as Syrian agents and forces infiltrated Beirut, Fadlallah received more courtesy calls from Ghazi Kan'an, the head of Syrian military intelligence in Lebanon. More rarely, Fadlallah met personally with Assad in Damascus. The Syrians knew the limits of Fadlallah's influence, but they could rely on him to communicate the message of cooperation precisely and persuasively, from the pulpit and behind the scenes.

To make that cooperation palatable, Fadlallah took a conciliatory view of Arab nationalism, the declared creed of Ba'thist Syria. Most of Hizbullah's clerics railed against Arab nationalism as secular self-worship, inspired by foreign example and bankrupted by the 1967 Arab-Israeli war. Not so Fadlallah. Islamic activism and Arab nationalism both sought to liberate Palestine and shake off great-power domination, he argued. Arabism could serve as an acceptable basis of identity, provided it also inspired action against imperialism. Fadlallah rejected only that variety of Arab nationalism which drew upon Marxism and socialism, and which dismissed Islam as something that issued from Muhammad rather than God.[213] These smooth words of ideological ecumenism, which deliberately obscured the conflict between Islam and Arabism, eased Fadlallah's efforts to recruit supporters from the diminished ranks of the Arab nationalists. But above all, they served to lubricate the relationship between Hizbullah and Syria.

Fadlallah also played a crucial role in the management of several crises that tested the broad understanding between Syria and Hizbullah. The most serious occurred in February 1987: Syria decided to extend its hold to West Beirut, symbol of Lebanon's disorder, where fighting then raged between Amal and the Palestinians. Some seven thousand Syrian troops entered West Beirut in force and issued an ultimatum to all of the armed factions—including Hizbullah—to evacuate their bases there. But something went awry, and, in a violent clash, Syrian troops killed twenty-three members of Hizbullah, whom they alleged had resisted the takeover of their barracks.[214] The Dahiya filled with rage; some fifty thousand persons attended the funerals of the dead, shouting, "Death to Kan'an!"[215]

Fadlallah made the claim of Hizbullah: "Not one shot was fired at the Syrians. It was a cold-blooded massacre."[216] But instead of calling for revenge, he demanded the trial of the Syrian troops who had committed the outrage. This was an artful dodge, suggesting that the episode could be attributed to undisciplined soldiers. It was unthinkable, of course, that the Syrians would allow any of their soldiers to stand trial. But they played along with Fadlallah, admitting in an elliptical way that an "error" had occurred. So rare were Syrian admissions of error in Lebanon that this had the immediate effect of mollifying Hizbullah. Assad then received Hizbullah's leaders in Damascus in a gesture of reconciliation, and Fadlallah announced that "the incident is closed."[217] But its lesson were not forgotten. Hizbullah had learned not to test Syrian resolve, and Fadlallah had again shown his unfailing skill as a navigator of treacherous waters. "We take a strategic view of relations with Syria," he said a few months later. "Naturally, differences do occur, but we believe these matters can be brought under control in a mature and conscientious manner."[218] There would be no more uncontrolled "differences" with Syria.

Yet Fadlallah still found an ingenious way to assert the movement's independence from Syria. Many in Hizbullah routinely denounced Lebanon as a "geometric box," created by imperialism for imperialism. For Fadlallah, such talk merely played into the hands of those who favored annexation to Syria, and he began to enumerate the merits of an independent Lebanon. Granted, the West may have used Lebanon as a launching pad for imported ideologies and political schemes. But in Beirut's tower of Babel, the voice of Islam could also speak. If Lebanon became a virtual province of Syria, the Islamic movement might be strangled in its infancy. So while Fadlallah advocated cooperation with Syria against Israel, he became the most paradoxical defender of Lebanese independence. Once asked about the possibility of future union between Lebanon and Syria, Fadlallah replied that ties between the two countries "should be distinctive and realistic."[219] In the code of Lebanese political discourse, this was a reply of great precision. By "distinctive," Fadlallah meant that Syria and Lebanon should be bound by a special relationship; by "realistic," that the two states should remain separate entities. He then projected this view upon the Syrians themselves: "I do not think that there is a Syrian decision to remain in Lebanon forever, or that Syria wants to annex parts of Lebanon, because Syria has no need to do so, and because it is unrealistic in the conditions that now prevail in the region."[220]

And this, in Fadlallah's view, was very much for the better. As the prospects for Lebanon's revival grew, Fadlallah began to explain to Hizbullah the country's many advantages. "If Lebanon were overthrown, the Arab region would be deprived of one of its very few democracies," he warned. "Lebanon's cultural wealth and variety gives it an ability to influence its environment which exceeds that of any other country in this region, and its openness to the outside world is greater than that of any other Arab country. All this would be lost if Lebanon disappeared."[221] So, too, would Lebanon's potential as an amplifier for the message of Islam. Unlike other countries in the region, Lebanon had a free press and freedom to organize. "This gives the Islamists in Lebanon the opportunity to continue their political activities freely." True, Lebanon's heterogeneity made an Islamic republic impossible in the near term. "But the Lebanese Islamists can support Islamist movements in other countries" where the obstacles on the road to power were fewer.[222] Lebanon's variety and openness, counted by many in Hizbullah as vices, suddenly flowered into virtues in Fadlallah's fertile mind.

Fadlallah still had to pay deference to the idea that America ran Lebanon: "In our view, Lebanon is governed by America, even in the smallest details, even in regard to administrative, political and economic affairs."[223] But even if Lebanon did serve an American interest, its continued existence also served its inhabitants. As the Lebanese civil war wound down, Fadlallah sounded increasingly like a Lebanese patriot. He drew "hope from the fact that even after fifteen or sixteen years of conflict, Lebanon as a state is still present on the ground. Not even all these terrible convulsions have been able to erase Lebanon from the map. This must tell us something about the essential strength of the nation."[224] It was a stunning shift. Before and during the war, Fadlallah had preached that foreign intrigue perpetuated Lebanon. Now he announced that Lebanon had survived the war because its own people had willed it—and that they were right. Here was Fadlallah once again steering the ship of Islam through storm and strait—the master navigator, who knew just when to tack his sail.

THE SHI'ITE *FITNA*

Much more treacherous waters separated Hizbullah from Amal. Fadlallah had always understood the potential for Shi'ite strife in the establishment of Hizbullah. To win men and women away from Amal, Hizbullah had stirred up old resentments that split Shi'ite families, neighborhoods, villages, and towns. Hizbullah preached resistance to foreigners, but it also played upon distrust of neighbors. The massive influx of arms, provided to Amal by Syria and to Hizbullah by Iran, added new volatility to old feuds. And after Israel withdrew to its self-declared "security zone," the two movements began to contest the south, the center of gravity of Lebanese Shi'ism. On more and more occasions, small-scale violence erupted, in the form of gunfire and kidnapping between Hizbullah and Amal.[225]

The conflict percolated upward in August and September 1987. Nabih Birri, head of the Amal movement, came to Tyre in the south to address a rally marking the ninth anniversary of Musa al-Sadr's disappearance. There he let loose a barb at the clerics who led Hizbullah: "It is not enough to put on a turban, like a religious man, so as to become a theologian. . . . There are only five religious leaders authorized to lay down the law in Lebanon," one from each confessional community. He did not have to spell it out: everyone knew that of the Shi'ite clerics, the state recognized only the fatwas of Shaykh 'Abd al-Amir Qabalan, officially recognized as the Shi'ite mufti of Lebanon. Qabalan also happened to be a zealous supporter of Amal and a sharp critic of Iran. Birri's remarks, for all their apparent subtlety, represented a frontal assault on Fadlallah's immunity. Fadlallah bit back; Birri's words, he said, would be taken as "a sign for those who thrive on fanaticism to give free reign to their attacks and insults against all the wearers of the turban."[226] The exchange drew lines that could not be crossed. Fadlallah was asked a month later if he and Birri had met to hammer out their differences. Fadlallah replied that Birri was too busy to do so, and so was he.[227]

The situation deteriorated dramatically in February 1988, when Hizbullah abducted Lieutenant Colonel William Higgins, a U.S. Marine Corps officer and deputy commander of the United Nations Truce Supervision Organization (UNTSO) in the south. Higgins was seized as he returned from a meeting with a local Amal chief in Tyre. Hizbullah claimed that Higgins was a CIA spy, and Fadlallah sanctioned his kidnapping, arguing that "there is a difference between his abduction and the abduction of a plain civilian."[228] But the kidnapping had been done in defiance of Amal, on its own ground in the south. Angry Amal militiamen stormed Hizbullah's southern centers searching for Higgins, and a Shi'ite civil war seemed imminent. Yet Fadlallah steadfastly maintained that fighting would not break out. "The day will never come when Shi'ites fight one another," he declared. Those who predicted fighting did not understand the Shi'ite community, its many mechanisms of mediation, and its strong taboo against shedding Shi'ite blood.[229] Was he sure Hizbullah and Amal would not fight? "I'm one hundred percent sure," he replied.[230]

Fadlallah was wrong. In April, the south exploded in battles between the two Shi'ite factions—clashes of such ferocity that they matched any past battle waged between Shi'ite and non-Shi'ite. Hizbullah and Amal slid into *fitna*—internal strife, the antithesis of sacred war—pitting brother against brother in violence that threatened to gut the Shi'ite community. Fadlallah groped for an explanation, at first attributing the fighting to "agents of darkness who have transformed red lines into green lights."[231] But no one who witnessed the sheer cruelty of the warring sides believed that foreigners had fomented the conflict. Fadlallah eventually admitted that the strife did "not necessarily reflect direct American inspiration," and originated in "local disputes."[232] Shi'ites were not a race unto themselves, he concluded ruefully; they had been infected by the same passions as other Lebanese.[233]

The fighting soon swept the Dahiya as well, and continued with varying intensity for more than two years, claiming the lives of over a thousand Shi'ites. The weekly newspapers of the two movements repeatedly published photographs of the bullet-torn bodies of the dead. For Fadlallah, the fighting, whatever its outcome, represented a defeat for the Islamic trend. It was also a personal setback. Where were Fadlallah's famous powers of persuasion, and his supposed following in Amal? Fadlallah did preach passionately from his pulpit against the fighting, and he issued several general appeals for an end to the strife. He made his strongest appeal in May 1988, when the killing swept across the Dahiya: "The continuation of these destructive battles, which kill innocent civilians, children, women, and elderly, is inadmissible. Many youths are falling—youths we want as a force to fight Israel. The residential areas are not a battlefield. You are free to fight among yourselves, but you are not free to fight among civilians. Stop this mad and futile carnage."[234] But he frankly admitted that his appeals had no effect. And Fadlallah did not test his influence by issuing formal fatwas against internecine killing. Doing so in these circumstances, he said, was not a "practical matter."[235] Trying to position himself above the fray, Fadlallah denounced the "reckless, crazy war," and counseled Hizbullah to end it quickly. But he also asserted that Hizbullah did not start it.[236] Amal responded by multiplying the personal attacks against Fadlallah, especially in its press. Although Fadlallah called for dialogue, he became so enraged that he refused to meet with Birri when Iran tried to bring them together in Tehran.[237] But Fadlallah did not descend into the morass of charges and countercharges that accompanied the Shi'ite civil war. That would have been undignified; he would not reply to "insults."[238] He answered his critics in the dignified manner of a man above politics, by receiving delegations of admirers who arrived from all over Shi'ite Lebanon to show their support for him.[239]

The successive rounds of fighting ended in mediated cease-fires, and finally in an agreement negotiated by Syria and Iran in late 1990. But the scars remained. In 1993, Fadlallah claimed that "extensive cooperation and coordination" had been established between the Hizbullah and

Amal. But he also admitted that "some time is needed before all the resid-
ual negative sentiments that surfaced due to the conflict can be erased."[240]
Vengeance was the deepest of these sentiments, and it became the ever-
present shadow of the Shi'ites. Fadlallah, for all his persuasive powers,
could do little to banish it, for it bypassed minds and appealed directly
to wounded hearts.

ISLAM AND WORLD ORDER

The world did not stand still while Shi'ite battled Shi'ite. Old ideologies
buckled under the weight of economics, old conflicts moved toward resolution. The Iran-Iraq war ended in 1988. The Eastern bloc collapsed in
1989. The Berlin Wall fell in 1990. The Soviet Union dissolved in 1991.
Hizbullah turned to Fadlallah to decipher the meaning of these events,
and he obliged, offering intricate commentary that fascinated the journalists, even when he proved to be wrong.

He certainly seemed to be wrong about the Iran-Iraq war. "One journalist has said that this war will continue another twenty years," he announced in October 1987. "I share his opinion."[241] In fact, the war lasted
only nine more months, until the cease-fire of July 1988. But Fadlallah
did not intend his remark to be read as a prediction. He wanted to suggest
the futility of the war, at a time when many in Hizbullah still awaited
an imminent Iranian offensive that would carry Islam to victory. They
were shocked when Iran accepted a cease-fire, but Fadlallah quickly
praised the decision as an act of sober calculation. To his mind, it was
time for Iran to advance to the more important business of building a
workable Islamic order at home. "The previous phase was one of war
and building the Revolution," he announced. "The current phase is one
of peace and rebuilding the country."[242] Fadlallah's idea of revolutionary
phases was itself revolutionary. Most of the clerics in Hizbullah explained
the course of Iran's revolution and their own struggle by some analogy to
the early history of Islam. Their victories were analogous to the Prophet
Muhammad's triumphs, their setbacks evoked the suffering of the Imam
Husayn. But Fadlallah preferred analogies to the great ideological revolutions of modern times, as though he were addressing a class in comparative revolution. From that perspective, a revolution was bound to shed
its early zeal. "Like all revolutions, including the French Revolution, the
Islamic Revolution did not have a realistic line at first," he lectured his
listeners. "At that time, it served to create a state, it produced a mobilization, a new religious way of thinking and living, with the aim of winning
Muslim autonomy and independence from the superpowers. [But] the

new phase which should now be reached is the normalization of relations with the rest of the world."[243] To speak of the Islamic revolution like any other revolution—as human history, not divine plan—suggested that Fadlallah, as political philosopher, perhaps owed less to Muhammad than to Marx, more to Hegel than to Husayn.

But could Khomeini make the transition to the next phase? Khomeini's fatwa of February 1989 against Salman Rushdie, the Indian-born British author of *The Satanic Verses,* threw up a sudden, massive obstacle to any "normalization" of relations between Iran and the West. The zealots of Hizbullah were ecstatic, filling the streets of Beirut and Baalbek, where they burned British flags and threatened Rushdie with death. Fadlallah, who had just returned from three weeks in Iran and a meeting with Khomeini, defended the fatwa—after a fashion. "The Imam Khomeini did not err in his ruling *[hukm]* on Rushdie, either in its form or its timing."[244] But Fadlallah skirted Khomeini's demand for the death of the author. The fatwa, he announced, had the desired effect of influencing publishing houses against the book. Beyond that, it did not matter whether Rushdie was executed or not. "The issue is not whether this man is killed or isn't, whether the decree is carried out or isn't."[245] It did not even matter that Rushdie was an apostate, for there were plenty of apostates in the world. It only mattered that the West had used Rushdie's book "to infiltrate its ideas of human rights into the Islamic world." Islam had a different concept of human rights, which entailed a respect for free debate but not for the defamation of the sacred. The fatwa thus represented an act of self-defense and would remind the West to respect the feelings of one billion Muslims.[246] In the meantime, Fadlallah argued that the West should not allow the fatwa to block improved relations with Iran, since Khomeini issued it as the leader of all the world's Muslims, not as the leader of Iran.[247]

In fact, Fadlallah's position on Rushdie smacked of casuistry. Fadlallah would never have issued a call for the death of the novelist, but neither did he dare to contradict Khomeini. And so, for once, Fadlallah visibly squirmed. He had made an art of escaping from intellectual culs-de-sac, but Khomeini's unambiguous text left too little room for an elegant getaway. In the end, the Rushdie affair demonstrated that as long as Khomeini lived, Fadlallah could be pinned down by surprises from Iran, and suddenly compelled to defend the judgment of a higher Shi'ite authority. After Khomeini's death in 1989, it almost seemed as though a weight had been lifted from Fadlallah's shoulders. "It is necessary to employ new and different methods from those employed while [Khomeini] lived," said Fadlallah, only six months later.[248]

Fadlallah preferred the soft line. There were some in the West, including intellectuals and analysts, who longed for a reconciliation with Iran and were even prepared to make apologies for movements like Hizbullah. They had to be cultivated with words of moderation, not fiery fatwas. This could best be done by avoiding wholesale condemnations of the West and sticking to criticisms of specific American policies. If the Islamic movement showed a friendly face, this would bolster all those in the West who favored the appeasement of its political demands. For their benefit, Fadlallah wrote several articles for foreign consumption, all couched in his most conciliatory tone. "We are not against the American people," he wrote in an article prepared especially for an American audience. "On the contrary, we have many friends in the U.S., and consider its inhabitants a naturally good, tolerant people. Yet we oppose the U.S. administration's policy, which has been the root cause of many of our problems and those of the American people."[249] Such statements won Fadlallah even more admirers abroad, especially among Americans who already opposed their government's Middle East policies. And Fadlallah did not always rule out the possibility of an eventual accommodation with Western governments. "I do not take a negative view of relations with the big powers," he stressed. "We, as a community that is part of this world, should have positive relations with all the world's countries." Those relations could be improved if the West simply understood that Muslims had interests too: "We appreciate that the U.S. and other countries have their interests in the world. We have no wish to jeopardize their interests, but it is our right not to allow their interests to destroy our interests."[250] This seemed reasonable enough, and Western testimonials to Fadlallah's "moderation" began to mount.

But to his Muslim audiences, Fadlallah provided a very different vision. A decade after Iran's revolution and Hizbullah's heroic sacrifices, the Americans seemed stronger than ever. The collapse of the Soviet Union left the United States as the sole great power, and its influence over the Middle East grew exponentially. Far from turning the tide against America, the famous bomb attacks in Beirut now looked like minor skirmishes. After Iraq invaded Kuwait in 1990, the United States showed its real power, quickly crushing an Iraqi army that Iran had failed to defeat in eight years of war. The victorious American president, who as vice-president had visited the smoldering ruins of the marines barracks in Beirut, announced that the United States would build a "new world order." "The U.S. is engulfing the world through its media," observed Fadlallah, "saying that it is master of the world."[251] There were some, even Islamists, who talked despairingly of the need to come to an accommodation with the "reality" of American power.[252] Fadlallah made it perfectly clear that he did not count himself among them.

"We believe that reports about the multifaceted and unrivaled strength of the United States are greatly exaggerated," he declared.[253] While America loomed large in the world, "its shadow is greater than its substance. It possesses great military power, but that power is not supported by commensurate political or economic strength."[254] Like the Soviet Union, the United States faced economic crisis, compounded by domestic divisions of race which exploded from time to time. There were differences between the Soviet Union and the United States, but in the final analysis they were both swollen politically and militarily, and diseases wracked their bodies politic.[255] "We therefore believe that the fall of global arrogance is possible," Fadlallah concluded.[256] "Here and there we see the chinks in the armor of the United States, and we can penetrate these chinks and enlarge them."[257]

But rising up against a great power required the building of Islam's own potential. That potential was immense. "We are powerful," declared Fadlallah,

> but we do not know how to mold our power, how to amass it. We are powerful, but we squander our power with our own hands, and we give the enemy power. As Muslims in the world, we are powerful in our natural resources, powerful in our numbers, powerful in our capabilities, powerful in our geographic situation—but we strive to weaken ourselves.[258]

What would it take to realize the potential of Islam? Strength of spirit— wedded, so Fadlallah imagined, to the tangible power conferred by arms. Fadlallah believed that Islam eventually would acquire enough of them to qualify as a great power in its own right. "We might not have the actual power the U.S. has," Fadlallah admitted. "But we had the power previously and we have now the foundations to develop that power in the future. We might wait 20, 30, or 40 years before we will be able to attain that power."[259] This could be read as an argument for an Islamic nuclear capability, and Fadlallah left little doubt that he favored it. "We see that many states have nuclear weapons, and it poses no great problem," Fadlallah complained. "But when it is reported that an Islamic country wants nuclear weapons to defend itself against another state that has them, the arrogant use all their pressure and power to prevent this state from acquiring weapons that would strengthen it."[260] In the present situation, the United States and Israel could intimidate the Muslims with threats that the next war would be a nuclear one, an argument "intended to defeat us before we even enter battle."[261] To stand up to such intimidation, Muslims needed their own weapons of mass destruction. And so while Fadlallah regarded Saddam Hussein as a criminal, he still rejected the destruction of Iraq's weapons after the Iraqi defeat: "We oppose the tyrant of Iraq, but Iraq's weapons are not the tyrant's property, they belong to the Iraqi people."[262] The destruction of these weapons had drained the power of the Muslims, who now had to find ways to restore, and extend, their power.[263]

It was obvious that Fadlallah regarded "normalization" and proliferation as complementary, not contradictory. Normalization would create political conditions in which Islam, led by Iran, could make, buy, or steal the keys to the power still locked in the atom. (There was ample precedent for such a pattern of acquisition, as when the United States, on the mere promise of normalization, sold arms to Khomeini.) And proliferation would finally create a true normalization—a balance of power between Islam and the West, superseding the abnormal state in which "global arrogance" commanded millions of times the destructive power of the combined forces of Islam. Fadlallah's idea of Islamic empowerment therefore went far beyond any simple modification of American policy in the Middle East. In the longer term of a generation or two, he envisioned a fundamental shift of world power in favor of Islam. "Power is not the eternal destiny of the powerful," he reminded his followers. "Weakness is not the eternal destiny of the weak."[264] The weak would obtain that power if, deep within themselves, they kept alive the spirit of rejecting global arrogance.[265]

Fadlallah had become the foremost philosopher of power in contemporary Islam. Beneath the soft line of normalization, he nurtured the vision of Islam's return to its proper status as a world power. If Islam were to avoid being destroyed, it would have to defend itself; if it were to realize its destiny, it would have to dominate others. The West could not be allowed to end history now, or to create a "new world order" resting on a gross disequilibrium in its favor. The West's own vision had to be resisted—and the first test would be the West's attempt to "normalize" the abnormality known as Israel.

THE THREAT OF PEACE

While Fadlallah explained the great world issues of the day, he kept one ear firmly to the ground of Lebanon. In the confrontation with "global arrogance," Lebanon's Muslims had the clearly defined task of driving Israel from Lebanese territory. This did not seem to be beyond even the limited power of the Shi'ites. In 1985, Israel had withdrawn from most of the south to a "security zone," largely as a result of guerrilla attacks by the Islamic Resistance. The following year, Fadlallah clearly stated Hizbullah's next objective: "We want the Israelis to withdraw from southern Lebanon without having to recognize Israel in return, as Egypt had to do in return for withdrawal from the Sinai."[266] This was to be achieved through a steady war of attrition against Israeli forces and the SLA—the South Lebanon Army, a client militia created by Israel to patrol the security zone.

The attrition proved anything but steady. From 1988 to 1990 Shi'ites shot at Shi'ites, and the Islamic Resistance launched only sporadic attacks against the Israelis. The struggle against Israel resumed only in late 1990, after Hizbullah and Amal reached an accord. By the spring of 1991, Fadlallah declared the Islamic Resistance back on course and ready for its mission. "It is not impossible to suppose that the Islamic Resistance could inflict such losses on the enemy as to force him to pull out of the 'zone,' just as the Israelis withdrew from the rest of the South between 1983 and 1985 as a result of Resistance operations."[267] From his pulpit, Fadlallah continued to preach resistance with all his persuasive force. He promised the fighters of the Islamic Resistance that they, not the diplomats, would write the next page of history. And he implored the inhabitants of the security zone to reject recruitment into the SLA and to rise up against occupation.

But the security zone held. The SLA, not Israeli forces, absorbed most of the attacks, and Israeli casualties did not mount fast enough to make a difference. Israel also rediscovered the power of artillery, raining down shells upon the villages just north of the security zone whenever they gave shelter to Islamic Resistance fighters. As a result, some in these villages charged the Islamic Resistance with callous disregard for their suffering. Other Lebanese also questioned the logic of resistance. Lebanon had previously rejected Israeli offers to withdraw from all of Lebanon in exchange for a peace treaty and security guarantees, invoking a 1978 United Nations Security Council resolution that called for a unilateral Israeli withdrawal.[268] But when Israel rejected the resolution and dealt out retribution of fire for attacks against it, the war-weary of Lebanon began to question the point of resistance. Would peace with Israel really be worse than continued Israeli occupation and retaliation? To argue that it would be, Hizbullah had to paint the blackest possible picture of Israel—at the very moment when many Arabs had begun to see Israel in its full complement of colors. The task of persuasion fell squarely on Fadlallah. Again he conjured up images of a voracious Israel—hungry not for territory but for economic domination. Israel's peace was far more threatening than Israel's war, for it would unleash a plague of Jews upon Lebanon's innocent Shi'ites: "Were it not for the Resistance, you would see all the Jews swarming over the South and the Bekaa in absolute freedom, corrupting the land and its people."[269] Recognition of Israel would open the door a crack, and Israel would rush in. The Islamists had to oppose peace with Israel "even if they remain the last rejectionist voice."[270] The villages of the south were the front line of Islam in this struggle for survival, and they had to shoulder the burden. Fadlallah called upon them to sacrifice, while Hizbullah promised ever-larger sums of money to help them stand steadfast against Israel.

But history lurched in a different direction. In October 1991, the United States orchestrated a stunning breakthrough: Israel sat down with Arab states, including Lebanon, in direct peace negotiations. Iran quickly summoned a conference to oppose the talks, which Fadlallah attended and addressed.[271] On this and every other opportunity, Fadlallah painted a grim picture of the likely outcome of the peace talks: "The Golan will remain occupied, the West Bank and Gaza will get municipal administration, but defense, security, and foreign affairs will all stay with the Jews."[272] In the end, the Palestinians would be reduced to a national minority, while Israel would receive Arab and Palestinian—perhaps even Islamic—recognition of its legitimacy.[273] Israel then would become the policeman of the entire Arab world.[274] The duty of the believers in these dire circumstances was clear: "We need to encircle this plan and foil it by active means, which force the re-creation of the Palestine problem in the consciousness of the Islamic nation as *the* central Islamic problem."[275]

Yet Fadlallah did not delude himself—or his followers. Syria also sat at the negotiating table opposite Israel, discussing a possible trade of occupied land for peace. Syria did not prevent the Islamic Resistance from launching operations, but it imposed more and more restrictions, especially limiting attacks during the negotiating rounds. Now that the cadence of the talks dictated Hizbullah's armed operations, it became impossible to sustain a guerrilla war that had any chance of driving Israel from its security zone. As one negotiating round followed another in 1992, Fadlallah's tone gradually changed: the forcible expulsion of Israel from the south faded into the distance. "The Islamic Resistance cannot expel the occupier in its present capabilities," he ruefully concluded, "unless God performs a miracle and shows His power. . . . We are a people who believes in miracles, but God has instructed us to act according to His law, and not to base our life on miracles."[276] What seemed possible only a few years earlier now required nothing short of divine intervention.

After the election of a new Israeli government in mid-1992, the cloud of peace over Hizbullah grew even darker, and Fadlallah's statements reflected a growing resignation. "Israel has now become an undisputed fact on the ground, indeed, one of the strongest facts on the international scene, whether we like it or not."[277] Syria would also come under pressure to make concessions, and "if Israel signs a peace agreement with Syria," he warned, "peace with Lebanon will also be achieved."[278] Fadlallah took no solace in the fact that the Syrian-Israeli talks seemed stalemated. "The talks are moving at a snail's pace in order to condition the Arab mentality to accept Israel through this continuous dialogue. This phase is one of normalization through negotiations."[279] Adepts who listened closely to Fadlallah might conclude that he thought peace inescapable. But Fadlallah did not despair. Hizbullah still had a vital role to play, even if Lebanon were forced to make peace with Israel:

> The battle which will commence after reconciliation with Israel will be the battle against the subjugation of the Arab and Muslim person to Israel, in politics, culture, economics, and security. In the vocabulary of the Qur'an, Islamists have much of what they need to awaken the consciousness of Muslims, relying on the literal text of the Qur'an, because the Qur'an speaks about the Jews in a negative way, concerning both their historical conduct and future schemes. The Islamists must deploy their Qur'anic and Islamic legal culture to combat normalization. Fatwas should be issued against purchasing Israeli goods and receiving the Israelis. The Islamists may not enjoy complete success, because not all Muslims are committed to Islam. But this will hamper much of the effort by Israel to encircle the region and become a natural member in it.[280]

In the past, planning for the eventuality of peace with Israel would have been considered defeatist. Now it seemed essential if Hizbullah were to survive. Fadlallah's thought reflected his dwindling expectations regarding armed struggle and a foreboding that the United States would succeed in cobbling together agreements between Israel and the regimes of the Arab world. When it did, Hizbullah would adopt a new strategy of political and social action against normalization—to prevent the peace between governments from becoming peace between peoples.

Fadlallah still preached Islamic resistance, and even backed a major escalation. In 1992, he sanctioned Hizbullah's decision to fire rockets into northern Israel in retaliation for Israeli shelling of villages. True, he had reservations about the use of rockets against civilian targets. But Hizbullah did not initiate the victimization of civilians: "Israel kills our children and elderly and shells our villages while it sits in safety. . . . It must be made clear to Israel that when one of our civilians is killed by its rockets, a Jewish civilian will also be killed by one of our rockets."[281] But eye-for-eye exchanges would never liberate the south. At best they might drain Israeli resources and perhaps give "the delegations conducting the negotiations cards to play."[282] Fadlallah expected that one day the Syrian and Lebanese governments would play just those cards, restraining the Islamic Resistance in return for American and Israeli concessions. In 1993, the Syrian and Lebanese governments did compel Hizbullah to stop the rocket firings against Israel, after a massive Israeli bombardment of the south; in the future, Fadlallah expected, they would force Hizbullah to lay down its arms altogether. But he urged Hizbullah not to despair when that day arrived. "If the Islamists freeze their military actions against Israel," he consoled them, "this will not mean they have sheathed their swords. It means they will seek every opportunity, however small, to continue the confrontation, even in a narrow margin, until the situation changes."[283]

Only if the Islamic movement adapted to change could it survive to fight another day. Fadlallah saw this clearly and spoke it frankly. Unless God worked a miracle, the United States would force Arab regimes to make peace with Israel, and the Islamic movement would have to translate the concept of Islamic resistance into a struggle for minds. But Fadlallah also assured the believers that their victory would come—and that it would come sooner if Hizbullah threw its turban in the ring of Lebanese parliamentary politics.

BALLOTS FOR GOD

In Lebanon, too, an era of domestic conflict drew to an end. The political and sectarian passions that had held the country in their thrall since 1975 began to loosen their grip. People were tired of war and the arrogance of militias; they longed to rebuild their lives and make money. Syria, Saudi Arabia, and the United States all sensed the exhaustion, and in 1989 they persuaded a majority of Lebanon's surviving parliamentarians to sign an agreement in the Saudi resort town of Ta'if. The so-called Ta'if Accord envisioned the eventual creation of a nonconfessional, democratic Lebanon, free of all foreign forces. But the interim stage provided for a revamped confessional order, based on Muslim-Christian parity. Syria guaranteed implementation of the agreement, which included the disarming of all militias, in return for a privileged standing that amounted to a shadow protectorate over Lebanon. The legitimacy of the new order was to be confirmed by general parliamentary elections, which had not been held since 1972.

Hizbullah was not a party to the agreement, and viewed it with apprehension. The movement had flourished like a weed in the untended garden of Lebanon, and its leaders shuddered at the prospect of a strong government in Beirut, backed by Syria. Furthermore, the agreement perpetuated confessionalism. How could an Islamic state ever be created if the Christian minority were guaranteed a virtual veto over the Muslim majority? Fadlallah added his voice to Hizbullah's denunciations of the accord. He portrayed it as "an American project which needed an Arab headdress and a Lebanese fez." The complex negotiations that had surrounded it were "mere theatrics."[284] By Fadlallah's reckoning, those who met at Ta'if represented only about a quarter of the Lebanese people, and their deal had entrenched Lebanon's "corrupt confessional framework." Fadlallah saw only two positive achievements in the plan: it "canceled" the war and put an end to calls for the country's partition.[285]

Of course, such criticism could only go so far. Given Syria's determination to enforce the accord, Hizbullah dared not try to block its implementation. But should Hizbullah boycott the parliamentary elections it called for? Some in Hizbullah thought the movement should have nothing to do with the rehabilitated state. Others pointed out that in other Arab countries, pressures from below had pushed regimes toward half-measures of democratization, and Islamic movements had decided to participate in the resulting parliamentary elections. Some of these movements had scored impressive results, despite the fact that regimes often rigged elections against them. Now that revolution in Lebanon had failed, might not Islam reach for power through democracy? As parliamentary elections drew nearer, Hizbullah agonized over its options—and turned to Fadlallah.

Fadlallah first considered general principles, contrasting the Islamic ideal with democracy and finding that the two could not be reconciled. "The idea of 'popular sovereignty' is an idea that is foreign to Islamic thought, because rule in Islam is a prerogative of God. It is God who appointed the Prophet; it is God who prescribed the general precepts for rule."[286] Therefore, Islam could not be reconciled with a form of government that "accords the majority the right to legislate in opposition to Islamic law."[287] No parliamentary majority, however large, could overturn the will of God, as codified in his law. "Naturally we are not democrats, in the sense that we would allow the people to legislate in contradiction to God's law."[288]

Still, there was a role for the people to play. They had to "develop a mode for dealing with political and social questions or filling gaps in Islamic law which Islam leaves to administrative discretion."[289] The instrument for filling the gaps was known as *shura,* or consultation. Even the Prophet took no action of war or peace without first consulting his companions. And although God did not require him to do so, the Prophet asked the Muslims for an oath of allegiance—a vote of confidence, as it were.[290] An Islamic system of government had to be based on such consultation. "The role of the consultative council is not to legislate," Fadlallah stressed, "but to investigate the Islamic laws at their sources, and to examine new matters of economic and political administration in relation to general Islamic legal rules." In Fadlallah's view, members of the consultative council could be elected by the people, as in Iran, all the way through the office of president.[291] These elected leaders had to act within "broad Islamic lines" and would be accountable to the people. They were not to be regarded as infallible, and would have to allow freedom for those advocating different strategies and tactics.[292]

How much freedom? Quite a bit, Fadlallah sometimes suggested. Political pluralism promoted the development of thought, he said, and could be reconciled with Islam. Some Muslims argued that Islam had to be protected from debate, but Fadlallah pointed out that, in historical experience, the denial of pluralism produced effects opposite to those that were intended. Islam would be better served by allowing this pluralism, "within limits that will protect the Islamic line, while not infringing on the freedom of people."[293] At times, however, Fadlallah narrowed those limits considerably. Parties and movements were the most effective means of political organization of the people, and they would be permitted— but only if they were Islamic. Islam gives the nation "the right to choose, but this does not mean unlimited choice. Rather, it is restricted to the content of Islamic thought."[294]

> As for non-Islamic parties and organizations, the Islamic view is that they can have no role in Islamic society or the Islamic state, because they represent an alternative to Islam in thought, law, and way of life. It is not natural that they should enjoy freedom, because that would mean granting freedom to overthrow the Islamic order, to weaken the appeal of Islam, and to allow unbelievers and the arrogant to infiltrate the Islamic nation and end its intellectual and political struggle, all by "legal" means. Islam cannot permit this on principle.[295]

Lebanon without freedom had no meaning, Fadlallah once declared: "Freedom is the table from which we all eat."[296] But he would restrict the country's heretofore varied political diet to that of Islam.

This was the Islamic ideal. But in the real world, it was the Islamic state that did not appear on the menu. And in these dire circumstances, even democracy could be made palatable. True, observed Fadlallah, democracy was deeply flawed. But it had some positive content: respect for others, the search for objective justice, and the rejection of tyranny. There were many forms of government that were far worse. Thus, even the principled rejection of democracy by Islamists

> should not prevent them from cooperating positively with democracy in states whose character has no Islamic content, if it is a matter of choosing between democracy and tyranny. Democracy should be chosen and tyranny rejected, because Islamists can then exercise their freedom to spread Islam and revive it, and rally the people around it, and so advance the cause of Islam or achieve total control by will of the majority. Islamists would have no such freedom under a dictatorial regime. This certainly does not mean recognition by the Islamists of democratic rule, either in thought or practice. It is accommodation to reality, and to the freedoms accorded to the Islamic movement (alongside non-Islamic movements) to contest one another.[297]

Accommodation to reality? Some in Hizbullah recoiled at the very idea of joining Lebanon's notorious political game, arguing that there was no way they could win total control. If they remained a parliamentary minority, their presence in parliament legitimated a non-Islamic state; if they gained a parliamentary majority, they would be crushed, as happened in Algeria. Better to concentrate on jihad and avoid the pollution of politicking. This view was championed by Shaykh Subhi al-Tufayli, one of the most senior clerics in Hizbullah, who enjoyed widespread support in the Bekaa Valley.[298]

Fadlallah strongly disagreed. History demonstrated that jihad movements that had no political dimension became stepping stones for others. Without a political dimension, "we would liberate the South, for example, but others would harvest the fruit of this liberation, according to their own political plans." And since the road of jihad was blocked, just what did his opponents propose? To "sit in their seats, waiting for the Prophet to send down angels to clear the way for them to take power here or there"?[299] Fadlallah favored complete immersion in politics, as the only way to break out of the growing encirclement of Islamic resistance and jihad.[300] In the context of Lebanon, this meant full participation in the parliamentary elections. Fadlallah believed that Lebanon's national assembly provided a powerful and protected platform for carrying the message of Islam: "Parliament represents an advanced propaganda podium for the Islamists. . . . In this way, you can pass a law for Islam here, and secure a position for Islam there."[301] A decade after Hizbullah's creation, Fadlallah urged the "party of God" to become a real political party, and its clerics to become candidates. The party's platform would be the welfare of the dispossessed and rejection of peace with Israel. Party politics also meant coalition politics, and Fadlallah began to meet with a remarkably wide range of political leaders, from communists to Phalangists.

Still, Fadlallah was in no rush to the ballot box. When Syria began to press for elections for the summer of 1992, Fadlallah hesitated. "If elections are to be free of any pressure," he announced, they should be conducted only after 1994.[302] Wary of Syrian manipulation of the polls, Fadlallah apparently presumed that Syria would allow a freer contest at a later date. But by summer he had changed his mind. If elections were postponed until after the withdrawal of all foreign forces—Syrian and Israeli—they might not be held for four or five years, by which time there might be an Arab-Israeli peace accord. It would be too late for Hizbullah to fight the peace in parliament. To those in Hizbullah who asked how Lebanon possibly could have free and fair elections under Syrian domination, Fadlallah pointed out that Lebanon had never in its entire history had such elections.[303]

This time, Fadlallah's persuasive power prevailed. Iran joined him in urging Hizbullah to contest the parliamentary elections scheduled for the summer of 1992, and the movement did just that, fielding candidates in all Shi'ite areas. Hizbullah's electoral machine mounted a slick campaign, more evocative of Tammany than Tehran. It spent money lavishly and struck preelection deals with Amal, the Progressive Socialist Party (Druze), two Sunni Islamic parties, and several independents. Given the limitations of the electoral system, the results were impressive. Hizbullah's candidates swept Baalbek and Hirmil, and took the most votes in Nabatiyya and Tyre. All eight Hizbullah candidates were elected to the 128-member body, making Hizbullah the largest single party in a parliament formed mostly of deputies who were personally subservient to Syria. There were rival blocs of deputies formed around one or another personality, such as Nabih Birri, but these remained unstable groupings. Hizbullah had the firmest foothold in the resurrected parliament.[304]

Hizbullah had every reason to be pleased with the results. But no decision ever came so close to precipitating an open rift in the movement. Tufayli resigned his position on the consultative council and returned to his home in the Bekaa Valley to sulk and grant interviews. The movement had lost touch with its militant principles, he maintained. Fadlallah never discussed the increasingly frequent reports of differences within Hizbullah, but he left no doubt as to his personal view of those who clung to old slogans. "It is unrealistic to talk about achieving complete power in Lebanon," Fadlallah said bluntly after the elections. So too was the idea that the Islamists could create an Islamic republic. None of the existing parties in Lebanon could make the country in its image; for the foreseeable future, Lebanon would remain "unstable," torn among conflicting visions. Still, the Islamists were as Lebanese as anyone, and could work within Lebanon's institutions to achieve some of their objectives.[305] It all made eminent sense. Yet paradoxically, while Fadlallah urged Hizbullah to narrow its ambition to Lebanon, he expanded his own ambition to encompass the globe.

THE GRAND AYATOLLAH

As Hizbullah took its place in the Lebanese "political club," Fadlallah positioned himself to join the pantheon of grand ayatollahs. Fadlallah never spoke of his own standing in contemporary Shi'ism. To do so would have been considered bad form, since convention demanded that a man of God always show humility. Yet on rare occasions his pride did show. "I am the one who established and set up in Lebanon 80 percent of the Islamic condition since I came to this country," he once boasted.[306] And he pointed to followers far beyond the narrow frontiers of Lebanon: "I am concerned with the Islamic level, not the Lebanese, and I have Islamic ties in the Arab world and perhaps in Europe, America, and Africa."[307]

This claim suggested the direction of his ambition. He did not want to be regarded as the guide, spiritual or otherwise, of Hizbullah; to hold any office conferred by the state of Lebanon; or to head the Supreme Islamic Shi'ite Council. Instead he aspired to winning recognition as one of the handful of Shi'ite clerics who could claim a universal following. Fadlallah was born and bred in a world where a few men, seated at the pinnacle of Shi'ism, commanded the unlimited respect and passionate veneration of believers from London to Lucknow. Everything in Fadlallah's long preparation had positioned him to assume the mantle of a grand ayatollah. To do so, he had to play by certain traditional rules. But by his time, the tradition had been bent so far out of shape that he could dare to manipulate it to his own advantage.

Khomeini had also bent tradition. Before him, the leading Shi'ite clerics had exercised an authority known as *marja'iyya*, from the Arabic root for "source." A few clerics who best knew Islam's sources became sources of guidance in their own right, usually after a lifetime of study in Shi'ite seminaries. Believers referred back to them for rulings on contested or ambiguous questions. Some of these questions might be political, but the clerics did not claim the authority to govern, only to guide. They admonished rulers to adhere to the precepts of Islam, but they did not see themselves as potential rulers. There were usually several clerics who were acknowledged widely as guides, so that the *marja'iyya* need not be concentrated in one hand. However, at times a wide consensus formed around one or another cleric, whose *marja'iyya* became virtually absolute.

It was Khomeini, during his years of exile in Iraq, who challenged the notion that clerics should leave government to others. He based his position on a saying attributed to the Prophet Muhammad which vested the clerics with another kind of authority, known as *wilaya,* or guardianship. Like all sayings, this one was open to multiple interpretations. Who precisely did the Prophet intend to place under the guardianship of clerics? Traditional Shi'ite interpretation held that the Prophet merely intended that clerics should serve as guardians for the orphaned and the insane. Khomeini, however, argued that the Prophet enjoined clerics to claim guardianship over the entire community of believers. Islam mandated not only the implementation of Islamic law, he argued, but also government by the most qualified Muslim jurisprudent, the *faqih.* This expansion of the guardianship of the jurisprudent, known as *wilayat al-faqih,* became Khomeini's revolutionary contribution to Shi'ite thought. He presented his views most systematically in lectures delivered in Najaf in 1970. Those Shi'ite clerics who accepted his premise became active claimants to power, denying the legitimacy of all existing governments. Khomeini personified his own doctrine. He personally led the political struggle for the overthrow of the Shah's regime, and when the revolution triumphed, he emerged as the constitutionally empowered "leader" of Iran. His foremost students left their seminaries for the highest positions in government.[308]

Yet not all of the leading Shi'ite clerics concurred with Khomeini's expansive view of their authority. Perhaps his most worthy opponent was Fadlallah's own teacher, Kho'i, who continued to teach in Najaf. Kho'i maintained that the most a cleric might do was to supervise government from afar, to assure that it conformed with the law of Islam. Clerics had no business exercising mundane political power, as Khomeini argued. Jurisprudents belonged in the Shi'ite seminaries, where they had a duty to preserve the inherited knowledge and learning of past generations. Kho'i himself set a personal example, refraining from any involvement in the politics of Iraq and avoiding all comment on contemporary affairs. His best-known treatises dealt with ritual purity. His traditional stand also had many supporters, and not just in Najaf: Kho'i's foundation presided over institutes in New York, Detroit, Toronto, London, Islamabad, Bombay, and Beirut, all supported by tithes from his followers worldwide.

By the time this debate began, Fadlallah had left Najaf for Beirut. But he could not escape the great dividing issue of contemporary Shi'ism, which soon divided Lebanon's Shi'ites as well. Khomeini's lectures appeared in a Beirut edition in 1979, and a noted Lebanese Shi'ite scholar quickly published a book that argued the opposing position.[309] Fadlallah faced a difficult choice. He had studied under Kho'i, whom he officially represented in Beirut. His aged teacher presided over a far-flung empire of influence, in which Fadlallah occupied a prominent place. Yet Fadlallah's own immersion in politics bound him to Khomeini, and his identification with Iran's revolution had made him into an influential player and an international celebrity. Although his stature had grown—after 1985, his followers began to address him as Ayatollah Fadlallah—the debate over *wilaya* involved the very definition of Shi'ism, and it could only be conducted by Khomeini and Kho'i, who were some thirty-five years his seniors.

Fadlallah accepted Khomeini's general authority, but by choice, not by obligation. In his eyes, Khomeini was not the sole authority, and other clerics could inspire "high esteem." Indeed, as a matter of theoretical principle, Fadlallah did not rule out the possibility that other clerics could exercise the same kind of authority as Khomeini, in other parts of the Muslim world. Fadlallah knew the arguments for the unity of leadership, particularly the examples of the Prophet Muhammad and the Imams, who had been entitled to exclusive obedience in every corner of Islam. Fadlallah also admitted the possibility that a multiplicity of leaderships might create chaos, as different clerics might rule differently on the same matters. "But there is another view," he stated gingerly,

> which holds that multiplicity in rule during the absence of the Imams is not a deviation from the theory, since the text which speaks about *wilayat al-faqih* does not speak about the exclusive, comprehensive dimension of guardianship, but instead speaks about a general principle that can be applied to many of the jurists, among whom these qualifications [to rule] are plentiful, so that each one of them is a deputy of the Imam.

In other words, if the Muslims of one land made a qualified person their ruler, "at the same time the Muslims of another land could agree on a different person who has the same qualities, and vest him with rule over their affairs." As to the argument that the most learned cleric was entitled to exclusive and universal authority, Fadlallah emphasized "a weak point in this argument: the difficulty of the community in agreeing on the definition of the most learned." Fadlallah thus concluded that "on the basis of the juristic data in our hands, we do not find any impediment to the multiplicity of states, and the multiplicity of leaderships."[310]

The far-reaching implications of Fadlallah's view were self-evident. If his argument was admissible, Lebanon's Muslims need not follow Iran's chosen "guardian." They were free to choose a guardian of their own, provided he combined the qualifications of a most learned jurisprudent. Indeed, the multiplicity of such authority constituted the natural order, for "in every generation there are two or three religious leaders in the Shi'ite community."[311] Such an argument clearly contradicted the message of Iran's emissaries, who insisted upon total submission to Khomeini and promised Lebanon's eventual inclusion in a vast "central Islamic state." Some in Hizbullah were scandalized by Fadlallah's views and sought to refute and rebuke him publicly. Only the better judgment of Iran's emissaries prevented an unseemly public debate over Fadlallah's ideas.[312]

Fadlallah thus gave himself room to maneuver on the most burning issue in contemporary Shi'ism. He put forth no comprehensive theory of his own, however, knowing that while Khomeini and Kho'i lived, they alone defined the terms of the debate. Khomeini died in 1989, at the age of eighty-six. Iran's Assembly of Experts elected Sayyid 'Ali Khamenei, Khomeini's most trusted student, to succeed him as Iran's "leader." Khamenei had impeccable revolutionary credentials, but he was not even an ayatollah at the time of his election, at the tender age of fifty. While Fadlallah formally welcomed the choice, his supporters let it be known that their man did not regard Khamenei as his better.[313] And Fadlallah himself was quick to point out again that there was no consensus about the meaning of *wilayat al-faqih,* especially on the point of its universality.[314] Fadlallah clearly expected that with Khomeini's passing, the *wilaya* of his elected successor would contract to the frontiers of Iran. He obviously welcomed that contraction.

Kho'i died in 1992, at the age of ninety-three, a virtual hostage of the Iraqi regime. This opened the wider question of the *marja'iyya,* a form of authority quite independent of the Iranian state, conferred by the informal consensus of clerics in the Shi'ite seminaries. Such a consensus soon emerged around Ayatollah Sayyid Muhammad Reza Golpayegani of Qom, also ninety-three, whose views on politics resembled those of Kho'i. Even before this, Fadlallah had begun to pay his respects to Golpayegani on his visits to Iran, positioning himself squarely in the old cleric's camp. When Kho'i died, Fadlallah did not hesitate: Golpayegani's name had "emerged strongly," said Fadlallah, "and we support his authority.''[315] But Golpayegani's advanced years assured that the question of the *marja'iyya* would be posed again shortly. Fadlallah positioned himself to provide an original answer.

He began by leveling criticism at the state of the great Shi'ite seminaries, the traditional incubators for the *marja'iyya*. The headship of such a seminary, either in Najaf or in Qom, had been the customary credential of any great *marja'*. Fadlallah now dismissed the seminaries as irrelevant to leadership. The schools in Najaf and Qom, he complained, taught only jurisprudence and its methodology *(furu'* and *usul)*. They did not offer proper instruction in such basic subjects as the Qur'an, Hadith (sayings and traditions attributed to Muhammad), theology, philosophy, general Islamics, and homiletics. From an organizational point of view, the academies were four centuries behind the times and their structure no longer met contemporary needs. Persons who spent only two years in study went out into the world as clerics, "doing harm to all Islam." Others lingered on as perpetual students. Fadlallah favored a sweeping reform: admission standards, curriculum reform, examinations, and formal graduation.[316]

In Fadlallah's view, the seminaries had specialized in questions "which no longer have great importance in the exercise of *ijtihad*."[317] The burning questions that faced Shi'ism were political and had to be handled by a figure versed, not only in the nuances of Islamic law, but in the complexities of world politics. Fadlallah pointed out that the remaining great ayatollahs, Khomeini's aged contemporaries, had differed with Khomeini over the active role of clerics, and were not up to the political task at hand. Future candidates for the *marja'iyya* from the seminaries were people who had never pronounced on politics. And few of their names resonated throughout Shi'ism. "It is necessary to specify new conditions for the elements that make up the personality of the *marja'*," Fadlallah concluded. This person would have to possess a commanding grip of world affairs "down to the last nuance."[318] No longer could the role be fulfilled by a scholar who knew only the life of the seminary: "I imagine that the *marja'* would have to be open to the entire world, as Islam is open to the world. He would have to be a person aware of events as they unfold daily down to the smallest details, either through reports submitted to him or direct experience."[319] And the *marja'* would not simply issue rulings on matters related to Islamic law. He would take political stands on every issue related to the general welfare of Islam.

Such a leader would have a global mandate. Now that Khomeini and Kho'i were gone, Fadlallah reversed his position on the "multiplicity of leadership." He knew the arguments for multiplicity—he had once made them—but now determined that the challenge facing Shi'ism could only

be met on a global scale. The tensions between Islamic schools, the relations with other religions, the great political and social issues—these
could not be dealt with by local clerics, since they affected the entire
Islamic world. The multiplicity of clerical authority constituted an obstacle to a unified approach: "With all its advantages, the disadvantages are
greater."[320]

Fadlallah envisioned a universal *marja'iyya,* established as a single
institution, with a permanent headquarters. It would house a collection
of documents of all the rulings of the previous incumbents, so that the
new *marja'* could begin precisely where his predecessor left off. He would
not remain at his seat, but would travel throughout the world, to speak
to people and open their minds. He would be assisted by experts who
would prepare studies of specific problems. He would have representatives in various countries, who would function like ambassadors. Fadlallah then drew a remarkable parallel:

> When I look for an example of how I imagine the role of the *marja',* I
> find the example of the papacy, which takes political, cultural, and social
> positions in accord with its comprehensive religious character. The papacy
> acts through representatives who deal with all the questions that arise in
> countries where there are Catholics or Christians, whether they concern
> internal affairs or relations with other Christian denominations and other
> religions, such as Islam, Judaism, Buddhism, and so forth.[321]

Fadlallah's idea of the *marja'iyya* represented so sharp a break with
Shi'ite tradition that he did not dare suggest it might have an Islamic
precedent. The only detail he did not provide was how such a *marja'*
would be selected. But perhaps it was no coincidence that the "personality" he described strongly resembled his own. Could any clerical candidate surpass Fadlallah in his knowledge of current affairs, his contacts
in diplomacy and journalism, and his experience in dialogue? Certainly
Beirut, not Qom, was a better base of operation for a leader with a global
mission. And the obviously demanding role of a traveling *marja'* could
only be filled by a vital man in his prime, not by a lingering nonagenarian.
This transformation of the Shi'ite *marja'iyya* seemed far-fetched. But Fadlallah often proposed the unattainable in order to achieve the attainable.
In this case, he seemed to aim at eventual recognition as one of Shi'ism's
two or three leading lights, with a sphere of influence encompassing Lebanon and the half of the Shi'ite world that lay outside Iran. Few doubted
that Fadlallah had the talent and drive to conquer this summit, and the
demise of each elderly ayatollah brought him still closer. His success not
only would represent a personal triumph, but would confirm the geo-

graphic redistribution of authority in Shi'ism. Najaf, groaning under the weight of the Iraqi Ba'th, had been ravaged. Beirut, emerging from the desperate years of civil war, seemed poised to flourish. Fadlallah, a transplant from Najaf, personified the emergence of the Dahiya as the new citadel of Arab Shi'ism. He would be its acknowledged master.

A LEADER IN ISLAM

"I learned that the slogans are not the cause," said Fadlallah of his early years, "but that the cause is reality. I learned to be pragmatic and not to drown in illusions."[322] Fadlallah owed his immense powers of persuasion to this quality. He allowed other clerics in Hizbullah to conjure up messianic visions of imminent redemption. His own preaching represented a steady mix of appeals for action and caution, on a long road toward the distant goal of Islamic power. That road was winding and sometimes treacherous. It offered no panoramic views of God's kingdom; at times, the believers would have to grope forward in pitch darkness. At those moments, the hands of the despised would seize Fadlallah's robe, imploring him to lead them. Sure of foot, he would steer them away from the precipice.

Fadlallah's own seemingly miraculous escapes from death created the impression that a divine light guided him. Fadlallah, of course, knew otherwise. Lebanon had a way of demanding the ultimate sacrifice before yielding the ultimate reward. He had seen other men of ability and ambition perish at the moment of their apparent triumph, so he could not avoid preparing himself for the possibility that he too would become a sacrifice. At some point, in the aftermath of one or another assassination attempt, he had faced the possibility of sudden death and had chosen not to flinch. "I have readied myself for martyrdom for thirty years. God has yet to grant it to me. I say to anyone who talks in such a way as to threaten: I do not fear death, because I have placed myself on a road bounded by dangers and will never go back."[323] In order to lead the "rebellion against fear," he had to suppress and banish his own fear, and above all the fear of violent, unexpected death. This he did by drawing upon inner reservoirs of vision, ambition, and faith—reservoirs whose depth could not accurately be judged from their surface appearances.

But having embarked upon a "road bounded by dangers," it was only prudent to advance slowly and to take every possible precaution. Fadlallah would have subscribed to Churchill's adage: "Although prepared for martyrdom, I prefer that it be postponed." Fadlallah deliberated over every move and every utterance, for a mistaken step, a wrong word, might spell disaster. He guarded his tongue as closely as his body-guards protected his person. And he urged the same caution upon Hizbullah as a whole. Hizbullah drew upon great tributaries of grievance, vengefulness, and ambition—the most elemental emotions. Yet Fadlallah warned that the raging flood of fervor would spend itself unless a dam were erected to manage its waters prudently, in the service of a higher purpose. Fadlallah would be that dam. By demonstrating exemplary self-control, he sought to control others. By speaking for the despised, he hoped to guide them. By calling upon Shi'ites to reach out for power, he attempted to grasp it. By the very ambiguity of his pose, he had come to personify the ambiguity of Hizbullah.

He had also come to personify a new kind of leadership in the contemporary movements that invoked the name of Islam. Their leaders no longer appealed to tradition. They themselves had repudiated it, re-creating their faith through a dialectic with the modern criticism of religion and Islam. Some did this at the University of London or the Sorbonne or the American University of Beirut, where they pursued doctorates in Western law and philosophy. But it could be achieved even in the seminaries of Najaf, as Fadlallah attested: "My studies, which were supposed to be traditional, rebelled against tradition and all familiar things."[324] These new leaders disarmed the devastating modern criticism of Islam by disowning large parts of Islam's tradition. And they attacked the West by replaying its own self-criticism, borrowed from the faculty lounges and scholarly journals of the Western academy. This postmodern polemic had a particular appeal for young Muslim students, whose egos had been battered by the very modernity they had successfully acquired.

But in the absence of tradition, what remained of Islam? For these leaders, and above all for Fadlallah, there remained Islam as a political identity, preoccupied with the pursuit of power. The absence of this power bred a deep yearning to repossess it, at almost any cost. Every tradition was submitted to one exacting criterion: did it bring Muslims closer to power? Every ritual was reexamined: did it inspire Muslims to battle? Those bits of Islam that contributed to the struggle became "true Islam." Other traditions and rituals, especially in Shi'ism, served only to heighten man's sense of intimacy with God. These were reworked, minimized, or discarded altogether. Fadlallah, like the leaders of similar movements, thus offered Islam perhaps its last chance to regain power in the world, by an unsparing effort to mobilize every resource and symbol in its reach. Fadlallah gave every assurance that this tremendous sacrifice would propitiate God. If it did, the reward would be great indeed for the domain of Islam. If it did not, the loss sustained by the faith of Islam would be beyond measure.

Acknowledgments

I researched this study at the Moshe Dayan Center for Middle Eastern and African Studies at Tel Aviv University. I am grateful to Haim Gal of its Documentation Center for guaranteeing the steady flow of Arabic press materials, and to my colleague Shimon Shapira for many discussions of sources and their meaning. A first draft was written during a year spent as a fellow at the Woodrow Wilson International Center for Scholars in Washington, D.C. I drew much encouragement from the Wilson Center's director, Charles Blitzer, and from my friends on its staff, Robert Litwak, Walter Reich, and Samuel Wells. The Harry Frank Guggenheim Foundation provided support at the research and writing stages, and I am especially grateful to Karen Colvard for including this project in the foundation's investigation of religion and violence. During final revisions, I benefited from a close association with the Fundamentalism Project of the American Academy of Arts and Sciences, and I owe the study's completion to the gentle prodding of Scott Appleby. Finally, I learned much from talks with Terry Anderson, Nora Boustany, George Nader, and Robin Wright, who shared with me their impressions of the Sayyid.

Notes

Place of publication of all newspapers, magazines, and journals cited is Beirut unless otherwise indicated at first occurrence. Hizbullah's weekly newspaper, *Al-'Ahd*, carried only an Islamic date in its first years of publication. In the following notes, these dates have been transposed to the Gregorian calendar; issue numbers are provided in the interest of accuracy.

1. *Al-Nahar al-'arabi wal-duwali* (weekly; henceforth *NAD*), 21 March 1988. At the time, prices of most prerecorded tapes ran between 250 and 350 Lebanese pounds (£L). Fadlallah's tapes sold for as much as £L500.

2. Bernard Lewis, "The Return of Islam," *Commentary* (New York) 62 (January 1976): 49.

3. On the emergence of Hizbullah and the role of Iran, see these studies by Martin Kramer: *Hezbollah's Vision of the West* (Washington, D.C.: Washington Institute for Near East Policy, policy paper no. 16, October 1989); "The Moral Logic of Hizballah," in Walter Reich, ed., *Origins of Terrorism: Psychologies, Ideologies, Theologies, States of Mind* (Cambridge: Cambridge University Press, 1990), 131–57; "Redeeming Jerusalem: The Pan-Islamic Premise of Hizballah," in David Menashri, ed., *The Iranian Revolution and the Muslim World* (Boulder: Westview Press, 1990), 105–30; "Hizbullah: The Calculus of Jihad," in Martin E. Marty and R. Scott Appleby, eds., *Fundamentalisms and the State: Remaking Polities, Economies, and Militance* (Chicago: University of Chicago Press, 1993), 539–56; and annual essays on Islamic affairs in the *Middle East Contemporary Survey*, commencing with volume 8 (1983–84). See also R. K. Ramazani, *Revolutionary Iran: Challenge and Response in the Middle East* (Baltimore: Johns Hop-

kins University Press, 1986), 175–95; Shimon Shapira, "The Origins of Hizbal-lah," *Jerusalem Quarterly,* no. 46 (Spring 1988): 115–30; James P. Piscatori, "The Shia of Lebanon and Hizbullah: The Party of God," in Christie Jennett and Randal G. Stewart, eds., *Politics of the Future: The Role of Social Movements* (Melbourne: Macmillan, 1989), 292–317; Andreas Rieck, "Abschied vom 'Revo-lutionsexport'? Expansion und Rückgang des iranischen Einflusses im Libanon 1979–1989," *Beiträge zur Konfliktforschung* (Cologne) 20, no. 2 (1990): 81–104; Augustus Richard Norton, "Lebanon: The Internal Conflict and the Iranian Connection," in John L. Esposito, ed., *The Iranian Revolution: Its Global Impact* (Miami: Florida International University Press, 1990), 116–37; As'ad Abu Khalil, "Ideology and Practice of Hizballah in Lebanon: Islamization of Leninist Organi-zational Principles," *Middle Eastern Studies* (London) 27, no. 3 (July 1991): 390–403; and Haleh Vaziri, "Iran's Involvement in Lebanon: Polarization and Radi-calization of Militant Islamic Movements," *Journal of South Asian and Middle Eastern Studies* (Villanova) 16, no. 2 (winter 1992): 1–16.

4. Fadlallah is not the yet the subject of a biography, although he has been briefly profiled. See Martin Kramer, "Muhammad Husayn Fadlallah," *Orient* (Opladen, Germany) 50, no. 2 (June 1985): 147–49; Fouad Ajami, *The Vanished Imam: Musa al-Sadr and the Shia of Lebanon* (Ithaca: Cornell University Press, 1986), 213–17; and Andreas Rieck, *Die Schiiten und der Kampf um den Libanon: Politische Chronik 1958–1988,* Mitteilungen des Deutschen Orient-Instituts, no. 33 (Hamburg: Deutsches Orient-Institut, 1989), 604–13. The Lebanese and Is-raeli press have also profiled him on occasion. For a sustained analysis of Fadlal-lah's early writings, see Olivier Carré, *L'Utopie islamique dans l'Orient arabe* (Paris: Fondation nationale des sciences politiques, 1991), 193–256.

5. For biographical details, see "Ayatollah 'Abd al-Ra'uf Fadlallah: Jihad al-'ulama wa-hayat al-salihin," *Al-Muntalaq,* no. 27 (February 1985), 88–96.

6. For an evocative descriptions of Najaf's academies at their height, see Fadil Jamali, "The Theological Colleges of Najaf," *Muslim World* (Hartford) 50, no. 1 (January 1960): 15–22.

7. *Al-Nahar,* 6 December 1984, has an account of the funeral in Beirut, and a photograph of the crowd of hundreds that saw him off at Beirut International Airport.

8. Fadlallah interview, *Al-'Ahd,* no. 421, 17 July 1992.

9. On the role of poetry in the life of Najaf, see Jacques Berque, "Hier à Nagaf et Karbala," *Arabica* (Paris) 9, no. 3 (October 1962): 334–36.

10. Fadlallah interview, *Al-Khalij* (Sharjah), 28 June 1986.

11. Fadlallah interview, *Al-Qawmi al-'arabi,* 3 December 1990. The cleric commemorated on the occasion was Sayyid Muhsin al-Amin; see Ajami, *Vanished Imam,* 76–80.

12. For an example, see Muhammad Husayn Fadlallah, *Ya Zilal al-Islam* (Beirut: Dar al-Ta'aruf, 1977), an extended poem in the classic form of the qua-train. It belongs to a genre of inspirational Islamic poetry, evoking the themes of jihad, resistance, and inner purification. See also the emotive poem he wrote upon the death of his mother, in *Al-Nahar,* 2 July 1992.

13. Fadlallah interview, *Al-'Ahd,* no. 421, 17 July 1992.

14. Fadlallah interview, Voice of Lebanon, 2 May 1992; FBIS DR, 5 May 1992.

15. See Muhammad Husayn Fadlallah, *Qadayana 'ala daw' al-Islam,* 2d ed. (Beirut: Dar al-Zahra, 1393 [1973]), in which his essays for the journal *Al-Adwa'* are collected.

16. On Baqir al-Sadr, see Chibli Mallat, *The Renewal of Islamic Law: Muhammad Baqer as-Sadr, Najaf and the Shi'i International* (Cambridge: Cambridge University Press, 1993); and T. M. Aziz, "The Role of Muhammad Baqir al-Sadr in Shi'i Political Activism in Iraq from 1958," *International Journal of Middle East Studies* (Cambridge) 25, no. 2 (May 1993): 207–22.

17. Fadlallah interview, *Al-'Ahd,* no. 425, 14 August 1992.

18. On the Bazzi family, see Waddah Chrara, *Transformations d'une manifestation religieuse dans un village du Liban-Sud (Ashura)* (Beirut: Centre de Recherches, Institut des Sciences Sociales, Université Libanaise, 1968), 47–52, 80–82.

19. Samir Khalaf, *Lebanon's Predicament* (New York: Columbia University Press, 1987), 263.

20. A certain Shaykh Rida Farhat, according to Ajami, *Vanished Imam,* 214.

21. Fadlallah sermon, *Al-'Ahd,* no. 77, 12 December 1985.

22. Ayatollah Al-Sayed Muhammed Hussein Fadl Allah, "The Islamic Resistance in Lebanon and the Palestinian Uprising: The Islamic Jihad Perspective," *Middle East Insight* (Washington, D.C.), March–April 1988, 6.

23. Fadlallah's discussion of Arab nationalism and Islam in *Al-Harakat al-Islamiyya fi Lubnan* (Beirut: Dar al-Shira, 1984), 260–63; Fadlallah interview, *Al-Shira',* 28 September 1987; and Fadlallah interview, *Al-Qawmi al-'arabi,* 8 May 1988.

24. This quote, and a fuller discussion of Sadr's ambivalence toward the Palestinians, is provided in Ajami, *Vanished Imam,* 161–64; see also Augustus Richard Norton, *Amal and the Shi'a: Struggle for the Soul of Lebanon* (Austin: University of Texas Press, 1987), 43–44.

25. Al-Sayyid Muhammad Husayn Fadlallah, *Mafahim Islamiyya 'amma* (Beirut: Dar al-Zahra, 1973), 3: 54–55.

26. Fadlallah sermon, *Al-'Ahd,* no. 184, 1 January 1988.

27. Fadlallah, *Mafahim,* 3: 42–49.

28. Ibid.

29. Fadlallah, *Mafahim,* 3: 54.

30. Fadlallah interview, *Nouveau Magazine,* 27 February 1988.

31. The Shi'ite dimension of the Nabaa episode is discussed by Shimon Shapira, "The *Imam* Musa al-Sadr: Father of the Shiite Resurgence in Lebanon," *Jerusalem Quarterly,* no. 44 (fall 1987): 138, and Rieck, *Schiiten und der Kampf,* 218–23.

32. Fadlallah interview, *Al-Afkar,* 29 October 1984.

33. Fadlallah interview, *Al-Afkar,* 29 October 1984.

34. Sayyid Muhammad Husayn Fadlallah, *Al-Islam wa-mantiq al-quwwa,* 2d ed. (Beirut: Al-Mu'assasa al-jam'iyya lil-dirasat wal-nashr, 1981).

35. On Bint Jubayl in the aftermath of the Nabaa exodus, see Ahmad Baydoun, "Bint-Jbeil, Michigan, suivi de (ou poursuivi par) Bint-Jbeil, Liban," *Maghreb-Machrek* (Paris), no. 125 (July-August-September 1989), 77–79.

36. Photograph in *Al-Muntalaq,* no. 3 (Ramadan 1398), 113. A much smaller branch was established in the Hirmil region; see the interview with its director, *Al-Muntalaq,* no. 24 (Jumada II 1401), 53–57.

37. *Al-Sharq*, 2 October 1987, and *Al-Nahar*, 30 September 1988, report Fadlallah addressing the graduation ceremony of the annual tutors' course.

38. Fadlallah interview, *Nouveau Magazine*, 27 February 1988.

39. Fadlallah interview, *Al-Wahda al-Islamiyya*, 4 March 1988.

40. Fadlallah interview, Voice of Lebanon, 2 May 1992; FBIS DR, 5 May 1992.

41. Al-Sayyid Muhammad Husayn Fadlallah, "Al-Thawra al-Islamiyya fi Iran: Ta'ammulat min al-dakhil," *Al-Muntalaq*, no. 8 (January 1980), 12–13, 16.

42. Al-Sayyid Muhammad Husayn Fadlallah, "Al-Thawra al-Islamiyya fi Iran bayna al-takhtit al-madi wal-isnad al-ilahi," *Al-Muntalaq*, no. 10 (June 1980), 10.

43. Fadlallah interview, *Monday Morning*, 15 October 1984.

44. *Al-Nahar*, 3 November 1980. Visits and statements of support for Fadlallah were reported in *Al-Safir*, 4 November 1980.

45. Fadlallah quoted in Robin Wright, *Sacred Rage: The Wrath of Militant Islam* (New York: Simon & Schuster, 1986), 96, where he speaks of four attempts from 1981 to 1982.

46. *Al-Safir*, 28 November 1980 (with photograph).

47. *Al-'Alam* (London), 1 October 1988, has article on the union. *Al-Haqiqa*, 4 September 1987, and *Al-'Ahd*, no. 169, 18 September 1987, have articles on a symposium sponsored by the union on the subject of the Islamic Resistance. In a session attended by Fadlallah, the editors of *Al-Muntalaq* described the history of the journal and asked for support to alleviate its financial troubles.

48. Fadlallah interview, *Al-Anwar*, 22 July 1985.

49. According to the analysis in *Al-Shira'*, 4 August 1986. See Fadlallah's clarification in response to this article, *Al-Shira'*, 15 September 1986.

50. Al-Sayyid Muhammad Husayn Fadlallah, "Harakat al-umma bayna al-qiyada al-marja'iyya wal-tanzim al-hizbi," *Al-Muntalaq*, no. 46 (August 1988), 5–15.

51. Fadlallah, "Harakat al-umma," 5–15.

52. Fadlallah interview, *Monday Morning*, 15 October 1984.

53. *Al-Nahar*, 3 October 1984.

54. Fadlallah interview, *Al-Musawwar* (Cairo), 20 October 1989. The press agency was the Agence France-Presse.

55. Fadlallah, "Ta'amulat Islamiyya," 9–10. See also Fadlallah, "Islam and Violence in Political Reality," *Middle East Insight* 4, no. 4 (1986): 13.

56. Fadlallah, "Ta'amulat Islamiyya," 11–12.

57. David B. Ottoway, "Sheik with Iranian Ties Is Suspect in Bombings," *Washington Post*, 28 October 1983.

58. David B. Ottoway, "Sheik's Involvement Never Proved," *Washington Post*, 26 May 1985.

59. Fadlallah interview, *Al-Afkar*, 29 October 1984.

60. Herbert H. Denton, "Sheik Named in Bombing Says He Is Nonviolent," *Washington Post*, 30 October 1983.

61. Fadlallah interview, *Al-Afkar*, 29 October 1984.

62. Fadlallah interview, *Al-Khalij*, 14 November 1983.

63. Fadlallah Friday sermon, *Al-Nahar*, 29 October 1983.

64. *Al-Nahar,* 4 November 1983.

65. Fadlallah, "Islamic Resistance in Lebanon," 5.

66. Fadlallah interview, *Politique internationale* (Paris), no. 29, autumn 1985.

67. Fadlallah interview, *Kayhan* (Tehran), 14 November 1985. In a similar vein, he declared that oppressed peoples "do not consider anything forbidden in the pursuit of these objectives. The legitimacy of every means stems from the legitimacy of the end sought." Fadlallah interview, *Al-Majallah* (London), 1 October 1986.

68. Fadlallah interview, *Middle East Insight,* June–July 1985.

69. Fadlallah interview, *Al-Khalij,* 2 April 1987; FBIS DR, 6 April 1987.

70. Fadlallah interview, *Al-Mustaqbal* (Paris), 6 July 1985; FBIS DR, 8 July 1985.

71. According to Sayyid Ibrahim al-Amin, those who blew up the marine barracks (and the Israeli military governate in Tyre) "did not martyr themselves in accord with a decision by a political party or movement. They martyred themselves because the Imam Khomeini permitted them to do so." Speech by Ibrahim al-Amin, *Al-'Ahd,* no. 135, 23 January 1987.

72. Fadlallah interview, *Revue d'études palestiniennes* (Paris), no. 16 (summer 1985), 40–41. The same revelation is made in the Fadlallah interview, *Al-Majallah,* 1 October 1986.

73. Fadlallah interview, *Al-'Ahd,* no. 421, 17 July 1992.

74. Ottoway, "Sheik with Iranian Ties."

75. Scarlett Haddad, a Christian Lebanese journalist who interviewed many figures in Hizbullah, interviewed Fadlallah in full chador; see the photograph in *Nouveau Magazine,* 17 October 1987.

76. Augustus Richard Norton, preface to Fadlallah interview, *Middle East Insight,* June–July 1985.

77. Fadlallah interview, *Time* (New York), 9 October 1989.

78. Fadlallah interview, Voice of Lebanon, 2 May 1992; FBIS DR, 5 May 1992.

79. Scarlett Haddad, preface to Fadlallah interview, *Nouveau Magazine,* 17 October 1987.

80. Johnny Munayyir, preface to Fadlallah interview, *NAD,* 12 December 1988; FBIS DR, 15 February 1989.

81. On the struggle, see Chris Mowles, "The Israeli Occupation of South Lebanon," *Third World Quarterly* (London) 8, no. 4 (October 1986): 1351–66; and W. A. Terrill, "Low Intensity Conflict in Southern Lebanon: Lessons and Dynamics of the Israeli-Shi'ite War," *Conflict Quarterly* (Fredricktown, New Brunswick) 7, no. 3 (1987): 22–35.

82. Fadlallah interview, *Monday Morning,* 14 September 1986.

83. Fadlallah interview, *Der Spiegel* (Hamburg), 1 April 1985; FBIS DR, 4 April 1985.

84. Al-Sayyid Muhammad Husayn Fadlallah, *Al-Muqawama al-Islamiyya fi al-Janub wal-Biqa' al-Gharbi wa-Rashayya: tatallu'at wa-afaq; Nass al-muhadara allati 'alqaha samahat al-'allama al-mujahid al-Sayyid Muhammad Husayn Fadlallah fi kulliyat idarat al-a'mal wal-iqtisad al-far' al-awwal, bita'rikh 19 Shawwal 1404 al-muwafiq 18 Tammuz 1984* (sermon published as pamphlet) (n.p., n.d.), 20–21.

85. Fadlallah interview, *Al-Watan al-'arabi* (Paris), 31 January 1992.

86. Fadlallah interview, *NAD*, 1 July 1985.

87. Fadlallah sermon, *Al-Nahar*, 24 June 1989.

88. Fadlallah, "Al-Quds fi al-dhakira al-Islamiyya," *Al-Muntalaq*, no. 77 (April 1991): 13.

89. Fadlallah, "Islamic Resistance in Lebanon," 9.

90. Fadlallah interview, *Der Spiegel*, 1 April 1985; FBIS DR, 4 April 1985.

91. Fadlallah Friday sermon, *Al-'Ahd*, no. 76, 6 December 1985.

92. Fadlallah speech, Voice of the Oppressed, 24 February 1992; FBIS DR, 24 February 1992.

93. Fadlallah interview, *Salam* (Tehran), 16 July 1991; FBIS DR, 31 July 1991.

94. Fadlallah interview, *Journal of Palestine Studies* (Washington, D.C.) 16, no. 2 (winter 1987): 5.

95. Fadlallah interview, *Al-Liwa'*, 9 April 1985.

96. Fadlallah, "Islamic Resistance in Lebanon," 9.

97. *Al-Nahar*, 9 November 1984 (with photograph).

98. *Al-Nahar*, 12 November 1984 (with photograph). Fadlallah was among those who credited Kissinger with ominous power. "Kissinger created the Lebanese crisis or at least planned it," Fadlallah repeated on another occasion. "Then Israel, with the approval of the U.S., invaded Lebanon." Fadlallah interview, *Middle East Insight*, June–July 1985. As late as 1989, Fadlallah expressed apprehension over Kissinger's persistent influence: "We are afraid that Henry Kissinger could be harmful to the Administration [of President George Bush]. We want them to be very cautious about Kissinger." Fadlallah interview, *Time*, 9 October 1989.

99. *Al-Nahar*, 19 November 1984 (with photograph).

100. See Yves Gonzales-Quijano, "Les interprétations d'un rite: Célébrations de la 'Achoura au Liban," *Maghreb-Machrek*, no. 115 (January-February-March 1987), 5–28.

101. Fadlallah speech, *Al-Nahar*, 27 September 1985. This was not simply an exhortation to action, but an attempt to undermine self-flagellation, of which Fadlallah disapproved. For an interpretation of the speech as a (failed) attempt to delegitimize self-flagellation, see *Al-Shira'*, 30 September 1985. The controversy among clerics over the practice is discussed by Werner Ende, "The Flagellations of Muharram and the Shi'ite 'Ulama," *Der Islam* (Hamburg) 55 (1978): 19–36. For Fadlallah's support of the earlier ruling against self-flagellation, see *Al-Bilad*, 28 March 1992.

102. Fadlallah lecture delivered on 18 July 1984, in Fadlallah, *Al-Muqawama al-Islamiyya fi al-Janub wal-Biqa' al-Gharbi wa-Rashayya*, pp. 16–19; lecture republished in Fadlallah, *Al-Muqawama al-Islamiyya: Afaq wa-tatallu'at*, pp. 48–51.

103. Fadlallah speech, *Al-Nahar*, 14 May 1985.

104. Fadlallah interview, *Monday Morning*, 16 December 1985.

105. Fadlallah, *Al-Muqawama al-Islamiyya fi al-Janub wal-Biqa' al-Gharbi wa-Rashayya*, 11.

106. Fadlallah interview, *Al-Hawadith* (London), 24 May 1985; FBIS DR, 29 May 1985.

107. Fadlallah lecture, *Al-Nahar*, 19 May 1985.

108. Fadlallah interview, *Monday Morning*, 14 September 1986.

109. Fadlallah speech at memorial service, *Al-'Ahd*, no. 177, 13 November 1987. Fadlallah returns to the positive example of the determination of the Jews in an interview in *Al-'Ahd*, no. 421, 17 July 1992.

110. Fadlallah interview, *Al-Anwar*, 22 May 1988.

111. Fadlallah interview, *Der Spiegel*, 1 April 1985; FBIS DR, 4 April 1985.

112. Fadlallah interview, *Al-Anwar*, 22 May 1988.

113. Fadlallah interview, *Der Spiegel*, 1 April 1985; FBIS DR, 4 April 1985.

114. Fadlallah interview, *Al-Ittihad al-usbu'i* (Abu Dhabi), 30 January 1986.

115. Fadlallah interview, *NAD*, 10 March 1986.

116. Al-Sayyid Muhammad Husayn Fadlallah, "Alamat istifham amama wahdat al-qiyada al-Islamiyya wa-ta'addudaha," *Al-Muntalaq*, no. 53 (April 1989), 17–18. This is the most systematic presentation of Fadlallah's thought on this subject. For an interview in which he makes some of the same points, see *Al-Shira'*, 26 May 1986.

117. Fadlallah interview, *Middle East Insight*, June-July 1985.

118. Fadlallah interview, *Monday Morning*, 15 October 1984.

119. Sayyid Muhammad Husayn Fadlallah, "Al-Dawla al-Islamiyya bayna al-Islamiyya wal-madhhabiyya," *Al-Muntalaq*, no. 40 (February 1988), 6–12.

120. Fadlallah interview, *Al-Shira'*, 28 September 1987.

121. *Al-Nahar*, 5 November 1984 (with photograph).

122. Fadlallah interview, *Monday Morning*, 15 October 1984.

123. Fadlallah interview, *An-Nahar Arab Report & Memo*, 29 April 1985.

124. Fadlallah, "Al-Dawla al-Islamiyya bayna al-Islamiyya wal-madhhabiyya," 13–14.

125. *Monday Morning*, 25 January 1993.

126. Fadlallah, *Al-Muqawama al-Islamiyya fi al-Janub wal-Biqa' al-Gharbi wa-Rashayya*, 35–36.

127. Fadlallah interview, *Shu'un al-awsat*, 14 December 1992.

128. Fadlallah interview, *Shu'un al-awsat*, 14 December 1992.

129. Fadlallah interview, Tehran Television Service, 27 September 1988; FBIS DR, 27 September 1988.

130. *Kayhan International* (Tehran), 12 March 1988; cf. Fadlallah interview, *Al-Shira'*, 18 January 1988.

131. Fadlallah interview, *Al-Kifah al-'arabi*, 23 November 1987. A photograph of the handbill appears in *Al-Shira'*, 18 January 1988. Also named as possible candidates in the handbill were Shams al-Din, Sayyid Sadiq al-Musawi, and Shaykh Sa'id Sha'ban.

132. *Nass al-risala al-maftuha allati wajjahaha Hizbullah ila al-mustad'afin fi Lubnan wal-'alam* (Beirut), 16 February 1985, 15.

133. Interviews with Fadlallah, *Monday Morning*, 19 August 1991, 10 August 1992; *Al-Bilad*, 24 October 1992. According to Fadlallah, Iran was also organizing an interfaith initiative that would involve him; Fadlallah interview, *Al-Bilad*, 31 October 1992.

134. Fadlallah interview, *Monday Morning*, 13 January 1992.

135. Fadlallah interview, *Al-Nahar*, 25 December 1991; reprinted in *Al-Bilad*, 11 January 1992.

136. *Monday Morning*, 25 January 1993.

137. Fadlallah interview, *NAD*, 12 December 1988.

138. Fadlallah, *Al-Muqawama al-Islamiyya fi al-Janub wal-Biqa' al-Gharbi wa-Rashayya*, 22.

139. Sadiq al-Musawi, article in *Al-Shira'*, 12 July 1993.

140. Fadlallah interview, *Middle East Insight*, June–July 1985.

141. Fadlallah interview, *Al-'Ahd*, no. 125, 14 November 1986.

142. Fadlallah interview, *Al-Shira'*, 18 March 1985.

143. Fadlallah interview, *Al-Hawadith*, 24 May 1985; FBIS DR, 29 May 1985.

144. Fadlallah interview, *La Vanguardia* (Barcelona), 9 November 1986; FBIS DR, 17 November 1986.

145. Fadlallah interview, *Al-Shira'*, 18 March 1985.

146. Fadlallah interview, *Le Quotidien de Paris*, 23 September 1986; FBIS DR, 30 September 1986.

147. Fadlallah interview, *Nouveau Magazine*, 17 October 1987.

148. Fadlallah interview, Radio Monte Carlo (Paris), 13 May 1988; FBIS DR, 20 May 1988.

149. Account of mass funeral, *Al-Nahar*, 10 March 1985.

150. Bob Woodward and Charles Babcock, *Washington Post*, 12 May 1985. For more details, see Bob Woodward, *Veil: The Secret Wars of the CIA, 1981–1987* (New York: Simon and Schuster, 1987), 393–98. There it is claimed that the attempt to kill Fadlallah was a joint initiative of the director of the CIA and the Saudi ambassador to Washington. The Saudis allegedly hired a British consultant, who trained the Lebanese team that planted the bomb.

151. Fadlallah interview, *Al-Nahar*, 10 March 1985.

152. Summary of Hizbullah's sixty-eight-page report, which also accused the group of many other bombings and assassination attempts, *Al-Nahar*, 4 March 1986. According to Woodward (*Veil*, 397), the members of the team were betrayed to Fadlallah by the Saudis, who thus sought to dissociate themselves from a deed they had initiated.

153. Fadlallah interview, *NAD*, 10 March 1986.

154. Article interviewing family members on the third anniversary of the bombing, *Al-'Ahd*, no. 194, 11 March 1988.

155. See the evocative photograph of Fadlallah arriving with his guards, in Marcel Coudari, *257 jours de détention au Liban* (Paris: Jacques Grancher, 1987), following p. 112.

156. The occasion was a visit to the Carlton Hotel following the death of the deputy Sulayman al-'Ali; *NAD*, 12 October 1987. The item does not name Fadlallah, but obviously refers to him.

157. The house as it appeared to a visitor in June 1988 is described by Gilles Delafon, *Beyrouth: Les soldats de l'Islam* (Paris: Stock, 1989), 88.

158. *Al-Nahar*, 13 May 1988; Fadlallah interview, *Al-'Ahd*, no. 203, 13 May 1988; *Al-Shira'*, 25 September 1989.

159. Voice of the Oppressed, 10 December 1989; FBIS DR, 11 December 1989; *Washington Post*, 10 December 1989.

160. *Al-Watan al-'arabi*, 20 October 1989, provided a convoluted account, which spoke of a ring of twenty to thirty persons. The incident concerned a

booby-trapped explosive discovered in the Imam al-Rida Mosque, an episode reported in *Al-Shira'*, 25 September 1989.

161. *Al-Nahar*, 2 September 1988, reported that Fadlallah's welfare bureau had given assistance to 1,122 families in Beirut and the Dahiya; 896 families in 156 villages in the south; and 406 families in 56 villages in the Bekaa and the Hirmil. In 1987 the bureau spent £L62 million in Beirut, £L35 million in the south, and £L26 million in the Bekaa, for a total of £L123 million in aid projects in Lebanon. *Al-Nahar*, 16 May 1989, reported that in 1988, the bureau spent £L260 million in Beirut, £L137 million in the south, and £L103 million in the Bekaa, for a total of £L501 million in aid projects in Lebanon.

162. 'Abd al-Majid 'Ammar was the nephew who ran the Beirut institute; 'Abd al-Muhsin Fadlallah, a first cousin, ran a seminary in Khirbat Islim.

163. See, for example, the Friday sermon delivered by 'Ali Fadlallah at his father's mosque, *Al-Diyar*, 4 February 1989. Fadlallah's name of endearment was Abu 'Ali.

164. Woodward, *Veil*, 397.

165. Fadlallah interview, *Monday Morning*, 5 October 1987. Fadlallah was asked why he did not sue if Woodward had slandered him. Fadlallah answered that Woodward had covered himself by attributing the words to a dead man, the late CIA director William Casey; Fadlallah interview, *Nouveau Magazine*, 17 October 1987.

166. Text of office's statement, *Al-Haqiqa*, 28 September 1987.

167. *Al-Dustur* (London), 30 May 1988. This hostile source also claimed that Fadlallah had secretly visited the United States three times, via Switzerland.

168. *Amal*, 10 February 1990.

169. On Shams al-Din, see Rieck, *Schiiten und der Kampf*, 314–15, 617–19; Norton, *Amal and the Shi'a*, 91–93.

170. Fadlallah interview, *Monday Morning*, 6 June 1988.

171. Fadlallah interview, *Al-Shira'*, 6 June 1988.

172. Fadlallah interview, *Al-Diyar*, 18 January 1989.

173. Eulogy in *Al-Muntalaq*, no. 27 (February 1985), 94–95; airport photograph in *Al-Nahar*, 6 December 1984.

174. Fadlallah sermon, *Al-Nahar*, 13 April 1985.

175. Text of Hizbullah statement, *Al-Nahar*, 29 June 1985.

176. *Al-Nahar*, 22 June 1985.

177. Fadlallah interview, *Al-Mustaqbal*, 6 July 1985. The hijacker was 'Ali 'Atwa.

178. Fadlallah interview, *NAD*, 1 July 1985.

179. Fadlallah interview, *Al-Sharq*, 1 July 1985.

180. Fadlallah sermon, *Al-'Ahd*, no. 76, 6 December 1985.

181. Fadlallah interview, *Kayhan*, 14 November 1985.

182. Fadlallah interview, *Kayhan International*, 23 May 1985.

183. The evidence is summarized by Ramazani, *Revolutionary Iran*, pp. 192–94.

184. For a comprehensive listing of Hizbullah's hostage holding, see Maskit Burgin et al., *Foreign Hostages in Lebanon*, Jaffee Center for Strategic Studies Memorandum, no. 25 (Tel Aviv: August 1988).

185. Fadlallah interview, *Al-Ra'y al-'Amm* (Kuwait), 3 April 1986; FBIS DR, 18 April 1986.

186. Fadlallah interview, *L'Express* (Paris), 10 July 1987.

187. Fadlallah interview, *Al-Anwar,* 24 March 1986.

188. For invocations of this verse, see Fadlallah sermon, *Al-'Ahd,* no. 76, 6 December 1985; Fadlallah interview, *Al-Majallah,* 25 December 1985; Fadl Allah, "Islam and Violence," p. 12. This appears in two places in the Qur'an, at 7:165 and 35:18.

189. Fadl Allah, "Islam and Violence," p. 12.

190. Fadlallah sermon, *Al-Nahar,* 14 December 1985.

191. Fadlallah speech, *Al-Nahar,* 1 April 1985.

192. Fadlallah statement, Agence France-Presse, 12 March 1986; FBIS DR, 12 March 1986.

193. Fadl Allah, "Islam and Violence," p. 12; Fadlallah statement, *Al-Nahar,* 17 May 1985.

194. Fadlallah interview, Tehran Television Service, 3 November 1988; FBIS DR, 4 November 1988.

195. Marie Seurat, *Birds of Ill Omen,* trans. Dorothy S. Blair (London: Quartet Books, 1990), 15.

196. *Le Monde* (Paris), 7 June 1985.

197. Fadlallah interview, *Kayhan International,* 23 July 1985.

198. Letter from Fadlallah to Anderson's sister, *Al-'Amal,* 31 January 1989.

199. Fadlallah interviews, *Al-Musawwar,* 24 October 1989 (where he speaks of forty mediation attempts), and *Time,* 9 October 1989 (where he mentions fifty appeals).

200. Fadlallah interview, *Al-Hawadith,* 27 March 1987; FBIS DR, 31 March 1987.

201. Between March and June 1987, a Lebanese survey asked Shi'ite students at the Lebanese University whether they approved of hostage-taking. There is no breakdown of response by political affiliation. However, since only thirty-five of those in the total sample, which included ninety-five adherents of Hizbullah, approved of hostage taking, the maximum possible rate of approval among Hizbullah's adherents was 37 percent. For the relevant table, see Hilal Khashan, "Do Lebanese Shi'is Hate the West?" *Orbis* (Philadelphia) 33, no. 2 (fall 1989): 587.

202. Fadlallah interview, *Time,* 9 October 1989.

203. Fadl Allah, "Islam and Violence," 12.

204. Seurat, *Birds of Ill Omen,* 16.

205. Revolutionary Justice Organization statement on "postponement" of the "execution" of Jean-Louis Normandin, *Al-Nahar,* 18 March 1987.

206. Fadl Allah, "Islam and Violence," 12.

207. Thomas L. Friedman, *From Beirut to Jerusalem* (New York: Farrar Straus Giroux, 1989), 506.

208. An unnamed diplomatic sources once claimed that a deal for the return of a West German hostage included four armored cars for Fadlallah. *Amal,* 17 September 1987.

209. Fadlallah interview, *Al-Qawmi al-'arabi,* 4 April 1990.

210. See Christin Marschall, "Syria-Iran: A Strategic Alliance, 1979–1991," *Orient* 33, no. 3 (September 1992): 433–46.

211. Fadlallah interview, *Politique internationale,* no. 29, Autumn 1985.

212. Fadlallah interview, *Al-Hawadith,* 24 May 1985; FBIS DR, 29 May 1985.

213. Fadlallah interview, *Nouveau Magazine,* 17 October 1987.

214. Ghazi Kan'an interview, *Le Quotidien de Paris,* 6 March 1987.

215. Account of funeral, *Al-Nahar,* 26 February 1987.

216. Fadlallah interview, *Libération* (Paris), 13 March 1987.

217. Fadlallah interview, *Al-Hawadith,* 27 March 1987.

218. Fadlallah interview, *Al-Hawadith,* 10 July 1987; FBIS DR, 13 July 1987.

219. Fadlallah interview, *NAD,* 1 July 1985.

220. Fadlallah interview, *Al-Nahar,* 4 December 1989.

221. Fadlallah interview, *Monday Morning,* 13 May 1991.

222. Fadlallah interview, *Kayhan,* 3 March; FBIS DR, 16 March 1993.

223. Fadlallah interview, *Monday Morning,* 19 August 1991.

224. Fadlallah interview, *Monday Morning,* 13 May 1991.

225. On the struggle between Hizbullah and Amal, see Martin Kramer, "Sacrifice and Fratricide in Shiite Lebanon," in Mark Juergensmeyer, ed., *Violence and the Sacred in the Modern World* (London: Frank Cass, 1992), 30–47.

226. Account of exchange, Agence France-Presse, 3 September 1987; FBIS DR, 4 September 1987.

227. Fadlallah interview, *Nouveau Magazine,* 17 October 1987.

228. Fadlallah interview, *Al-Wahda al-Islamiyya,* 4 March 1988.

229. Fadlallah interview, *NAD,* 21 February 1988.

230. Fadlallah interview, *Nouveau Magazine,* 27 February 1988.

231. Fadlallah interview, *Nouveau Magazine,* 4 June 1988.

232. Fadlallah interview, *Al-Qawmi al-'arabi,* 9 April 1990.

233. Fadlallah interview, *Nouveau Magazine,* 4 June 1988.

234. Fadlallah appeal, Radio Beirut, 9 May 1988; FBIS DR, 9 May 1988.

235. Fadlallah interview, *Al-Shira',* 6 June 1988.

236. Fadlallah interview, *Al-Ra'y* (Amman), 1 December 1988.

237. Fadlallah interview, *Nouveau Magazine,* 16 September 1989.

238. Fadlallah interview, *Al-Shira',* 5 December 1988.

239. Report on visits of support by delegations, *Al-'Ahd,* no. 207, 10 June 1988.

240. Fadlallah interview, *Kayhan,* 3 March 1993; FBIS DR, 16 March 1993.

241. Fadlallah interview, *Nouveau Magazine,* 17 October 1987.

242. Fadlallah interview, *Time,* 9 October 1989.

243. Fadlallah interview, *La Republica* (Rome), 28 August 1989.

244. Fadlallah speech, *Al-Nahar,* 3 March 1989.

245. Fadlallah speech, *Al-Nahar,* 3 March 1989.

246. Fadlallah interviews, *Al-'Ahd,* no. 245, 3 March 1989; *Al-'Ahd,* no. 246, 10 March 1989.

247. Fadlallah interview, *Al-'Ahd,* no. 244, 24 February 1989.

248. Fadlallah interview, *Al-Nahar,* 4 December 1989.

249. Fadl Allah, "Islam and Violence," 13. "We are not against the American and European peoples, and we wish to be friendly with all nations, because this

is one of the commandments of Almighty God. We will confront American and European policies, however, because these policies are based on crushing oppressed nations." Fadlallah sermon, Radio Tehran, 21 June 1985; FBIS DR, 21 June 1985.

250. Fadlallah interview, *NAD*, 1 July 1987.

251. Fadlallah speech, Voice of the Oppressed, 24 February 1992; FBIS DR, 24 February 1992.

252. Al-Sayyid Muhammad Husayn Fadlallah, "Qira'a Islamiyya lil-mutaghayyirat al-siyasiyya fi al-saha al-duwaliyya," *Al-Muntalaq*, no. 63 (February 1990): 15–16.

253. Fadlallah interview, *Salam*, 17 July 1991; DR, 31 July 1991.

254. Fadlallah interview, *Monday Morning*, 1 February 1993.

255. Fadlallah interview, *Shu'un al-awsat*, 14 December 1992.

256. Fadlallah interview, *Shu'un al-awsat*, 14 December 1992.

257. Fadlallah interview, *Salam*, 17 July 1991; FBIS DR, 31 July 1991.

258. Fadlallah sermon, *Al-'Ahd*, no. 449, 29 January 1993.

259. Fadl Allah, "Islamic Resistance in Lebanon," 6.

260. Fadlallah sermon, *Al-'Ahd*, no. 417, 19 June 1992; cf. sermon, *Al-'Ahd*, no. 418, 26 June 1992.

261. Fadlallah interview, *Filastin al-Muslima* (London), April 1993.

262. Fadlallah speech, Voice of the Oppressed, 19 March 1992; FBIS DR, 24 March 1992.

263. Fadlallah interview, *Al-'Ahd*, no. 446, 8 January 1993.

264. Fadlallah interview, *Al-Nahar*, 19 October 1987.

265. Fadlallah, "Qira'a Islamiyya lil-mutaghayyirat," 16.

266. Fadlallah interview, *Le Quotidien de Paris*, 23 September 1986; FBIS DR, 30 September 1986.

267. Fadlallah interview, *Monday Morning*, 13 May 1991.

268. UN Security Council Resolution 425, dating from Israel's first major incursion in 1978, called upon Israel to "withdraw forthwith its forces from all Lebanese territory." For the text and context of the resolution, see Ramesh Thakur, *International Peacekeeping in Lebanon: United Nations Authority and Multinational Force* (Boulder: Westview Press, 1987), 337; and Fida Nasrallah, *The Questions of South Lebanon* (Oxford: Centre for Lebanese Studies, 1992), 33.

269. Fadlallah sermon, *Al-'Ahd*, no. 414, 29 May 1992.

270. Fadlallah interview, *Al-Diyar*, 30 September 1992.

271. Jean-François Legrain, "La conférence de Téhéran," *Maghreb-Machrek*, no. 134 (October–December 1991), 124–27; Fadlallah speech, *Al-Anwar*, 21 October 1991; speech also in *Filastin al-Muslima*, November 1991.

272. Fadlallah sermon, *Al-'Ahd*, no. 419, 3 July 1992. At the very most, Israel might withdraw from the Gaza strip; Fadlallah interview, *Monday Morning*, 19 August 1991.

273. Fadlallah interview, *Al-Watan al-'arabi*, 31 January 1992.

274. Fadlallah quote, *Monday Morning*, 24 January 1993.

275. Fadlallah message to an Islamic conference in Chicago, *Al-Bilad*, 25 January 1992.

276. Fadlallah interview, *Al-'Ahd*, no. 421, 17 July 1992.

277. Fadlallah interview, *Monday Morning*, 1 February 1993; cf. interview, *Al-Bilad*, 24 October 1992.

278. Fadlallah interview, *Ettala'at* (Tehran), 28 January 1993.

279. Fadlallah interview, Voice of Lebanon, 2 May 1992; FBIS DR, 5 May 1992.

280. Fadlallah interview, *Shu'un al-awsat*, 14 December 1992. "If the regimes must make peace, the people should not make peace, should not purchase Israeli merchandise, should not receive any Israeli tourist, and should not give Israel the feeling of stability. The question is one of struggle for existence with what we perceive as the Jewish octopus, which is linked to more than one arrogant global octopus." Fadlallah interview, Voice of Lebanon, 2 May 1992; FBIS DR, 5 May 1992.

281. Fadlallah sermon, *Al-Nahar*, 31 October 1992.

282. Fadlallah interview, *Al-Watan al-'arabi*, 28 August 1992.

283. Fadlallah interview, *Shu'un al-awsat*, 14 December 1992.

284. Fadlallah interview, Voice of Lebanon, 2 May 1992; FBIS DR, 5 May 1992.

285. Fadlallah interview, *Al-Qawmi al-'arabi*, 4 April 1990.

286. Fadlallah interview, *Shu'un al-awsat*, 14 December 1992.

287. Sayyid Muhammad Husayn Fadlallah, "Qira'a Islamiyya sari'a li-mafhumay al-hurriyya wal-dimuqratiyya," *Al-Muntalaq*, no. 65 (April 1990): 18.

288. Fadlallah interview, *Al-Ribat* (Amman), 4 May 1993.

289. Fadlallah interview, *Al-Ribat*, 4 May 1993.

290. Fadlallah interview, *Shu'un al-awsat*, 14 December 1992.

291. Fadlallah interview, *Al-Shira'*, 26 May 1986.

292. Fadlallah, "Qira'a Islamiyya sari'a," 16.

293. Fadlallah interview, *Shu'un al-awsat*, 14 December 1992.

294. Fadlallah, "Qira'a Islamiyya sari'a," 16.

295. Fadlallah, "Qira'a Islamiyya sari'a," 15. This reiterated his well-known position against freedom for "parties of unbelief and atheism," first made in *Al-Islam wa-mantiq al-quwwa*, 217.

296. Fadlallah interview, *Al-'Ahd*, no. 463, 7 May 1993.

297. Fadlallah, "Qira'a Islamiyya sari'a," 18.

298. See Tufayli interview, *Nouveau Magazine*, 11 June 1993, for a concise exposition of his view.

299. Fadlallah interview, *Filastin al-Muslima*, April 1993.

300. Fadlallah interview, *Al-'Ahd*, no. 425, 17 July 1992.

301. Fadlallah interview, *Filastin al-Muslima*, April 1993.

302. Fadlallah interview, Voice of Lebanon, 2 May 1992; FBIS DR, 5 May 1992.

303. Fadlallah interview, *Al-Watan al-'arabi*, 28 August 1992.

304. On the elections, see Joseph Bahout, "Liban: les élections législatives de l'été 1992," *Maghreb-Machrek*, no. 139 (January–March 1993), 53–84; A. Nizar Hamzeh, "Lebanon's Hizballah: From Islamic Revolution to Parliamentary Accommodation," *Third World Quarterly* 14 (1993): 321–37.

305. Fadlallah interview, *Shu'un al-awsat*, 14 December 1992.

306. Fadlallah interview, *Al-Musawwar*, 20 October 1989.

307. Fadlallah interview, *Al-Anwar*, 22 July 1985.

308. On Khomeini's position, see Gregory Rose, "Velayat-e Faqih and the Recovery of Islamic Identity in the Thought of Ayatollah Khomeini," in Nikki R. Keddie, ed., *Religion and Politics in Iran* (New Haven: Yale University Press, 1983), 166–88.

309. Muhammad Jawad Mughniyya authored this tract; see Chibli Mallat, *Shi'i Thought from the South of Lebanon* (Oxford: Centre for Lebanese Studies, 1988), 21–25.

310. Sayyid Muhammad Husayn Fadlallah, "'Alamat istifham amama wahdat al-qiyada," 12–18.

311. Fadlallah interview, *Sabah al-Khayr*, 17 June 1989.

312. According to *Al-Shira'*, 4 August 1986, the Iranian embassy in Beirut intervened and prevented a riposte to the interview with Fadlallah in *Al-Shira'*, 25 June 1986, where he explained his concept of the multiplicity of leadership.

313. *Al-Shira'*, 10 July 1989.

314. His most comprehensive post-Khomeini discussion of the question appears in Fadlallah interview, *Al-Diyar*, 10 July 1989.

315. Fadlallah interview, *Al-Sharq al-awsat* (London), 11 February 1993.

316. Fadlallah interview, *Al-Bilad*, 26 September 1992.

317. Fadlallah interview, *Al-Bilad*, 19 September 1992.

318. Fadlallah interview, *Al-Bilad*, 19 September 1992.

319. Fadlallah interview, *Al-Bilad*, 26 September 1992.

320. Fadlallah interview, *Al-Bilad*, 19 September 1992.

321. Fadlallah interview, *Al-Bilad*, 26 September 1992.

322. Fadlallah interview, Voice of Lebanon, 2 May 1992; FBIS DR, 5 May 1992.

323. Fadlallah interview, *Al-'Ahd*, no. 194, 11 March 1988.

324. Fadlallah interview, Voice of Lebanon, 2 May 1992; FBIS DR, 5 May 1992.

THREE

GLOBAL ISLAMIC AWAKENING

OR SUDANESE NIGHTMARE?

The Curious Case of Hassan Turabi

Judith Miller

At the Ottawa airport in May 1992, Hashim Badr al-Din, a Sudanese martial arts champion, saw a man he never expected to meet in his recently adopted land. A few paces ahead of him in the departure hall was Hassan Turabi, the de facto leader of the Islamic movement that has ruled Sudan since the military coup of 1989. Badr al-Din, a political exile who blamed Turabi for Sudan's profound misery, took the opportunity to attack the man he considered a tyrant.[1]

"He gave me four blows—that black belt in karate!" Turabi told me in an interview in Khartoum two years later, in the summer of 1994. "The doctors said that the first chop—just above the right ear—should have killed me! The second came right across the middle of my forehead. The third and fourth I don't even remember. And yet I survived! And now I'm even more famous. I have become a symbol of Islam."

Throughout more than forty years of political life, Hassan Abdallah al-Turabi has turned such savage assaults, many of which would have destroyed weaker or less fortunate men, to his advantage. But Turabi is a survivor. He has come to interpret his own political—and now physical—survival as evidence of both God's favor and the inevitability of the triumph of Islam in the Middle East and throughout an increasingly troubled and rudderless world.

Ever since a small group of junior army officers inspired by Islam and led by General Omar Hassan al-Bashir took power on 30 June 1989 in a coup against the democratic but monumentally ineffective government of Sadiq al-Mahdi, Hassan Turabi and his Muslim disciples have been trying to transform Sudan, an impoverished land almost one-third the size of the continental United States with a population of twenty-six million people, into an Islamic success story.

During its first six years in power, the regime has been bitterly and widely condemned by Western governments, international human-rights groups, the United Nations' special rapporteur, and Sudanese dissidents at home and abroad as antidemocratic, a violator of human rights, and a supporter and promoter of international terrorism. As early as 1991, four of the country's senior Christian leaders accused the government of systematically violating both the United Nations Charter on Human Rights and its own declarations assuring non-Muslim citizens of equality under law. The government was guilty, they said, of arresting and harassing priests, expelling missionaries, closing and destroying churches, fomenting hatred of non-Muslims among Muslims, and using food and other aid to promote conversion to Islam.[2]

The director of the Washington, D.C., office of Human Rights Watch/Africa, a privately funded human-rights organization, called the ostensibly Islamic regime Sudan's most brutal government since independence.[3] Gaspar Biro, special rapporteur to the United Nations Human Rights Commission, accused the regime of atrocities that border on genocide against the black, non-Arab, cattle-herding tribesmen of the Nuba mountains and non-Muslims of southern Sudan, where the fierce, protracted civil war rages on.[4] Amnesty International accused the Khartoum government of engaging in systematic torture to quell dissent. Not even children have been spared; street children, Amnesty says, have been subjected to "cruel, inhuman, or degrading treatment."[5] In 1993 the United States added Sudan to its list of countries that sponsor and assist international terrorism, a decision which led to a further reduction in international relief and development assistance to the desperately poor country, whose per capita income in 1994 was less than one hundred dollars a year, the lowest in the Arab world.

Despite these harsh verdicts many young Arabs throughout the region, and Muslims far beyond it, have been captivated by Sudan's transformation and Turabi's Islamic experiment in the only Sunni Arab state so far to have embraced absolutist, militant Islamic rule. Arab university students study Turabi's few books and other writings and debate his speeches and pronouncements at Islamic conferences, particularly those sponsored by the Khartoum-based Popular Arab and Islamic Congress, which Turabi created and led in the wake of the Gulf crisis.

Detractors have described Turabi as a "villain,"[6] "ruthless,"[7] "Machiavellian,"[8] "Islam's Lenin," a "calculating opportunist," and the "godfather of international terrorism."[9] Ostensibly neutral observers have called him "forceful," a man with a "charismatic personality," and a "skilled strategist." To his admirers, he is a "genius," the "preeminent pioneer and spokesman of the Islamic revival."[10] Few are indifferent to him.

Who is Hassan Turabi, and why does he arouse such hatred and devotion among so many Arabs? Is the Dr. Turabi who presides over the brutal Islamic regime in Sudan the same man who holds advanced degrees from the University of London and the Sorbonne in Paris—the liberal, tolerant Islamic theologian who once promoted Islamic emancipation of women, the triumph of Islam through persuasion rather than force, individual dignity and the right of dissent, and the obligation of citizens to question and challenge their rulers? Is this genial and learned man simply misunderstood by his critics? Or is he in fact the spokesman and supreme guide of a heartless and intolerant regime that has extinguished freedom in once-democratic Sudan?

IN PREPARATION

Hassan Turabi was born in Kassala, Eastern Sudan, on 1 February 1932, one of four sons and four daughters born to his father's first wife, who died when Turabi was very young. His family had a long tradition of Islamic learning and Sufism, a heritage, he has said, that was critical to his intellectual formation. "My grandfather was a famous scholar. He worked for public life and welfare, and he struggled against the government of those days."[11] Turabi's grandfather was imprisoned for seven years for opposing the Anglo-Egyptian condominium that ruled Sudan for forty-two years. "I inherited his tendency for detention," jokes Turabi, who has spent more than a thousand days in jail under three different military regimes.

The young Turabi also inherited other qualities—a passion for law, a peripatetic existence that acquainted him with many parts of his vast country, and intimate knowledge of his religion. All three came from his father, who was a member of the first graduating class of Sudan's first religious college, El Ma'had al-Ilmi, in 1934. As a shari'a judge, his father was transferred often from one region to another. Though his father's village was Wad al-Turabi, about fifty miles south of Khartoum in the Gezira cotton-growing district that the British had delineated in 1925, Turabi spent little time there as a boy. He received his elementary education in western Sudan, in Kordofan; his intermediate school years were spent in Medani and Dofar, in central Sudan; and he attended secondary school in Handub, in Medani, at one of only three such schools in the country at the time. Though the schools were English-speaking, secular, and British-run, Turabi learned the Qur'an at home from his father, who taught his intellectually precocious son the traditional religious curriculum of Cairo's Al-Azhar, the Arab world's oldest Islamic university, and Khartoum's el-Ma'had al-Ilmi, as well as Arabic language and literature, especially poetry. "That explains a lot about my character," Turabi said. Though a product of secular colonial schools, "I had another culture. I thought critically. And as I listened to my father, I learned to think critically because I had a double source of education." This dual training would eventually serve him well, for Turabi, unlike many other leading Islamic militants, is comfortable addressing both Western and non-Western audiences.

Turabi attended Gordon Memorial College, named in honor of the eccentric British governor-general killed in 1885 by the forces of Mohammed Ahmed ibn Abdullahi—the man known as the Mahdi (a national messianic religious and political leader, the Mahdi had briefly unified the Sudan and founded one of the region's first modern, militant Islamic states). In 1955 he graduated from the college (since renamed the University of Khartoum) with a law degree, but he did not wish to practice law. "I never liked the bar association, and I knew that justice was not an independent value," Turabi explained. "Whoever paid your fees, you argued his case. Even in those early days, I didn't like that."

In 1949 the Egyptian-based Muslim Brotherhood founded a chapter in Sudan, of which some students at the Handub secondary school became early members. Turabi did not become active in Islamic student politics until 1951, however, when the charismatic, well-spoken young man became the head of the Brotherhood branch at Gordon College. The communist National Liberation Movement and the Islamic Liberation Movement, a branch of the Ikhwan (Muslim Brotherhood), were the two student movements of consequence in the days before independence. The two groups were bitter rivals and have remained so. In 1953, the Ikhwan won nine out of ten seats on the student union executive committee—a significant victory for the young movement and a blow to the better established communists. When asked about the relation of the Sudanese branch of the Brotherhood to the mother organization in Cairo, Turabi downplayed the ties. Though the Sudanese branch was always "fairly independent," he said, the communists played up its links to Cairo in order to discredit the Ikhwan in the eyes of many Sudanese, who still resented Egypt's protracted occupation of their country. "And Nasser was all against the Muslim Brothers—he was slaughtering them and jailing them. The communists controlled the media; they called us Muslim Brothers and we accepted the name. We said: why not?" But Turabi recalls the Egyptian Muslim Brotherhood as being "a little paternalistic towards us," something he always resisted.

Not knowing what he wanted to do professionally, Turabi went to England in 1955 to continue his studies at the University of London. He completed his master's degree in law in 1957 and in 1959 went to France, where he obtained his Ph.D. from the Sorbonne in 1964, one of the first Sudanese graduates of Gordon Memorial College to do so. He decided to study in Paris partly "to learn another language, another culture," and also because the British, who had recently ended the condominium, did not want Sudanese to be educated in the land of England's historic enemy. "They wanted you to learn English, to study and think in English," Turabi said. His doctoral dissertation compared the executive powers of France and Britain during a state of emergency, a subject that would be useful some thirty years later when his own Islamic group ruled in a perpetual state of emergency. In both London and Paris he remained active in Islamic student politics.

Turabi toured the United States in the summer of 1960 and a year later married Wissal al-Mahdi, the sister of Sadiq al-Mahdi, the great-grandson of the Mahdi. Sadiq would eventually lead the Ansar ("helpers") movement that his great-grandfather had created. He and Turabi were great friends when they were students together in England—Turabi in London and Sadiq at Oxford. But despite the family bond created by Turabi's marriage to Sadiq's sister, they were destined to be fierce rivals. Turabi returned to Khartoum in the summer of 1964 to teach at the Law Faculty of the University of Khartoum. His status as one of the first Sudanese holders of a doctorate enhanced his standing and made him an instant superstar within the ranks of the Ikhwan, which was marginalized and intensely faction-ridden when he arrived on the scene.

Abdelwahab el-Affendi, a gifted, British-educated disciple of Turabi and the author of a comprehensive (and highly sympathetic) portrait of his mentor, describes two incidents that reveal the young Turabi's political inclinations.[12] Both occurred before Turabi's full-time return to Khartoum and involved a debate within the Ikhwan in the late 1950s and early 1960s over its own political role and its relations with Sudan's traditional political parties—the Umma Party, founded by Sadiq al-Mahdi's family and based largely on membership in the Ansar sect, and the Union Party, which drew mainly on the Khatmiya, the largest Sufi religious sect, founded in the nineteenth century by Mohammed Othman al-Mirghani, a charismatic Muslim who gained a large following in northern and eastern Sudan. Turabi's position in this debate demonstrated what was to be a lifelong preference for political pragmatism or, as el-Affendi and Turabi prefer to put it, for moderate, inclusive policies.

In 1958 the Brotherhood was divided over whether its members should run for Sudan's democratic parliament and, if so, whether they should run as members of their own, independent political party or in alliance with the large traditional parties. Turabi, by now a member of the Brotherhood's executive committee, supported a proposal by a leader of an Ikhwan faction who wanted to run on the Umma Party's ticket. The committee, however, rejected the proposal; Muslim Brotherhood doctrine favored providing an alternative to traditional Arab politics, which the Brotherhood considered corrupt.

In 1962, after the military had seized power and ended Sudan's first experiment in democracy, Turabi proposed that the Ikhwan work not as a formal political party but as "an intellectual pressure group" to build support within existing parties for an Islamic state. This, too, was rejected by his Brotherhood peers. At the same meeting, however, the Brotherhood approved another Turabi initiative, one that would shape the movement's strategy even in its proponent's continuing absence in Paris. Turabi held that the Ikhwan should oppose the ruling military government, as a matter of principle, because its goals were "in no way those of Islam" and because its reign was based on "tyranny, oppression and espionage" and on the denial of *shura* (consultation between the ruler and the ruled). In addition, Turabi argued, the regime hampered "the work for Islam," caused "decline in the moral standards of the people, corruption in their transactions," and harmed "the country's interests." Turabi proceeded to outline a strategy for opposing the unpopular regime of General Ibrahim Abboud. Opponents of the junta could topple it, he maintained, by forming a broad, united front of Sudan's traditional political parties and the southern political factions with whom the north was then waging a fierce civil war. A united opposition could weaken and ultimately defeat the Abboud regime, Turabi argued, through a protracted, peaceful resistance that would include mass strikes, protests, and propaganda outside and inside the country.

These early stances reflect Turabi's preference for gaining political experience whenever and wherever the Brotherhood could do so, even if that meant diluting the group's exacting dogma and abandoning its tightly knit, elitist approach to organization and recruitment. By the time Turabi returned to Sudan from the Sorbonne in the summer of 1964, General Abboud's government was being subjected to the very measures he had recommended two years earlier. Unfortunately for the Brotherhood, however, much of the resistance was coordinated by the larger and better-organized Sudan Communist Party, then the largest communist party in Africa.

The opposition's opportunity to topple the government came in October 1964; the episode was triggered by students at Khartoum University, a traditional source of political activism in postcolonial Sudan. In a well-publicized debate at the student union Turabi called for an end to military rule. In response the junta arrested several students and banned all political meetings on campus. When students staged another political debate in defiance of the ban, the police intervened, and one student was killed. The funeral for the slain student prompted mass strikes, street protests, and the resignations of university staff and judges. As a result support for the junta waned within military circles. These events, now known as the October Revolution, led to the resignation of the junta leaders. The uprising ushered in another round of democratic politics and a second, ultimately unsatisfactory effort by Sudan's traditional political parties and groups to solve their country's pressing economic and political problems through coalition rule.

Though Turabi maintained a high profile during the October Revolution—transporting wounded students in his car, advising on how to maximize the emotional appeal of the slain student's funeral, lobbying traditional politicians to attend the funeral—el-Affendi acknowledges that Turabi was stunned by the breadth and ferocity of the opposition to the junta. The Ikhwan could do little more than keep up with the popular uprising; the Ansar, Khatmiya, and even the communists played far more important roles in mobilizing support for an end to the regime. But due to his dramatic student-union appeal for an end to military rule and the restoration of democracy, Turabi became known throughout Sudan.

One month after the October Revolution, Turabi, now dean of the law faculty at Khartoum University, was named secretary-general of the Ikhwan, a new position that directly challenged the group's previous insistence on collective leadership. But Turabi, an effective orator and now an Islamic celebrity, managed to circumvent the Ikhwan ruling elite and win Brotherhood support for his leadership through shrewd parliamentary maneuvering and by reaching out to younger members of the country's emerging elite.[13] His actions, however, outraged older militants who had long disagreed with him over tactics and substance. Turabi had returned to Khartoum from London and Paris to champion what many of them regarded as dangerous "Western" ideas: voting rights for women and other forms of emancipation consistent with Islamic law and practice, democracy in government, an independent judiciary. He also advocated ending the civil war with the non-Muslim, non-Arab south through peaceful restoration of their constitutional rights. Most of these ideas were anathema to traditional Ikhwan members, who had inherited both their radical, uncompromising Islamic doctrine and the group's exclusive, elitist structure from Egypt.

As Turabi's control over the Brotherhood tightened and his own prominence soared, he repeatedly maintained that he was being dragged unwillingly into politics and that he would have "preferred a nonpolitical role."[14] This position foreshadowed another consistent strand in Turabi's conduct—his curious insistence to this day that he holds no formal post in the putative Islamic fundamentalist government and plays no official role in the regime.

In November 1964, Turabi formed the Islamic Charter Front (ICF), a coalition of religious individuals and groups through which he would press for a peaceful solution to the war in the south and for the adoption of an "Islamic" program, including the imposition of shari'a as the law of the land.[15] Though neither the Umma Party nor the Unionists joined the ICF, relations between Turabi and Sadiq al-Mahdi's Umma Party remained close, which further fueled suspicions about Turabi's true motives and goals among more orthodox, radical members of the Brotherhood. After the end of the military rule, however, Sadiq al-Mahdi and leaders of the traditional parties saw little utility in cooperating with the ICF, since they viewed the Ikhwan as marginal. The elections of 1965 confirmed their assessment: while the Islamic Charter Front won seven seats—including one for Turabi, thanks mainly to his personal prominence—the communists won eleven.

External opposition from the communists proved easier for Turabi to quell than the growing opposition within the Brotherhood, but his actions against the communists raised serious questions about the depth of his commitment to democracy. Less than a year after the military regime was overthrown, the Ikhwan lobbied for and secured from Al-Azhar, the highest Islamic authority in Egypt, a ruling that all communists should be regarded as "nonbelievers." Within Sudan Turabi capitalized on the public furor surrounding a Communist Party member's insulting remarks about the Prophet Muhammad, winning support for constitutional amendments that banned the Communist Party in Sudan and expelled the eleven communist members from the parliament. "More damaging to his democratic credentials," wrote Peter Nyot Kok, an ardent critic of Turabi and the current military regime, "was his prominent role in mobilising the Assembly to defy the High Court, which had ruled in favour of the unseated members by declaring the constitutional amendments as unconstitutional."[16] Such infighting resulted in a pattern of parliamentary paralysis, debilitating feuds, and a loss of public confidence in democratic politics in Sudan—disenchantment that would set the stage for yet another military coup four years later.

Meanwhile, the long-standing feud within the Brotherhood over how to create an Islamic state in Sudan was reaching a boiling point. Turabi, the leader of what el-Affendi described as the "political school" within the Ikhwan, continued to press for building a broad coalition of forces sympathetic to an Islamic revolution and participating whenever possible in government to gain experience and contacts. The hard-line "educationalist school," galvanized by Muhammed Salih Omar and Gaafar Idris, argued that an Islamic state could be brought about only by an uncompromising militant elite devoted to the Brotherhood's discipline and credo, and by Muslims operating in relative isolation from mainstream Sudanese politics and society, a position consistent with orthodox Muslim Brotherhood doctrine. When the Islamic Charter Front fared poorly in the general elections of 1968, the educationalists decided the time had come to limit Turabi's power and return the Ikhwan to its more traditional goals and tactics. Omar and Idris were determined to impose their political line on the ICF, which the Ikhwan executive committee supposedly controlled, but Turabi's faction resisted. In April 1969 an Ikhwan general congress was convened to settle the dispute. Thanks in part to his personal charisma, Turabi won the support of the majority of Brotherhood members in what is generally regarded as the fiercest dispute within the ranks of the Sudanese Brotherhood.

That, at least, is el-Affendi's version of the struggle. Gaafar Idris, the Muslim Brotherhood ideologue, who now lives in Virginia, paints a less glowing portrait of Turabi's maneuvers. Idris characterizes the dispute as not only one of ideology, but also of personality. "Many of us did not trust Turabi," Idris said in a recent interview. "We felt that he was not honest and was not truly committed to an Islamic state, that what he really wanted was power."[17]

When Turabi insisted on including the Umma Party in the Islamic Charter Front and continued to cooperate with his brother-in-law, Sadiq al-Mahdi, after that plan was rejected, Turabi's detractors within the Ikhwan suspected him of forming a secret alliance with Sadiq. Was Sadiq, they wondered, trying to use Turabi to neutralize the fledgling Brotherhood as a potential challenger to the Umma? Was Turabi willing to sacrifice Islamic principles to secure personal power? Turabi's restructuring of the Brotherhood in the 1970s further fueled their suspicions. Under the old structure, Brotherhood chapters throughout the country elected representatives to a biennial general congress, which included some three hundred to four hundred representatives. The congress then elected a *shura,* or consultative or parliamentary group of sixty people, which in turn elected an executive committee of ten members. The executive committee, of which Idris had been a member, elected the national leader. But through a series of parliamentary maneuvers, Turabi reversed the process: the shura would henceforth elect the leader, who would then handpick his executive committee. Later Turabi won approval of another change: the congress itself would elect the national leader. Since Turabi was a dynamic orator and by far the best-known member of the Brotherhood elite, these ostensibly procedural changes helped him solidify control of the group. Whenever his leadership or prerogatives were challenged, concludes Idris, Turabi did not behave like the liberal he pretended to be. Being "liberal in religious doctrine did not make you a liberal in politics," he said. "Some of us wanted more than simply for Islam to come to power in Sudan; we wanted Islam to succeed in power."

Turabi's "victory" in the April 1969 Brotherhood general congress soon appeared Pyrrhic. One month later, General Gaafar Nimeiri and a group of leftist, nationalist military officers seized power in a mostly bloodless coup. Turabi, other senior Ikhwan members, and other traditional party leaders, including Sadiq al-Mahdi, were initially imprisoned as Nimeiri's government cracked down on groups that opposed his rule. While repressing political challengers in the north, however, Nimeiri managed to end the costly and protracted civil war with the south in 1972 by guaranteeing southerners freedom of religion, regional autonomy, and a greater share of national resources. Nimeiri, who came to power as a radical Arab nationalist, gradually came to believe—particularly after the communists nearly succeeded in overthrowing him in 1971—that he had less to fear from religiously based opponents than from leftists. In 1977, when Nimeiri undertook "national reconciliation" talks with the major political parties and the Ikhwan, Turabi ended his opposition to Nimeiri's rule and joined the military government, at first holding a minor post, but gradually advancing to jobs of greater importance. In 1979 Turabi became Nimeiri's attorney general and in 1983, his adviser on legal and foreign affairs. In addition Nimeiri put his former rival in charge of a committee to study ways of making Sudan's legal code conform with Islamic law.

Nimeiri's new-found confidence in him enabled Turabi to install Brotherhood members in key posts throughout the government, including the army and security services, something he had been unable to do during Sudan's two previous forays into democratic, parliamentary politics. He came to understand, however, that his strategy was not without risk. As corruption increased in the military regime and Nimeiri proved unable to solve his impoverished country's desperate economic and social problems, Turabi and his party shared the blame. Although Turabi's committee had nothing to do with drafting the harsh Islamic penal code that Nimeiri made the law of the land in 1983, Turabi was also blamed for the extreme punishments dispensed by Nimeiri's emergency courts— cross amputations of a left foot and a right hand for repeated theft, flogging for drinking alcohol, and death for apostasy.

The implementation of these laws enraged the largely non-Muslim south and helped rekindle the insurgency that Nimeiri himself had ended earlier in his rule. It not only generated widespread opposition within Sudan but also outraged the West. Sadiq al-Mahdi opposed Nimeiri's legal code as "un-Islamic," but Turabi, a government member—though not an important one, he now insists—defended the laws and the harsh punishments. Though flawed, Turabi maintained at the time, Nimeiri's Islamic penal code was a step toward making "shari'a the law of the land and creating a truly Islamic society."[18] In addition, Turabi had persuaded Nimeiri to permit the opening of the Faisal Islamic Bank and other Islamic financial institutions, though Turabi was always careful in interviews to distance himself from these institutions. Thanks to their creation in the late 1970s, the Ikhwan had access to the capital, credit, and financial resources that it had always lacked.

Ironically, Turabi's political standing and credibility were saved at the last moment—inadvertently—by Nimeiri himself. Suspecting that Turabi and his Brotherhood were not to be trusted, Nimeiri had Turabi arrested and imprisoned in 1985. Shortly thereafter, upon his return from an official visit to the United States, Nimeiri was overthrown in another bloodless military coup by a group of officers determined to restore democratic politics in Sudan and end the bloody, ever more costly civil war. Turabi and other political leaders, including Sadiq al-Mahdi, were released from prison, and Turabi was able to claim that he, too, had suffered under Nimeiri's erratic, repressive rule.

With military rule ended once more, Sudan's traditional political parties relaunched their historic feuds and petty personal struggles in what passed for democratic politics in Sudan. The Ikhwan, now more than ever under Turabi's leadership, formed the National Islamic Front (NIF) to run for elections. In the 1985 elections the Brotherhood won less than 20 percent of the national vote—the last objective measure of its true public support. This was a far better showing than the 5 percent it had won in 1965, but far less than it needed to claim the right to rule Sudan exclusively. Sadiq al-Mahdi, whose Umma Party won the largest share of the vote, became prime minister, forming a coalition government with the Union party that excluded Turabi and the NIF. Plagued as usual by paralyzing infighting and rivalry, however, Sadiq was forced to form a new coalition with his brother-in-law Turabi and several small southern parties in 1988. Again Turabi assumed the offices of attorney general and justice minister; later he became deputy prime minister and minister of foreign affairs.

But neither Sadiq al-Mahdi nor Hassan Turabi trusted the other. Turabi was using his participation in the coalition to continue to press for shari'a and the formation of an Islamic society, a goal that in his view superseded whatever obligations he had undertaken to his coalition partners.[19] While Turabi pressed his agenda on an increasingly resistant but utterly ineffectual Sadiq, he also, again, placed Brotherhood members in key positions throughout the government he had vowed to uphold. In 1989, more than four years after Nimeiri's expulsion, with the economy in tatters and the civil war raging out of control in the south, Sudan experienced two military upheavals, the second of which brought the NIF to power.

In February 1989 150 military officers handed Sadiq al-Mahdi a memorandum demanding that he expand his government to include parties other than the NIF and either take steps to end the civil war or give the army sufficient resources to win it. At first Sadiq, as usual, dithered. Finally, largely in response to the army's threat of a coup d'état, he arrived at an understanding with southern leaders and northern political parties on a formula to end the debilitating conflict. The understanding called for the abrogation of Sudan's Islamic penal code—what Turabi had repeatedly called "God's law"—and the granting of autonomy once again to the non-Muslims of the south. When Turabi's NIF balked at the formula, Sadiq expelled the Brotherhood from his coalition, formed a new government, and prepared to implement the agreement. This prompted army officers in the Brotherhood to stage a coup d'état.

The new military regime's political inclinations and Turabi's importance to that regime were initially obscured by General Omar Bashir's decision to imprison all of Sudan's traditional political leaders, including Turabi. By the time Turabi emerged from prison five months later, however, it was clear to at least some Sudanese analysts—if not to Western government representatives in Khartoum—that Turabi and his NIF were in charge (though the party itself would soon be officially disbanded along with all existing political parties.) General Bashir, it turned out, had long been a member of the Muslim Brotherhood; he was seen by NIF leaders as an effective, pliable officer who could be relied upon to carry out orders.[20] Yet again Turabi had accomplished through a military coup what he had been unable to obtain through Sudan's democratic process—exclusive political control of his fractious country.

"In the third liberal democratic era (1985–1989)," which Peter Kok called Turabi's "finest hour," Turabi "spoke not only affirmatively about his commitment to democracy, but took an oath on becoming a minister in May 1988 to uphold and defend the democratic order prescribed by the Transitional Constitution of 1985 (amended 1987). A year later, his party cadres in the armed forces overthrew that constitution."[21]

Since the early stages of the ensuing regime, which marked its fifth year in power as this essay was written, Turabi has consistently denied that he is running the government. In the wake of the 1990–1991 Gulf war, he founded and became head of the Popular Arab and Islamic Congress (PAIC), an "independent" association that brings together militant Islamic groups throughout the Middle East and the Muslim world for meetings and conferences aimed at revitalizing Islamic thought and responding to political and social challenges posed by modernity. But apart from the Congress, which is staffed by younger, mostly Western-educated Brotherhood members, he claims no official leadership role. In an interview in 1992, Turabi described himself as a "mere house husband with no public office in the state," rather than, as Kok described him that same year, "the *éminence grise* of the present regime." "The policies of the government are basically NIF's and al-Turabi's policies," Kok concluded, a view shared by most western analysts.

IN POWER

How has Turabi's thinking evolved since the coming to power of the militant fundamentalist government—the goal for which he has struggled

throughout his political life? And how does Turabi square his liberal pronouncements of the 1970s with the political realities of Sudan today?

In some ways, Turabi has remained remarkably consistent. He has
rarely rejected an opportunity to broaden his Islamic coalition or participate in a government—military or civilian—that would enable him and
his group to gain administrative experience and useful contacts. To el-
Affendi this demonstrates Turabi's "consummate pragmatism"; to critics,
it is proof of what Sadiq al-Mahdi called his "Machiavellianism" and
opportunism. Turabi clearly believes that the end justifies the means—a
conviction shared by all secular or religious absolutists. Thus, the goal
of implementing shari'a and establishing an Islamic society must take
precedence over constitutional vows or other pledges to uphold democratic rules. Freedom and democracy were useful to Turabi when they
advanced his cause; they have clearly proven dispensable when they do
not. So while the Turabi of 1965 championed democracy as a way of
ridding Sudan of a leftist military regime that opposed implementing
shari'a and his Islamic program, the Turabi of 1995 had no problem
defending another military junta that was committed to implementing
God's law on earth.

Another respect in which Turabi remains consistent becomes evident
when one compares his views before and after the current military regime.
In both periods he presents militant Sudanese Islam, which he has led for
more than twenty years, not as merely a variation on the programs of
earlier Islamic pioneers, but as original. According to his writings and
interviews, Turabi has little respect for Mohammed Ahmed ibn Abdullahi, the nineteenth-century Sudanese messianic figure who claimed to
be the Mahdi, the "expected one" who would appear one day to defeat
oppressors and free the world in the name of Islam. The Mahdi left a deep
imprint on the modern Sudanese national and religious consciousness: he
united Sudan for the first time, expelled its Egyptian-Ottoman occupiers,
and established for thirteen years a Mahdiya, an Islamic entity that some
analysts regard as Islam's first modern militant state.[22] Nonetheless, Turabi does not see the Mahdi as his intellectual or political predecessor,
nor the Mahdiya as a prototype of the military regime in power today.
Like many Sunni Muslims, Turabi has only disdain for the Mahdi's claims
to leadership, which were based on what he alleged was a special relationship with the Prophet. Moreover, leadership in the Mahdist movement
quickly became dynastic and hence, according to militant Sunni doctrine,
inherently un-Islamic. "People would vote for the Mahdi," Turabi said,
referring to his traditional rival, Sadiq al-Mahdi, the Mahdi's great-
grandson, "because of his great-grandfather, because of his achievements

in the nineteenth century. . . . His followers are indifferent to what he thinks today, and what he would do, and would never ask him questions about the way he conducts politics. They would vote for him whether he goes left or right or whether he makes a mess of the government."[23]

When asked who had most influenced his religious and political thinking, Turabi mentioned no Muslim philosophical predecessors. He seems to perceive Sudanese Islam as a truly inventive model that Sunni Muslim groups in other countries would do well to imitate, despite the growing chorus of complaints about the military government's human rights record. In many ways, however, Turabi's thinking mirrors that of the well-known group of militant Islamic thinkers who became prominent once Kemal Atatürk vanquished the Ottoman sultan-caliph after Turkey's defeat in World War I. Turabi views the Islamic revival of the last seventy years as a reaction to the "real secularization and de-Islamization of public life" resulting not from modernity per se, but from "Western imperialism" following the collapse of the Ottoman Empire and the abolition of the caliphate. "They established, in the place of shari'a, positive laws: French, English, or whatever, and secular institutions: army, civil service, and economic system," Turabi told a small group of scholars in Tampa, Florida, during his 1992 tour of North America. The first phase of the public response to this "disestablishment" of Islam," he argued, was directed against "the advent of colonialism," whose demise Turabi readily attributes mainly to the secular Arab nationalist movements. But once independence was achieved, he said, the public understood that the nationalists were not prepared for anything else, that they had no program. Independence to the secular Arab nationalists, he said, meant putting a Sudanese administrator in the place of a British one. "Once independence was achieved, these movements looked bankrupt."[24]

The more "mature" response to Western imperialism, according to Turabi, was the Islamic revival that grips much of the modern Middle East. "I remember those early days, the 1940s," he told the mostly sympathetic academicians. "The most important thing about Islamic movements was that slogan that Islam is a state and a religion (*Islam din wa dawla*). We had forgotten it completely; religious people all over, even though they had wielded political influence, had stayed away physically from politics." Turabi credits the Muslim Brotherhood of Egypt, its creator Hassan al-Banna, and "early populist movements in Iraq and Syria" with reengaging in politics and lobbying for Islamic constitutions and Islamic laws. He blames the Arab governments of the same era for repressing these movements and driving them underground. In Turabi's view, this led "traditional" Islamic movements, such as the Muslim Brotherhood and Pakistan's Jama'at-i-Islami, to work in great secrecy, concentrate on education, recruitment, and indoctrination, and "shy away from politics." In the late 1970s and 1980s, the "newer" Islamic movements—those in Iran or Algeria—were popular movements that sought "masses and quantity" right away rather than "elitism or obsession with quality."

But the Sudanese "model," Turabi asserted, was neither totally "traditional" nor "popular"; rather, it was a synthesis of the two—a movement that began in traditional Brotherhood fashion with an elite corps, but that later developed "a popular dimension and became politicized."

Turabi has little use for armchair Islamists. "People are not interested in detail," he told the Tampa gathering. "That's why slogans like 'Islam is the solution,' are very important. You don't develop a program by sitting in an ivory tower and writing out an economic program or a social program," he opined. "You develop it in public life through interaction with public opinion." And he does not hesitate to disparage the classical Muslim Brotherhood's structure, its "antidemocratic" organization and operating style, and its former leaders. Hassan al-Banna, he said, led the Brotherhood "in the typical manner of a 'shaykh' with followers; there was little that was democratic about it." Nor is Turabi impressed with Sayyid Qutb, the Muslim Brotherhood leader and author of the manifesto of the modern militant Muslim revival. Qutb's most influential work— the creed, so to speak, of many young Islamic militants—is a slender book entitled *Signposts on the Road*. It argued that true Muslims had to break with the *jahiliyya* society of the contemporary Arab world, for it was spiritually similar to societies that existed during the period of "ignorance" and "barbarism" before the Prophet Muhammad founded his state in Arabia. Even rulers who claimed to be Islamic were not so unless they ruled by the laws of Islam. Asked whether Qutb had influenced his own thinking, Turabi dismissed Islamic fundamentalism's most influential theorist as just another revolutionary—"too dogmatic" and "too opposed to the regime, rather than thinking about what would come after."

Revolutions inevitably bred such negative thinking, Turabi lamented in a previous interview with this author—"the American, French, the Russian, Iran . . . it's always just destroy, destroy." That was one reason why the Iranian revolution had failed to achieve its promise, Turabi said, noting that Khomeini had been limited by historical circumstances and his sect's dogma. Like the early Christians, said Turabi, Shi'ite Muslims, a minority in Islam, had developed a church to protect them because they were persecuted. "When you are a minority, especially under persecution and suppression," Turabi said, "your leadership and private organizations become a most important thing." While he personally opposed such structures as "intellectual barriers in thinking about Islam," Turabi understood why they had developed among the Shi'ites, descendants of Islam's first great schism.

"I don't want to be a holy man, a pope. Journalists from the West always misunderstand me," Turabi said, "because they think that Islam equals Christianity. So I am a black pope. The pope of Islam. And I really don't like it. In a lecture, wherever I go, people respect me. All over the world, people know me. But I sit down with them and talk on the same level. And even if I know that I have a much richer legacy of knowledge, I still speak to them as if they were my equals." In the future, he said, he hoped that all of the titles of the Shi'ite "church"—"the ayatollahs, or marjas, or whatever—will disappear from their society." Clerics or scholars could be rulers, but without any claim of "divine right." In one respect, Turabi said, his role is similar to that of the late Ayatollah Khomeini, whose revolution, if not revolutionary doctrine, Turabi championed in Sudan: neither he nor the late Khomeini were day-to-day rulers. "They thought Khomeini was running the country; he wasn't," Turabi said. "He was a very influential person, yes. He was a symbol of the revolution. People had to respect him. But he only interfered in things that were strategic. Sometimes he interfered in things that were not that important, but he wasn't managing the country, economically or otherwise."

This is one possible explanation of Turabi's unwillingness to be described as Sudan's leader, or even as an important arbiter of disputes within the government. "I'll say that I'll have a role in society rather than in government," Turabi told the scholars in Florida.[25] And society, he stressed, was "the primary institution in Islam, far more important than the state." Through shari'a, God's binding law, Islam limits the power of government by investing it in society, that is, in the people, through commanding the obligation to ordain "what is good" and forbid "what is improper." Moreover, Turabi thinks of himself, as Khomeini did, in far grander terms—as a symbol of his country's revolution, an Islamic internationalist whose vision cannot be limited to his hopeless land, so isolated from regional and international power centers, that fate has designated as the site of militant Sunni Islam's first official experiment. "I don't want to become a nationalist," he told me. "I must carry a passport, yes. But when I go to America, or anywhere, I hope people will treat me as a human being, not a Sudanese. Yes, they have to see passports, check visas. But I am not narrowly nationalist. Muslims are all like that."

The Popular Arab and Islamic Congress, therefore, is a vehicle consistent with Turabi's self-perception in that it permits him to provide guidance on the wide range of problems confronting Muslims in many far-flung lands. Another reason for Muslims to reject state borders, Turabi told the scholars in Tampa, was that the national frontiers were "not of their making; it was the British, French, and Belgians who made them in the first place. . . . If you have noticed, the Sudan is going a little bit international." Nonetheless, he denied his neighbors' charges that Sudan was trying to export its revolution to them: "It's just that people don't really believe that a frontier is relevant. There are people on the other side of the frontier in the Sudan that are of the same ethnic stock, in all directions: north, east, west. So the Sudan is now opening up frontiers toward Ethiopia, to Chad."

Turabi, more than many militants, acknowledges and respects the legitimacy of the nation-state and its borders. But the notion of the nation-state as an obstacle to the spread of Islam is also a consistent theme in his thinking. In the early 1970s, when the Brotherhood was still being harassed and repressed by Nimeiri's regime, the Sudanese Ikhwan was largely sustained by contributions and assistance from official and private supporters in Saudi Arabia, whom Turabi visited frequently during his years in exile.[26] In 1989 when he was Sadiq al-Mahdi's foreign minister, Turabi created a diplomatic furor with the Soviet Union when he recognized the Mujahadeen of Afghanistan—then based in Peshawar, Pakistan—as Afghanistan's "legitimate government" and permitted them to open an embassy in Khartoum. Similarly, the current military government, from its early days, has provided safe haven for Islamically inspired "liberation" groups and given diplomatic passports to leading Islamic militants wanted by conservative Arab governments, including Rashid Gannouchi, the leader of the Tunisian militant movement an-Na'ada.

The PAIC, in sum, gives Turabi a vehicle for offering opinions on the myriad debates among Islamists, and for mediating disputes in countries from Afghanistan to Algeria. Through this forum he is able to assert himself as an adjudicator in domestic and international policy quarrels within the *umma*, the global Muslim family.

Another journalist who visited Turabi in 1994 argued that Turabi's "strangely transparent" denials of playing any role in government were not aimed at persuading his visitor as much as they were a way of reassuring himself, of deceiving himself, as it were, and of tuning out the unpleasant realities of modern-day Sudan, perhaps to enable him to continue dreaming of a prosperous, successful Islamic model that would spread across the globe. "Turabi," the journalist wrote, "is an observant man and a student of history. As a Muslim, he has to accept the frustrations of his fate: to have been born ambitious and idealistic—and Sudanese. Perhaps in his most private thoughts he knows already that he will die disillusioned. There will be no reforming of distant lands, let alone his own."[27]

This interpretation, though charitable, is not supported by the indignation with which Turabi responds to the burgeoning charges against the regime, or by his impressive ability to weather political storms in pursuit of his Islamic agenda, or by the way in which he claims to view his accomplishments. "I've achieved more than I ever dreamed of," Turabi told this author. "But I'm still dreaming of more things. . . . I don't want to call them my dreams. I call them ideals. And I plan towards them. I draw my path towards them. My very life." These are not the words of a disillusioned man. Turabi knows that he is not being honest when he downplays his importance in Sudan or denies abuses that observers, including this one, know firsthand to be true. His false modesty and reflexive denial of the obvious are useful to him.

In late 1994 some careful students of Sudanese politics asserted that the military regime in Khartoum was out of control—that the Ikhwan and its government had become hopelessly factionalized, its policies and actions rendered incoherent by competing Islamic power centers within the military, the security services, and government ministries. Turabi may no longer be able to influence decisions and provide the direction and unity he once did, a well-placed Sudanese official has said.[28] It is possible, in such a situation, to see Turabi's distancing of himself from the regime as a sort of insurance policy, in that it permits him both to claim credit for the regime's successes and to evade responsibility for its many failures. For as Turabi learned during the Nimeiri years, too close an association with an unpopular regime may have severe costs; only his arrest during the last days of that regime, which he served as attorney general and adviser, saved the Ikhwan from being held culpable for its role in Nimeiri's oppressive, quixotic rule. By fostering ambiguity about who makes decisions in Sudan, then, Turabi maintains a fall-back strategy, by means of which he may retain some claim to power when and if the Sudanese decide they have had enough of the Islamic militants' rule and, either collectively or through another group of disgruntled army officers, expel the Brotherhood from power.

What has recently taken place is harrowing, particularly by the standards of Sudan, where prisons, as Turabi himself once told me, were places in which he managed to read, reflect, and even finish several long essays, where family was permitted to visit on weekends, and where torture was uncommon, if not unknown. Prisons in Turabi's regime, by contrast, are filled with political prisoners and are supplemented by the now notorious "ghost houses," where people suspected of opposing the regime are subjected to "severe torture" for weeks and months on end, "completely cut off from the outside world," according to the final report of the United Nations special rapporteur, Gaspar Biro, published in February 1994. Biro expressed "deep concern" about the "grave and widespread violations of human rights by government agents and officials," as well as by the southern Sudanese army, the SPLA, which carries out Khartoum's "jihad" against Christians and other non-Muslims in the south. He accused Khartoum of "large numbers of extrajudicial killings, summary executions, enforced or involuntary disappearances, systematic torture and widespread arbitrary arrest of suspected opponents," as well as abuses committed against women and children, such as "abduction, traffic, enslavement and rape."[29] In the south, churches have been burned, priests and Christian villagers abducted and mowed down by the army, women raped, and children taken from their parents, and these violations have not been confined to the war zone. Freedom of conscience, expression, association, and peaceful assembly are also being "seriously infringed," the report states, noting that several people who had the courage to tell Biro what was happening in Sudan were "subjected to reprisals" for having met with him. The government's treatment of the non-Arab tribes in the Nuba Mountains, he added, is so harsh and its violations of such a "grave nature" that "the fate of the Nuba communities in the area may be in question," which in the dry language of such UN reports, virtually accuses the government of what is more commonly called ethnic cleansing and genocide.[30]

Nor did the human-rights situation improve after the special rapporteur's visits. In October 1994, Human Rights Watch/Africa issued an equally searing condemnation of Turabi's regime, accusing it of "massive violation of human rights and humanitarian law," "systematic terror" in quelling dissent, and taking "extraordinary measures" to prevent the world from learning about what is taking place in the country. Although Islam prohibits coerced conversion—but only of Christians and Jews—the report documented case after case in which children living in shantytowns in and around Khartoum were rounded up and sent to Islamist camps, where they were beaten, given new names and Muslim identities, and at age fifteen, incorporated into the government's militias to fight fellow non-Muslims in the south.

In an effort to "disempower, marginalize and relocate" the 1.9 million people who have been officially displaced by the civil war in the south and drought in western Sudan—40 percent of whom now live in and around Khartoum—the government has bulldozed and razed thousands of homes in "brutal" nighttime raids and moved people under pain of death into "unsuitable sites"—tent camps well outside the city with limited access to food and water, no sewage or sanitary facilities, and no stores or transportation into town. Those who resist the government's "urban renewal," as the Housing Minister called the practice in an interview with this author, have been killed. Moreover, the government enacted laws that prescribe the death penalty for "apostasy," and regulations that permit the police to punish women by severe flogging for brewing alcohol, selling tea at roadside stands after 5 P.M., or "immodest dress." In 1995 Sudan, which once enjoyed one of the freest presses in sub-Saharan Africa, with over forty journals and newspapers, tolerated no opposition press. The country's once professional civil service—the judiciary, foreign service, army, security forces—has been thoroughly purged, and all political parties have been banned, as have most non-Islamic cultural and social associations.[31]

DEFENDER OF "WOMEN'S RIGHTS"

Turabi has long taken pride in his desire to "liberate" women of conservative Arab societies from cultural constraints that have little basis in Islam.[32] El-Affendi has argued that Turabi's attitude toward women has created a "far-reaching revolution" within Sudan. The place of women in society is "a vexed one for Sudanese Islamists and the modern Islamist movement generally," since Islamists were "torn between their sympathy for the demands for a better lot for women and their perception of what Islam taught and tradition dictated."[33]

The Sudanese Ikhwan has included women in its membership since its creation in 1949. But it opposed the formation of the Women's Union in Sudan in 1952 despite the fact that the group designated an Islamist woman as its leader. El-Affendi acknowledged that women recruits to Ikhwan were "hard to come by" in the group's early years. But there is little doubt that Turabi was an early supporter of their inclusion and promotion within the Brotherhood. He created a furor within the organization in 1957 during a visit from England when he endorsed the principle of women's liberation. Turabi lobbied hard for and in 1965 won a platform within the Islamic Charter Front that endorsed a woman's right to vote.

In his 1973 pamphlet "The Woman in Islamic Teachings," Turabi outlined his Islamic rationale for the emancipation of women from, on the one hand, un-Islamic conservative traditions and, on the other, Western exploitation and enslavement to men as sexual objects.[34] A woman, Turabi wrote, had not just a right but an obligation to defy her family if necessary in order to fulfill her religious duties. "The family is not the unit of accountability on the Day of Judgment," el-Affendi's translation states. Given the fact that this principle is enshrined in shariʻa, it was "very strange" that traditional Muslim societies had flagrantly defied both the letter and the spirit of Qur'anic law.

Turabi interpreted the repression of women in Muslim lands as another reflection of "religious decline and decadence." Traditional Islamic thinkers who insisted on rigid and uncompromising submission to the holy Qur'an's teachings on most issues, Turabi wrote, had become uncharacteristically "flexible" in seeking excuses and pretexts to waive and diminish the rights that the Prophet Muhammad had explicitly guaranteed women. Islamic principles, Turabi insisted, demand "full participation" of women in public life, "subject to reasonable safeguards and provisions allowed for in Shariʻa. . . . Whatever the potential damage that may arise from the free mixing of the sexes, this should not be used as an argument to deprive women of the benefits of participation in public life . . . which outweighed by far the alleged danger." Turabi countered Muslim arguments that women should be kept at home since their main duty in life was to raise children and take care of the home, by arguing that women who were "totally isolated from life" were not adequately prepared to raise children and educate them for life. Whether or not Muslims accepted it, he maintained, the liberation of women was a fact of modern life. Modernization, urbanization, and growing economic pressures made it inevitable that women would want to work. And once they did, their enslavement to men would be replaced by enslavement to "material needs and sexual desires" as well as commercial manipulation. So rather than resist the inevitable, enlightened Islamists should seek to improve women's status "in a truly Islamic manner."

"The acceptance of Turabi's arguments in the ranks of the Sudanese Ikhwan," el-Affendi wrote before the Islamist coup of 1989, "led to the transformation that Turabi aimed for: the adaptation of the movement to make it a major beneficiary of the rapid process of social modernization."[35] More than a decade after writing the pamphlet, Turabi had not altered his views on women in public life. The NIF election manifesto of 1986 reaffirmed the Ikhwan's commitment to encouraging women to "escape social oppression and discrimination and to play a full part in building a new society."[36]

In 1992, three years after his NIF had come to power in Sudan, Turabi elaborated his views on women in Islam to a large audience at a think tank in Washington, D.C. He insisted that Islamic rule in the Sudan would provide "authentic women's liberation."[37] Western feminism, by contrast, emphasized rights at the expense of "duties and responsibilities," an error that resulted in numerous social tragedies—promiscuity, divorce, and the disintegration of family life. Women, in Turabi's interpretation of Islamic doctrine, had a right to work in public life, in fact, an obligation to do so. What they could not do, he added, was be "out of sight together in a room with men if they are not related."

The Qur'an focuses on family more than any other institution, certainly more than the state, he said. Therefore, since family is at the heart of an Islamic system, *shura,* or consultation, within the family is essential. But unless he is "financially irresponsible," the father is the head of that group or unit; women could not lead families, Turabi said. And while women could lead "smaller institutions and businesses," they could not lead a state. (Turabi's injunction would come as news to Pakistan's current ruler, Benazir Bhutto, and former Turkish prime minister Tansu Ciller.) Modern Sudan was applying his Islamic feminism, he told the group. There was no reason why women could not be active in society— as workers, civil servants, and judges. They could even lead men in prayer as they had done in the time of the Prophet. Islam, he said, encouraged the liberation of all individuals—male and female alike.

These noble pronouncements are not, however, reflected in Sudanese government policy. Women have been prime targets in the government's campaign to root out un-Islamic conduct and transform Sudanese society. In November 1991 General Bashir banned dancing between the sexes and decreed that all female students and women who enter government offices in the north must dress according to traditional Islamic standards. Women were lashed for inappropriate dress even before a new dress code was formally announced.[38]

That same year, the government announced a new criminal code based on shari'a, the centerpiece of the new, ostensibly Islamic order and a document that, according to government spokesmen interviewed at the time, reflected Hassan Turabi's interpretation of Islam's injunctions.[39] The code includes corporal punishments mandated by the Qur'an—the so-called *hudud* penalties for specific offenses—including the death penalty, amputations, lashings, and even crucifixion. For women, the code is particularly onerous. A married female convicted of adultery can be stoned to death; an abortion that is not required to save the mother's life or to end a pregnancy resulting from rape can result in up to three years in jail and a fine; "gross indecency," defined as "any act contrary to another person's modesty," can bring forty lashes, and the same penalty applies to someone who wears an "indecent or immoral uniform which caused annoyance to public feelings." Finally, while Sudan's laws with respect to marriage and divorce rights for women were, before 1983, among the most liberal in Africa or the Arab countries, the new penal code permits polygamy and limits a husband's obligations and a woman's rights in event of divorce.[40]

As of 1995 women retain the right to vote, to hold government posts—even that of judge—and to run for the parliament, although those rights remained theoretical since there were no national elections in Sudan between 1988 and 1994. Several women have been appointed to the regime's transitional parliament, but there are no women within the regime's senior decision-making ranks. Sudanese women, moreover, are now barred from leaving the country without the permission of a husband, a father, or another male guardian who is legally and officially responsible for them. Transportation is officially segregated, with women, of course, consigned to the back of trucks and buses. And hundreds of women have been dismissed from government jobs and even private offices for un-Islamic views or for failing to conform to the government's dress code, which requires that women wear the *hijab,* which covers them from head to ankles. The traditional Sudanese wrap—the thobe—a long piece of material that is wrapped around the hair and the body, is not considered sufficiently "modest"; but resistance to abandoning the thobe has been so widespread among Sudanese women that the government has had to compromise by permitting women to wear a head scarf underneath their thobes.

The current regime has restricted women's participation in other ways as well. The Public Order Act of Khartoum State, enacted in 1992, bars women from selling peanuts, making tea in street stands, and engaging in other forms of small commerce between 5 P.M. and 5 A.M., effectively ending a source of income upon which many abandoned or otherwise impoverished women depended to support their families and make ends meet.

How does Turabi defend such policies? Usually he has denied that there is any problem. Asked about the Islamic dress code in January 1992, for example, Turabi maintained that only "moral education" was being used to change dress habits.[41] Turabi dismissed as "hostile propaganda and gibberish" the statements of several doctors who told this author that they had treated young women who had been lashed for "improper attire," often without being formally charged or tried, at police stations and in security offices as early as 1991.

When the scholars in Tampa questioned Turabi about the regime's attitude toward women, also in 1992, he defended the Islamic dress code. "In the Qur'an and in the Sunna," he said, "there is definitely a prescription, not for the mode, but how much you should cover." In society, he added, "you are always under some form of pressure when it comes to dress." (Segregation of women, however, was "unjustified." He was not asked why, then, the government was trying to segregate public transportation.) He then equated the government's requirement that women be wrapped up in confining clothing in Sudan's intense heat with the dress rules of clubs and restaurants in the West. "If I go without a necktie, there are many places where I can't be admitted," he said. Women, of course, were often subjected to "much more pressure" than men. Unlike Saudi Arabia, Sudan did not permit any organization to stop women or to arrest or harass them for dressing immodestly, "unless someone goes completely naked, [for] that would be obscenity." Harassment, Turabi insisted, "is definitely objectionable in Islam," and abusing an immodestly dressed woman was "definitely not allowed in Islam"; he thereby dismissed as fiction charges by numerous human-rights groups, Western governments, and the United Nations that the rights and status of women have been adversely affected by his ostensibly Islamic regime.[42]

Turabi also told the scholars that no Islamic code could outlaw polygamy. "There is no way that can happen because it is categorical in the statements of the Qur'an," he said, suggesting that he would also support the implementation of other Qur'anic discriminations against women. These include the declaration that a woman's testimony is inadmissible, or has half the value of a man's, in certain criminal and civil proceedings; the notion that women should expect less than an equal share of an inheritance; and the ease with which a man can divorce his wife.[43] Turabi himself has only one wife—Sadiq el-Mahdi's sister—but maintains that polygamy is probably unavoidable because "the whole world is going polygamous de facto if not de jure. English law now recognizes cohabitation as a legal relationship with legal consequences, so why bother about this?" In an interview with this author, Turabi offered a lengthy and unusually candid justification of polygamy on biological and sexual grounds:

The fertile age of women is between fifteen and forty. The fertile age of men is between fifteen and the end of your life. Women are normally more anxious than men about children, about having them. It's their nature. I would like all women to be able to have children. And I know that if a woman has two children, and her husband dies, she wouldn't mind if nobody remarries her. But a man, he's interested in sex more than family. I'm sorry to say that. So, if you calculate it this way and know that women have a monthly period, when you can't have sex with them . . . and then if she's very pregnant, you want to avoid [sex]—or when she's just given birth to a child. So although numerically there are as many men as women, there are more men who are sexually active than there are women who are sexually active. So in principle, I don't mind polygamy.

There is another good reason for allowing polygamy, he continued. "She's fifty and she doesn't care about you. And she has children. And of course, when women are about forty to fifty, they become very active in society—in hospitals, schools—so if someone wants to take another lady regularly . . . but I would want it to be regularized. I don't want mistresses; I'm against extramarital relationships."

With respect to women, Turabi argues, Sudan's penal code "borders on being liberal." "I don't claim to have read it closely myself," he contended, distancing himself from a document that many Sudanese insist he helped draft. But the new laws "borrowed freely from all sources of Islamic jurisprudence, Sunni or Shi'ite or whatever." "I can't judge the new code definitely," he repeated, "but I assume it is as you would think, perhaps a development of the earlier practice in the Sudan." The military government's record with respect to women has been excellent, Turabi asserted at the Florida gathering. Several women had been appointed to the regime's transitional parliament and as ministers; and the former resentment of "some clerics and traditional-minded Sudanese" was "no longer felt anywhere." Furthermore, Sudan guaranteed equal pay for men and women; and education, though segregated in secondary schools, was now coeducational at the elementary and university levels. "We don't have any more problems," Turabi declared.[44]

Islam and Democracy

Turabi's position on democracy has usually reflected a tough-minded calculation about whether or not it will advance his cause. As previously indicated, though he became publicly known in Sudan for championing democracy, individual freedom, and an end to General Abboud's harsh military rule, he joined Nimeiri's undemocratic, single-party military government when he felt it would enhance the prospects of his then-marginal Islamic group. When Nimeiri's dictatorship was ousted in 1985, Turabi once again became a champion of democracy, until his Islamic movement was positioned to seize power in its own military coup in 1989.

Turabi's writings, or documents that he inspired, are littered with references to the importance of freedom and democracy. The charter for the ICF, issued in 1965, reflects "the philosophical style which is Turabi's trademark," and repeatedly stresses that democracy and individual liberty are basic values of Islam.[45] Turabi's brand of Islam, el-Affendi asserts, always preferred "an imperfect democracy to any form of dictatorship," because "avenues for reform and criticism at least remain open within a democracy."[46] El-Affendi thus has some difficulty explaining Turabi's decision in 1976 to join Nimeiri's dictatorial government. Before accepting Nimeiri's offer of reconciliation and access to state power, el-Affendi argues, Turabi invited Sadiq al-Mahdi's Umma Party and the Unionists to join forces with his Ikhwan in a common Islamic front that would either force Nimeiri's regime to accept an Islamic program or drive him from power. When the traditional parties spurned this proposal, the Muslim Brothers under Turabi's leadership concluded that working with Nimeiri might be preferable to restoring democracy, in that "the restoration of democracy would do no more than allow them to exercise the role of a junior actor in an order dominated by the two traditional parties." Without acknowledging any contradiction between Turabi's alleged commitment to democracy and the Ikhwan's new strategy, el-Affendi concludes that after the events of 1976 — a failed insurrection led by the Umma Party and the collapse of Turabi's National Front—the Brotherhood's new "central strategy" called for the building of an Islamic movement that would be "capable of taking over power in Sudan on its own." From that point on, el-Affendi maintains, "all political initiatives were to be geared to serve this purpose, rather than the earlier one of restoring democracy."[47]

Though el-Affendi asserts that a belief in democracy is central to Turabi's Islamic ideology, Turabi's definition of democracy has always differed from its commonly accepted meaning in the West. A clear grasp of Turabi's concept, however, is essential to understanding not only his decision to join the undemocratic government of Nimeiri, but also his ardent defense of the present ostensibly Islamic military regime. Turabi says that Islamic democracy is based on the Qur'anic concept of *shura*, or consultation. In and of itself, shura is not democracy as westerners understand it; Turabi has described the differences in his own writings and at greater length in interviews over the years.[48] The major difference, he has argued, is that in Islamic democracy, sovereignty lies not in the people, but in God. This is hardly a new or revolutionary concept in militant Islam: it permeates the thinking of virtually all modern Islamic literalists and underlies their inherent suspicion of man-made legislative and judicial institutions. Turabi's concept of shura differs theoretically from that of his militant predecessors only in that he insists that Islam requires it be obligatory and binding; consultation with the ruled is, in his view, not something that the ruler undertakes at his discretion or to cloak in Islamic legitimacy a decision he has already made.[49] Under true Islam, a ruler cannot be a dictator, Turabi maintains, because he, too, is bound by shari'a, Islam's framework and the binding legal codification of God's will. "Whereas the Prophet was appointed by God, the caliph was freely elected by the people who thereby have precedence over him as a legal authority," Turabi wrote in 1983. The caliph, therefore, must be subject "both to the Shari'a and to the will of his electors."[50]

One problem with this stance, as noted by Ahmed An-Na'im, the Sudanese jurist and human-rights advocate, is that there are too few precedents for such genuine contractual consultation in Islamic history. Such statements, An-Na'im argues, are not only "hopelessly vague and liable to create intolerable abuse and corruption because of the uncertainty and controversial nature of the relevant rules of Shari'a"; they also reflect, in his view, either hypocrisy or ignorance of Islamic law and history. "There are numerous disagreements between Muslim jurists," he writes, "especially with reference to many public law issues. Therefore, to speak in categorical terms of Shari'a as a definite and well-settled code of law which directly limits the power of the caliph, or as the arbiter between social order and individual freedom, is grossly misleading."[51]

Turabi further argues that the jurisdiction and authority of the government and the legislature, like that of the ruler, are limited because shari'a is a higher law. Shari'a functions like a constitution, albeit a detailed one, he told the Tampa scholars and this author in separate meetings. "Government is chosen through consultation, *shura* as we call it. . . . And lawmaking is ultimately based on shura and ijma [consensus]." The difference between shura and democracy is that "the higher law in Islam is so intensive that the legislature has much less to do or say. The legislature, the Congress or Parliament or whatever, is not sovereign at all. The Shari'a governs so much. Sometimes the rules are categoric and certain and you can do very little about them. Sometimes there are principles which guide you and curtail you, but there is a lot to do within those limits."[52]

Turabi's concept of democracy has never afforded a place of honor to political parties. "There is no legal bar to the development of different parties," he wrote in 1983 and has repeated on numerous occasions. "However a well-developed Islamic society would probably not be conducive to the growth of rigid parties wherein one stands by one's party

210 / JUDITH MILLER

whether it is wrong or right." This "factionalism," as he called it, could be "very oppressive of individual freedom and divisive of the community," and therefore "antithetical to a Muslim's ultimate responsibility to God and to umma." So while an Islamic system might include several political parties, an Islamic government, in Turabi's view should promote the development of consensus "rather than a minority/majority system with political parties rigidly confronting each other over decisions."[53]

Over time, Turabi's antipathy to political parties has intensified. "I don't think parties are essential to the democratic process in the West," he told the Tampa scholars in 1992. Political parties in the United States, Turabi told me in 1994, were little more than a reflection of financial interests. "America is less democratic because money plays a very important role in your elections," he asserted. "Money!" he emphasized, "not the choice of the voter!" In Sudan, he said, parties were reflections of family, sectarian, and tribal groups: the Umma Party was the modern political expression of the Mahdi's Ansar; the Union Party was the political organ of the Khatmiya religious sect. And all except the Ikhwan, Sudan's only "modern" group (he did not mention the communists), were dynastic. Traditional political parties usually produced debate and division rather than discussion and consensus. Sudan, he said, had produced a "new" system:

> It looks like a single party but there is no party; there is no central leadership anywhere. It is "government by convention," they call it. Many people suspect that it must have been inspired by the experience of the National Islamic Front because it was based on convention. People assemble freely, without any inhibition, with nobody being ostracized or exiled from the political process, and then they elect their leaders, they determine their strategy, and they elect a council, a Parliament, a local council, a regional Parliament or a national Parliament. This is the fundamental nature of the regime, but it's more sophisticated.[54]

At the moment, the process Turabi describes is also nonexistent. Soon after coming to power, the military regime banned all political parties, trade unions, and in effect, any unauthorized political gathering. It suspended the constitution and declared a state of emergency and martial law. The government held "local elections" in 1992 in which Islamic candidates approved by the regime were elected to powerless offices. In 1993 General Bashir, the only candidate, became "President" Bashir. In 1995 all political dissent in Sudan continues to be suppressed, the official press is censored and papers not approved by the government are banned, thousands of the country's elite have been forced to flee or live underground, and thousands more have been imprisoned or threatened because of their political views. Turabi's nonparty, consensus Islamic entity has all the characteristics of a garden-variety police state. What makes Turabi's police state unusual in the Arab world is its Islamic vocabulary.

HUMAN RIGHTS AND THE "ISLAMIC AWAKENING"

In addition to focusing on the role of women, human-rights debates within Sudan have invariably concerned the status and rights of non-Muslims (about one-quarter of the population) and non-Arab peoples (roughly half of Sudan), as well as the treatment of Sudanese political prisoners, dissidents, and others who run afoul of the political system.

At this stage, one can say categorically that never before in its modern history has Sudan been accused of such deliberate and widespread violations of human rights. Many of the charges have focused on the government's activities in southern Sudan and the Nuba mountains in connection with its conduct of the country's savage, protracted civil war. In Turabi's defense, the military government did not initiate this long-running conflict; it inherited it. Between 1985 and 1989, the Ikhwan's political program called for a peaceful solution to the civil war through administrative decentralization, the exemption of the predominantly non-Arab and non-Muslim south from shari'a, and federalism. Moreover, the military government launched peace talks with the south, which stalled in 1994 and seemed unlikely to produce a breakthrough. But while the government repeatedly expressed its desire for a peaceful resolution, southerners, northern Sudanese dissidents, and neutral diplomats agreed that the its words matched its deeds no better in this sphere than in any other: though Khartoum continued negotiating, it also continued to pursue a war that cost the bankrupt government an estimated one million dollars a day. In 1994 and 1995 it certainly seemed as if the government, despite its rhetoric, was seeking a military victory.

Given Sudan's ethnic and religious diversity and its large number of pagans (who are not entitled even to the limited rights afforded Jews and Christians), the issue of how non-Muslims should be treated is of paramount importance to the country's future. Yet Turabi has often been vague or evasive when asked about non-Muslim rights in an Islamic state, and his position on how an Islamic state would treat minorities has shifted over time. Consider first his position on whether non-Muslims should be allowed to serve in leadership posts in government. In the early 1960s, when the Ikhwan was weak and seeking to develop an image as a defender of democracy against the Abboud regime, Turabi insisted that the group abandon its demand that all key government posts be held by Muslims. His ICF charter did not address the issue, nor did he state a view in his 1983 essay on what constitutes an Islamic state. He had avoided this thorny issue for Islamic fundamentalists because, he wrote, "I did not want to complicate issues."[55] During a debate, however, he admitted that in his view shari'a prohibited an Islamic state's being ruled by a non-Muslim.[56] In 1987 Turabi switched positions again and argued in the Ikhwan's Islamic charter that no citizen should be barred from any post in government because of his religion. Peter Kok points to this shift as yet another indication of Turabi's opportunism. "By adopting this position," he wrote, "al-Turabi was not changing direction but only changing lanes towards state power."[57]

Turabi has also been evasive about the legal standing of non-Muslims in his Islamic state. In his essay on the hallmarks of such a state, Turabi argues that non-Muslims should welcome its creation because the "historical record of Muslims' treatment of Christians is quite good especially compared with the history of relations between different religions and religious denominations in the West." Muslims, he added, did not like the term *minorities*, preferring "People of the Book (*ahl al-kitab*), the '*dhimmi*,' or protected people." These non-Muslims, he said, had a guaranteed right to profess and defend their own religious convictions and even to criticize Islam and engage in dialogue with Muslims. "Non-Muslims also have the right to regulate their private life, education, and family life by adopting their own family laws. If there is any rule in the Shari'a which they think religiously incompatible, they can be absolved from it." Moreover, he added, "Muslims are bound to relate to non-Muslims positively . . . to be fair and friendly in their person-to-person conduct . . . and treat them with trust, beneficence, and equity." Turabi conceded that there "may be a certain feeling of alienation because the public law generally will be Islamic law." But because Islamic law was fair and just and devoted to the "general good," even a non-Muslim would "appreciate its wisdom and fairness."[58]

There are several problems with Turabi's formulation. First, most of Sudan's non-Muslims are not "People of the Book." The designation applies only to Jews and Christians, members of religious groups the Prophet and the Qur'an specifically mention as spiritual predecessors of Islam. It does not apply to animists or to pagans, who constitute the largest group of non-Muslims in Sudan; the Qur'an offers these groups no religious or civil protection. None of the prohibitions—such as the ban on forcible conversion—apply to them, nor is their religion protected by Islam as it was under Sudan's 1973 secular constitution, which afforded equal status to people of all religions, even those who held what the document tolerantly called "noble spiritual beliefs."[59] Second, as An-Na'im argues, Turabi's statement that members of protected minorities, or dhimmis, can be exempted from any rule in the shari'a they find religiously incompatible is both "inaccurate and misleading." As Turabi well knows, findings of incompatibility must be based on interpretations by Muslims, and not by non-Muslim citizens, of shari'a itself. "Thus," An-Na'im writes, "whereas non-Muslims may be exempt by Muslim authorities from the Shari'a's prohibition of intoxicating beverages because the Shari'a itself accepts this exemption, they may not be exempt from, say, the amputation of the right hand as punishment for theft because that exemption is not allowed by Shari'a."[60] Finally, while Turabi and the government have agreed to exempt the south from shari'a if southerners agree to end the fighting, Turabi himself has often stated that the one to two million southerners now living in Khartoum and elsewhere in the north would be bound by the Islamic code, despite the fact that it would deny them legal standing equal to that of their Muslim counterparts.

In his wide-ranging condemnation of the military government's human rights abuses, Gaspar Biro called for the repeal of Sudan's Islamic code, an appeal that Turabi rejected with great vehemence. Biro's criticism of the military government, Turabi told this author, indicated that he was not only a "lousy lawyer" but greedy and anti-Islamic as well. No one would force non-Muslims in northern Sudan to live under Islamic law, as the majority clearly desired, he said. But non-Muslims in Khartoum had to respect the will of the majority; if they felt that strongly about being exempted, they were free to return to the war zone in the south.

Peter Kok, who comes from a prominent southern family, argues that the Ikhwan's offer of autonomy to the south is not credible to southerners given Turabi's political history. In 1968 peace negotiations nearly collapsed over the insistence of Turabi's group that the country's constitution state that "the Sudan is an Islamic Republic."[61] During those times when the south was strong—from 1972 to 1976 and from 1985 to 1989—it bolstered the "forces of secularism" in Sudan. In response the Ikhwan sought to weaken the south, to decouple it from the rest of the Sudan. When the north had the upper hand and was able to pursue its goal of Islamizing and Arabizing the south, it favored unity. In short, Kok charges, Turabi has always opposed meaningful autonomy for the south. "Turabi was behind the emasculation of the regional self-rule for the south resulting in the subdivision of the south into three regions in June 1983." This manipulation, along with the introduction of shari'a, "contributed to the outbreak of the present war."[62] Turabi has dismissed these criticisms of the military government, as well as those made by Amnesty International and other widely respected human-rights groups, which he portrays as "biased" and guilty of imposing "western standards of criminal justice and human rights" on Islamic systems.[63]

Turabi's "liberal" Islamic code also provides, in accordance with Islamic law, a death penalty for Muslims convicted of "apostasy." The issue is particularly sensitive given Sudanese history and the human-rights community's preoccupation with the Ayatollah Khomeini's fatwa calling for the death of British writer Salman Rushdie on grounds of apostasy, a ruling that Iran has repeatedly refused to withdraw. Turabi has repeatedly denied any responsibility for either the imposition of President Nimeiri's harsh Islamic code or his regime's execution of Mahmoud Mohamed Taha for apostasy in January 1985, both of which severely undermined Nimeiri's internal support and international legitimacy. But Turabi neither denounced the code when it was imposed nor opposed Taha's execution. Taha, he told this author and others at the time, was executed for the wrong crime. "He actually waged a political campaign against Nimeiri," Turabi told the group in Tampa. Taha was arrested and charged with sedition, not apostasy, which was not formally in the penal code, Turabi said; but the judge, knowing that shari'a was then the law of the land, took it upon himself to cite shari'a as the grounds for execution. This was "a bad decision," concluded Turabi, thereby objecting not to the execution per se but on procedural grounds.[64] Turabi still detests Taha and appears to uphold the state's right to eliminate such troublesome figures. "He claimed that he was Jesus Christ," Turabi told me.[65] "Then he said that he had a second message after Mohammed—a refinement—and then towards the end of his life, he promoted himself to a god." But should he have been executed because of that? this author pressed him. "They killed him not because of his apostasy, but because he attacked Nimeiri. Because he circulated his leaflets all over the place. Because if you're Mahmoud Mohamed Taha and you are a god, and someone else claims that he is God, how can you tolerate it? It's not like saying you're a congressman."

Sudan had now "solved" the apostasy issue, Turabi claimed, by insisting that "to become punishable by death, it has to be more than just intellectual apostasy. It would have to translate into not only sedition, but actually insurrection against society. That is how it is defined. . . . It is just like treason; it reads like treason." Rushdie would not be subject to the death penalty in Sudan for two reasons, Turabi stated: first, because he did not take active steps to undermine any Islamic state's constitutional order and, second, because, although Islam is "very universal in its implications, it does accept territory as the basis of jurisdiction. Thus those living abroad are not subject to Islamic law, but to international treaty obligations between states."[66] In fact, the definition of apostasy in the current Sudanese penal code, according to an English-language version provided by the government, is not that narrowly drawn, defining as apostate "every Muslim who propagates the renunciation of the creed of Islam, or publicly declares his renouncement thereof, by an expressed statement or conclusive act."

Turabi was also evasive when questioned at the Tampa meeting about repeated charges of systematic torture of political dissidents and other violations of human rights by the military regime. Perhaps there were a few cases of torture following the coup, Turabi conceded, but no longer. Torture, he insisted, was not Islamic, so it did not exist in Sudan. Perhaps Sudanese prisoners, he said, who "call harsh words torture," or "a strong light in one's face," were overly "sensitive to their dignity."[67]

INTERNATIONAL CONFLICTS

As criticism of the Sudanese regime mounted, Turabi grew increasingly hostile toward the West. In his 1992 tour of the United States, he tried to assure Americans that "the West is no longer our preoccupation" and that Islamists were mainly interested in the "constructive regeneration of our societies by mobilizing our souls and our minds, not fighting 'Great Satan.' "[68] Since then, however, he has been persuaded that the West, and America in particular, is instinctively if not irrevocably "anti-Islam." Spurred on by "Zionists" and other powerful lobbies, "America has done everything it could with the United Nations, with Europe, with the Arabs to stop aid to the Sudan," Turabi has complained. Nevertheless, in 1994 he still had "some hope" of improved relations in the future. "Americans are pragmatic," he said. "They will try and try and try to undermine this government so that they can nip it in the bud before it goes international and becomes contagious, and endangers the Gulf and Saudi Arabia and all that oil." But after repeated effort and failure, he predicted, the United States, and then Europe, would start a dialogue with Sudan.

The stance Turabi's regime took in response to Iraq's invasion of Kuwait and the subsequent U.S.–led war to evict the Iraqis suggests how uncertain Turabi was regarding his own government's prospects. Fourteen of the twenty-one members at the Arab League meeting in early August 1990 condemned the Iraqi invasion but cautioned against any foreign intervention in Arab affairs. Sudan abstained. When the group met a week later Sudan, joining Jordan and Mauritania, supported (with reservations) a proposal to send troops to help defend Saudi Arabia and other Gulf states against Iraq. When the United Nations imposed a naval embargo against Baghdad, Sudan, along with Jordan, Libya, Tunisia, and Yemen, kept shipping spare parts for critical machinery and other high-value items to Iraq.[69] In 1991 Turabi joined a small group of Islamic leaders who met with Pakistan's leader to demand, unsuccessfully, that Pakistan recall its eleven thousand troops from the multinational force in Saudi Arabia and back Iraq "in its steadfastness."[70]

Thus Sudan, under its Islamic leadership, became increasingly opposed to the American-led effort to expel Iraq from Kuwait by force, a policy that led Washington to suspend most of the aid that had not already been suspended after the military coup of 1989. Turabi took a somewhat more nuanced stand, however, with respect to the post–Gulf war peace process led by the United States. Though Sudan was the only Arab country to boycott the American-brokered Madrid peace conference, neither Turabi nor the Sudanese government condemned the Arab states or players that joined the negotiations.

Turabi has also wavered on other important regional issues, telling his interviewers what he thinks they want to hear. Whereas most Islamic militants hold that peace with Israel is unacceptable on religious and political grounds, Turabi has not taken that position. There is nothing inherently "anti-Islamic" about peace between a Jewish state and the Arabs, he told me. The Prophet himself, after all, approved a "constitutional document" between his state and the Jews of Medina. Yet two months after he made that statement, he told a French journalist that no Arab could ever accept Israel. "I do not question the existence of Jew—but of Israel, yes."[71] On Jerusalem, however, Turabi has been consistent. There can be no compromise on Jerusalem, he has cautioned; reconciliation would be impossible unless "the Jews" gave Jerusalem back to the Palestinians, from whom it was "taken by force." "Not a single Muslim all over the world would say: well, let us be pragmatic on that."

Turabi, however, astonished and infuriated many Islamic militants at a gathering of Islamists that he sponsored in late 1993 by arguing against and ultimately blocking a resolution to condemn Yasir Arafat and the Palestine Liberation Organization for their peace accord with Israel. The proposal, Turabi argued after the fact, would have served "no purpose" but to further divide Muslims. Moreover, it would have damaged Turabi's (as yet unsuccessful) efforts to mediate a truce between the PLO and Hamas, thus carving out a role for himself and Sudan, albeit a marginal one, in the peace process. Turabi did object to the peace accord Arafat signed on the White House lawn in September 1993. "The U.S. is very powerful now; the Arabs are very weak. So it is not very likely that the process will proceed towards recognition of a Palestinian state without an unforeseen development in world history," Turabi said. Had Arafat asked his advice in advance, Turabi added, he would have urged the PLO chief not to accept the deal. But Arafat had not asked. Turabi observed that the accord itself, and the way in which it was negotiated, did not strengthen Arafat's position within the PLO nor that of the PLO within the Palestinian movement. As a result, Hamas grew ever stronger. "History is moving towards Hamas," Turabi said.

The addition of Sudan to the short list of countries that the United States has officially accused of aiding or sponsoring international terrorism has infuriated Turabi. Though Washington accused Khartoum of harboring every radical terrorist organization in the region, Turabi consistently denied their presence in his country, even though this author interviewed representatives of Hamas, Hizbullah, and other groups that he claims have no official presence in Khartoum. "The evidence is simply overwhelming," said Don Pederson, Washington's ambassador to Khartoum in an interview in the summer of 1994.

Turabi has also maintained that Sudan had nothing to do with the plot to bomb New York's World Trade Center in 1993 or with a related scheme to blow up New York bridges, buildings, and tunnels in subsequent attacks. According to American investigators, Shaykh 'Umar 'Abd al-Rahman, the Egyptian cleric who inspired and blessed the operations and was convicted of conspiracy by an American court in January 1996, spent several weeks in Sudan at Turabi's invitation, an allegation Turabi flatly denies. He also denies any link between his government and the five Sudanese nationals arrested for their involvement in the planned attacks, although American investigators have documented numerous contacts between several of the suspects and two Sudanese diplomats assigned to the United Nations mission.[72] Turabi has denied knowing any of the suspects, adding that the young men were clearly framed by the Egyptian agent the U.S. government hired to uncover this alleged Islamic threat to New York; he has provided no evidence, though, to substantiate his allegation.

Turabi's protestations of innocence notwithstanding, Sudan has taken steps to get its name removed from America's list of states supporting terrorism. In August 1994, the Sudanese government turned over to

France, with which it does substantial trade, a terrorist wanted for more than two decades in several European countries—Ilich Ramirez Sanchez, better known as "Carlos." While the American State Department officially praised Khartoum's actions, they said privately that Sudan would have to do far more before its status on the list would be reconsidered. Hassan Turabi had no comment on the incident.

CONCLUSION

If the Palestinians, as Abba Eban once observed, were a people who never missed an opportunity to miss an opportunity, Turabi's Ikhwan is a movement that has never missed an opportunity. Whether this demonstrates Turabi's pragmatism, or mere opportunism, it is clear that Turabi has been consistent in at least one important thing: his pursuit of power. While his supporters argue that Turabi has sought power in order to implement his "liberal" Islamic ideas and agenda, the military government in power in Khartoum today bears virtually no resemblance to the theoretical Islamic government that Turabi outlined in his earlier writings and which he continues to promote.

Despite his government's appalling human-rights records, its pariah status in most of the West, the American conviction that it supports state terrorism at home and abroad, its failure to build either a productive economy or to end the devastating civil war, and its systematic suppression of all dissident views—even contrary Islamist opinions—Hassan Turabi has somehow maintained a reputation as one of modern militant Sunni Islam's most influential political leaders and prominent theoreticians. Throughout the Middle East and far beyond it, young Muslims look to him for guidance on how to combine modern techniques and terminology with ancient principles to transform their religion into a vehicle of revolutionary change. For Turabi Islam is a rebellious call to arms—a command to implement God's law through the creation of truly Islamic states, not states that merely emulate Western models and call themselves Islamic.

His assertions notwithstanding, Turabi's brand of Islam is not new. Throughout the fourteen hundred years of Muslim history, many men and movements have challenged the dominant interpretation of the faith, starting with the fanatical Kharajites of the seventh century, who rejected arbitration of a succession dispute because, in el-Affendi's words, it would give "men a say in matters already resolved by God." Throughout Muslim history, since the time of the seventh-century caliph Muawiya, such rebels have rejected the interpretation that Islam demands total submission not merely theoretically to God, but to temporal rulers as well. The eighteenth-century Wahabis in Arabia and, much closer to home, the Mahdist movement of the nineteenth century in Khartoum, zealously pursued a purist, revolutionary vision of Islam, a sort of Muslim liberation theology in which the ruler would have to return to Islam's original inspiration, its sources and roots, or risk repudiation. And though Turabi vehemently rejects the comparison, his National Islamic Front state resembles, more than other current Islamic model, the Mahdiya established briefly in Sudan by the Mahdi and his even more ruthless military leader and successor, the Khalifa. The Mahdi was much more an Islamic innovator than his French- and English-educated spiritual descendant.

Turabi sees himself as the latest addition to an impressive line of militant Islamic philosopher-kings. He rejects the Ayatollah Khomeini's clerical rule, however, perhaps because, like his Sunni Muslim counterparts Hassan al-Banna and Sayyid Qutb, he is not a cleric. But what has he added to militant Islamist ideology? El-Affendi argues that by espousing an activist, but ostensibly tolerant, pluralistic Islam more reminiscent of Locke and Jefferson than Khomeini, Turabi has elevated the role of the individual in Islamic life at the expense of the state. By maintaining that authority resides in *ijma,* or public consensus, not solely with the clerics or the rulers of the state, Turabi has emphasized individual freedom and dignity. Turabi, he argues, has "elevated the state to the role of religious adjudicator," but has also "subordinated it to popular will."

That is the theory. But there is no public consensus or individual ijma in Sudan today. Human Rights Watch describes Turabi's Sudan as a "military regime" with an "exclusivist ideology alleged to be founded on religion that flouts minority rights." That is neither new nor a dramatic departure from Middle Eastern tradition. It is, rather, all too familiar—an ostensibly Islamic version of the autocratic Arab states ruled by armies and security men, states created during the heyday of socialist, secular Arab nationalism. A police state with God.

What is really new in Turabi's thinking? Surely not his determination to combine Islamic theory and practice. In mingling thinking and doing, Turabi partakes of a long Muslim tradition that includes not only such modern activist philosophers as al-Banna, Qutb, and Khomeini, but also the Prophet Muhammad himself. Nor is his description of the "Islamic awakening"—his defiant, anti-Western epistemology—truly original. The Muslim Brotherhood began, as did most other modern Muslim militant movements, in opposition to the West—first to colonialism, and later to a less tangible but equally powerful and pervasive Western "imperialism," namely, the seemingly relentless spread of Western concepts, ideals, and culture to non-Western societies.

Like several of his more prominent predecessors in the Muslim Brotherhood, Turabi's attitude toward the West is ambivalent. Having been educated in England and France, he is all too aware of the power of the ideas and culture that underlie its dominant technology. Turabi's advantage as an anti-Western preacher of fundamentalist "Islamic" values is his ability to attack the West fluently, and often perceptively, in at least two Western languages. Like Sayyid Qutb, who also traveled widely in America and was horrified by what he considered its lax morality and rampant individualism, Turabi did not like much of what he saw in the United States in the early 1960s. But his ability to address Western audiences in their own language and portray his Islamic vision in terms that Westerners find reassuring has been advantageous in promoting his reputation as an Islamic trailblazer.

In other words, Turabi has justified his regime's authoritarianism by translating it into language and concepts that appeal both to Westerners and to young Arabs, men and women raised on television, telephones, airplanes, and cars—in sum, on a steady exposure to the fruits of Western ingenuity and culture, if not to the West itself. He has cloaked "Islamic values" in the largely Western jargon of human rights, pluralism, and democracy, whereas in fact the Qur'an does not dwell on these (and in the case of democracy, does not even mention it). He has tried to demonstrate that although his Islamic precepts are different from the "good government" models espoused in the West, they are not antithetical to Western ideals. But as any visitor to modern Sudan can attest, what Turabi has created in his isolated, impoverished country, and what he wholeheartedly defends, has nothing to do with the individual dignity, enlightenment, or freedom he says Islam cherishes.

Turabi has bluntly warned his opponents that they will pay a price for opposing him—or his version of Islam. Western and Islamic interests need not be at odds, he has said consolingly, despite their superficial differences. A clash is only inevitable, Turabi told the group in Washington, if the West attempts to crush or resist the "Islamic awakening." Revolution, with its violent excesses, is the fundamentalist's only resort if other means of coming to power are blocked. Through this formulation, Turabi not only justifies Iran's notorious violations of human rights; he also blames those excesses on the West. By his logic, the United States is responsible for the Iranian revolution with all its accompanying horrors for having supported the corrupt Shah and resisted means of peaceful change. But ultimately, in Turabi's view, it matters little whether Islam comes to power "through the ballot box or the barricades," though he claims to prefer the ballot box. What matters is that history be permitted to take its course. Islam, he declared in Washington and consistently repeats, is the future: "The West will have to accommodate Islam."

In fact, Turabi's main contribution to the radical Islamist project has been largely tactical. He is responsible for one single innovation; never before has a radical Islamic regime come to power through a military coup. Iran, at least, had a genuine revolution, however ugly and repressive it ultimately became. Islamic fanatics took power in Afghanistan following a devastating war with the Soviet Union and then a civil war. Militant Islamists in Algeria tried, but failed to use the ballot box. Muslim radicals in Egypt have tried a variety of stratagems—infiltrating the system and, lately, urban terrorism and economic warfare aimed at robbing the regime of tourism revenue, among its largest sources of foreign currency.

Thus the Sudan is unique, but not for the reasons Turabi claims. For the Islamic project in Sudan reversed the formulation he espoused in Washington: having been unable to secure power through the ballot box or the barricades, the NIF resorted to the boot—a military coup, its only resort. But even this, alas, is all too conventional in Sudan and the modern Middle East. The only really new element in Turabi's regime is its Islamic vocabulary. What makes recent history in Sudan particularly tragic is that the country had dabbled with Western-style democracy, albeit unsuccessfully. Before its current Islamic dictatorship, Sudan had thriving political parties, a lively press, a generous, infinitely patient, and truly devout people. Only when Turabi could no longer use democracy to advance God's rule, as he interpreted it, did he jettison the democratic experiment he had joined and vowed to uphold in favor of a less innovative, but more reliable approach. The Sudanese deserved better. So does Islam.

Notes

1. See two interviews with Hashim Badr al-Din, in *al-Sharq al-Awsat*, 28 May 1992, and the London-based *al-Hayat*, 29 May 1992. Translation by *Mideast Mirror*, a daily summary of press reports from throughout the Middle East that is published in London.

2. "The Truth Shall Make You Free," joint pastoral letter written by four members of the Sudan Catholic Bishops Conference, 16 November 1991. The government of Sudan ordered the requisition of all copies on 15 January 1992.

3. Interview with Abdullahi Ahmed An-Na'im, *Human Rights Watch/Africa,* June 1994.

4. Gaspar Biro, "Situation of Human Rights in the Sudan," interim report submitted to the United Nations General Assembly, New York, 18 November 1993 (published, with subsequent final report, 1994).

5. "Amnesty International Report, 1994" (London: Amnesty International Publications, 1994), 272–75.

6. Edward Mortimer, *Financial Times* (London), 29 April 1992, 7.

7. Gill Lusk, "Reunited SPLA Rides High," *Middle East International,* no. 427, 11.

8. Sadiq al-Mahdi, interview with the author, Khartoum, January 1992.

9. All three terms appeared in Alex de Waal, "Turabi's Muslim Brothers: Theocracy in Sudan," *Covert Action,* summer 1994. De Waal is codirector of the London-based Africa Rights. I am indebted to Taiser M. Ali for pointing the article out to me.

10. Arthur L. Lowrie, ed., "Islam, Democracy, the State and the West," roundtable with Dr. Hassan Turabi, 10 May 1992, Clearwater, Florida (World and Islam Studies Enterprise, 1993), 9. World and Islam Studies Enterprise is hereafter cited as WISE.

11. Unless otherwise indicated, quotes from Turabi are based on tape-recorded interviews with the author, conducted in Khartoum on 3–5 June 1994. Turabi spoke in flawless, idiomatic English.

12. Abdelwahab El-Affendi, *Turabi's Revolution, Islam and Power in Sudan* (London: Grey Seal, 1991).

13. The following account is based on interviews with Brotherhood members of differing ideological bents. Some of them are identified; others have preferred to remain anonymous.

14. El-Affendi, *Turabi's Revolution,* 76.

15. The ICF included several important Muslim clerics, or ulema, the disciplined, Riyadh-oriented Ansar al-Sunna group, a variety of Sufi groups, and other religious and tribal notables.

16. Peter Nyot Kok, "Kurzbiographien," *Orient* 33 (1992): 186. Kok's vivid, penetrating, and highly critical article is the best biography of Turabi available in English.

17. Telephone interview with Gaafar Idris, 1995.

18. Author's interview with Hassan Turabi, January 1985.

19. Kok, "Kurzbiographien," 192.

20. Interview with Brotherhood members who requested anonymity.

21. Kok, "Kurzbiographien."

22. John O. Voll, "Fundamentalism in the Sunni Arab World: Egypt and the Sudan," in Martin E. Marty and R. Scott Appleby, eds., *Fundamentalisms Observed* (Chicago: University of Chicago Press, 1991), 352–54.

23. Lowrie, "Islam, Democracy, the State and the West," 26.

24. Ibid., 15. In 1995 the administrative director of WISE, Ramadan Abdullah Shallah, who also taught Middle Eastern politics at the University of South Florida, moved to Damascus and announced that he was the new leader of the Islamic Jihad, a violent Islamic group that claims credit for murdering dozens of Israelis in suicide attacks.

25. Ibid., 23.

26. Interviews with Saudi and former Sudanese officials who wish to remain anonymous.

27. William Langewiesche, "Turabi's Law," *Atlantic Monthly,* August 1994.

28. Interview with official who, given the nature of the regime, understandably wishes to remain anonymous.

29. Under shari'a law, infidels captured in a declared jihad may lawfully be enslaved and, if female, used as concubines. Theoretically, therefore, the exercise of this right does not constitute rape. But the war against the south had not been formally declared a jihad by ranking Sudanese clerics (Turabi lacks religious authority to do so since he is not an *alim.*) Moreover Turabi denies that there are human rights abuses in the south.

30. Gaspar Biro, "Situation of Human Rights in the Sudan," report submitted to the United Nations Economic and Social Council in accordance with Commission on Human Rights resolution 1993/60, E/CN.4/1994/48, 1 February 1994 (42 pages).

31. Human Rights Watch/Africa, "In the Name of God: Repression Continues in Northern Sudan," October 1994, vol. 6 (77 pages).

32. Interviews with the author and numerous statements.

33. El-Affendi, *Turabi's Revolution,* 162.

34. Ibid., 173–75.

35. Ibid., 175.

36. Kok, "Kurzbiographien," 189.

37. Address to the Center for Strategic and International Studies, 12 May 1992, Washington, D.C.

38. Judith Miller, "The Islamic Wave," *New York Times Magazine,* 31 May 1992. See also Human Rights Watch/Africa's reports on Sudan and treatment of women, 1992 and 1993, and the U.S. State Department Report on Human Rights, 1993.

39. Author's interviews with Sudanese officials, including the ministers of justice, of housing, and of foreign affairs, in January 1992.

40. Sudanese Justice Ministry, official translation of its penal code, issued March 1991.

41. Jane Perlez, "A Fundamentalist Finds a Fulcrum in Sudan," *New York Times,* 23 January 1992; interview with the author, January 1992.

42. See, among many other sources, Biro, "Situation of Human Rights in the Sudan," interim and final reports.

43. Abdullahi Ahmed An-Na'im, *Toward an Islamic Reformation* (New York: Syracuse University Press, 1990).

44. Lowrie, "Islam, Democracy, the State and the West," 46.

45. El-Affendi, *Turabi's Revolution,* 157–59.

46. Ibid., 160.

47. Ibid., 164–65.

48. See, in particular, Hassan Turabi, "The Islamic State," in John L. Esposito, ed., *Voices of Resurgent Islam* (New York: Oxford University Press, 1983), 241–51.

49. See An-Na'im, *Toward an Islamic Reformation,* 97, for a comparison of

Turabi's views with the draft Islamic constitution prepared by al-Azhar University in 1978, which does not make shura binding or obligatory.

50. Turabi, "Islamic State," 243.

51. An-Na'im, *Toward an Islamic Reformation,* 40.

52. Lowrie, "Islam, Democracy, the State and the West," 25–26.

53. Turabi, "Islamic State," 245.

54. Lowrie, "Islam, Democracy, the State and the West."

55. Turabi, "Islamic State," 250.

56. This point is acknowledged by El-Affendi, who does not provide an explanation for or background to Turabi's admission. A fuller account of the confrontation that finally ended Turabi's evasions is found in "The Elusive Islamic Constitution: The Sudanese Experience," *Orient* 26(1985).

57. Kok, "Kurzbiographien," 188.

58. Turabi, "Islamic State," 250.

59. See An-Na'im, *Toward an Islamic Reformation,* on the 1973 constitution.

60. Ibid., 42.

61. Mohamed Omer Beshir, *The Southern Sudan, from Conflict to Peace* (Khartoum: Khartoum Book Shop, 1975), 33.

62. Kok, "Kurzbiographien," 191.

63. Interview in the London-based *Al-Hayat,* 14 May 1992, 8, also cited by Peter Kok in his penetrating examination of Turabi's political career in *Orient.*

64. Lowrie, "Islam, Democracy, the State and the West," 44.

65. Abdullahi Ahmed An-Na'im, a former follower of Taha and a widely respected lawyer and analyst of the Taha's reformist Islam adamantly denies that Taha ever made such a claim. "There is simply no proof, none whatsoever," Na'im said in a recent interview, "of Turabi's claims about Taha."

66. Nathan Gardels, "The Islamic Awakening's Second Wave" (interview with Hassan Turabi), *New Perspectives Quarterly,* summer 1992.

67. Lowrie, "Islam, Democracy, the State and the West," 95.

68. Turabi, quoted in Gardels, "Islamic Awakening's Second Wave."

69. Lawrence Freedman and Efraim Karsh, *The Gulf Conflict,* 1990–1991: *Diplomacy and War in the New World Order* (Princeton: Princeton University Press, 1993), 150.

70. Mumtaz Ahmad, "The Politics of War: Islamic Fundamentalisms in Pakistan," in James Piscatori, ed., *Islamic Fundamentalisms and the Gulf Crisis* (Chicago: The Fundamentalism Project, 1991), 184 n. 35.

71. Olivier Rolin, "Al-Turabi on Carlos, F.I.S., Israel,and Islam," *Le Nouvel Observateur,* 31 August 1994; translated by Middle East Intelligence Report.

72. A rare specific reference to the allegations appears in *Mideast Mirror,* 19 August 1993, 8.

FOUR

SHAYKH AHMAD YASIN AND THE ORIGINS
OF HAMAS

Ziad Abu-Amr

Shaykh Ahmad Yasin, a handicapped Palestinian refugee who has resided in the Gaza Strip since the establishment of the state of Israel in 1948, is the founder of the most influential Islamic movement in recent Palestinian history. Hamas—an abbreviation of Harakat al-Muqawama al-Islamiya (Islamic Resistance Movement)—may be compared to Hizbullah, although it occupies a more central place in Palestinian society than Hizbullah does in Lebanon. The establishment and consolidation of Hamas, furthermore, marks a radical shift in Palestinian history: for the first time in decades, a political group that espouses Islam as an ideology has effectively challenged the dominant secular nationalist trend, embodied since 1964 by the Palestine Liberation Organization (PLO). In the 1990s Hamas—the brainchild of Ahmad Yasin, whose declared aim is to restore Islamic fundamentals and character to Palestinian society—has engaged in a fierce struggle for the spirit of the Palestinian people, as a first step in asserting its leadership and its control over Palestinian identity.

Yasin is a modest man in every sense of the word. But he was in the right place at the right time; his particular genius for plumbing and revolutionizing traditional Islamic discourse emerged at the same moment as an apparent shift toward Islamic revival. In fact, Yasin helped trigger that shift, for he shrewdly exploited not only his personal talents and charisma, but also the failures of others and the inherent appeal of Islam as an alternative for the disaffected Palestinian masses.

A REFUGEE TURNS TO ISLAM

Ahmad Yasin was born in 1936, the second youngest of nine children, six boys and three girls. His father, Ismaʿil Hasan Yasin, was a farmer and local dignitary from the village of Jora in the northern part of the Gaza district in mandate Palestine. An illiterate man who married four women, he was a middle-level landowner and, by the standards of his village, well-to-do. Five years after Ahmad was born, his father died, and an older brother assumed the responsibilities of providing for the family. The violent clashes between Palestinian Arabs and Zionist Jews, and between Israel and the Arab armies, that followed the establishment of the Jewish state in May 1948, caused Yasin's family to flee Palestine. Like many other displaced Palestinians, they settled in a refugee camp in Gaza. The uprooting of his family was to have a lasting impact on Ahmad.

The refugees who came to Gaza in 1948 needed a few years to settle and absorb what had happened; adjusting to the loss of their homeland was not easy. As a result of the Palestinian exodus, the population of what would later be known as the Gaza Strip, previously about ninety thousand, tripled almost overnight. The crowded strip of land bordering on the Sinai peninsula simply did not have the resources and services to accommodate the new population; the establishment of refugee camps by the United Nations was a humanitarian response to the situation. The Palestinian refugees believed that their exile was temporary, an attitude encouraged by the neighboring Arab states, which remained at war with Israel. The status of Palestinian refugees in these states was generally unpleasant, as they were unable or not allowed to assimilate into society. Yet the Arab states, especially Egypt, espoused a Pan-Arab nationalist ideology, which nurtured Palestinian political and national consciousness—as did the adverse conditions under which the refugees lived in these countries. Except for Jordan, which annexed the West Bank in 1950 and granted the Palestinians Jordanian citizenship, the Arab countries preserved the Palestinians' refugee status. In later years, the Palestinians themselves, especially those in the Gaza Strip, strongly resisted refugee resettlement plans.[1]

For a time the refugees relied on modest food rations and health and educational services provided by the United Nations Relief and Works Agency. Socioeconomic conditions in the refugee camps were harsh and the refugees had to struggle to eke out a living. Some joined the work force in Gaza, while others went to Saudi Arabia and other Gulf states to seek employment. The story of Yasin's experience as a refugee in Gaza was a typical one of deprivation and a constant struggle for survival. Poverty prevented him from pursuing higher education and required him to seek employment to help provide for his family.

Only two political organizations existed in Gaza when Yasin's political awareness began to crystallize: the communist League for National Liberation and a Palestinian branch of the Egyptian Muslim Brotherhood. Communism was not appealing, not only because it was alien to the conservative Muslim population of Gaza, but also because of the communists' stands on the issue of Israel and Palestine. The communists had endorsed the 1947 United Nations plan for the partition of Palestine, which called for the establishment of two states, one Jewish and the other Arab. The Gaza communists' attitude echoed that of their patron, the Soviet Union, and coincided with the position of the Israeli Communist Party. But it drew severe criticism from an uncompromisingly nationalist Palestinian population, which believed that the whole of Palestine belonged to the Arabs and that the Zionists had no right to any part of it. The communist attitude, visionary but insensitive to Palestinian bitterness, undermined the nationalist credibility of the already small and weak communist political organization, lending resonance to the claim that communism was an alien ideology.

By contrast, the Muslim Brotherhood's history in Palestine, dating back to 1936, lent it credibility as a popular resistance movement. During the 1948 war, the Brotherhood sent volunteers from Egypt, Syria, and Jordan and recruited Palestinians from Gaza and elsewhere in Palestine to fight alongside it against the Zionists. Despite its limited scope, the role of the Muslim Brotherhood in the war was highly publicized. Much of the Palestinian population was aware of its mission and the views of the volunteers. No other organized political group engaged in such activity. It was therefore natural that nationalist youth, like Ahmad Yasin, would seek to join the Brotherhood.[2]

While still in his teens, Yasin became politically conscious. Like many Palestinians at the time, he associated the misery of his family with the refugee camp, which would be his world for twenty-five years. The camp served as a constant reminder of the loss of his family's home and property in their village, and the loss of his country as a whole. Many other

Islam + Pal. nationalism compatible

Comm. + Pal nat not.

But central struggle was restorative justice of Pal. cause: past land displacement.

youths made similar associations and began to look for means to retrieve their country from the Zionists. Yasin and his contemporaries were thus willing recruits when political organizations raised banners protesting the plight of displaced Palestinians. They were recruits, however, who came to the Palestinian cause already committed to a higher cause defined by religious belief.

?

A religious orientation had prevailed in Yasin's family from the days in Palestine before 1948; now in Gaza, Yasin spent much of his time in a mosque that housed a center for the Muslim Brotherhood. In this center, he and his young colleagues were exposed to the teachings of Muslim leaders and thinkers such as Hassan al-Banna, the founder and Supreme Guide of the Muslim Brotherhood Society in Egypt. He was also influenced by schoolteachers who were active in the Gaza Brotherhood, the most prominent among them being his headmaster, Mohammad Mahmoud al-Shawwa.[3] Furthermore, Lajnat al-Wa'z wal-Irshad (Mission of Admonition and Guidance), an association involved in spreading the Islamic call in Gaza, used a Muslim Brotherhood front organization called Jam'iyat al-Tawhid as a religious learning center and a place to hold meetings, lectures, discussions, and other activities. Yasin started frequenting this society when he was still in the sixth grade.

In 1952, at the age of sixteen, Yasin fell and broke his back while playing on the beach, an accident that resulted in an almost total paralysis of his limbs. The paralysis likely accelerated his religious evolution; it was not unusual in the environment in which Yasin was brought up for individuals who became handicapped to turn to religion for solace or a means of addressing feelings of helplessness.

Yasin was being treated in a Gaza hospital when the 23 July 1952 Egyptian revolution took place. This revolution ended the monarchy in Egypt and brought to power the Free Officers, a group of military officers headed by Muhammad Najib, but effectively led by Gamal Abdel Nasser. A number of the Free Officers were linked to the Egyptian Brotherhood, which supported the revolution and thereby gained influence for a time in Egypt.

The change in the political regime in Egypt also had ramifications in the Gaza Strip, which was administered by the Egyptian government: the Gaza Brotherhood now enjoyed the sympathy of the Egyptian administration and tried to expand its numbers and its influence. The Brotherhood in Cairo, in coordination with the Egyptian government, supported the Mission of Admonition and Guidance in Gaza, frequented by Yasin and his friends. Leading elements of the Muslim Brotherhood in Egypt were selected for leadership roles at the mission, the members of which, in addition to their work as religious teachers and preachers, acted as liaison officers between the Muslim Brotherhood societies in Egypt and Gaza. After the Egyptian revolution, the Islamic trend thus became dominant in the Gaza Strip.

The relationship between the Muslim Brotherhood leadership in Egypt and the revolutionary government of Nasser deteriorated in 1954, however, following the government's endorsement of the Evacuation Treaty between Britain and Egypt. The Brotherhood opposed the treaty, the terms of which it deemed unjust to the Egyptians. An attempt was made on the life of Nasser, in which the Muslim Brothers were accused of being complicit. The Brotherhood was consequently banned in Egypt as well as in Gaza, causing it to become secretive in its activities. After enjoying the sympathy of the government and freedom of movement and organization, the Muslim Brothers were now subject to persecution.

The mother organization in Egypt received another devastating blow following an abortive attempt by the Brotherhood to seize power in 1965. Sayyid Qutb, a leading figure in the Brotherhood, was executed in 1966, and many others were arrested. A campaign of arrests in the Gaza Strip followed. Among those detained was Ahmad Yasin, now thirty years old and working as a teacher of religion and Arabic language. He spent forty-five days in jail but was released by the Egyptian administration, as were many other members of the Brotherhood, on the eve of the 1967 war in which Egypt, Syria, and Jordan were defeated by Israel. The resulting Israeli occupation of Gaza changed the situation on the ground, ending the Egyptian presence in the Strip as well as the Egyptian government's harassment of the Brotherhood.

After their release, the Brotherhood in Gaza and its leaders needed time to recuperate. But Yasin immediately resumed his religious activities in the Gaza mosques, working to spread Islamic awareness through meetings and discussion sessions and the establishment of modest libraries in mosques. Because these activities had no explicit political character, they were of no concern to the Israel military occupation, which was preoccupied with consolidating control over the Palestinian population and suppressing an emergent armed resistance movement backed by the Palestine Liberation Organization.

At this point Yasin was merely continuing the Muslim Brotherhood pattern of religious activities. He had no distinct agenda, no grand plan or strategy to challenge Israeli occupation. On the contrary, he and his fellow Islamists—small in number and lacking a real, functioning organization—deliberately avoided Israeli attention. Over time, Yasin and his associates adopted an unprovocative, gradualist approach, designed to build a social network focused in the first instance on religious activities. The rise of the Palestinian armed resistance movement immediately after 1967, inside Palestine and in neighboring Arab countries, was an eye-opener for Yasin. But he and the other Palestinian Islamists felt they were too weak to match the PLO factions' style of resistance to the Israeli occupation. They were also wary of the PLO's secular ideology and believed that the organization was created in 1964 on the behest of their deadly enemy Nasser. Accordingly, Yasin and his followers refused to participate in the armed resistance. As a result Yasin was not particularly well known on the popular level in the late 1960s; the time was not ripe for his talents to be made manifest.

The relative weakness of the Muslim Brotherhood continued for about a decade after 1967. While the PLO factions continued to be involved in acts of violence and resistance to the Israeli occupation, the Brotherhood turned to what it described as "the upbringing of an Islamic generation," a program of religious education that precedes transition to the next phase of jihad in the Muslim Brotherhood scheme. As a substitute for a direct political strategy, however, this program was not very convincing to a nationalist population seeking salvation from a foreign occupation. Moreover, by 1967 the field of competitors for popular allegiance in Gaza had grown. In addition to the communist and Brotherhood organizations, two Pan-Arab nationalist groups, the Ba'th Party and the Arab Nationalist Movement, had been founded, in 1953 and 1958, respectively. These two organizations had, at various times, enjoyed the support of the Nasser regime in Cairo and the Egyptian administration in Gaza. In the latter half of the 1950s, the Fatah movement also began to emerge. This proliferation of political organizations contributed to the relative weakness of the Gaza Brotherhood in the late 1960s, as did the Egyptian administration's antipathy toward the organization. Many of the group's leading figures and activists fled the Gaza Strip seeking employment or refuge from Egyptian harassment, often in Saudi Arabia and the other Arab Gulf states. In the late 1970s, however, this situation began to change.

RELIGIOUS REVIVAL IN THE 1970S

The 1970s proved a propitious moment for a religious revival in the occupied territories, and Yasin's skill in exploiting political openings in Palestine enabled him gradually to build and consolidate a viable Islamic force. One such opening emerged when the Palestinian resistance movement began to stumble. A 1970 war in Jordan between the Palestinian guerrilla movement and the army of King Hussein led to the expulsion of Palestinian armed groups from the country. Until then Jordan had been the movement's primary base for launching attacks against Israel and infiltrating the West Bank, and had been a major source of logistical support. At the same time, Israel implemented effective and extensive measures to counter and fight the PLO in the West Bank and Gaza.

The PLO was also forced to deal with the implications of the October 1973 war, which demonstrated the limitations of the Arab military option and of Palestinian armed resistance as a strategy for liberation. (The war, celebrated initially as a major Arab victory as Egypt and Syria launched a surprise attack against Israel to retrieve Sinai and the Golan Heights, ended with Israel occupying more Arab land across the Suez Canal and on the Golan Heights. These lands were returned to the Arabs after the disengagement treaties of 1974–1975 between Israel and both Egypt and Syria.) The convening of the Geneva Peace Conference of 1973 signaled the new possibility that the Arab-Israeli conflict might eventually be resolved not by armed resistance but by peaceful negotiation. As the PLO faced these new realities, a sense of disillusionment began to spread among the Palestinian population in the occupied territories. The people gradually became more amenable to alternative political or ideological approaches to the Palestine question.

By the late 1970s the Brotherhood was the only clear alternative to the nationalists. The Arab defeat in the 1967 war had weakened secular, nationalist, and socialist thinking in the Arab world and had led to a rise in the influence of Islamic-oriented states. Islamic trends and groups, including Yasin's, began to enjoy the material and moral support of Saudi Arabia and other Gulf states whose wealth had accumulated from oil exports.

The 1979 revolution in Iran also played a critical role in consolidating the Islamic revival in the occupied territories, inspiring Palestinian fundamentalists by demonstrating the ability of revolutionary Islam to overthrow mighty enemies like the Shah. Such valor in the name of Islam made it increasingly difficult for the Muslim Brotherhood in the West Bank and Gaza to remain passive in the face of Israeli occupation. Militant trends started to appear within Palestinian Islamic groups, especially on West Bank university campuses after Brotherhood activists visited the campuses and praised the Iranian revolution as a model for the struggle to rid Palestine of its Israeli oppressors.

Subsequently, other external factors forced the Islamic movement to redefine its role in the occupied territories. Some Muslim activists interpreted the Islamic revival in the Middle East and the world at large as a prelude to and precondition of a holy struggle to free Muslim societies from subjugation and alienation through Westernization and to restore their Islamic character. The 1981 assassination of Egyptian president Anwar Sadat, in the aftermath of his signing the Camp David Accords with Israel in 1979, emboldened and radicalized Islamic groups. The rise of the Islamic resistance against Israel in southern Lebanon following the Lebanese war of 1982 also provided a model and posed a challenge to the Muslims of the occupied territories.[4]

The specific domestic context for the rise of the Islamic movement came from the continuing Israeli occupation of the West Bank and Gaza, which was perceived as an immediate and direct threat to both the national and Islamic character of the Palestinian society. The growth of fundamentalist Jewish and rightist tendencies within Israel itself, which had led to occasional impingements on Muslim holy places, heightened the sense of fear and anxiety among the Palestinians.[5] Furthermore, supporters of the Islamic movement spread the belief that Israel's victory was the result of the Jews' adherence to their religion and that the Arabs' defeat was an outcome of their failure to adhere to Islam.[6] Ironically, the occupation of the West Bank and the Gaza Strip in 1967 provided the Muslims of these territories with additional geographic and demographic depth. Numerous Muslims in Israel received their religious education in Palestinian institutions in the West Bank and Gaza, and in the process established links between Islamic groups in Israel and in the Palestinian territories. Palestinian Islamists in both communities have exchanged visits and participated in joint religious, social, and political activities. Shaykh Yasin has supported this development, arguing that Islam calls for cooperation with Muslims both inside and outside of Palestine.[7]

But the primary domestic factor accounting for the rise of the Islamic movement in the occupied territories was the weakening of the secular nationalist movement led by the PLO. After twenty years the PLO seemed to be going nowhere. It had successfully revived the question of Palestinian national identity and had articulated three objectives for the Palestinian people: self-determination, statehood, and the right of return. But the PLO failed to realize any of these objectives. To the contrary, it had been expelled from Jordan in 1970 and from Lebanon in the aftermath of the Israeli invasion of 1982. These expulsions deprived PLO forces of immediate proximity to Palestine. Yasin and his associates watched carefully and missed no opportunity to capitalize on these setbacks and failures; they immediately attributed the failures of the PLO to the secular line the organization adopted.

Yasin and the Brotherhood also profited from Israel's policy of tolerance toward the Islamic movement. Israel hoped to use radical Islam as a counterforce to undermine the influence of the PLO. While there is no solid evidence of deliberate coordination between the two sides—and the Brotherhood categorically denies any complicity with Israel in return for material support—it is nonetheless true that throughout Israel's relentless war against the PLO, the Brotherhood was left to operate freely. Furthermore, the Israeli authorities extended legal status in 1979 to the Islamic Center, which Yasin had established in 1973, and a former Israeli military governor of the Gaza Strip claimed that his government had given money to the mosques.[8] Israeli tolerance of the Islamists may, however, have been merely a coincidence of interest, since the two sides sought to undermine the PLO, though for different reasons. But Yasin and the Brotherhood did not challenge the PLO in order to serve Israeli purposes; to the contrary, they were very keen to establish their own nationalist credentials as an alternative to the PLO. The Israelis for their part were concerned that a rise in Islamic influence could become a real problem in the future. Their concerns were justified, but Yasin was able to avoid repression until his movement became powerful enough to challenge the Israelis.

Yasin did not succeed solely by default. Rather, while Israel's campaign against the PLO weakened his secular Palestinian rivals, he hastened to make the Gaza branch of the Brotherhood a serious contender for their mantle, turning his attention to the task of building an Islamic infrastructure in Gaza. In 1973 he had established al-Mujma' al-Islami (the Islamic Center) in Gaza as a front for Muslim Brotherhood activities. In 1979 the Israeli authorities granted Yasin a legal license to operate the center, and by the mid-1980s it was one of the most powerful institutions in the Gaza Strip, boasting a number of affiliated mosques, libraries, kindergartens, and clinics. Through these institutions it worked to reform the Palestinian community from within and to combat secularism.[9]

The establishment of the Islamic Center provided Yasin and the Brotherhood with unprecedented political clout, as well as social leverage. Yasin began to be included in deliberations about major issues and events pertaining to the Palestinian population of the West Bank and Gaza. He and the center became a key factor in ensuring national consensus in the Strip. The mosque in particular played an important role as a platform for Yasin, whose frequent sermons made him a popular figure. The sharp increase in the number of mosques in the West Bank and Gaza reflected the growing popularity of the Islamic idea. Between 1967 and 1987, the number of mosques in Gaza more than doubled, from 77 to

160, and in the West Bank new mosques were built at a rate of forty per year.[10] Yasin turned the mosque from a place of worship into a center of learning and a place for political organization. The number of people who frequented mosques established by his Islamic Center increased considerably. As a result other indices of religious observance also increased. More Palestinian women covered their heads and wore veils or robes over their clothes. "Young men grew beards and wedding ceremonies returned to their traditional modest format. Even sports came into play as karate clubs sprang up in the mosques and soccer teams formed to join the Islamic League, whose players wore long pants and never let a curse slip past their lips."[11]

As he became more prominent in the Palestinian community, Yasin displayed his unique personal qualities. Known for his intelligence and sharp sense of humor, he was also a tireless worker. He knew his environment well, was firm in his leadership, and was judicious in meting out both praise and criticism to his followers among the youth of Gaza. These qualities appeared almost miraculous in a man paralyzed in over half of his body. Yasin's combination of intelligence, humor, sharp wit, dedication, and iron will—unbridled by the squalor and difficulty of life in Gaza as a handicapped man—fascinated his followers, and made them see in him something more than an ordinary preacher.[12]

Employing his unique talents and circumstance with great dexterity, Yasin extended the Brotherhood's control over the Islamic University and the *waqf* (religious endowment) authority in Gaza. The Islamic University, founded in 1978, was the only university in Gaza and quickly became the Muslim Brotherhood's principal stronghold. Through it, Yasin wielded considerable influence; its five thousand students provided a power base for the Brotherhood, especially in its relations with other political groups. In the 1980s the university began to provide local mosques with preachers loyal to Yasin and thus served as a primary source for the dissemination of his religious ideas and political views. As for the *waqf,* this religious institution controls an extensive network of property, which it leases to the local inhabitants. The *waqf* constitutes at least 10 percent of all real estate in Gaza—"hundreds of shops, apartments, garages, public buildings, and about 2,000 acres of agricultural land belonged to its trusts, and the *waqf* employed scores of people, from preachers and other clerics to grave-diggers."[13] Yasin's influence in the *waqf* provided him and the Brotherhood with a certain legitimacy in the eyes of the population, which credited the Brotherhood for the variety of services rendered.[14]

THE FOUNDING OF HAMAS

Like so many other significant events in Yasin's career as an Islamist, the founding of the Islamic Resistance Movement (Hamas) was a response to a particular set of conditions and openings in the sociopolitical environment of the occupied territories. On 9 December 1987, Yasin called the most prominent leaders of the Islamic Center to his home to discuss the appropriate response to an incident of the previous day: a number of Palestinian workers had been killed when an Israeli truck hit two cars carrying workers from Gaza. The popular masses were outraged; Gaza was at a boiling point. At the meeting Yasin pondered ways to exploit the situation for the benefit of the Islamic movement; discussion with his associates—also present were Dr. 'Abd al-'Aziz al-Rantisi, Dr. Ibrahim al-Yazuri, Shaykh Salah Shihada, Issa al-Nashshar, Muhammad Sham'a, and 'Abd al-Fattah Dukhan—revolved around the need to manipulate the event so as to arouse religious and nationalist sentiments and create popular disturbances.[15]

On 14 December the Brotherhood leaders issued a statement calling on the people to stand up to the Israeli occupation in a protracted uprising that would come to be known by its Arabic name, *intifada*. Hamas was born. The new movement subsequently considered this statement to be the first in a series of leaflets promulgating its ideology and program of action. As the disturbances in Gaza and the West Bank expanded, Yasin and his colleagues continued to meet, and Yasin established contact with Shaykh Jamil Hamami, one of the young preachers of Al-Aqsa Mosque in Jerusalem. Hamami, who acted as a liaison between the West Bank and Gaza, formed a parallel leadership body for Hamas in the West Bank.

Hamas, as we have noted, is an acronym for Harakat al-Muqawama al-Islamiya (Islamic Resistance Movement); the word also means "enthusiasm" or "zeal." Hamas's emergence in tandem with the intifada reflected a turning point in the evolution of the Palestinian Muslim Brotherhood, for it provided the organization with an opportunity to engage in the national resistance and to establish its nationalist credentials. Yasin declared that the establishment of Hamas was his duty as a human being, as a Muslim, as an Arab, and as a Palestinian, since he and large segments of his people "have for decades been suffering under the yoke of an intruding and oppressive occupation."[16] Although his natural constituency was religious, Yasin argued that Hamas was basically a political movement with its primary goal being to secure the legitimate and natural rights of the Palestinian people.

Of course the religious appeal of Hamas cannot be overstated. The popular turn to Hamas reflected not only a political decision but also a search for the psychological strength and endurance that a religious worldview usually provides. "When all other doors are sealed," as Yasin put it, "Allah opens a gate."[17] Yasin and Hamas offered the Palestinian population a more appealing combination of goods than did the PLO, according to one observer: "The fundamentalist groups offered a special kind of activism that combined patriotism with moral purity and social action with the promise of divine grace. Shaykh Yasin offered the young Palestinian something far beyond Arafat's ken: not just the redemption of the homeland, but the salvation of his own troubled soul."[18]

It may well be that Yasin the religious leader was forced by events to become Yasin the religiopolitical activist. He was initially cautious in endorsing full-fledged Brotherhood participation in the intifada, for he was not very keen on dragging the Islamic Center and the Brotherhood as a whole into an uncertain confrontation with the Israeli occupation. Yet he realized that a moment of crisis had arrived, a moment that would shape his destiny in one way or another. He could not sit on the sidelines ignoring the pressures within his movement and the unprecedented events taking place around him; nor could he avoid making serious and risky decisions.

Nonetheless, Yasin the calculating and astute politician managed to do things his own way. Until the day the intifada erupted he insisted that his movement was still going through the phase of Islamic upbringing and preparation; that the time had not yet come for the actual jihad. A seemingly new framework such as Hamas was therefore necessary to justify the abrupt ideological shift represented by the intifada. In creating Hamas Yasin devised a strategy to join the intifada without placing the Brotherhood and the Islamic Center in the direct line of fire. Should the intifada fail, Hamas would take the blame. But if it persisted, the Brotherhood could claim Hamas as its own. This it did a few months later, when the charter of Hamas was issued declaring the Islamic Resistance Movement as a wing of the Muslim Brotherhood Society in Palestine.[19]

Yasin was also mindful of other considerations. He had always sought to maintain his movement's position vis-à-vis other political factions in the occupied territories; participation in the intifada therefore seemed necessary if the Brotherhood was to play a role in any future political negotiations or settlement. Like the PLO, the Brotherhood needed a parallel resistance body. Accordingly, Yasin envisioned Hamas as the Brotherhood's parallel to the PLO's newly established Unified National Leadership of the intifada (UNL). In response to the PLO nationalists' predictable claims that the Brotherhood joined the intifada late and under pressure, Yasin boasted that the Brotherhood was responsible for the very eruption of the intifada, and that he had developed its leadership. When asked if the intifada was spontaneous (that is, not preplanned), he replied, "I believe it happened as something destined by God. There is nothing called spontaneous in Islam."[20]

Yet the intifada could not be contained within any one ideological framework, and the PLO stood to benefit from the popular uprising no less than the Brotherhood. To differentiate the Islamic approach from that of the PLO, Yasin strove to articulate the political objectives of the Muslim Brotherhood. The two movements shared the goal of ending the Israeli occupation of the West Bank and Gaza, of course, but the views of the Brotherhood and the PLO diverged on most other issues, and Yasin became quite vocal in underscoring this divergence. The founding and steady growth of Hamas allowed Yasin to throw political caution to the winds, with almost no negative political consequences for his larger Islamic movement. As leader of Hamas, he could openly challenge the PLO and its leadership, which had previously faced no political rival as representative of the Palestinian people; in this way Yasin and the Brotherhood began to contend with the PLO for the representation of the Palestinians in the occupied territories and managed over a relatively short period of time to become a force that could not be ignored.

In the late 1980s Hamas attacked the PLO secular line and its specific policies on more than one occasion.[21] For example, Hamas scorned the Palestinian National Council's resolutions of November 1988, which recognized Israel, accepted United Nations resolutions 242 and 338, and renounced terrorism. Hamas argued that the PLO was wrong in making such declarations and that it had no right to do so. Similarly, in response to the Unified National Leadership's call to the Palestinians in the West Bank and Gaza to hold mass rallies to celebrate the convening of the nineteenth PNC session and the declaration of independence, Hamas appealed to the people to turn the days the PNC was in session into "days of confrontation, opposition and rejection of peace with the murderers. . . . Let us tear down all appeals for capitulation and let us put an end to toying with the [Palestinian] cause by weaklings and those who are betting on the enemy's elections."[22] Shaykh Yasin judged the PLO declaration of independence, which was announced in the session, to be premature:

> We have not liberated any part of our country upon which we can found our state. We are still under occupation, and we have not yet put an end to it. In what place will we establish the state? . . . We must have land

upon which we can stand in freedom and establish our state without prior conditions and without concession.[23]

In sum, the establishment and growth of Hamas triggered a process that changed the balance of forces in the occupied territories. Some of Hamas's influence was earned by the movement's active endeavors, but much was gained by default, due to the failures of the PLO to deliver on its promises. The growth of Hamas's influence vis-à-vis that of the PLO was reflected in its emergence as a rival force, the expansion of its popular support and power base, and its success in winning the elections in a number of professional associations and trade unions in the West Bank and Gaza.

The Imprisonment of Yasin

The evolution of the Palestinian Muslim Brotherhood and the emergence of Hamas mirrored Yasin's own evolution from a religious advocate of reform into a skillful politician and a fundamentalist Islamic leader. Despite their claims to the contrary, the eruption of the intifada caught Yasin and his movement by surprise. Hamas's rapid consolidation of its influence and success in establishing its credibility and legitimacy became apparent, however, when scores of Gaza inhabitants began to frequent Yasin's home on a daily basis, requesting assistance for their various problems. This practice began with the intifada and continued until the day the shaykh was arrested in 1989. The visitors to Yasin's home included the religious and the secular, the poor and the well-to-do, the educated and the uneducated, merchants, businessmen, and even Palestinian Christians.[24] People paid tribute to Yasin during these visits but mainly came to seek mediation or arbitration. Yasin conducted these mediations effectively, aided by his charismatic character and down-to-earth nature. His success as a mediator also resulted in generous financial donations to the Brotherhood institutions and later to Hamas itself.

The resort to Yasin grew out of the absence or lack of credibility of the authority structures in Palestinian society. During the intifada, most law-enforcement institutions, such as courts and the local police, were practically shut down because of the widespread daily disturbances. Moreover, these structures, which were controlled by the very Israeli military occupation the Palestinians were struggling to dismantle, were seen by the Palestinians as sources of oppression and persecution. Thus Palestinian members of the Israeli-controlled local police resigned in solidarity with the intifada, and Palestinians, rather than turning to the courts, sought to settle their differences in informal settings. The secrecy of the PLO factions and their lack of spiritual authority or high moral standing increased the demands for arbitration of disputes by the Hamas leader. Yasin thus enjoyed a double reward for his years of leadership: while the resort to Hamas undermined the authority of the occupation, it also undermined the authority of the PLO and other secular institutions.

The emergence of Hamas also changed the Muslim Brotherhood's tactics toward the Israeli occupation. The Brotherhood's participation in the intifada marked the transition within Palestinian society to a systematic, planned confrontation with the Israeli occupation. Thus the activities of the Brotherhood were no longer officially restricted to spreading the Islamic call and building a Muslim generation.

Yasin had tried to set the stage for violent resistance to the occupation, but it was not until the days of rage of the intifada that violent tactics were employed systematically. In 1983 Yasin had formed two paramilitary units, al-Majd and al-Mujahidun. Al-Majd was an intelligence unit entrusted with the surveillance and punishment of drug dealers, prostitutes, and—most importantly—collaborators with Israel. Al-Mujahidun consisted of commando groups entrusted with forming underground cells, gathering information on Israeli targets, conducting training, and carrying out military operations.[25]

It was also in 1983 that the Israeli authorities charged Yasin with establishing an Islamic organization dedicated to waging jihad against Israel and establishing an Islamic state in its place. Sixty rifles were found in his home, and he was sentenced to thirteen years in prison. In May 1985, after ten months in jail, he was released as part of a prisoner exchange between the Israeli government and the Popular Front for the Liberation of Palestine—General Command. When he left prison, the Israeli authorities, wary of his intentions, did not allow him to resume his position as chairman of the Islamic Center. As leader of the Muslim Brotherhood Society in Gaza, however, Yasin continued to work to raise religious consciousness among the Palestinians through education and social action. But he remained dedicated to the use of violence against the Israelis. During the intifada he was implicated in the kidnapping and killing of two Israeli soldiers and other violent acts against Israelis and against Palestinians suspected of collaborating with them. In May 1989 Yasin was taken to jail, where he awaited trial for several years; he was later sentenced to fifteen years imprisonment.

From the foundation of Hamas in 1987 to his arrest in 1989, Yasin was in charge of drafting the leaflets that defined the activities of the intifada. In so doing he would consult his colleagues in the leadership of

Hamas, who have since taken on this duty in his absence. Yasin may have continued to lead the movement at times, even after his imprisonment, by smuggling out instructions as he did during the earlier jailings. Because of Israeli security restrictions and Yasin's poor health and physical condition, however, it is likely that the movement and its leaders inside and outside the occupied territories have had to rely largely on themselves. These leaders are generally highly educated individuals, intellectuals and professionals who have gained considerable leadership experience since the arrest of Yasin. In any case, second-tier leaders of Hamas exercised practical, day-to-day leadership on the ground and issued the orders all along—Yasin's actual role may have been largely symbolic. In that sense Yasin and Hamas are no longer identical; the dynamics of a movement go beyond a founder who is no longer actively involved. After Yasin's arrest, a number of significant developments led Hamas to ever more dramatic acts of extremism.

THE RADICALIZATION OF HAMAS

Hamas emerged intact after the Gulf crisis of 1990–1991; indeed, its shrewd refusal to vocally support Saddam Hussein won Hamas the financial support of Saudi Arabia. Its influence among the Palestinians in the occupied Territories subsequently increased, even as the PLO opted to participate in the Madrid Peace Conference (October 1991) and subsequent negotiations leading to the Palestinian-Israeli accord of September 1993. In line with Yasin's ideology, Hamas voiced fierce opposition to the peace process, and in 1994, 1995, and 1996 the world saw an escalation of the group's obstructionist activities, including suicide bombings against Israeli targets. These spectacular attacks, staged inside Israel, claimed the lives of scores of Israelis and injured hundreds more; one of the most serious took place in Tel Aviv 19 October 1994, killing twenty-two Israelis and injuring over forty more. In January and February 1996, fifty-eight Israelis died in a series of suicide bombings conducted by militant factions of Hamas. Such attacks were carried out by Kata'ib al-Shahid 'Izz al-Din al-Qassam (Brigades of the Martyr 'Izz al-Din al-Qassam). Although the formation of these brigades in 1991, two years after Yasin's imprisonment, marked the actual radicalization of Hamas and the adoption of violence as its principal tactic, Yasin was a source of inspiration. Indeed, many of the activities undertaken by al-Majd and al-Mujahidun, the paramilitary units he founded, were inherited by the Qassam Brigades.

The violent attacks of the Qassam Brigades were designed in part to put pressure on the Israeli government to release Yasin and other Hamas leaders, and in part to maintain Hamas's visibility in the absence of Yasin. Hamas's adoption of suicidal attacks may also have been influenced by the Islamic militants of Hizbullah; Israel's yearlong expulsion of 415 Hamas and Islamic Jihad activists to southern Lebanon in 1992 put these activists in direct contact with Hizbullah.

Hamas has suffered noticeably for lack of Yasin's charismatic, independent leadership. The decision-making activities of the Qassam Brigades are believed to be somewhat autonomous of the Hamas political leadership. Furthermore, Hamas has had to rely on input from leaders outside the occupied territories, especially in Jordan. Other Hamas leading figures are to be found in Syria, Lebanon, Sudan, Saudi Arabia, some Arabian Gulf states, Iran, Europe, and the United States. Yasin had been the primary figure in the movement; after his arrest, therefore, it was a matter of necessity that the movement change its leadership style and rely on a more collective leadership. The shift to a collective leadership has transformed Hamas in significant ways. In the 1990s the movement has begun, for example, to adopt a nationalist rhetoric, reflecting the Muslim Brotherhood's desire to expand its sphere of influence. Acting on this desire entailed the admission that the Brotherhood had participated in the intifada and had established Hamas as an act of nationalist fervor—admissions, in short, designed to enhance the influence and popularity of the Islamists.

Yasin's ideological leadership, even from an Israeli prison cell, remained a factor for the collective leadership to consider, however. After his incarceration in May 1989, Yasin made a number of appearances on Israeli television and was allowed to give newspaper interviews. On one occasion (December 1992) he was briefly shown on Israeli television appealing to Hamas kidnappers of Nassim Toledano, an Israeli border police officer, not to kill their hostage. In an interview in 1995, however, Yasin categorically rejected "reconciliation with the Jews" as "a crime for those who effect it . . . if it legitimized the occupation, recognized its right to exist on our usurped land, and kept the Palestinian people dispersed outside its country."[26] In that interview Yasin also rejected the Oslo Declaration of Principles of September 1993 between Israel and the PLO, arguing that jihad was the only way to foil the peace agreement. To this end, he endorsed the suicidal attacks carried out by the Qassam Brigades—for they "terrify and confuse the Jews"—but reminded the brigades to observe Islamic principles of war, according to which women, the elderly, and children should not be killed unless they carry arms and engage in the fight.[27]

While Yasin rejected reconciliation with the Jews, he argued that Islam does permit a truce or a cease-fire when the enemy is powerful and the Muslims are weak and need time to build their power. Such a truce, according to Yasin, should last no longer than ten years; ending it requires the awakening of the Muslim *umma* (nation). Yasin argued, however, that pursuing a truce in the current Palestinian-Israeli situation would not be appropriate because it would involve a recognition of the enemy's legitimacy and its pillaging of Palestine.[28] Despite his poor health Yasin has repeatedly rejected offers of early release in return for his renunciation of violence.

THE IDEOLOGY OF YASIN

What made Yasin and Hamas distinctive in the Palestinian society were their views on the nationalist issue—views which developed over time. Yasin's initial position was derivative, inspired by that of the Muslim Brotherhood societies in Jordan and Egypt, and of the international Islamic movement as a whole. Since the establishment of the state of Israel, the theoretical and ideological stance of the Muslim Brotherhood has been that all of Palestine is Muslim land, and that no one has the right to concede any part of it. The rights of the Muslims in Palestine, furthermore, are both historical and religious in nature. On the constant defense of this right depends the integrity of anyone who would claim to be a true Muslim—or so the "fundamentalist" version of political Islam has it.

In drawing upon this fundamentalist credo, Yasin took full advantage of his strategic setting in Palestine, the symbolic if not the actual center of worldwide Islamist resistance. He taught his followers that the way to regain Palestine is through the exercise of jihad, in the sense of a holy war against external enemies. When asked about his willingness to resort to jihad as a means to realize his aspirations, Yasin asked me, in turn, "What is the other alternative available to those who cannot regain their rights by peaceful and nonviolent means?"[29] The Palestinian people would prefer to realize their objectives peacefully and not through violence, Yasin assured me; if they resort to violence it is in self-defense, because the Israeli occupier understands only the language of violence and force. Under such circumstances, "the gun is the only means that should be used in addressing the enemy."[30] As a people under occupation, the Palestinians, according to Yasin, choose the means of resistance that are available to them. This attitude stood behind the various pragmatic tactics, violent and nonviolent, used by Hamas during the intifada.

According to Yasin, Hamas's use of violence had but one objective: the removal of oppression and corruption and the establishment of justice. Those who defend oppression and try to sustain it are deplorable in the eyes of Islam, he said, regardless of their religion or beliefs, yet the goal of violence is not the destruction of the human beings who engage in these practices.[31] Nonetheless, Yasin's statements on the issue of jihad sometimes contradicted each other. He argued, for example, that jihad should start after the Islamic transformation of Palestinian society is complete, but he also taught that Muslims who remain silent about the occupation of Palestine commit a sin because Islam requires them to engage in a holy war. Yasin contended that failure to act constitutes "fatal treason," and any philosophy that justifies submission and does not urge the sacrifice of souls and resources is "heretical."[32] If Muslims do not fulfill their obligations with respect to the exercise of jihad, he said, time is bound to change the situation.

Yasin believed, further, that the liberation of Palestine would require the efforts of the world Islamic movement; the Palestinians alone could not reconfigure the political map in the Arab and Muslim worlds according to the demands of justice, as defined by the Islamists. Thus the Brotherhood advocated the establishment of an Islamic state, society, and regime in one of the Arab countries neighboring Israel, such as Syria, Egypt, or Jordan. Yasin articulated this goal in the late 1980s. This entity would function as a base for the Islamic movement in Palestine, he said, and was a prerequisite to the realization of the general goal embodied in the victory of the Islamic call. It should be ruled by an elite committed to Islam as a constitution and a way of life and elected by a people who are also committed to Islam. The ruler of this state would, over the course of a decade, unite and prepare the *umma* for "the decisive battle with the Jews."[33]

Although he acknowledged the nationalist dimension to the struggle, Yasin did not embrace nationalist rhetoric prior to the 1990–1991 Gulf war. The concept of nationalism, he warned in the late 1980s, has geographic boundaries, and commitment to land alone, in the absence of Islamic doctrine, is a grave mistake, since one piece of land can be replaced with another. It is evident that the views of Yasin on nationalism (*Wataniya*) were inspired by those of Hassan al-Banna, considered the delineator of the Muslim Brotherhood's doctrinal and political views on such critical issues as the Islamization of state and society, political rule and the means to attain it, the question of nationalism, and Pan-Arabism.[34] Failure to make the Palestine question part of a broader Islamic concern, according to Yasin, amounts to treason in that it excludes millions of Muslims from the struggle against Israel. Palestine, he recalled, was liberated from the crusaders under the banner of Islam. Thus attributing the defeats Arabs and Palestinians had suffered to the fact that their leaders did not raise the banner of Islam, Yasin rejected the secular program of the PLO.[35]

Finally, Yasin opposed the teaching of some Palestinians during the early stages of the intifada, that people should postpone making specific ideological or doctrinal commitments until national liberation was realized. This advice was flawed, Yasin held, because genuine liberation cannot be achieved without the commitment to Islam, which provides the necessary ideological and psychological preparation.

Yasin remained critical of the PLO because "it is an organization that does not serve God."[36] "The PLO is secularist. It cannot be accepted as a representative unless it becomes Islamic."[37] But while Yasin and his movement clearly desired to become the alternative leadership of the Palestinian people, they initially denied harboring such ambitions. Instead Yasin voiced positions suggesting moderation and compromise. A studied ambiguity colored his pronouncements: "We do not differ with the PLO. We have an idea, and the PLO has an idea, and the sole arbiter is the people. What the people decided is acceptable to us."[38] On another occasion, when asked if he supported certain steps taken by the PLO, Yasin replied, "I support them and I oppose them. I support having a state, and I oppose the conceding of the rest of the land of my homeland, Palestine."[39] Such ambivalence stemmed from Yasin's awareness that the PLO still constituted the major Palestinian force in the occupied territories and enjoyed the largest popular support among the Palestinian people: "Being a prudent man, he was careful to explain that the PLO was not evil, merely misguided; the yardstick for judging Arafat, like every other Muslim, was not nationalist fervor but religious piety."[40]

This same awareness of the other underscored Yasin's ambiguous statements regarding Israel. When questioned about negotiating with Israel, he replied:

> Yes, if Israel acknowledges our full rights and recognizes the Palestinian people's right to live in its homeland in freedom and independence. But the Islamic movement will not negotiate as an alternative to the PLO. . . . I do not want to destroy Israel . . . we want to negotiate with Israel so the Palestinian people inside and outside Palestine can live in Palestine. Then the problem will cease to exist.[41]

This circumlocution was also motivated by his fear of the occupying power, Israel. The concept of *taqiyya* in Islam justifies concealing the true beliefs if expressing such beliefs would harm the Muslims.[42] The following excerpts of an interview given by Yasin reflect his mastery of political ambiguity:

> *Interviewer:* Do you want a Palestinian state from the river to the sea?
>
> *Yasin:* I want a Palestinian state.
>
> *Interviewer:* What are its boundaries?
>
> *Yasin:* Palestine has well-known boundaries; these are the borders of the Palestinian state.
>
> *Interviewer:* Where is Israel then?
>
> *Yasin:* Israel is in Palestine.
>
> *Interviewer:* Can you clarify your concept of the Palestinian state?
>
> *Yasin:* The Palestinian state must be founded on every inch of Palestine that we liberate, but without conceding the rest of our rights.
>
> *Interviewer:* Do you recognize Israel?
>
> *Yasin:* If I recognized Israel, the problem would be finished, and we would have no rights left in Palestine.
>
> *Interviewer:* But if Israel withdrew from the West Bank and the Gaza Strip, would you recognize it?
>
> *Yasin:* When it withdraws, I will say.
>
> *Interviewer:* But at that time, should it be recognized?
>
> *Yasin:* I leave this matter to the representatives of the Palestinian people.
>
> *Interviewer:* Who are they?
>
> *Yasin:* Those whom the Palestinian people will elect.[43]

Yasin thus rejected the political objectives embraced by the PLO. He remained opposed to its willingness to establish an independent Palestinian state on only part of Palestine and to its attempts to reach a political settlement with Israel on this basis. Yasin and his movement rejected the idea of holding an international or regional peace conference or negotiating any accord or agreement with Israel. According to Yasin, the convening of a peace conference is "sheer mirage and a waste of time." He was (and remains) equally opposed to any PLO concessions to Israel under pretexts of alleviating the suffering of the Palestinian people by means of a political settlement: "Suffering is no reason for conceding rights. When a human being is unable to attain his rights, he does not concede them."[44]

As for negotiations with Israel, Yasin argued that it would not be right to negotiate given an imbalance of power in which the Israeli counterpart "can imprison me, deport me, or kill me. It is therefore logical that negotiations do not take place." Although Yasin's attitude toward negotiations was motivated by doctrinal convictions, he calculated the political angle as well. When asked if a Palestinian state and an Israeli state can live in peace side by side, he replied, "No. This situation will be temporary. If that happens, the conflict will be resumed after a while in a more intense fashion. Palestine is a holy place for the Jews, the Christians, and the Muslims. The solution therefore, lies in living together in one state."[45]

Clearly, Yasin taught his zealous young followers that any Palestinian state must comprise the area of Israel, the West Bank, and Gaza. Hence the reference to "from the river [Jordan] to the [Mediterranean] sea." These are the borders of Palestine as defined in nationalist as well as Islamic literature. This state must also be an Islamic state, in which the "People of the Book," the Jews and the Christians, are treated according to Islamic teachings: "I personally prefer that Islam dominates in a state like this one." When asked if he hated the Israelis or the Jews, Yasin replied, "Islam calls for the love of all people. What forces me to hate the Jews is the fact that they have deprived me of my rights. And I hate whoever deprives me of my rights."[46] Since Yasin rejected reconciliation with Israel, it is natural that he would not support political solutions that leave the Jewish state intact, let alone dominant. For Yasin, granting autonomy or self-rule to the Palestinians of the occupied territories meant that the Jews "will get everything, while the Palestinians will get nothing." Yasin argued that autonomy does not satisfy the present or future aspirations of the Palestinian people.[47]

On the related issue of elections in the occupied territories, Yasin told his followers that elections are possible and right only if they are conducted under international supervision or after the Israeli withdrawal from the West Bank and Gaza. Yasin meanwhile conveyed his desire for a confederation with Jordan: "Islam calls for unity. When we commit ourselves to Islam, we do not reject any unity, but this unity should be predicated on correct and equal basis."[48] Again, Yasin's position reflected a measure of political calculation: a Palestinian-Jordanian confederation would doubtless strengthen the Muslim Brotherhood vis-à-vis the PLO. Yasin also depended on support for Hamas operations from the Brotherhood in Jordan.

On more than one occasion after the founding of Hamas, Yasin indicated to his followers that a democratic state with a multiparty system would be acceptable: "Whoever wins will be entitled to assuming authority. Even if the communists win, I will respect the will of the Palestinian people."[49] It is not clear, however, how Yasin intended to reconcile this prodemocracy position with his determined stand on the necessity of establishing an Islamic state in Palestine. Presumably, Yasin's talk about a multiparty system was tactical since the Qur'anic states explicitly the Islamic rejection of political parties that do not derive their principles from Islamic doctrine. Muslims who interpret Islam's position towards political parties otherwise are considered by militant fundamentalists to be guilty of doctrinal misinterpretation or diversion. In Iran and Sudan, where Islamic rule is established, non-Islamic parties are outlawed.

When Yasin and other leaders of Hamas talk about elections, their purpose is to find out who represents the Palestinian people. This interest in "the will of the people" should not be taken, however, as an endorsement of the Western notion of democracy. Yasin, Hamas, and the Brotherhood have avoided talking about this issue with any degree of specificity.[50] Yasin has condemned Western democracy as a tool to "remove Islam and the faithful Muslims from the leadership of the Muslim people." Using the victory of the Islamic Salvation Front in Algeria's 1991 parliamentary elections as an example, he noted how this victory was stolen from the Islamists by the Western-backed Algerian government. During his current imprisonment in Israel, Yasin has continued to admonish the Palestinian people not to trust the talk about embracing Western democracy as a means to end occupation, imperialism, and the control of secular governments.[51] In sum, it is safe to say that Yasin and other Muslim Brotherhood leaders would tolerate democracy only as a phase leading to *shura* rule, the closest Islamic analogue to democracy.[52]

COPING WITH THE PEACE PROCESS

During the course of the intifada, Hamas issued a series of leaflets that elaborated its political goals, spread its slogans, and provided the agenda for its daily activities. The leaflets usually began with, or contained, Qur'anic verses and were full of Islamic historical and religious references, announcements of Islamic memorial days, and commentary on morality, conduct, spirituality, and the observance of religious practices. Instead of promising material rewards, Hamas spoke of spiritual compensation: "the building of a new identity for the people as an army of believers for whom the gates of Paradise were about to open." But this spiritual compensation was matched by less-publicized material rewards, including social services and financial support to the followers of the movement.

Ahmad Yasin's fundamentalist brand of liberation theology, as articulated in these leaflets, was somewhat crude and improvised. Less a function of formal intellectual or doctrinal training than of the handicapped preacher's own situational interpretation of Islam, it drew on a highly selective reading of the Qur'an and other traditional Islamic sources, a reading guided by the contemporary sloganeering of Islamists calling for jihad in the Muslim cause, resistance to the Israeli occupation, and, on a more strategic level, a holy struggle to liberate Palestine and establish a Muslim state in it. Hamas preached this crude gospel to a people frustrated by decades of living in squalor under a corrupt and ineffective "national" leadership. The Islamic resistance employed the discourse of the streets, using graffiti to express its views and positions on political issues and developments: "The land of Palestine is an Islamic *waqf*, Islamic law forbids its abandonment or bargaining over it"; "The Qur'an is the sole legitimate representative of the Palestinian people"; "Islam is the way to return [to Palestine]"; "Islam is the solution"; "The destruction of Israel is a Qur'anic imperative"; "O Jews, leave our land."

On 18 August 1988, Hamas issued a charter outlining its philosophy and raison d'être. It is not clear how much input Yasin had in the drafting of this charter, but it contained the major themes of his teaching. According to the charter, the "Islamic Resistance Movement is a distinct Palestinian movement that gives allegiance to God, takes Islam as a way of life, and works to raise the banner of God over every inch of Palestine."[53]

> Initiatives, so-called peaceful solutions, and international conferences to solve the Palestinian issue are at variance with the doctrine of the Islamic Resistance Movement. Abandoning any part of Palestine is an abandonment of a part of religion. The patriotism of the Islamic Resistance Movement is a part of its religion. Only the jihad can solve the Palestinian issue. Initiatives, proposals, and international conferences are a waste of time and an exercise in futility. The Palestinian people are too precious for anyone to play with their future, their rights, and their destiny.[54]

Regarding Hamas's position toward other Palestinian Islamic groups, the charter announces that the Islamic Resistance Movement "looks at the other Islamic movements with respect and esteem" and considers that those movements are "covered by the principle of *ijtihad* [Islamic legal judgment conducted independently by religious scholars] as long as they are sincere and intend well, and as long as their actions remain within the bounds of the Islamic framework." The Islamic Resistance Movement, the charter continues, considers these movements an asset and prays to God for divine guidance for all. "Hamas will continue to raise the banner of unity [of all Islamic resistance groups] and try hard to achieve it on the basis of the Qur'an and the Sunna."[55]

As regards the PLO, the charter's studied ambiguity reflects a degree of evolution from Yasin's previous hard-line Muslim Brotherhood position. On the one hand, the charter "considers the PLO to be the closest to the Islamic Resistance Movement and regards it as a father, brother, relative, or friend. Can the Muslim be alienated from his father, brother, relative, or friend? Our nation is one, our misfortune is one, our destiny is one, and our enemy is one." On the other hand, it observes that the PLO endorses secular ideas "and secular thought is incompatible with religious thought, completely incompatible. Upon ideas are based positions, and actions and decisions are made." Accordingly, "despite our esteem for the PLO . . . and what it may evolve into, and without belittling its role in the Arab-Israeli struggle, we cannot abandon the present and future Islamism of Palestine, in order to endorse secular thought." The Islamism of Palestine is a part of our religion, the charter continues, "and those who abandon their religion will lose."[56]

Finally, the charter asks the Arab states surrounding Israel to open their borders to the *mujahidun* (holy warriors engaged in the practice of jihad) of the Arab and Muslim peoples, "so that they can play their role and add their efforts to the efforts of their brothers, the Muslim Brothers in Palestine. . . . As for the other Arab and Islamic nations, they are asked to facilitate the mujahidun's movement. This is the very least to be done."[57]

An accurate reading of the Hamas charter reveals that some of its cleverly written sections and ideas are capable of being interpreted in different ways by different parties. Although it is not known specifically who drafted the document, Yasin's evasive and ambiguous style can be discerned therein. Of course evasiveness or ambiguity is a usual characteristic of oppositional political discourse, especially that of the Muslim Brotherhood societies in Palestine, Jordan, and Egypt. Yasin made use of this style in his statements vis-à-vis the PLO and Israel; since his arrest, this style has been less visible in Hamas statements—especially those concerning Israel.

This early ambiguity afforded Hamas an advantage over its secular rival. As the situation warranted, Hamas could claim that while the liberation of "Muslim Palestine" remains the ultimate goal and jihad the ultimate means, the circumstances confronting the umma at any given time necessitate a temporary and tactical halt or retreat. (Yasin's Muslim Brotherhood did just that for many years.) The PLO, by contrast, cannot afford such ideological flexibility; if it were to suggest to its following that self-determination, statehood, the right of return, and PLO representation were no longer feasible and needed to be postponed until further notice, it would definitely lose some of its supporters to Hamas. After all, these objectives—not pursuing the will of Allah—have been the raison d'être of the PLO.

After the establishment of the Palestinian Authority in 1994 a debate ensued within Hamas as to how to relate to this authority. Some Hamas leaders believed that the Oslo agreement marks a new phase in the Palestinian situation and that the movement should embrace the change. This trend in Hamas relies on Yasin's teaching that the Islamic movement should adapt to every new development in order to maintain its force, growth, and expansion. In this context, an element within Hamas called for the establishment of a political party to cope with the change. But the militant faction in the movement saw no need to create such a party; according to Yasin, "The time is not appropriate to create a party because this phase is one of jihad against the enemy, and the establishment of a party requires the existence of an independent state."[58]

In a March 1995 interview Yasin argued that it was possible for the Islamist movement to coexist with the Palestinian Authority if the Authority did not undertake hostile steps against the Islamists. Hostile steps he defined as the establishment of a dictatorial Palestinian authority and the suppression of the Qassam Brigades, whose attacks are intended to "evict the Jews from the settlements and restore the territories the Palestinian Authority hoped to restore by signing the Oslo Agreement." If the Palestinian Authority ever opened fire on the Islamic forces, "becoming thus a wing of the Israeli army and its intelligence services," Hamas would "fight the Palestinian Authority without leniency the way we fight the Jews."[59] Yasin also reminded his followers of Hamas's dictum that the struggle of the Islamists made it possible for the Palestinian Authority to come to Gaza and Jericho.

A transition of Hamas from militancy to accommodation is less likely, of course, if the movement splits into radical factions, as was the case in the early 1980s when the Islamic Jihad Movement split from the Muslim Brotherhood Society. The evolution of the PLO toward moderation in its dealings with Israel in the early 1990s, made Hamas's positions appear, by contrast, exceedingly radical; indeed, its refusal to endorse or participate in the peace process cast Hamas in an obstructionist role in the public eye, despite the fact that this had always been the Hamas position. And when PLO participation in the intifada subsided, Hamas's continuation with intifada-style operations was also considered a sign of its uncompromising radicalism. For Hamas, however, the refusal to shift to moderation was the movement's way of asserting that there is a major Palestinian force that opposes the peace process and cannot be ignored.

After Yasin's arrest differentiation within the movement strengthened Hamas's radical element. The politically seasoned Yasin had played a calculated moderating role in the movement; on more than one occasion, for example, he had called on Hamas militants not to kill Israeli hostages. But, because of Israeli measures against Hamas, the movement experienced a new wave of reaction since Yasin's arrest in May 1989. About 260 Hamas activists, in addition to Yasin's close aides, were arrested in the early 1990s and hundreds more were arrested by the Israeli security forces in the West Bank, as well as by the Palestinian Authority after the latter's establishment in Gaza and Jericho.

In light of these reprisals and the weakening of its leadership Hamas could have followed one of two courses. The first was to regroup and shift back from armed resistance to building infrastructure and consolidating its influence within Palestinian society (as the PLO factions did when armed struggle stumbled in the mid-1970s). At this writing, such a regrouping has not occurred. Instead, Hamas has taken the second road, that of marked radicalization. Its tactics have become more militant; the use of firearms, bombings, and suicidal attacks against Israeli targets are now more common. It remains uncertain in 1996 whether Hamas can sustain this violence, given Israel's much greater resources, its own declining influence in the face of arrests and other restrictive measures imposed by the Palestinian Authority and Israel, and a reduction in outside support for the movement due to measures undertaken by the surrounding governments. The Jordanian government, for example, officially prohibits support for Hamas in Jordan, and is also bound to honor the spirit and letter of its peace treaty with Israel. Jordan has therefore expelled a number of Hamas leaders from its territory, including, in 1995, Dr. Musa Abu-Marzuq, head of Hamas's political bureau. Abu-Marzuq was arrested later that same year in the United States, where he is still awaiting trial. Hamas's suicidal attacks against Israeli targets have continued after the arrest of Abu-Marzuq.

The question of popular support for Hamas is also a vexed one. Not only is there lingering skepticism about the movement's viability as an alternative to the PLO, but Hamas's conservative social outlook creates anxiety among large segments of the Palestinian population. Moreover, Hamas is not homogeneous; it includes fundamentalist, political, and merely opportunist elements. Radicalization—which can be seen as a response to popular desperation and frustration with the lack of progress in the peace process—was politically rewarding to all three elements, as it increased Hamas's popularity and influence.

Hamas and its mother organization, the Muslim Brotherhood Society in the occupied territories, constitute an integral part of the world Islamic movement. But this may be a liability as well as an asset to Hamas, in that the movement as a whole, and in particular the Muslim Brotherhood societies in Jordan, Egypt, and elsewhere, at times restrains its Palestinian counterpart in the occupied territories because of external considerations. Since the society in the occupied territories lacks the decision-making status the other societies enjoy, it relies on guidance from them on the major issues and continues to some extent to abide by their decisions. Restraining decisions made by the Muslim Brotherhood societies abroad naturally take into account not only factors in the occupied territories, but also the circumstances of Islamic movements throughout the region and the world.

CONCLUSION: THE SITUATIONAL LEADERSHIP OF SHAYKH YASIN

While Yasin became the most prominent Islamic figure in the Gaza Strip and the West Bank, the underlying causes of his prominence were political. His emergence as a rival to the previously uncontested secular PLO brought him attention initially; his later decision to have his movement engage the Israeli occupation through participation in the intifada increased his visibility. Yasin's leadership was strictly situational—creative, indeed, but entirely a response to his environment. He was not a Khomeini, a Fadlallah, a Shari'ati, not an al-Banna or a Qutb. His prominence derived neither from any unique theological or doctrinal contribution nor from his regional or global leadership, but primarily from his role within the political context of the Palestine issue.

Yasin is indeed a Islamic fundamentalist, but his brand of fundamentalism differs from that of other Palestinian fundamentalist leaders. While Yasin is in no way a conformist, Hamas under his leadership was but partially revolutionary and partially reformist, especially when compared to the ultramilitant and revolutionary Islamic Jihad. While Yasin occasionally equivocated, for political reasons, his counterparts in the Islamic Jihad Movement were categorical in their rejection of Israel and its right to exist. They were also avowedly committed to changing the existing order within the Arab and Muslim worlds.

The Islamic Jihad stands for speedy and revolutionary change, a position reflected in its articulations and tactics. Shaykh As'ad Bayud al-Tamimi, a prominent Islamic Jihad leader, came to the fore in the wake of Yasin's arrest, iterating his argument that Israel's destruction is inevitable. Tamimi's wing of the Islamic Jihad Movement was responsible for the January 1990 attack on an Israeli tourist bus on the road from Ismailiya to Cairo in Egypt, in which nine Israelis were killed and a dozen others injured. Another key leader of the Islamic Jihad in Palestine, Dr. Fathi al-Shiqaqi, was assassinated in Malta in October 1995. In his book *Al-Khomeini: Al-Hall al-Islami wal-Badil* (Khomeini: The Islamic solution and alternative), Al-Shiqaqi provided an exposition of the significance of the Islamic revolution in Iran as a model for changing a corrupt order and establishing an Islamic state.

Unlike Islamic Jihad, the Muslim Brotherhood has been around for several decades and embraces a strategy for long-term change. This and its pragmatism have ensured the Brotherhood's longevity. Much of the credit in this regard goes to Yasin; after his arrest, Hamas grew closer to the Islamic Jihad in terms of tactics and revolutionary intent. This is not to say, however, that Yasin, the situational leader, would have responded any differently than his successors. Hamas has proven susceptible to outside influences, including changes in the strategies, agendas, and priorities of other Islamic movements. But Hamas also stands to benefit from the presence of other Islamic states in the region. Currently both Iran and Sudan are considered close allies of the movement, extending to it material, logistical, doctrinal, and political support.

This dual emphasis on home-grown radicalism and international Islamic awareness is Yasin's legacy. Ironically his movement, Hamas, has grown in influence and popularity since he left the scene. The rise of Hamas in the early 1990s bears comparison to that of the Palestinian resistance movement in the late 1960s and early 1970s, when that movement enjoyed a great deal of support among the Palestinians and in many quarters in the Arab world. It remains to be seen whether Hamas will have a better luck in sustaining and building on this support, or if its support will diminish over time as did support for the PLO.

Hamas's response to the intifada broke the barrier of fear the Islamists felt toward Israel. It had taken the PLO over two decades to earn the degree of credibility, popularity, and legitimacy that Hamas, under Yasin's militant leadership, won for the Brotherhood in less than four years. Through participation in the intifada and the sacrifices that participation entailed, Yasin argued, he and his Brotherhood were building a tradition of resistance that would inspire future Muslim generations.

In sum, then, the intifada and Hamas provided Yasin and the Islamic movement with renewed doctrinal conviction and credibility. Putting the Islamic principle of jihad into practice had a revivifying effect on the followers of the Brotherhood, as well as on other Islamic movements outside the occupied territories. Yasin believed, in fact, that he was transforming Islam, long accused of conformity to the status quo, into a type of liberation theology. History alone will decide whether he was correct.

Notes

1. For discussion of this subject see Ziad Abu-Amr, *'Usul al-Harakat al-Siyasiya fi Qita' Ghaza* (The origins of political movements in the Gaza Strip) (Jerusalem Dar Al-Aswar: Acre, 1987), and L. M. Burns, *Between Arab and Israeli* (London: George G. Harrap, 1962).

2. Ziad Abu-Amr, *The Islamic Movement in the West Bank and Gaza: The Muslim Brotherhood Society and the Islamic Jihad Movement* (in Arabic) (Jerusalem Dar al-Aswar: Acre, 1989), 24.

3. Author's interview with Shihda Isma'il Yasin, Ahmad Yasin's older brother, Gaza, 10 July 1991.

4. Ali E. Hillal Dessouki, "The Islamic Resurgence: Sources, Dynamic, and Implications," in Ali E. Hillal Dessouki, *Islamic Resurgence in the Arab World* (New York: Praeger, 1982), 23.

5. Abu-Amr, *Islamic Movement,* 14.

6. The author has often heard this argument from religious figures in the occupied territories, as well as from common believers. See, for example, Mu'min 'Abd al-Rahman, *The Islamic March between the High and Low Tides* (in Arabic) (n.p., n.d.), 81–82; this publication was distributed in the occupied territories.

7. Author's interview with Ahmad Yasin, Gaza, 2 May 1989.

8. David Shipler, *Arab and Jew: Wounded Spirits in a Promised Land* (New York: Penguin, 1987), 177.

9. Elie Rekhess, "The Iranian Impact on the Islamic Jihad Movement in the Gaza Strip," paper submitted to the conference "The Iranian Revolution and the Muslim World," held in the Dayan Center, Tel Aviv University, 4–6 January 1988, 5.

10. Ze'ev Schiff and Ehud Ya'ari, *Intifada: The Palestinian Uprising—Israel's Third Front* (New York: Simon and Schuster, 1989), 225.

11. Schiff and Ya'ari, *Intifada,* 226.

12. Indeed, Yasin's physical speech deteriorated in the years after he rose to prominence. When I met him for the last time, a few days before his final arrest in May 1989, he spoke with difficulty. And of course, he could not write (his hands are paralyzed). So Yasin did not, unfortunately, leave any recorded or written material to give the readers a flavor of his rhetoric.

13. Schiff and Ya'ari, *Intifada,* 224.

14. In the early 1990s a PLO-backed split in the Islamic University resulted in the establishment of the pro-PLO Al-Azhar University. This split ended the Brotherhood's monopoly over higher education in Gaza. Pro-PLO faculty and students joined the new university, which is currently controlled and supported by the Palestinian Authority (PA) of the autonomy rule led by PLO chairman Yasir Arafat. The establishment of Al-Azhar University has provided PLO supporters and the PA in particular with a parallel power center to counterbalance the influence of the Islamists. After the establishment of autonomy rule, the PLO

controlled Palestinian Authority in Gaza and the West Bank assumed control of the *waqf*, which is bound to gradually weaken the grip of the Islamists on this important Islamic institution.

15. Author's interview with Dr. Ibrahim al-Yazuri, executive director of the Islamic Center in Gaza and a founder of Hamas, Gaza, 9 July 1991.

16. Ahmad Yasin, reply to the charges of the Israeli Military Court in Gaza, case no. 115, 25/89.

17. Schiff and Ya'ari, *Intifada,* 227.

18. Ibid.

19. *Mithaq Harakat al-Muqawama al-Islamiyya (Hamas)* (Charter of the Islamic Resistance Movement, Hamas), 18 August 1988, 5.

20. *Ila Filastin,* no. 30, 25 March 1988.

21. The antipathy of Yasin and his followers toward secularism should not be taken to imply that the Palestinian Islamists have common cause with religious, antisecular Jews; the contradiction between Palestinian Islamists and secularists is by far less significant than that between the Islamists and the Zionist Jews, who are considered national enemies.

22. Islamic Resistance Movement (Hamas), appeal to the nineteenth session of the Palestine National Council, 10 November 1988.

23. Interview with Shaykh Ahmad Yasin, *Al-Islam wa-Filastin,* 10 November 1988.

24. Yasin and Hamas refer to the Palestinian Christians as brothers and have only kind words to say about them as an integral part of Palestinian society and as partners in the national struggle. The long tradition of religious tolerance in Palestinian society provides the context for these views. But Hamas, which espouses Islam as a doctrine and ideology, has no Christians in its leadership or following.

25. Ahmad Rashad, *Hamas: Palestinian Politics with an Islamic Hue,* Occasional Paper Series no. 2, United Association for Studies and Research, December 1993, 9, 10.

26. *Filastin al-Muslima,* March 1995, 24.

27. Ibid., 25, 26.

28. Ibid., 25.

29. Author's interview with Ahmad Yasin, Gaza, 2 May 1989.

30. Ahmad Yasin, reply to the charges of the Israeli Military Court in Gaza, case no. 115 25/89.

31. Ibid.

32. *Al-Da'wa,* November/December 1985, 14.

33. Ahmad Bin Yousef, *Harakat al-Muqawama al-Islamiya* (The Islamic Resistance Movement) (Carbondale, Ill.: Islamic Center for Research and Studies, 1990), 125.

34. For further discussion of these issues, see Hassan al-Banna, *Majmu'at Rasa'il al-Imam al-Shahid Hasan al-Banna* (Collected messages of the martyred Imam Hassan al-Banna), (n.p., n.d.).

35. Author's interview with Ahmad Yasin, Gaza, 27 April 1987.

36. *Al-Fajr,* 29 April 1984.

37. Author's interview with Ahmad Yasin, 27 April 1987.

38. *Al-Sha'b,* 11 September 1988.

39. Interview with Ahmad Yasin, *Al-Nahar*, 30 April 1989.

40. Schiff and Ya'ari, *Intifada*, 225.

41. Ibid.

42. It is true that the concept is primarily a Shi'ite strategy. But it also remains Islamic, and Sunnis can use it if it suits their purposes; there are numerous verses in the Qur'an that justify the concealing of one's intentions if that serves the interests of the Muslims.

43. Schiff and Ya'ari, *Intifada*, 225.

44. Ibid.

45. Author's interview with Ahmad Yasin, Gaza, 2 May 1989.

46. Ibid.

47. Ibid.

48. Ahmad Bin Yousef, *Ahmad Yasin: Al-Zahira al-Mu'jiza wa-Usturat al-Tahaddi* (Ahmad Yasin: The miraculous phenomenon and the myth of challenge) (Carbondale, Ill.: Islamic Center for Research and Studies, n.d.), 40.

49. Interview with Ahmad Yasin, *Al-Nahar*, 30 April 1989.

50. When Yasin was asked about the authority he relied upon to implement his arbitrations, he said that he "does not implement arbitration, but rather helps the oppressed"; author's interview with Ahmad Yasin, Gaza, 2 May 1989.

51. *Filastin al-Muslima*, March 1995, 24.

52. For a more detailed discussion of the attitude of Palestinian Islamists on the questions of pluralism and democracy, see Ziad Abu-Amr, "Palestinian Islamists, Pluralism and Democracy," in Edy Kaufman, Shukri B. Abed, and Robert L. Rothstein, eds., *Democracy, Peace, and the Israeli-Palestinian Conflict* (Boulder: Lynne Reinner Publishers, 1993). For an exposition of diverse Islamic views of democracy, see John L. Esposito and James P. Piscatori, "Democratization and Islam," *Middle East Journal* 45, no. 3 (summer 1991).

53. *Mithaq Harakat al-Muqawama al-Islamiyya*, 7.

54. Ibid., 14–15.

55. Ibid., 26.

56. Ibid., 29–30.

57. Ibid., 31.

58. *Filastin al-Muslima*, March 1995, p. 25.

59. Ibid., 25.

FIVE

FUNDAMENTALIST PREACHING AND ISLAMIC
MILITANCY IN UPPER EGYPT

Patrick D. Gaffney

In June 1980 Karam Zuhdi, a student leader of the Jama'a Islamiya (Islamic Society) of Minya in Upper Egypt, approached Shaykh 'Umar 'Abd al-Rahman, a blind Islamic scholar and preacher in his early forties, with the request that he serve as the mufti, or legal counselor, for the newly formed secret network Tanzim al-Jihad (Jihad Organization), which Zuhdi and other radicals had recently constituted. Since 1973 the shaykh had been a professor at the Azhar Institute in Asyut, where he had developed a reputation for strict religious observance and support for the views of the outlawed Muslim Brotherhood, which sought to replace the secular state with an Islamic order.[1] 'Abd al-Rahman honored Zuhdi's request and provided the legal authorization to these militants, thereby allowing them to carry out acts of violence against non-Muslims, specifically Egyptian Christians.

A decade later, in July 1990, Shaykh 'Umar 'Abd al-Rahman arrived in the United States from the Sudan and took up residence in New Jersey. He had left his native Egypt after years of intermittent arrests, imprisonments, and trials because of his links to the militant Islamic underground that had, among other acts of terrorism, assassinated President Anwar Sadat in 1981. It did not take very long for 'Abd al-Rahman to resume his violent activism in the United States. In 1992 he allegedly approved a plan to plant a massive car bomb beneath New York's World Trade Center. Subsequently, in October 1995, he and several others were found guilty of conspiring to launch a larger campaign of bombings and assassinations. Following his arrest for plotting the New York bombings 'Abd al-Rahman argued that "the principles of Islam are revolution, the destruction of tyranny and the extermination of oppressors, . . . yes, war, for as long as the oppressors seek to destroy us."[2]

As a preacher at the al-Salam Mosque in Jersey City, 'Abd al-Rahman was indeed continuing the work he had been doing in Egypt for the past decade. Among his listeners in New Jersey he found a number of Egyptian expatriates who felt demeaned, marginalized, and alienated—feelings similar to those of the Egyptian Muslims who had responded to his message in their homeland. 'Abd al-Rahman was, in effect, playing a familiar role, and his new followers reacted in a predictable fashion.

Needless to say, Shaykh 'Umar 'Abd al-Rahman came to prominence at a particular time and place. He was substantially formed—and radicalized—by the formidable shifts in Egyptian society that occurred during the late 1970s after Sadat's peace initiative with Israel. His roots, in effect, ran parallel with the developments elsewhere in the region. 'Abd al-Rahman was an active participant in, and a major producer of, a vibrant oral culture in Upper Egypt. Ideas such as those he advocated were not his alone; rather, they were part of a wider mentality that other preachers shared and around which the discourse of radical Sunni Islam developed.

This chapter examines that discursive system by presenting the case of Shaykh Ahmad Isma'il, a contemporary of 'Abd al-Rahman in the hinterland of Upper Egypt. Shaykh Ahmad's story is a paradigm of the potent and protean nature of fundamentalist preaching. Minya, the provincial city in which he resided and preached, was one of the early breeding grounds for Islamic fundamentalism in Egypt and remains one of the nation's most volatile sites of religiously motivated unrest. By probing the conditions under which Shaykh Ahmad exercised influence in the region, by analyzing his fundamentalist discourse and the way it helped to constitute an Islamic movement in Minya, and by demonstrating the complex relationship between Shaykh Ahmad and his followers, this chapter seeks to illuminate the larger story of the rise of Islamic militance in Upper Egypt in the 1970s and 1980s—a development with worldwide repercussions to this day.

Shaykh Ahmad Isma'il

Shaykh Ahmad Isma'il, who died in 1985, was a retired schoolteacher and a vigorous septuagenarian when he took over as *khatib,* or preacher, at the largest private mosque in the city of Minya in the early 1970s. Minya is the capital city of a rural governorate of the same name, situated 250 kilometers south of Cairo. It has a population of approximately two hundred thousand and serves as the hub for administrative, economic, medical, educational, and other services for an immediate area with over a million more residents, primarily peasants who live within a few hours' walking distance. Although these figures are small by the standards of the more densely urbanized delta to the north, Minya is second in size only to Asyut in the Sa'id, or Upper Egypt, the long ribbon of fertile land that extends along the Nile from Giza to Aswan. But the Sa'id is not only a geographic designation; it also refers to a vivid set of Egyptian social patterns and cultural stereotypes. While the Cairenes may scorn Sa'idis as bumpkins and brutes, the image of the tough, shrewd, self-reliant villager, firmly rooted in religion, quick in the defense of honor, and unstinting in generosity evokes deep pride among the people of Upper Egypt themselves.

The preaching of Shaykh Ahmad Isma'il in Minya during the late 1970s is noteworthy for its appeal and its effects on local youth, many of whom were just beginning to acquire a political consciousness and to display activist tendencies. But his enormously popular sermons also played a major role in the formation of a broader collective awareness, shared not only by those later identified as religious extremists but also by many others in the community who did not join them on the front lines but who expressed sympathy with their ultimate, largely utopian aspirations. The heavy proportion of students and other youth from Minya who took part in the bloody uprising in nearby Asyut following Sadat's assassination testifies to the effective buildup of this local fundamentalist movement, in which Shaykh Ahmad's pulpit was key.[3] But even before this assault, the week of sectarian violence that erupted during the summer of 1981 in the neighborhood of al-Zawiya Hamra in Cairo had roots in this distant mosque; that outbreak had triggered the cycle of escalating reprisals Sadat sought to bring under control through mass arrests in mid-September. A Coptic priest then living in the riot-torn area remarked that "most of the trouble began after the arrival of rural migrants from Minya."[4]

Nor has this pattern of interconfessional tension faded in Upper Egypt, although the media spotlight continues to focus largely on Cairo.

When Muhammad Islambouli, whose brother Khalid was the soldier who led the team of assassins against Sadat, was released from prison in the mid-1980s, where he was being held for involvement in earlier Islamist violence, he settled in Minya. Today, a decade and a half after the assassination and riots brought these fundamentalist extremists to the forefront of world attention, Minya remains a center for their militant activism. Periodic bouts of sectarian and antigovernment conflict continue to erupt in and around the city, while a few local mosques still echo with the puritanical thunder of that earlier moment when the confidence of the Islamic movement seemed unbounded.[5]

In Minya from December 1977 until September 1979 I witnessed the rapid growth and consolidation of a militant group that was in the process of becoming one of the most assertive student-based Islamic Societies in the nation.[6] The Minya group's emerging stature was confirmed on a national level by the sudden recognition accorded it by the Muslim Brotherhood's monthly magazine al-Da'wa, which contained a regular feature dedicated to "news of youth and universities."[7] Minya was also selected as the site of the first National Congress of Islamic Societies in late March 1979, a meeting that brought together representatives from campuses all over the country. During this same period, a surge of local excitement swirled around Shaykh Ahmad, who began to be treated as a sort of cult figure, with a growing number of followers attending his weekly sermons. Given the concurrent events in Paris and Iran, local admirers in Minya quickly dubbed Shaykh Ahmad the Ayatollah Khomeini of Egypt.

As with all ritual rhetoric, the full meaning of Shaykh Ahmad's preaching is not conveyed by the preserved text alone, which fails to capture symbolic cues and veiled references to events external to the mosque of which members of the congregation would have been well aware. The contextual referents of the preacher's coded allusions became increasingly transparent as the gap between political and religious expression in Egypt narrowed. Given the prevalence of Islamic references in Sadat's own rhetoric, it became harder to distinguish speeches from sermons, and the relationship of authority to power, as expressed in each idiom, become blurred.

In the light of this sometimes confusing interplay of factors affecting the social identity of preachers, especially that of an extraordinarily public figure like Shaykh Ahmad, a note about the institutional background of mosques is helpful. At this time in Egypt, two basic types of mosques were ordinarily recognized by Muslims. One type was called a "government" (hukumi) mosque and the other a "private" or "popular" (ahli) mosque. The difference was not always evident in the mosque's outward appearance, although certain architectural features were more commonly associated with one type than the other, whereas the same basic Islamic rituals were performed in each. But one difference, which gained significance in the 1970s, made them, in principal, quite distinct. This concerned the formal character of the preacher, or more precisely the relationship of the preacher to the state on the one hand and the local congregation on the other. According to the general conception, government mosques were fully subsidized by the government through the Ministry of Religious Endowments and consequently were staffed by imams who were essentially civil functionaries. Private mosques, however, were built and supported entirely by local initiatives, and their pulpits were filled by preachers chosen by the communities themselves.[8]

Shaykh Ahmad was the preacher in what was technically a private mosque affiliated with the Shari'a Cooperative Society of Followers of the Book and the Sunna of Muhammad, a loose national network of mosques and associated social-welfare centers. The mosque in Minya was usually called merely the Sunna Mosque or, more commonly at this time, the "mosque of Shaykh Ahmad." Founded in 1913, the Shari'a Cooperative Society had a mission that included a range of social as well as religious objectives. Its charter, however, envisioned the provision of religious and social services quite apart from political activity, which it renounced and supposedly strictly avoided.[9] Thus combining, as it were, religious reform and social activism with traditional piety, it survived and flourished while a good number of other activist groups failed to attract adherents or, as in the case of the Muslim Brothers, were officially suppressed. Shaykh Ahmad had apparently long been a member of this Sunna society in Minya but had only recently been chosen by its local membership to serve as the chapter's president. His chief public function was to preach at the Friday noon prayers. Although he was roughly seventy years old at the time of his election, his forceful personality and remarkable gift for populist oratory had made him a favorite particularly among younger members of the society, who were eager to replace his slightly older predecessor, a kindly, reserved, owlish figure who had been a merchant prior to his retirement.

Upon my first exposure to Shaykh Ahmad's preaching, I concluded that I was hearing a virtuoso of the popular pulpit whose public manner and indeed whose entire performance indicated long experience in this role. Occasional autobiographical anecdotes punctuating his sermons contributed to the impression of a man whose life had been fully devoted to the fundamentalist cause he enthusiastically embodied. I surmised that his biography probably included arrests and perhaps imprisonment under Nasser or maybe a period of self-imposed exile, for these episodes were quite typical for Muslim militants of his generation. Random inquiries among his youthful admirers indicated that they shared my preliminary assumptions about this preacher. But subsequent probing among certain older residents who were less sympathetic to the shaykh's views revealed that the facts of Shaykh Ahmad's past contrasted starkly with the image he projected. Senior preachers in local government mosques tended to regard him as a rival who was, in professional terms, at best an annoying interloper and at worst a rabble-rousing fraud.

As it turned out, Shaykh Ahmad's conversion to militant Islam was quite recent. A skilled and well-practiced popular orator, he had begun his career as a primary school teacher in the late 1920s, when free education modeled on Western learning had only begun to replace the traditional *kuttab*, or Qur'an school, in the region. He stemmed from poor rural origins and had first received a kuttab education, then earned the equivalent of a rudimentary high school degree, which was the prerequisite for teaching in the new modern, compulsory elementary school system. He was soon drawn by the pressures of his expanding profession to become a vocal participant in the newly established syndicate for primary school teachers; eventually he rose from local to regional and then to national prominence in the ranks of this burgeoning professional association. Older teachers remembered him well for a series of pugnacious speeches in the 1940s opposing the leadership of the Ministry of Education over issues of salary and status. He became a sort of celebrity and a popular leader by virtue of his ferocious advocacy for the interests of his fellow teachers, whom he depicted as an unesteemed guild facing a corrupt and irresponsible central government. Education in Egypt was undergoing a process of nationalization; the established private and foreign-language schools were depicted, by the likes of Shaykh Ahmad, as privileged institutions at odds with the needs and cultural traditions of Egypt.[10]

After 1952 Shaykh Ahmad became an equally vociferous proponent of Gamal Abdel Nasser's popular appeal. In the early years after the republic replaced the monarchy, the shaykh's speaking engagements were so many and his rousing message so uncompromising that he became known throughout the region as *khatib al-thawra,* or "spokesman of the revolution." At one point the shaykh was reportedly offered a post in Nasser's cabinet as Minister of Guidance but declined it. During this period he also had the opportunity to travel abroad with official delegations organized by the ruling Arab Socialist Party. Mention of this international experience occasionally surfaced in his sermons, especially when he was pontificating to his congregation on the moral conditions of the wider world. Almost invariably, however, these brief eyewitness accounts took the form of wholly negative summary judgments. He was fond of making outraged allusions to the purported shamelessness, excesses, and hypocrisy of these non-Muslim lands that showed negligible acquaintance with the actual countries in question. Nevertheless, this bit of foreign travel was a rare adornment that enhanced the preacher's status and bolstered his credibility among the people of Upper Egypt who came to hear him. Related to this limited perspective was the shaykh's chauvinism with regard to the Arabic language, a theme he often raised in the course of his preaching. He knew no other languages. Clearly, in his frequent sweeping comparisons between nations, religions, and cultures, it was his version of Arab Islam that served as the standard. Before it, by divine appointment, all else pales.

Shaykh Ahmad's career suffered with the declining fortunes of Nasserism and began to recover only after he took an Islamic tack in the early 1970s, a turn toward religion that matched a sea change in the wider society. Thus the shaykh I initially took to be Minya's aging colossus of undeviating, flint-edged fundamentalism had actually only recently fitted himself with this mantle. Interestingly, Shaykh Ahmad's rapid rise to this stature was likely related to the lack of other local contenders. Another respected shaykh in Minya, a man of the same generation who enjoyed a much more solid reputation for his bold Islamist preaching, had died in January 1979 after a lingering illness. This man, Shaykh Mahmud, had also been a schoolteacher, but the private mosque in which he preached was an independent foundation that he and his devoted following had, over the years, built up from nothing. Furthermore, Shaykh Mahmud's career had been marked by long and faithful dedication to the principles of the Muslim Brotherhood. For his beliefs and this involvement he had been imprisoned on four separate occasions, coinciding with each of the great crackdowns launched against the society beginning in 1949. Shaykh 'Umar 'Abd al-Rahman, later of Asyut, expressed the highest regard for Shaykh Mahmud in an autobiographical account published a decade later in which he sought to explain his beliefs and justify his involvement with militant groups.[11] The weakness of orators from the student Islamic Society also contributed to an overall lack of genuine rhetorical competence in the city.

The late 1970s and early 1980s was a time of growing unrest and uncertainty, with rising social, economic and political expectations on a collision course with limited opportunities and resources. Government spokesmen trumpeted assurances that peace would also bring prosperity, blaming the patent liabilities of a bloated and inefficient public sector and the poor performance of agricultural cooperatives on the exigencies of the long-standing "war" with Israel, which had been institutionalized decades before. But the promised prosperity would elude most Egyptians; while some few would enjoy new opportunities for wealth, most would feel excluded. The complex process of reshaping systems of production and redistributing wealth could hardly follow as painless a course as that set out in official declarations. Polar shifts in the nation's ideological orientation and economic structure were suddenly further accelerated by Sadat's stunning peace initiative in late 1977.

One area of immediate concern, especially for ambitious youth, was the changing character of the employment market. For decades a post in the government service had provided both prestige and a secure basis sufficient for the support of a family. This ideal combination of security and status, already in slow decline, eroded steadily during the decade of Sadat's liberalizations. By the mid-1970s, the gap between a government functionary's salary and the actual cost of living had widened to such a degree that the salary no longer constituted a suitable wage. Although it had long been illegal for civil servants to hold second jobs, the practice now became the norm. Pressure mounted for women to join the workforce to augment family income.

At the same time, the under-the-table payments required to make the administrative wheels turn promptly and effectively felt the effects of inflation at all levels of the bureaucracy. In schools the problem took the shape of teachers withholding basic material from classroom discussion so as to benefit from expensive "private lessons" after hours. The exorbitant fees charged by repairmen and craftsmen whose services were in high demand were also widely reported and disparaged as a sort of national scandal by traditionalists unreceptive to explanations that evoked the logic of a free market. Concomitantly, a massive housing shortage, provoked by a broad range of inefficient and manipulative practices, was also a constant source of complaint and anxiety, especially among young men. Since Egyptian custom normally requires that a couple have a permanent dwelling before they marry, this lack of accessible space, especially notable in urban settings, forced a large proportion of the population to postpone marriage, a phenomenon that demonstrably added to the restlessness of youth.

Coloring the situation in Sadat's later years was the sensational boom of the petroleum-rich Gulf states. Among its consequences was a wholesale labor migration; hundreds of thousands of Egyptians found employment in various capacities abroad, with millions more eager to follow. This migration, unprecedented in recent Egyptian history, had many repercussions, among the more obvious being a rapid and selective influx of new wealth. The money and status that flowed back into the country as laborers returned after several years of saving could not but prompt a wave of social disjunctures. Such instant riches also fed a cycle of real estate speculation, together with a burst in imports of such products as automobiles, appliances, and electronics. Complicating the moral commentary from the mosques on these changes was the fact that so much of the petroleum was located in lands that had not developed into modern secular societies. Many Egyptians saw a connection between this vast wealth and the maintenance of an explicit Islamic identity.

This convergence of pressures, opportunities, and anxieties, had created a sort of moral vacuum by the late 1970s. Mosque preaching, which was enjoying a revival among newly converted enthusiasts, served as a powerful channel for the formation of opinion, sometimes to stunning effect, when, as happened in Minya, a preacher capable of responding to the sense of urgency among his hearers was at hand.

MINYA

The local urban geography provided several important spatial dimensions of the fundamentalist movement as it evolved in Minya in the late 1970s. The mosque in which Shaykh Ahmad regularly preached and the university campus, the base for the Islamic Society, were located at opposite ends of this oddly shaped city, which consists of a long, narrow strip bounded by the Nile River on the east and the Ibrahimiya Canal on the west. Although located on the same street, the two institutions were more than two miles apart, with most of Minya stretched out longitudinally between them. The mosque lay at the far southern end of the city, just beyond the old, densely populated warren of mud-brick construction that had been the core of the premodern town. The mosque, quite large by local standards, was part of a complex that also included a school, a day-care center, a dormitory for female students, a consulting office, an auditorium, and a playing field; apart from the mosque, however, which opened onto the main street, most of these facilities were seldom used and remained closed most of the time. The entire complex comprised an area of two and a half hectares, about the size of a city block, and was surrounded by a high wall. It stood in a crowded popular quarter with uneven new housing connected by unpaved streets. The population consisted largely of first- and second-generation migrants from villages, who were incompletely integrated into the urban society.

The neighborhood at the northern end of Minya, where the university was located, was the city's most exclusive residential quarter, on the edge of the modern commercial center graced with broad boulevards, parks, and plazas. In the immediate area were the province's elite institutions, including its most prestigious secondary schools, ministry offices, corporate headquarters, hospitals, hotels, banks, and sport clubs. Nearby was the center of municipal government, the palace of culture, the tourist information office, and the city library.

Minya University in the late 1970s did not consist of a single campus. Established only in 1976, in response to intractable popular pressure for wider access to higher education, the university was created by simply uniting five preexisting educational facilities—teachers' training colleges, technical institutes, and extension facilities of Asyut University, scattered about the city—under a single administration and labeling the resulting entity a university. Between 1972 and 1976 Sadat had opened seven such universities, six in the Delta and one, that of Minya, in Upper Egypt. This led to a precipitous jump in the number of university students on the national level, from roughly 229,000 in 1973 to over 415,000 in 1977.[12] But the demographic change in Minya was even more pronounced: in 1975 approximately 5,000 students attended the city's various advanced schools; two years later, these same schools, now formally designated a university, were flooded with an enrollment that totaled 10,742 students, without any additional buildings having been constructed or made available to accommodate the twofold increase.[13]

A large majority of these students were concentrated in just two colleges, that of arts and that of education, which shared the single campus located in the middle of the middle- and upper-class neighborhood described above. It was there that the Islamic Society most aggressively established its presence, even though its leadership consisted almost entirely of students from the colleges of commerce and engineering, both of which were situated far afield. Sheer physical distance, therefore, in a city where walking was the major mode of transportation, obviously played a major part in the interaction between Shaykh Ahmad, with his mosque at one end of the city, and the student Islamic Society, whose center of gravity was at the other end.

Social distance was also a factor as these two forces arose to form an energetic, if sometimes awkward, Islamist axis. At times competing, at times acting in tandem, they advanced into the public arena from their different angles in the heady days of the late 1970s. Only in mid-1979 was the momentum of the fundamentalist movement checked, first by a series of local measures in Minya and then, in late summer, by a presidential decree that effectively banned the Islamic Societies from Egypt's universities. This banishment deprived the groups of their sheltered meeting grounds and thus severely hampered their recruitment, indoctrination, and mobilization capacities. But it did not by any means eliminate the presence of a solid nucleus of militants, nor, as time would show, did it weaken their resolve.

On the contrary, tensions escalated to new heights in the following year, as Islamists shifted their focus and struck out more pointedly at sectarian targets, that is, those associated with Coptic Christians. Their confrontational tactics led to a chain reaction of increasingly violent incidents and eventually arrests that culminated in an all-night siege of Minya's main police headquarters in April 1980. A mob supporting those who were being detained had gathered and was on the verge of setting the building on fire. More serious trouble was averted only by direct orders from Cairo that several local Islamist leaders being held for their part in fomenting sectarian violence be released. These individuals quickly went underground to avoid being rearrested, only to reappear fully armed in the assault at Asyut in October of the following year. Gilles Kepel, in his detailed account of the Tanzim al-Jihad, refers to these events in Minya as a "curtain raiser" and a "dress rehearsal" for the killing of Sadat and this insurrection in Asyut, which cost more than seventy lives.[14]

FUNDAMENTALIST PREACHING

To avoid conflating fundamentalism with political violence one must attend to the context in which Islam's multivalent symbols are given concrete associations, namely, in the verbal performances of mosque oratory. The preaching of Shaykh Ahmad Isma'il played an essential part in the ideological formation of the members of Minya's Islamic Society. His sermons are expressions of what it means for a community to acknowledge such paradoxes as those of being Egyptian and Muslim, Arab and African, traditional and modern, young and old, proud and dejected. His sermons represented the shaping of this collective identity in the effort to come to terms with the contours of creedal and moral realities.[15]

The master metaphor for Shaykh Ahmad's preaching was the revealed book of Islam, the Qur'an. A focus on this sacred text might seem thoroughly conventional for a Muslim preacher, but the extent to which Shaykh Ahmad used it in his sermons and the manner in which he incorporated it was exceptional and, to some degree, original. Traditional sermons molded after classical prototypes, like those heard regularly on the broadcast media or found reprinted in standard anthologies and contemporary religious periodicals, normally include some citations from the Qur'an. Ordinary preachers may also adopt a Qur'anic vocabulary, imitate its prose cadences, and refer obliquely to familiar passages and recognizable figures. But the idiom of traditional sermons constitutes a distinct literary genre, a subdivision of *balagha,* or eloquence, which is governed by clearly defined models that set out the structure, style, form, content, and sources for mosque preaching appropriate to the needs of different occasions.[16] Within this genre the Qur'an has an important but fixed and restricted place.

Shaykh Ahmad's sermons, however, were hardly the products of such academically correct craftsmanship. Rather, they were syncretic compositions that broke out of this formal mold in ways that were at once idiosyncratic and astute. His sermons were also conspicuously longer than those of his professional peers; whereas few preachers in today's government mosques orate for more than twenty minutes, with a third or more of that time given over to formulas that change little from one sermon to the next, Shaykh Ahmad would typically hold forth for an hour and a half or more.

He also rejected many of the visual accoutrements that characterize the office of the state clergy. In particular, he avoided their distinctive tasseled red fez rimmed by a low and tight muslin turban, which many amateur preachers imitate, for it carries the approximate symbolic weight of a Roman collar among Western Christians. Instead, he typically wore a distinctly chic version of the sort of cap widely associated with the fundamentalist movement, usually a rather large and lush off-white brimless felt cap or fez, around the base of which he wrapped a broad white cotton band, taking care to allow one end to dangle over the back of his neck in the manner, it is said, prescribed by the Sunna. He also trimmed his white beard according to the precedent of the Prophet, that is, leaving it to ring the chin while removing the mustache.

When Shaykh Ahmad preached he did not mount a platform as is the custom. He preferred rather to speak standing before a microphone at floor level, avoiding even the simple low dais, a deliberately reduced version of the traditional *minbar,* or Islamic pulpit, that stood in his Sunna Mosque. The congregation of course was seated on the floor before him. He invariably opened his sermons with a long grandiloquent recitation, apparently of his own composition, studded with ample Qur'anic citations. Then he would launch into the body of the sermon, choosing his own direction. He might, for instance, break this spell of formalism and momentarily turn chatty. Or he could sustain the high pitch of solemnity and perhaps play the schoolmaster or patriarch. Regardless of his tactic, he displayed an array of mesmerizing rhetorical devices in the process. His pacing was varied although he normally followed a patterned trajectory. He would begin slowly, dispassionately, then gradually work toward a peak of excitement, managing along the way a broad range of moods, including comedy, parody, melancholy, and especially righteous rage. He was a master at holding his listeners' attention and moving them from a tense calm to agitated outpourings of enthusiastic resolve. At times, his rhetorical questions virtually invited collective response and the congregation would affirm him with repetitions of "Allah" or "amen." In other situations, he might also summon his listeners, who were all males, of course, to chant exclamations such as "there is no god but God" or to repeat Islamist slogans that also had currency in street demonstrations.

In another noteworthy departure from normative preaching, Shaykh Ahmad spoke almost entirely in the colloquial dialect rather than the *fusha*, or literary Arabic, that forms the universal standard medium of oratory in Islamic worship in Egypt. This lowering of the linguistic register would ordinarily deprive a preacher of much of the putative authority associated with *'ilm* (knowledge) and validated by the competent display of canonical eloquence. But, for several reasons, this popularization seemed to produce the opposite effect in Shaykh Ahmad's case. First, there is the matter of degree. While the Arabic he employed was much closer to everyday speech than to the classicisms that typify the sermons of a trained shaykh of al-Azhar, it was not the vulgar argot of the street. He spoke rather in a composite, intermediate idiom that was elevated enough to sound refined to a marginally literate listener but was unencumbered by the staid and archaic tokens of erudition that were commonly retained at the expense of a cogent and colorful delivery. He could also affect a musicality that tended toward *fortissimo* and *vivace*, and was capable of masterful extemporaneous demonstrations of prosody, rhyme, and alliteration, as well as parallelism, symmetrical repetition, and other tropes. In short, he was a verbal athlete whose skillful manipulation of the morphological, phonological, and lexical particularities of different levels of Arabic appeared effortless.

No less important a dramatic element was his extraordinarily frequent and fluid resort to the Qur'an. In an all but inimitable fashion, Shaykh Ahmad would recite strings of verses from the Qur'an in such abundance that some sermons seemed as much recitation as commentary. He also had a facility for reciting rapidly, like a tape speeded up, achieving an effect that inevitably won admiring oohs and aahs from the congregation. Clearly this sacred text—which he learned as a child and then taught to three generations of children—or at least large parts of it, was so familiar to him that he could punctuate his sermons with citations that provided verification or pious emphasis to fit any occasion. In the popular Muslim culture of Egypt, where respect for a *hafiz*, one who has memorized the whole Qur'an, exceeds the veneration for scientists, Shaykh Ahmad's ostentatious competence in this regard was no small factor in the constant projection of his implicit religious authority.

Sometimes Shaykh Ahmad's scriptural citations merely provided a proof text to seal a specific point. For example, in a sermon delivered on 27 October 1978, he rounded off a sweeping condemnation of any who would ape the fashions, behaviors, and attitudes of outsiders—meaning Europeans—as irreligious by intoning this verse: "Is it not sufficient for them that We have revealed the Book to you which is read out to them?" (29:51).[17] Later in this same sermon, he embarked on a diatribe against the leaders of the nation by citing the famous Sura of the Unbelievers: "I do not worship what you worship. Nor do you worship what I worship" (109:1-2). Then he piled on an assortment of other lesser-known verses suggesting a divine reprimand for idolatry. He then confronted his listeners angrily: "I will leave you and those you evoke apart from God" (19: 48). And finally, he offered solace: "They had almost led you astray from what had been revealed to you" (17:73). As these illustrations suggest, his typical maneuver was to seize upon a few key words, which he then connected by various rhetorical stratagems to make plain to whom the pronouns in the citations were meant to refer.

Extrapolations on selected fragments of the sacred text could also be employed in the construction of lengthy and complex rhetorical bulwarks. Highly charged words drawn from a given Qur'anic citation might be strung together with contemporary allusions on the basis of their related or contrasting semantic elements. Shaykh Ahmad started a later section of this same sermon, for example, by citing a well-known Qur'anic validation for the taking of vengeance: "In retribution there is life" (2:179). But then he lifted the word "life" *(haya)* from the sentence and linked it to an odd set of references, juxtaposing bits of the jargon of modernization with charged terms from the lexicon of traditional morality. He equated life with planning *(takhtit)*, protection *(himaya)*, development *(tanmiya)*, improvement *(tarqiya)*, and purification *(tanqiya)*, all of which, he declared, are inextricably connected: "These words encompass each other, are consecutive with each other, fit together, and are coordinated in their meanings, each complementing the others." He also defined life as conscience *(dhamir)* and conscience as equivalent to power *(quwa)*, to faith *(iman)*, and to Islam. Islam, in turn, was comprised of what is written *(maktub)*, which he further glossed as "creation" *(khalq)*. He proceeded to discuss the application *(tatbiq)* of God's "plan," recovering this term from earlier in the sequence. He thus built up to a summary term that appears nowhere in the Qur'an but rather comes from the widely echoed fundamentalist slogan calling for application of shari'a as law. Finally, the shaykh wove his way toward a conclusion by incorporating yet another Qur'anic phrase often used to discredit supposedly alien influences by framing them as temptations.

Such dense and verbose rhetorical layering had the effect of redefining both traditional moral concepts and the vocabulary of public sociopolitical discourse. By fusing selected value-laden terms with what he insisted were the imperatives of God's book, the shaykh sought to undermine the implicit distinctions that separate different spheres of authority and their respective systems of institutional reproduction. In the process, he appropriated a variety of notions that had become catchwords in the state-sponsored ideology—notions he then skillfully tied to the Qur'an and to emotionally charged religious slogans. A reference to east and west, for instance, which climaxed one portion of this sermon, alluded to the cold war and thereby reinforced a divine injunction that Muslims reject communism as well as capitalism.

Shaykh Ahmad's recourse to the Qur'an also produced ample eschatological imagery. Warnings about the dire punishments that await sinners on the last day were repeated in tones of urgency. Depictions in the Qur'an of divinely ordained catastrophes, such as fires, floods, and earthquakes, were mixed with intimations of impending judgment aimed at those who govern apart from God's law. The shaykh singled out rulers *(hukkam)* who have failed to hear God's word as being mainly responsible for the world's present disorder; upon them, he assured his rapt audience, the worst punishments are destined to fall.

In addition to these nimble manipulations of the Qur'an as a polemical tool and as proof text, Shaykh Ahmad engaged in a considerable discussion of its exalted status and miraculous character. He expounded at length upon the uniqueness of the book, its unsurpassed excellence in both form and content, its clarity, its irreproachable orderliness, and its sublime refinement of expression, which endows each word, each single letter, with a beauty and potency that makes the smallest of them indispensable. These claims can be seen, in one sense, as simple restatements of the familiar orthodox doctrine of the Qur'an's inimitability as the uncreated word of God.[18] Shaykh Ahmad's motive in stressing these claims, however, did not derive merely from a concern to recall one of the tenets of the faith. Rather, the Qur'an served as a symbol that represented the Muslim community, whose moral superiority, by virtue of the book, was to be translated by divine right into history. A sermon delivered on 8 December 1978, for instance, took the unity of the Qur'an as its major theme and was framed as a defense of the book against "the enemies of Islam"—those who contend there are "differences" or "disparities" *(ikhtilaf)* within the sacred text. Shaykh Ahmad embarked on an elaborate concatenation of images, setting out his basis for a comparison between the Gospel *(injil)*, the Torah, and the Qur'an. The gist of the shaykh's prolix remarks, which concentrated most heavily on the Gospel, was that some passages did not correspond or harmonize with others, a fact which he declared to be proof that some were inauthentic and the whole was therefore untrustworthy.

Needless to say, this polemical exercise is virtually as old as Islam itself, although the shaykh made these assertions without any reference to older authorities. He spoke with an air of amazement, as though his own research had led him to these discoveries. Curiously, however, he cited only one specific phrase from the New Testament; most of the episodes he related for the purpose of demonstrating and denouncing the irreconcilability of the gospels are not found anywhere in the New Testament but seem to derive from certain apocryphal sources whose content rarely surfaces apart from occasional Muslim polemical tracts.[19] On one level, the shaykh set out to present a contrast between the Qur'anic Jesus and the Jesus of the New Testament, which was clearly to the detriment of the latter. But more practically and forcefully, within the context of an Upper Egyptian city, he launched an attack on the faith of Christians or, as he referred to them, Crusaders *(salibiyin)*. His outraged commentary left little doubt that his target was the believers and not the text itself.

These anti-Christian themes, thinly disguised by the pretext of comparing books, reflected the current intensification of sectarian tensions in and around Minya. Shaykh Ahmad exacerbated these tensions by providing an ideological basis for them; the students of the Islamic Society supplied the organizational framework and the physical force to match his booming voice. Although the shaykh never, to my knowledge, mentioned the Islamic Society by name in his formal preaching, he indicated his unambiguous approval of them and their activities through frequent, encoded mentions of the Islamic "youth" *(shabab)*. This avoidance of direct references to persons and events reflected discretion and corresponded to the traditional protocol of the mosque pulpit, which normally forbids the singling out of factions or individuals by name. Hence, in a sermon delivered in January 1979, Shaykh Ahmad lauded the local youth extravagantly while condemning their elders, who should also be their betters:

> Who among you, as Muslim, as Egyptian, as a human, in whatever position would not encourage youth to act as they do? . . . We urge them on because they are strong in the principles of God and strong in imitation of the Prophet. They are models, flourishing examples, instant exemplars, set before every ruler who has not found the way, not yet turned toward knowledge. . . . This indeed is Islam. But the nation doesn't want Islam at all! For we see them order what is forbidden [munkar] and depart from what is good [ma'aruf]. . . . And so, my brothers, youth, you people of right reason, you who are eager for God's reward and forgiveness, rejoice for paradise is yours! Make your place where you belong and may you be brought to it despite your enemies, for God will expose them.

THE IMPACT OF FUNDAMENTALIST PREACHING

The first serious public outburst of sectarian conflict in Minya occurred in late spring of 1978. On Easter Sunday, a band of militant Islamists openly vandalized a church under construction in a middle-class neighborhood not far from the "university city," an overcrowded male student housing complex. No official reaction followed their symbolic assault but anger, anxiety, and vigilance were palpable, especially throughout the local Coptic community. In the months that followed, other confrontations reflected the animosity of the Islamic Society members toward Christian symbols and Coptic institutions. Targets also included objects generally identified as products of corrupting Western influences such as foreign banks or movies. Local Islamists often tarred the two with the same brush, blaming the government's failure to enact religious law for the immorality that purportedly resulted.

One day in November 1978, for instance, rumors spread through the city that Shaykh 'Abd-Hamid Kishk, Egypt's most renowned dissident preacher, was to be in Minya that evening to deliver an address under the sponsorship of the Islamic Society. A crowd began to gather an hour prior to the designated time; hundreds and soon thousands of people milled about the campus in excited anticipation. Shaykh Kishk was well known for his critical posture toward the government, but he was also prone to offending the Copts. Although he was banned from access to the state-controlled press and broadcast media, his books and, particularly, cassette recordings of his sermons made him a great celebrity among fundamentalists.[20] Shortly after the specified hour had passed, a student leader of the Islamic Society rose to announce that Shaykh Kishk would not appear because he had been forbidden to leave Cairo. The student then delivered a speech blasting the government for its oppression of Islam and summoned the immense crowd to pray the evening prayer, although only a couple hundred of those in attendance, mostly those identified with the Islamic Society, complied. After the prayer ended, another student orator rose and sought to rally what remained of the crowd to show their zeal by joining in a protest march. Striking up a chant, he led a column of a few hundred persons, with the recognized militants at the fore, out the gates of the campus and down the main street toward the city center. This fairly large demonstration was met a few blocks away by ample ranks of the Central Security Forces, equipped with the helmets, shields, and batons of a riot squad. Well before the two groups came into contact the potential clash between them dissipated into a sudden melee of running, pushing, and shouting, which soon left the downtown streets clear. Thereafter, it was not uncommon to see police vehicles and handfuls of troops stationed at strategic points around the university during times when Islamist meetings were being held there.

Demographic factors were notably pertinent to this escalation of sectarian tensions. For historical reasons, the central part of Upper Egypt constitutes a sort of "Coptic belt";[21] according to official figures, Christians constitute roughly 20 percent of the population in the province of Minya as well as in Asyut and Sohaj, the two neighboring governorates to the south. Nationwide, only 6 to 8 percent of Egypt's residents are members of the Coptic minority, though this estimate is subject to dispute.[22] Furthermore, owing largely to the lingering influence of European mission schools in the region, the rate of formal education continues to be somewhat higher among Copts than among Muslims. Not surprisingly, then, Copts are disproportionately represented in such prestigious professions as medicine and pharmacy, as well as in the academic world. By consequence, the ratio of Copts to Muslims among university students in Minya, though never officially published, would almost certainly show that Christians made up at least a quarter of the student body. In short, a thinly veiled premise of economic inequity and class conflict often lurked behind Islamist attitudes toward their Christian countrymen.

As a practical matter, Coptic Christians within the university milieu tended to give Islamic militants a wide berth. But Copts were growing increasingly apprehensive, and they inevitably voiced support for a secular society in which religion and politics were separate domains. At this time, President Sadat was addressing himself to this domestic unrest with the same vision, calling for "no religion in politics and no politics in religion," but the government at large was leaning strongly in the Islamist direction, having announced, for instance, timetables for the completion of work to overcome the last legal technicalities that stood in the way of Egypt's complete "Islamization."[23]

By late November, Shaykh Ahmad's verbal assaults on Christianity had escalated beyond sham comparisons of the Qur'an and the Gospel. In one sermon he decried the enormous publicity accorded to reports a few years earlier of apparitions of the Virgin Mary at a church in Zaytun, a suburb of Cairo.[24] "How is it," he asked, "that I can speak for hours and only a few people hear me and then leave here and forget, whereas the papers can print anything at all and suddenly everybody believes it? Is this Islam? Is this the truth?" He blamed, first, Muslims whose faith was so weak that they would believe such claims and go off to see it for themselves. But he held up for still greater rebuke the heathen credulity of Christians. Turning to a comic mode, he recalled other reports of appearances of the Virgin, in Lebanon and in Europe, all amounting to nothing but ridiculous hoaxes, he said. Finally, pointing to the nation's neglect of the Qur'an, he lamented the lack of regard for the sacred book, which would bring freedom from all such folly: "If I were to say that a statue moved, people from Alexandria to Aswan would come pouring in here to see it. More people would believe that than believe me now."

When Shaykh Ahmad turned his sights on Judaism and the Torah, the pretext of merely comparing sacred texts or exposing superstition masked as faith soon disappeared, to be replaced by more direct attack. The Jews, he proclaimed, stood first on the list of enemies of Islam. Some remarks in this vein were undoubtedly carried over from the slightly earlier period when Egypt and Israel were at war. As he continued, vague allusions to Qur'anic accounts of Jewish hostility to the mission of the Prophet were freely incorporated into jingoistic rhetoric that frequently omitted fine distinctions between Judaism and Zionism, the past and the present.[25] After Sadat's monumental initiative toward Jerusalem and the meetings at Camp David were declared a triumph for Egypt, guaranteeing prosperity through peace, such attacks upon Jews no longer suited the nationalist consensus. Therefore, while Shaykh Ahmad continued to depict Jews as perennial liars and traitors, he pointed not to political but to literary evidence. He insisted that certain medieval Jews of Muslim Spain had established the foundations for all later attacks upon the Qur'an. For this outrage, above all others, the preacher scorned the Jews.[26]

Interestingly, although Shaykh Ahmad did occasionally refer to Palestine and to Palestinians, always with sympathy, his harangues against Jews virtually never focused on Zionism specifically. He associated Jews on a grand scale with imperialism, colonialism, and warmongering, at times lumping them together with America and Russia as chief among those spreading corruption upon the earth. By contrast, he said, Muslims have never engaged in any such activities; they have only suffered their consequences. On a lower plane, he stigmatized the Jews of Egypt, who had only departed over a decade before, as haughty, stingy, and disloyal.

In the sermon of 17 November 1978, Shaykh Ahmad developed these themes from another angle, alleging that Egypt's Arab and Islamic character had been contaminated by the institution of the *dada,* the foreign governess or nanny who was a fixture in aristocratic households until the revolution. By the preacher's account, these European nannies, some of whom were Jews, actively subverted the minds of children while they served in the houses of Egypt's elite, "turning these homes into schools where rulers and ministers were diverted from following God to [follow-ing] the path of godlessness." Fortunately, honest peasants, he recalled, had no such nannies.

Explicit in this particular attack was the shaykh's rejection of foreign language learning, which he saw as playing a particularly pernicious role in the process of corruption. This view also occasionally extended to a slighting of "foreign learning" generally, a slighting he justified, charac-teristically, by insisting on the prerogatives of the Qur'an over other sources: "Do you want me to leave the Qur'an? Give me a better book. . . . When I'm with the Qur'an I'm with all books. Why should I leave the whole and take a part?" This rejection of foreign influence stemmed from a vision of the world that, in so far as it consists of unbelievers, is bent on evil:

> For you know that all nations, every one of them, every people that is not Muslim, are united and consolidated in their hostility toward Islam and in their enmity toward Muslims and Arabs. We see too that they have lost their way politically; they have lost their way economically; they have lost their way socially; they have lost their way in terms of behavior with respect to brotherhood, friendship, and the military. They have lost their way in terms of science too. We see them battered and bruised in every nation, an object lesson for others by what they do and by their errors, torn by their divisions, their factions, and all because they have left the book of God.

It apparently detracted little from the rousing force of this philippic that Shaykh Ahmad began by declaring that Islam's enemies were acting in concert yet finished by depicting them as broken and divided. The logic at work here was devoted not to analysis but to the stirring of feelings that would call for a counterattack. The shaykh ended this particular oratorical volley by returning again to the Qur'an. He choose a familiar verse, one that had served as a rallying cry during Muslim uprisings against colonial invaders for the last century and a half: "Hold on firmly together to the rope of God, and be not divided among yourselves" (3: 103). Thus in calling his listeners to unity he was also summoning them to action. The noun *i'tisam,* or "holding firm," which corresponds to the verb used in the imperative at the head of this verse, is itself a highly charged catchword. It was, in fact, the name of the second and more radical of the two glossy monthly magazines the government temporarily allowed Islamic fundamentalists to publish during the late 1970s. Roars of enthusiasm from those in the mosque instantly greeted the shaykh's declaration. In this sermon, many heard an affirmation of the mandate to go beyond words in the quest for an Islamic order.

This was a time of anxious speculation in the realm of international relations as Egyptians followed the mercurial course of the negotiations between their leaders, Israel, and the United States in anticipation of some sort of peace settlement. The ultimate outcome of these talks was still uncertain, and Egypt was feeling considerable regional pressures to withdraw from the process. In early November 1978, months before it was clear whether or not the Camp David agreements of the previous September would be ratified, Egypt's role and its concessions were formally condemned at the Arab summit held in Baghdad. Diplomatic traffic was also extremely active, as Cyrus Vance, then the American secretary of state, arrived in Cairo the following month. This marked his third trip to Cairo in less than a year and would be followed some weeks later by President Jimmy Carter's sensational visit, which brought the negotiations to their climactic end.

Just prior to Vance's December visit, President Sadat had staged a triumphant tour of Upper Egypt that culminated with three days in Minya. Such state visits to the region seldom occur, and thus it was a very special occasion that fixed national attention on the city. Minya's main streets were transformed into a spectacular forest of banners, posters, streamers, bunting, and polychrome tent-arches bearing variations on the slogan "Sadat, hero of peace." These trimmings were commissioned almost entirely by the party apparatus; they were not spontaneous products of local enthusiasts. Thousands of troops were also on hand for the visit, and special trains and buses were chartered to ferry peasants in holiday spirits from surrounding towns and villages.

One of the signal events of Sadat's visit, according to the national media, centered on Minya's most prominent government mosque. This centrally located place of worship, which served as a sort of cathedral for the city, was named for its putative patron, Shaykh al-Fuli, whose tomb was housed in an elaborate domed shrine attached to the mosque. Here, the president and his sizable entourage, joined by local notables, had chosen to attend the Friday noon prayer, bringing with them a flurry of limousines and cameras unlike anything ordinarily seen in these precincts. The local imam who preached the sermon delivered an unusually patriotic homily, which was, of course, broadcast live on the radio, as was usually the case when Sadat was in attendance at a mosque. Images of the president at prayer were frequently displayed in the official media, as though in reply to fundamentalists who sought to depict the "believer president" (al-ra'is al-mu'min) as an enemy of religion. Thus the fact that Sadat used Minya as a stage from which to project not only the pomp and power of the state but also what they regarded as his pious pretensions greatly irked local Islamic militants. They did not risk any open protest during the visit itself for they were undoubtedly warned against it and probably kept under surveillance. But soon after, they began to move in the direction Shaykh Ahmad was already encouraging.

The smoldering tensions on the university campus soon erupted into a dispute concerning an attempt by the college of arts to set up a small cafe for students just within the campus gate. A local merchant, who himself showed Muslim fundamentalist leanings, had received the contract and was on the verge of opening for business when Islamic Society activists announced on 1 January 1979 they were occupying the site to prevent the cafe from opening: the facility, they insisted, would allow for illicit social contacts between men and women. After this occupation had persisted loudly for two days, some twenty students who were frustrated and angered by these high-handed tactics staged a counterdemonstration, barricading themselves into a second-floor classroom and demanding a hearing before university officials to discuss the issue. Later that night, a large band of Islamic militants, armed with clubs and sticks, broke into the classroom and assaulted the students who supported the cafe. This violent incident sent shock waves through the student grapevine. Within an hour, hundreds of agitated students had descended on the campus. The dean of the college of arts was roused out of bed and all but dragged back to his campus office, where he took part in an angry and impromptu mass meeting that ran through most of the night. During the course of the meeting, he promised to initiate formal disciplinary procedures against those responsible for attacking and beating the students involved in the counterdemonstration. The decision marked the first significant official check on the spreading influence of these youthful religious activists, who were in turn outraged at these measures.

In his sermon of 5 January, Shaykh Ahmad launched a stinging rebuke of those who presumed to challenge "the divine mandate," raising several familiar themes to a new pitch by emphasizing a litany of the starkest polarities: light and darkness, justice and corruption, truth and falsehood, Islam and godlessness. The congregation roared its approval as the shaykh stepped up his refutation of the charges brought against the Islamic Society activists. Nothing less than the integrity of the Qur'an and the ultimate choice of right over wrong was at stake, he insisted. After contrasting the saintly early converts to Islam with the benighted academics of today, the charismatic preacher turned sharply upon the highest symbol of Egypt's Coptic community. Abandoning the traditional protocol that proscribes naming names, he shouted direct rebukes at Shanuda III, the Coptic pope, reprimanding him first in rage and then in mocking tones for refusing to acknowledge Muhammad as the Prophet and to convert to Islam. Then the shaykh roared out a list of the nations of the world that he declared are besieging the Prophet, followed by an overlapping series of nations over whom the Prophet is destined to triumph. At the very end came the Vatican, a name the shaykh proclaimed in a loud stage whisper after a dramatic pause.

But the shaykh did not stop there. He then went on to indict the president himself. After mentioning Sadat by name several times, in elliptical asides that suggested the shaykh had himself recently been called in for questioning by local authorities, he proclaimed defiantly: "As for being charged with an attack upon the president of the republic, what I really fear and consider significant is an attack on the Lord of creation." Then seizing upon two of the ideological pillars of Sadat's regime, he said:

> As for patriotic peace [al-salam al-watani] and national unity [al-wahda al-qawmiya] these are things about which every citizen knows his rights. [One should] help to maintain and protect neighbors from ruin. But if it comes to patriotic peace and national unity at the expense of the Qur'an, then no; at the expense of Islam, then no; at the expense of the Prophet, then let me repeat, no, no, no!

The crowd, tense with excitement, responded with shouts of righteous defiance.

Building toward a climax, the shaykh echoed the basic tenets of Sayyid Qutb, the Muslim radical whose writings shaped the views of Egypt's most extreme militants.[27] Our age is an age of ignorance (jahiliyya) worse than the first age of ignorance before the Prophet, declared Shaykh Ah-mad. Accordingly, he continued, it is a time of *takfir,* that is, the practice of accusing fellow Muslims of being "unbelievers" *(kafir).* This practice of naming the unbeliever was also becoming common in the preaching of Shaykh 'Umar 'Abd al-Rahman, 'Abd al-Salam Faraj (the ideologue of the Tanzim al-Jihad), and many other radical fundamentalist preach-ers.[28] On this occasion Shaykh Ahmad implied that President Sadat him-self was an unbeliever: "There is no Muslim president or subject, ruler or ruled, who can hear an insult against the book of God and remain silent. If he does remain silent, he is a hypocrite. If he approves, he is an unbeliever." The audacity of such remarks, especially coming from a pul-pit, was extraordinary; officially they were held to border on sedition. Sadat himself had begun to call for an end to critical remarks of this kind by public figures who opposed the government. He spoke of the need for a sweeping "law of shameful conduct," which was eventually enacted early in 1980. This statute "made failure to uphold the regime's view of the values of religion, family, national unity, and social peace a criminal act"[29] and provided for the establishment of a special court, juridical pro-cedures, and punishments to be applied against anyone found to have offended against "shame" *('aib).*

This new directness on the part of the shaykh was soon reinforced by monumental events in Iran, namely, the arrival of the Ayatollah Kho-meini in Tehran and the declaration of an Islamic republic. In Minya, as elsewhere, this news sparked a heady mixture of fascination, bewilder-ment, and horror. For some Islamic militants in Egypt, the triumph in Iran stirred up zeal to hasten the local movement's progress in the same direction. On 10 February 1979, a group of such militants carried out a symbolic operation, an "outrage for God" *(ghadbah l-allah),* when they broke into the municipal building of Minya and claimed to be holding it as a first step toward the founding of an Islamic Republic in Egypt. After the first employees arrived and discovered them, they were quickly removed from the premises and detained by police.

Each in their own way, Shaykh Ahmad and the Islamic Society main-tained this aggressive stance throughout the early months of 1979. But the physical distance as well as the social and cultural gaps between mosque and campus made it increasingly difficult for them to stage con-certed actions. This was to change, however, at the end of March. On 27 March, while Carter, Begin, and Sadat were signing the Camp David accords in Washington, D.C., members of the Islamic Society in Minya placed themselves at the gates of the different colleges of the university in order to block the way of students and keep them from entering. They declared the university to be closed for the day in protest against the dishonorable treaty. They also posted insults against President Sadat, an action certain to anger the authorities. One memorable poster, for instance, bore an ode beginning with the line "O you who have sold out your religion and your country." This daylong student strike was judged largely successful by its organizers. Since they had not been prevented from setting up their blockades, nor was their boycott forcefully interrupted once under way, their confidence was visibly bolstered. But the action caused consternation among the university officials and the local authorities.

Although there was no immediate official response, three days later, on Friday, the other shoe fell, not on campus, but on the doorstep of Shaykh Ahmad's mosque. Well before worshipers began arriving for the customary Friday noon prayer, a large police detachment arrived and took up positions around the mosque, sealing it off and announcing that it was closed for the day. Among those turned away were many student members of the Islamic Society. Apparently, Shaykh Ahmad and the Islamic Society had planned a demonstration in which student militants would lead the sizable crowd gathered for prayer on a march from the mosque into the city, gathering strength along the way. The security forces were acting preemptively, as they had failed to do at the university earlier in the week.

It was then the turn of the Islamic Society to react. A group of perhaps two hundred youths, most of them students, gathered at Shaykh Ahmad's mosque that evening. They marched toward the city, moved onto an important bridge adjacent to a major commercial street on the south side of town, and occupied the roadway there to perform their evening prayers, cutting off all traffic and prolonging the delay with supererogatory devotions. This protest marked a milestone in the conflict. A few days later, the police arrested several of the leaders of the Islamic Society. University authorities implemented a new security procedure and advertised it by placing on the campus streets squads of soldiers in army vehicles, armed with rifles and bayonets, unmistakably prepared for trouble. Furthermore, the extraordinary disciplinary committee that had been convoked to hear the case of the beatings in January expelled the accused Islamic activists.

As might be anticipated, the convergence of these arrests and expulsions sparked additional demonstrations and skirmishes. Mobilizing their membership and sympathizers, the Islamists seized control of the male student housing blocks, taking hostage some thirty Coptic students who resided there. The militants then demanded the release of their leaders in exchange for the safety of the Christian students. After a few days, when initial, informal efforts to resolve the standoff failed, the local police moved in. The possibility of a major confrontation increased the next day when over a thousand troops arrived in Minya by train and proceeded to surround the complex, cutting off its water and electricity. After three tense days, a settlement was reached and the Copts were released. But from then on police posts were permanently set up at the entrance of "university city" and at the entrances to all colleges of the university.

In the midst of these events, on 6 April, Shaykh Ahmad, who had been forcibly barred from his pulpit the previous Friday, returned with a vengeance to denounce what he regarded as onslaughts against Islam. Much of what he said in the long, scathing sermon he preached that Friday had been prefigured earlier, but on this occasion he lashed out unrelentingly. To President Sadat's name he now added the names of two of his ministers, accusing them all of failing to accept Islam. Nor did Shaykh Ahmad hesitate to draw the unsettling conclusion that flows from this denunciation. He explicitly sanctioned, in the name both of Islam and of democracy, the disobeying of orders from such illegitimate authorities. The following citation from this sermon, delivered with sober and excited force, illustrates concretely one technique by which the shaykh made his point. Note how he mixes voices, achieving great dramatic effect as he mounts his assault. Interestingly, he concludes these remarks by manipulating the pronouns in his staged dialogue in such a way that, using the first person singular, he ends up speaking in the persona of God. Except in quoting from the Qur'an, such divine personification is an unusual trope, one that is not at all standard in Muslim preaching:

> The ultimate independence of the nation, the ultimate independence of society, the deepest meaning of democracy is this: The foundation of democracy is that no one, neither my president, nor my wife, nor my father, nor my brother can come and say to me, "Do such and such!" And if you say, "That's wrong!" And he says, "You're fired!" [You say,] "Hey, listen, no, no, no, it's okay! I'll do whatever you want, sir. I'll do whatever you want even if you want me to kill my wife, I'll kill her. Just leave me to eat my bread, sir, for God's sake!" Is this the good citizen or functionary? No! the ultimate independence is that I can say to the president: "This is Truth, I accept it, and this is Falsehood, I reject it." That's the deepest meaning of democracy if that's what the president wants. Why? Because that same president is responsible on the Day of Judgment. Listen, you give a speech that lasts for three hours or four or five, and ears perk up to hear it all over the earth. But what do you want with all your speech making? Do

you want what I want or do you want something I do not want? Our Lord, exalted be He, says I made your ears so that you could hear everything that is said. So did you listen to what I wanted or did you listen to what I did not want? I made your hands and your feet to take you to what I want and not to what I do not want. Well, then, did you strive for what I wanted or for what I did not want?

The shaykh's bombastic volleys from his popular pulpit were approaching a threshold of serious provocation. The sense of an impending collision grew palpable in Shaykh Ahmad's relentless and uncompromising jeremiads before weekly crowds that spilled over from the mosque itself to its courtyard and onto the street. Rumors of confrontations with the law ran rampant, seemingly feeding on each other and so threatening to spark additional outbursts.

A feud mentality and the related impulses of clanlike solidarity became evident, not only dividing groups along confessional lines but also pitting the government and fundamentalists against each other. Feeling unfairly besieged in the first alignment and caught in the middle in the second were the Copts. Many of them, including those at university, deeply resented the abuse they had to suffer as their cries for protection went largely unheeded by state authorities. Not surprisingly, then, some elements in the Coptic community sought to rally their coreligionists to active defiance and to organizing for their own defense. Unwilling to remain pawns in what they perceived as a bidding war, which had the government and the fundamentalists each claiming to be more Muslim than the other, advocates for a Coptic resurgence began to surface publicly. One dimension of this Christian response was articulated through the official Coptic Orthodox hierarchy, most notably by Pope Shanuda III, who began to challenge the regime's religious policy quite boldly at this time. But Egypt's Copts also had their fringe groups, well represented in Upper Egypt, some of whose members did not hesitate to advance a fanatical chauvinism that, perhaps ironically, mirrored the aggressiveness of Islamic militancy.[30]

The mounting tension that stemmed from the Islamic Society's continued hold on the campus and Shaykh Ahmad's shrill appeals from the pulpit finally broke the following week, in a most unexpected way. On very short notice, the faculties of the universities of Minya and Asyut were summoned to attend a public discussion on 14 April with President Sadat, held on the Asyut campus. Sadat called this peremptory gathering a "town meeting," invoking the spirit of the traditional American forums recently made famous by his "good friend" Jimmy Carter in the United

States. The nearly three-hour session, consisting mainly of Sadat's stern speech and his responses to questions, was treated as a national priority; it was broadcast live on radio and television and rebroadcast in its entirety several times over the next few days. The following day it was the headline story in the press, and a verbatim transcript of the president's extensive remarks appeared in full in *al-Ahram,* the government's semi-official newspaper. At the meeting Sadat first addressed the academics and administrators about the values of freedom and security, religion and politics with regard to universities. He upbraided students of the Islamic Society and all others who were mixing politics and religion, arguing that they were undermining Egypt's educational institutions. At several points, he elaborated on events in Minya, frequently reading directly from a police dossier that included exact dates, places, and the names of those involved. He spoke at length of large sums of money that had been discovered in the possession of leaders of the local Islamic Society, thereby insinuating that these students were acting as agents of an unspecified foreign power that was using them to destabilize Egypt and to obstruct the peace process. Then he opened the floor for comments and questions, all of which were likewise reported in the media coverage. The disruptive activities of the Islamic Society on the two campuses was clearly the key issue under consideration.[31]

The impact of this evening of presidential revelations on the people of Minya, especially the Copts, was exhilarating; it cast a new light on all that had been happening over the past year and a half. For many months, amid increasing anxiety, threats, and fears, it had seemed that the government was somehow indifferent to or tacitly complicit with the surge of fundamentalist militancy that had brought havoc to the new university and was now spilling over into the streets. While reports of fundamentalist agitation and sectarian violence had appeared in leading European newspapers, including *Le Monde* and the *Guardian,* as much as six months earlier, and a large number of well-established rumor networks ensured that no one with family links in or around Minya was completely unaware of these problems, Egypt's official print and broadcast media had not, until that moment, publicly acknowledged the provocations, demonstrations, and closings, the hostage-taking incident, and other confrontations. Now, in a surprising coup de théâtre, the "father of the Egyptian family," as Sadat was fond of calling himself, revealed not only that he had been watching these ordeals with concern, but that henceforth he would oversee their resolution.

Although the legal measures that officially suppressed the Islamic Society, banning it from the campuses, would follow in stages and be completed a year later, from this day on the fundamentalist organization in Minya effectively lost its potency in the wider student community. Islamic activism centered elsewhere in the city also came under new scrutiny. Within forty-eight hours of Sadat's address, senior deputies from the ministries of the interior, of justice, and of religious endowments had descended on Minya to issue new directives in accord with the president's address.

Shaykh Ahmad was to all appearances brought to heel by these measures. His leadership of the cooperative society affiliated with his Sunna Mosque was called into question. Even as he drew enormous crowds on Fridays, it was now pointed out that virtually all the other facilities associated with the society had been sorely neglected. The condition of the buildings was in decline, and the social programs lacked staff and resources to the point that they were largely token exercises. Shortly after Sadat's speech, Shaykh Ahmad disappeared from sight and the report went about that he was in Cairo undergoing medical treatment. He eventually returned home, but his profile in the city steadily diminished. Having been forced to back down in the face of mounting official pressure, he seemed to lose much of his credibility; this in turn diminished his usefulness to the increasingly aggressive militants. By the time he died in 1985 he had become peripheral to the Islamist protest movement. Events had passed him by. During his decline, funds from a number of modest state assistance programs were allotted to other leaders associated with the mosque formerly called by his name. Most notably, the construction of a new building was approved after the provincial governor paid an official visit to the mosque, a gesture that would have been altogether incongruous a few months earlier.

At about the same time Shaykh 'Umar 'Abd al-Rahman was also showing unusual signs of temperance. Contrary to all expectations, he announced in 1987, in the course of the political campaigns for the People's Assembly, that he supported the ticket of the Social Labor Party, which was serving as a front for Muslim Brotherhood candidates.[32]

CONCLUSION

The triumph and the collapse of Shaykh Ahmad's career as a mosque preacher, and the relative ease with which the aging preacher was dismissed, demonstrate the essential interdependence of the sermon and the wider society as well as the limitations of the preaching that had momentarily cast him in the role of Islamist folk hero. His capacity to arouse and channel collective emotion through his pulpit oratory was impressive,

but it was limited to a specific ritual setting; he was not so adept at lis-
tening to the often delicate voices of the complex and changing real world
beyond the ritual space. His ability to organize and direct the zeal he
excited toward cogent, realistic, and practical objectives, to oversee routine administration, or even to mobilize resources for an effective grass-
roots movement was negligible.

Moreover, the coincidence of Shaykh Ahmad's decline and the rise
of Shaykh 'Umar 'Abd al-Rahman as the new, often sotto voce mentor
of the Islamist students of Minya, now increasingly drawn to Asyut,
should not be overlooked. If one speaks of a passing of the mantle, one
must also note a change of tactics, both in the pulpit and in the clandestine
meeting room. Shaykh Ahmad would not have flourished in the underground. His primary points of reference seem rather to have become increasingly removed from that everyday realm just outside the doors of
the mosque as he set his compass by the poles of a utopian order where
all colors faded to either black or white.

Clearly many who listened and who were following this same course
as Shaykh Ahmad were moved by his vision. Others were apparently persuaded, at least for a time, that he did speak for the holy book, and they
adopted his views with that same rigid fervor. And finally, there were a
few who would carry his convictions forward into symbolic deeds entail-
ing considerable violence. Militants who heard and approved of his
preaching seem to have concluded, however, that the learning and the
applying of God's book, though different activities, could not really be
separated. Both must occur in the sanctum of the mosque and amid the
confusion of an imperfect world. Therefore the message they heard from
Shaykh Ahmad was but one half of a whole.

By 1992 Hosni Mubarak's tenure in office had equaled that of President Sadat. But Egypt had still by no means resolved the key dilemmas
posed by Islamic fundamentalism. On the contrary, that year the Islamist
cause took a sudden violent turn, which included attacks on foreign tourists, to which the government security forces responded ferociously.
While the regime has so far largely succeeded in preventing the emergence
of an open and consolidated Islamist opposition, the cost has been great.
In 1992 the total number of casualties, including activists, police, and
civilians, was 322; it rose to 659 in 1994.[33] At this writing, in 1995, the
Islamic militants are certainly on the run or in hiding. For all the periodic
assurances by security officials that the tide has been turned, however, it
remains unclear when or how these confrontations will end. In January
1995 alone, there were eighty-seven reported deaths in Upper Egypt due
to violence perpetrated by Islamic militants and police raids in response.[34]

In addition, it appears to many observers that the legitimacy of the regime and its base of support is continuing to shrink, not specifically due to popular admiration for Islamic extremists, but because of a perception that the Islamic agencies are more dedicated and effective than those of the government in serving the needs of the lower classes. Contrary to the official Islam, a new "social Islam" has been emerging which has little investment in the formal institutions of government and looks instead to informal networks largely centered in the burgeoning local and national religious networks.[35] During the massive American-led intervention in defense of Kuwait in the 1991 Gulf war, for example, the semilegal Muslim Brotherhood felt compelled to refrain from active opposition to Egypt's prominent role as an ally against Iraq.

Nevertheless, elsewhere, in underground activities the crisis demonstrated the assertiveness of the violent extremist fringe of the movement.[36] The early 1990s witnessed a steady stream of assassinations and assassination attempts targeting current or past government officials who sought to counter these disruptive elements. Diplomats, police, journalists, intellectuals, and finally tourists have also been victims of attacks. Furthermore, the fatal bombing of the Egyptian embassy in Pakistan in November 1995 may indicate the militants' intention to extend their campaign of violence to foreign soil as it becomes more difficult to pursue domestically. Until recently the state has tended to react as though it were dealing with large criminal gangs rather than politically motivated insurrection. Although government security forces have gathered considerable data on the organizational character, size, degree of coherence, and proximate objectives of this violence-prone underground, much remains shrouded in secrecy.

The immediate and widespread public outcry against the June 1992 shooting of Faraj Foda, a prominent Muslim thinker who championed social tolerance and political secularism, seemed to point to a growing rejection of religiously justified terrorism among the general public. This response underscored the paradoxical situation in which the radical cells of the Islamic movement find themselves. On the one hand, the general public, even those groups and syndicates that support the drive for a genuine Islamic order in Egypt, has demonstrated an unwillingness to endorse anarchic violence and terrorism in the pursuit of this goal. On the other hand, this lack of popular support, matched with a dearth of organizational planning and ideological coherence, has further marginalized and alienated the radical groups, which have responded by resorting to even greater acts of violence.

By the same token, preachers find it increasingly difficult to perform today in the manner that was possible for Shaykh Ahmad a decade ago. Firebrand pulpit rhetoric has by no means disappeared in Egypt, but overall it has been both tempered and circumscribed. Nevertheless, the prevalence of cheap audiocassettes as a medium for preaching has increased phenomenally in recent years. In Minya, the spacious mosque where Shaykh Ahmad preached continues to function, but it no longer serves as the magnet for local Islamist enthusiasm. Instead, the visible focus for this trend has moved into the center of the city. A new mosque has been founded, scarcely a block from the main square, that is actually little more than a converted storefront. Today, it is in and around this new mosque that one sees and hears the public display of ardent fundamentalism. At Friday noon, for instance, the devotees of *masjid al-tawhid,* the "mosque of [God's] unity," gather regularly. They perform the prayer and hear a sermon not in the mosque, but on the major street facing it, which they cover with mats in a highly ostentatious fashion. Two government mosques within a minute's walk of this pious demonstration would accommodate the worshipers if they merely sought to fulfill their ritual obligations. Typically the sermon, proclaimed over a loudspeaker that can be heard throughout the neighborhood, bears some of the familiar traces of Shaykh Ahmad's defiant and accusatory oratory.

Given the current context, however, the political and social implications of this preaching are substantially different from the sermons of a decade ago.[37] In the present circumstances, the preacher seems to be addressing the converted, rather than appealing to the uncommitted or indoctrinating the well-disposed as was the case in Shaykh Ahmad's mosque. The age of those participating in this public Islamic movement today tends to be greater; this reflects both the retention of earlier activists, who have aged, and a falling off in the number of young recruits. Further, the ideological orientation of activists is incorporated into a set of identifiable accoutrements. Virtually all of those participating in this prayer on the street, as I observed them in the summer of 1991, were dressed in white, and most had beards. The impression of uniformity and routinization apparent in this ceremonial garb announces the solidarity and the separateness of the movement in ritual terms.

But this view of an aging and tamed Islamic congregation does not fully convey the changing character of the more militant ranks of this movement. The Ibn Khaldoun Center for Development Studies in Cairo has published figures indicating that, whereas the average age of Islamic activists arrested in the 1970s and 1980s was twenty-five to twenty-seven, the average age in 1995 is twenty-one. While 64 percent of those arrested in the 1970s had university degrees, only 48 percent had degrees in the

1980s and only 30 percent of those arrested in the 1990s fall within this category.[38]

The containment of militant elements in Minya, at least provisionally, is not, however, only a matter of the systematic censoring of preachers; at least two other major local developments have contributed. First, the capacity of student activists to mobilize has been reduced by stricter measures within the university and the city. Second, a decisive physical displacement has taken place. In 1980, an entirely new campus for Minya University was opened on agricultural terrain about five kilometers north of the city; the move abruptly eliminated student activists' proximity to the centers and symbols of power—the administrative center of the governorate and the residences of its elite—that were concentrated in the school's former neighborhood. No less telling has been the recent completion by the ministry of the interior of a colossal new complex, set on the site of Minya's central police post. This huge, eight-story building dominates the skyline and stands as a cogent reminder of the amplified vigilance of the state. Nor is this facility sealed off: it extends its presence into the community by assorted transparent gestures. For instance, on Friday afternoons, shortly after the fundamentalists have completed their long and demonstrative ritual at the new midtown mosque, troops from the Central Security Forces, stationed at the post, can be seen and heard jogging in formation on the near-empty streets, passing conspicuously and more than once within a hundred yards of the mosque.

In retrospect, the role played by Shaykh Ahmad's preaching in the formation of fundamentalist cadres—cadres which continue to exercise considerable influence—was both representative and exceptional. It was representative—even prototypical—in that it successfully fused articulations of the rage, excitement, frustration, and longing of a large sector of the population with potent religious images. The oratorical virtuosity with which Shaykh Ahmad dressed vaguely understood national and international issues in Qur'anic terms was a key factor in the generation of a popular Islamist consciousness in the region and, perhaps more important, in the initial extension of an aura of legitimacy to the militants, among a congregation that would otherwise have tended to shun direct involvement in student-led demonstrations. The emergence of this distinguished and definite voice, steeped in the tradition and capable of translating its tenets into an idiom of action, was indispensable in the effective mobilization of major Islamist movements.

Shaykh Ahmad also profited, however, from exceptional circumstances, which permitted or, perhaps, propelled him to adopt a posture of leadership in a mounting confrontation that eventually proved to be beyond his control. His mastery of the ritual forum, as rousing as it was at the time, ultimately paled beside the explosive consequences that were unfolding in the streets. The conflict took on a life of its own, quite apart from his performances, with an escalation of provocation and violence that resulted in clashes with authorities and a fragmentation of the Islamist movement in Minya—part of it accepting the compromising legal restraints, part persisting as a public but formally unrecognized protest movement, and part hardening into underground extremist cells.

Thus the government's successful censoring or silencing of preachers such as Shaykh Ahmad may not signal a real decline in the trend they embody, especially when their activities as preachers, despite appearances, are structurally distinct from the actual planning and direction of strategic operations. This was the case in Minya in the late 1970s and early 1980s. Indeed, such pulpit personalities, for all their mass appeal, often play the role of mouthpiece or propagandist, rather than the genuine leader, in "movements" in which ideology and organizational structure are relatively uncoordinated. Unlike the Ayatollah Khomeini, who unified in his person the religious and political properties of the imam, Shaykh Ahmad represented a charismatic but characteristically Sunni exponent of the relation of state power to divine law. Furthermore, Shaykh Ahmad did not have the status of the doctorate from the Azhar, a credential that figured very significantly in the authority of Shaykh 'Umar 'Abd al-Rahman.

As the Islamist tendency in Egypt and elsewhere gains more experience and adapts to changing social and political circumstances, it will almost certainly continue to rely on the support of populist preachers like those who were so instrumental in the movement's early growth. Figures with such special talents as Shaykh Ahmad will rise again when determined activist groups appear, giving organizational backing and concrete force to their sermons. When and as this occurs, observers would do well to note whether the pattern described in this essay—of a disjuncture between the pulpit and the street leading to the dismemberment of a movement with wide popular appeal but little organizational depth—is repeated.

One conclusion is clear: the revival of Islamic preaching as a medium of relevant political discourse has been introduced at the heart of a protracted crisis of legitimacy that surfaces in many forms throughout the contemporary Middle East. The remark of Shaykh 'Umar 'Abd al-Rahman, made in 1989 shortly after his trial in Cairo opened, will undoubtedly continue for some time to elicit a sympathetic response as it is repeated from pulpits: "The ruling regime is against us because we speak of the looting in Egypt, which has given ministers and rulers big accounts in Western banks."[39] By issuing such indictments preachers have displayed a potency that points to their growing significance both for the evolution of fundamentalism and for the direction of societies and nations throughout the region.

Notes

1. Prior to this appointment, Shaykh 'Abd al-Rahman had worked in Minya, where he retained close contacts. "Egypt's Khomeini," *Guardian Weekly,* 14 March 1993.

2. Celhia de Lavarène, "Je suis un terroriste, si . . .," an interview with Shaykh 'Abd al-Rahman, *Jeune Afrique,* 5–11 October 1995, 33.

3. Saad Eddin Ibrahim, "Islamic Militancy as a Social Movement: The Case of Two Groups in Egypt," in Ali E. Dessouki, ed., *Islamic Resurgence in the Arab World* (New York: Praeger, 1982), 117–37.

4. Hamied Ansari, "Sectarian Conflict and the Political Expedience of Religion," *Middle East Journal* 3, no. 3 (1984): 397–418.

5. "Religious War Rends a Cairo Slum, Pitting the Muslims against the Copts," *New York Times,* 22 October 1991, A4.

6. The material presented here on Shaykh Ahmad, his preaching, and his relationship to local Islamic militants derives principally from field observations obtained while I was engaged in ethnographic research. In addition to numerous interviews with Shaykh Ahmad, I attended his mosque as a guest. There I was able to record a number of his sermons on audiocassette, just as many in the congregation customarily did. These recordings were later transcribed for more careful study.

7. See especially *al-Da'wa* issues of March, July, and August 1979.

8. In fact, this sharp dichotomy between government and private mosques is misleading insofar as a variety of quasi-official subsidies were widely available to private mosques. See Morroe Berger, *Islam in Egypt Today: Social and Political Aspects of Popular Religion* (Cambridge: Cambridge University Press, 1970), and Patrick D. Gaffney, "The Changing Voices of Islam: The Emergence of Professional Preachers in Contemporary Egypt," *Muslim World* 81, no. 1 (1991): 27–47.

9. The society's mission is given as follows: "To spread religious teaching and combat superstitions; establish Koran-teaching departments and mosques; issue a religious magazine as well as religious books; extend aid to the needy, provide burial facilities and establish a hospital for underprivileged Moslems" (Isis Istiphan, ed., *Directory of Social Agencies in Cairo* [Cairo: Social Research Center, American University at Cairo, 1956], 185).

10. Judith Cochran, *Education in Egypt* (London: Croom Helm, 1986), 22–40.

11. 'Umar 'Abd al-Rahman, *Kalimat al-Haqq* (Cairo: Dar al-i'tisam, n.d. [1985]), 14.

12. Arab Republic of Egypt, *The Year Book, 1977* (Cairo: Ministry of Information and State Information Service), 165.

13. M. Martin, "Egyptian Students: University Expansion and Student Life," in *Islamic Law and Change in Arab Society*, CEMAM Reports (Beirut: Dar El-Mashreq, 1978), 189.

14. "Une répétition générale" and "une scène d'exposition préalable"; Gilles Kepel, *Le Prophète et Pharaon: Les Mouvements Islamiques Dans l'Egypte Contemporaine* (Paris: La Découverte, 1984), 158 (*Muslim Extremism in Egypt: The Prophet and Pharaoh* [Berkeley: University of California Press, 1986]).

15. Sermons provide the preacher with an occasion to transmit and transform power and authority. Or as Max Weber put it: "It is the specific means of legitimate violence as such in the hand of human associations which determines the peculiarity of all ethical problems of politics." Max Weber, "Politics as a Vocation," in H. H. Gerth and C. Wright Mills, eds., *From Max Weber: Essays in Sociology* (New York: Oxford University Press, 1946), 124.

16. Ahmad Ahmad Badawi, *Asas al-Naqd al-Adabi 'ind al-'Arab* (Cairo: Dar Nahdha Misr, 1979), 639–51.

17. Translations of the Qur'an are taken for the most part from *Al-Qur'an: A Contemporary Translation*, Ahmed Ali, trans. (Princeton: Princeton University Press, 1984).

18. Fazlur Rahman, *Islam* (Garden City: Doubleday, 1968), 29 ff.

19. Most Christians would be unfamiliar with the episodes attributed to the life of Jesus by Shaykh Ahmad. The dim underworld of vulgar prejudice and provocative religious polemics, which has, however unfortunately, an important place in the total economy of contemporary Islamic fundamentalism in Egypt, is rarely explored in any detail by scholars. A recent and illuminating exception is contained in an angry and candid book by the former correspondent for *Le Monde* in Egypt. Jean-Pierre Péroncel-Hugoz, *The Raft of Mohammed*, George Holoch, trans. (New York: Paragon House, 1988), 81 ff.

20. M. Tosy and B. Etienne, "Le modÈle Kichkiste et son impact," in Olivier CarrÈ and Paul Dumont, eds., *Radicalismes Islamiques* (Paris: L'Harmattan, 1986), 2: 17–32; Emmanuel Sivan, "Eavesdropping on Radical Islam," *Middle East Quarterly*, March 1995, 13–24.

21. Maurice Martin, "Note sur la communauté Copte entre 1650 et 1850," *Annales Islamologiques* 18 (1982): 193–215.

22. B. L. Carter, *The Copts in Egyptian Politics* (London: Croom Helm, 1986), 5 ff.

23. Nazih N. M. Ayubi, "The Political Revival of Islam: The Case of Egypt," *International Journal of Middle Eastern Studies* 12, no. 4 (1980): 481–99.

24. Cynthia Nelson, "Religious Experience, Sacred Symbols, and Social Reality: An Illustration from Egypt," *Humaniora Islamica* 2 (1974): 253–66.

25. Ronald L. Nettler, *Past Trials and Present Tribulations: A Muslim Fundamentalist's View of the Jews* (New York: Pergamon Press, 1987), 11–24.

26. The figure Shaykh Ahmad cites as his villain is Samuel Ha-Levi (d. 1056), a native of Granada renowned as a poet, scholar, and diplomat who mastered both Hebrew and Arabic. See R. A. Nicholson, *A Literary History of the Arabs* (Cambridge: Cambridge University Press, 1969), 428–29.

27. Yvonne Haddad, "Sayyid Qutb: Ideologue of Islamic Revival," in John

L. Esposito, ed., *Voices of Resurgent Islam* (New York: Oxford University Press, 1983), 67–98.

28. The doctrine was later, of course, subjected to official scrutiny during the trial of the conspirators, and the Azhar specialists condemned it as heretical. Johannes J. G. Jansen, *The Neglected Duty: The Creed of Sadat's Assassins and Islamic Resurgence in the Middle East* (New York: Macmillan, 1986), 1–35.

29. Raymond W. Baker, *Sadat and After: Struggles for Egypt's Political Soul* (Cambridge: Harvard University Press, 1990), 46.

30. See, for instance, the remarks of Dr. Fu'ad Jirjis of Cairo University in Kepel, *Muslim Extremism in Egypt,* 167–69.

31. An abridged version of Sadat's remarks was published at the time in English. See Foreign Broadcast Information Service, Daily Report: Middle East and North Africa, "President As-Sadat Addresses Asyut Governorate Leaders," 17 April 1979, D1–D6.

32. Mona Makram Ebeid, "The Role of the Official Opposition," in Charles Tripp and Roger Owen, eds., *Egypt under Mubarak* (London: Routledge, 1989), 35.

33. Nemat Guenena, "Islamic Activism in Egypt," *Civil Society* 4 (June 1995): 8.

34. Mohamed Sid-Ahmed, "Menaces sur l'Egypte," *Le Monde Diplomatique,* March 1995.

35. Sami Zubaida, "Islam, the State and Democracy: Contrasting Conceptions of Society in Egypt," *Middle East Report* (November–December 1992), 2–10.

36. See Gehad Auda, "An Uncertain Response: The Islamic Movement in Egypt," in James Piscatori, ed., *Islamic Fundamentalisms and the Gulf Crisis* (Cambridge, Mass.: American Academy of Arts and Sciences, 1991), 109–30.

37. Author's field research notes, Cairo and Upper Egypt, 1991.

38. Guenena, "Islamic Activism in Egypt," 7.

39. "Cairo Frees Fundamentalist Cleric Pending Hearing on Role in Strife" *New York Times,* 11 August 1989.

SIX

THE FATHER, THE SON, AND THE HOLY LAND

The Spiritual Authorities of Jewish-Zionist

Fundamentalism in Israel

Gideon Aran

Israeli fundamentalism is embodied in the hard core of Gush Emunim (the Bloc of the Faithful).[1] This movement, in turn, is an extension of Kookism, a comprehensive religious-political subculture encompassing the lives of a few thousand cadres who constitute the stable, militant avant-garde among the settlers in the disputed areas of the West Bank and Gaza.[2] Kookism is an original mystical-messianic system whose three cornerstones are Rabbi Kook the father, Rabbi Kook the son, and the Merkaz HaRav Yeshiva in Jerusalem. This essay focuses on two elements of the Jewish-Zionist fundamentalist triad—the two rabbis Kook, the spiritual authority of Gush Emunim.[3]

Kook the son is a difficult figure to reconstruct. He was not famous most of his life, and by the time his leadership became recognized, access to him was almost impossible. He did not leave behind a written legacy of significance, and most of the published material about Gush Emunim

294

was written after his death.[4] In contrast, Kook the father is the subject of innumerable studies, though most are in Hebrew.[5] The senior Rabbi Kook's reputation is formidable among students of contemporary Jewish thought who are impressed by the rich and seminal legacy he left behind. After all is said and done, few Jewish activists deny that he was a great man. Lacking in objectivity and critical perspective, the literature about Kook the father borders on the hagiographic. This is conspicuous both in the myriad biographies of the rabbi and in the unquestioning way his approach is integrated into the cultural policy of the state of Israel, as is evident in the curriculum guidelines promulgated by the Ministry of Education.[6] Few studies examine Kook in terms of his connection to Gush Emunim, however, although the connection is taken for granted by scholars as well as the general public.[7] Do the teachings of Kook the father convey the message of Gush Emunim? Are Gush activities driven by the words of Kook? The relation between the rabbi and the movement is strong but complex.

In this chapter I will distinguish between the senior Rabbi Kook and Kookism, and then examine the affinity between them. To a certain extent the Kookist complex of ideas and moods developed independently of Kook, as an effort to grapple with and react to him. Kookism places Kook in the center, but this very act tends to modify the source. The transfer of the rabbi's teachings to the public realm altered their intent and character by popularizing them and making them an ideological medium and a cult object. Kook's esoteric religious system has a certain logic and appeal on the theoretical level, but it was also interpreted— and vulgarized—for the rank and file in a selective and somewhat misleading way.

Kookism, furthermore, involves not just Kook the father but also Kook the son: the father is generally seen through the prism of the son, and the son, with the halo of the father. The link between the two Kooks is the key to understanding Gush Emunim, which discovered first the son and later, through him, the father.

THE FATHER

Abraham Isaac Kook (1865–1935) was born in Latvia and studied in Volozhin, the model of a prestigious new type of yeshiva in Eastern Europe that reflected the transition from a traditional Jewish society to early modern Orthodoxy. Around the turn of the century, Kook held pulpits in several European cities. From an early stage, he was a mixture of a Lithuanian yeshiva man and a Hasid: a *posek* (rabbi who gives halakhic

rulings), erudite in the Talmud and strictly observant of the commandments, yet at the same time of mystical temperament, spontaneous and
fervent in his religiosity. In addition to his Torah scholarship and broad
knowledge of classical and contemporary European thought, Kook apparently had visions; prophetic powers bordering on the supernatural
were attributed to him. The older he became, the more he acted out of
an intense experience of intimacy with the living God; later in his life
he was acutely aware of an imminent messianic presence under which
inspiration he composed his writings and took part in public affairs. Even
some of his halakhic rulings were influenced by his messianic sensibility.
After all, he said, while "the hope for Redemption is the force that sustained Judaism in the diasporic past, the present Judaism of the Land of
Israel is the very Redemption."

Rabbi Kook was original, creative, and unusually prolific. He produced dozens of books, hundreds of articles, and thousands of letters, an
endless and disjointed flood, all written in a close and messy hand.[8] Their
publication—mostly after his death—required great efforts; some are still
not edited, and several have never even been made public. His printed
words, in many volumes, are rich and varied; they are ethereal, replete
with innuendo, entangled and vague in method and in style. Thus one
can find in the teachings of Kook a great deal, including statements that
could easily be interpreted in different and contradictory ways. Gush
Emunim views itself as the implementer of these teachings, but even
among those who oppose the movement, one finds experts in and admirers of Kook's teachings. The debate for and against Gush Emunim has
taken place in terms of different readings of Kook; drawing on various
passages of his writings, or even disparately interpreting the same passage, one can cull, for example, both a humanistic universal and a chau-
vinist Jewish message.[9]

As evidenced by his talmudic reasoning, kabbalist references, and the
ascetic regimen of his private life, Kook was deeply immersed in the world
of traditional Judaism, a fact expressed symbolically in his mode of attire.
Yet in his mystical-philosophical writing, his correspondence, his polemical writing, and his several public initiatives, he evinced modernist tendencies that deviated from the sanctioned norm. In his decisions regarding
Torah questions as well as matters for which there is no explicit law but
merely convention, he was thoroughly conservative and somehow also a
daring revolutionary. For example, he came out against coed schooling
and women's right to vote, as do the ultra-Orthodox, but he approved
the practices of cultivating the body through sports and military activity
and of working the land during a sabbatical year—when Jewish law pre-

scribes that it lie fallow—to strengthen the economy of the Yishuv. This last decision caused the ultra-Orthodox to vilify him.[10]

In Kook's relations with individuals and groups there was also a mixture, sometimes difficult to explain, of radical harshness and radical leniency. Even his demanding rulings and wrathful remonstrations were shaped by his modesty, kindly ways, and likable personality. Toward contemporary secularity in general and the national Zionist enterprise in particular, he was of two minds—open and sympathetic but also isolationist and critical.

Kook immigrated to Palestine in 1904 upon his appointment as rabbi of Jaffa and the surrounding agricultural settlements, a position he held until 1914. In that capacity he was in charge of the religious institutions for a community that included the vanguard of the fundamentally secular Zionist pioneers. Under those circumstances, he cultivated his "affair" (as it was later described in idealized retrospective) with the pioneers of the second and third aliyahs, mainly socialists who professed atheism. In contrast with what might be expected from an Orthodox Jewish authority upholding stringent religious precepts, Kook had generally friendly contacts with his secular flock and aspired to provide them with guidance and patronage. Following this innovative approach, Kook gave legitimacy to the idealization of Jewish pioneers and defenders of the land of Israel, even those who publicly and deliberately desecrated the Sabbath. The religious non-Zionists of the "old Yishuv," who were the forebears of the haredim (the ultra-Orthodox), reacted harshly to Kook's embrace of the secular Zionists. Despite their opposition, however, Kook was appointed by the British mandate authorities, with the consent of the national Jewish establishment, to be the first chief Ashkenazi rabbi of Palestine (1921–1935). In this key position he sought to bring together religion and Zionism by advocating the sanctification of secular Zionists. Behind this seminal position were feelings of personal sympathy for the Zionists as well as a shrewd strategy and, above all, deep faith and a clear doctrine.

At the time most of Jewish Orthodoxy rejected the nationalist enterprise because it was initiated and implemented by secular Jews and was therefore fundamentally secular in nature. Jewish political nationalism, in other words, was based on a belief in the power of man and the nation, rather than faith in divine providence. Thus it was bound up with forces that promoted abandonment of the traditional way of life and desecration of the Torah commandments. The Orthodox accused Zionism of hubris and viewed Zionists as heretics and sinners who presumed to usher in the messianic era on their own terms, without waiting for God. Although some Orthodox did come aboard late in the development of the modern nationalist movement, they did so only after stripping Zionism of religious significance and making a clear distinction between nationalist political affairs and divine, halakhic affairs. At most, they accorded Zionism a very narrow religious significance; it certainly was not messianic. The ultra-Orthodox, perceived by themselves and by other Jews to be the steadfast faithful of religious tradition, became the sworn enemies of Zionism. They segregated themselves from the secular Jews of Israel, boycotted participation in the institutions of the collective, and even sabotaged nationalist projects. Against this backdrop Kook was indeed a daring figure. One can perhaps understand why the haredim hated him, even though he was very close to them in his way of life.

The religious radicalism of Rabbi Kook, and the fulcrum of his public involvement, was located precisely in his quest to reverse the Orthodox attitude toward Zionism and the Zionists. His form of religious nationalism was based on the belief that God was leading Jews, the secular no less than the religious, to return to the Holy Land. "The spirit that beats today in the people of Israel is suffused with the holy dew, and the movement for return to Zion is motivated by a divine yearning," he wrote. "In the depths of its soul, the nation wishes to return to the faith, but the will to return is yet concealed in the innermost reaches of its soul." Kook believed that the return to Israel was the first step in the reconversion of the Jewish people. As chief rabbi of Palestine in the prestate era, he sanctified Jewish migration to Palestine with the doctrine that "return to the land carries the light of full return to the faith." "This is an internal return, but it is covered with many separating masks," he wrote. "In the final analysis, however, the holy will be revealed even from within the profane, and even from within the frenzied freedom the beloved burden will be taken on."[11]

Kook thus developed a unique nationalist theology within which the special status of Jewish identity was emphatically reaffirmed. Among gentiles, he taught, nationalism stems from a material and cultural aspiration, "while for Israel, the nationalist spirit is the divine quality that exists in the nature of their souls." The national feeling of Israel "is in and of itself holy and lofty," despite the fact that some of the Jews possessed of that feeling are, religiously speaking, "impure." Nonetheless, "Israel will never become completely impure." The impurity of the nonobservant Jews "can act on the nation, it can blemish it, but it can never sever it completely from the source of the living God."

Central to this Kookist doctrine was the notion that secular Jews, however confused and uncertain they might be about their true place in the divine plan, are nonetheless an essential part of that plan. They are, so to speak, unknowing agents of God:

> Many adherents of the newly awakened nationalist revival claim that they have no need of the divine spirit. But what they really want, they themselves do not know. The revival of Israel is so closely linked to the spirit of God, that the divine spirit resides even in those who claim they want only the revival of Israel, despite themselves. The individual can cut himself off from the source of life, but the House of Israel as a whole cannot, and therefore the divine spirit exists in everything that is cherished from a national point of view, such as land, language, customs. . . . Thus when the national idea takes root in the heart of the people, it will bear with it the noble goal and the children of Israel will again seek the Lord their God.[12]

Another key element in the Kookist vision was the conviction that Israel's chosen status among nations is betokened and even guaranteed by its true inner character as an Orthodox Jewish nation. "It is a grave error to be insensitive to the distinctive unity of the Jewish spirit, to imagine that the Divine stuff which uniquely characterizes Israel is comparable to the spiritual content of all the other national civilizations," Kook warned. "This error is the source of the attempt to sever the national from the religious element of Judaism. Such a division would falsify both our nationalism and our religion, for every element of thought, emotion, and idealism that is present in the Jewish people belongs to an indivisible entity, and all together make up its specific character."[13]

Because the divine character of the nation depends ultimately on God, not man, the unfolding of Jewish history in the messianic era carries a certain inevitability, Kook proclaimed:

> The spirit of God can be buried under heaps of filth, wantonness, and corruption of customs, hidden under mounds of false knowledge whose content is wicked and leads the imagination astray, but the divine impression will not be obliterated from the essence of the nation. . . . Eretz Israel is part of the very essence of our nationhood; it is bound organically to its very life and inner being. Human reason, even at its most sublime, cannot begin to understand the unique holiness of Eretz Israel; it cannot stir the depths of love for the land that are dormant within our people. What Eretz Israel means to the Jew can be felt only through the Spirit of the Lord which is in our people as a whole, through the spiritual cast of the Jewish soul, which radiates its characteristic influence to every healthy emotion. This higher light shines forth to the degree that the spirit of divine holiness fills the hearts of the saints and scholars of Israel with heavenly life and bliss.

For Kook, Eretz Yisrael was not merely a tool for establishing national unity—or even for sustaining religion in the Diaspora. Such worthy but penultimate goals followed from the true identity of Eretz Yisrael as a spiritual force capable of opposing the cosmic powers of darkness:

> The merit of the holiness of the Land—when the nation maintains its courageous link with it—has the power to reverse evil and to raise it to the highest vaults of holiness. And the divine quality of the nation can be revealed and shine in the world only when the nation will gather in its land, united in spirit.
>
> Secular nationalism in Israel does not yet recognize its roots or its mission: Its eyes are on the land, and it does not yet lift its gaze to the heavens. It pursues courage and bravery, but is truly all holiness and divinity. *Indeed, the sparks of holiness are released by the practical work in Eretz Israel.* . . .
>
> In these days of the threshold of the coming of the Messiah, the soul of the criminals of Israel—those who connect with love to the House of Israel and the Land of Israel and the revival of the nation—is more whole than the soul of those who observe Torah and the commandments, but who do not work on behalf of the People and the Land.[14]

Kook's revolutionary attitude toward Zionism developed in the context of his broad mystical-messianic approach, which can be termed a theology of the profane. This theology is an ambitious attempt, from a religious perspective, to grapple with the challenge of modern Western secularity, which had permeated Judaism, carrying off many of the best and the brightest. Kook did not deny the contemporary world, but rather recognized and took an interest in it, affirming and glorifying it. This was an effort to rescue religion from crisis and to return to it its previous supremacy; by sanctifying the profane environment, religion could appropriate a tempting and threatening rival. Thus Kook wished to incorporate everything into religion, to apply the sacred to all existence. Kook declared that the ancient must be modernized and the modern sacralized. This sacralization of being, especially the Judaization of Zionism, he saw as a step toward redeeming the entire cosmos. His proposed revolution by way of the profane was not an escape from religion but a way to revive it.

Kook fought the profane only insofar as it conceived of itself as original and autonomous and aspired to hegemony. That is, he did not negate the profane but only its pretension to sovereignty, its view of itself as having an independent raison d'être, and its claim to explain and regulate religion. Neither did Kook confront Zionism per se, but only the prevalent view that "Zionism has nothing to do with religion." According to Kook, the profane in the world is but a derivation and manifestation of the sacred—hidden, strange, and cunning though it may be. The profane conceals the germ of the sacred. Profanity fills a mystical and messianic function in Kookist thought, and secular Zionism is seen to be truly a religious movement fulfilling a holy mission.

Kook found positive qualities in many phenomena of the world: philosophy, science, art, movements for social justice and human rights. Nor could he dismiss the effort of secular Jews to attain security and independence for the Jewish people in its land. All that is good and beautiful in the world Kook tried to restore to the Jewish religion by claiming that everything has its origin in Judaism. Reality is Jewish in its innermost being, fulfills a Jewish calling, and will reveal its Judaism after having fulfilled its mission. The task at hand for Kook's followers, then, was to expose the religious Jewish nature of things in order to return things to their place, to themselves. This is the revival of religion and the redemption of the world. Evil, then, means viewing things as authentically separate from and external to the total unity. The profane awareness of independence is an illusion, for the harmonious whole in which everything is contained is the sacred. The movement of the world reveals the tendency of everything to return home. History by definition, and modern Jewish national history in particular, is a movement toward repentance and redemption. The profane emanates from religion and yearns to return to it, to realize itself and to complete its mission. This is even true of cases that appear to oppose religion and insist that they are areligious or antireligious. Accordingly, heresy has both truth and value; and the heresy of Jewish nationalism is actually part of the search for God. Furthermore, Zionists who take pride in an exemplary secularist ideology are more noble than those whose secularity is casual. The pioneers who were dedicated to revival of the nation and the land, even though they rejected the Torah and desecrated its commandments, were "righteous despite themselves." Kook's followers often cite this quote and find in it inspiration for radical behavior.

According to Kook's somewhat pantheistic approach, the sacred is dispersed throughout the world, but there is an especially high degree of religiosity in Israel, and the Jewish nation is the most sacred reality, the very incarnation of the sacred. The difference between Israel and other nations is not quantitative but qualitative. Israel is the axis of the harmonious totality from which everything emanates and to which it returns, "a heavenly creature carrying the seal of God on its forehead." Its holiness is a *segula*—an essential attribute that cannot be denied or changed. No false consciousness or effort can dislodge Israel from its basic nature. Hence a Zionism confident and proud of its secularity will ultimately admit the truth of its religiosity and understand that it was placed upon earth in secular garb to fulfill a vital sacred purpose. At this moment in history only that which appears profane can fulfill the mission because religion is itself limited and partial—here Hegel's concept of the "cunning of history" comes to mind. While religion currently sets itself apart from the Zionist enterprise, the latter has the obligation and even the privilege of redeeming the people and the land. When this secret religious mission is complete, Jewish nationalism will return to an open and conscious religiosity. Then religion will also begin to see the light and will embrace nationalism.

Actually, Kook's mystical-messianic move was dialectical—a synthesis of opposites whose outcome is greater than the sum of its parts. The objective is a meeting of the spiritual with the material, of current religion with current nationalism. When they fuse, the longed-for total harmony will be created. According to Kook, this redemptive synthesis is taking place before our very eyes. The secular Zionists should be joined and applauded; that they are violating halakhic norms should not deter. On the contrary, this intimates that the final messianic stage is about to begin. After all, tradition relates that the dawn of redemption will coincide with the height of profligacy among people and impertinence toward God.

The rehabilitation and glorification of sinners and apostates stems from a mystical view that seeks to penetrate their interior and from a sense of messianic presence that fills one with absolute certainty. But for Kook himself—and for his Gush Emunim heirs—it was hard to bear the obligations of this theology. Applying the implications of the Kook school of mystical messianism—sanctifying that which appears grossly opposed to religion—is an almost impossible task; hence, there was vacillation about the contemporary world and ambivalence toward Jewish nationalism in the land of Israel. This had dramatic manifestations. Kook was the last great original Jewish thinker who aspired to create a spiritual authority for Judaism that would bridge the division between believers and nonbelievers, yet it was during his time that the schism between the two camps widened and was perpetuated. His desire to bring together the religious and the secular under the canopy of his mystical messianism did not succeed. The two groups remained alienated from each other and hostile or apathetic to Kook and his system. They shared only a refusal to acknowledge his authority. The religious rejected Kook blatantly, founded their own rabbinic institutions, and declared that only these were authentic and legitimate. The secular Jews flirted with him but never carried on a real dialogue: all contacts remained superficial and subject to misinterpretation.

Behind the reservations of the secular Jews was a discomfort with the fact that Kook was not interested in a relationship based on equality, mutuality, and compromise but wished to bring nationalism more in line with religion. Indeed, it is doubtful that Kook really understood or respected secularity per se. Rather than accept the pioneers' self-definition, he forced an alternative definition on them out of his belief that he knew them better than they knew themselves. Perhaps it was not the Sabbath-desecrating pioneers that the rabbi loved and wanted to bring nearer, but the holy spark that he attributed to them against their will. In the final analysis, the secular had no desire to be part of an expanded religion, while the religious did not respond to Kook's call to expand religion. Thus Kook remained isolated.

The failure of Abraham Kook to realize his dream of uniting the religious and the secular Jews doomed the institution of the chief rabbinate, which he had founded. The chief rabbinate was intended to be the supreme spiritual authority for all segments of Israel. In reality, those faithful to tradition openly rejected its authority while the nonreligious accepted it for instrumental and shallow ritualistic purposes only. In fact, Kook failed in all his enterprises. The religious movement that he tried to create—Degel Yerushalayim—never got off the ground, while the original pretensions of the yeshiva that he founded were not realized during his lifetime. This was the Yeshiva HaMerkazit Ha'Olamit, which eventually came to be known as the Merkaz HaRav Yeshiva. Under Kook's stewardship, and for one or two generations following, the situation of the yeshiva was dismal: it had few students, second-rate scholarship, scarce resources, and little prestige. Even there, Kook's writings did not gain stature, and outside the yeshiva they were virtually unknown. Indeed, very few of his writings were printed and disseminated in his time.

Outside a small circle of admirers, Kook never held halakhic or general spiritual authority. Only after his death was he discovered and awarded glory. In the Israel of the 1960s, Kook became a cultural hero and, among religious Zionists, an idolized spiritual guide. This happened after Gush Emunim claimed him, posthumously, as their forefather and founder, and devoted themselves to carrying out his legacy. The late rabbi then became the axis of the Kookist spirit and supplier of the Kookist doctrine. The movement turned him into a saint. Mythologizing the man and his work, Gush Emunim sought to monopolize his spiritual heritage and control its interpretation. All hard-core Gush activists know Kook's anthology of quotes by heart.

THE SON

The mantle of Rabbi Abraham Kook was inherited by his only son, Rabbi Zvi Yehuda Kook (1891–1982). The son did not win respect and influence in his father's lifetime; nor did he head the yeshiva founded by and named for his father, even after his father died, until the terms of several other rabbis had ended. For many years Zvi Yehuda Kook was a marginal figure in a marginal institution. The secular had never heard of him; rabbinic authorities disdained him; the ultra-Orthodox and most of the neo-Orthodox saw him as a curiosity. He was not known as a public figure, and he met none of the traditional criteria for rabbinic excellence: he was not a Gemara scholar, issued no halakhic rulings, and composed no original system of organized religious thought. The only writings he left behind were freewheeling sermons—deemed substantially inferior to his father's works even by the elder Kook's worst detractors—that combined Aggadah and ethics with quotes from his father and comments on current political affairs. These were edited by his students and originally appeared in newspapers or were passed around as leaflets. The posthumous legacy of Kook the son is contained almost entirely in two anthologies of such sermons.[15]

Despite all this, Kook in his later years became an influential figure. Senior politicians took an interest in and respected his opinions, a broad nationalist public avidly imbibed his instructions, and the militant Gush Emunim movement turned him into a guru. Since his death, the distinction between father and son has become increasingly blurred, and they have tended to fuse into one great authority. For a while, the two occupied the supreme throne side by side, with a certain division of labor between them: the spirit of the father, with his deep, wide-ranging philosophy, was translated and popularized through the focused and decisive presence of the son.

Kookists tried to dismiss the differences between father and son or to explain the son's position as an extension of and complement to that of the father. They emphasized the strong affinity between the two: a consistent doctrine, identical values, personal closeness—even a supernatural spiritual connection that continued as the dead father was revealed to his son in dreams. An important similarity in their religious outlooks—both assumed a position that was simultaneously ultratraditionalist and ultrarevolutionary—became one of the distinguishing features of Kookism. On the one hand, they held a tough, defensive, if not reactionary attitude about adherence to the halakha; on the other hand, their approach was so daring and innovative that it threatened to transgress the boundaries of traditional rabbinic Diaspora Judaism's teachings concerning messianism and hence Zionist politics.

Kook the son cultivated the association with his father and used it effectively. His charisma was to a great extent inherited; he exploited every opportunity to mention his father, alluded to the intimacy between them, and quoted the father incessantly. In fact the son's oral and written words were largely compilations and paraphrases of his father's. Zvi Yehuda Kook's interpretation of his father's legacy was comparatively elementary, as well as selective; some aspects of Abraham Kook's teachings were emphasized and others not mentioned at all—portions of the father's writings, the son ensured, would never see the light of day. Rhetorical and didactic talent and the halo effect ensured that the son's interpretation would be the one to endure. He was particularly artful when explaining current affairs in terms of his father's philosophy, thereby giving it vitality, albeit at the price of superficiality and bias.

In collaboration with Gush Emunim, the son claimed the role of his father's authoritative interpreter. A systematic and violent campaign to discredit dissenters and rivals ensued, abetted by the son's control over his father's manuscripts. Legal possession gave him moral validity and a capacity for manipulation; he could conceal documents or monitor their release for publication. Doctored excerpts appeared, with summary comments or connecting sentences added but not acknowledged as additions. From the end of the 1960s and throughout the 1970s, the son had almost no raison d'être apart from his connection with the father, at least in Kookist circles, and the father never appeared except in the version processed and presented by the son. Indeed, several faithful members of Gush Emunim who had been admirers of the father and experts in his teachings were regarded with suspicion and even harassed for analyzing his texts directly, thereby circumventing the son's lessons and writings. The unmediated interpretation of the father's teachings—especially those relating to nationalist-religious matters with political implications—was considered particularly grave. It is, therefore, no coincidence that from a plethora of the father's writing, the son chose to collect and publish a group of articles that distilled Judaism to Zionism by means of messianism. This book, entitled *Orot* (Lights), has been by far the most widely read of Kook's writings and the most decisive in determining his practical influence.[16] It became the "red book" of the Gush Emunim cadres, carried everywhere and read at every opportunity, especially during breaks in operational activity. Among many Kookists, this book is identified with its editor, the son, no less than its writer, the father.

The aspiration of Kook the son to personify the legacy of his father did not, however, conceal the differences between them. These were pronounced, manifested in temperament, style of expression and behavior, and even handwriting. The father's hand was round and soft; the son's was compressed, sharp, and aggressive. The lyrical romantic impulse of the father was replaced in the son by defiance and a preoccupation with power. The aspiration to unite or be swallowed up turned into instinctive rejection and an obsession with conquest. Besides being simplified and categorized, the teachings of the father underwent fundamental changes of content and method that can be summarized as qualification and contraction of the mystical-messianic quality of the system.

First, the son introduced a shift of emphasis inward. As noted before, Abraham Kook wished to incorporate into Judaism all the human treasures that fascinated him, especially modern secular Jewish nationalism, whose drive he envied and achievements he admired. He brought this into the realm of religious Judaism by revealing the Jewish essence ostensibly hidden there. Out of a belief in the Jewish religious nature of the entire universe, the father derived his avid interest in the apparently nonreligious world around him. The son adopted this same faith but stood it on its head, reversing the original implications: If everything is actually Jewish at root, then Judaism is everything; that is, the unified totality in the universe is sacred. One can therefore turn inward and go directly to the place where this sacredness is concentrated, dismissing the periphery—all that is not Jewish—and rejecting the notions of inclusiveness, affinity, and harmony so dear to the father. Hence the centrifugal nature of the father's teachings becomes centripetal in the son's, and everything shrinks to a closed, haughty, and antagonistic point. Kookists seek unending riches within the four walls of religious Judaism.

Second, Zvi Yehuda Kook shifted the emphasis of the teachings from the general and universal—the great diversity of human civilization—to the particularism of narrow Jewish nationalism. This revised theology of the profane implies the narrowing of the realm of the sacred. While the father sanctified all the manifold elements in the universe, the son sanctified one specific field—that of Jewish nationalism. The son's exclusive focus on an isolated fragment of the profane, ignoring the other large expanses, necessarily reduces the sacred to something partial. Everything not conventionally considered Jewish or religious remains outside the realm of relevance or legitimacy, including the treasures of secular culture, both international and Israeli. Only Jewish secular nationalism is charged with the sacred, and thus it becomes the whole world.

In essence, these transformations concentrate all religious energy into two spheres: religious Judaism of the old type and the new Israeli Judaism. In place of the all-embracing unity a strange coupling emerges: an emphasized Orthodoxy summed up by Torah and commandments and, at its side, an emphasized nationalism suffused with messianism. Two parallel avenues evolve for religious self-realization: the traditional option, which resembles haredi (ultra-Orthodox) Judaism, and the revolutionary option, which appears Zionist. Between the two, of course, there is great tension.

There is also a third transformation in the son's teachings, a dismantling of the synthesis between the mystical and the messianic that had characterized the father's teachings. Under the son, the mystical is greatly diminished, leaving the messianic virtually alone and dominant, though less complex and refined. For the father, there had been an inherent affinity between the mystical and the messianic: redemption was identified as the return of things to their true nature, to total harmony, to God. This cosmic dynamic could be traced by a probing of the interior of things. In the absence of special sensitivity to the mysterious dimension of the world, things are grasped simply as they appear and redemption is identified with a concrete reality. The sense of messianic urgency is no less intense, but it searches for conspicuous and unequivocal objects. From the moment the key to unraveling our precise location in the continuum of messianic progress is no longer symbolic and secret, but forces itself upon us, it is impossible to find positive value in the contents of secular culture such as literature and art. At that point the messianic interest gravitates toward politics and is firmly focused on various aspects of the state. Because the signs of redemption are expected to be interwoven in a simple historical reality, messianic fervor turns into an obsessive search for parallels between verses from the sacred texts and specific manifestations in real life. Hence the emphasis on the practical components of the land of Israel—economy building, a police force, and so on—in the vision of redemption.

This politicization of the father's mystical-messianic vision found its natural expression in the elevation of the conquest of territories to the status of authorized and accurate index to the unfolding messianic plan of redemption. The concretization of messianic signs in turn brought about a fundamental change in the contents of redemption. The search, conducted by Kookist enthusiasts, for correlations between ancient verses and contemporary events led the true believers, ironically, to nontraditional conclusions. In the new reality of the modern Jewish state, it was hard to find evidence to support the classical notion of redemption, identified with ideals of the traditional faith and ethics. The milieu in which the Kookists were struggling in the 1970s was characterized by a marked drop in Orthodox standards of Torah study and adherence to commandments. This same milieu, however, fostered nationalist values that have from time immemorial been considered part of the messianic future, although in practice virtually nothing had ever been done to realize them. The emphasis thus was shifting from values traditional Judaism practiced rigorously to values to which it paid ritual obeisance but never really took seriously.

Kookism sacralized Zionist reality, strong in its agricultural achievements and weak with regard to the status of the rabbinate and prevalence of a halakhic way of life. This in effect, said Zvi Yehuda Kook, is the reality of redemption; after all, "the Bible and the Talmud speak of planting trees in the holy land and not the establishment of yeshivas."[17] The antinomian potential of such an attitude is obvious. This revolution could have been derived, on principle, from the philosophy of Abraham Kook; with his son it is sharper and more central.

In the unified religious system of the Kooks, then, the traditional relation of redemption to repentance, and of the future to the present, is completely reversed, a shift that entails a basic change of values. In the rabbinic tradition, which opens with the ancient sages and continues through to contemporary Orthodox authorities, redemption is usually dependent upon repentance. It is incumbent upon the people of Israel to improve themselves with respect to relations with others and relations with God, as a result of which personal redemption and the redemption of the world are ensured. Among the Kookists, however, redemption will be fulfilled first and repentance before God will follow. According to an influential Kookist view, repentance takes place within redemption, and because redemption is already at its peak, repentance has also naturally begun and will soon be visible.

Neo-Orthodox and especially ultra-Orthodox critics of the rabbis Kook were incensed and outraged at this innovation: such an approach, they claimed, would destroy all motivation for religious improvement and moral betterment, legitimizing the continuation of an ethically disastrous situation. To this argument, Kook the son responded more explicitly and radically than his father: A sovereign Jewish state *is* redemption; the ancient heritage does not promise that the righteous will rule in this commonwealth. Thus, the vision of redemption gradually took on a character that was more and more concerned with nationalism and statism.

For Zvi Yehuda Kook, the politicization of redemption reached the point of a one-to-one correspondence between messianic elements and details in the current state reality. Abraham Kook lived and wrote in circumstances completely different from those facing his son. The father could speak of the ideal state of Israel and project a hypothetical future; the son faced the more daunting challenge of accounting for the concrete reality of Israel. Indeed, this was the reality to which he referred in setting the ideal. In one of the three most important articles published by Kook the son, "The State as Realization of the Vision of Redemption," he declared that the state, as is, meets the criteria set by the biblical prophets.[18] Even though the state is patently profane, it is sacred.

The father had asserted that the state is the foundation of the reign of God in the world, but he may have entertained the hope of a future return to religion; the son did not have this luxury. Nevertheless, without denying reality, he took his father's conclusion a step further. The secular state became the arena in which true Judaism was realized. The symbols of Zionist nationalism and sovereignty, such as the flag and the anthem, took on supreme religious value, became media for the worship of God. In his yeshiva, Kook the son established the celebration of Independence Day as a key religious event, at the center of which was a sermon he preached. This innovation became the trademark of Kookism: classifying Independence Day as a religious holiday distinguished the rabbi and his pupils from secular Zionism, from anti-Zionist haredism, and even from those religious nationalists who did not go so far as to endow the state with the highest messianic import.

Jewish sovereignty, valued as both the fulfillment of a commandment and the proof of redemption, became a tenet in the messianic system of the younger Kook. Jewish sovereignty is revealed in the Israeli concept of *mamlakhtiut*—Zionist-style statism—which for Kookists is the current embodiment of the biblical kingdom; as befits a kingdom, the state must flaunt Jewish authority over the people and Jewish supremacy over other nations. Fundamental religious importance is also ascribed to national pride and the ceremonies that cultivate it. Kookist culture relates that Kook the son never humbled himself before Orthodox rabbis or honored them even by rising from his chair; yet he received generals and Israeli cabinet members—even the pork eaters and skirt chasers among them—with dances performed by his pupils and the song "Lift up your heads, oh gates, that the king of glory may enter," part of the ceremony for welcoming a Torah scroll into a synagogue.

Kook the son over time shifted the focus of his teaching toward power politics and a statist hawkishness quite similar to positions taken by Israeli ultranationalists. Some ascribe this shift to his closeness to the prestate underground and the right-wing parties or to his having been shunned by the ruling political establishment. But this establishment, despite its secularity and its shortcomings, remained the subject of religious awe for the followers of Kook.

If the elder Kook's central theme was the religionization and messianization of nationalism, his son's emphasis was on the nationalization of religious messianism. As a result, the father's loving wish to embrace the world was displaced by a series of burning hatreds felt by the son, who was not satisfied with emphasizing the qualitative difference between Israel and the other nations but insisted on the other nations' contemptible inferiority. Zvi Yehuda Kook transformed the verse "Lo, a people dwelling alone, and not reckoning itself among the nations" from descriptive to prescriptive.[19] He was particularly incensed at attempts by the gentile world to meddle in Israel's affairs and influence it morally and politically. Kook took an interest in the official policy of the state and was especially sensitive to its sources: if the motivation of the policy makers emerged from purely Israeli concerns, and hence could be regarded as indigenous and authentically Jewish, then it sanctified God's name; if it was tainted in the slightest way by foreign interference, no matter how subtle, then it profaned God's name.

In this spirit, Kook the son launched an assault on all public manifestations in Israel that were not of purely Jewish origin. He focused criticism on the judicial system—based on the Ottoman and British legal heritage—and on the elementary school system and universities in which the literature and philosophy "of Christians" are taught. Kook was one of the few Israelis—religious or secular—who dared to express publicly a hostility toward Christianity. In his opinion, Christianity was a greater enemy of Israel than Islam. It is with Christianity that a tough account must be settled, after Israel frees itself from the more pressing but less significant rivalry with its Arab neighbors. Although an ultimate confrontation with the church on both theological and historical planes was postponed, Kook channeled the activist energies of his followers, even before the subject of the land of Israel arose, into violent actions against missionary institutions in Jerusalem and against Israeli Jews who enjoyed concerts of Christian music.

One expression of the younger Kook's messianic chauvinism was his placement of militarism and war high on the scale of political and religious values. The Israeli army embodied for him what is morally and spiritually noble in Judaism. After establishment of the state, Kook the son was asked by yeshiva students whether it was permitted to watch the military parade on Independence Day. The haredim had absolutely forbidden this: the Israeli army, they asserted, reflects the secular Zionist chutzpah that forcefully interfered in a messianic process without any concomitant moral and religious improvement, violates halakhic norms by failing to rest on the Sabbath or to separate the genders, and, worst of all, expresses the hubris of faith in the deeds of man and material power, rather than trusting only to spirit and God. Yet Kook's answer was unequivocal: not only may one watch the parade, but watching it is a religious duty, because the army is sacred. Soldiers are just as righteous as scholars of the Torah, and weapons—even those manufactured by gentiles—are as sacred as a prayer shawl *(tallit)* and phylacteries *(tefillin)*.[20]

Redemption, then, becomes a function of politics, and politics not just a means but a good unto itself. Abraham Kook spoke about entering world politics under duress; Zvi Yehuda Kook spoke enthusiastically of involvement in politics. Their different attitudes toward politics took on special meaning considering the different political realities in which they lived: the father worked in the absence of Jewish sovereignty; for the son, this sovereignty was a given. Thus it is hardly surprising that the son's application of his father's words to the current situation sometimes seemed anachronistic. Note, for example, the different contexts in which the Kooks sanctified those Jews who desecrated the Sabbath and violated the laws of kashruth. The secular Jews in Palestine in the first decades of the century were not like those of recent generations. The former were devout and active Zionists, idealists with authentic culture and high moral standards, who sacrificed on behalf of the national collective. Their secularity was a conscious choice, an expression of an original and courageous position. The secular Jews of the son's generation, on the other hand, held a casual, mechanical, and purely formal brand of Judaism. They lacked ideological tension and were selfish and materialistic, indifferent to the needs of their people and country. The world around Israel was also different: the son lived in an era of constant bloodshed with the Palestinians and the Arab states; the father seems not to have been keenly troubled by or even fully aware of the existence or potential for what was called in Zionist jargon "the Arab problem."

Abraham Kook was by nature optimistic, the era in which he worked characterized by Woodrow Wilson's Fourteen Points and the Balfour Declaration; his messianism was a reflection of the zeitgeist. The era of Zvi Yehuda Kook, by contrast, was burdened by the disappointments and grief of the Holocaust, cruel wars with the Arabs, and moral decline; his messianism was, understandably, more pessimistic, as was his political outlook. Yet the optimistic teachings of the father were successfully absorbed and implemented in the disillusioned period of the son. For the son, much more than for the father, there is a special kind of politics, Zionist politics, that is of itself messianic. Modern Jewish national politics has a priori religious value; it is sacred even if its objectives and achievements do not appear to advance religious interests. Since Israeli politics is sacred, the deeper one enters it, the higher the pinnacles of the sacred that one can attain. Thus preached Kook the son to his disciples, even though he evinced political naiveté. In his later years, Kook identified redemptive Israeli politics with a particular political line: vehement opposition to withdrawal from any territories of the greater land of Israel. Settlement and annexation of the territories he equated with truth, justice, and religious fulfillment.

Before publishing the charter of the Land of Israel Movement, immediately after the Six Day War of 1967, its initiators, many of whom were close to Kook the son, asked him to add his signature to the list of founders, but he refused. Kookists most often explain this refusal with the argument that the greater land of Israel was still not in the hands of the state of Israel; were Kook to sanctify the borders of the most recent conquest, his signature could have been construed as relinquishing claim to territories on the eastern bank of the Jordan River, which are included in the promised biblical borders. Another version holds that, at this early stage, the connection between the conquered territories and redemption had not yet been fully drawn by Kook and was not of paramount interest to him.

Despite the official Kookist argument, the authenticity and indispensability of the "greater land" motif in Kookist consciousness is not at all self-evident. It is unclear whether the biblical towns that became Palestinian cities were originally at the center of the system developed by Kook and his disciples.

Shortly before the Six Day War, on the nineteenth Independence Day of the state of Israel, Kook was giving a sermon in the yeshiva when he suddenly interrupted himself with a sobbing scream, enunciated as both a rhetorical question and a jeremiad: "Where is our Hebron, Shechem, Jericho, and Anathoth [historical sites sacred to Judaism], torn from the state in 1948 as we lay maimed and bleeding?" This outcry did not merge organically with his sermon, nor did it fit any context familiar to the body of disciples. The words were surprising and obscure. A few of those present attributed the strange reference to the land of Israel to the rabbi's sympathy for right-wing, revisionist (Herut) circles, whose rhetorical repertoire included ritual mention of the greater land.

In retrospect, it is also possible to see this expression of affinity for the land of Israel as a ritual repetition of another important element in the spiritual legacy of Abraham Kook. The elder Kook, from the time of his immigration to Palestine during the period of the Yishuv, had emphasized settlement of the land, not just to fulfill the commandment in the Torah and not just because it made possible the fulfillment of other important commandments that had been forgotten in two thousand years of exile, but primarily because of the land's inherent sacredness. Kook the father thereby iterated an ancient concept that ascribed to the land a mystical-messianic dimension that imbues its soil and air with a miraculous effect; yet he did not refer to a particular geopolitical area or to any specific aspect. Even the physical dimension of the land that aroused such fervor in him was grasped as an abstract value; Zionist agriculture and construction were infused with sparks of holiness in the best tradition of kabbala. The father had no interest in a formal or concrete definition of the land, and hence did not address national or international implications of the issue of borders. By contrast the son focused on the size and integrity of the land, and to the religious importance of the land of Israel, he attached a clear strategic criterion: territorial completeness is a reflection of and a factor in the completeness of Judaism. Thus, each grain of earth has supreme value, and conquest or defense of any square kilometer is worship of God.

Three weeks after that sermon, the Six Day War broke out. The land was conquered and the ancient cities whose names the rabbi had cried out were transformed from a dream to an immediate reality. The Kookists then declared the Independence Day sermon to have been a prophecy and exploited every opportunity to glorify Kook as possessing both historical perspicacity and metaphysical sensitivity. Further, they portrayed the sermon as proof that an interest in the greater land of Israel had played a key role in the thought of both Kooks, in the pre-1967 period. As one might expect, this sermon—"The Nineteenth Psalm to the State of Israel"—was recognized as a cornerstone of Gush Emunim and subsequently attained mythological proportions. The sermon is known by heart to every Kookist, and the original tape became a ritual accessory at every religious Zionist ceremony.[21] Seven years passed after the 1967 war, however, before Kook was popularly recognized as the champion of the greater land of Israel. When the possibility of withdrawal from conquered territories first publicly arose in 1974–1975, he issued the authoritative call "Be killed rather than transgress." This is the most far-reaching rabbinic injunction, reserved in the halakha for the most extreme cases: incest, idol worship, and murder. Yet this became the war cry for the radical settlers of Gush Emunim, led by Rabbi Kook, during their struggle with the government.

Zvi Yehuda Kook based his extreme views about territory on the Torah and an imposing dynasty of rabbis, from the Nachmanides to his own father, and could quote experts on foreign affairs and security; nonetheless, a tone of artificiality crept into his references to the subject. His own lack of familiarity with the actual land—its sights, smells, and details, the inhabitants and their lives—was evident on the rare occasions that he left his house or the yeshiva. Some of his close disciples claimed that his opposition to withdrawal stemmed not from a love of the land and the sanctification of its wholeness, but from the belief that withdrawal would mean succumbing to outside pressure, a violation of Jewish sovereignty—a subject dear to the rabbi's heart. As for Kook's obsession with the precise location of the borders, this was largely the influence of those surrounding him, who, although they admired him as saintly, actively manipulated him and decided his public positions.

After the war of 1973, Kook aged rapidly and became sickly and exhausted. Because of a disability in his legs, he was confined to his room and left it only rarely—actually borne aloft—to visit yeshivas and settlements. A speech disability caused him to stutter and lisp, making it hard to figure out what he was saying. These limitations on his mobility and communication were most severe in the period that Gush Emunim was at its height. In circumstances where his ability to judge and cope with reality was dubious, he appeared particularly authoritative and categorical; a wide periphery of admirers obeyed his pronouncements to the letter.

A number of would-be usurpers of Kook's charismatic authority appeared in the growing gap between the rabbi and the outside world, where they began to mediate between the rabbi and his disciples and the Israeli environment in general. A few gradually gained strategic positions, monopolizing access to the rabbi, supplying him with information and counseling him, and publicizing and interpreting his conclusions. But although Kook, in the final and most significant decade of his life, was less autonomous and responsible for his decisions, his facade of authority remained: deliberations were generally carried out in his presence, an effort was made to win his blessing for the decisions, even if retroactively, and the "great calls" that issued from his home as handwritten notes set the agenda of religious Zionism in general and radical settler activism in particular. Even the fragments of quotes from the acknowledged interpreters were the basis for Gush Emunim goal setting and calls to action.

Even those who opposed Kook found it hard to ignore his charisma. His influence stemmed not merely from association with his father, but also from his personal qualities. He excelled as a pedagogue and was charming in intimate gatherings. A modesty that reflected a life of absti-

nence also contributed to his aura. Kook had almost no physical or material life, and his dedication to the Torah and the nation was absolute.
But although he was completely alienated from the daily life of modern
Israelis, he did not refrain from voicing outspoken opinions on social and
political issues. Here he was known for his stubbornness.

At the end of his life, in his eighties and nineties, Kook the son was
the focus of Kookist culture; according to the Kookists themselves, he was
the center of the cosmos—an *axis mundi*. The believers and the cadres
surrounded him; they had a clear interest in inflating the status of the
rabbi beyond all proportion, as their own power and prestige derived
from their proximity to him. In the last two decades of his life, Kook
underwent a process that might be called "admorization";[22] he was
turned into a religious leader in the style of a Hasidic rebbe with absolute
magical powers. An inalienable part of the dynamics of this form of leadership are the intrigues of the court and the rituals of the community
focused on the rabbi.

Other characteristics of the Hasidic authority marked the leadership
of Kook late in his life: He was considered a mediator between heaven
and earth, between simple believers and their God. Religious realization
could be achieved through him. He was not just a channel, but a recepta-
cle that itself contained holiness. Therefore he was credited with all sorts
of miraculous qualities, such as the ability to see the future. At the same
time, he allegedly excelled in human qualities, such as empathy for those
in distress. The very fact of being in his presence, studying his appearance,
and imitating his way of life—these "observances" were imbued with the
quality of worship. An important role was assigned not just to his teachings, but also to his personality and behavior, which also became tenets
of faith. Moreover, contrary to what was acceptable in rabbinic religious
Judaism, especially among the Lithuanians, religious authority for Rabbi
Kook was not Torah-based, but spiritual. He was judged not according
to his command of the Gemara and his ability to make halakhic rulings
but according to his inspiration. Application of his religious authority
was not confined by halakhic norms and ritual, but was particularly expressed in affairs that were traditionally considered irrelevant to Torah
and commandments: Kook was consulted about what name to give a
newborn or for which party to vote.

The words of Kook the son were gradually given the status of *da'at
Torah,* literally "Torah wisdom." This concept had once been understood
according to its simple Talmudic rendering: as a rabbinic ruling based
on a textual analysis of the holy sources. But with the tendency over
recent decades to increased orthodoxy, this traditional meaning has been

completely reversed and now refers to the authority of a rabbi to issue binding directives to believers without giving an account of them and without basing them on valid Talmudic evidence. Rather than being justified in terms of the rules of the Torah, the pronouncement now derives its authority from being Torah-inspired. This paradoxical phenomenon characterizes the non-Zionist ultra-Orthodox, such as those of Agudat Israel, who give full obedience to the "Torah Sages." From there, the phenomenon passed to the super-Zionist Orthodox Jews in Gush Emunim, who were completely deferential to Rabbi Kook. Needless to say, the haredi Jews were quite disturbed by this development.

The younger Kook's leadership also assumed other characteristics of charismatic haredi authority: His *da'at Torah* authority—like that exercised by the Lithuanian haredi leaders, the Hazon Ish, Rabbi Schach, and Hasidic *admors* like the Lubavitch and Satmar rabbis—was ex cathedra rather than based on sanctioned halakhic precedent. But it also sought to stimulate followers through the arousal of passionate, intense emotion rather than through persuasion and rational means. There is, moreover, no display of Talmudic dialectic in his pronouncements, but only reference to stories of the Bible and the Aggadah or lessons from the kabbala and *makhshava* [Jewish thought]. In Kook's preaching, Sophist Talmudic legalism was replaced by the pathos and didacticism of the homiletic genre.

In addition, Kook's charismatic rabbinic leadership deviated from the tradition in that it took a stand primarily with regard to public matters rather than the ritual norms of the private domain. Gradually, Kookist leaders—again, like the haredi authorities—entered extrahalakhic realms that in the past had not been subject to rabbinic decision. From time immemorial, rabbis had weighed religious-political factors in their decisions, taking into consideration the interests of religion in the circumstances of a changing dominant environment; but they always distinguished these interests from '*ikkarei hadin* (legal tenets). In the case of Kookism, decisions based on religious politics were enforced as if they were full halakhic rulings.

This double transformation, once described as the papalization of Judaism,[23] reflects an adaptation of radical religion to the trying circumstances of the modern Western, fundamentally secular world and reveals a rather typical fundamentalist predicament. In traditional society, the role of the halakha sage had been much simpler. The entire community regulated its life according to the halakha, which was taken for granted. Routine was the organizing principle for private and public existence; few questions were asked and there was little need for guidance and authoritative decisions. But when the halakha faithful become a besieged minority within a threatening and tempting world, and when circumstances change so drastically, questions proliferate. When the believer is no longer in a homogeneous, isolated community automatically following the conventions of the immediate environment, dependence on the rabbi increases. Furthermore, the believer comes to expect from the rabbi not just directives on practical matters, but also intellectual and emotional aid for the spirit, to help justify clinging to a life of halakha, despite the visible and rather attractive alternatives. From a solver of specific problems, the rabbi becomes one who inspires to stronger faith in times of distress.

The religious leadership of Kook the son thus became absolute and diffuse—free of the need to justify decisions and applicable to matters that had not previously fallen within the jurisdiction of the Torah. A division of labor thus arose between two kinds of rabbinic authority. For classic normative-ritual matters, one turned to the haredi rabbis, even though their position on matters of Zionism and messianism was unacceptable to the Kookists. And for broad matters of faith and general Israeli issues, one consulted Rabbi Kook. Thus, regarding the kashruth of a chicken or a mezuzah or a matter of the menstrual impurity of a woman, the Kookist sought out the authority of the ultra-Orthodox enclave of Mea Shearim. Meanwhile, Kook took questions such as "Should one obey the orders of the Israeli police and army when they evacuate settlers from Nablus and Jericho?" On this question two lofty religious-political values clash: the holiness of the state and the holiness of the land.

In such circumstances, Kook's authority was strengthened; indeed, it became infallible. It was thus expected that his death would provoke a crisis, organizationally and spiritually, particularly since there was no heir to the Kookist dynasty: Kook had been a widower and childless, and despite pressure from various directions had declined to name a successor. The moment of succession in religious and political systems based on charismatic leaders—such as the Kookist system—is a particularly vulnerable point. But in 1982, when Rabbi Kook died, no such crisis ensued, even though the end of the Kookist dynasty coincided with a political-religious ordeal in Gush Emunim, precipitated by its defeat in the struggle to prevent retreat from the Yamit area in the Sinai as stipulated by the peace accords with Egypt. Shortly thereafter, members of the Jewish terrorist underground were arrested after exposure of their plot to blow up the mosque on the Temple Mount in Jerusalem. The Kookists viewed the conjunction of these events as a heavenly sign.

Contrary to the expectations of observers, the Kookists, both in Merkaz HaRav and within Gush Emunim, adapted to the new situation. With the death of the rabbi, however, the distance between the yeshiva and the movement widened. No leader appeared to lead both the yeshiva and the movement, and each institution grappled with leadership problems of its own. Radical Kookism was weakened, though the believers gave no evidence of moderation. Rather, a separation between their Judaism and their Zionism, between their religion and their politics, took place in the decade after Kook's death. Both Gush Emunim and Merkaz HaRav became less messianic and much less mystical. To a degree the religious Judaism of the settlers returned to its conventional Orthodox mien, while their politics deemphasized religious and Jewish elements but clearly remained extreme, right-wing, and hawkish.

THE THIRD LEG OF THE KOOKIST TRIANGLE

The influence of the Kookist triangle—the teachings of Kook the father, the standing of Kook the son, and the Merkaz HaRav Yeshiva—moved from nadir to zenith within one generation. In the last two decades of the Yishuv and at the beginning of the first decade of the state, the teachings of the elder Kook were considered aberrant and known to very few, Kook the son was isolated and considered eccentric, and Merkaz HaRav was a small, forgotten institution powerless to compete with other yeshivas in material resources, educational achievements, or Torah authority. The beginning of the triple revolution took place shortly after the founding of the state and long before the Six Day War.

An embryonic version of Gush Emunim—the roots of the zealotry of the 1980s and 1990s—appeared in the early 1950s when about a dozen students from a religious high school staged a rebellion against their parents, their teachers, the religious Zionist establishment, and the Israeli ethos in general.[24] The incident is not generally known to the Israeli public or even to many in Kookist circles, but some twenty-five years later, when the religious-nationalist revolution was complete and Gush Emunim at its height of power, these youths, who had then been fourteen years old, had become the leading Kookist rabbis, famous in Israeli society.

Their youthful initiative emerged out of frustration with the humiliating status of religion in Israel. Reacting especially to the progressive abandonment of Orthodoxy and the lowering of Orthodox standards, the youths adhered more strictly to halakhic norms and dedicated themselves to the study of Torah in a yeshiva. The few who swam against the tide turned to excessive Orthodoxy. But while they tended somewhat toward haredi Judaism, these boys were not willing to surrender their Israeli identity or participation in the heady enterprise of building a modern, independent state. On the contrary, parallel to their increased religiosity, they sought to deepen their nationalism; they were the first to realize in practice a pioneering Zionism through Torah Judaism. They called the semiformal framework that they set up Gahelet. Literally *gahelet* means "glowing ember," which stood as a symbol of preserving the tradition; as an acronym, it stands for "core of pioneer Torah students." Their intermediary goal, on the way to realizing a larger religious national revolution, reflected the uneasy combination of Torah and pioneerism: a kibbutz, in the best tradition of heroic romantic Zionism, at the heart of which would be a yeshiva, an institution that belonged to another world entirely. In their naive dream, the boys would study Gemara day and night, and the girls would make the desert bloom and worry about livelihood and services.

Spontaneously and independently, these youth took on a harsh religious regimen, which they then tried to thrust on their families and fellow students. In addition to their commitment to religious studies, they demanded morality and asceticism. They insisted on modest dress, clean language, and separation of the genders and forbade free time, recreation, gossip, and small talk, thereby fostering a gap between themselves and other young sabras. They also set up draconian means of social control: *musar* (morality) lessons, public confessions, trials for transgressors, and even ostracism. Within two or three years, the small group had solidified and gained prominence among circles of religious Zionist youth. As requests to join them increased, they established stringent criteria for membership. They became charged with a sense of mission and left their boarding schools to spread the word in other schools and B'nai Akiva branches throughout Israel.

Gradually, the emphasis in their dual identity shifted from the pioneering to the Torah element. Breaking with convention, they first added another year of school to devote more time to study of the Torah. Later they really turned the tables when they chose to convert their *Nahal* army service—a framework that integrated frontline duty with life on a border kibbutz, the classic service of elite Israeli youth in those years—into study in an advanced yeshiva, the classic career of elite haredi youth. The leaders of the religious-nationalist establishment put many obstacles in their path and viewed this reversal of priorities as the outcome of an educational failure. The stubborn instigators now had to choose between sparse offerings; in those days, there were few yeshivas in Israel, and the vast majority were apathetic to or rejected Zionism. The three remaining yeshivas were disappointing in their low level of morality and religiosity, and after a year of study, the young men found that their Zionism was also inadequate. Their attempt to penetrate an existing yeshiva, to take control from within and to redirect it, had failed. By chance several members of Gahelet, frustrated in their search, met with Kook the son, and it appeared that they had found exactly what they were looking for. Their friends, dragged to meet him, also fell under the charm of the rabbi. It was a love at first sight that developed into a long-lasting bond. Each side discovered what it had been missing, its complement, in the other. The young people found a rabbi who supplied an organized system, the weight of tradition, rabbinic guidance, a home, and fatherly support. And the forgotten old man finally found disciples, admirers, and implementers. Meetings between them became more frequent until they decided to settle permanently in Jerusalem. They did not like the type of students who were then in the yeshiva or its general spirit, but they soon became the dominant force and reshaped it in their image. When this clicked in Merkaz HaRav, the age of Kookism dawned.[25]

The ideal formulated as a dictum notes, "Take unto yourself a rabbi." To a large extent, the youths of Gahelet not only took but made for themselves a rabbi. According to them, they uncovered a hidden just man, a genius who had not achieved the influence and glory that he was worthy of. In a fairly short time, Kook the son became a towering figure with an irresistible magnetism that could not be explained by those who had known him in the past. Only at this late stage of their unwavering path, through talks and lessons with Kook the son, did the young people first learn about the teachings of Kook the father. They immediately adopted his thought as their ideology and presented it as if it had motivated them from the very beginning of their quest. The teachings of Kook provided an original and appealing explanation for their authentic religious experience; it refined, systematized, and deepened what they had intuitively understood. The Kook teachings opened for them channels they had never before imagined, allowing them to spread their wings and soar. While the teachings increased the youths' ambition and charged them with high spiritual tension, the students revealed dimensions of the teachings that had never previously been known. The individualistic, rather esoteric theology that had previously been accessible only to virtuosos now became a potent ideology for a young and enthusiastic public. A complex mystical-messianic Torah became filled with vitality, also of the fundamentalist variety.

In the early 1960s, Merkaz HaRav spawned a second generation of students. This group embodied a distinct and crystallized Kookism, one at peace with itself. The new Kookists completed their studies and dispersed throughout Israel to spread the tidings as rabbis and educators. And then the war of June 1967 broke out. Just over ten years had passed since the Gahelet members met Kook the son and through him Kook the father, and now their moment in the sun arrived. On the seventh day of this six-day war, they were already calling it the "war of redemption." These were days of euphoria in Israel, accompanied by anomie and great confusion. Like other Israelis, these religious youngsters were bewildered after the war, but at their disposal was a religious system that allowed them to digest the extraordinary events relatively quickly. Rather than develop a new theology to fit the unforeseen events, these events were woven into the existing mystical-messianic scheme related to the rabbis Kook. It was a perfect match.

A religious method of hitherto limited influence provided a persuasive rationale for the incomprehensible new historical circumstances, while these circumstances gave the religious system new layers of meaning, relevance, and validity, making it more attractive and empowering its followers with greater confidence. Following the war, messianic urgency was added to the original Kookist philosophy, and the holiness of the greater land of Israel became central. A revitalized Zionist religion ripened, within which Gush Emunim would burst upon the scene as a militant religious-political movement.

CONCLUSION

What, then, is the nature of the relationship between the Jewish fundamentalist leader and the movement, between the rabbis Kook and the Kookist community? One phenomenon that illuminates this relationship is the existence of gaps in the biographies of the radical religious leaders; episodes in their lives that are problematic for the movement are omitted. The biography of the fundamentalist leader thus takes on a mythological or hagiographic quality, serving as a behavioral model whose details carry ideological significance. Shadowy areas, common in the biographies of saints, are symptomatic of those of charismatic religious and political leaders in general; Jewish fundamentalist groups provide some prominent examples.[26]

In fundamentalist movements, the standing of the authority is a matter of great sensitivity. The leading figure should be perfect, with a pure and consistent biography. Those close to the leader sometimes feel the need to hide or correct details, tailoring the image presented to the faithful and to the public at large to avoid undermining faith in the leader and the teachings. If this is not achieved during the leader's lifetime, it can be taken care of after his death. The relationship between Kook the father and Kook the son, for example, is a delicate matter for religious Zionist followers of both men. Existing testimonies are contradictory, and even well-informed hypotheses can lead in opposite directions. There is evidence that the father greatly respected his son, and also evidence that the father scorned him. Sometimes the same information serves opposite claims, such as the fact that the son was a Bible teacher in his father's yeshiva. The haredi opposition notes that in the world of tradition, the Bible is inferior to the Talmud in practice; thus they conclude that the father assigned his son a relatively minor role as an expression of his lack of trust. In contrast, Merkaz HaRav faithful point out that the innovative approach of Kook the father entailed an effort to change the priorities of the rabbinic curriculum, to return to the Bible the seniority that had been taken from it by the Talmud—a kind of quasi-Karaism—and therefore he assigned this difficult and important task to his best person, his son.[27]

Several strategies exist for coping with the gaps in sacred biographies. One is obfuscation, concealment, or denial. Another is apologetic sophistry. A third is rewriting, plain and simple. Kookists in recent years have tended to omit or obscure the fact that Kook the son never issued halakhic rulings, which could be viewed as embarrassing. When pushed into a corner, they appeal to a rationalization with rather heretical potential, namely that rulings are petty legalisms that are "too small for the giant stature" of the rabbi. The physical infirmities of the rabbi they handled with a slightly different technique. When the infirmities became impossible to hide, Kookists found in them secret positive qualities of the highest order. The rabbi's stutter, for example, took on fabled qualities; it was said to be caused by "the bounteous pearls of wisdom that welled up from within him and crowded together in his narrow throat, wanting to illuminate the world, bumping into each other in their struggle to emerge first." In many ancient religions, physical disability evoked fascination and the attribution of supernatural qualities that transformed one into a holy figure.

This example recalls an additional strategy, more singular and revealing than the previous one: the magnetic attraction of the believers to the allegedly weak points in the biographies of the charismatic leader. The true believers give a revolutionary new interpretation of these weak points, suggesting a new quality of their leader hidden therein. Kook the son, for example, was once involved with the League Against Religious Coercion, an anticlerical group that operated in

Israel in the 1950s and 1960s, espousing a militant secular ideology. Once this secret was unearthed, the Kookists capitalized on it. They publicized the story and searched for more witnesses to corroborate it, as evidence of the wonderful qualities of their rabbi and the paradoxical nature of his teachings. According to the rationalization used for this affair, Kookism does not share the isolationist and antagonistic approach of the Orthodox; it transcends the distinction between religious and secular, asserting that the secular may conceal within it a religious essence of great holiness.

To take another example, the Kooks were reputed to have been in intensive and sympathetic contact with "foreign culture" through study at the Sorbonne. To this day some of their disciples try to hide this fact, but other eminent Kookists boast about this "flirtation" with secular, Western modern culture and elaborate details of the rabbis' accomplishments in competing with the secular on their own turf. These Kookists manipulate the gaps in information rather effectively, using evidence of the rabbis' secular learning to demonstrate, first, that the attitude of radical religion toward secular culture is based on intimate acquaintance, not ignorance—renouncing and rejecting a culture that one has mastered is particularly compelling—and, second, the virtuosity of their radical religious leaders: they pushed back the boundaries, tested the limits, approached the dangerous brink, tottering like an acrobat at the edge of the abyss, and were able to return. The leader is revealed as daring, as one who faced great temptation, one to whom a certain mystique is attached. This episode also betrays the obsessive preoccupation of fundamentalism with the modern profane.

The obsession with the profane on the part of the Kooks and their first disciples is woven like a scarlet thread through their lives and writing. As we have seen, however, the militant interpreters of the Kooks, the hard core of the Jewish settler movement Gush Emunim, shrank from the potentially universalistic and radically inclusive vision of these rabbinical spiritual authorities of Jewish-Zionist fundamentalism. The hard-core religious Zionists needed to resolve the dialectic tension in the Kookist system in order to pursue an exclusivist right-wing politics in which the profane was devalued and identified with the secular enemy. Thus Gush Emunim tended to play down a key theme of the Kookist system. Even scholars have tended to ignore it, despite its great importance. Yet this element, it can be argued, captures the essence of the theological revolution of Kookism and could have had far-reaching political implications. The radical potential of Kookism, realized only partially in the "fundamentalism" of Gush Emunim, is couched in these words of Rabbi Kook the father:

> As the soul of man is higher and deeper than the angels, and because of its very greatness has descended to the depths and will ascend from there in great and mighty power and prepare the entire world for the supreme height, so too *the holy within the profane that descended to absolute profanity, is more lofty and more holy than the holy within the holy,* but it is thoroughly concealed. And there is no end to the repair of the world that will ensue from all the good that comes from the profane who sees and reveals the glory and splendor in its joy . . . and before the light of the Messiah will appear, the power of the holy within the profane will be awakened.[28]

The idea expressed here, when taken to its full conclusion, could have brought the political religion of Gush Emunim to a point of self-contradiction. In a very real sense the concept of the holiness of the profane threatens fundamentally to undermine traditional religion—and thus to rob extremist political religion of its religious base. Gush Emunim was therefore careful to avoid overadherence to Kookist ideas and moods and managed to avoid facing the truly radical implications of Kookist doctrine. The activist believers in Israel knew how to contain the revolutionary fervor that erupted from the theology of the rabbis Kook and to channel it into the spheres of foreign policy and security, investing Kookist passion almost exclusively in the matter of settlement in the territories. Thus they fundamentally transformed the geopolitics of the Middle East, while carefully remaining within the limits of Jewish orthodoxy.

Notes

1. Gideon Aran, "Jewish-Zionist Fundamentalism," in Martin E. Marty and R. Scott Appleby, eds., *Fundamentalisms Observed* (Chicago: University of Chicago Press, 1991). For other works on Gush Emunim in English, see E. Sprinzak, *The Ascendance of Israel's Radical Right* (New York: Oxford University Press, 1991), chaps. 2–5; Eliezer Don-Yehiya, "Jewish Messianism, Religious Zionism and Israeli Politics," *Middle Eastern Studies* 23, no. 2 (1987): 215–35; David Newman, ed., *The Impact of Gush Emunim: Politics and Settlement in the West Bank* (New York: St. Martin's Press, 1985); and Myron J. Aronoff, "Gush Emunim: The Institutionalization of a Charismatic Religious-Political Revitalization Movement in Israel," *Political Anthropology* 3, no. 4 (1984): 62–84.

2. I coined the term "Kookism" to denote a new phenomenon whose birth I attended and whose development I have followed ever since. When I first used the term in the presence of activist believers most resented it, considering it a slight. Others accepted the designation with a touch of humor, and some even

read into it a measure of esteem and friendliness. Gradually, increasing numbers of "Kookists" withdrew their objection to the appellation. I recently found evidence that the term had been adopted within the movement and the Merkaz HaRav Yeshiva, indicating perhaps acquiescence to a fait accompli or perhaps a retroactive assertion of proprietorship and control.

3. For a comprehensive review and critical analysis of the Kookist complex, see Gideon Aran, "From Religious Zionism to Zionist Religion: The Origins and Culture of Gush Emunim, a Messianic Movement in Modern Israel," Ph.D. dissertation, Hebrew University, Jerusalem, 1987. For particular aspects of Kookism, see Gideon Aran, "The Gospel of the Gush: Redemption as a Catastrophe," in Emmanuel Sivan and Menachem Friedman, eds., *Religious Radicalism and Politics in the Middle East* (New York: State University of New York Press, 1990), 157–75, and Gideon Aran, "A Mystic-Messianic Interpretation of Modern Israeli History," *Studies in Contemporary Jewry* 4 (1988): 263–75.

4. No solid firsthand research has been published about Kook the son, as far as I know. My dissertation contains a long chapter about him based on extensive fieldwork: participant-observations, long personal conversations with him, and study of his teachings as interpreted by his students.

5. For an introductory presentation of Kook's religious system, see Z. Yaron, *The Philosophy of Rabbi Kook* (Jerusalem: World Zionist Organization, 1991). For a general short survey of Kook's thought, see Shlomo Avineri, *The Making of Modern Zionism* (New York: Basic Books, 1981), and Arthur Hertzberg, *The Zionist Idea: A Historical Analysis and Reader* (New York: Harper & Row, 1966). See also *The World of Rav Kook's Thought* (New York: Avi-Chai, 1991), presentations from a conference held in Jerusalem, 1985. For a list of about fifty items on Rabbi Kook in Hebrew, see B. Ish-Shalom, *Rabbi Kook: Between Rationalism and Mysticism* (Tel Aviv: Am Oved, 1990).

6. For an example of an idealized biography in English, see J. Agus, *Banner of Jerusalem* (New York: Bloch Publishers, 1946). In the official guidelines issued in the 1980s by the director-general of the Ministry of Education concerning the curriculum of state elementary and secondary schools, the topic of religious Zionism is emphasized and more or less equated with Rabbi Kook's thought.

7. For an authoritative work relating the ideology of Gush Emunim to Rabbi Kook's theology, albeit lacking a sociological perspective, see Aviezer Ravitzky, *Messianism, Zionism and Jewish Religious Radicalism* (in Hebrew) (Tel Aviv: Am Oved, 1993), chap. 3.

8. The main works or collections of Abraham Kook are *The Letters of Rabbi Kook*, 4 vols. (1985); *The Offering of Rabbi Kook* (1985), *The Lights of the Holy* (1985), and *The Lights of Repentance* (1987). All are published in Hebrew by Mosad HaRav Kook in Jerusalem. For a translated selection, see Ben Zion Bokser, ed., *The Essential Writings of Abraham Isaac Kook* (Amity, N.Y.: Amity House, 1988), or A. I. Kook, *Lights of Penitence, Lights of Holiness: Essays, Letters and Poems*, trans. B. Bokser (New York: Paulist Press, 1978). For the convenience of the readers, I have limited myself in this essay to quotations from Rabbi Kook, most of which appear in English translation and have relatively wide circulation. Many of the quotations here are taken from Hertzberg, *Zionist Idea*, 414–31, a volume accessible to an American audience.

9. Movements opposed to Gush Emunim, such as Netivot Shalom, have also published collections of the writing of Rabbi Kook the father.

10. On the controversy surrounding the permission granted to engage in agriculture during a sabbatical year *(shmita)*, see M. Friedman, "The Meaning of the 'Shmita' Debate 1909–1910," *Shalem: Studies in the History of Eretz Israel,* no. 1 (Jerusalem: 1974), 455–80.

11. A. I. Kook, quoted in Hertzberg, *Zionist Idea,* 419 ff.

12. Ibid.

13. Ibid.

14. Ibid.

15. The main writings of Rabbi Kook the son appear in a two-volume anthology in Hebrew, *Li-Netivot Yisrael* (Jerusalem: Menora Publishing, 1967/1979) and *Or Lenetivati* (Jerusalem: Rabbi Z. Y. Kook Institute, 1983); see also his articles "And Let There Be No Hope for the Schematics" (on Christians and Christianity), "Chapters on the Messiah," and "Independence Day." All are published in Hebrew by Ateret Kohanim Yeshiva in Jerusalem. For a translated collection, see Z. Fishman, ed., *Torat Eretz Israel: The Teachings of Z. Y. H. Kook* (Jerusalem: Torat Eretz Israel Publisher, 1992).

16. A. I. Kook, *Orot* (Lights) (in Hebrew), 2d ed., ed. Z. Y. H. Kook (Jerusalem: Mosad HaRav Kook, 1985). Innumerable extracts from this book have been distributed by the movement through the yeshivas and the national religious school system. They have been reproduced in a variety of formats, from easily portable booklets and lists of passages for memorization to wall posters and billboards.

17. Z. Y. Kook, "The Nineteenth Psalm" (in Hebrew), *HaTsofeh,* 23 June 1967.

18. Z. Y. Kook, *Li-Netivot Yisrael,* 188–95.

19. Numbers 23:9.

20. Z. Y. Kook, "Nineteenth Psalm."

21. The sermon was first published in *HaTsofeh,* the daily newspaper of the National Religious Party, several days after the end of the Six Day War. Since then, it has been reprinted in innumerable locations, including A. Ben-Ami, ed., *All of It: The Book of the Greater Land of Israel* (in Hebrew) (Tel Aviv: Madaf, 1967).

22. *Admor* is an acronym for the Hebrew sequence of titles *Adonenu, Morenu, Rabenu,* that is, Our Master, Teacher, and Rabbi.

23. Jacob Katz, a social historian of medieval and modern Jewry, was the first to use this term for Judaism. See his *HaHalakha BeMeitzar* (Jerusalem: Magnes Press, 1992).

24. Gideon Aran, "The Roots of Gush Emunim," *Studies in Contemporary Jewry* 2 (1986): 116–43.

25. For a detailed study of this transformation, see Aran, "From Religious Zionism to Zionist Religion."

26. Peter Brown, *The Cult of the Saints* (Chicago: University of Chicago Press, 1981). On the life stories of contemporary "saints" in Israel, see Y. Bilu and E. Ben-Ari, "The Making of Modern Saints: Manufactured Charisma," *American Ethnologist* 4 (1982): 672–87. On the issue of spiritual leadership in one Jewish fundamentalist group, Habad, and particularly in the analogous case of the char-

ismatic but problematic authority of the last Lubavitch rebbe, see Menachem Friedman, "Habad as Messianic Fundamentalism: From Local Particularism to Universal Jewish Mission," in Martin E. Marty and R. Scott Appleby, eds., *Accounting for Fundamentalisms: The Dynamic Character of Movements* (Chicago: University of Chicago Press, 1994), 328–59.

27. G. Aran, "Return to the Scriptures in Modern Israel," *Bibliothèque de l'École des Hautes Études Sciences Réligieuses* 99 (1993): 101–32.

28. Kook, *Orot*, sect. 45, "Lights for Rebirth"; emphasis added.

SEVEN

GUIDES OF THE FAITHFUL

Contemporary Religious Zionist Rabbis

Samuel C. Heilman

Provide for yourself a rabbi
and acquire for yourself a companion.

Talmud *Mishna Avot* 1:6

"The Temple Mount is in our hands." With this simple phrase, General Mordecai Gur, who led the June 1967 assault on Jerusalem's old city, passed the word to his superiors and the nation that, after nearly two thousand years, Jews were once again in control of the symbolic center of their national capital. Since May 1948, Jews had been in possession of a homeland in the sovereign state of Israel, with its capital in Jerusalem. Yet this return as conquerors to the site of King Solomon's ancient Holy Temple seemed to complete the restoration. Like most of his fellow citizens, Gur was a thoroughly secular Israeli; to mark this military victory, however, he chose terms that resonated with collective religious—even messianic—significance. He was not alone. In those days, even toughened paratroopers and secular government ministers were rushing to the foot of the Temple Mount to "pray" at the Western Wall, that sacred remnant of the Temple complex.

The scope of the victory and its swiftness were stunning, both militarily and emotionally; only a few days before, facing the massive Arab armies arrayed against them, the Israelis had seemed on the edge of a second holocaust. The significance of this extraordinary turn of events—an unexpected victory, a return to the holiest of places, and what seemed a religious reawakening among the secular—was not lost upon those Jews who had long sought to find religious meaning in Zionism and its accomplishments. Their ideological forebear, the late Rabbi Abraham Isaac Kook (1865–1935), had seen signs of redemption in the earliest Zionist achievements and asked: "Who is so blind that he does not see in this the Lord's hand guiding us, and does not feel obligated to work with God?"[1] Now they too saw, in the events of 1967, evidence of God's will, a giant step toward redemption. Infused with a belief that the Zionist enterprise was religiously legitimate and the state it spawned was religiously significant, they felt obligated to work with God, and more than ever they rejected the ultra-Orthodox notion, held by the haredim, that the "heresy" of Zionism was forcing the hand of God, who had decreed exile as a punishment for Jewish sin.[2]

Among the religious Zionists none was readier to build on what they believed God had handed them than a group of rabbis who had studied or taught in Kook's Merkaz HaRav Yeshiva, and who saw themselves as disciples and colleagues of his seventy-six-year-old son and yeshiva dean, Rabbi Zvi Yehuda Kook. These rabbis included Ya'akov Ariel, Shlomo Aviner, Haim Druckman, Moshe Levinger, Dov Lior, Zalman Melamed, Avraham Shapira, and Eliezer Waldman, men who would become influential leaders and guides for an expansive and self-assured religious Zionism in the years ahead. Except for Shapira, who was a generation older, most were in their thirties in 1967. Aviner, an immigrant from France, had studied at the Sorbonne. Waldman came from the United States. The others were born in the land of Israel. All had their nationalist consciousness formed in the heady first years of statehood and identified deeply with the idea of a new sovereign Jewish state. Most had been part of the B'nai Akiva, the religious Zionist youth movement begun in 1929, which tried to marry the pioneering ideals of Zionism and a commitment to Orthodox Judaism and Jewish tradition.[3]

During the 1950s most of them had studied in the newly established yeshiva high schools—most prominently K'far Haroeh, a B'nai Akiva–sponsored school that took its name from the initials of Rabbi Kook's name and was headed by a thirty-year-old Polish-born rabbi and Kook disciple, Moshe Zvi Neria. Some also became involved in a newly formed group called Gahelet (Embers), made up of teens who sought to rescue Zionism from secularity and Orthodoxy from political irrelevance while exploring the messianic meaning of the new Jewish state.[4] Gahelet became part of the extracurricular student life at K'far Haroeh, and its ideas remained embedded in its graduates when they later moved to Merkaz HaRav. There they were joined in their enthusiasms by Haim Druckman, who had once been their B'nai Akiva youth leader but now became a follower.[5]

These young men adopted Kook's formulation that, whatever else one did or did not do as a Jew, by facilitating the return of the Jewish people to their homeland and to sovereignty one engaged in action that had redemptive and messianic meaning. That God might act through secular Jews, who were the primary instruments and movers behind Zionism and the state, was puzzling but not impossible. Indeed, they believed, as Kook had, that God was creating a situation in which, as redemption neared, these secular Zionists would have their eyes opened to the true meaning of their actions and would return not just to the land but also to the Jewish tradition, its holy practices, and true beliefs. Thus common cause with secular Zionism was not only permissible but required of the religious. These rabbis, in short, were deeply imbued with Zionist ideals, which they framed with religion.

With sovereignty newly extended to sites deeply rooted in Jewish religious consciousness and collective memory, these ideas took on added significance. The elder Kook had hoped that some day secular Israeli Jews would comprehend that there was no real difference between cultural or historical attachments and religious ones. Now, in June of 1967, they saw "the first blossoms of the redemption," a movement of Jewish return, both geographic and spiritual, a Jewish renaissance.[6]

Swept up in these convictions some of these rabbis, on the sixth day of the war, carried their aging teacher, Rabbi Zvi Yehuda, past the tanks and battlements to the foot of the Temple Mount, where, beside the Western Wall, he declared: "We announce to all of Israel, and to all of the world that by a divine command we have returned to our home, to our holy city. From this day forth, we shall never budge from here."[7] The younger Rabbi Kook had seemed to prophesy this moment, when, during a sermon at the yeshiva a few days before the war, he had mysteriously blurted out, "Where is our Hebron, Shechem, Jericho, and Anathoth, torn from the state in 1948 as we lay maimed and bleeding?"[8] Now those places were in Jewish hands. In the six-day campaign the heartland of Jewish heritage, the area called "Samaria and Judea," was suddenly (miraculously, Kook's followers believed) under Jewish control. The religiously significant cities of Bethlehem, Jericho, Shechem (Nablus), and Hebron, cut off from Jews since 1948, were accessible again.

THE EMERGENCE OF MOSHE LEVINGER

Perhaps no one was more energized by these events than Rabbi Moshe Levinger, thirty-two at the time. He was a man who, as his brother would later explain, believed it was "his duty—a *mitzvah* [commandment] from the Torah" to rebuild the kingdom of Israel.[9] As he saw it, this was a Jewish return that at last gave real purpose to Zionism:

> Samaria and Judea belonged to the Jewish people even before 1967. We've known that they belong to us throughout all history. . . . It's God's will. No Jew prayed three times a day that he'd come back to Tel Aviv or Haifa, but for centuries we did pray to come back to Jerusalem, Hebron and Nablus. The tombs of Abraham, Isaac and Jacob are here. Hebron was David's capital. And until the Arabs slaughtered the community of scholars in the 1920s, there were Jews in Hebron during all the years of the Diaspora.[10]

Levinger was not alone in his convictions. "I believe that God brought us back to Judea and Samaria just as He brought us back to the Galilee and the coastal plains," said Rabbi Eliezer Waldman.[11] The sentiment was echoed by the other graduates of Merkaz HaRav.

In these Zionist rabbis' minds, Kook's religious endorsement of secular Zionist attainments could finally be replaced. As Shlomo Aviner put it, a religious Zionism was now being built on the wreckage of the "simple and superficial nationalism" of secular Zionism.[12] While most Israelis largely ignored religious attachments, practices, identity, and beliefs, replacing them with secular citizenship—hence implicitly advancing an alternative definition of a Jew—these rabbis sought to reverse the trend.[13] As Levinger expressed it, Tel Aviv and Haifa, the great urban centers, the creations of secular Zionism, were in this *religious* Zionist vision far less significant than Jerusalem, Hebron, and Shechem. Zionism was not just a national liberation movement or a quest for a sovereign state by a people who for two thousand years had lived as a barely tolerated minority in a precarious, dispersed existence. It was rather an expression of religious return. In a formulation that would become a popular slogan of Gush Emunim, the so-called Bloc of the Faithful, the movement these rabbis guided: "There is no Zionism without Judaism, and no Judaism without Zionism."[14]

Every settlement, every link to place, would recall religion. As the Israeli army rolled into Nablus, these religious Zionists recalled the words of Genesis (11:7) in which Abraham, standing near a terebinth tree overlooking this same city, heard God's promise: "To thy seed will I give this land." They marveled as the army of the Jewish state retraced the footsteps of children of Israel, and as they watched they heard the echo of the divine voice that assured them that "every place whereon the soles of your feet tread shall be yours" (Deuteronomy 11:24). And when Gur and his paratroopers came to the Temple Mount, where David and his son Solomon had established a national and religious capital, they felt the full weight of Jeremiah's prophecy: "Behold, days are coming, says the Lord, when I will raise to David a righteous offshoot, and he shall reign as king and prosper. . . . In his days shall Judah and Israel dwell in security . . . returning from all countries in which I have driven them and they shall dwell in their own land" (23:5–8).

To these rabbis the biblical text was a living and legal document, and these promises were not to be dismissed as literary heritage or poetry. The Bible constituted their title to the land and provided a blueprint for settlement action. To bring the text's promises to life was holy activity, they believed; it was speeding the redemption, bringing on the messiah. And no one was in a greater hurry to do so than Levinger. "Zionism will wither away if you cut it off from its mystical-messianic roots," he would later explain. "Zionism is a movement that does not think in rational terms—in terms of practical politics, international relations, world opinion, demography, social dynamics." He went on, dismissing the very essence of the realpolitik Zionism had learned in its state building. For Levinger, as for all these rabbis, Zionism had to operate "in terms of divine commandments. What matters only is God's promise as recorded in the Book of Genesis."[15]

Moreover, if it was true, as Abraham Kook had written, that anyone who attached himself to this movement of return "had a soul equal to the supreme *zaddik*," the most righteous of Jews, then Levinger and those who shared his perspective could rest assured that in hastening this return, they were supremely right, blessed, in all they were doing.[16]

Levinger had not come to these ideas alone. Along with his rabbinic colleagues, he had grown up convinced that the Torah was relevant to every issue and could therefore serve as a blueprint for Zionism. Born in Jerusalem in 1935, two years after his parents fled from Hitler's Germany, Levinger had been forged in the pioneering spirit of a nascent Israel. He attended the Horev school in Jerusalem, where the German–Jewish Orthodox ideals that married secular and Jewish study were the pedagogic organizing ideals.[17] Young Levinger was a member of the Jerusalem branch of Ezra, the Orthodox Jewish youth movement sponsored by Poaley Agudat Israel, which traced its origins to Germany and was dominant at Horev at the time. In Israel, Ezra was "absorbed in the cultural life and educational outlook of the new community" of pioneering religious Zionism and nationalism, the outlook that dominated the larger B'nai Akiva.[18]

Like his religious Zionist peers, Levinger searched for role models and guides, leaders who, convinced that the exile was over, could help retrieve from the Torah (including its talmudic elaboration and legal codes, or halakha) the lessons that in the emergent Jewish society and state would make them whole—both full-fledged Jews and full-fledged Israelis or Zionists. In those days, the ideas of Rabbi Abraham Kook, who died the year Levinger was born, were important but not yet popularized, and were probably too abstruse for Levinger and his fellow teens. Rabbi Zvi Yehuda Kook, already in his sixties in the 1950s, devoted himself to working on his father's notes and had not yet captured young people's attention. Indeed he and his institution seemed part of another Orthodox world, engaged more in traditional study and less in expansionist Zionism.

As Michael Rosenak has explained, the young religious Zionists who made up the rank and file of B'nai Akiva and Ezra were in the years just before and after statehood often left to their own devices, for they "found no rabbinic authorities who had the clout, courage, or even the inclination to interpret the Torah as they perceived it."[19] Accordingly, their enthusiasms led them first and foremost to one another, to a solidarity born of youth. After 1940 it also led some of them, including Levinger, to the newly founded K'far Haroeh. This school, loosely affiliated with B'nai Akiva, from which it drew its students, combined traditional yeshiva Torah education with a few hours of general high school studies in the afternoon or evening, a curriculum that enabled its graduates to be wedded to the Orthodox Jewish world of learning and values, yet still prepare for the government's matriculation exams and hence enter into Israeli society and culture. K'far Haroeh was actually the second such high school yeshiva; it was preceded by the Yeshiva of the Yishuv Hechadash, founded and led by Rabbi Moshe Avigdor Amiel (1883–1946), chief rabbi of Tel Aviv.[20]

Essentially religious boarding schools, these yeshiva high schools created what Gideon Aran has called a "hothouse" effect.[21] They took youngsters who were going through the natural adolescent transition from childhood and the rebellion associated with that transition, detached them from their families and home communities, and threw them together with other young people who, like themselves, wanted to be part of the new Jewish society being forged through Israeli statehood. In these yeshivas—filled with people who bounced between the ideals of traditional talmudic study, the enthusiasms of religious Zionism, and the excitement of state building—teenage boys who had grown up together in youth movements like B'nai Akiva studied side by side and built a new identity upon their shared commitment to Orthodoxy and Zionism. This enhanced their already powerful feelings of solidarity and amplified these dual attachments. The only adult voices of authority in this setting were rabbis, at least some of whom were haredim and not quite ready to embrace Zionism. These ultra-Orthodox rabbis informed their students that "you cannot evaluate Torah with your own faculties, but must accept [the sages'] explanations of every word, every letter of the Torah." Accordingly, these youngsters grew up convinced that "the authority of the rabbi-teacher is absolute." [22]

At first, these rabbis who sat next to the youngsters for hours on end in the study hall, poring over talmudic and scriptural texts in the time-honored fashion, demanded only that they hold to strict standards of Orthodox practice and religious devotion and guide their lives by their judgments. But something else was communicated as well; there were also powerful religious Zionist expressions that reviewed Scripture as a certificate of title. The following assertion by Rabbi Amiel of Yishuv Hechadash Yeshiva, although made in 1937, is exemplary:

> It is hard to find a halakhic dispensation for us to agree to relinquish the greatest portion of the land of Israel, that it no longer be the Land of Israel but rather the Land of Ishmael. . . . Renunciations such as these can occur with other nations and other lands, but not in connection to the eternal connection that exists between [the people of] Israel and its land, which is not only its national homeland but also a holy land. [23]

Statements such as this resonated not only with the young men's obvious attachment to the entire land of Israel; they also reflected the self-assurance of the new religious-based Zionism that was in the air in these high school yeshivas and even more a part of the B'nai Akiva movement. With their conviction that Jewish exile was over, men like Rabbi Amiel, Rabbi Neria, his counterpart at K'far Haroeh who spouted Kookist ideas, and their students, concluded that in the land of Israel there was "no longer any need to modify the all-inclusive cultural demands of the Torah; the halakha could now be fully carried out, in its own environment, in its own land." [24]

Influenced by their religious Zionism, by their high school teachers, and, perhaps most importantly, by one another, these young men began to look with disdain at their parents' religious moderation and compromises. They sought to be more completely Jewish, became more religiously observant—some might say extreme—and chose to become rabbis. But they longed to be more Zionist too. Being more observant was easy, but being more Zionist was difficult, since the settlement process was nearly complete, or so they believed in those early years.

Upon graduation, many of these young men, like other Israeli high school graduates, felt a commitment to the state and to the army that defended it. They were committed to rigorous Orthodox practice and Jewish learning but, unlike the non-Zionist Orthodox, were unwilling to claim the complete exemption from military service that the government offered for yeshiva students. Infused with the Kook-inspired conviction that even a secular institution like the army was an instrument of messianic redemption, they were ready, even eager, to serve. In the words of Shlomo Aviner, once part of this circle, "We have no quarrel with the Israel Defence Forces. The army is us and we are the army."[25]

For Moshe Levinger, the doctor's son who chose to become a rabbi, military service meant joining Nachal, the so-called Fighting Pioneer Youth. Nachal was a program that combined army service with the social and ideological preparation necessary for forming a kibbutz or cooperative agricultural settlement. Nachal units were commonly organized by cohorts of particular youth movements who at eighteen entered the army with their peers, each forming a *garin*, a group that would comprise the nucleus of a unit and of the kibbutz it would become. Because the regular army was a leveling and secularizing institution in which religious practices and outlook were often undermined and crushed, a place where in practice teens might be swept out of the orbit of their faith, Nachal became popular among the religious Zionist youth. Levinger went in with an Ezra *garin*. As part of a Nachal unit, he could fulfill most of his army service with others who shared his religious outlook and practices. Moreover, he would learn practically how a religious settlement was established from scratch, a skill that would later serve him well. In 1953–1954, Levinger was sent to Kibbutz Sha'alabim, located in the Ayalon valley on what, until 1967, was the border with Jordan. Sha'alabim, never a very successful kibbutz, would come to be associated with Poaley Agudat Israel, a party infused with a peculiar and not always consistent amalgam of German-Jewish intellectuality that mixed Orthodoxy, socialist labor values, and an attachment to Israeli pioneering—the same amalgam that was characteristic of Ezra. A yeshiva was established there, and its students often joined kibbutz members and soldiers in the defense of the settlement against Arab attacks from across the border.

Around the time Levinger chose Nachal, other religious Zionist youth—especially those who had become attached to the yeshiva life— were discovering that they were not interested in using the army to launch them into a kibbutz life. Instead, they sought some arrangement, or *hesder,* that would enable them to continue yeshiva study as part of their army service. Among them were some of Levinger's peers, the high school seniors at K'far Haroeh, who helped restructure a yeshiva near the religious kibbutz at Yavneh. This institution, founded in 1954 and called Kerem Beyavneh, aimed at first simply to provide an additional year of study after high school but before army service.[26] In 1965 Kerem Beyavneh became the first official hesder yeshiva; along with the twenty others that followed (including one at Sha'alabim), it would ultimately allow students to combine their obligatory military service with yeshiva study. Indeed, by the 1980s many of these hesder yeshiva men, with yarmulkes on their heads, went on to join the officer corps (of which they now constitute about 40 percent) and the most elite army units, a course Israelis had come to associate with best of the nation's youth. The hesder boys perceived themselves to be the true children and heirs of Zionism. In 1990, in what must have seemed to some a confirmation of that perception, the government awarded the state's highest award, the Israel Prize, to Moshe Zvi Neria, on behalf of the hesder system.

After completing his army service in 1957, Levinger chose not to stay on at Sha'alabim and instead enrolled at Merkaz HaRav Yeshiva, where he again found graduates of K'far Haroeh and members of Gahelet. Kook's yeshiva wooed graduates of the yeshiva high schools, seeking to assemble a cadre of the best and most dedicated among them. Initially these young men had rejected Merkaz HaRav as being too much like the old-style haredi yeshivas.[27] However, several meetings with Rabbi Zvi Yehuda Kook, who deeply impressed them, and the fact that Kerem Beyavneh suddenly found itself without a rabbinic head, led them to gravitate to Merkaz HaRav. Although he was aging and infirm and his speech was difficult to understand, Rabbi Kook became for them the charismatic leader they had been seeking. Besides reworking and publishing his father's papers, he expressed strong feelings about the land and a prophetic vision calling for expanded Zionist settlement. Although most of these rabbis had left Merkaz HaRav by 1967, they always saw it and the rabbis Kook as the wellspring of their faith.

For Levinger, the years after Merkaz HaRav were a time of some wandering. After marrying Miriam, an American-born woman from the

Bronx, he served as a rabbi at the religious Zionist kibbutz Lavi, an agricultural settlement founded by British and North American Jews in 1949 in the lower Galilee. In 1966, he left there to became a rabbi of Moshav Nehalim, a religious Zionist farming settlement of about seven hundred inhabitants near Tel Aviv. By 1968, the biblical heartland beckoned powerfully, to Levinger and to many of the other Merkaz HaRav graduates, giving them at last a chance to be more Zionist than their parents. In April of that year, on Passover, the holiday of Jewish redemption, Levinger led a small vanguard group (including Aviner) to the Park Hotel inside Hebron. What began as a Passover visit to this holy city evolved into the first settlement in what they called the city of Abraham, when Levinger and many of those who had accompanied him refused to leave. For at least some Israelis, this act of daring settlement was inspiring.

"Hebron is still awaiting redemption," David Ben-Gurion, the first prime minister of the state and by then an old man, reputedly wrote to Levinger at the Park Hotel. "And there is no redemption without extensive Jewish settlement."[28] The mantle of Zionist pioneering was being passed. The Labour government of Levi Eshkol tried unsuccessfully to extract Levinger, his family, and his supporters. But these settlers stubbornly refused to leave what they said was a neighborhood from which the Arabs had in 1929 chased away the Jews. Two years later, after a bomb wounded Jewish worshipers at the Cave of the Patriarchs in Hebron, Levinger was instrumental in forming a larger settlement on the heights above the city. Called Kiryat Arba, the biblical name for Hebron, it grew into a city of over five thousand by 1972, and the Labour government listed it provisionally as a rural settlement.[29] Levinger would play an increasingly large role in guiding and sometimes prodding the faithful to establish Jewish settlements throughout the newly conquered territories. But that would come later, after the Yom Kippur war.

Gush Emunim

While the events of 1967 had galvanized Levinger and Aviner to move into Hebron, the 1973 Yom Kippur war, during which Israel snatched victory from the jaws of defeat, was even more crucial to the creation of a settlement movement. Perceiving that Israel had in this last war come close to losing all that had been gained in 1948 and 1967, many of the religious Zionists rabbis and their followers were moved to greater activism, lest history steal away the unique opportunity for redemption God had given the nation. If after 1967 most, except for Levinger and Aviner, were prepared to wait for God to point the way, after 1973 they believed God had warned them to act lest they lose everything.[30]

Three months after the end of the war, Gush Emunim (Bloc of the Faithful), an offshoot of the National Religious Party, the political voice of mainstream religious Zionism, tried—with Levinger's active involvement—to establish a Jewish settlement at a railroad depot near Shechem. They called it Elon Moreh, the city's biblical name. As part of their settlement effort, they sat down in the depot and began to study sacred texts, turning it into a kind of yeshiva.[31] In April 1975, Levinger led a march of twenty thousand Jews into Samaria and was hoisted on the shoulders of young boys in the crowd when the Labour government agreed to accommodate thirty of the Elon Moreh settlers at a nearby army camp. Levinger had led the "battle" and, from his "war situation room" in a tent, negotiated with Shimon Peres.[32] The Gush Emunim saw this as a major victory. Under Levinger's leadership, they saw themselves as doubly faithful—faithful to God and to Kook's idea (which had reinforced their own youthful B'nai Akiva enthusiasms) of the messianic meaning in the Jewish return to the land of their biblical forebears. Levinger was the face of that faith for many. He was the rabbi who might at last wrest Zionism from its secular past and outlook. "Levinger symbolizes the return of Zionism," said Geula Cohen, one of the founders of the Tehiya ("renaissance") party, whose goal was to encourage greater settlement. "He is standing like a candle in Judea and Samaria. He is the leader of the Zionist revolution."[33] The thin, balding man, with bad teeth, thick, black-framed glasses, big black skullcap, and unkempt beard—the rabbi in search of his calling—had been transformed into a charismatic revolutionary, the protector of Zionism.

While the struggle for Elon Moreh was protracted, other settlements followed with greater ease. Nachal outposts were established in the territories and after 1974 began to be transformed into civilian settlements, often affiliated with religious Zionist parties or populated by their members, the bloc of the faithful. Throughout the rest of the 1970s and into the 1980s, the general population supported these settlers' ideals and actions. "The passion for pioneering that characterized the left in the first half of this century is now found among the Gush Emunim religious movement," wrote Israeli political scientist Asher Arian. The movement seemed to bring "to the prospect of settlement and redeeming the land of Israel the same kind of youthful excitement, dedication, and self-sacrifice that early generations identified with the kibbutz movements."[34]

Although many of these first settlements were established under a Labour government, headed by Yitzhak Rabin and Shimon Peres, the growth of Gush Emunim's political involvement and influence coincided with the Likud's rise to power in 1977. Likud, dedicated to territorial expansion and opposed to the "re-partition of the Land of Israel," created a felicitous political atmosphere for expansionist religious Zionism. Under Menachem Begin, who was an outspoken supporter of Levinger, Likud often used religious imagery and language to accompany its nationalist politics of territorial expansion. Thus rabbis like those of Merkaz HaRav felt more at home in alliance with them (even when they chose to affiliate themselves with smaller parties that took a more aggressive and religious settlement policy). This alliance affected both groups: while the Likud appeared to become more religious in its outlook, Gush Emunim became more right-wing in its politics.

Levinger was not the only rabbi from Merkaz HaRav encouraging active settlement. Prominent among the others were Shlomo Aviner and Haim Druckman. In 1978 the soft-spoken, university-educated Aviner (who had gradually become more religiously observant as an adult and, after studying at Merkaz HaRav, had served as rabbi in the same Galilee kibbutz as Levinger) set up a yeshiva in the Muslim quarter of Jerusalem's old city. Built with funds from American Jews and Christian evangelicals, it was called Ateret Cohanim, the Crown of Priests. Its purpose was to provide a place within sight of the Temple Mount for the study of ancient priestly talmudic texts, in anticipation of the coming of the Messiah and the imminent rebuilding of the Temple.[35] In 1990 Ateret Cohanim sought to enlarge its territory by placing some of its students in the Saint John's Hospice in the old city's Christian quarter, a place they called Neot David (Oasis of David); in 1991 they tried to move the students into homes purchased in the Arab village of Silwan, site of the City of David, the ancient Jerusalem. Aviner, who for a time may have been engaged in work for Israel intelligence, subsequently became chairman of the rabbinical council of Judea, Samaria, and Gaza and rabbi of the Bet-El settlement north of Jerusalem, in addition to being head of Ateret Cohanim.

Druckman, the erstwhile B'nai Akiva leader and founding member of Gahelet, had in 1967 established a yeshiva high school in the south of Israel, enrolling many Sephardic Jews of Middle Eastern origin from the surrounding rural settlements. By 1978 he had expanded his student base and established a hesder yeshiva at Or Etzion, which he headed. Later, he also became a National Religious Party member of parliament. But by 1981, wanting to press harder for increased Jewish settlement in the territories, he set up his own party, Morasha ("heritage"). Druckman wore the trademark large knit skullcap and, like all the rabbis, sported a bushy beard; an extraordinarily serious man, he had become a kind of conscience for religious Zionism, a counselor no less than he had been in B'nai Akiva.

Yet Aviner, Druckman, and Levinger still looked to *their* teacher for guidance. While the prophets claimed to speak with God, rabbis only claimed to be able to understand his intentions by means of careful plumbing of the sacred texts, the Torah. This scholarship endowed them with something additional, *da'at Torah,* the capacity to intuit the Torah's position (and hence divine will) on issues on which the Torah appeared to be silent. This interpretation was passed from generation to generation. To the rabbis of Gush Emunim, concerned with the messianic and religious significance of Jewish settlement, the *da'at Torah* that mattered most was that which related to the land of Israel, especially the territories of Judea, Samaria, and Gaza (Yesha, in its Hebrew acronym). Yesha (which can also be translated "salvation") was, after all, the place where Jewish faith was being renewed most vigorously, where settlement motivated by religious Zionism was the dominant dynamic. And no one's opinion about Yesha mattered more than Rabbi Zvi Yehuda Kook's. Kook's pronouncements thus took on the character of doctrine.

In a statement, widely quoted among the Gush Emunim, Kook asserted what is perhaps the fundamental *da'at Torah* of religious Zionist settlement policy:

> All this land is assuredly ours, everyone of us, and it is not permissible to give it to others . . . therefore, once and for all let it be clear and resolved that there is no question here of any Arab territories or Arab lands, but lands of Israel, the eternal settlements of our forefathers . . . and we shall never leave them or be cut off from them.[36]

It was an idea that would echo endlessly among his students throughout the years ahead and would guide the faithful until the end. Levinger, his wife, and his children echoed this sentiment when, along with a few other families, they moved into Beit Hadassah, a building in the center of Hebron's Casbah, the bazaar in the center of the city. Levinger claimed it as part of the Jewish heritage and would not move out. "The Arabs don't understand," he explained to a reporter, "that our connection to Hebron is no less strong than it is to Tel Aviv."[37] They would never leave Hebron, he said.

CAMP DAVID AND ITS AFTERMATH

The 1979 Camp David Accords signed by Menachem Begin and Anwar Sadat were the first sign that the road to redemption might be filled with obstacles. Not only did the agreement vow a withdrawal from Sinai, it also promised that the settlement of Yamit, on the Mediterranean coast, would be relinquished; the Egyptians demanded that the territory there be cleared of Jews and that autonomy be negotiated for the Palestinians in Yesha. That commitment, unprecedented in the life of the state, carried on with the approval of the nation and the assistance of the Israeli armed forces, led to personal and national uncertainty for the faithful. How could Jews dismantle a settlement? How could the prophecies of eternal Jewish return not be fulfilled?

To Moshe Levinger this accord infected Zionism with "the virus of peace."[38] He would have none of it. In a 1979 television interview Miriam Levinger expressed her family's abiding commitment to stay in Beit Hadassah and added, "Hebron will no longer be *judenrein*."[39] Her choice of the Nazi word for "cleared of Jews" to characterize the government's policies was a calculated slap at the Camp David Accords.

In the spring of 1982, in a classic response to the cognitive dissonance between their beliefs and political reality, Levinger led many of the faithful—quite a few of whom moved into the abandoned homes of Yamit in protest against the withdrawal—staving off anxieties that redemption might *not* be at hand by engaging in even greater activism.[40] He was joined by, among others, Yisrael Ariel, brother of Ya'akov and a rabbi in the hesder yeshiva in Yamit. It was a battle they lost. Yamit was the first Jewish settlement voluntarily dismantled by the sovereign state. Ariel became yeshiva head in Neve Dekalim in Gaza and later head of an institute studying the objects that would be used in the Holy Temple of the future; Levinger returned to Hebron.

There was another crisis that year: Rabbi Zvi Yehuda died. The faithful felt orphaned, and in a sense closer to one another. No single rabbi emerged as his successor as the voice of the faithful, and the mantle of rabbinic leadership settled on the men of the hesder yeshiva, most of whom had some connection to Merkaz HaRav or K'far Haroeh. Levinger, Druckman, and Aviner were among the most prominent and active, but others were growing in stature. Dov Lior, at first a rabbi at K'far Haroeh, became chief rabbi of Kiryat Arba, the largest of the Gush Emunim settlements. Zalman Melamed became head of the yeshiva at Bet-El and subsequently chairman of the board of Arutz-7, the radio station of the settler movement. And Eliezer Waldman, after working at Yeshivat Or Etzion with Haim Druckman, became head of the yeshiva in Kiryat Arba; he also became a member of parliament during the 1980s, representing the right-wing Tehiya party and acting as a spokesperson for the settler movement. For moral support these rabbis leaned on the transitional generation of rabbis that followed Kook, elders like Avraham Shapira, head of Merkaz HaRav, and Moshe Zvi Neria of K'far Haroeh.

In Zvi Yehuda's absence, the rabbis were compelled by a desire to be even more zealous, as if to prove themselves worthy of their precious legacy. By focusing their energies on extending settlements in the territories, they sought to deny that the utopia of messianic redemption might be on the verge of disappearance; the aim was to take control of Jewish destiny once again. Often the role played by the rabbis in the settlements was to inject them with religious meaning. To retreat from these territories would be a betrayal of the faith.

Yet while their enthusiasms and faith remained undiminished, it became increasingly difficult to square the course history was taking with the notion of an unswerving movement towards messianic redemption. Moreover, there was abundant evidence that the great religious awakening they had supposed would lead the secular majority in Israel to support the new religious Zionist settlers and their efforts was *not* happening. Camp David, with its unprecedented cession of land and agreement to dismantle a Jewish settlement, shook the confidence of the faithful. And the nation's general support of these provisions further distressed the believers, for it suggested that their pioneering settlements were perceived as less essential than those in the rest of the nation. Tel Aviv might be more important to the nation than Hebron, in other words.

Those who wanted to deny this disappointing reality could still point to the fact that the Sinai and the area around Yamit were not part of the biblical land of Israel. Yesha, however, would be something else; there the line would be drawn.

THE UNDERGROUND

In Yesha, especially in Hebron, settlers experienced a deteriorating political situation and growing insecurity, including attacks on them by Arabs. In reaction to one such attack, in May 1980, when six yeshiva students were killed and sixteen others wounded in Hebron, some of the settlers organized what came to known as the Machteret, the Jewish Underground. This group tried to change the course of events by engaging in extreme and violent actions—attacking an Islamic college in Hebron, blowing up the cars of Arab mayors in the territories, and conspiring to clear the Temple Mount of its mosques in preparation for the rebuilding of the Temple. No one had suspected that these putatively religious people were capable of such activity. Settlement alone had seemed their goal. But now they went further. They concluded, in social analyst Eliezer Don-

Yehiya's words: "We shall no longer depend on miracles. The Holy One, blessed be He, expects us to act, that we bring the Redemption with our own hands."[41] That apparently required aggressive acts of violence as well.

Many in the nation assumed, when members of Machteret were arrested in 1984, that such religious men would never have acted without the approval of their rabbis. The question was, which rabbis? While most of the rabbis were silent, sixteen rabbis, including Dov Lior and Eliezer Waldman, circulated a petition within the Merkaz HaRav community in June 1984 protesting the criticism of the Underground that had been voiced in Merkaz HaRav circles.[42] Even though Waldman was careful to separate himself from the most extreme of Machteret's actions—he had been accused, though never convicted, of giving encouragement and support to the perpetrators—he argued for the release or pardon of those arrested, a goal which was achieved by July 1991. (Waldman's colloquial English made him a favorite of American journalists who sought rabbinic spokesmen for the settlers.)

Yet perhaps no one was more zealous and outspoken on the subject of the Underground than Moshe Levinger. Among those arrested were his son-in-law, three of his neighbors, and five who were with him at the Park Hotel. Levinger was initially arrested too but was released after ten days. Although he was never prosecuted for involvement in Machteret's activities, he was named as a coconspirator by at least one of its leaders, Menachem Livni. According to Livni, Levinger told him that recruits to the Underground should be "people who are deeply religious, people who would never sin, people who haven't got the slightest inclination for violence."[43] Dan Be'eri, another Underground member, claimed, "Levinger said he would not try to prevent the group from carrying out such an operation [as blowing up the mosque on the Temple Mount], although he personally believed the nation had to be prepared in advance for such a thing."[44]

To be sure, not all the settlers' rabbis, or even a majority, supported the aims and activities of the Underground. Shlomo Aviner, for example, focusing on the plot to blow up the mosques on the Temple Mount, published a lengthy series of statements and articles arguing that while "the Temple symbolizes the ultimate return of the Jewish people to its land," its rebuilding should be a national enterprise, carried out in accordance with the wishes of the *entire* people as well as the state, and only after the kingdom of Israel is restored in accordance with the Torah and the instructions of a prophet."[45] Yet for all of Aviner's moderation, he, no less than Levinger, was far from moderating his conviction, as he had put it in 1982, that Jews "must settle the whole Land of Israel, and over all of it establish our rule."[46]

The general population did not, however, accept Aviner's and Waldman's intricate arguments. With the discovery of the Underground and the rabbis' apparent involvement with it, Israelis and Jews worldwide came to perceive these men as unrelenting ideologues whose single-mindedness no longer represented pioneering Zionism but instead bespoke intolerance, an image far closer to the popular perception of haredi rabbis. The idea that religious Zionism was the repository of the best spirit of Israel, holding to the highest moral standards, was called into question. Suddenly, the idealistic settlers who had so caught the imagination of the Israeli public only a few years earlier were threatened with delegitimation and marginalization. The possibility that such cataclysmically violent acts had been carried out with the support of religious Zionist rabbis suggested, moreover, that at least some of these leaders and holy men were no different from the mullahs of the Islamic Jihad. After all, the same moderate Aviner who had declared that it was the Jews' religious obligation to "not abandon the land to any other nation," citing a medieval biblical commentary of Nachmanides, had added: "If that is possible by peaceful means, wonderful, and if not, we are commanded to make war to accomplish it."[47]

Moshe Levinger, ubiquitous in his presence at settler protests and rallies, went further. As at Yamit and in Hebron, he militantly marched, blocked entry or egress, pushed and shoved, always "to tell the world that Eretz Yisrael [the land of Israel] is Jewish."[48] Like the best Israeli officers in battle, more often than not he led the charge; he was with his fellow believers on the ramparts. He had to convince the rest of the nation that Yesha—that is, Judea, Samaria, and Gaza—was intrinsic to the entire nation, no more expendable than Jerusalem or Tel Aviv. Reflecting Levinger's sentiments, the slogan Yesha Is Here began to appear on bumper stickers produced and displayed by the settlers. The slogan played on the double meaning of "Yesha": First, it asserted that the territory indicated by the acronym was *in* and *of* Israel proper. It was this sentiment that resounded at a rally at the Kiryat Arba Sports Center, when Rabbi Lior exclaimed for all the nation to hear: "Without all of Eretz Yisrael there is no life in Israel." Second, the slogan resonated with redemptive promise: *yesha*—salvation—is here, and there is no need to lose the faith; Yesha could not be permitted to go the way of Yamit. But salvation did not come. Instead, the Arabs began an uprising, the intifada. With stones and fires, they tried to chase Israelis away.

"Every day," Levinger told a reporter, as rampaging Arabs made life in the settlements more dangerous, "hundreds of stones are thrown at the army and Jews traveling the streets of Judea, Samaria, and Gaza. The government has the power to quiet the Arabs but lacks the will to do so."[49] Levinger did not lack the will. He battled government policies and Arab stone throwers alike, and not just with words or rabbinic judgments. In 1988, after he was stoned while driving through Hebron with two of his sons, a daughter, and a granddaughter, he began firing a pistol. He later claimed he had shot into the air to frighten his attackers, but others asserted that he left his car and shot directly at the attackers. A stray bullet struck down Khayed Salah, who stood near his shoe store. Seven months later, Levinger was indicted on manslaughter charges. Nine months into the trial, the charge was bargained down to criminally negligent homicide. Sentenced to five months in prison, he was released after ten weeks. "You know," Levinger told his lawyer, "if Moses had to pay because he killed an Egyptian without permission from God, maybe I have to pay, too."[50] And though he maintained during the trial that he had not murdered anyone, he also stated that he wished he had "the honor of killing an Arab."[51] Clearly, Levinger's example indicated that a rabbi was no longer just a moral guide or ideological leader; he could also be a violent activist who would take up a weapon.

Later in 1989, Levinger entered the home of his Arab neighbor, Abdel Rahman Samua, and attacked his family—in retaliation, Levinger later claimed, for attacks on him and one of his eleven children. "I won't behave like Jews in the *Galut* [the Diaspora], who say it's raining when a *goy* [Gentile] spits at a Jew," he explained. "I won't let that happen in Israel."[52] For this act of violence, Levinger was convicted of assault in January 1991 and sentenced to four months in jail. In response, he accused the court of being "a tool of Yasir Arafat," an outburst that made the judge add ten days to his sentence.

Levinger grew increasingly shrill, portraying himself as the last defender of the faithful and the protector of those who were continuing to settle the biblical territories. When he felt the nation and army were abandoning him, he became even more aggressive. "When I traveled to Hebron," he explained, "there awakened within me raging spirits that did not give me peace."[53]

Nor did Levinger give his nation peace. Perhaps no rabbi would plummet so far in Israeli public opinion. The man who had received encouragement from Ben-Gurion and later Begin, whom Geula Cohen had called "the leader of the Zionist revolution," was described by Peres as a "Napoleon." At the same time, however, he remained one of the most dedicated of the beleaguered settlers—still a beacon, a guide for the faithful, a spokesman for and embodiment of the despised religious Jews. He was the person who, one of them said in 1991, "gives us our sense of direction."[54] But his direction was increasingly at odds with that of the nation and the government.

The Union of Rabbis for the People and Land of Israel

The return of the Labour Party to power under Yitzhak Rabin in 1992 marked a watershed. As Levinger and his peers surveyed the scene, they saw a government, the heir of the socialist Zionists, that had no religious parties in its coalition and no Orthodox Jews in its cabinet, headed by a man who was known to have little sympathy for or understanding of Orthodox Judaism or Jewry. Rabin's election—the "revolution," as the Israeli press headlined it—made it clear that a majority of the voters no longer supported the settlement aims of the new religious Zionism.

"The great anger at Rabbi Levinger," said Zvi Katzover, head of the Kiryat Arba council, had led many mainstream Israeli voters to vote for parties in the Labour coalition. By his violent militance "Levinger stabbed us in the back," some settlers were quoted as saying.[55] But Levinger's faith remained intact. He reacted with the calm certainty that this electoral shock would move the opposition closer together and closer to him on the extreme, "and all will turn out well."[56]

But all did not turn out well. The Labour government's agreement with the Palestine Liberation Organization was of course the greatest threat of all, signaling the decision to give up Yesha forever, to relinquish Jewish sovereignty over lands that God had manifestly promised his people. To many of the rabbis and their faithful, this was a pact made by unbelievers. Although it included no immediate agreement to abandon Jewish civilian settlements, it would lead to an accord requiring that the Israeli army be withdrawn from bases in the territories. These would be turned over to the Palestinian Authority and its police force; weapons would be allowed in the hands of Arabs.

Levinger was incensed, as were the other rabbis, and as Levinger had predicted they came together, forming a new organization, the Ichud Rabbanim L'Ma'an Am Yisrael V'Eretz Yisrael (Union of Rabbis for the People and Land of Israel), with a presidium consisting of the elders Avraham Shapira, Moshe Zvi Neria, and Shaul Yisraeli (among the Kooks' veteran pupils) and including rabbis Aviner, Druckman, Melamed, Levinger, Lior, and Waldman. The Union issued a number of dramatic public statements, starting with a general declaration that asserted the basic principles of religious Zionism and applied them to the specific and

changing political realities, thereby wrapping their political stand in the
mantle of religion and a rabbinic *da'at Torah:*

> According to Torah law, it is a positive commandment to move to the Land
> of Israel, to settle there, to conquer it and to take possession of it. And
> since it is a positive commandment to do so, the Jewish position is that to
> act contrary to this would be not only a sin, but [would have] no chance
> of succeeding ultimately[. Advocating such a course] is bad counsel. There-
> fore, any directive to cancel out Jewish settlement in the land of Israel is
> both a sin and bad counsel, and this is the Rabbinic opinion, of Rabbis in
> the Land of Israel and in the United States, against the Oslo accords.[57]

The rabbis were asserting that the Jewish people of Israel were standing
at a crossroads between redemption and apocalypse; their direction
would be determined by the choices made by the nation and its government. If the land was given away to an odious enemy, destruction and
apocalypse were inevitable. But if the land was retained, if settlement
continued unabated, the relentless march toward redemption would continue.

As the government took action that appeared to be directed toward
large-scale withdrawal, these rabbinic opinions were issued with greater
urgency. The rabbis needed to alert and persuade the faithful that the
government's course did not just amount to bad counsel or sin; it jeopardized Jewish security and life, both in the disputed territories and in Israel
proper. Boundaries had disappeared, they asserted, echoing the slogan
Yesha Is Here. To stress the risks to the entire nation, the rabbis focused
on the arms that the Palestinians would have:

> It was clear to everyone that people [i.e., Arabs] in the autonomy must not
> be given arms because then the neighbors of this autonomy would have no
> security. Giving the people of Gaza access to weapons endangers [the Jew-
> ish settlements in] Gush Katif, Ashkelon, Kiryat Gat, and Ashdod. Arms
> in the hands of the Arabs of Jenin, Tul Karem, and Ramallah endanger
> Kfar Sava, Petah Tikva, and Jerusalem. Jewish citizens would be attacked
> and stabbed, and security would be jeopardized throughout the country.

Gush Katif was in Yesha; Ashkelon, Kiryat Gat, and Ashdod were in
Israel proper, as were Kfar Sava, Petah Tikva and Jerusalem. In arguing
that "security would be jeopardized throughout the country," the rabbis
sought to remind the general population that those who supported Yesha
were protecting the whole nation.

To say that Jewish life was being threatened also opened the door
to an important new religious argument: holding onto the territories and

opposing the Oslo accords was a matter of *pikuach nefesh,* the concept of threat to life which, according to Jewish law, is ultimate in importance. According to halakha, in the face of *pikuach nefesh* nearly all laws may be broken, all actions taken. Concluding their statement, the rabbis urged: "Jews! Wake up. Show your opposition to this unfortunate agreement as forcefully as you are able! It is matter of life for every Jew!"

No one was more aware that he needed to awaken all Jews than Avraham Shapira, who had just concluded a term as Ashkenazic chief rabbi of the state. As a young man, Shapira had been a student in the Hebron Yeshiva, a branch of the renowned Slobodka Yeshiva of Lithuania, which relocated to Jerusalem after the Jews were chased out of Hebron in the Arab uprising of 1929. From there he had been invited by Rabbi Zvi Yehuda Kook to become a head at Merkaz HaRav; gradually transformed into a religious Zionist rabbinic guide, he inherited Kook's position in 1982, although he lacked the charisma and stature of his predecessor. In 1983 he was selected as Israeli chief rabbi, following the far more outspoken and prominent Shlomo Goren. Now, in his late seventies, he at last had a chance to make his mark in public. Although portly and cherubic-looking in his satin caftan, snow white beard, and curly earlocks, he had already publicly demonstrated his religiously extreme points of view: In 1987 he had demonstrated against the opening of movie theaters on the Sabbath in Israel; in 1988 he had criticized American Jewry for calling for liberalization of the Israeli law defining who was a Jew, endorsing the most rigorous of Orthodox decisions; and in March 1989 he had called for a ban on Salman Rushdie's *Satanic Verses.*

In a 1994 address to the Ichud Rabbanim, Shapira made the *pikuach nefesh* argument even more explicit. The assertion that the government was endangering Jewish survival was a calculated one. Among the relatively few rabbinic doves (including some in the haredi community, most notably Ashkenazi Rabbi Menachem Schach and Sephardi Rabbi Ovadia Yosef), this same principle had been used to argue in favor of territorial withdrawal. That is, if withdrawal could vouchsafe even one additional Jewish life, it was worthwhile. In a classic rabbinic dissertation drawing upon prior rabbinic literature and Judeo-legal decisions, Shapira countered that argument, explaining that the Jewish obligation to conquer and settle all of the land of Israel overrides consideration of *pikuach nefesh:* in the very command to conquer there is an obligation to put one's life at risk if necessary. But beyond that, he explained, if one were using *pikuach nefesh* as an argument, the greater danger to Jewish life came not from remaining on the land but from withdrawal. "Any withdrawal of our security forces from parts of Eretz Yisrael and giving autonomy to our

Arab enemies, who have suckled their hatred from their youngest infancy, increases the danger," he wrote. "All their declarations and signatures are utterly worthless."

Finally, Shapira, the aged sage, added his own version of Kook's claims: "We are confronted here with the Mitzvot of not foregoing any part of Eretz Yisrael, of settling Eretz Yisrael, and the prohibition of not giving goyim [other nations] a foothold in any part of Eretz Yisrael by transferring it from Jews to goyim." This was a three-step argument: the God-given command to settle the land of Israel assumed dangers to life; withdrawal from conquered and settled land presented the greatest of all dangers to life, for Arabs could not be trusted to make peace; and, beyond everything else, it was sinful to relinquish Jewish sovereignty over the Holy Land to other nations.

God himself had shown the Jews that they were meant to hold to this land; hence the government that sought to relinquish it could not be correct. Having already tried to usurp Zionism from its secular origins, Shapira and the other rabbis of his union had now taken an enormous step away from Abraham Kook's conception that the secular leaders of Zionism could be acting on behalf of God. This was a significant step towards their religious as well as political delegitimation, or even demonization. Suddenly the secular leaders of the government were defined as criminals, bad counselors, equivalent to the goyim, the Arabs. The declaration continued, in words that echoed many of Levinger's most volatile statements:

> There are Jews that agree to the goyim's claim that we are thieves. We are preventing these poor unfortunates from creating their own state in Eretz Yisrael. Unfortunately, many of these Jews are part of the government and the government rests on such circles. Some are Arabs; others are communists that never recognized our right to Eretz Yisrael; and still others are extreme leftists that never wanted a Jewish state but a binational one. They don't believe in the Tenach [Scripture] and claim that the book of Joshua which describes how Joshua conquered Eretz Yisrael, should be expunged from the Tenach that is taught in the schools.

In contrast to these Jews stood the rabbis and their audience, "observant G-d fearing Jews that keep the whole Torah, oral and written, from beginning to end. We are willing to sacrifice our lives for every single Jewish custom. Thus, we cannot agree to forgo even one square inch of our holy land." This sort of commitment was true Zionism, and those who did not share it were no longer acting on behalf of the Jewish people.

Rabbi Shapira's speech, however, did not call for direct action but instead concluded with a vague and typical rabbinic call: "Let us close ranks and work for the annulment of the decree and rely upon our 'Father in Heaven' who will have mercy on His nation and His land. May we be privileged to experience a great redemption speedily in our time." To be sure, some might draw their own conclusions as to what action these words called for, but the truly observant would never take concrete initiative without approval or at least guidance from the rabbi they considered their personal religious authority. The counsel they received, however, would depend upon which rabbi they asked, although properly one asks questions only of one's rabbinic decisor (yeshiva students normally choose the head of the yeshiva in which they studied). In practice, though, one asks a question only when one is already certain of the response and has decided to accept and be bound by that answer. In short, the rabbi's judgment is often simply a ratification of a prior personal decision. By voicing and supporting these sentiments, the rabbis of the Ichud Rabbanim made clear their opinion on direct action. They had only to wait for the question to be asked before issuing a halakhic judgment. That would come in time.

Whether these rabbis, including Levinger, intended to initiate violence or only to ratify it among the faithful is not clear, just as their relation to the Underground had been uncertain. In general the abiding question is whether the fundamentalist rabbis are leaders or simply collective representations, symbolic reflections, and religious expressions of those who place trust in them. What is most likely is that these rabbis synergistically reacted to and directed the activities of their followers. Even Levinger needed the support and encouragement of his followers, his faithful.

Declarations by the Ichud Rabbanim notwithstanding, the peace process moved forward relentlessly, without protest from the majority of the Israeli population. The rabbis next decided that a rabbinic *psak,* a binding judgment based on halakha, was required. On 11 November 1993, three days after Arabs fired on Haim Druckman's car and killed his driver, the Ichud Rabbanim, meeting in a Jerusalem hotel, issued decisions, presumably in response to inquiries from their flock, restating "the fact that the Jewish people are the only legitimate owners of the Land of Israel" and expressing "fear that the 'agreement' will endanger the lives of all the inhabitants of Israel." Key among the decisions reached at this meeting was the fourth one:

> According to the laws of the Torah, it is forbidden to relinquish the political rights of sovereignty and national ownership over any part of historic Eretz Yisrael to another authority or people. All of historic Eretz Yisrael which

is now in our possession belongs to the entire Jewish people past, present and future, and therefore no one in any generation can give away that to which he [alone] does not have title. Therefore any agreement to do so is null and void, obligates no one, has no legal or moral force whatsoever.

The rabbis were legally undoing the Oslo accords. Moreover, they were not just interested in the territory for its own sake. Holding on to it was identical with holding fast to the faith, the Jewish way. The Oslo accords were not just about land but were part of an ongoing culture war between the religious and the secular, between those who were guided by faith and heavenly covenants and those who rejected God and his promises. Relinquishing territory was equated with that other cardinal sin, assimilation, a loss of Jewish identity. Both assimilation and territorial compromise undermined the all-important Jewish continuity. Hence, decision number eleven:

We are extremely concerned over the present trend that aims to create a secular culture here which is to blend into "a new Middle East"—a trend which will lead to assimilation. We have a sacred obligation to strengthen and deepen our people's connection to the Torah and to Jewish tradition as passed down through the generations.

And what did this require of the faithful? For this, the rabbis provided their twelfth decision:

We support the continuation of protests, demonstrations, and strikes within the framework of the law. In addition, we encourage educating and informing the masses in order that they may realize the falseness of this "peace." We hope that our wide range of actions will prevent the government from carrying out damaging policies.

This was a call for action, a clear message that echoed Levinger's sentiments most powerfully. Men and women must act on God's behalf and save the land and the Jewish people. Only barely did it stop short of endorsing the violence that Levinger had modeled.

Response in Israel was swift and broad. Instead of rallying the general population, the Union's decisions incensed it; the Rabin government saw in them a rabbinic call to insurrection. Only the fact that the rabbis represented so small a segment of the population, coupled with a desire to keep the lid on passions, prevented government action against them. The conflict between the rabbis and the state grew, however, as the peace accords moved closer to fruition and Israel withdrew from Jericho and Gaza. Before his death in December 1995, Moshe Zvi Neria, who five years earlier had received the Israel Prize, urged a change in the standard prayer for the state of Israel recited in synagogues worldwide: instead of praying for the protection *of* its leaders, he suggested a text that asked for protection *from* its leaders.

In May 1994 the Ichud Rabbanim, restless about events, issued another set of resolutions, contending that the PLO-government agreements were "creating deep spiritual and social divisions, while creating an atmosphere of civil war." Again they called for protests against what they labeled "the criminal act of signing this agreement." This was a far cry from the Kook viewpoint that secular Zionists might be instruments of God's plan. Criminals, after all, cannot act on God's behalf, cannot bring the redemption or do God's bidding; criminals can only be punished. To make sure these lessons were learned, moreover, the declaration called on "rabbis, heads of yeshivot and educators" to "dedicate hours of study devoted to explaining the living link between the nation and the land of Israel."

Finally, in July 1995 the most definitive rabbinic ruling was handed down by Shapira and fourteen of his associates on the executive of the Ichud Rabbanim. Among the signers were rabbis Ya'akov Ariel (now chief rabbi of Ramat Gan), Druckman, Lior, Melamed, Neria, Nahum Rabinovitch (head of the hesder yeshiva in Ma'ale Adumim), and Waldman. The revolutionary aspect of this ruling lay in its claim that "there is a prohibition from the Torah to evacuate [army] camps and transfer the location into the authority of Gentiles." That is, the rabbis, five of whom were from hesder yeshivas, were telling soldiers (and in particular their hesder student soldiers, many of whom headed units charged with evacuating the camps) that they were prohibited from following the directives of their secular government leaders and superior officers when it came to relinquishing the "area within which the I.D.F. [Israel Defence Forces] is located and controls." This was because "a permanent army camp is also in and of itself a Jewish settlement in all respects," and the prohibition on dismantling Jewish settlements had already been established in the May ruling.

This edict, for the first time, explicitly put the rabbis and the secular government, and especially the army, on opposing sides; direct and open conflict was inevitable. The very soldiers, the hesder boys, suddenly became suspect. Twenty years before, they had been considered the most dedicated, the elite; their religious morality had been so stringent that in Lebanon in 1982 they had called their rabbis to find out whether they could eat cherries off Lebanese trees without asking permission of their owners. To whom did they owe their greatest allegiance: their flag, government, and army or their Torah and the rabbis who called the govern-ment criminal and its orders sinful? The choice confronting these soldiers was between loyalty to values on which their lives were based and mili-tary orders.

The outcry from the Israeli public and government was sharp and immediate. President Ezer Weitzman said, "[The ruling] undermines the basic principles on which the I.D.F. is based and could invalidate the democratic foundation of the state."[58] Prime Minister Rabin called on the attorney general to determine whether the rabbis had breached the law and were fomenting sedition. Not only Levinger but the entire Union might now be acting illegally. This ruling was not like encouraging civil disobedience and protest demonstrations; this directive was aimed at the army—once the great integrative institution of Israeli society—and had the potential to cause a civil war. Government ministers Shulamit Aloni and Yossi Sarid called for the disbanding of the hesder yeshivas, the very system that in 1990 had been honored with the Israel Prize. The same rabbis who, following Kookist ideology, had once asserted that the state and its army were holy instruments of God's will, were now distancing themselves from and endangering that state and army.

To be sure, this change was not effected hastily. The rabbis were keenly aware of the momentous implications of their decision. As one described the moment of their decision: "The atmosphere in the room reflected the historic nature of the gathering, which was conducted with majestic dignity."[59]

Even the National Religious Party was thrown into confusion by the rabbis' decision. Yigal Bibi, one of its members of parliament, whose son was then in the army, announced, "I will not be able to instruct my son to disobey orders."[60] Rabbi Yehuda Amital, head of the Har Etzion hesder yeshiva, announced his complete disagreement with the ruling, arguing that it was wrong to use halakha for political purposes. This edict, he added, put the Jewish people in far greater jeopardy than most of the territorial withdrawals the army had planned.

Retreating somewhat in the days ahead, some of the signers of this declaration explained that their decision was only binding on those who actually asked for their counsel and personally accepted their authority. But as much of the nation realized, these were prominent rabbis whose following was broad and deep. Their decisions would not easily be dis-missed. A new rabbinic argument was also beginning to be heard. If the withdrawals were truly endangering life, then the Jews who were making and implementing these life-threatening agreements might be defined as a *rodef* or a *moyser*. According to Jewish law, a *rodef* (pursuer) is some-

354 / Samuel C. Heilman

one who threatens the life of a Jew or through his action puts the life of a Jew in danger, while a *moyser* is one who hands Jews over to their enemies. The law asserts that one must, or at least may, kill the *rodef* and punish the *moyser*.

These arguments had been circulating in yeshiva circles since at least 1993. In December of that year, on the heels of the Ichud Rabbanim's conclave, the chief rabbi of Ramat Gan, Ya'akov Ariel, reflected on the question of whether Prime Minister Yitzhak Rabin might be classified halakhically as a *rodef*.[61] Not prepared to designate Rabin a *rodef,* since that would also place all his supporters in the same category, a situation that would create the conditions for violent civil war, Ariel concluded that Rabin was an "indirect pursuer." While "a pursuer is subject to death, an indirect pursuer is not subject to death," Ariel stated; then he added, as a codicil, "yet in order to be saved from him it is permissible to hurt him" but only if doing so assured "redemption from danger." In the case of the prime minister, Ariel concluded, "an attack on indirect pursuers will not prevent the danger."

Yet what if one concluded that hurting the prime minister *would* assure redemption from danger? At some B'nai Akiva meetings during 1995, there were discussions about shooting at Israeli soldiers attempting to take Jews out of settlements.[62] Dror Adani, a B'nai Akiva member and later one of the suspects in the conspiracy to assassinate Prime Minister Rabin, has said, "We would sit and talk politics. We had to stop the [peace] process. Inside of me, I feared that our actions may bring about a civil war. We had our doubts. Both Rabin and Peres were classified as *rodefim* and therefore had to be killed."[63] At Ramat Gan's Orthodox Bar Ilan University, some students were likewise debating the question of whether the prime minister deserved "to die for his deeds."[64]

The rabbis had opened the door for these judgments. Yigal Amir, former student at the hesder yeshiva in Kerem Beyavneh, army veteran, and student at Bar Ilan, walked through it. Amir (whose first name means "Redeemer") felt compelled to prevent the withdrawal of Jews from the land of Israel. After assassinating Yitzhak Rabin on 4 November 1995, he claimed that "my whole life, I learned Jewish law" and that that law permitted him to kill the enemy, the prime minister.[65] Later, perhaps reflecting on Ariel's arguments, he claimed in court that he had meant only to paralyze the prime minister and not to kill him.

Amir, however, did not need to point to a particular rabbi who had given him sanction to harm the prime minister. The air had been filled with rabbinic opinions. Shlomo Aviner reported that Margalit Har-Shefi, a Bar Ilan student who was detained for questioning after the Rabin murder, had come to him several weeks before the shooting requesting "that I provide her with counterarguments that she could use in debating" those who like Amir called for the prime minister's death.[66] While Har-Shefi looked for debating points, Amir took gun in hand. While some pointed to Lior and Rabinovitch as the ones who offered approval, others singled out Ariel or Waldman, who had been so understanding of the violence perpetrated by the Underground. But it did not really matter which rabbi, if any, Amir had turned to for approval. The ground had been prepared by the Ichud Rabbanim: the government were criminals and sinners, their actions would lead away from redemption, and they had to be stopped.

"Provide for yourself a rabbi and acquire for yourself a gun," the largest circulation Israeli newspaper quipped in a headline at the time, satirizing the well-known talmudic adage.[67]

THE INFLUENCE OF MEIR KAHANE

Another rabbi who had sought to guide the faithful, and whose impact was also felt, posthumously, in the turn toward violence, was Meir Kahane. Shaped by the ethnic and racial tensions of his New York background, Kahane came to Israel and embraced the ideals of Zionism, which he wed to his own militancy, theology, and politics of confrontation. Underscoring the implicit ethnocentrism of Zionism and mixing it with the biblical idea of a separate and superior Jewish people, he formed the idea that for Israel to be a Jewish state demanded that it actively rid itself of Arabs, whose very presence undermined the purity and promise of the Jewish character of Israel. In places like Kiryat Arba, the Jewish settlement adjacent to Hebron, Kahane and his Kach party won support on the city council. Their support grew in the days of the Arab stone throwing and uprising. Many soldiers, worn down by the Lebanese war and the grinding battle against the Arab uprising, were among those receptive to its message. (As a soldier in the elite Golani brigade, Yigal Amir had been ardent in beating Arabs whom he caught participating in violence.)[68]

Kahane's goals were not easily distinguishable from Levinger's. Though they have not been identified with each other, Levinger attended Kahane's funeral in November 1990, and Levinger's son's house in Hebron was "festooned" with Kahane posters.[69] Like Kahane, Levinger had no love for Arabs. Levinger, however, called not for their transfer but only for their subordination.

Kahane wanted not just to transfer Arabs out of the Jewish state but to transform Israel into an Orthodox Jewish entity. After the Arabs, his quarrel, like that of the ancient Maccabee zealots, was with the Jews who compromised their Judaism—"hellenizers," as he called them. Kahane counted as contemporary hellenizers those Israelis who had assimilated secular values and lifestyles and, long before the Ichud Rabbanim, connected assimilation and territorial compromise. Moreover, Kahanism, like the religious rulings that the rabbis made, included an animosity to democracy, which it viewed as a doctrine that allowed the people rather than God to decide what was right. If democracy could allow the state to be taken over by a secular and heretical government that gave Jewish land to Arabs, endangering Jewish life and the Jewish future, democracy had to be set aside. This idea took on a life of its own after Kahane's death, especially in the Kahane Chai (Kahane Lives) party and among its supporters. It infected a number of Orthodox Jews who felt that contemporary events and actions by the hellenizing government, seen as absorbed by American culture and American goals, were threatening the Jewish future. Kahanism captured some of the Orthodox in the same net in which it caught extreme nationalists. Suddenly, even for some of the religious Zionists, democracy became a questionable ideal.

As the peace process moved swiftly forward, all these groups found themselves pressed into common cause. Kahane Chai and small allied groups like Zu Artzeynu (This Is Our Land) and Eyal (Organization of the Jewish Fighter) were the most extreme, but the settlers and their rabbis, and even some of the haredim, became convinced that the current secular-dominated government was the great enemy. At the same time, those Orthodox who still valued the ideals of democracy, tolerance, and pluralism became silent, lacking leadership and nerve as they watched many of their rabbis and children swept up in the religious right.

THE RABBINIC COUNTERARGUMENTS

And then came the shots that killed Yitzhak Rabin. Amir, son of a Torah scribe from Yemen, could not easily be separated from his act or background. Rabbi Aaron Lichtenstein, a Harvard Ph.D. in English literature and a head of the Har Etzion Yeshiva, appraised Amir in a talk to his students in the aftermath of the assassination:

> Here was a man who grew up in the best of our institutions. A day before the murder, he could have been cited as a shining example of success and achievement, and a source of communal pride. Coming from a 'deprived' background, he studied in a yeshiva high school, attended a great yeshivat

hesder, and was accepted to the most prestigious division of Bar-Ilan University.

As Lichtenstein concluded, the choices Amir made were "not 'despite' but, at least partly, 'because' " of his belief and Jewish education.

Lichtenstein's colleague, Rabbi Yehuda Amital, who in 1968 had taken twenty young men and formed a yeshiva in the Etzion region in the territories and who, within days of the Rabin murder, was appointed a minister in the new government of Shimon Peres, added his voice to those in the religious Zionist camp who sought to retrieve their young followers from the extremism of Levinger, Kahane, and Amir. He argued that "halakha is too volatile to be left in the hands of youth," adding that no individual can say, "I will decide for everyone, and I have the right to assault the anointed of God, chosen by the people, a man who dedicated his entire life to the Jewish people." Citing the rabbinic tradition, he concluded that "our sages tell us even a sinful idolater cannot be put to death unless the highest judicial authorities condemn him." Then he added, "the populist use of halakha in political debates must be stopped"[70]

In a widely distributed talk, Amital also cited Maimonides, the great medieval rabbinic authority, who explained that "whomever the Jewish people choose to lead them is the choice of God, for if God would not have approved, the election would not have succeeded." This statement recalled Rabbi Abraham Kook's belief that God can and does act through secular authorities. Echoing that judgment, Rabbi Yoel Bin-Nun, head of the high school for girls in the West Bank city of Ofra and one of the founding voices of Gush Emunim, wrote in December 1995 in *Yediot Acharonot*, "The peace process is a heavenly decree."[71] In a similar vein, rejecting the Kahanist and haredi notion that secular Jews are the absolute "other," Lichtenstein asserted, "they are our flesh and blood."

Even Shlomo Aviner expressed this sentiment in his call for "loving someone with opposing views":

> Disagreements are legitimate, and sometimes even necessary. One is obligated to wage a forceful intellectual confrontation against ideas that may destroy the Jewish people. But this is a far cry from an obligation to hate the person expressing those ideas. Divided opinions—yes; divided hearts—no. We must understand that even when an idea is hateful, the man expressing it is not. . . .
>
> It is incumbent upon us to separate in our minds between the man, and the opinions that he holds. For if we don't, but instead form stereotypes,

and create mental caricatures blowing this one aspect of his personality way out of proportion, this distorted portrait replaces our knowledge of him as a human being created in the image of God, and we begin to view him as a foreign object, a "political animal." From here easily arises the (mistaken) dispensation to hate, and to attack, and, who knows, even to murder.[72]

Zalman Melamed, responding to accusations that Arutz-7, the radio station he headed, was fomenting hatred and shared part of the responsibility for the assassination, bemoaned the dissipation of "feelings of a common destiny, national brotherhood, and mutual love." Drawing on the Kook ideological heritage, he urged his listeners to "the recognition that all of us, together, belong to a special nation with a unique mission—different than all other nations." He called on the faithful "to renew and rebuild the togetherness that is the essential hallmark of the Jewish nation, adding that "this, of course, requires mutual consideration of the highest order. Any course of action that touches upon the fundamental nature of our nation must be decided upon only by a wide national consensus. We must spare no effort to improve the relations between the religious and non-religious sectors. We must carefully safeguard that which allows all of the various groups within our people to live together as one nation."[73]

Yet for all these calls for soul-searching and unity from some of the hesder yeshiva rabbis, the divisions between the expansionist religious Zionists and secular Israel began to reappear as the initial shock of the assassination wore away. In late November 1995, Israeli police investigated Rabbi Dov Lior of Kiryat Arba on suspicion of incitement, suggesting he may have given rabbinic approval for acts of violence. Religious affairs minister Simon Shetreet called for Ya'akov Ariel's removal from his post as Ramat Gan chief rabbi for similar reasons. Parliament member Ran Cohen called for an end to government funding of a military academy affiliated with Rabbi Haim Druckman's Or Etzion yeshiva on the grounds that it was unacceptable to support a school whose dean signs rabbinic rulings telling soldiers to disobey orders issued by the army. And in early December, deputy defense minister Ori Orr called for the shutdown of the hesder yeshiva system, arguing that it was necessary for all soldiers to serve in a standard way. Although Prime Minister Peres countermanded this proposal (as had Rabin before him), more and more Israelis had come to perceive these institutions as sanctuaries for the spokesmen of insurrection.

As for Moshe Levinger, he was again sentenced to prison for violent

activities, with an admonition by the judge that "Rabbi Levinger has chosen the path of 'an eye for an eye' and this is unacceptable."[74] In January
1996, the Jerusalem District Court turned down his appeal of the conviction, and Levinger turned himself over to police to begin serving his sentence. In the meantime, the diminished hard core of his supporters, the
Hebron Jewish community, issued a statement:

> We deplore the decision by the Israeli courts that sentenced Rabbi Moshe
> Levinger to a prison sentence for disturbing the peace at a time when hun-
> dreds of Arab terrorists are being set free by the Israeli government. Even
> murderers are being set free. The Levinger family have been a pillar of He-
> bron and have given their lives for the Jewish people.[75]

Following the withdrawal of the Israeli forces from Shechem in mid-
December 1995, Ichud Rabbanim issued yet another reminder that withdrawal from the territories and their deliverance "on a silver platter" to
Arab gentiles was a sin and placed the Jewish people in *pikuach nefesh,*
mortal danger.[76] The ruling was again signed by, among others, Shapira,
Ariel, and Druckman. Druckman furthermore asserted that his student
soldiers "cannot be expected to act against their way of life, their religious
beliefs or their conscience," and added, "I would hope the I.D.F. will not
place these men in a position in which they are forced to disobey an
order."[77] Comparisons were drawn by some of Druckman's supporters
between the rabbis' decisions to order their students to refuse to assist
in the withdrawal of Jews from the territories and the earlier demands
by "left-wing" parliament members who had urged soldiers to refuse to
carry out commands to uproot Arabs from their settlements during harvest time.[78]

Those who tried to steer a middle course, to remain true to the faith
but loyal to the state, its government, and its democratic apparatus, were
caught in the middle. They were not taken seriously by the general public—Amital was labeled "merely window dressing"[79]—and were abandoned by erstwhile allies, who saw them as quislings; in planning a National Religious Party rally for 16 December 1995, a decision was made
to include Druckman among the invited speakers but not to invite Amital.[80] Rabbi Bin-Nun was provided with a twenty-four-hour complement
of guards after violent threats were made against him.

To the public at large, the overarching question at the beginning of
1996 was where it would all end. Would Amital, Lichtenstein, Bin-Nun,
and others like them become the dominant voices and rabbinic guides of
religious Zionists, or would Levinger and the Ichud Rabbanim emerge
as their ultimate authorities and spokesmen? Would peace eventually

reign in Israel? Or would the next stage fulfill the cynical prophecy that the war between the Jews and the Arabs will be followed by a war among the Jews themselves over the Jewish state?

Notes

1. A. I. Kook, *Rav A. Y. Kook: Selected Letters,* trans. Tzvi Feldman, letter 35.

2. For a full discussion of the haredi Jews, see Samuel Heilman, *Defenders of the Faith* (New York: Schocken, 1992).

3. Michael Rosenak, "Jewish Fundamentalism in Israeli Education," in Martin E. Marty and R. Scott Appleby, eds., *Fundamentalisms and Society* (Chicago: University of Chicago Press, 1993), 392.

4. Gideon Aran, "The Roots of Gush Emunim," in Peter Medding, ed., *Studies in Contemporary Jewry,* vol. 2 (Bloomington: Indiana University Press, 1986). See also the essay by Aran in this volume.

5. Aran "Roots of Gush Emunim," 142 n. 23.

6. Benjamin Ish-Shalom, *Rabbi Abraham Isaac Kook: Between Rationalism and Mysticism* (Tel Aviv: Am Oved, 1990), 11.

7. Quoted in Robert I. Friedman, "The Messiah Complex," *Vanity Fair,* July 1991, 135.

8. Anathoth, the village from which Jeremiah came, is in northern Jerusalem, just beyond the 1948 armistice line.

9. Friedman, "Messiah Complex," 134.

10. Quoted in *U.S. News & World Report,* 4 April 1988, 30.

11. Quoted in Martin E. Marty and R. Scott Appleby, *The Glory and the Power* (Boston: Beacon Press, 1992), 118.

12. Shlomo Aviner, "A Double Crisis: The Body of Israeli Nationalism and Its Soul," *Nekuda,* no. 14, 15 August 1980, 12.

13. See, for example, Ish-Shalom, *Rabbi Abraham Isaac Kook,* 29.

14. See Aran, "Roots of Gush Emunim," 120. For a fuller description of this group, see Gideon Aran, "Jewish Zionist Fundamentalism: The Bloc of the Faithful in Israel (Gush Emunim)," in Martin E. Marty and R. Scott Appleby, eds. *Fundamentalisms Observed* (Chicago: University of Chicago Press, 1991), 265–344.

15. Friedman, "Messiah Complex," 137.

16. A. I. Kook, *Arpalay Tohar,* quoted in Ish-Shalom, *Rabbi Abraham Isaac Kook,* 185.

17. These ideals were most prominently associated with German rabbi Samson Raphael Hirsch, whose sons-in-law, the Breuers, played a key role in the leadership of Horev.

18. See Aran, "Roots of Gush Emunim," 142 n. 23; Menachem Friedman, *Hevrah Ve Dat* (Jerusalem: Yad Ben Tzvi, 1978), 52.

19. Rosenak, "Jewish Fundamentalism," 393.

20. "Yishuv Hechadash," new settlement, was the name used to identify the settlement of Zionists. It stood in contrast to the "Yishuv Hayashan," old settlement, associated with those few Orthodox who lived passively in the Holy Land, quietly waiting for the Messiah and living off the dole from Jewish communities

abroad. A yeshiva that identified itself with the new settlement was essentially identifying itself with the new active Zionism.

21. Aran, "Roots of Gush Emunim," 132.

22. Aaron Kotler, "How to Teach Torah" (Lakewood, N.J.: Rabbi Aaron Kotler Institute for Advanced Learning, 1972), 3. See also Yochanan Ben-Yaakov, "Religious Youth and the Manner of Its Education," *Amudim* 467 (Heshvan 5745/November 1985): 83.

23. *Kol Ha'Aretz* (Jerusalem: Chug Shollelei HaChaluka [Group against the Partition], 1947), cited in Yoseph Shilhav, "The Peace Process as an Educational Problem," unpublished manuscript, 1.

24. Rosenak, "Jewish Fundamentalism," 396.

25. Shlomo Aviner, "Our Principles of Faith," in the Israeli daily *Ma'ariv*; republished on the Internet by Ateret Cohanim, the Jerusalem Reclamation Project, at gopher://gopher.jer1.co.il:70/oo/relig/ateret/rav/faith.

26. Aran, "Roots of Gush Emunim," 134.

27. Aran, "Roots of Gush Emunim," 142 n. 26.

28. Robert I. Friedman, "Making Way for the Messiah," *New York Review of Books,* 11 October 1990, 45

29. Encyclopedia Judaica Yearbook 1975–1976, 305.

30. Aviv Lavi, "Analysis," *Ha'Ir,* 17 November 1995, 51–55.

31. See the photo of the settlers in Encyclopedia Judaica Yearbook 1975–1976, 313.

32. See Friedman, "Messiah Complex," 135.

33. Quoted in Milton Viorst, *Sands of Sorrow* (New York: Harper and Row, 1987) p. 158.

34. Asher Arian, *Politics in Israel: The Second Generation* (New York: Chatham House, 1985), 97.

35. Robert I. Friedman, "The Settlers," *New York Review of Books,* 15 June 1989, 55.

36. Quoted in Zvi Ra'anan, *Gush Emunim* (Tel Aviv: Sifriyat Poalim, 1980).

37. Quoted in Friedman, "Messiah Complex," 134.

38. Viorst, *Sands of Sorrow,* 223.

39. Quoted in Friedman, "Messiah Complex," 135.

40. For the classic discussion of this process, see Leon Festinger et al., *When Prophecy Fails* (New York: Harper, 1956).

41. Quoted in *Ha'Ir,* 17 November 1995, 53.

42. "Friends, Heed Your Words," *Tzfiya,* no. 1 (August 1984), 41–42.

43. Friedman, "Messiah Complex," 135–36.

44. Friedman, "Messiah Complex," 136.

45. Shlomo Aviner, *Shalhevetyah: Pirkei Kodesh Unikdash* (Torch of God: Chapters on the holy and the sanctified) (Bet El: Sifriyat Hava, 1989), 13.

46. Friedman, "Making Way for the Messiah," 47.

47. Friedman, "Making Way for the Messiah," 47.

48. Friedman, "Settlers," 50.

49. Friedman, "Messiah Complex," 99.

50. Friedman, "Messiah Complex," 137.

51. Friedman, "Messiah Complex," 137.

52. Friedman, "Messiah Complex," 98.

53. Friedman, "Messiah Complex," 135.

54. Friedman, "Messiah Complex," 137.

55. Zvi Singer, "Dismay among the Settlers: Great Anger at Levinger and Parties of the Right," *Yediot Acharonot,* 24 June 1992, 13.

56. Singer, "Dismay among the Settlers," 13.

57. The argument regarding "bad counsel" had, ironically, originally been made by the Orthodox (haredim) in opposing Zionism. Many of these documents have now been posted on the Internet; see the Jerusalem One site (particularly the home page of the Union of Rabbis for the People and Land of Israel, http://www.jer1.co.il/orgs/ichud/irindex.htm, and the Opinion page for Arutz-7 radio, http://www.jer1.co.il/media/arutz7/opinion.html) and the Mail-Jewish Torah and halakha discussion list (particularly its collection of rabbinic statements relating to the Rabin assassination, http://shamash.nysernet.org/mail-jewish/rabin.html).

58. Jerusalem Post News Service, 13 July 1995.

59. Rabbi Sholom Gold, "More on the IDF Controversy," open letter posted on the Internet (archived at http://shamash.org/mail-jewish). Gold, formerly of the United States, is now rabbi in congregation Zichron Yosef in Jerusalem.

60. *Yediot Acharonot,* 13 July 1995, 14.

61. For a discussion of Ariel and the withdrawal from Yamit, see Eliezer Don-Yehiya, "The Book and the Sword," in Martin E. Marty and R. Scott Appleby, eds., *Accounting for Fundamentalisms: The Dynamic Character of Movements* (Chicago: University of Chicago Press, 1994). The article by Ariel appeared in *Hatzofeh,* a religious Zionist newspaper on 31 December 1993.

62. *Yediot Acharonot,* 11 December 1995, 14.

63. Quoted in *Yediot Acharonot,* 11 December 1995, 5.

64. Shlomo Aviner, letter to Edmond I., Esq., 20 December 1995, in "Seeking Truth and Justice: An Exchange of Letters," posted on the Arutz-7 Opinion page on the World Wide Web (http://www.jer1.co.il/media/arutz7/aviner2.htm).

65. "Killing for God," *Time,* 4 December 1995.

66. Aviner, "Letter to Edmond I. Esq."

67. *Yediot Acharonot,* 17 November 1995.

68. *New York Times,* 19 November 1995, 1.

69. Friedman, "Messiah Complex," 97.

70. *Ha'aretz,* 9 November 1995.

71. *Yediot Acharonot,* 14 December 1995.

72. Shlomo Aviner, "Loving Someone with Opposing Views," December 1995, posted on the World Wide Web (http://shamash.nysernet.org/mail-jewish/Rabin/Aviner 1.txt and http://www.jer1.co.il/media/arutz7/loving.htm).

73. Zalman Melamed, "In the Wake of the Assassination," December 1995, posted on the World Wide Web (http://www.jer1.co.il/media/arutz7/mel1.html).

74. *Ma'ariv,* 12 December 1995, 18.

75. Shomron News Service, 17 January 1996.

76. Israel Radio, 15 December 1995.

77. Shomron News Service, 15 December 1995.

78. *Yediot Acharonot,* editorial, 27 June 1990.

79. Jacob Schreiber, "Window Dressing or True Voice," *Jewish Week,* 8 December 1995, 55.

80. *Ma'ariv,* 12 December 1995, 23.

EIGHT

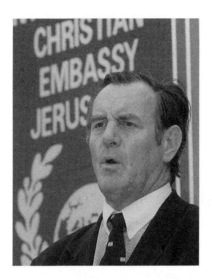

A CHRISTIAN FUNDAMENTALIST VISION
OF THE MIDDLE EAST

Jan Willem van der Hoeven and the International

Christian Embassy

Yaakov Ariel

In 1985 a Zionist conference took place in Basel, Switzerland, commemorating the first Zionist congress convened in that city by Theodore Herzl
almost ninety years earlier.[1] This congress was sponsored, not by the
World Zionist Organization or any of its affiliates, nor by the state of
Israel, but by the International Christian Embassy (ICE), an institution
established and run by Christian supporters of Israel. This Christian
Zionist congress, the first of its kind, was a manifestation of the self-
perception of the leader of the Embassy, Jan Willem van der Hoeven,
and his associates as true followers of the Zionist ideal of the ingathering
of the entire people of Israel and the building of a Jewish commonwealth
within the historical boundaries of the Land of Israel. In their eyes they
were indeed an embassy, representing true Christianity and working to-

wards the realization of God's plans for the end of age and the ushering in of the messianic kingdom.

In October 1992 the Embassy organized its yearly Tabernacles gathering in Jerusalem, with thousands of supporters from all over the world. Israel's prime minister, Yitzhak Rabin, addressed the opening at Binyanei Ha'Uma, the major concert hall in Jerusalem, conveying the government's greetings and commending the audience for their love and goodwill towards Israel. Rabin's speech at this gathering signified the special connection that has developed between ICE and the government of Israel, a country van der Hoeven views as fulfilling an essential role in the realization of the kingdom of God on earth.

MESSIANISM AND CHRISTIAN ZIONISM: IDEOLOGICAL ROOTS OF THE INTERNATIONAL CHRISTIAN EMBASSY

Belief in the imminent return of the Lord characterized Christianity in its early generations but was largely abandoned by the church in the fifth century. The attitude of the major Christian churches since then could be described as mainly amillennial: passages in Scripture containing messianic overtones have been interpreted allegorically and symbolically. A number of groups adhering to a belief in the imminent arrival of Jesus to establish the kingdom of God on earth did, however, appear in Western Christianity in the Middle Ages and the early modern period.[2] Some of these groups recognized in the Jews the historical Israel and expected their return to their ancient homeland as part of the events presaging the end of time. A resurgence of messianic expectations occurred in the 1640s and 1650s in England at the time of the English Revolution. Such hopes played a part in the decision to allow Jews—who had been expelled in 1291—to reenter the realm.[3]

A new wave of messianic hopes arose in English religious life in the early decades of the nineteenth century. Among its ardent advocates was the seventh Earl of Shaftesbury, who viewed the Jews as the historical Israel and the object of biblical prophecies. In 1840 Shaftesbury approached the minister of foreign affairs, Lord Palmerston, with the suggestion that Britain initiate the establishment in Palestine of a Jewish commonwealth.[4] Other British and American evangelicals as well as European pietists also advocated the idea of the Jewish restoration to Zion and the establishment of a Jewish commonwealth.[5] Perhaps the most noted among them was William Hechler, who befriended Theodore Herzl, the father of the political Zionist movement, and helped him approach some of Europe's rulers. The International Christian Embassy sees itself as heir to this Christian Zionist tradition, a view reflected in the Christian Zionist congresses it organized in Basel in 1985 and 1988, and in its publications, which often refer to the deeds and contributions of earlier Christian supporters of Jewish restoration.[6]

Messianic expectations became widespread in American religious life relatively late. Movements such as the Mormons and the Millerites, which arose in the 1820s and 1830s, were ostracized by the mainstream churches. The messianic hope become an accepted and popular component of evangelical Christianity in the United States only in the decades following the Civil War, when it gained ground among members of major churches, such as the Baptists, Methodists, and Presbyterians. By the end of the nineteenth century premillennialist belief had become characteristic of conservative American Protestantism, notably among the rank and file of the emerging fundamentalist movement. Premillennialism fit well with fundamentalism's system of biblical hermeneutics and served as its philosophy of history. Many of the leading figures in the new fundamentalist movement were ardent propagators of the messianic hope. Since the late nineteenth century, most of America's noted evangelists have accepted the messianic conviction and have used it in their public speeches and sermons. It has given a sense of urgency to their appeals to accept Christ.[7]

Although the International Christian Embassy has primarily represented European evangelical premillennialist supporters of Israel, its messianic vision has been the American fundamentalist one. Van der Hoeven identifies Lance Lambert, a British-American evangelist who concentrates almost exclusively on Israel's role in history and its position as a key to the fulfillment of biblical prophecy, as the most acceptable exponent of that belief.[8]

The messianists of the early nineteenth century held to a "historical" school, which identified current events with messianic prophecies, and frequently predicted specific dates for the appearance of the Messiah. A new messianic school, dispensationalism, crystallized in Britain in the 1830s in the teachings of John Darby (1800–1882), the leader of the Plymouth Brethren, and eventually became dominant. Adherents of this school, which did not set an exact date for the arrival of the Lord, assert that history is divided into a number of eras, for each of which God has a specific plan for humanity. According to their beliefs humanity is now at the end of the penultimate era, to be followed by the millennium, the righteous reign of Jesus on earth for a thousand years.[9]

A noteworthy element in Darby's teaching is his belief in the "secret any-moment rapture of the Saints." According to this doctrine, which has become central to dispensationalists, Jesus' arrival on earth will take part in two stages. The first will begin with his coming to meet the true believers in the air, where he will remain with them for seven years. This rapture of the saints is to be expected at any moment, yet no one can know with certainty when it will actually take place. For those who remain on earth, the seven years between the rapture and Jesus' descent with the saints will be known as "the Great Tribulation," a period of natural disasters—floods, earthquakes, and volcanic eruptions, famines and plagues—as well as wars, civil unrest, and the emergence of tyrannical regimes.[10]

For the Jews, this period will be known as "the time of Jacob's trouble." The Jews will return to their land "in unbelief," that is, without accepting Jesus as their savior, and will build a state. This state is not expected to be the desired kingdom but merely a necessary instrument in preparing the way for the arrival of the Messiah and the building of the kingdom of God on earth. During the Great Tribulation, the Jews will be ruled by Antichrist, a Jewish impostor of the Messiah who will rebuild the temple, reinstate the sacrifices, and institute a reign of terror; those who come to accept Jesus as their savior in those times will be persecuted or martyred. A series of enemies will try to invade Israel. This tumultuous period will end with the arrival of Christ and the righteous believers, who will destroy Antichrist and usher in the kingdom of God on earth. According to the dispensationalist scheme, the Jews who survive the turmoil of the time of Jacob's trouble will recognize Jesus as their savior and welcome his arrival. In the millennial kingdom each nation will live in its land, and the Jews will dwell within the boundaries of the ancient kingdom of David. Jesus will establish his capital in Jerusalem, David's city, as the center of the world's government. The Jews, as God's covenant people, will assist him in his righteous administration.[11]

Since the beginnings of the movement, premillennialist fundamentalists have shown great interest in the fate of the Jewish people and the prospect of their return to Palestine. They viewed the Jewish national revival and the rise of the Zionist movement as "signs of the time" indicating that history is developing according to schedule, with Jesus' return imminent. These Christians welcomed the establishment of the Zionist political movement, the rejuvenation of the Hebrew language, and Jewish immigration and settlement in Palestine. Dramatic events such as the Balfour Declaration in 1917 and the birth of the state of Israel in 1948 strengthened premillennialists in their belief that they have read the Bible correctly and that their perception of history is accurate. Such events have served to reaffirm their critique of culture and society as well.

Since the French Revolution and the Napoleonic wars, no single political-military event has stirred the imagination of messianists so strongly as the Six Day War between Israel and its Arab neighbors in June 1967. Israel's victory, and particularly its takeover of historical sections of Jerusalem, strengthened the premillennialist view of Israel as having been created for a special purpose in God's plans for the end of age. The war happened to coincide with a marked growth in the influence and confidence of the evangelical-fundamentalist camp in American Protestantism. Through the lobbying groups of the "new Christian right," fundamentalists and right-wing evangelicals have attempted to shape the character and policies of the American government. Fundamentalists are among Israel's most ardent supporters in the American political arena. In the 1970s and 1980s, dozens of pro-Israel fundamentalist organizations were established in the United States, and Christian fundamentalists lectured on Israel in churches, distributed published material and videocassettes, and organized tours to the Holy Land.

In some respects Jan Willem van der Hoeven calls to mind the Christian Zionists who advocated the Jewish return to Palestine in the nineteenth and early twentieth centuries. The International Christian Embassy, however, is the result of the post-1967 Christian fundamentalist relationship to Israel, which has brought about the establishment of permanent organizations to promote the Zionist-Israeli cause.

The Emergence of a Christian Zionist

Jan Willem van der Hoeven was born in March 1940 in Haarlem, a mid-size city in central Holland near Amsterdam.[12] The second son of a successful attorney, he grew up in a middle-class family of four boys. His parents were religiously committed people; his father was a Mennonite and his mother's family belonged to the Dutch Reformed Church. The family, however, did not belong officially to either of these churches. The children occasionally accompanied one of their parents to either a Mennonite or a Dutch Reformed service but more often the family prayed at home. This lack of commitment to a particular denomination had a decisive influence on the way van der Hoeven was to view denominations and their role, or, from his point of view, their lack of any positive purpose in Christian life. For the founder of the International Christian Embassy, church membership does not equate to sincere spiritual Christian commitment. "'Churchianity' is not Christianity," he repeatedly claims. His antagonism to established church life was nourished throughout the years by his disagreement with the positions taken by the mainline churches on a number of issues, among them the Arab-Israeli conflict.

Van der Hoeven's father, also named Jan, was an attorney, but he acquired fame as an author. His best-known book, *Slant Eyed Angel,* told the story of his family and his youngest son, who was born with Down's syndrome.[13] The Dutch queen Juliana was deeply impressed by the book; in 1957 she invited Jan van der Hoeven to serve as her private secretary. Moving from Haarlem to the queen's residential town of Soest-dyk, the van der Hoevens became acquainted with the royal family and the queen's social circle. Jan Willem's personal acquaintance with the queen later served him well as a Christian Zionist. Queen Juliana ac-cepted an invitation to participate in one of the Tabernacles celebrations organized in Jerusalem by the International Christian Embassy, giving the occasion an aura of legitimacy and respectability.

Upon graduation from high school, Jan Willem left for England, where he studied at the Bible College of London University. His decision to become a minister came after many years of keen interest in religious and spiritual matters. According to his own and his father's account, his inclination towards a Christian religious life began very early in his life, and he was instrumental in bringing about the conversion of his third brother.[14] Religious trends in the decades following World War II also made their mark on the young man. In the late 1950s and early 1960s conservative German, Scandinavian, and Dutch Protestants, adopting the terminology and characteristics of American evangelicalism, began to in-sist on the need to be "born again" in order to be saved. In London van der Hoeven absorbed a literalist biblical and premillennialist outlook from British and American evangelists who were making inroads in pietist circles in Holland and other parts of Western Europe.

At the Bible College van der Hoeven also met his future wife, Widad, a Lebanese Arab from Beirut, who grew up in a Protestant evangelical environment. Like Jan Willem, she tended towards a literal reading of the Bible.[15] Her family, like most Lebanese Christians, identified with Arab national sentiments and were hostile to the Zionist movement and to the establishment of the state of Israel. Widad, however, came to share her husband's positive view of the Jewish national revival in Israel. The young couple married upon van der Hoeven's graduation in 1962 and settled in Holland. Widad's Lebanese origin brought the van der Hoevens on tours to the Middle East, and Jan Willem, who did not identify himself with the Dutch Reformed Church or other mainline churches, was or-dained in the Armenian Evangelical Church in Beirut. For all his criticism of "Churchianity," ordination was a must for van der Hoeven. It was, after all, the only way he could receive recognition and establish his au-thority as a minister.

During his travels in the Middle East the new minister was offered the position of warden of the Garden Tomb in Jerusalem. This archaeological site, situated near the northern wall of the old city of Jerusalem, not far from the Damascus Gate, was excavated in the late nineteenth century by noted British evangelical figures (among them Charles George Gordon, a British general who had helped suppress the Taiping Rebellion and who died fighting the Mahdi in Sudan) and was accepted by many Protestant evangelicals as the burial site of Jesus Christ. Evangelicals noted that the Holy Sepulcher in the old city of Jerusalem—divided for hundreds of years between Roman Catholics, Greek Orthodox, Armenians, Copts, and Ethiopians, with Protestant churches having no legal standing—is inside the city wall; since it was forbidden to bury the dead inside city boundaries, they concluded, the Holy Sepulcher could not have been Jesus' burial site. They then pointed out that the hill on which the Garden Tomb is located resembles a skull *(golgolet)* and argued that it was the biblical Golgotha, where Jesus was crucified and buried in the family tomb of Joseph of Arimathea.

Many of those who visited the Garden Tomb between 1968 and 1975 were struck by the young, enthusiastic, and compassionate Dutch minister who spent long hours showing tourists around, explaining what he considered to be the historical significance of the place, the meaning of Jesus' death and resurrection, and his understanding of current Middle East politics, which he connected with Jesus' role in history. During these tours he would pray, raise his hands, and cry. In these years van der Hoeven began to associate himself with the charismatic wing of evangelical Christianity, whose representatives became increasingly predominant in Jerusalem's local Christian community. He felt at home with Christians who shared his manner of prayer and his conviction that he had a direct manifestation of the divine in his life. His association with charismatics is evident in the International Christian Embassy; most of the institution's staff and supporters are charismatics.

The Pentecostal-charismatic movement became part of evangelical Christianity early in the twentieth century, but for many decades it was small, not very influential, and in many ways unacceptable to the larger mainline elements of evangelicalism. The late 1960s and 1970s, however, witnessed a dramatic change in the size and role of Pentecostal-charismatic groups. They grew in influence, attracting millions of new members, many of them middle class, in the United States and elsewhere, particularly South America and South Korea. Many of the leading evangelists in America in the 1970s and 1980s were charismatics; some became premillennialists and settled in Jerusalem, where they built the largest evangelical congregations in the city. Most of these congregations featured mild forms of charismatic worship—closing the eyes and raising the hands during prayer, for example—a style that van der Hoeven found congenial.[16]

During his years as warden of the Garden Tomb, van der Hoeven also came to view the right-wing Israeli political parties as ideologically closer to his own vision of the role Israel should play in Middle East politics. They had, he felt, a better grasp of the Jewish mission in history. Van der Hoeven, who has lived in Israel most of his adult life, has gained a good grasp of Israeli society, culture, and morality. He is not fluent in Hebrew, nor has he acquired a solid systematic education in Judaic studies, as have many Israel-based Christian ministers, both liberals and conservatives, but he has nonetheless made social contacts with many Israelis in public life, traveled extensively within the country, and dealt constantly with Israeli bureaucrats and national and municipal government officials. Both his son and his daughter served in the Israeli army, and he built his home in a Jewish neighborhood. On a personal level, van der Hoeven has been recognized by both friends and foes as an honest man devoid of personal greed. His lifestyle has always been modest. Although colleagues who have broken with him have accused him of tyrannical practices, an inability to share power and prestige, and a lack of tolerance for opposing views within his own enterprise, they have also remarked on his friendliness and kindness.

For a time after leaving his position as warden of the Garden Tomb, van der Hoeven did not hold any official position and relied for his livelihood on private donations from supporters of Israel in Europe and North America, a common practice among evangelical activists residing in Israel. In the late 1970s, together with others who shared his convictions, he laid the foundation for his future organization. His natural allies were premillennialist evangelicals with charismatic leanings who, like himself, saw Israel as fulfilling a role in the events of the end times. Calling themselves the Almond Tree Branch, this group of evangelical supporters of Israel sponsored a number of activities that would later become characteristic of the International Christian Embassy.[17]

Among the founders of both the Almond Tree Branch and the Embassy was Robert Lindsey, then pastor of the Baptist House congregation in Jerusalem. A Southern Baptist from Oklahoma, Lindsey had come to Jerusalem in the 1930s and studied at the Hebrew University. He completed his graduate studies in the United States, then returned to Israel at the end of World War II. By the late 1960s Lindsey was the central figure in the Baptist community in Israel and well known to the Israeli public. Sponsored by the Department of Missions of the Southern Baptist Convention, he served as senior missionary in Israel and eventually enjoyed the closest connections to the Israeli government of any Protestant representative in the country. During Lindsey's tenure the Southern Baptists became the largest evangelical church in Israel, with a dozen congregations, seven of which were in Arab communities. Under his authoritarian leadership, the Baptists of Jerusalem became charismatic, a transformation that was quite rare among Baptist congregations worldwide.

Lindsey wrote and published extensively, using in his Hebrew writings an Israeli literary name. His major scholarly effort was the translation of the New Testament into modern Hebrew. He developed a theory that large parts of the original text of the New Testament were written in Hebrew, and later translated into Greek. The primary manuscript, he claimed, was devoid of anti-Semitism. Some Jewish scholars joined Lindsey and others to form the Jerusalem School of New Testament Studies. The Jewish scholars concentrated mainly on tracing the Jewish roots of Christianity. Van der Hoeven did not join the school, however, and has never shown any scholarly inclinations or interest in academic discussion. He sees Judaism and Christianity as two distinct religions and is uncomfortable with those who emphasize similarities between early Christianity and the Judaism of those days.

Other Bible believers flocked to the ranks of the new movement. David Bivin, a Southern Baptist associate of Lindsey, was also active in the Almond Tree Branch and participated in the Jerusalem School. Bivin made his living in those years by running a Hebrew school for interested Christians, and van der Hoeven studied there for a short while.[18] Bivin, too, is a charismatic evangelical. Another noted member of the group was Douglas Young, a former president of Trinity Evangelical Divinity School in Deerfield, Illinois. In 1958 Young founded the Holy Land Institute, an evangelical institution of higher education and research in Jerusalem. An ardent premillennialist—certain that Israel is to play a dominant role in God's plans for humanity— Young also founded Bridges for Peace, a noncharismatic pro-Israel organization, in 1978. He lent his support to the Almond Tree Branch (and later to the International Christian Embassy) since he felt there was room for an organization more intimate and charismatic in style. An associate of Young, George Giakumakis, has directed the Holy Land Institute since 1978, and was also among the active participants in van der Hoeven's group of pro-Zionist Jerusalemite evangelicals. Other activists were Marvin and Merla Watson, from Canada, who lived in Jerusalem in the 1970s and early 1980s. Merla composed "Davidic music," which was later performed at the Embassy's gatherings, and advocated building a center in Jerusalem where evangelical Christians could come to learn about Jews and Israel.

The Almond Tree Branch, in short, was something of a fellowship. The participants met weekly at the Watsons' home in Motza, a suburb of Jerusalem, where they prayed, sang, and discussed various issues. Van der Hoeven emerged as its outstanding activist, since Lindsey and Young were busy with other activities. It was van der Hoeven's idea to organize large annual gathering of Christian supporters of Israel on Sukkoth, the Jewish harvest festival commemorating the tent sanctuaries, or tabernacles, used during the Exodus. His theological rationale was twofold: First, according to the Bible (Zechariah 14:15) gentiles were also commanded to gather in Jerusalem during the festival. Second, he pointed out that whereas Christians celebrate two of the "pilgrimage festivals" commanded in the Bible—Easter (at the season of Passover) and Pentecost—there was no general Christian celebration of Sukkoth. In 1979 he led the Almond Tree Branch to launch the yearly Tabernacles festival, a weeklong assembly of Christian supporters of Israel, highlighted by a march through the streets of Jerusalem. These early gatherings served as the foundation for the creation of the Embassy.

THE ESTABLISHMENT OF THE INTERNATIONAL CHRISTIAN EMBASSY

In 1980, the Israeli Knesset passed the "Jerusalem Law," which declared the whole of the city to be the capital of the state of Israel. In protest, almost all countries with embassies and consulates in Jerusalem moved their diplomatic staffs to Tel Aviv. This evacuation provided a dramatic point at which to announce the creation of the International Christian Embassy, which was presented as a spontaneous act of sympathy and support for Israel on the part of true Christians at a time when even friendly or neutral countries betrayed her.[19] The Embassy chose as its logo two olive branches hovering over a globe with Jerusalem at its center. "This symbolizes the great day when Zechariah's prophecy will be fulfilled, and all nations will come up to Jerusalem to keep the Feast of Tabernacles during Messiah's reign on earth,"[20] the Embassy's leaders announced.

The new organization was welcomed and encouraged by Israeli officials—including the prime minister's liaison for the Christian evangelical community, the director of the Department for Christian Churches and

Organizations of the Ministry of Foreign Affairs, and Jerusalem mayor Teddy Kollek—who noted the propaganda value of the Embassy's creation; it made the point, they believed, that even though many countries had removed their embassies and consulates from Jerusalem due to Arab pressure, the Western Christian world backed Israel and endorsed the unification of Jerusalem under Israeli rule.[21]

Struggling to establish and maintain itself financially, the Embassy received support from Jacques Fischer, a Jewish cosmetics manufacturer and millionaire, who helped the Embassy obtain its first headquarters and financed the beginning of its activity. But the friendly relationship did not last long. The Embassy's leaders rejected what they considered attempts by Fischer to interfere with their work and policies.[22] Raising funds from Christian supporters, they returned Fischer's donation and severed their connections with him. The clash with Fischer was illustrative. The Embassy's leaders insisted on building and running their organization on their own terms. Although the Embassy's Christian financial supporters have not always fully agreed with its policies, it has never been willing to compromise its views to keep all supporters happy or to enlarge its base of support.

Since the Embassy's founding, van der Hoeven has held the seemingly modest post of ICE spokesman. Yet he is the Embassy's undeniable leader and its chief ideologue. The Embassy chose Johann Luckhoff as its administrative director. A South African of Afrikaner descent, Luckhoff had served for a few years as pastor of the Afrikaner Dutch Reformed Church in his native country He had come to Jerusalem some time before the establishment of the Embassy, been involved with the Almond Tree Branch and its Tabernacles celebration, and, like van der Hoeven, had no secure job. But unlike his Dutch comrade, he did not look upon the Embassy's work as a life vocation. His admitted dream in the early 1980s was to become a politician of the ruling Afrikaner party in his homeland. He nonetheless remained with the Embassy, where he has proved to be an able organizer. The Embassy since its inception has had close ties with white Dutch Reformed groups and churches in South Africa and has received substantial financial support from them. Van der Hoeven and Luckhoff have worked well together. Luckhoff is a private person who does not attract much attention, and he has shown little interest in the ideological matters, which are handled by van der Hoeven. The person in charge of the Embassy's financial matters has been, from the start, Tim King, a rather modest and unassuming American liked by van der Hoeven. The Embassy staff in 1992 consisted of about fifty-five workers.

Some received salaries, but most were volunteers. The Embassy paid the volunteers' rent and medical insurance and provided them with one meal a day and pocket money to cover their basic expenses.

The Embassy's major work has been to spark interest in Israel among evangelicals worldwide and to promote various philanthropic programs in Israel. The two tasks are closely related: its promotional efforts are also fund-raising opportunities. While its main supporters are European Protestants, the Embassy wishes to represent "true Christianity" worldwide and has made a great effort to open branches and gain supporters in as many countries as possible. In the United States, its branches are mainly situated in the Bible Belt, that is, the southern states.[23] In Europe, representatives of the Embassy can be found in Finland, Denmark, Norway, Sweden, Holland, Germany, Switzerland, and the United Kingdom. There are also volunteers for the Embassy in the predominantly Catholic countries—Spain, Portugal, France, and Belgium. In recent years, representatives have also worked for the Embassy's interests in Eastern Europe—Russia, Poland, Hungary, the Czech Republic, Slovakia, and Romania. Australia, New Zealand, South Africa, Zaire, and Nigeria also have representatives; the last two countries do not provide much financial support, but they enhance the international image of the Embassy, enabling it to claim that true Christians everywhere support Israel. ICE has also received support from Latin American countries, including Mexico, Guatemala, Columbia, Brazil, El Salvador, and Costa Rica, and has made special efforts to garner support from the growing number of Latin American premillennialists, thousands of whom participate in the annual tours of the Holy Land sponsored or initiated by the Embassy. There has also been an attempt to attract supporters in South Asia.

The Embassy's international work focuses on lecturing, mostly in churches, about Israel's role in history and the work of the Embassy on behalf of Jewish immigration and settlement. "Embassies" distribute ICE journals, brochures, leaflets, and cassettes of "Davidic music" and van der Hoeven's sermons. Embassy representatives also recruit pilgrims for the annual Tabernacles gathering and collect money for the Embassy's philanthropic enterprises in Israel. The day-to-day work of the Embassy in Israel is devoted to this international mission; the Jerusalem headquarters supervises the work of the representatives in various countries, administers the finances, maintains public relations and publications departments, and oversees the production of video and audiocassettes in a number of languages—in addition to English chiefly German, Dutch, Finnish, Spanish, and Russian. A special department produces material for Latin American countries in Spanish and Portuguese. The radio department prepares a special program, *A Word from Jerusalem,* which is broadcast to evangelical radio stations, mostly in North America. The Embassy also provides welfare services in Jerusalem, distributing money and goods to new immigrants as well as other needy Israelis. Aware that many Jews are suspicious of Christian charitable enterprises, ICE often distributes its parcels through Israeli public agencies.[24]

The Embassy's basic annual budget as a rule has not exceeded a million dollars, which pays for day-to-day activities, maintenance of the office building in Brenner Street in the fashionable and central neighborhood of Talbia, employees' salaries, some travel expenses of the staff, and the preparation of publications. The figure does not include the budget for special operations, such as the transportation of immigrants from Russia, which runs much higher; the ICE has also offered direct financial support to the Israeli government for the absorption of Russian Jews. In 1991 the Embassy's budget for philanthropic operations in Israel reached the sum of five million dollars, and the overall cost of the feast of Tabernacles in 1992 was over ten million dollars. Each of the six thousand pilgrims who participated paid $1,300 to $1,800 for air fare, hotel accommodations, and the festivities in Jerusalem.[25] Van der Hoeven and Luckhoff spend much of their time fund-raising in evangelical communities around the globe. A considerable amount of funding has come from Germany.[26]

The Embassy's policy of raising money for Zionist and Israeli causes is something of a novelty. American evangelicals and fundamentalists have endorsed the expanded financial aid the United States has offered Israel since 1967, but have neither given money directly to the Israeli government nor taken upon themselves activities normally paid for by the Israeli government.[27] The Embassy is the first Christian evangelical institution that has systematically donated money to Jewish Zionist enterprises. Most Christian Zionists, by contrast, have supported missionary agencies that aim at converting Jews. The Embassy has thus set new norms in the relationship between Christian fundamentalists and Israel.

The Embassy does not regard itself as a religious community and does not provide regular church services, but it holds prayer meetings every Wednesday evening, with van der Hoeven preaching the sermons whenever he is in the country. The Embassy's employees attend services on weekends at the various charismatic congregations in the city: the King of Kings (a charismatic congregation sponsored by Canadian Pentecostals), the Baptist House, and Christ Church, an evangelical charismatic Anglican church located near Jaffa Gate in Jerusalem's old city.

DISAGREEMENT AND DISSENT

Some activists who participated in the Embassy's founding assumed that they would have a share in shaping its character and ideology, but it became evident by the mid-1980s that the Embassy's priorities and opinions were almost synonymous with those of van der Hoeven.[28] In the fall of 1985 more than half the Embassy's employees and volunteers and a few members of its board of directors resigned. Many of them objected to van der Hoeven's dominance in these areas and to his "very authoritarian style of leadership."[29] Some thought his views on various issues, which often became the Embassy's declared positions, to be too radical and political. Such an attitude, his critics claimed, alienated many moderate Christians. Some disagreed with the Embassy's policy of refraining from missionary work. Others found its explicit charismatic atmosphere not to their liking.[30]

Significantly, most of the resignations were those of supporters and employees from English-speaking countries: the United States, Canada, and Britain. Among other things, the 1985 crisis reflected a difference in character and style between European members and those from Britain and North America, the latter being used to a more open and democratic atmosphere.[31] Some representatives of the Embassy in English-speaking countries also resigned, for similar reasons, and those branches virtually closed down.[32]

There is no doubt that the Embassy suffered from the resignations and desertions, yet it survived and overcame the crisis. It recruited new workers, raised sufficient funds to continue its activity at the same level as before the crisis, and, perhaps most significantly, retained its position as the most prominent pro-Israel organization among evangelical Christians. Yet the 1985 resignations marked a turning point in the Embassy's history. It became a controversial institution even among evangelical supporters of Israel, many of whom openly criticized its character and policies. The Embassy's base of support became narrower; its policies no longer represented the general views of evangelical-fundamentalist supporters of Israel who shared the messianic hope, but only specific attitudes within this larger group: those of charismatic, predominantly European, mostly Dutch, German, and Scandinavian supporters of Israel, whose leadership advocates right-wing, hard-line politics.[33]

Since the late 1980s, van der Hoeven has made efforts to broaden the Embassy's base of support. Realizing how important it was to gain a stronghold among American evangelicals, he set out on a series of lecture tours in the United States. In his attempt to build connections with evangelical leaders and churches there, he enlisted the support of Rabbi Yechiel Eckstein, head of the Holy Land Fellowship of Christians and Jews, an organization established by Eckstein in Chicago in the early 1980s to promote Jewish-evangelical relations. The Chicago rabbi encourages evangelical Christians to donate money for various enterprises in Israel. Impressed with van der Hoeven, he considered the work of the Embassy to be beneficial for Israel and for the evangelical-Jewish encounter.[34] Eckstein accompanied van der Hoeven in some of his travels in the United States, introducing him to pro-Israel evangelical activists. Building a new network of supporters and branches in America did not prove an easy task. Whereas in Europe, the Embassy is often the only pro-Israel Christian organization, in the United States there are other, better established organizations of that sort. To promote its cause the Embassy hired workers with expertise in public relations and established a small office in Washington, D.C. Ted Pantaleo of Bradenton, Florida, serves as the Embassy's coordinator in America.

The Embassy made a major attempt to gain ground in the United States with the "Washington for Israel Summit," a pro-Israel conference it organized in September 1992 in Washington, D.C. In taking this initiative, van der Hoeven hoped to make the International Christian Embassy better known in evangelical pro-Israel circles, to build a closer relationship with pro-Israel evangelical leaders and organizations, and to create momentum for establishing a network of support for the Embassy in America. ICE found willing support in the Israeli embassy in Washington; the policy of Israel's foreign ministry has long been to encourage Christian evangelicals in pro-Israel activity. Official sponsors of the event included such pro-Israel evangelical organizations as the Christians' Israel Public Action Campaign (CIPAC), established in the 1980s as a Christian counterpart to AIPAC (America Israel Public Affairs Committee, the pro-Israel lobby in Washington). One of the leaders of CIPAC, the only official evangelical pro-Israel lobby, is Senator Jesse Helms of North Carolina, with whom van der Hoeven established a cordial relationship. As far as van der Hoeven was concerned, however, the most prestigious participant in the conference was the Reverend W. Criswell of the First Baptist Church in Dallas, Texas; the premillenialist minister, then eighty-three years old, had long been an ardent supporter of Israel. In addition to lectures, group discussions, and prayer meetings, the conference included a "march for Israel" in Washington and the broadcasting of video movies on Israel and the Embassy's activities there. A special session was devoted to a prophetic understanding of Israel's role in history.[35]

Despite van der Hoeven's satisfaction with the conference, it demonstrated the Embassy's weak position in the United States. The number of attendees did not exceed two hundred, including reporters and Israeli guests. Few of the pro-Israel evangelical leaders and organizations in America showed interest in participating; most of them have no contact with the Embassy and see no need to promote its activities. Yet the Embassy continues in its attempts to broaden its base of support in the United States.

Van der Hoeven's Vision of Israel

Being neither a systematic theologian nor a professional writer, Van der Hoeven has published no books on his theological and political views. But the Embassy's many popular brochures and van der Hoeven's frankness in expressing his creed and political understanding leave little room for misinterpretation as to his stand. Van der Hoeven's understanding of the role and purpose of Israel, of its future historical developments, and of his own mission emerge from his eschatological messianic hope. He and other leading activists of the Embassy adhere to a premillennialist dispensationalist conviction that serves also as a system of biblical hermeneutics and a philosophy of history.

Van der Hoeven shares the premillennialist-dispensationalist vision of Israel as a transitory but necessary vehicle on the messianic road. Although, according to that view, the Jewish political entity will exist in rebellious unbelief until the arrival of Jesus, its existence and security is a positive, even reassuring development in the unfolding of history, and it is therefore pertinent to protect Israel against forces that would undermine it. Christian fundamentalists have usually seen Arab hostility toward the Zionist enterprise as an attempt to jeopardize the advancement of God's plans. Van der Hoeven has repeatedly insisted that there is no room in the country for Arabs who militate against Israel's existence. Arabs who are "true believers" support the Israeli cause, he says, as do his wife and a number of other Arab Christians.[36] Yasir Arafat and the Palestine Liberation Organization are instruments of Satan.

Yet van der Hoeven's attitude toward the Jews is ambivalent. He firmly believes that the Jews are the heirs of biblical Israel, God's chosen people, destined for a glorious future in the messianic age; but he also harbors negative attitudes toward Jews, including feelings of frustration, disappointment, and anger. He has expressed bitterness, for example, that so many Israelis are unwilling to support the political agenda he advocates. In order to be accepted by liberals, he complains, they are willing to compromise their national aspirations,[37] and in so doing, they betray their historical role, their purpose in God's plans for the end of age. For example, in a speech delivered during the Embassy's 1989 Tabernacles celebration, he attacked moderate and left-wing Israeli politicians, declaring that giving up the territories Israel had occupied since 1967 would mark the second time the Jews reject God.[38]

To the founder of the International Christian Embassy, "land for peace" is not merely a pragmatic political decision aimed at enhancing the well-being of the state; such a decision has disastrous cosmic implications and would impede the divine plan for human redemption. The Jews are not just another people who can make choices according to their political needs; they have a burden to carry, a duty and purpose in history. For the Jews to refuse to play their role would constitute unforgivable treachery toward all humankind. Van der Hoeven's words convey the bitterness felt by many fundamentalists regarding the Jewish refusal to accept Jesus Christ; in their view, the Jews should have been the first to recognize him as their savior. A second refusal to accept him, or to prepare the ground for his arrival, would be even worse than the first, for the Jews would miss their second opportunity for redemption. In a sermon delivered in one of the Wednesday prayer gatherings at the Embassy, van der Hoeven prayed that Israel's prime minister would listen to God and not to the American secretary of state and would refuse to give up territory.

Like many premillennialist supporters of the Zionist movement, van der Hoeven is disappointed at the secular character of Israeli life and morals. He points to the sexual promiscuity of many Israeli officials and public figures. He sees no intrinsic value in much of the Jewish religious tradition, in its rites and institutions or its spiritual perceptions. Like other fundamentalists, he sees the Jewish religion as instrumental in keeping the Jewish nation alive and ready to fulfill its historical role, but following the ministry, death, and resurrection of Jesus, observance of the Law is now unnecessary, in fact futile. Accordingly, van der Hoeven has little respect for the rabbinate. "Had Moses been a rabbi," he repeatedly claims, "he would not have led the Jews out of Egypt, but would have built synagogues and yeshivoth, established a rabbinate and declared himself a chief rabbi." "The rabbis still insist on living according to the old covenant," complained van der Hoeven, "whereas God has graciously offered us a new one."[39] In his view, there is no real Judaism without recognition of the messiahship of Jesus Christ. As long as the Jews have not accepted Jesus as savior, the most basic and profound element is missing from Jewish life.[40] One must conclude that van der

Hoeven's good will toward the Jewish people and his activity on their behalf derive almost exclusively from his messianic hope, which in its turn represents an entire worldview, conservative and reactive in nature. His pro-Israel attitude and his keen concern for the physical well-being of Jews worldwide derive from the function of the Jews in the advancement of history toward the arrival of the Lord.

Van der Hoeven shares with many fundamentalists a negative attitude toward Western culture. In its open pluralistic and permissive society he sees the advancement of un-Christian forces, the impact of Satan on planet earth. To him the current immoral society represents an inevitable stage before the arrival of the Lord. Only the appearance of the Messiah can change this sordid reality and bring salvation to all. Yet van der Hoeven is not a pessimist; he looks to the future with great hope, enthusiasm, and zeal, assured that history will develop according to the divine plan as revealed in Scripture. He sees himself as a worker in a great cause, the greatest of all—the advancement of the messianic age and the establishment of the kingdom of God on earth. His sense of mission is intimately connected with his understanding of the role of the Jewish people and Israel in history; he sees himself as helping to restore the Jews to their ancient homeland, thereby preparing the ground for the arrival of the Lord.

In van der Hoeven's eyes almost all mainline churches have gone astray and no longer carry the divine message. Only he and his associates and supporters realize the true significance of the historical developments taking place in the land of Israel. The International Christian Embassy is thus not only an embassy of Christian supporters of Israel, but the embassy of true Christianity, the one house and center in Jerusalem that represents the word of God and works toward realization of God's plans for humanity.

THE FEAST OF TABERNACLES

The Feast of Tabernacles serves as the focal point of the year for the Embassy. A major convocation of thousands of supporters from around the world, it provides an opportunity to present the Embassy and its message to the Israeli public. Activities include tours of the country for the "pilgrims," a march through Jerusalem's main streets, a "biblical meal" served and celebrated on the shore of the Dead Sea, and assemblies in Jerusalem. Some of the gatherings take place in Binyanei Ha'Uma, the largest convention hall in Jerusalem; booths exhibit publications and feature programs and enterprises promoted by the Embassy. Of special interest in the early 1980s was Stanley Goldfoot's Temple Mount Foundation booth.

The high point of the Tabernacles festival is a mass gathering at the Sultan's Pool, a reservoir constructed during the Ottoman period, which in the late 1970s was converted into an open-air amphitheater. In addition to the Christian pilgrims, hundreds of Israelis are regularly invited: government officials, academics, journalists, and new immigrants. At the gathering in September 1991 thousands filled the renovated pool. Although Embassy supporters are predominantly European, the participants included Christians from around the globe, including North and South America and East Asia. At the beginning of the spectacular event twelve flags, representing the tribes of Israel, were brought from within the crowd to the platform. Each flag was embroidered with traditional symbols of one of the tribes, and with the motto "Arise and Shine." This short phrase indicates the Embassy's message to the Jewish people—the Jews should recognize their historical role and work toward its fulfillment. They will then flourish and prosper both as individuals and as a nation. After the flags were placed on the platform, the choir sang "Davidic music," often based on verses from Psalms, calling upon Israel to arise and fulfill its historical role. Song titles included "Arise, O Children of Israel;" "Awake, Awake O Zion;" and "Awake, O Israel." Other songs, such as "Hine Yeshua, Yeshuat Israel" (Here is Jesus, the redeemer of Israel), emphasized the role of Jesus in the redemption of Israel, asserting that he is the key to the Jewish national restoration and it is for him that the Jews should yearn.[41] A dance company performed, with men and women dancing separately. Johann Luckhoff, administrative director of the Embassy, said a few introductory words, followed by a major presentation by Jan Willem van der Hoeven.

In his speech the Dutch minister expressed his opinions on the latest developments in the life of the Jewish people and the prospects for its future. Ethiopian and Russian Jewry have poured into Israel, he observed, and the rest of world Jewry would follow them "even if it would require anti-Semitism in America to bring that Jewry over here." Referring to President George Bush's unwillingness to provide loan guarantees for Israel, the Embassy's leader promised that Israel will get more than it ever hoped for. "We are better Zionists than you are," declared van der Hoeven, directing his words to the Israeli audience, many of whom responded by laughing, assuming that the speaker was referring to the expansionist, right-wing political outlook of the Embassy.

During the praying and singing that followed, many in the crowd lifted up their hands, as the charismatics often do, held hands, joined in the singing, or danced. Another flag was brought to the platform after the introductory speeches; on one side it read "Messiah" and on the other, in Hebrew, *mashiach*. The crowd cheered. The flag holder left the stage, and the flag reappeared a few seconds later on the roof towering over the platform, the amphitheater, and the crowd, a waving reminder of the underlying belief of the Embassy that the return of the Jewish people to the land of Israel and the building of a Jewish commonwealth are necessary steps preceding the arrival of the Lord. Many of the Israeli guests cheered along with the evangelicals, apparently unaware that the Embassy's messianic scheme differs considerably from their own; indeed, for many Israelis who hold messianic hopes, the International Christian Embassy seems a Christian endorsement of their own messianic and nationalist vision. Teddy Kollek, the mayor of Jerusalem, addressed the audience, remarking that he had spoken at every gatherings since the establishment of the Embassy and inviting everyone to return to Jerusalem the following year. The Tabernacles festival helps raise the city's morale and offers hope, he declared.

Celebrations of the 1992 Feast of Tabernacles were considered extremely successful by the Embassy's leaders, with more than six thousand pilgrims taking part. The Jewish festival of Sukkoth fell rather late that year, 12 through 19 October.[42] It was therefore decided not to hold the main gathering at the Sultan's Pool as in previous years, but at Binyanei Ha'Uma, near the western entrance to Jerusalem. On the night of 12 October thousands of pilgrims filed into the building; some were ushered into a small auditorium to watch the events on large screens. The singing of Davidic music, the dancing by young men and women in biblical costumes, the Israeli songs, the march with the banners of the twelve tribes and the flag proclaiming "Messiah" in English and Hebrew were all similar to the ceremonies and events of past years. Prime Minister Yitzhak Rabin spoke to the gathering, offering greetings to "Israel's Christian friends." He was warmly welcomed by the cheering crowd, though many of the pilgrims were certainly unfamiliar with Israeli political debates and accepted Rabin primarily as the leader of a country they viewed as having a special mission in God's plans for humanity. Rabin's visit and speech demonstrated that the Labour government had opted to continue the policy of the previous Likud government in encouraging the kind of political support offered by the International Christian Embassy. The Embassy, for its part, showed its willingness to work with the Labour government as it had with the Likud.

Even the large Binyanei Ha'Uma building could not accommodate the many Christian pilgrims and the Israeli guests the Embassy had invited. Special gatherings were organized for Israeli guests, including officials and public figures as well as many new immigrants from Russia and Ethiopia. Four such events, each with more than a thousand invitees, were scheduled at the Ramada Renaissance hotel located near the convention center. The evenings for the Israeli guests followed the familiar pattern, with Davidic music, dancing, and Israeli folk songs. Van der Hoeven's speeches were translated into Hebrew and Russian. The presence of so many immigrants from Russia, he declared, was a positive sign of the fulfillment of biblical prophecies. Mass immigration of Jews from other countries such as the United States was just a matter of time.

Van der Hoeven has often pointed out that in the Bible the Feast of Tabernacles is the one holiday for which all nations are commanded to gather in Jerusalem. He has further speculated that the apocalyptic events will begin at one of the Tabernacles gatherings.[43] Jesus, he claims, was born during that holiday;[44] Christmas, originating from a pagan holiday, has no basis in Scripture.[45]

BUILDING THE TEMPLE

In van der Hoeven's understanding of salvation history, the downfall of Islam and the destruction of the Temple Mount mosques are to precede the arrival of the Messiah. Like other Christian fundamentalists, the Embassy's leader does not regard Islam as a legitimate religious belief. Allah, he claims, is merely a god the Arabs worshiped even before the rise of Islam, which he therefore regards as an idolatrous religion that does not recognize the divinity of the one almighty God of Israel. He sees the Muslim resurgence and the rise of extremist Islamic groups as rebellions against God. During the Gulf war, van der Hoeven prayed to God "to crush the power of Allah," and bring about the downfall of Islam.[46] The fact that the Arab enemies of Israel are mostly Muslim and that Muslims have opposed both Jewish resettlement of the land of Israel and the spread of Western Christianity is only one factor in his negative perception; he accords no place to a religious belief which does not accept Jesus as savior. Islam's "pretense" of being a God-abiding religion only demonstrates its diabolic nature and allows one to assume that it will be associated with Antichrist and the reign of terror of the end of age. The Embassy's publications during the Gulf crisis and war in 1990–1991 suggested that Saddam Hussein's Iraq was the "northern power" that, according to their understanding of biblical prophecies, was bound to declare war on Israel, attempt to invade the country, and eventually be crushed. When Iraq was defeated without its having invaded Israel, the Embassy speculated that the northern power might instead be Assad's Syria.[47]

The Temple Mount mosques symbolize for van der Hoeven an idolatrous dominance of the sacred site on which the Temple will be rebuilt in the days of the Great Tribulation preceding the millennium. In his opinion these mosques must be destroyed to prepare the way for the arrival of the Lord. To that end, the Embassy has established contacts with both Christian and Jewish advocates for rebuilding the Temple. Following the Six Day War, many Christian fundamentalists, encouraged by some Jewish Orthodox groups' preparations for the rebuilding of the Temple and the reinstating of its ritual works and sacrifices, expected its imminent reconstruction as part of the events of the end of the age.[48] A new interest arose in certain fundamentalist circles in the Temple building, its interior plan, and its sacrificial works, as well as in the priestly garments and utensils. A few books on these subjects enjoyed popularity in evangelical-premillennialist circles.[49] In the 1970s and 1980s a few evangelical leaders and organizations openly advocated the rebuilding of the Temple. Chuck Smith, a noted minister and evangelist whose Calvary Chapel in Costa Mesa, California, is one of the largest and most dynamic evangelical churches in America, secured financial support for physicist Lambert Dolphin and the California-based Science and Archaeology Team to research the exact site of the Temple. Using sophisticated technology they concluded that the Temple had been located, not on the site of the Dome of the Rock, but on an empty space on the Temple Mount; thus it could be rebuilt without destroying the mosque—a "peaceful solution" to the problem of building the Temple on a site holy to Muslims.[50] Van der Hoeven, however, remained firm in his conviction that the mosques must be destroyed before the end of days.

For a few years the Embassy had a cordial relationship with Stanley Goldfoot's Temple Mount Foundation.[51] Goldfoot's enterprise has been in many ways a one-man institution. Born in South Africa, Goldfoot emigrated to Palestine in the 1930s, making his living as a journalist and businessman. During the 1940s he was a member of Lechi, an underground organization that used terrorism as a means of forcing the British to leave the country, and served as its speaker and liaison for the foreign press. A secular Jew with artistic inclinations, Goldfoot advocated a right-wing outlook on Israeli politics in an English-language satirical magazine he published in Tel Aviv in the 1960s and 1970s. Once retired, he established the Temple Mount Foundation, which he operates from his handsome Jerusalem home, and became the Israeli contact of American Christians advocating the rebuilding of the Temple.

The Embassy's relationship with the other Jewish group promoting the restoration of the Temple, the Temple Mount Faithful, has been less amicable. The Embassy adopted the tactics of the Temple Mount Faithful in 1984, however, when Embassy leaders planned a march of Christian pilgrims to the Temple Mount as part of the Tabernacles festival to demonstrate that the site belongs to Christians and Jews and that true Christians yearn to see the Temple rebuilt and the coming of the Messiah thereafter. Mayor Teddy Kollek, anxious to avoid interreligious confrontations, exercised his influence on the Embassy's leaders, however, and the march was canceled.

CONTEMPORARY CHRISTIANITY AND THE EMBASSY

Over the years the International Christian Embassy has become one of the most controversial of the Christian groups and agencies that work in the Middle East or take an interest in its fate. Eastern churches, as a rule, have no contact with the Embassy and reject its message and its activities. Eastern Christianity generally holds to "replacement theology," the claim that the Christian church is the continuation and heir of biblical historical Israel and that Judaism has no further purpose in God's plans for humanity. Most of these churches also have large Arab constituencies and are sympathetic to Arab national feelings, including the Palestinian demand for national liberation; with the exception of the Coptic and Armenian churches, which for political reasons have not joined in condemning Israel, all eastern churches have openly opposed the Israeli occupation of territories taken over from Jordan in 1967 and have expressed support for the PLO and the Palestinian uprising. They see the Embassy as an institution offering one-sided support for Israel in its struggle against the Arabs and, as members of the Middle East Council of Churches, have signed petitions condemning its activities.

The Roman Catholic attitude toward the Jewish people and their role in history has undergone a revolution in the last quarter of a century. Since the Second Vatican Council, which ended in 1965, the Catholic church has recognized the legitimacy of the Jewish religion and has entered into a dialogue with Jews, taking steps to combat old prejudices and animosities. In 1994 the Vatican established diplomatic relations with Israel. Rome has also expressed sympathy for the plight of the Palestinians and endorsed the demand for a Palestinian state. The Pope has met with Yasir Arafat, and the Vatican interceded in favor of PLO activists imprisoned in Israel, such as the Greek Catholic archbishop Hilarion Capucci. The majority of lay Catholics in the Middle East, including Israel, are Arabs, and the Catholic hierarchy, traditionally European in origin, has been replaced in the past two decades by Arab prelates. Thus Catholics have little appreciation for the Embassy's activities. In turn, the attitude of the Embassy's leaders combines the traditional Protestant fundamentalist outlook on "papalism" with additional bitterness over the Catholic outlook on Middle East politics. Van der Hoeven refrains from attacking Roman Catholics, however, because some of them are supporters of Zionism and the state of Israel. In a few instances, Catholics have participated in Embassy activities or sent donations.[52]

Like the Roman Catholic church, most mainline Protestant churches have undergone a radical change in the last generation and now regard Judaism as a legitimate religious tradition. Protestant churches in Europe and North America have come out with their own declarations acquitting the Jews of accusations of deicide and expressing sorrow over the persecution of Jews throughout the centuries, culminating in the horrors of the Holocaust, and have participated in Jewish-Christian dialogue and appointed liaisons for interaction with the Jewish people. Catholic and liberal Protestant theological seminaries have introduced Jewish studies during the past two decades. These liberals do not hold premillennialist messianic convictions and do not consider Israel to be a necessary vehicle in God's plans. Mainline Protestant churches have also made a strong commitment to social and political justice worldwide, supporting movements of national liberation and expressing sympathy for the Palestinians' quest for independence from Israeli rule; in their opinion Israel should be judged, like all other countries, on the basis of political justice and morality.[53] Since the International Christian Embassy represents hard-line supporters of right-wing Israeli politics, it arouses resentment among many liberal Protestants, who have little patience for fundamentalist Christianity and the premillennialist messianic conviction.

The Middle East Council of Churches (MECC), an institution affiliated with the World Council of Churches, has also opposed the Embassy's Christian Zionist agenda, fearing that the Embassy might succeed in raising support for Israeli political causes. In its May 1988 meeting in Cyprus it discussed ways to combat the Embassy. In denouncing one-sided Christian supporters of Zionism, the MECC declared, "The consultation was referring here especially to the western fundamentalist Christian Zionist movement and its political activities conducted through the self-declared International Christian Embassy in Jerusalem."[54] The very name "International Christian Embassy," which implies that the Embassy represents all Christians, aroused anger in the MECC.[55] Among other things, they decided to systematically collect material on the Embassy and its activities, in order to combat its influence.

Widad van der Hoeven's pro-Zionist stand has been virtually unique among Christian Arabs. Although Christian Arabs have been at times ambivalent in their attitudes towards Arab nationalism, they have vehemently opposed the Zionist movement and its political aspirations. Only a few premillennialist Arab Christians have raised their voice in favor of the Zionist agenda of a Jewish commonwealth in Palestine.

Although the International Christian Embassy claims to represent all "true Christians" and is often regarded as the representative of evangelical and fundamentalist premillennialist supporters of Israel, many evangelicals and fundamentalists do not identify with the Embassy's views and methods. Some find its open support of right-wing politics too extreme. Many object to its willingness to refrain from missionizing Jews as a condition of establishing a close relationship with the Israeli government. *Mishkan,* a Jerusalem-based English-language magazine associated with various Christian evangelizing groups in Israel, dedicated a special issue to criticizing the nonmissionary policy of the Embassy.[56] This policy obviously has touched a nerve among evangelicals who, while supporting Israel, remain firmly committed to proselytizing the Jews. For the pro-Israel evangelical premillennialist organizations engaged in missionary work among the Jews, mustering political support for Israel does not take precedence over spreading the Gospel. For institutions such as the American Messianic Fellowship or the Friends of Israel, the two aims are inseparable.[57] Their premillennialist convictions motivate both their Zionism and their zeal to evangelize God's chosen nation. An important part of their work is lecturing in churches and distributing written material in which they advocate their outlook on the Jewish people and praise Israel's historical role and the importance of "sharing" with the Jews, that is, evangelizing them. For them, giving up proselytizing would mean giving up their raison d'être. It would also contradict their conviction that the Gospel was intended first and foremost for the Jews.

Taking care to avoid being identified with missionary groups, the Embassy has often refrained from establishing close contacts with missions to the Jews. In the United States such agencies serve as promoters of support for Israel; in addition to their evangelization efforts, they organize tours to Israel, lecture on Israel in churches, distribute material, and collect donations as an expression of interest in and concern for the Jews. Paradoxically, in order to establish itself as a credible agent in Jewish eyes, the Embassy, which seeks to represent all Christian supporters of

Israel, has given up any relationship with the agencies that represent the bulk of evangelical support for Israel. The ICE has continued, however, to enjoy support from many conservative Protestants, mostly in northern Europe. These Protestants may not be fully aware of the details of the Embassy's credo, but merely regard it as an evangelical institution that supports Israel, a country they view as fulfilling a role in the divine plans.

In sum, the International Christian Embassy is viewed in an unfavorable light by most nonevangelical Christians, and even among conservative evangelical Protestants, far from representing the majority position, it is a controversial establishment.

THE ISRAELI COMMUNITY AND THE INTERNATIONAL CHRISTIAN EMBASSY

For many Israelis the International Christian Embassy is the only Christian evangelical institution they know. Dozens of articles on the Embassy have appeared in Israeli newspapers and the Embassy tries to make itself known in Israeli society. But despite all the publicity, few are aware of the Embassy's motivation and nature. Most Israelis who know about it regard it as merely a pro-Israel Christian group convinced that the establishment of the state of Israel is a fulfillment of biblical prophecies.[58]

Many government officials who interact with the Embassy also understand this to be the nature of this group. Over time, Israeli officials have relied on the Embassy more and more as a vehicle to reach the Protestant Christian community, apparently believing that it represents a large segment of Christianity; its actual base of support, however, is much more limited. Prime Minister Yitzhak Shamir, for example, wrote that "the Christian Embassy . . . [carries] a message which cannot be overlooked or discounted by governments and statesmen in all five continents."[59] Subsequently, Israeli leaders met several times with Embassy leaders and granted the ICE permission to hold gatherings in the courtyard of the Knesset as part of its Tabernacles celebrations.[60] In April 1990, the speaker of the Knesset presented the Embassy with the Quality of Life Award, for its positive role in Israeli life. The access of the Embassy's leaders to the Israeli leadership, as well as their good record and connections with Israeli government ministries, has helped the Embassy to establish its reputation as the leading institution of Christian supporters of Israel. Protestant supporters of Israel who belong to mainline churches have often been frustrated by what they consider to be the preference the Embassy has enjoyed among Israeli officials who consider the Embassy's activities to be important in promoting the Israeli cause.[61]

Most Israelis view the International Christian Embassy as an institution representing millions of Christians worldwide and embodying goodwill and support towards Israel.[62] For the most part, they are totally unfamiliar with the details of the Christian evangelical premillennialist eschatology that motivates the Embassy's leaders and supporters; nor are they aware of van der Hoeven's complicated attitude toward Judaism, Jews, and Israeli society, of his radical political stance, or of his own and the Embassy's position within the general Christian community in Israel. Some Israeli officials, such as the directors of the Department of Christian Affairs in the Ministry of Religious Affairs, have been well acquainted with the character and motivation of the various Christian groups and organizations, but this has not always been the case with officials responsible for Israel's relationship with Christian churches and organizations in the foreign office or the prime minister's office.[63]

Naturally the Embassy's friends are in the nationalist-religious wing of Israeli society. Van der Hoeven has little regard for moderate, centrist, or left-wing Israeli politicians, whom he sees as betraying their nation's historical mission, and he openly criticizes their views. Convinced that Israel must keep the territories that it took over from Jordan in June 1967, he has attacked Israeli leftists and moderates for their willingness to give up land for peace and thus to jeopardize the realization of the kingdom. On the personal level, he has found fault with many Israelis he has encountered, including those from the nationalist and religious wing. Although they are fulfilling a heroic historical mission, he contends, their behavior has been morally wanting. The Dutch minister is particularly taken aback by the sexual promiscuity of Israeli public figures and political activists.[64]

Van der Hoeven has had contacts over the years with right-wing political parties and politicians. According to one source, he showed up in the Likud headquarters in Jerusalem on the night of the election in 1984.[65] According to another source, he endorsed the politics of the late Meir Kahane, who was blocked from running for office in the 1988 election on account of his racist views and attempted to establish contacts with the Kach leader; this overture, however, was rejected by the xenophobic Kahane.[66] In July 1991 the liberal Jerusalem weekly *Kol HaIr* published an article claiming that the International Christian Embassy was conducting welfare activities and distributing money to needy new immigrants in the offices of the Likud (the major ruling party) and Moledet (a small right-wing nationalist party that advocates the "transfer" of the Arabs from Israeli territories to Arab countries as a solution for the problem of Palestinian-Israeli hostility).[67] In 1988 the magazine *Nekuda* (Settlement), an organ of the Jewish settlements in Judea and Samaria, which reflects the ideology of Gush Emunim, published a favorable article on the Embassy entitled "Without Inhibitions: Christians Committed to Judea and Samaria." In it the Embassy's people were described as pro-Israel Christians who realize that the Bible authorizes the Jews to settle their land.[68] *Nekuda* emphasized that the Embassy had no missionary intentions. Other religious nationalists, such as former Chief Rabbi Shlomo Goren, have also accepted the Embassy as a genuine friend and supporter of their cause.[69] Only a few have voiced reservations.[70]

The Embassy has succeeded in establishing a positive image among the Zionist Orthodox Israeli Jews but not among the *haredim,* the non-Zionist Orthodox Jews; in spite of its attempts to assure Orthodox Jews that it refrains from missionary activities, many of them remained suspicious of the Embassy and its intentions. In one incident, swastikas were painted on the Embassy's building, presumably by Jewish extremists for whom the Embassy appeared as yet another alien proselytizing institution.

Yad LeAchim ("a hand for our brethren"), established in the 1970s to combat the activities of groups set on capturing Jewish souls, has not been impressed with the Embassy's stated nonmissionary policy. One of its main activities has been the collecting of material on groups considered dangerous in order to "expose" their covert missionizing nature. A report of this sort on the ICE was prepared by Sylvia Soester, a former employee of Yad LeAchim, and sent to a number of Israeli government officials. In the document Soester claimed to have proofs of the Embassy's missionary nature. She had examined the publications of the Embassy, as well as speeches and sermons of van der Hoeven, and, unfamiliar with Christian premillenialist rhetoric, had concluded that the Embassy's program was nothing less than a plan "to take control and win Jerusalem for the Christian church."[71]

In attempting to demonstrate that it refrains from missionizing Jews, the Embassy has limited its interactions with Israelis to its annual Tabernacles celebrations and does not encourage Israelis to visit its center. Its publications are not intended for the Israeli public, and it tends to carry out its welfare work through Israeli organizations. Its workers' day-to-day contacts with Israelis are limited to officials, political activists, and agencies from which the Embassy buys services. The Embassy has been careful not to associate itself too closely with groups and communities of Jewish converts to Christianity, since such an association could be interpreted as advocating missionary work. As a rule, it does not employ Jews (including Jews who have accepted Christianity), nor does it encourage Jewish converts to join in its activities.[72] This is not to say, of course, that the Embassy disapproves of missionary work among Jews by other groups, or that its leaders look unfavorably upon Jewish conversion to Christianity. On the contrary, van der Hoeven looks upon Jews who accept Jesus as their savior as both perfect persons and Jews; in his eyes they have fulfilled their true selves. He does invite converted Jews to speak in closed gatherings organized by the Embassy, but not at large public events such as those at the Sultan's Pool. Nor does the Embassy quote converted Jews or advertise their messages in its publications.[73]

Van der Hoeven was unhappy with the results of the 1992 Israeli elections. The victory of Yitzhak Rabin's Labour Party and its coalition with Meretz, a left-wing party headed by Shulamit Aloni, worried him. He felt much closer to the Likud's right-wing ideology and policies, and had not hesitated, during the Likud tenure in government, to demonstrate that preference. The Embassy had been established during a Likud administration and had acquired a unique position as the Christian organization most trusted by the Likud government, a position van der Hoeven and his friends wished to retain. In spite of his criticism of Rabin's policies, van der Hoeven accorded the prime minister great deference as the head of the country on whose behalf he and his friends at the Embassy had been laboring so hard. Rabin was invited to speak at the Tabernacles gathering, and his photograph appeared in Embassy publications.

The years 1993 to 1995 were not very happy ones for the leader of the International Christian Embassy. His wife Widad fell ill and eventually died. Israeli government policy also gave him reason for frustration. Van der Hoeven did not hide his dissatisfaction with the peace agreement signed by Rabin's government and the PLO, in which Israel promised to withdraw from Judea and Samaria.[74] He and his colleagues also expressed their fears that Israel might give back the Golan Heights in the process of reaching a peace agreement with the Syrian government, which the Dutch minister viewed as diabolic.[75] The Embassy's newsletter even tried to stir public opinion against giving up the Golan, quoting Rabin's own word on the importance of the Golan for Israeli security.[76]

Upset as he has been with the government policy, van der Hoeven has refused to look upon it as an intermission or a retreat in the advancement of history. In a twisted way, the new developments might even mean that the end of this age is near and the great events that are to precede the messianic age are soon to occur. The Labour government, led by Shimon Peres in the aftermath of the November 1995 assassination of Rabin by a Jewish extremist, is pursuing a careless, naïve policy toward the Arabs, van der Hoeven believes. But that policy might just bring about a catastrophic political situation that would serve as the beginning of the "time of Jacob's trouble." At the end of 1995 Van der Hoeven remained firm in his conviction that the messianic age was near.

CONCLUSION

The International Christian Embassy is a product of the religious and political atmosphere of our days. It reflects the hopes, beliefs, and historical understanding of Christian fundamentalists, as well as their perception of the place and role of the Jews and Israel in God's plans for humanity. It similarly reflects the political situation of the Israeli state and its dilemmas in the years following the Six Day War (1967), the Yom Kippur War (1973), and the war in southern Lebanon (1982). Israel's eagerness to find support in the Western Christian world has played no small part in shaping the Embassy's activities and reputation. The Embassy's special relationship with the Israeli government reflects, albeit indirectly, the attitudes of nonfundamentalist Christians towards Israel as well. The reserved, critical, and at times hostile relationship of most eastern, Orthodox, Catholic, and mainline Protestant churches towards Israel and its political choices has helped turn the Embassy into the Christian organization closest to and most trusted by the Israeli government as well as into a controversial body insofar as Christians' attitudes towards the Arab-Israeli conflict are concerned.

Politics make strange bedfellows; the relationship between the Israeli government and the International Christian Embassy is a marriage of convenience, based on the Israeli belief that the Embassy is instrumental in mustering support for Israel in the Christian world. The Embassy, in turn, sees in the Israeli state a necessary vehicle on the eschatological road. Whereas not all Israeli officials are aware of the Embassy's real attitude towards the Jewish people and Israel, the Embassy's leaders have had no illusions as to the Israeli attitudes toward them. As a necessary step to gain Israeli trust, they refrain from missionizing, a concession other pro-Israel evangelicals have seen as willful neglect of an essential Christian duty. Thus the Embassy has become a controversial institution even within evangelical circles.

Those associated with the Embassy felt encouraged by the immigration to Israel of Russian and Ethiopian Jewry and by Jewish settlement in the occupied territories of Judea and Samaria, developments that indicate a Jewish commitment to inhabit the entire boundaries of the Davidic kingdom. Such events offered proof that their eschatological belief, biblical hermeneutics, and critique of culture are correct and that history is advancing according to their predictions. In 1994 and 1995, however, they expressed alarm at the willingness of the Rabin government to give up land in exchange for peace, which they viewed as a betrayal of the Jews' historical mission. At other times as well, van der Hoeven has not concealed his disappointment and bitterness at the fact that the Jewish people fail to understand the historical significance of their national revival and thus fail to live up to his expectations on both public and private levels. Because the Jews have not accepted Jesus as their savior, in his eyes, they remain spiritually and morally deprived.

Thus Christian Zionism entails a unique relationship between religious communities in which one community plays a crucial role in the messianic expectations of another. Most Christian groups do not share van der Hoeven's fascination with the future of the Jewish people and their national revival. Developments in the life of the Jewish people, particularly the birth of the state of Israel and the Six Day War with its territorial conquests, have helped intensify Christian messianic expectations and the belief that the Jewish people are to play a dominant role in the events of the end times. What will happen if people such as van der Hoeven are ultimately disappointed by developments in the Middle East and in the life of the Jewish people—and conclude, therefore, that the Jews have jeopardized the fulfillment of the messianic hope—remains to be seen.

Notes

1. *International Christian Zionist Congress, Basel, 27–29 August* 1985 (Jerusalem: International Christian Embassy, 1985); *Christian Zionism and its Biblical Basis* (Jerusalem: International Christian Embassy Jerusalem, 1988).

2. Norman Cohn, *The Pursuit of the Millennium* (New York: Oxford University Press, 1970); George Williams, *The Radical Reformation* (Cambridge: Cambridge University Press, 1964).

3. David Katz, *Philosemitism and the Readmission of the Jews to England* (Oxford: Oxford University Press, 1981).

4. Barbara Tuchman, *Bible and Sword* (London: Macmillan, 1982), 175–207.

5. Ibid.; Lawrence J. Epstein, *Zion Call* (Lanham, Md.: University Press of America, 1984).

6. See, for example, "Christian Zionism" and "Rev. William Hechler," in *International Christian Zionist Congress*, 6–10.

7. William G. McLaughlin, *Modern Revivalism from Charles Grandison Finny to Billy Graham* (New York: Ronald Press Company, 1959).

8. Interview with Jan Willem van der Hoeven, 5 December 1990. On Lance

Lambert's understanding of Israel and its role in history, see his book *The Uniqueness of Israel* (Eastbourne: Kingsway Publications, 1980).

9. On Darby, the Plymouth Brethren, and dispensationalism, see Clarence B. Bass, *Background to Dispensationalism* (Grand Rapids: Eerdmans Publishing Company, 1960); Dave MacPherson, *The Incredible Cover-Up: The True Story of the Pre-Tribulation Rapture* (Plainfield, N.J.: Omega Publications, 1975); Ernest R. Sandeen, *The Roots of Fundamentalism* (Grand Rapids: Baker Book House, 1978).

10. For details of the premillennialist-dispensationalist scheme, see, for example, Hal Lindsey, *The Late Great Planet Earth* (Grand Rapids: Zondervan Publishing House, 1971).

11. Jan Willem van der Hoeven, "If I Forget Thee O Jerusalem," Sukkoth brochure (Jerusalem: International Christian Embassy, 1984), 9.

12. There is no biography of Jan Willem van der Hoeven. Most of the information was provided by him in a series of interviews with the author.

13. Jan van der Hoeven, *Slant Eyed Angel* (Gerrards Cross: Colin Smythe, 1968).

14. Ibid., 14–18.

15. The information on Widad van der Hoeven and her background was provided by her husband.

16. On the place of charismatics in current evangelicalism, see, for example, Randall Balmer, *Mine Eyes Have Seen the Glory* (New York: Oxford University Press, 1989).

17. Information on the Almond Tree Branch was provided in interviews with David Bivin, Jerusalem, 28 October 1992; Menahem Ben Hayim, Jerusalem, 25 June 1991 and 14 October 1992; and Marvin and Merla Watson, Jerusalem, 16 October 1992. All were members of the group.

18. Interview with David Bivin, Jerusalem, 28 October 1991.

19. James McWhirter, *A World in a Country* (Jerusalem: B.S.B. International, 1983), 160–74; interviews with Marvin and Merla Watson, Jerusalem, 16 October 1992, and Menahem Ben Hayim, Jerusalem, 14 October 1992.

20. Van der Hoeven, "If I Forget Thee O Jerusalem," 4.

21. Interview with Haim Schapiro, correspondent for religious affairs of the *Jerusalem Post,* Jerusalem, 6 October 1992.

22. Interviews with David Bivin, Jerusalem, 28 October 1991, and Joseph Emmanuel, Jerusalem, 3 October 1991. Emmanuel, who was the director of the Israel Interfaith Association, served as a mediator between Fischer and the Embassy.

23. A typewritten list of ICEJ international representatives, February 1992, included representatives in Florida, Georgia, Mississippi, South Carolina, Texas, Maryland, California, and Wyoming.

24. On the various activities of the Embassy, see its brochure, "The Ministry of the International Christian Embassy Jerusalem" (Jerusalem: International Christian Embassy, 1992).

25. Arlynn Nellhaus, "Go Tell It On the Mountain," *Jerusalem Post Magazine,* 9 October 1992, 6–7.

26. In 1991, for example, Germans offered more financial support for bringing Russian Jews to Israel than supporters in any other country. "Wohnungsbau

fur Sowjetische Juden," *Ein Wort aus Jerusalem,* March–April 1992. As premillennialism and messianism are not strong among German Protestants this may be attributed to guilt and a wish to help the Jewish state, regardless of its role in the events that precede the arrival of the Messiah.

27. See, for example, Ruth W. Mouly, *The Religious Right and Israel* (Chicago: Midwest Research, 1985).

28. Interviews with David Bivin and David Pileggi, Jerusalem, 14 October 1991; and Joseph Emmanuel, Jerusalem, 3 October 1991.

29. "Statement on the International Christian Embassy in Jerusalem," circulated by the United Kingdom Branch of the International Christian Embassy, Jerusalem; New Malden, Surrey, 1 June 1985.

30. Interviews with David Bivin, David Pileggi, Joseph Emmanuel, and Menahem Ben Hayim. Cf. "Christian Embassy Suffering," *Jerusalem Post,* 2 October 1985, 3.

31. Interview with David Pileggi, former volunteer at the Embassy. Cf. "Statement on the International Christian Embassy in Jerusalem."

32. One group of those who resigned established a new organization, the Christian Friends of Israel. This group, headed by Ray Sanders, is also headquartered in Jerusalem and aims to promote Israeli causes. It is, however, a more conventional institution, in line with other pro-Israel evangelical organizations. Among other things it does not advocate radical political views and engages in missionary activities.

33. A list of donors providing for flights of Russian Jews to Israel through the middle of 1991 is instructive. Donors from Germany paid for ten flights, Finland three, Switzerland two, Holland one, Denmark one, Norway one, South Africa one, the United States two, Canada one, Australia one, and New Zealand one. "Flugzeuge Fur Sowjetjuden," *Ein Wort aus Jerusalem,* Marz–April 1991.

34. Interview with Rabbi Yechiel Eckstein, Chicago, 1 September 1992.

35. On the conference schedule and participants, see *Washington for Israel Summit* (Jerusalem: International Christian Embassy, Jerusalem, 1992).

36. *Le Maan Tzion Lo Echeshe* (in Hebrew) (Jerusalem: International Christian Embassy, 1990), 13.

37. Interview with Jan Willem van der Hoeven, Jerusalem, 19 August 1991.

38. Interview with Reverend Michael Krupp. See also Michael Krupp, "Falsche Propheten in Jerusalem," 3 October 1988, sent to the Protestant religious press in Germany.

39. Interview with Jan Willem van der Hoeven, 19 August 1991.

40. Van der Hoeven recalls, in a sermon delivered at the International Christian Embassy, Jerusalem, 14 August 1991, a conversation he had with two yeshiva students in the mid-1970s. He tried to point out to them the enormous void that characterizes a rebuilt united Jerusalem that has not yet let the true Messiah reign and dwell in its midst.

41. "Songs of Celebration," in 1985 Sukkoth brochure (Jerusalem: International Christian Embassy, 1985), 28–38.

42. The Jewish calendar is based on solar-lunar calculations; hence the holy days do not correlate with the solar Gregorian calendar but vary from year to year.

43. In a sermon, "Getting Tender before the Lord," 17 July 1991, audiocassette E-282 (Jerusalem: International Christian Embassy, 1991).

44. Jan Willem van der Hoeven, "A Greater Fulfillment," in *Succot* 1985, 15–16.

45. Interview with Jan Willem van der Hoeven, Jerusalem, 5 August 1991.

46. See, for example, a sermon given 22 August 1990, audiocassette E-251 (Jerusalem: International Christian Embassy, 1990).

47. Jan Willem van der Hoeven, "Will Syria's Assad Be the Next Saddam Hussein?" *Middle East Intelligence Digest* 2, no. 4 (July 1991); this journal is a publication of the ICE.

48. See, for example, Raymond L. Cox, "Time for the Temple?" *Eternity* 19 (January 1968), 17–18.

49. See, for example, C. W. Sleming, *These Are the Garments* (Fort Washington, Pa.: Christian Literature Crusade, n.d.); Doug Wead, David Lewis, and Hal Donaldson, *Where Is the Lost Ark?* (Minneapolis: Bethany House Publishing, n.d.).

50. Yisrayl Hawkins, *A Peaceful Solution to Building the Next Temple in Jerusalem* (Abilene, Tex.: House of Yahweh, 1989).

51. Interview with Stanley Goldfoot, Jerusalem, 12 November 1990.

52. Interview with Father Marcel Dubois, Jerusalem, 1 January 1992. See also Alting von Geusau, "The Testimony of a Catholic Christian Zionist," in *Christian Zionism and Its Biblical Basis,* 24–25.

53. Some liberal and mainline churches, such as the Quakers and Lutherans, have worked in the West Bank and Gaza and, in protests and actions, have expressed their commitment to the Palestinian cause. In some cases, such as in Holland, mainline Protestant church members often have more positive attitudes towards Israel than their leadership; consequently the Embassy, which is regarded as representing pro-Israel sentiments, enjoys support even when the church establishment is hostile towards its activities. Interview with Reverend Simon Schoon and Reverend Geert Cohen-Stuart of the Dutch Reformed Church, Southampton, 14 July 1991.

54. "Signs of Hope," 1988 annual report of the Middle East Council of Churches, Cyprus, July 1989.

55. *What is Western Fundamentalist Christian Zionism?* (Limosol, Cyprus; The Middle East Council of Churches, April 1988; rev. ed., August 1988). The second, revised edition is somewhat more moderate than the first

56. *Mishkan,* no. 12 (1990).

57. Interview with Reverend William Currie, former head of the American Messianic Fellowship, Jerusalem, September 1991. Currie has little appreciation for the Embassy.

58. "A Different Kind of Embassy," *Jerusalem Post,* 2 November 1982, 20; "A Mission of Friendship," *Jerusalem Post,* 8 December 1984, 4.; Yossi Klein Halevi, "Balancing Act," *Jerusalem Report,* 26 December 1991, 10–14.

59. "Israel's Leaders Greet the Embassy," in *Prepare Ye the Way of the Lord* (Jerusalem: International Christian Embassy, 1991).

60. For a photograph of such a gathering, see Tzipora Luria, "LeLo Tasbichim: Notzrim Mechuiavim LeYesha" (Without inhibitions: Christians committed to Judea and Samaria), *Nekuda,* no. 128, 17 March 1989, 31.

61. Interview with Reverend Geert Cohen-Stuart, representative in Jerusalem of the Dutch Reformed Church, Southampton, 14 July 1991.

62. Interview with Noemi Teasdale, Southampton, 14 July 1991. Teasdale was the liaison of the mayor of Jerusalem for Christian affairs. Explaining the amicable relations that have developed between the Embassy and the municipality of Jerusalem, Teasdale remarked that the city inhabitants derive great encouragement watching Christians march in their support through the city's streets. Teasdale's words reflect the attitude of Israeli officials towards the Embassy, as well as that of many in the Israeli public who hear or read about the Embassy or watch its marches through Jerusalem. It further reflects the large gap between image and reality.

63. In 1985, Michael Pragai, then head of the Department for Christian Affairs at the Foreign Ministry, published a book on Christian supporters of Zionism and Israel; Michael Pragai, *Faith and Fulfillment* (London: Vallentine Mitchell, 1985). The book clearly reveals both the author's inability to differentiate between the motivations of the various supporters of Israel and his lack of knowledge as to the history, theology, and character of the various Christian groups.

64. Interviews with Jan Willem van der Hoeven, Jerusalem, 5 and 9 August 1991 and 29 September 1992; interview with David Pileggi, Jerusalem, 14 October 1991.

65. Interview with David Pileggi, Jerusalem, 14 October 1991.

66. Interviews with Menahem Ben Hayim, Jerusalem, 15 July 1991, and Reverend Andrew White, Birmingham, 11 July 1991.

67. Yael Eshkenazi, "HaKesher HaNotzri Shel Moledet" (The Christian connection with Moledet), *Kol HaIr*, 1 November 1991, 30.

68. Luria, "LeLo Tasbichim," 30–34.

69. *Le Maan Tzion Lo Echeshe*, 14.

70. See Halevi, "Balancing Act."

71. Sylvia Soester, "A Report on the Work of the International Christian Embassy, Jerusalem and Its Proselytizing Programme to the Jews," September 1990, 1.

72. Interview with Gertrude Weiss, Jerusalem, 25 October 1991.

73. Interview with Menahem Ben Hayim, Jerusalem, 25 June 1991.

74. See, for example, *Middle East Intelligence Digest* 5, nos. 8 and 9 (August and September 1994).

75. *Middle East Intelligence Digest* 5, no. 10 (October 1995): 3.

76. Ibid., 1.

CONCLUSION

The Measure of a Fundamentalist Leader

R. Scott Appleby

Our comparative study has produced two general conclusions that at first glance seem contradictory. On the one hand, the various profiles confirm the centrality of strong male charismatic leadership in the formation and growth of the most powerful fundamentalist movements of the Middle East. In the Islamic world these are radical protest movements of the economically and politically marginalized—the masses of underemployed and seemingly forgotten people known throughout the region as the "downtrodden." These people, hailing from various backgrounds, feel despised and betrayed both by secular political leaders and by religious officials, who have failed to challenge the corruption, mismanagement, and moral laxity popularly associated with godless ideologies and development programs indifferent to religious and cultural values. The radical Jews of the region are also despised, by their fellow Israelis and Arab neighbors, for their tenacious ultra-Orthodox religiosity and extremist political views. The Protestant fundamentalists of the International Christian Embassy are merely ignored by the majority of Arabs and Israelis in the Holy Land, while Israeli and Arab politicians sometimes try to manipulate them as pawns in the domestic political game. In each of these cases, the charismatic fundamentalist preacher is the catalyst for the hardening of resentment into organized opposition.

As an authoritative interpreter of religion, the only cultural system still capable of articulating popular outrage and tapping reformist idealism, the fundamentalist preacher or religious scholar occupies an inherently powerful position in the local community. He speaks for the despised, proclaiming and subtly reinterpreting their sacred history and destiny—a story of imminent or eventual redemption that amuses or scandalizes skeptical outsiders. In so doing he skillfully redefines the bonds and boundaries of the traditional community, mobilizing its most courageous members for revolutionary action.

On the other hand, the authors point to the waning or shifting importance of the charismatic religious leader in the period following his success in establishing or giving religious sanction to a radical protest movement. The fundamentalist leader initially mobilizes disaffected masses and attracts or recruits a core of ideological and organizational chieftains, who build a viable and multilayered organization. Ironically, this development creates a situation in which charismatic religious leadership itself may become little more than one among several elements at work in a fundamentalist organization. The charismatic leader is then forced to contend with, because he cannot not entirely control, the creature he has called into being.

This tension gives rise, in the cases examined in this volume, to various patterns of relation between the leader and his movement. Patrick Gaffney's portrait of Shaykh Ahmad Isma'il delineates a pattern of charismatic leadership outstripped by the devotion of its followers and undermined by the *lack* of an organizational infrastructure and second-tier leadership capable of channeling revolutionary energies into effective operations and institutions. A gifted preacher, Shaykh Ahmad galvanized the Muslim population and university students of Minya, in Upper Egypt, in the late 1970s. During a heady eighteen months of militant activism, his followers staged provocations and demonstrations, engineered a hostage taking, forced public closings, and otherwise caused havoc. In this case, however, the charismatic leader was not an operational or organizational leader, and he did not have a cadre of deputies on which to rely for the long term. His Friday sermons at the Sunna Mosque attracted overflow crowds, but the buildings of the associated cooperative society were in decline, its social programs understaffed, its financial resources poorly managed and dwindling. Thus when President Sadat became annoyed with the flare-ups in Minya and decided to suppress the militants, Gaffney tells us, "from this day on the fundamentalist organization in Minya effectively lost its potency in the wider student community." Shaykh Ahmad quickly became peripheral to the Islamist protest movement, which fragmented and sought other forms of leadership.

A second pattern finds the charismatic leader overwhelmed by the very success of his organization. Hamas provides perhaps the most dramatic example of an Islamic movement of resistance that has evolved beyond its local base, and beyond the original vision of its founder, to become an international organization with a diverse leadership. Ziad

Abu-Amr describes the differentiation and internationalization of Hamas's infrastructure and leadership after its charismatic founder, Shaykh Ahmad Yasin, was jailed by the Israelis in 1989. Yasin's successors honored and extended some aspects of his legacy, Abu-Amr points out. The Qassam Brigades, Hamas's militant wing, recapitulated the mission of the militant cadres Yasin had established prior to the intifada and the creation of Hamas itself. But the Qassam Brigades also adopted new methods and sometimes engaged in the type of undisciplined violence that Yasin had warned against; and when Israel deported 415 Hamas activists in December 1992, dumping them on a barren, snowy hillside in Lebanon, the deportees likely came into contact with members of Hizbullah, from whom they learned the fine points of suicide bombing and other terrorist tactics.

Leadership inevitably became diffuse after Yasin was imprisoned, as lower-ranking leaders of Hamas attempted to fill the gap created by his absence. Mohammed Mousa Abu Marzook, an American-educated engineer and native of Gaza, restructured the movement, transforming Hamas into a formidable international organization with a network of operatives that extends beyond the Middle East to the United States and Europe. Abu-Amr notes the financial support Hamas received, especially in the aftermath of the Gulf war of 1990–1991, from the Muslim Brotherhood in neighboring Arab states, Palestinians living abroad, prominent figures in Saudi Arabia and other oil-rich Gulf states, and the Iranian government. In the mid-1990s much of the money was being channeled through Jordan, where the Muslim Brotherhood remains strong.[1]

Hamas was never a one-man show, of course. Several dozen fiery shaykhs preached rebellion against Israel in the mosques of Gaza. But Yasin had been the central figure, his political judgment sought out precisely because he was the local hero who had built an elaborate social service network of mosques, schools, orphanages, clinics, and hospitals. With his arrest and the internationalization of the movement, however, the leadership structure changed, with different bureaus overseeing political activities, religious and charitable missions, and clandestine military operations. In the religious sphere, for example, the Council of Religious Sages, comprising more than 150 Muslim clerics in the occupied territories, coordinated sermons so that similar political messages were heard in mosques throughout the region and circulated audiocassettes with titles like "P.L.O. High Treason: The Oslo Accords and Beyond."[2]

The Israeli crackdown, in response to the radicalization of the movement, further splintered Hamas's leadership. When Marzook was arrested at Kennedy Airport in New York, on 28 July 1995, Emad Al-Alami, an engineer from Gaza but now based in Damascus, assumed his position. By this time, however, the charismatic leadership once wielded by one man, Yasin, had become diffused and routinized. Thus Al-Alami found it necessary to share power with the local political leader in Gaza, Mahmoud El-Zahar (subsequently imprisoned by Israel), and the military leader Yahya Ayyash (subsequently assassinated, reportedly by Israel). At times, the three wings of the movement acted in an uncoordinated fashion.

The growth and differentiation of the movement made Hamas nearly ungovernable. Yet Yasin remained a powerful symbol of unity. The shaykh's absence from the scene eroded his control over the movement's day-to-day operations; yet remarkably, despite imprisonment and deteriorating health, he continued to function in a general supervisory capacity. In February 1996, for example, one of Yasin's deputies, Sayyid Abu Musamih, invoked the shaykh's recent pronouncements when offering a rationale for a string of Hamas-engineered suicide bombings designed to jeopardize the peace process.[3] In other situations, Abu-Amr tells us, Yasin has spoken through the media in an attempt to restrain the excesses of the militant wing.

Sayyid Muhammad Husayn Fadlallah of Lebanon tried to remedy the problem of diminishing influence by reversing the pattern of internationalization: he would keep the movement, Hizbullah, strictly Lebanese, while making the leader—Fadlallah himself—an international Islamic "pope." The oracle of Hizbullah kept himself at arm's length from the movement; indeed, Martin Kramer tell us that Khomeini's emissaries, not Fadlallah, founded Hizbullah. From the beginning Fadlallah was wary of restricting Islam's political reach and power by excluding Muslims who did not fulfill Hizbullah's explicit membership requirements. Whereas Yasin derived his authority strictly from his local roots and neighborhood identity, Fadlallah cultivated the international media, projecting the image of a transnational ayatollah who was somehow above the fray. At the same time, Fadlallah was a political realist with a firm grasp of the incomparable aspects of the Lebanese situation—especially the abiding confessional pluralism—and the resulting limited range of possibilities for political Islam. Thus he resisted the Iranian emissaries who spoke vaguely of an Islam without borders, and he pushed Hizbullah to participate in parliamentary elections, carving a niche for itself in the complex political environment of the Lebanese state.

POLITICAL REALISM

In the introduction I characterized fundamentalists as dualists and absolutists who divide the world into realms of good and evil, and refuse to compromise with "impure" outsiders. In the preceding chapters we have seen this belligerent and zealous attitude on display in the cadres of Hizbullah and the Muslim Brotherhood, in Hamas and its Jewish counterpart Gush Emunim. Significantly, however, the charismatic leaders are the most flexible of the fundamentalists, the ones least likely to take a consistent hard-line position; indeed, they have often attempted to restrain young militants or doctrinaire clerics whose absolute devotion to the ultimate goal of religious sovereignty was untempered by political realism.

Daniel Brumberg's profile of the Ayatollah Khomeini, like Kramer's portrait of Fadlallah, provides a striking example of the "utilitarian" element in effective charismatic leadership. Both of these ayatollahs shared an unstinting devotion to the sovereignty of Islam, and each identified the rise of his own star with this ultimate political goal. As a result, they spoke vividly, with undeniable conviction, when describing the plight of the oppressed, the mendacity of Islam's enemies, and the glory of the Qur'an and the Hadith of the Prophet, which contained the blueprint for a just society. Yet neither man was so caught up in the rhetoric of Islamic triumphalism as to be blind to the practical necessities of leadership in a fallen and compromised world. Khomeini recognized the importance of consolidating the revolution and feared the imprudence, born of unchecked zeal, of some of his clerical disciples in the Iranian government. In the last years of his life, as he prepared his last will and testament and delivered major speeches on his legacy, he therefore ensured that the absolutists would not inherit his mantle. He denied them the power to undermine his considerable if flawed political accomplishments with their single-minded devotion to "pure" Islam. Fadlallah likewise demonstrated his pragmatic realism in numerous ways, as detailed by Kramer: in extending the hand of friendship and collaboration to the Sunni Muslims of Lebanon, whose support political Islam needed; in advancing a realistic appraisal of Israel's staying power in the region; in his careful diplomatic relations with Syria and Iran.

A shrewd pragmatism also informs the charismatic leadership of Hassan Turabi, the éminence grise of the current Sudanese regime. Judith Miller traces Turabi's infallible instinct for political survival to his early days as a member of the Sudanese branch of the Muslim Brotherhood. In 1958 the Brotherhood's executive committee opposed a Turabi-backed proposal allowing Brotherhood candidates to run for parliament on the

Umma Party ticket, refusing—in standard fundamentalist fashion—to allow impure elements to infect the righteous. In 1962, however, Turabi's pragmatism triumphed, when he convinced the Muslim Brotherhood that a coalition of Sudan's traditional parties, joined with southern political factions normally inimical to the Muslim Brotherhood, could topple the unpopular and un-Islamic regime of General Ibrahim Abboud. This was just the first of several effective coalitions Turabi has built during the course of career devoted to Islam—but to an Islam conceived of not as an abstract ideal but as a workable political solution for the oppressed of the earth.

In 1996, the thirteenth year of Sudan's civil war, Turabi once again proved himself a survivor. On 24 March the results of the Sudanese elections held earlier in the month were announced. As expected, Omar Hassan al-Bashir, the fifty-two-year-old military strongman who had appointed himself president in 1989 after overthrowing Sadiq al-Mahdi's democratically elected government, celebrated a landslide victory over forty little-known candidates. The newly elected president vowed to keep the country ruled by "Islamic law and dignity," with no return to party politics. "We have fully returned power to the people," General Bashir proclaimed. Leaders of the Sudan's main opposition parties, disbanded when Bashir took power, boycotted the presidential and parliamentary elections; Sadiq el-Mahdi called the elections a cheap attempt by the government to buy legitimacy. Turabi, however, was elected to a seat in the new parliament, along with twelve Islamist clerics. He could reasonably expect widespread support for his programs in the 400-member body, especially from the 125 members appointed three months earlier, at Turabi's prodding, by progovernment committees known as national congresses. "The power behind [Bashir's] Government [continues] to be the militant Muslim cleric Hassan Turabi," the Reuters news agency reported.[4]

The story of Jewish radicalism narrated by Gideon Aran and Samuel Heilman presents a somewhat different picture of charismatic leadership under pressure. In this case political realism on the part of the fundamentalist leaders created a climate of religious extremism fueled by desperation. In the end that extremism proved to be beyond the leaders' control.

The charismatic Jewish rabbis who formed the Ichud Rabbanim— the Union of Rabbis for the People and Land of Israel—did so in order to consolidate and sanctify opposition to the government of Israeli prime minister Yitzhak Rabin, whose policies Gush Emunim saw as a direct threat to its brand of religious Zionism. Samuel Heilman recounts a sequence of rabbinic rulings amounting to a religious declaration of war on the government, which was said to have become "a threat to Jewish life." In the minds of zealous leaders of Gush Emunim like Rabbi Moshe Levinger, the Oslo Accords implemented by the Rabin government constituted a particular threat to religious Zionism, which had gambled its very existence on the belief that secular Zionists would never betray Judaism by uprooting the settlements in Judea and Samaria. Thus the radical rabbis handed down rulings legitimating a strike against the secular leadership. One of the most fascinating aspects of Heilman's essay is his account of the rabbis' response after Yigal Amir acted upon their lead. Their evasions, denials, and mutual recriminations were obviously motivated in part by a wish to live another day as Israeli citizens in order to continue the religious Zionist campaign. But this status was undeniably threatened by repulsion at the deeds they had legitimated.

THE SITUATIONAL CHARACTER OF FUNDAMENTALIST LEADERSHIP

What we discover, in short, by nuancing the categories "fundamentalist" and "charismatic" through biographical studies, is that the measure of a charismatic fundamentalist is the effectiveness of his situational leadership. This effectiveness lies in his ability to react creatively to crisis situations, to make choices that expand his influence over the religious community and the larger political culture of his society, and to mix and match ideological and organizational resources as the situation demands. He cannot alter long-term social structures, which determine the range of possibilities available to him and his followers; nor can he predict the occurrence of short-term chance events—military invasions, crop failures and famine, the death of leaders—which may affect such questions as timing, location, scale, and militance of his movement's activities. All he has is the power of his own free choices, which are responsive and creative actions, and hence unpredictable. But if he is indeed charismatic, these choices may be enough to unlock the transformative or revolutionary potential of the true believers. From that point on, the fundamentalist leader must practice cautious forbearance and resourceful timing of his interventions and mobilizations. He must temper religious zeal with practical judgment. "I learned that the slogans are not the cause," said Hizbullah's Fadlallah of his early years, "but that the cause is reality. I learned to be pragmatic and not to drown in illusions."

Being pragmatic means being aware of the opportunities for and constraints on religiopolitical activism; the long-term structures or characteristics of the host society constitute the raw material, so to speak, available to the fundamentalist leader.[5] Religion is one such characteristic: the religious complexion of the society as a whole, and the fundamentalist's host religion. The nature of the host religion—its theology, its organizational structure, its vitality—is obviously of great importance in determining the form of fundamentalism that will emerge. Does the host religion have a semihierarchic structure as in Shi'ism, or a congregational one as in Protestantism and Sunni Islam? How is the religious leadership supported financially—by individual contributions, by the state, by an international organization? What does the tradition teach about the relation of religion to politics and temporal affairs in general? Does the theological tradition harbor a rich apocalyptic imagination—an expectation that the righteous will suffer terrible injustices until the dramatic intervention of God, who will overturn history and vindicate the true believers?

The fundamentalist leader—be he a Muslim, Christian, or Jew—is both constrained and empowered by the particularities of his tradition; he becomes an effective leader in large part by exploiting the political and/or revolutionary potential of its religious symbols and traditions. The Dutch Reformed minister Jan Willem van der Hoeven, for example, appropriated and magnified one element of traditional Christian theism— the expectation of the Messiah's imminent return—to gain a foothold for Christian fundamentalists in the Middle East.

It was no mere coincidence that the first successful Islamic *revolution* of the twentieth century was led by a charismatic Shi'ite jurist, for historically Shi'ism has been suspicious of temporal political leadership, anticipating true justice only at the hands of the Hidden Imam. Thus Shi'ism has remained politically passive for much of its history, depending religiously on its clerical leaders and politically on eventual deliverance by Allah. But the tradition nonetheless contains revolutionary elements— narratives of holy martyrdom, symbols of defiance, rituals like 'Ashura— which, interpreted in a certain way, could be retrieved and recast by a charismatic leader. Once the Shi'ite clerics, led by a brilliant innovator like Khomeini, justified the recourse to political activism with the doctrine of the Rule of the Jurist, the mobilization of the masses became possible. Shi'ism, in other words, provided the necessary ingredients for revolutionary political Islam—Shi'ite fundamentalism—but the actual mounting of a Shi'ite revolution required the action of a charismatic religious leader having or mobilizing the support of associates and lower clergy and claiming the authority to displace the temporal ruler (in this case, the Shah of Iran).

One feature shared by all three host religions of Middle Eastern fundamentalisms is patriarchy, according to which God intended society to be governed by men and the home to be ruled by the father. Defending

406 / R. SCOTT APPLEBY

and reasserting traditional gender roles is a hallmark of Jewish, Christian, and Islamic fundamentalisms; indeed, some scholars have argued that fundamentalism is best understood as a patriarchal protest movement dedicated to eliminating feminism and restoring male dominance to what is perceived as a feminized society.[6] Religious fundamentalists are not the only types of social conservatives opposing feminism, of course, but the fundamentalists make their distinctive contribution to antifeminism by claiming a divine origin for the patriarchal structures of traditional Judaism, Islam, and Christianity.

Already we have noted that fundamentalist leaders, in their defense of traditional religion, are the masters of paradox: they are strict but innovative, uncompromising in principle but surprisingly flexible in practice, and pragmatic when necessary. Their approach to women reflects this balancing act. In 1989 Ayatollah Khomeini, the master of the vivid symbolic action, condemned to death two radio producers in Tehran for broadcasting an interview with a young woman who rejected Fatimah, the Prophet Muhammad's daughter, as a role model for Iranian women. (The young woman preferred the "liberated" heroine of a Japanese television serial popular in Iran.) Khomeini also sought to repeal Iran's Family Protection Law (1967), which afforded women certain rights and minimized a man's unilateral right to divorce. The most immediate and noticeable change in the status of women after the 1979 revolution was the requirement of veiling. At the same time, Khomeini acknowledged the significant role of women in the revolution: Muslim religious scholars had encouraged women to participate in demonstrations against the Pahlavi regime and to join the fight against oppression in the spirit of Zainab, the Prophet's granddaughter who avenged her martyred brother, Imam Husayn, in the aftermath of the tragedy of Karbala. And despite the rhetoric about the lofty status of veiled women in an Islamic society, the dependence of Khomeini's movement on women activists during and immediately after the Iranian revolution "ushered in a new role model for women, one that proved to have widespread appeal to urban women."[7]

Hassan Turabi, in his public pronouncements, projects unambiguous support of an expanded role for women in an Islamic regime. Indeed, he portrays himself as a kind of champion of women's rights, a claim Judith Miller reports but does not quite accept. Turabi characteristically blames the repressive sexual practices of Muslim men not on Islam but on local customs that have crept into Muslim practice over time. He wants only to eradicate these corrupt local practices, he told Miller, so that the transformative power of fundamental, purified Islam can restore the kind of harmonious relations between men and women that flourished early in the history of the faith community. In various writings and speeches Tu-rabi has outlined "an Islamic rationale for the emancipation of women from un-Islamic conservative traditions, on the one hand, and from West-ern exploitation and enslavement to men as sexual objects, on the other." This type of rhetoric, it must be said, does not deter Miller from reviewing the long record of gender-discriminatory practices and human-rights abuses that have occurred under the Sudanese regime.

The Jewish radicals of Gush Emunim actually promoted a woman to a position of real power in the organization. In 1984 the "founding fathers, intellectuals, and rabbis" who formed the core of Gush leadership "surprisingly resolved" to appoint Daniela Weiss—mother of five, home-maker, and charismatic spokesperson for the settler movement—to the important post of secretary-general. Weiss became the darling of the Is-raeli media and revitalized the secretariat of the Gush, emphasizing its uplifting cultural and educational activities. She proposed an impressive reorganization of the entire movement, calling for an executive council of ten people to handle the day-to-day affairs and a supreme council of fifty "wise men" to recommend long-range strategies. In 1987 Weiss, a disciple of Rabbi Moshe Levinger, participated prominently in a Gush raid on the Arab town of Kalkiliya, in violent retaliation for the fire-bombing of a settler's car. Israeli television showed her throwing rocks and leading the attack, an image that stuck in the public imagination and transformed the profile of the fundamentalist Jewish activist.[8] Despite her prominent role in Gush Emunim, however, Weiss continued to take or-ders from and defer to the male rabbinic leadership of the movement.

Other fundamentalist movements relied heavily on women but re-sisted the language or practice of equality. Unlike Sudan's Turabi, Shaykh Yasin did not distinguish between "purified Islam" and traditional gender roles when he recruited only young men for the militant cadres of the Palestinian Muslim Brotherhood and, later, Hamas. Women provided es-sential social and familial support along the way, however, and eventually began to complain when they sought to join the ranks of the suicide bombers but were excluded from the company.

The fundamentalist leader is constrained not only by his own reli-gious tradition, however, but also by the larger religious and political environment in which that religion is embedded: Is the religious context a homogeneous one, or are there other, competing significant religions? Does religion coincide with ethnolinguistic differences? What is the his-toric pattern of relations among ethnoreligious groups? Which religion or sect has the advantage in obtaining access to the resources of the state? Considering these questions helps us understand, for example, why Fad-

lallah, though trained in the same traditional milieu as Iran's Khomeini—
and sharing with him a basic worldview and ideological vision, as well
as the canon of Shi'ite scriptures, symbols, and rituals—exercised a very
different brand of fundamentalist leadership amid the confessional pluralism and sectarian politics of Lebanon than Khomeini did in Shi'ite
Iran. In Fadlallah's setting, ambiguity in political discourse is a mark of
the seasoned veteran. Islam, declared Fadlallah, constitutes a framework
in which all Lebanese—Shi'ite Muslims, Sunni Muslims, Maronite Christians, Greek Orthodox Christians, Armenians, and Druze alike—could
live in harmony, regardless of their religious affiliation. Yet when pressed
to explain how Islam would achieve this, Kramer tells us, "Fadlallah let
ambiguity reign." There could be no rule of the supreme jurist in Lebanon.

In addition to the religious setting, the fundamentalist leader must
take into account other social structures: the form of government, the
educational system, the various levels of economic and social stratifica-
tion, and the relative strength of the civil society (voluntary associations,
free press, labor unions, and other collective entities independent of government control). The authority structure of a state, the legitimacy of its
institutions and leadership, the extent to which the state penetrates the
society, the level of popular participation, the degree of partisan polarization—all of these factors inevitably shape the nature of movements arising in that society. Different political and constitutional arrangements
may be associated with differences in the goals and tactics of fundamentalist movements. The emergence of two distinct types of Jewish fundamentalism—that of the non-Zionist haredim, or "ultra-Orthodox," and
that of the religious Zionists of the Gush Emunim settler movement, described in this volume by Aran and Heilman—was made possible by their
existence in an open, democratic society. Indeed, the structure of the Israeli political system, in which small, sectarian parties may exercise influence disproportionate to their size, encouraged the politicization of the
fundamentalist Jews.

Other long-term social structures also have a bearing on the direction
taken by fundamentalist leaders. As in the case of Lebanon, the subordination and exploitation of one ethnic or religious group by another will
create grievances in the long term and violent clashes in the short term.
Changes in government policy toward education may also serve as precip-
itants for fundamentalist movements; the Israeli government's decision
to grant army deferrals to yeshiva students provided the necessary condition for the emergence of the haredi "society of scholars" and, ultimately,
for a Jewish fundamentalist movement. Finally, trends in media develop-

ment—the spread of print, the rise of mass-circulation newspapers, the development of cinema, radio, and television—have had implications for political religion and the rise of fundamentalism. In the hands of the secular world these new and powerful media spread information, knowledge, and moral standards seen as threatening to religious beliefs and practices; but later generations of religious leaders, and particularly the fundamentalists among them, have discovered that they may use the media to their own ends.

Indeed, as the preceding chapters demonstrate, fundamentalist leaders excel in manipulating the media to disseminate their ideology and their politically charged interpretations of unfolding events. The ability to seize the moment is the sine qua non of charismatic leadership. Each of the fundamentalists profiled in this book underwent formal theological training and profound spiritual formation, usually from an early age and often characterized by a powerful assimilation of both the mystical and rational-legal elements of their host religions. Yet philosophical or theological originality was not their most striking quality; rather, an uncanny sense of timing and the shrewd application of ideas contributed more to their ultimate success. Abu-Amr notes that Shaykh Ahmad Yasin's theological ideas were derivative, for example, and Aran portrays Rabbi Zvi Yehuda Kook as an effective manipulator of his father's legacy but not an original thinker himself. Nonetheless Yasin exploited the popular rage following a traffic accident in which an Israeli truck hit a car carrying Palestinian workers, killing several of the Palestinians. The incident thus triggered the Palestinian uprising (intifada), which has had such historic consequences. And Kook's radical interpretation of the meanings of the Arab-Israeli wars of 1967 and 1973, bizarre though it seemed to many Orthodox Jews, has served to consolidate the radical settler movement known as Gush Emunim.

Fundamentalist leadership, in other words, is a matter of practical rather than theoretical intelligence, of political savvy as much as spiritual insight. The fundamentalist leader must choose the appropriate time to act; the opportunity is provided him by unexpected occurrences that temporarily or permanently change the facts in the field. These short-term "triggers" are events that allow the weaknesses or lines of cleavage in the structures of a society to be exploited, creating an opening for social protest movements to consolidate or expand their influence in the society. In such cases the rhetoric of the charismatic leader—at times incendiary, at other times restraining in its effect—may convert these grievances into collective awareness and action. The triggering event might be a depression, a famine, a deteriorating economic situation, a riot over migrant labor, a sudden population movement, an ethnic clash, a sharp change in government policy, a war or other international event—or a tragic traffic accident.

One such event, which changed the lives of all of our subjects, was the 1967 Six Day War and the resulting capture of East Jerusalem by Israel. The Arab attack that launched the war, though it flowed naturally from the long-term geopolitical situation in the Middle East, was a surprise and thus unpredictable; the results—stunning defeat for Egypt and the Arab world, a major victory for Israel—provided an exhilarating moment for Jews and premillennialist Christians and a deep shock for Muslims everywhere. Fundamentalist leaders of all three religions saw the event as an opportunity to mobilize their forces and expand their influence: Muslims claimed that Israel had won the war because the Arab world had abandoned Islam in favor of secular Arab nationalism; the religious Zionists who joined Gush Emunim in Israel viewed the victory of 1967 (and the subsequent narrow escape of the 1973 Yom Kippur War) as irrefutable evidence of the brilliance of Kookist ideology and as divine warrant to establish settlements in the occupied territories; Christian fundamentalists saw it as one of the prophesied events leading to the return of Christ to the Holy Land.

Such chance events mobilize people along structural lines of cleavage in a society; they may or may not be the triggers for the rise or consolidation of a fundamentalist movement. That requires the special genius of a charismatic leader who knows how to exploit the new circumstances and who matches the organizational and ideological resources at hand to the situation. This kind of leadership is expressed through the talents both of ideological catalyzers, such as the elder Rabbi Kook, Turabi, and Khomeini, and of organizers and coalition builders like the younger Rabbi Kook, Yasin, and Jan Willem van der Hoeven. Fundamentalist movements invariably draw on both ideological and organizational types of leadership.

THE INTERNATIONALIZATION OF FUNDAMENTALISM

Most fundamentalisms worldwide are associated with religions in which authority and legitimacy are concentrated in local congregations or independent religious communities—settings, that is, in which fundamentalist breakaway is relatively low in cost, where a congregation or community may simply go fundamentalist, or where new ones may be easily formed. This has led to the proliferation of fundamentalist movements, but in the past it has also tended to inhibit them from gaining revolutionary momentum.

Yet our authors point to a new trend on the horizon, which has been gaining momentum since the mid-1980s: the aforementioned internationalization of fundamentalist movements. The international political environment has long been the raw material of fundamentalist preaching; one cannot overestimate the role of "Western imperialism" as a narrative trope in the ideologies of indigenous fundamentalist movements in the Middle East, which display nationalist and anti-imperialist tendencies in addition to religious ones.[9] But the growing ability of technology to erase boundaries and shrink time and space is making the international political environment an increasingly significant factor in the organizational planning of the fundamentalist leaders as movements establish bases of operation far from the homeland.

The new fundamentalist geopolitics allows leaders to stretch or even overcome the traditional theological or organizational barriers to effective political activism. In the 1970s and 1980s, for example, the relatively centralized Shi'ite organization lent itself more readily to takeover by a radical faction than did the diffuse organizational and authority structures of Sunni Islam and Protestant Christianity. In the 1990s, however, both Protestant Christian and Sunni Muslim fundamentalists are striving to overcome these structural inhibitions by emphasizing and bolstering international connections. The International Christian Embassy in Israel, described by Yaakov Ariel, exploits the strong relationship between the United States and Israel, even as it becomes involved in partisan Israeli politics by supporting those who would reclaim "the whole land of Israel"—a precondition, as these Christian fundamentalists see it, for the return of Jesus Christ in glory. And the Sunni Muslim fundamentalists profiled in this volume, especially Shaykh Ahmad Yasin and Hassan Turabi, rely rhetorically and materially on the growing salience of Islam as a transnational political force. Yasin, who began his career with eyes set solely on the local situation, eventually recognized that the liberation of Palestine would be accomplished, not by Palestinians alone, but by a coordinated effort of Muslims everywhere (and especially in Jordan, Saudi Arabia, and other nations of the Middle East). Turabi, Miller tells us, recognized that Sudan's "experiment" in political Islam makes sense only if it is seen as an initial, and partial, contribution to a much more significant historical development: the politicization and unification of the umma—the worldwide Islamic community.

Internationalization is well underway in the world of Islamic fundamentalism, as was made apparent by a meeting held in Damascus in February 1996 to discuss the impact of the string of bus bombings in Jerusalem that month. In attendance were Hassan Habibi, the vice-president of Iran; Hussein Sheikholeslam, an Iranian Foreign Ministry official who was among the hostage takers at the American embassy in Tehran in 1979; Emad Al-Alami, the main leader of Hamas at the time; Ramadan Abdullah Shalah, the leader of Islamic Holy War; and leaders of Hizbullah. According to published reports, money exchanged hands at the meeting; afterwards, Sheikholeslam boasted to the Iranian news service, I.R.N.A., that "the Islamic resistance movement [around the world] is in for a glorious future" as a result of such unprecedented collaborative efforts.[10]

Internationalization may, of course, undermine the authority of the charismatic leader, for this authority is locally rooted. In the fundamentalist enclave, this book demonstrates, the crucial moment in the dialectic of the charismatic process usually begins with an extraordinary local situation, which may be political, economic, or religious in nature, followed by the "calling" of the potential leader and his request for obedience from the potential following. The bridge between the charismatic leader and his followers is built on the ruins of a violated social compact through which society and personality were previously assumed "to be integrated on the basis of common values and norms." Thus one expects a charismatic leader in such a situation of crisis "to be a man who seems to know how to confront this double task" of reconstituting personal and societal integrity, and fusing the two, often through the medium of his own person.[11]

Fundamentalist leadership, like charismatic leadership in general, is thus primarily ethical and cultural. The leader must be the true bearer and interpreter of the mature culture of his people. He must be capable of decisions based on a cultivated and specifically noble reflection on history. In his impassioned but pragmatic advocacy for the dispossessed of his community the fundamentalist leader finds both the source of his inspirational power and the limits of his ability to direct the actual operations and development of the fundamentalist movement when it moves beyond the enclave. The charismatic leader, as a local figure, is capable of entering into political negotiations and making compromises with outsiders—without sacrificing the integrity of his followers or giving up the greater goal of Islamization or Christianization or Judaization, as the case may be. If he becomes primarily an international figure, however, the fundamentalist leader may lose the most potent source of his power: the support of the despised and dispossessed.

Policy makers and educators who consider the findings of this book may be surprised and also strangely comforted to realize that the charismatic preacher, minister, or rabbi—who may have "caused" the fundamentalist "problem" in the first place—is also the figure with the power to moderate the movement, to force it to consider the power of the enemy, and thus to constrain its most radical elements. He enjoys this power only as long as he is beholden primarily to the enclave, the local religious community of true believers. Ironically, we may one day mourn the passing of the charismatic fundamentalist leader, especially if he is succeeded by an extremist whose zeal is untempered by a religious commitment to the least of his brothers and sisters.

Notes

1. John Kifner, "Alms and Arms: Tactics in a Holy War," *New York Times*, 15 March 1996, A-6.

2. Ibid.

3. Joel Greenberg, "Hamas Blames Killings by Israel for New Bombings," *New York Times*, 27 February 1996, A-2.

4. "Islamic Rule Is Reaffirmed by Sudan Chief," *New York Times* (Reuters), 24 March 1996, A-13.

5. Gabriel A. Almond, Emmanuel Sivan, and R. Scott Appleby, "Explaining Fundamentalisms," in Martin E. Marty and R. Scott Appleby, eds., *Fundamentalisms Comprehended* (Chicago: University of Chicago Press, 1995), 425–43.

6. See, for example, Martin Riesebrodt, "Fundamentalism and the Political Mobilization of Women," in Said Amir Arjomand, ed., *The Political Dimensions of Religion* (Albany, N.Y.: State University of New York Press, 1993), 243–71; Helen Hardacre, "The Impact of Fundamentalisms on Women, the Family, and Interpersonal Relations," in Martin E. Marty and R. Scott Appleby, eds., *Fundamentalisms and Society* (Chicago: University of Chicago Press, 1993), 129–50. See also, John Stratton Hawley, ed., *Fundamentalism and Gender* (New York: Oxford University Press, 1994).

7. Shahla Haeri, "Obedience vs. Autonomy: Women and Fundamentalism in Iran and Pakistan" in Marty and Appleby, *Fundamentalisms and Society*, 202.

8. Ehud Sprinzak, *The Ascendance of Israeli's Radical Right* (New York: Oxford University Press, 1991), 157–59.

9. See Mark Juergensmeyer, *The New Cold War? Religious Nationalism Confronts the Secular State* (Berkeley: University of California Press, 1993).

10. Kifner, "Alms and Arms," A-6.

11. Luciano Cavalli, "Charisma and Twentieth-Century Politics," in Scott Lash and Sam Whimster, eds., *Max Weber, Rationality, and Modernity* (London: Allen and Unwin, 1987), 322–23.

CONTRIBUTORS

ZIAD ABU-AMR is associate professor of political science at Bir Zeit University in the West Bank. He holds a Ph.D. in comparative politics from Georgetown University. Professor Abu-Amr is the author, most recently, of *Islamic Fundamentalism in the West Bank and Gaza: Muslim Brotherhood and Islamic Jihad.* In 1996 he was elected from Gaza to the Palestinian Council.

R. SCOTT APPLEBY is associate professor of history at the University of Notre Dame, where he directs the Cushwa Center for the Study of American Catholicism. From 1988 to 1994 he was the codirector, with Martin E. Marty, of the Fundamentalism Project of the American Academy of Arts and Sciences. With Marty he coedited a five-volume series on religious fundamentalisms published by the University of Chicago Press. Appleby is also the author or coauthor of five books, including the forthcoming *The Ambivalence of the Sacred: Religion, Violence, and Reconciliation.*

GIDEON ARAN is senior lecturer in the department of sociology and anthropology, Hebrew University, Jerusalem. He is the author of numerous articles and books, including *The Land of Israel: Between Politics and Religion* and the forthcoming *Zealotry: A Study in Politics and Religion.*

YAAKOV ARIEL teaches religious history at the University of North Carolina at Chapel Hill. Formerly he taught at the Hebrew University, Jerusalem, where he was voted outstanding lecturer on three occasions. Professor Ariel is the author of *On Behalf of Israel: American Fundamentalist Attitudes towards Jews, Judaism, and Zionism, 1865–1945.*

DANIEL BRUMBERG is an assistant professor in the department of government at Georgetown University. Previously he was a visiting professor in the department of political science at Emory University and a visiting fellow in the Middle East Program in the Carter Center. He has published articles on the political economy of reform in the Arab world, Islamic fundamentalism, and Iranian politics. He is currently working on a book on Islam and democracy.

PATRICK D. GAFFNEY, C.S.C., is associate professor of anthropology at the University of Notre Dame, where he serves as a fellow of the Joan B. Kroc Institute for International Peace Studies. He is the author, most recently, of *The Prophet's Pulpit: Islamic Preaching in Contemporary Egypt*.

SAMUEL C. HEILMAN is Harold Proshansky Professor of Jewish Studies and Sociology on the faculty of Queens College and the Graduate Center of the City University of New York. He is the author of numerous articles and reviews as well as seven books: *Synagogue Life*, *The People of the Book*, *The Gate behind the Wall*, *A Walker in Jerusalem*, *Cosmopolitans and Parochials: Modern Orthodox Jews in America* (with Stephen M. Cohen), *Defenders of the Faith: Inside Ultra-Orthodox Jewry*, and, most recently, *Portrait of American Jews: The Last Half of the Twentieth Century*.

MARTIN KRAMER is director of the Moshe Dayan Center for Middle Eastern and African Studies at Tel Aviv University. He has held visiting professorships at Cornell University, the University of Chicago, and Georgetown University. Dr. Kramer is the editor of *Shi'ism, Resistance, and Revolution* and *Middle Eastern Lives: The Practice of Biography and Self-Narrative*. He is the author of *Islam Assembled: The Advent of Muslim Congresses* and, most recently, *Arab Awakening and Islamic Revival: The Politics of Ideas in the Middle East*.

JUDITH MILLER has been a correspondent for the *New York Times* since 1977; she was the newspaper's Cairo bureau chief and its special correspondent during the Gulf war. Miller is the author of three books: *Saddam Hussein and the Crisis in the Gulf* (with Laurie Mylroie); *One, by One, by One*; and, most recently, *God Has Ninety-nine Names: Reporting from a Militant Middle East*.

PHOTO CREDITS

INDEX